The 2008 edition of the Michelin Eating out in Pubs guide contains details of over 550 pubs. As ever, the crucial factor for selection in the guide is the quality of the food served, and though the style of cooking and the menus may vary from one pub to the next, our independent inspectors ensure that each and every pub listed reaches the requisite gastronomic standards.

In this, the first decade of the 21st Century, cooking in British pubs has reached new heights, and there is an enormous amount of choice now available to diners. Some pubs are travelling proudly down the organic route, with the support of small local suppliers, while others focus more on regional specialities and long-established local recipes. Some serve creative, contemporary cooking with more of an international flavour, but equally, there are plenty of places offering traditional British favourites too.

If you're having trouble choosing where to go, the descriptive texts give an insight into the individual character of each pub, highlighting what we found to be most memorable and charming therein, and the accompanying pictures reveal a little bit more of their personality – as well as ensuring that you don't end up at the wrong place by mistake. Smoky environments are now a thing of the past following the recent change in the law banning smoking in all pubs.

Some of these pubs serve their food by the fireplace in the bar; others may have a more formal dining room, but whatever their style, they all have one thing in common: carefully prepared, flavoursome food made from fresh, quality ingredients. We've done the research; now all you have to do is enjoy.

Readers of the Michelin guide to Eating out in Pubs write thousands of letters and emails to us every year, praising or criticising current entries, recommending new entries or simply making suggestions for the guide itself. Please keep these coming - and help us to make the next edition even better. You can also fill in and return the readers' questionnaire form at the back of this guide; either way, we look forward to hearing from you.

contents

SCOTLAND
NORTH EAST
NORTHERN IRELAND
YORKSHIR
&
THE HUMBE
ISLE OF MAN
IRELAND
NORTH WEST
REPUBLIC OF IRELAND
ENGLAN
WALES
WEST MIDLANDS
SOUTH WEST
ISLE O
WIGHT
CHANNEL ISLANDS

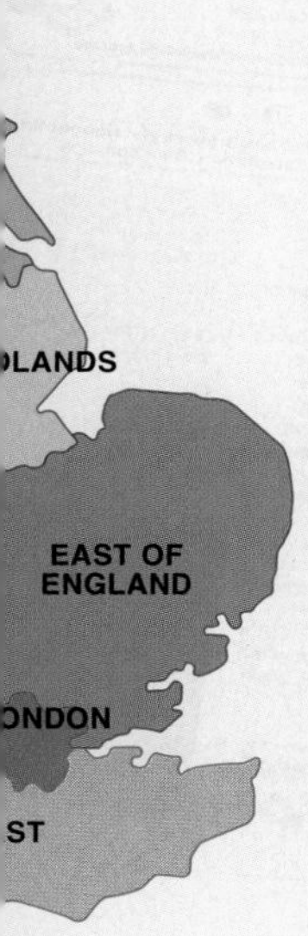
LANDS
EAST OF
ENGLAND
ONDON
ST

COUNTRY OR REGION & COUNTY NAMES

ONE OF OUR FAVOURITE SELECTIONS

TOWN/VILLAGE NAME

NAME, ADDRESS, TELEPHONE, E-MAIL AND WEBSITE OF THE ESTABLISHMENT

001

ENTRY NUMBER

Each pub or inn has its own entry number.

This number appears on the regional map at the start of each section to show the location of the establishment.

COLOURED PAGE BORDER

- Introduction
- East Midlands
- East of England
- London
- North East
- North West
- South East
- South West
- West Midlands
- Yorkshire & The Humber
- Scotland
- Wales
- Northern Ireland
- Republic of Ireland

East of England • Bedfordshire

Bolnhurst

001 **The Plough at Bolnhurst**

Kimbolton Rd,
Bolnhurst MK44 2EX
Tel.: 01234 376274
e-mail: theplough@bolnhurst.com - Website: www.bolnhurst.com

Batemans XB, Potton Village Bike and 1 guest ale: Hobgoblin, Wychwood, Great Scot, Caledonian, Deuchars IPA

Razed to the ground two decades ago, the pure white Plough has been lovingly and sympathetically restored to something like its original 14th century glory and reopened several summers ago. The charming interior offers an inglenook, thick rustic walls and wood and stone floors in three main seating areas with reassuringly low ceilings and exposed beams. You can't help but feel utterly relaxed. Step outside and there's a duck pond, spacious gardens and two extensive terraces. Local produce is keenly sought and carefully prepared on menus which also pay due homage to the seasons. There's an eclectic feel to what's on offer: modern dishes like Thai salads or chargrilled squid, as well as old favourites that have stood the test of time, like steak and kidney pudding or bangers and mash. Often deservedly busy, as well as the food, it's the smooth, assured and friendly service which keeps people coming back time and again.

Food serving times

Tuesday-Saturday:
12pm-2pm, 6.30pm-9.30pm

Sunday:
12pm-2pm

Closed at New Year, first 2 weeks in January

Prices

Meals: 16.00 (3 course lunch) and a la carte 25.00/37.00

Typical Dishes

Yellow split pea bro
Char-grilled calve liver
Lemon tart

7mi North of Bedford by B660, on South side of village. Parking.

52

HOW TO FIND A PUB

There are 3 ways to search for a pub in this guide:
- use the regional maps that precede each section of the guide
- use the alphabetical list of pubs at the end of the guide or
- use the alphabetical list of place names also at the end of the guide

PUBS WITH BEDROOMS

For easy reference, those pubs that offer accommodation are highlighted. in blue This theme is continued on the regional maps that precede each section of the guide.

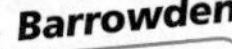

Barrowden

Exeter Arms

026

28 Main St,
Barrowden LE15 8EQ
Tel.: (01572) 747247 - Fax: (01572) 747247
e-mail: info@exeterarms.com - Website: www.exeterarms.com

VISA MC

Beach Boys, Bevin Boys, Hopgear, Winterhop, Attitude

Handily placed just off the A47, this family run pub exudes much of the rural charm associated with the area close to Rutland Water. It's a 17C inn of light stone idyllically rooted in a sleepy village overlooking the green with its little pond and duck house. Inside is warm and welcoming: the yellow painted walls see to that. Beers here are a must. They come from the pub's own micro-brewery housed in an old rear barn, and you can't sup them anywhere else in the country. If you're eating you can choose a seat wherever takes your fancy, be it the stone-walled dining room or the bar with its cosy open fire. Either way, you won't forget where you are, as old photos of the pub crop up on all walls. You'll remember this hostelry, too, for its well-executed cuisine, classic dishes given an updated, international twist, with Asian influences inspiringly conspicuous. Three neat and tidy bedrooms offer pleasant country views.

Food serving times
Monday:
7pm-9pm
Tuesday-Saturday:
12pm-2pm, 7pm-9pm
Sunday:
12pm-2.30pm, 7pm-9pm
Prices
Meals: a la carte
20.65/29.45
3 rooms: 37.50/75.00

Typical Dishes
Sautéed foie gras
Braised wild rabbit
Honey pannacotta

11mi South West of Oakham by A6003 and A47. Parking.

East Midlands • Rutland

43

SYMBOLS

 Meals served in the garden or on the terrace

 A good range of wines served by the glass

 A particularly interesting wine list

 No dogs allowed

 Visa accepted

 American Express accepted

Diners Club accepted

MasterCard accepted

REAL ALES SERVED

A listing to indicate the number and variety of regular and guest cask beers usually served.

OPENING HOURS FOOD SERVING TIMES PRICES ROOMS

Approximate range of prices for a three-course meal, plus information on booking and annual closures.

Some inns offering accommodation may close in mid-afternoon and only allow guests to check in during evening hours. If in doubt, phone ahead.

Room prices range from the lowest-priced single to the most expensive double or twin.

The cup and saucer symbol and price relate to breakfast; if no symbol is shown, assume it is included in the price of the room.

Prices are given in £ sterling, except for the Republic of Ireland where €uro are quoted.

HOW TO GET THERE

Directions and driving distances from nearby towns, and indication of parking facilities and any other information that might help you get your bearings.

THE BLACKBOARD

An example of a typical starter, main course and dessert, chosen by the chef.

Whilst there's no guarantee that these dishes will be available, they should provide you with an idea of the style of the cuisine.

The Pub of the year

Our team of Michelin inspectors have eaten, drank, and slept their way around the British Isles, in a search for the 550+ pubs worthy of inclusion in this year's Guide. Each has been selected for the quality of its food – that much is a given. But what is it that merits the title of Pub of the Year? There's the choice of beers and wines, the warmth of the welcome and the service. The location is important, as is the ambience; but the number one spot can only go to a pub with real star quality: that extra ingredient which you can't quite put your finger on – but which you'd travel to experience, and which is recognisable almost as soon as you step through the door.

The pub was converted from three farm-workers' cottages and the story of the conciliatory gesture behind this transformation helps explain the origin of its name. The pub was originally situated next to the farmer's house - but so fed up did he become with the late night noise that he closed it down. The farm workers subsequently went on strike – the problem only being resolved when the workers agreed to swap; they would live in the old pub and the cottages would become the pub.

Several distinct areas are still in evidence, each one cosy and characterful, with blazing log fires and church pew seats. Champagnes and wines are available by the glass, as is refreshing homemade lemonade; and the choice of real ales includes the pub's own label - the infinitely gluggable 'Olive Oil'. The ambience is unhurried and informal, and the shelves, chock-full of empty wine bottles and cookery books, provide a hint to the pub's gastronomic credibility.

A passion for good food means that high quality produce and seasonal ingredients are at the base of every dish served here; a local map on the menu lets you know exactly where your food has come from. There's a flexibility too; dishes are not divided into starters and mains, so you can have as little or as much as you like. This is simply and carefully prepared food; unfussy, fresh and full of flavour – and their cookbook, 'Full English and other pub recipes', means that you can even attempt to recreate it at home.

Across the road in Beech House are six beautiful bedrooms with names like Chocolate, Double Cream and Biscuit. Furnished with antiques and contemporary fabrics, every little extra has been thought of, like the homemade biscuits, magazines and flowers. Breakfast is served by the log fire in the barn: feast on eggs from the local farm, fruit smoothies and homemade preserves. A charming all-rounder, our Pub of the Year for 2008 is…

The Olive Branch & Beech House

Main Street, Clipsham, LE15 7SH

Tel: (01780) 410355 – Fax: (01780) 410000

e-mail: info@theolivebranchpub.com – website: www.theolivebranchpub.com

see page 44 for more details

All the pubs in this guide have been selected for the quality of their cooking. However, we feel that several of them deserve additional consideration as they boast at least one extra quality which makes them particularly special.
It may be the delightful setting, the charm and character of the pub, the general atmosphere, the pleasant service, the overall value for money or the exceptional cooking.
To distinguish these pubs, we point them out with our "We most liked" Bibendum stamp.
We are sure you will enjoy these pubs as much as we have.

EAST MIDLANDS

EAST OF ENGLAND

LONDON

NORTH EAST

NORTH WEST

SOUTH EAST

SOUTH WEST

WEST MIDLANDS

YORKSHIRE AND THE HUMBER

SCOTLAND

WALES

NORTHERN IRELAND

REPUBLIC OF IRELAND

Beer in the U.K. and Ireland

As most pub-goers know, beers in Britain can be divided not only into Ales and Lagers – which differ mainly in their respective warm and cool fermentations – but also according to their means of storage. Keg beer is filtered, pasteurised and chilled, and then packed into pressurised containers from which it gets its name, while cask beer or "Real Ale", as it is often called, continues to ferment and mature in its barrel.

Brewers rightly insist that the final flavour of a beer depends on all sorts of elements, from the variety of yeast to the minerals in the local water, not to mention storage in the pub, but there are three stages of brewing which particularly influence the character of the beer in your glass.

The malting, the way the germinating barley is dried, roasted and milled to make it fermentable, affects the flavour, the 'body' and the colour of the drink: a hotter kiln means a darker malt. This malt is then soaked in hot water to form a porridge-like mash; time and temperature are crucial here. Perhaps most importantly, the addition of hops gives a familiar, faintly astringent tang, with different strains of plant lending different overtones to the final pint. For extra aroma, bunches of hop flowers, called cones, can be added to the beer later, at the end of its vat fermentation or even in the barrel, a process known as "dry hopping".

Traditional Styles

Of the several distinct beer styles in the British Isles, **bitter** is the most popular traditional beer in England and Wales, although now outsold by lager. No precise definition exists and the name is loosely used, but bitters are usually paler and dryer than Mild with a high hop content and, of course, a slightly bitter taste and bouquet, from flowery to citrus, depending on the hop variety.

Mild is largely found in Wales, the West Midlands and the North West of England. The name refers to the hop character as it is gentle, sweetish beer, generally lower in alcohol and often darker in colour.

The great dry **stouts** are brewed in Ireland and are instantly recognisable by their black colour and creamy head: they have a pronounced yeast flavour and sometimes a faint smoky taste. Reddish-black **porter** was revived by the renewed interest in real ale and is still something of a rarity. Originally known as 'entire', this slightly lighter though still substantial beer was said to have been a favourite with London's market porters and deliverymen when it was first brewed in the 18th century.

In Scotland the beers produced are typically full-bodied and malty and are often known simply as Light, **Heavy** or **Export**, which refers to the body and alcoholic content of the ale. The old shilling taxes were levied by roughly the same scale, at rates of 60/- to 80/- and beyond, and still survive in some beer names.

The Continental Connection

Many great European styles are now imitated by UK producers, with greater or lesser success, and publicans are also becoming increasingly discerning in their choices of European imports. Drinkers in Britain's dining pubs might come across fizzy, hazy, tan-yellow **Weizenbier** from southern Germany which can accompany anything from full-flavoured white meats to seafood, or one of the crisp, bitter-edged **lagers** produced in the north, where they are sometimes served with fish.

Belgium's spontaneously fermenting **lambic** is aged in wine barrels for up to three years; when flavoured with fruit and bottle-matured it becomes **gueuze**, a sweet-sharp, bubbly beer quite unlike anything in the British tradition. The great **abbey beers**, traditionally produced by the Belgian Trappist orders, are usually rich, effervescent and complex and need similarly robust flavours to complement them, while cloudy **white beers** make a refreshing accompaniment to light meals and summer salads. Top-fermented then cold-stored like lagers, **bières de garde** from northern France and Wallonia are sometimes sealed with a Champagne-style wired cork. These amber or nut-brown beers are typically strong and characterful and go well with cheeses or slow-cooked meats.

A tour of the region begins with a well-kept secret: the rural beauty of the east. Towards the coast lie acres of silent fens, the gentle countryside of the wolds, and the magnificent silhouette of Lincoln Cathedral, rising above the old city. Nottingham, Derby and the nearby towns shot to fame as centres of industry and science and remain the powerhouses of the region. With Leicester they form an old industrial heartland, regenerated by the first plantings of the National Forest and bordered by rural Rutland, "independent" again since 1997. Then to the west, sombre moors, the pretty 'White Peak' downlands, the Derwent and dramatic Dovedale form some of the country's most picture-perfect landscapes, while Peak architecture reflects every mood and era of its history: Matlock's mills and the moving monuments of Eyam village, Georgian Buxton and the stately archetypes of Chatsworth and Haddon Hall. In the region's pubs, there's a strong local flavour on tap – even Rutland brews its own beer – as well as on the plate. Bakewell tarts, or puddings, are a point of local pride, while only the rich, blue-veined cheese from three East Midlands counties can lay claim to the name of Stilton.

Yorkshire & the Humber
North West
West Midlands
EAST
South East
Bolton
Wigan
Leigh
Oldham
Huddersfield
Holmfirth
Wakefield
Barnsley
MANCHESTER
Ashton-under-Lyne
Glossop
Stocksbridge
Peak District
Conisbrough
Doncaster
Rotherham
Altrincham
Hyde
Stockport
SHEFFIELD
High Peak
Castleton
Maltby
Bawtry
Knutsford
Wilmslow
Whaley Bridge
Chapel-en-le-Frith
Northwich
National
Dronfield
Worksop
Macclesfield
Buxton
Baslow
Staveley
Chatsworth House
Chesterfield
Middlewich
Congleton
Bakewell
Park
Sandbach
Little Moreton Hall
Clay Cross
Hardwick Hall
Tuxford
Ollerton
Crewe
Kidsgrove
Leek
Matlock
Alfreton
Mansfield
Sutton-in-Ashfield
Southwell
Newcastle-under-Lyme
DERBY
Ashbourne
Ripley
Heanor
Hucknall
Audlem
STOKE-ON-TRENT
Belper
NOTTINGHAM
Market Drayton
Stone
Ilkeston
Derby
Uttoxeter
West Bridgford
Bingham
Eccleshall
Sudbury
Long Eaton
Stafford
Abbots Bromley
Burton-upon-Trent
Rempstone
Newport
Rugeley
Shepshed
STAFFORD
Swadlincote
Loughborough
Cannock
Ashby de la Zouch
Gailey
Brownhills
Lichfield
Coalville
LEICESTER
Walsall
Tamworth
WOLVERHAMPTON
Sutton Coldfield
Oadby
Dudley
Atherstone
Hinckley
BIRMINGHAM
Nuneaton
Market Harborough
Stourbridge
Bedworth
Lutterworth
Kidderminster
Halesowen
Solihull
Bewdley
COVENTRY
Husbands Bosworth
Rugby
Stourport
Bromsgrove
Kenilworth
Rothwell
Wells
Redditch
WARWICK
NORTHAMPTON
Royal Leamington Spa
Wellingborough
Henley
Droitwich
Warwick
Worcester
Alcester
Daventry
Southam
WORCESTER
Stratford-upon-Avon
Great Malvern
Evesham
Ettington
Upton
Pershore
Shipston-on-Stour
Chipping Campden
Towcester
Banbury
Broadway
Wolverton
Tewkesbury
Moreton
Brackley
Milton Keynes
Winchcombe
Stow-on-the-Wold
Chipping Norton
Buckingham
Bletchley
Gloucester
Cheltenham
OXFORD

Scunthorpe
Immingham Dock
Immingham
Kilnsea
Grimsby
Spurn Head
Cleethorpes
Brigg
Humberside
Caistor
Rotterdam
Zeebrugge
Gainsborough
Market Rasen
Louth
Mablethorpe
Sutton-on-Sea
Wragby
Alford
Lincoln
Horncastle
Partney
Woodhall Spa
Spilsby
Skegness
MIDLANDS
Sleaford
Boston
Grantham
Hunstanton
Wells-next-the-Sea
The Wash
Donington
Sutterton
Sandringham House
Holbeach
Long Sutton
Bourne
Spalding
King's Lynn
Oakham
Stamford
Crowland
Wisbech
East Dereham
Swaffham
Eye
Guyhirn
Outwell
Stradsett
Peterborough
Downham Market
Corby
Whittlesey
March
Mundford
Weldon
Oundle
Chatteris
Littleport
Brandon
Kettering
Ramsey
Thetford
Thrapston
Ely
East of England
Huntingdon
Earith
Soham
Higham Ferrers
St. Ives
Rushden
Godmanchester
St. Neots
Newmarket
Bury St.
Eltisley
Sandy
Potton
Cambridge
Bedford
Newport Pagnell
Biggleswade
Haverhill
Clare
Ampthill
Shefford
Saffron Walden
Sudbury
Royston
Woburn Abbey
Letchworth
Baldock
Hitchin
Buntingford
Finchingfield
Halstead
Leighton
N. LINCS
N.E. LINCS
LINCOLN
RUTLAND
NORFOLK
CAMBRIDGE
NORTHAMPTON
BEDFORD
SUFFOLK

001 Bramhall's

6 Buxton Rd,
Ashbourne DE6 1EX
Tel.: (01335) 346158
e-mail: info@bramhalls.co.uk - Website: www.bramhalls.co.uk

   VISA

 **Bass**

It's been all change at Bramhall's – the original Bramhalls have departed and this former coaching inn has been taken over by a couple of civil engineers. Only time will tell if they're as good at gastronomy as they were at designing buildings…The tiny bar is now hidden away at the back, and there's a lounge to relax in, but the majority of floor space is now given over to dining, with one of the rooms more formal than the other. Starters on offer might include ham hock and black pudding terrine or smoked chicken and guacamole salad, with main courses ranging from steak and chips and rack of lamb to braised venison casserole or artichoke, cherry tomato and black olive papperdeli (sic). Stay overnight in one of ten comfortable bedrooms, and take advantage of the pub's position at the gateway to the Peak District National Park to go riding, shooting, climbing, fishing or walking – or whatever other activity takes your fancy.

Food serving times

Monday-Sunday:
12pm-2.30pm, 6.30pm-9.30pm

Closed Sunday dinner November to Easter

Prices

Meals: 13.95 (3 course lunch) and a la carte 13.95/24.95

10 rooms: 50.00/90.00

Typical Dishes

Chicken liver parfait

Fillet of Derbyshire steak

Vanilla crème brûlée

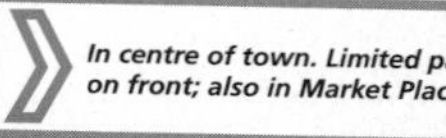

In centre of town. Limited parking on front; also in Market Place.

002 Rowley's

Church Street, Baslow DE45 1RY
Tel.: (01246) 583880
e-mail: info@rowleysrestaurant.co.uk
Website: www.rowleysrestaurant.co.uk

 **London Pride, Thornbridge**

The people who run the Michelin Star-encrusted Fischer's at Baslow Hall have now 'set up shop' along the road with this classy second venture. It's based in a quiet village in one of its quietest positions: surrounded on three sides by graveyard and church! Nothing funereal about the ambience here, though: a full makeover in 2006 introduced chrome tables and chairs and large dark brown banquettes to this old stone pub. There are three dining areas and, under the watchful eye of a bubbly manager, waiting staff skim across the blond wood floors providing excellent and personable service. Dishes are in the modern British category, and most ingredients have a Derbyshire accent: matured steaks are a particular speciality. Close by is Chatsworth House, an ideal destination for anyone making a day of it in the Peak District.

Food serving times

Monday-Thursday:
12pm-2.30pm, 6pm-9.30pm

Friday-Saturday:
12pm-2.30pm, 6pm-10pm

Sunday:
12pm-2.30pm

Prices

Meals: a la carte
21.25/36.50

Typical Dishes

Parsnip tarte Tatin
Fillet of seabream
Sticky toffee pudding

4mi North of Bakewell by A619.
Parking.

The Devonshire Arms

003 The Devonshire Arms

Devonshire Square, Beeley DE4 2NR
Tel.: (01629) 733259 - Fax: (01629) 733259
e-mail: enquiries@devonshirebeeley.co.uk
Website: www.devonshirebeeley.co.uk

John Smith's cask ale, Theakston's Old Peculier, Timothy Taylor's Landlord, Peak Ale's OPA, Swiftnick, Bakewell Best

Part of the famous Chatsworth estate, this historic stone inn has two distinct parts to it: one side is decidedly rural in character, typified by its low ceilings, oak beams and inglenook fireplace, while, by contrast, light streams in through the floor to ceiling windows in the brightly furnished, modern extension. Upstairs, stylish contemporary bedrooms complete the picture. Far from typical pub rooms, they have been styled by the Duchess of Devonshire and are named after the nearby Dales. Food is also far from typical, and although classics like bangers and mash and prawn cocktail are on the menu, other dishes offered might include confit duck terrine, warm salad of wood pigeon or lobster, with most of the fresh, seasonal ingredients coming from local sources and from the estate itself. Wine lovers are also well-catered for with an impressive wine list containing over 300 bins, housed in a glass-fronted cave.

Food serving times
Monday-Sunday:
12pm-3pm, 6pm-9pm

Prices
Meals: a la carte
17.95/27.95

4 rooms:
145.00/165.00

Typical Dishes
Crab mayonnaise
Roast fillet of beef
Sticky toffee pudding

5mi South East of Bakewell by A6 and B6012. Parking.

004 The Druid Inn

Main St,
Birchover DE4 2BL
Tel.: (01629) 650302
Website: www.thedruidinn.co.uk

Druids Ale and guest ales including Dovedale, Goldings, Hairy Helmet

Taking its name from the mysterious and ancient Druid Rocks above it, the Druid Inn, in the heart of the Peak District countryside, has been a hill-walkers' landmark for many years. Much extended since the 19C, it still has plenty of true rural character in the old bar, which has kept its tiled floor, chunky furniture and flickering firelight, and is that bit more authentic-feeling than the smarter modern dining rooms. Considerate and informal staff somehow keep track of a large menu that ranges from daily pastas and risottos, hot and cold lunchtime sandwiches and pints of prawns, by way of enjoyable and substantial modern classics. This is more than food to keep the cold out: it may not be elaborate, but it's marked by true, balanced flavours and sound culinary understanding, with sensible prices to match.

Food serving times

Monday-Saturday:
12pm-2.30pm, 6pm-9.30pm

Sunday:
12pm-3pm, 6pm-9.30pm

Prices

Meals: 16.00 (3 course lunch and dinner weekdays only) and a la carte 25.00/35.00

Typical Dishes

Assiette of Gressingham duck
Seared sea scallops
Chocolate fondant

7.5 mi Northwest from Matlock by A6 and 5.5 mi from Bakewell. Parking.

005 The Chequers Inn

Froggatt Edge,
Hope Valley S32 3ZJ
Tel.: (01433) 630231 - Fax: (01433) 631072
e-mail: info@chequers-froggatt.com - Website: www.chequers-froggatt.com

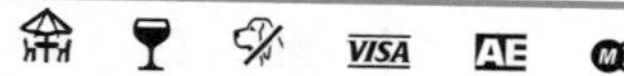

Greene King IPA, Black Sheep, Charles Wells Bombardier

On the eastern edge of the Peak District National park, in the heart of the Derbyshire countryside, this traditional 16C country inn is ideally set for nourishment and refreshment before or after a hike, and even has a direct path from its pretty woodland garden right up to the glorious views at Froggatt Edge. Beware when leaving by the front door, however, as the main road is right outside. Inside, clocks and farm implements decorate the walls, there's a large room with a bar, and a quieter, cosier room on the other side of the hall. Menus are chalked up on blackboards, and you place your order at the bar – satisfying favourites such as sausage and mash and pot roasted lamb shank will recharge your batteries, and – named after the nearby market town - Bakewell pudding and custard makes a fitting dessert. Weary walkers staying the night will find bedrooms comfortable – go for one at the back to avoid noise from passing traffic.

Food serving times

Monday-Friday:
12pm-2pm, 6pm-9.30pm

Saturday:
12pm-9.30pm

Sunday:
12pm-9pm

Closed 25 December

Prices

Meals: a la carte
21.15/27.85

5 rooms: 70.00/90.00

Typical Dishes

Belly pork
Venison and mushroom pie
Doughnuts with ice cream

Situated on the edge of the village. Parking.

006 The Crown Inn

Riggs Lane, Marston Montgomery DE6 2FF
Tel.: (01889) 590541 - Fax: (01889) 591576
e-mail: info@thecrowninn-derbyshire.co.uk
Website: www.thecrowninn-derbyshire.co.uk

Marston's Pedigree, Timothy Taylor's Landlord, Guinness and regularly changing guest beer

Just up the road from Alton Towers, life flows at a rather more sedate pace in the hamlet of Marston Montgomery, and nowhere more so than in this traditional creeper-clad pub, its low-beamed bar furnished with comfortable leather sofas; real ales ready to pour. The lunchtime menu is classic in its simplicity, with three choices at each course and a few specials chalked up on a blackboard. In the evenings, the menu becomes more lengthy and adventurous, with dishes such as cold pressed game terrine, crab linguine or pan seared scallops to start, and mains which create an interesting blend of different flavours, like seabass fillets with squid ink tagliatelle, crab and baby spinach, or paupiettes of sole with sunblush artichoke risotto and orange and caper beurre noisette. Outside there's a small terrace and garden, while the pub's seven bedrooms are simply furnished, with whitewashed walls.

Food serving times

Monday-Saturday:
12pm-3pm, 7pm-9.30pm

Sunday:
12pm-3pm

Closed 25 December and 1 January

Prices

Meals: 14.95 (3 course lunch) and a la carte 20.00/30.00

7 rooms: 50.00/75.00

Typical Dishes

Tomato and pork meatballs

Rack of Derbyshire lamb

Coconut and lemongrass pannacotta

7.5mi Southeast of Ashbourne by A515. Parking.

007 **The Queen's Head**

2 Long St,
Belton LE12 9TP
Tel.: (01530) 222359 - Fax: (01530) 224860
e-mail: enquiries@thequeenshead.org - Website: www.thequeenshead.org

 **Fuller's Discovery, Marston's Pedigree**

A renovation of the old village inn has left little if any trace of a 19C pub; even Her Majesty's severe, Penny-Black profile on the monochrome pub sign looks like a tribute to a design classic rather than a touch of Victorian detail. But it's fairer to appreciate the place for what it is. The transformation, into a smart bar, bistro and restaurant has been complete and thorough: calm whites and creams, chocolate suede and polished wood give a feeling of all-over modernity. It's no surprise to find similar attention to detail in the various seasonally- evolving menus, where proud use is made of local produce. Dishes such as breast of guinea fowl, pan-fried brill or roast loin of venison are served at dinner; with bring-your-own wine evenings on the first Wednesday of every month. Bedrooms are a mix of shapes and sizes; individually furnished, spacious, contemporary and bright.

Food serving times

Monday-Thursday: 12pm-2.30pm, 7pm-9.30pm

Friday-Saturday: 12pm-2.30pm, 7pm-10pm

Sunday: 12pm-4pm

Closed 25-26 December and 1 January

Prices

Meals: 17.00 (3 course lunch and dinner) and a la carte 18.00/35.00

6 rooms: 65.00/110.00

Typical Dishes

Tian of crab & smoked salmon

Roast fillet of beef

Chocolate brownie

6mi West of Loughborough by A6 on the B5234. On the Diseworth/ Breedon rd. Parking.

008 The Three Horseshoes Inn

Main St,
Breedon-on-the-Hill DE73 8AN
Tel.: (01332) 695129
e-mail: ian@thehorseshoes.com - Website: www.thehorseshoes.com

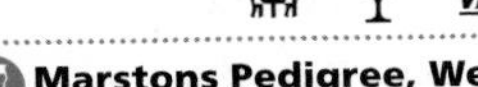
Marstons Pedigree, Websters Yorkshire Bitter

A 230 year-old former farriery, The Three Horseshoes is one third of a stalwart trio in a noteworthy village, famed for its church perched atop a quarry cliff visible for miles around, and opposite an 18th Century lock-up. It's a welcoming pub: there's a locals bar with an open fire, where you can quite happily mingle and enjoy a pint. Food, though, is the main emphasis here. Apart from the bar, there are two dining areas with coir matting, walls filled with a variety of pictures, crafts and artefacts, and plenty of space to take it all in. Large mismatched dining tables and odd chairs complete the quirky picture. Nothing quirky about the menus…large blackboards offer ample choice of carefully sourced and combined ingredients in dishes more akin in style to restaurant than pub, like blackened swordfish with crème fraîche and lime, pheasant with Savoy cabbage and whisky or sliced fillet of beef in Cajun spices with tzatziki dressing.

Food serving times

Monday-Saturday:
12pm-2pm, 5.30pm-9.15pm

Sunday:
12pm-2pm

Closed 25-26 December and 1 January

Prices

Meals: a la carte
25.95/33.35

Typical Dishes

Potted pork
Braised local lamb shank
Chocolate whisky trifle

4mi Southwest of Castle Donington by Breedon rd off A453. Parking.

Bruntingthorpe

009 Joiners Arms

Church Walk, Bruntingthorpe LE17 5QH
Tel.: (0116) 247 8258
e-mail: stephenjoiners@btconnect.com
Website: www.thejoinersarms.co.uk

   VISA

 **Greene King IPA**

Home to a former RAF base now used as a racing track, the hidden hamlet of Bruntingthorpe also houses this charming 18C inn. You might well drive past it at first, however, unaware of the sign swinging slowly and silently in the breeze, shyly announcing its status as a public house. Inside, the style is smart with exposed oak beams, terracotta floor tiles and modern artwork giving the place a contemporary feel. Sit out on the small front terrace or in the large main bar or eat at one of the wooden tables in the informal dining area. Classic, hearty food has been well-chosen to make up the compact menu and you can also choose from the daily-changing blackboard specials which often involve the best kind of seafood – fresh and simply prepared. Locals who frequent this inn join with those who've made a longer trip to sample the appealing cooking, and the friendly, efficient service ensures the smiles stay on everyone's faces.

Food serving times

Tuesday-Saturday:
12pm-2pm, 6.30pm-9.30pm

Sunday:
12pm-2pm

Closed 25-26 December

Booking essential

Prices

Meals: 12.50 (set price lunch) and a la carte 20.00/26.00

Typical Dishes

Dorset crab cakes
Shoulder of lamb noisette
Créme brûlée

Between Leicester and Husbands Bosworth off A5199. Parking.

010 Tollemache Arms

48 Main St, Buckminster NG33 5SA
Tel.: (01476) 860007
e-mail: enquiries@thetollmachearms.com
Website: www.thetollmachearms.com

 VISA AE MC

 **Timothy Taylor's Landlord, Ruddles County**

In the heart of Rutland, something's cooking…and the small village of Buckminster is reaping the dividends. The Tollemache was gutted in 2004 (as were many of the villagers when it happened) but the refurbished Arms has gone a mighty long way to redress the balance. Admittedly, it now bears little resemblance to its late Victorian coaching inn origins. In fact, the wood floor, stainless steel topped bar, huge leather sofas and contemporary colour scheme are about as far removed from 'traditional' as it's possible to get. But regulars and visitors alike have taken to the 21st century version, not least due to the cooking qualities of chef Mark, who for three years was chef de partie at the famous Le Manoir in Oxfordshire. His menus are modern British, but nothing too complicated to upset a consistent level. Simple, good value rooms await those staying overnight.

Food serving times

Tuesday-Saturday:
12pm-2pm, 7pm-9pm

Sunday:
12pm-2pm

Prices

Meals: 14.00 (3 course lunch & dinner) and a la carte 20.00/37.50

5 rooms: 50.00/70.00

Typical Dishes

Crayfish risotto
Loin of venison
Strawberry vodka milkshake

Off the A1 at Colsterworth, 3.75 mi West on the B676. Parking.

011 The Fox and Hounds

6 Somerby Rd,
Knossington LE15 8LY
Tel.: (01664) 454676 - Fax: (01664) 454031

Greene King IPA, Marston's Pedigree and guest beer Fuller's London Pride

This lovely, ivy clad 18C former coaching inn makes an ideal refuelling stop after a visit to Rutland Water. Set in a small, pretty village, it's the very picture of a rural Leicestershire pub, with low ceilings, beams and wood tables at the front for al fresco meals. Drinkers relax on stools at the bar; diners make for one of two coir-carpeted rooms with polished wood tables and a choice of cushioned chairs or pew-style banquettes. Daily changing menus comprise good value, modern rustic dishes with local produce in much evidence. Try, perhaps, breast of chicken with chick peas, broad beans and lentils, or grilled calves liver with green beans and tapenade. Warm attentive service is a pleasant plus.

Food serving times

Tuesday-Saturday:
12pm-2.30pm, 7pm-9.30pm

Sunday:
12.30pm-2.30pm, 7pm-9pm

Booking essential

Prices

Meals: a la carte
19.95/30.00

Typical Dishes

Chicken liver parfait
Local rib of beef
Vanilla pannacotta

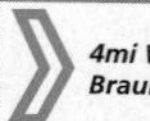

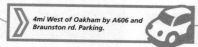

4mi West of Oakham by A606 and Braunston rd. Parking.

012 Red Lion Inn

2 Red Lion St,
Stathern LE14 4HS
Tel.: (01949) 860868 - Fax: (01949) 861579
e-mail: info@theredlioninn.co.uk - Website: www.theredlioninn.co.uk

We most liked

  VISA 

 **Fuller's London Pride, Brewester's Marquis, Exmoor Gold**

The Red Lion Inn lies at the heart of the village of Stathern and the emphasis here is firmly on food; ingredients are locally sourced, the menus change everyday according to what produce is fresh in - and a map provided on their reverse shows exactly where and from whom the ingredients for your dishes have come. Lunch might see ox tongue terrine or eggs Benedict on offer, while dinner might include pigeon breast or smoked haddock. A good value set menu is available at lunch but booking is essential whenever you wish to eat. Saturdays in the summer months mean barbeques and Pimms on the terrace; in winter, a fireside seat has to be best. Taken a liking to your chair? Chances are it's for sale, as are many of the pieces of furniture and pictures on the walls - ask a member of staff – prices are negotiable. Home made preserves are also for sale too, plus a cookbook from its sister pub, the Olive Branch at Clipsham.

Food serving times

Monday-Saturday:
12pm-2pm, 7pm-9.30pm

Sunday:
12pm-2pm

Closed 25 December (dinner) and 1 January

Booking essential

Prices

Meals: 13.50 (3 course lunch) and a la carte 25.75/32.50

Typical Dishes

Tempura tiger prawns
Chargrilled rib-eye steak
Hot chocolate fondant

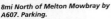

8mi North of Melton Mowbray by A607. Parking.

Thorpe Langton

013 The Bakers Arms

Main St,
Thorpe Langton LE16 7TS
Tel.: (01858) 545201 - Fax: (01858) 545924
Website: www.thebakersarms.co.uk

 **Langton Brewery - Baker's Dozen Bitter**

The Langtons are well signposted off the A6, so you should have no trouble tracking down this popular thatched inn – situated on the village's quiet main street. Inside, it's traditional décor all the way, with floral and chintz in abundance; and several comfy, softly lit seating areas and a snug help to create a warm and cosy atmosphere. The oft-changing blackboard menus offer classic dishes such as steak, kidney and ale pie, breast of duck and sausage and mash. Fish also have pride of place on the menu – and more so on Thursdays, for fish night - while all mains come with fresh vegetables and what has become the pub's trademark: dauphinoise potatoes. Cooked using fresh, carefully-sourced and seasonal ingredients, flavours are natural and clearly defined. Jan from a few doors up provides the puds, of which the dessert plate for two is a favourite. Service sometimes takes a while to warm up, but is efficient nonetheless.

Food serving times

Tuesday-Friday:
6.30pm-9.30pm

Saturday:
12pm-2.30pm, 6.30pm-9.30pm

Sunday:
12pm-2pm

Booking essential

Prices

Meals: a la carte
21.00/31.00

Typical Dishes

Pan fried scallops
Lamb chump with herb crust
Vanilla brûlée with oranges

3.75mi North of Market Harborough by A4304 via Great Bowden. Parking

014 Houghton's at the Pear Tree

8 Church Hill, Woodhouse Eaves LE12 8RT
Tel.: (01509) 890243 - Fax: (01509) 890243
e-mail: david@houghtonspeartree.co.uk
Website: www.houghtonspeartree.co.uk

VISA 

 **Pedigree, Adnams, Black Sheep, Green King IPA**

This attractive pub is named after the chef's maternal ancestors; his grandmother used to frequent it during the war and his mother was also proposed to by her second husband here, so you could say it is a building close to the family's heart. With early 19C roots, it's apparently the oldest pub in the village, but has been given a new and modern look, typified by its decked terrace and bold floral wallpaper. Chocolate brown tables and burgundy tones give the place a warm feel, and service from a team dressed in black is sleek and attentive. Despite the contemporary conversion, there's still a bar area for drinkers, and the dining room upstairs is popular with local business parties. Menus offer plenty of choice, with full-flavoured dishes ranging from bar menu classics such as burgers and spicy meatballs through to Stilton and spinach turnover or poached fillet of brill; and they even do a partridge salad in The Pear Tree.

Food serving times

Tuesday-Saturday:
12pm-3pm, 7pm-9.30pm

Sunday:
12pm-3pm

Closed 25-26 December and 1 January

Prices

Meals: 16.00 (3 course lunch/dinner) and a la carte 20.50/34.00

Typical Dishes

Roast scallops
Pan-fried duck breast
Iced praline parfait

5mi South of Loughborough by A512 West and minor road South. Parking.

015 The Blue Bell Inn

1 Main Rd,
Belchford LN9 6LQ
Tel.: (01507) 533602

Nobody really knows how old this pub is; they're even less sure about the origins of the huge blue bell that hangs outside the place. Either way, it adds a unique dimension to the pretty exterior. Run by a friendly husband and wife team (he cooks, she looks after customers), the Blue Bell's a warm and inviting place in the heart of the Wolds. Clearly, this is a dining pub, though you'll still see locals at the bar at weekends when all the fuss over lunch and dinner has died down. Comfy armchairs in front of the bar provide a relaxing place to peruse the menu: you can choose to stay where you are and eat at the bar or go through to the similarly decorated restaurant. Take your time over the blackboards – there are six in all! – and you'll find a healthy share of accomplished and adventurous modern British dishes amongst the standard pub favourites.

Food serving times

Tuesday-Saturday:
12pm-2pm, 6.30pm-9pm

Sunday:
12pm-2pm

Closed 25 December, 1 January, 2nd and 3rd weeks in January

Prices

Meals: a la carte
15.00/30.00

Typical Dishes

Goat's cheesecake
Rack of lamb
Chocolate & pecan nut brownie

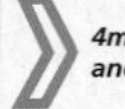

4mi North of Horncastle by A153 and righthand turn East. Parking.

016 Wig & Mitre

30-32 Steep Hill,
Lincoln LN2 1LU
Tel.: (01522) 535190 - Fax: (01522) 532402
e-mail: email@wigandmitre.com - Website: www.wigandmitre.com

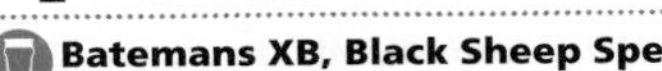
Batemans XB, Black Sheep Special

This pub stands between the castle, which is still used as a court - hence the wig - and the cathedral - hence the bishop's mitre. Open all year round and serving food all day, the owners also run the adjacent wine shop and each dish on the à la carte has a wine recommendation, with even Krug champagne being sold by the glass. Part 14C, part 16C and part 20C extension, the Wig and Mitre is certainly a unique building. Downstairs, there's a small cosy bar with scrubbed tables at the front and lounge style seating at the rear, while upstairs there's another small bar, two smaller period dining rooms, plus a light and airy beamed restaurant with pictures of old judges on the walls. The same menus are served upstairs and down and might include smoked salmon and scrambled eggs for breakfast, sandwiches and other light meals at lunch, with perhaps a caviar starter, followed by steak or duck breast in the evening.

Food serving times
Monday-Sunday:
8am-12am

Prices
Meals: 13.95 (3 course lunch) and a la carte 22.75/37.50

Typical Dishes
Baked cheese soufflé
Fillet steak
Stilton parfait with figs

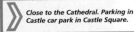

Close to the Cathedral. Parking in Castle car park in Castle Square.

Surfleet Seas End

017 The Ship Inn

154 Reservoir Rd,
Surfleet Seas End PE11 4DH
Tel.: (01775) 680547 - Fax: (01775) 680541
e-mail: info@shipinnsurfleet.com - Website: www.shipinnsurfleet.com

    MC

Adnams Bitter, Tom Woods, Pedigree, Cottage and Slaters

Despite the name of its location, The Ship's actually a dozen or so miles from the briny! Newly rebuilt, it stands on the 17C foundations of a pub once used by Irish navvies building local drains, and offers good views over the surrounding creek and Fenland. As such, this is a busy meeting place for sailors and walkers alike. The popular pubby bar on the ground floor has nautical paraphernalia; upstairs a slightly more formal restaurant boasts a wonderful balcony where you can eat and watch the boats. The menu is based around very seasonal, well-sourced local ingredients; dishes might include homemade pork and leek sausage with mash, pan fried venison steak or leek and potato pie. The bedrooms are large, comfy and up-to-date – best of all, they have long-distance views over the Fens. Join the pie club for a discount on your pie meal and a free pie on your birthday.

Food serving times

Monday-Sunday:
12pm-2pm, 7pm-9pm

Closed lunch October-April

Bar lunch

Prices

Meals: 8.95/12.00 (3 course lunch / dinner) and a la carte 15.00/25.00

4 rooms: 55.00/70.00

Typical Dishes

Ham hock and duck egg terrine

Roast fillet of beef

Sticky toffee pudding

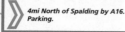

4mi North of Spalding by A16. Parking.

018 The Chequers

Main Street,
Woolsthorpe-by-Belvoir NG32 1LU
Tel.: (01476) 870701
e-mail: justinnabar@yahoo.co.uk - Website: www.chequers-inn.net

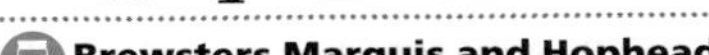
Brewsters Marquis and Hophead

The Chequers still has the feel of a village pub: locals sit supping real ale on their stools at the bar and the fixtures for matches on the adjacent cricket pitch hang by the front door, while framed menus from famous restaurants and cruise liners, and the framed Mouton Rothschild labels are a clue to the owners' passion for good food and drink. Made with locally sourced ingredients wherever possible, cooking is simple yet modern, and menus might include classics such as sausage and mash or Stilton pork pie, or for the more adventurous, dishes like clam, squid and salmon risotto or roast rabbit leg. Close to the famous castle in the Vale of Belvoir, this part-17C pub has several areas in which to dine; sit at one of the long tables in the bar or try the more intimate dining room - the cosiest seat in the house is the leather banquette next to the wood burning stove. Four bedrooms are situated next door
in the converted stable block.

Food serving times

Monday-Saturday:
12pm-2.30pm, 6pm-9.30pm

Sunday:
12pm-4pm, 6pm-8.30pm

Closed dinner 25-26 December, 1 January

Prices

Meals: 15.00 (3 course lunch and dinner) and a la carte 21.50/32.00

4 rooms: 49.00/59.00

Typical Dishes

Salt cod croquettes
Roasted rump of beef
Rice pudding and compote

7.5mi West of Grantham by A607. Parking.

The Collyweston Slater

019 The Collyweston Slater

87-89 Main Road, Collyweston PE9 3PQ
Tel.: (01780) 444288 - Fax: (01780) 444270
e-mail: info@collywestonslater.co.uk
Website: www.collywestonslater.co.uk

Everards: Slaters Ale, Tiger, Original

Refurbished in 2006, this country pub now pulls off the feat of feeling light and modern but without having lost touch with its rustic roots. Rural charm aplenty remains in the form of solid wood and slate floors, exposed beams and the numerous photos of the local area in times past which decorate the walls. You'll receive a friendly welcome from the staff, and, although you can eat in the dining area or the bar, a seat in the latter guarantees an intimate and relaxing atmosphere. Like the décor, there is also an appealing mix of the modern and traditional on offer on the menu. No nouvelle cuisine here; just wholesome manly food, such as suet pudding and game, made using fresh and locally sourced ingredients. If you need a place to lay your head, the rooms – named after English vineyards - are comfortable and elegant, and you can even put a bit of 'ooh la la' into your life with a game of boules in the authentic floodlit alley outside.

Food serving times

Monday-Saturday:
12pm-2.30pm, 6.30pm-9.30pm

Sunday:
12pm-2.30pm

Closed 25-26 December

Prices

Meals: 15.00 (3 course lunch) and a la carte 20.00/30.00

5 rooms: 60.00/100.00

Typical Dishes

Seabass fillet with salad
Braised lamb shank
Pistachio crème brûlée

3mi Southwest of Stamford by A43. Parking.

020 The Snooty Fox

16 Main St,
Lowick NN14 3BH
Tel.: (01832) 733434
e-mail: the.snooty.fox@btinternet.com - Website: www.snootyinns.com

Green King IPA, Potton Village Bike, Hopback Summer Lightning, Everards Tiger

This spacious stone built pub has everything a village pub should have: a charming village location, a garden for al fresco summertime dining; even a picket fence. The owner cooks, rustling up British favourites such as cottage pie and Scotch beef and kidney pudding, as well as drawing on more international influences, with offerings such as bresaola or garlic soup on the constantly evolving menu. The speciality here is the rotisserie and grill; meats and fish are displayed in a chilled cabinet - choose your steak and it will be cut and cooked to order. The pub runs over two levels; downstairs you'll find the main bar and restaurant, while the contemporary upstairs dining room, with its deep burgundy décor, is popular at weekends, and there's even a romantic hideaway for two with its own door tucked away on the corner. Wine is taken seriously here, and there's ample opportunity for tastings, at various wine and jazz evenings.

Food serving times

Monday-Sunday:
12pm-2pm, 6pm-9.30pm

Closed dinner 25-26 December, dinner 1 January

Set price dinner 6pm-7pm only

Prices

Meals: 14.95/12.95 (3 course lunch / early dinner) and a la carte 18.00/25.00

Typical Dishes

Warm potato shrimps
Scotch beef & kidney pudding
Hot chocolate fondant

8mi South East of Corby by A6116. Parking.

021 The Falcon Inn

Fotheringhay,
Oundle PE8 5HZ

Tel.: (01832) 226254 - Fax: (01832) 226046
e-mail: falcon@cyberware.co.uk

  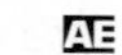  

Adnam's, Barnwell and a local including Potion, Nethergates

As you enter the village of Fotheringhay and catch a glimpse of its magnificent floodlit church, you might well be surprised at its size, until you know that this village was once an important centre – and that the now razed castle was both the birthplace of Richard III and the deathplace of Mary, Queen of Scots. Antique pictures celebrating these links hang on the walls at The Falcon Inn, and the 15C bell clappers on show further emphasise its historical credentials. You enter the stone inn through the bottle-green front door, into the bar with its open log fires; the conservatory at the rear, with its views of the church, is a popular place in which to dine. There's a freshness and light touch to the cooking here; flavours are kept clean and the kitchen uses ingredients when they're at their seasonal best. Locals tend to drink in the tiny tap bar at the back, and the adjacent cottage room is popular for private parties.

Food serving times

Monday-Saturday
12pm-2.15pm, 6.15pm-9.15pm

Sunday:
12pm-2.15pm

Prices

Meals: a la carte
12.00/35.00

Typical Dishes

Chargrilled asparagus
Pork chops stuffed with apple
Caramelised lemon tart

3.75mi North of Oundle by A427 off A605. Parking.

022 Caunton Beck

Main St,
Caunton NG23 6AB
Tel.: (01636) 636793 - Fax: (01636) 636828
e-mail: email@cauntonbeck.com

  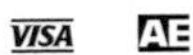  

 **Batemans Valiant, Websters Yorkshire, Marston's Pedigree**

Ducks breed on the banks of the Beck, which runs behind this pretty brick pub, and if you approach from the north, you'll make a splash through a ford on you way into the village. There's been a pub at this site for over 300 years, at one point in a state of semi-ruin, but these days, it's modern, welcoming, well-run, and popular with the locals, who enjoy sampling the cask ales. Like its sister pub, the Wig and Mitre, it opens from 8 a.m., and it's a particularly popular destination for breakfast at weekends. The menu offers mostly classic dishes; maybe steak and ale pie, lamb chop or sausage and mash, and daily specials and set menus are chalked up on a blackboard. The restaurant boasts period furniture, beamed ceilings and decorative antique cartoons, but don't dismiss a meal in the stone-floored bar, especially if you're after something lighter. In better weather, try the large front terrace with its colourful flower baskets.

Food serving times
Monday-Sunday:
8am-12am

Prices
Meals: 13.95 (3 course lunch) and a la carte 22.75/33.50

Typical Dishes
Cheese soufflé
Grilled fillet of beef
Lime and Tequila pannacotta

7mi North West of Newark by A616, 6mi past the sugar beet factory. Parking.

023 The Martins Arms

School Lane,
Colston Bassett NG12 3FD
Tel.: (01949) 81361 - Fax: (01949) 81039

   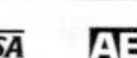 

Bass, Adnams, Black Sheep, Marston's Pedigree, Greene King IPA, Timothy Taylor's Landlord, Woodforde's Wherry

Warm, welcoming and well run, The Martins Arms has the sort of appearance and atmosphere you'd like to expect from a village pub. Its white façade wears a cloak of creepers, while inside, the traditional décor takes in copper, brass and carpet; plus several pieces of furniture rescued from the village manor house, including a fine Jacobean fireplace. If it's a cosy corner you're after, try the candlelit snug, or for more formal service and surroundings, head for the dining room. With an appealing mix of the traditional and the more modern, the menus contain something for everyone. The owner is a keen hunter, so expect some local game; other choices might range from Ploughman's with Colston Bassett Stilton on the bar menu, to duck liver and foie gras parfait on the à la carte. The large, neatly lawned garden provides a pleasant setting for al fresco dining should the sun decide to spread its love as far north as Nottinghamshire.

Food serving times

Monday-Saturday:
12pm-2pm, 7pm-9.30pm

Sunday:
12pm-2pm

Closed dinner 25-26 December

Prices

Meals: 16.95/22.95 (3 course lunch/dinner) and a la carte 30.00/45.00

Typical Dishes

Asparagus & mushroom linguini
Seared seabass, potato rösti
Mille feuilles

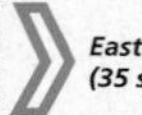

East of Cotgrave off A46. Parking (35 spaces only).

024 Waggon and Horses

The Turnpike, Mansfield Rd, Halam NG22 8AE
Tel.: (01636) 813109 - Fax: (01636) 816228
e-mail: info@thewaggonathalam.co.uk
Website: www.thewaggonathalam.co.uk

 **Thwaites Lancaster Bomber, Thwaites Original, Thwaites Smooth, Wainwrights**

A blooming marvellous display of flowers in various boxes and hanging baskets greets the eye on arrival at this village pub. Inside, it's small and cosy with wooden floors and beams, chunky furniture and an extensive display of cricket prints and memorabilia. The laminated lunch menu isn't in danger of winning any prizes for innovation this side of Christmas, but the specials board offered alongside creates more interest, while the daily-changing set three course menu represents good value for money. Wait until evening and you'll find more substantial dishes from which to choose; perhaps some sautéed calves liver, local partridge and rabbit terrine or slow roast lamb shank. Originally a local boy, chef-owner Roy Wood likes to keep the emphasis on regional produce, so meat is from Derbyshire, fruit and vegetables come from nearby farms and the bread from the local bakery. Wizzard.

Food serving times

Monday-Saturday:
11.30pm-2.30pm, 5.30pm-9.30pm

Sunday:
11.30pm-2.30pm

Closed 25-26 December and 1 January

Prices

Meals: 15.00 (3 course lunch and dinner) and a la carte 20.00/30.00

Typical Dishes

Pan fried red mullet
Slow cooked blade of beef
Warm chocolate and pecan tart

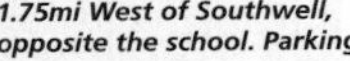
1.75mi West of Southwell, opposite the school. Parking.

025 Cock and Hoop

25 High Pavement, Nottingham NG1 1HE
Tel.: (0115) 852 3231 - Fax: (0115) 852 3223
e-mail: cockandhoop@lacemarkethotel.co.uk
Website: www.cockandhoop.co.uk

  MC

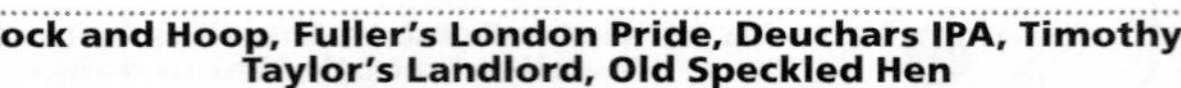
Cock and Hoop, Fuller's London Pride, Deuchars IPA, Timothy Taylor's Landlord, Old Speckled Hen

Known by many names over the last two centuries, the Cock and Hoop has at last come full circle. The cobbled streets of the redeveloped Lace Market have had a change in fortune too, and the refurbished pub fits in well: an old-fashioned front of mullioned windows and brick-and-timber between two dignified 18C neighbours. Inside is a clutch of tables by a brass-edged bar and, downstairs, a much larger lounge and dining area, panelled in pale modern wood. The familiar modern British cuisine works in a few daily variations, but the core of the menu is tasty and substantial cooking in fair quantity – it's the kind of place where you can have one or two courses and feel well satisfied. Pleasantly chatty staff, all in black, keep the place running smoothly.

Food serving times

Monday-Sunday:
12pm-10pm

Closed 25 December

Prices

Meals: a la carte
20.00/30.00

Typical Dishes

Duck and mushroom risotto
Braised lamb shank
Sticky toffee pudding

Adjacent to Lace Market Hotel. Fletchergate car park and free on-street parking in offpeak hours..

026 **Exeter Arms**

28 Main St,
Barrowden LE15 8EQ
Tel.: (01572) 747247 - Fax: (01572) 747247
e-mail: info@exeterarms.com - Website: www.exeterarms.com

VISA MC

Beach Boys, Bevin Boys, Hopgear, Winterhop, Attitude

Handily placed just off the A47, this family run pub exudes much of the rural charm associated with the area close to Rutland Water. It's a 17C inn of light stone idyllically rooted in a sleepy village overlooking the green with its little pond and duck house. Inside is warm and welcoming: the yellow painted walls see to that. Beers here are a must. They come from the pub's own micro-brewery housed in an old rear barn, and you can't sup them anywhere else in the country. If you're eating you can choose a seat wherever takes your fancy, be it the stone-walled dining room or the bar with its cosy open fire. Either way, you won't forget where you are, as old photos of the pub crop up on all walls. You'll remember this hostelry, too, for its well-executed cuisine, classic dishes given an updated, international twist, with Asian influences inspiringly conspicuous. Three neat and tidy bedrooms offer pleasant country views.

Food serving times

Monday:
7pm-9pm

Tuesday-Saturday:
12pm-2pm, 7pm-9pm

Sunday:
12pm-2.30pm, 7pm-9pm

Prices

Meals: a la carte
20.65/29.45

3 rooms: 37.50/75.00

Typical Dishes

Sautéed foie gras
Braised wild rabbit
Honey pannacotta

11mi South West of Oakham by A6003 and A47. Parking.

027 The Olive Branch & Beech House

Main St, Clipsham LE15 7SH

Tel.: (01780) 410355 - Fax: (01780) 410000

e-mail: info@theolivebranchpub.com

Website: www.theolivebranchpub.com

 **Grainstore 1050, Batemans XB**

Locals are to be found at the bar of our 2008 Pub of the Year sampling the real ales and soaking up the friendly atmosphere, while the shelves full of cookery books above the church pew seating will also give any newcomers a clue to the pub's gastronomic bent. Their provenance detailed on the menu, dishes might include cottage pie, langoustine ravioli or venison casserole; the kitchen here confident enough to keep things simple and let the quality ingredients speak for themselves. Don't leave without dessert; they are a speciality and definitely worth leaving room for. Six bedrooms in the delightful building across the road have equally delicious-sounding names and every extra has been thought of from homemade biscuits to a DVD player, magazines and books. Breakfast by the fire is also a treat, with freshly squeezed orange juice, and homemade everything, including the fruit compotes and the brown sauce.

Food serving times

Monday-Saturday:
12pm-2pm, 7pm-9.30pm

Sunday: 12pm-3pm, 7pm-9pm

Closed 25 (dinner), 26, 31 (lunch) December, 1 January

Booking essential

Prices

Meals: 18.50 (set price lunch) and a la carte 21.50/33.85

6 rooms: 75.00/150.00

Typical Dishes

Artichoke & beetroot risotto

Roast Herdwick lamb

Bramley apple crumble

9.5mi Northwest of Stamford by B1081 off A1. Parking.

028 Finch's Arms

Ketton Rd,
Hambleton LE15 8TL
Tel.: (01572) 756575 - Fax: (01572) 771142
e-mail: finchsarms@talk21.com - Website: www.finchsarms.co.uk

  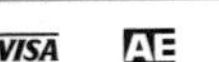

Bass, Timothy Taylor's Landlord, Greene King, Abbot Ale,

With its bird's eye view of Rutland Water, this country pub is a Mecca to ornithologists and oenophiles alike. Its front is prettily framed by trees, but it's the rear terrace and garden which cause people to flock here whenever the temperature rises slightly above lukewarm. Whatever the weather, the staff maintain a sunny outlook, and there's always plenty of them around, pleased to help. The emphasis here is on seasonal, locally sourced and traceable produce, with traditional, frill-free yet flavourful dishes created using a minimal number of ingredients. Drinkers are made to feel as welcome as diners and tend to congregate in the traditional beamed bar. The garden room with its bold wallpaper and fresh flowers is more contemporary in style and has a distinctly Mediterranean feel. Six bedrooms blend French country décor with the more modern; several have stunning views over the water and one has its own balcony.

Food serving times

Monday-Sunday:
12pm-2.30pm, 7pm-9.30pm

Closed 25 December

Prices

Meals: 13.95/15.95 (3 course lunch/dinner) and a la carte 13.95/20.00

6 rooms: 65.00/75.00

Typical Dishes

Pan-fried crayfish
Pan-fried Seabass
Lemon tart

3mi East of Oakham by A606.
Parking.

029 Old White Hart

51 Main Street,
Lyddington LE15 9LR

Tel.: (01572) 821703 - Fax: (01572) 821965

e-mail: mail@oldwhitehart.co.uk - Website: www.oldwhitehart.co.uk

 **Greene King IPA, Greene King Abbot, Fuller's London Pride**

A warm welcome awaits at the 17C Old White Hart and from the moment you step inside this country pub, with its low beams, stone walls and open fires, it's a cosy feel that envelops you. The owners are well-established and their friendly team are always around but never obtrusive. The chef-owner used to be a butcher, so you know the meat will have been carefully sourced, and whole beasts are delivered to the kitchen. Sausages are homemade and fish are also well-represented on the blackboard menu. Cooking here is classic in style but with a French slant so rump steak and grilled loin of pork share space on the menu with dishes like seared foie gras with homemade brioche. What may look like a random collection of the usual pub paraphernalia actually has deeper meaning to the owners, staff and regulars; like the pipe collection donated by a regular after he'd kicked the habit, and the dragon from a local boat race won by the staff.

Food serving times

Monday-Saturday:
12pm-2pm, 6.30pm-9pm

Closed 25 December

Closed dinner September-April

Prices

Meals: 12.95 (3 course lunch & dinner) and a la carte 20.50/33.50

6 rooms: 60.00/90.00

Typical Dishes

Roast oak-smoked salmon

Rack of lamb

Hot sticky toffee pudding

1.5mi south of Uppingham off A6003. By the village green. Parking.

030 The Jackson Stops Inn

Rookery Lane,
Stretton LE15 7RA
Tel.: (01780) 410237

   VISA

 **Greene King IPA, Abbot, Adnam's Bitter, Adnam's Broadside, Marston's Pedigree**

Cosy, intimate rooms with exposed brickwork, low ceilings and beams make this thatched, 17C inn a great place to dine on a date – get all hot under the collar in the inglenook room with its large fireplace, or snuggle up in the bakery room where the original oven is still in the wall. For the romantically disinclined, the white room at the other end of the building, with its small bar counter and decorative farm implements, might be more suitable. You can dine in all areas, and the choice ranges from a good value two-course set lunch menu to a more elaborate evening à la carte, plus a full English or baguettes for Sunday brunch. Evenings and weekends can get especially busy, so it's best to book ahead. And if you're wondering about the name; it's not some obscure reference to Michael, but because way back in 1955, the Jackson Stops estate agency left their sign outside for so long that the pub itself became known as the Jackson Stops.

Food serving times

Tuesday-Saturday:
12pm-2pm, 6.30pm-9pm

Sunday:
12pm-2pm

Closed 1st week in January

Prices

Meals: 10.00 (2 course lunch) and a la carte 30.00/50.00

Typical Dishes

Crab mayo lettuce rolls

Fillet steak

Vanilla, apricot crème brûlée

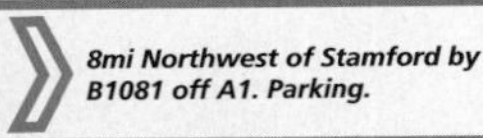

8mi Northwest of Stamford by B1081 off A1. Parking.

With culinary tastes ranging from fresh samphire-shoots to cockles, smoked eel and Cromer crab, it's easy to get a flavour of the East of England. It's a region with strong brewing traditions and some of England's most charming pubs, but it's also a place of rich historic roots and a deep attachment to rural life. Here you'll find the medieval wool towns of Lavenham, Coggeshall and Saffron Walden and the old trading centres of Norwich and King's Lynn, Ely's distant tower and the Palladian splendour of Holkham Hall. Be part of the world-famous Aldeburgh music festival or the first Classics of the racing season at Newmarket; cast off into the waterways of the Norfolk Broads or lie back in a punt and drift down the Cam past the beautiful Cambridge colleges. Stroll through the fields of a lavender farm or strike out into the wilds, under the great open sky of the coast and the salt marshes, and spot basking seals, a flight of curlew or the rare wildlife of the broadland meadows. Wherever you go exploring, it's bound to be an inspiration. "They made me a painter and I am grateful", Constable once said of the walks along the Stour near his boyhood home. We can't guarantee the same for everyone, but you'll certainly work up an appetite along the way…

East Midlands
South East
London
Boston
Grantham
Peterborough
Huntingdon
Cambridge
Bedford
Luton
Stevenage
Hertford
Harlow
Chelmsford
Brentwood
Basildon
Watford
Northampton
Leicester
Kettering
Wellingborough
Milton Keynes
Aylesbury
High Wycombe
Stamford
Spalding
Wisbech
Ely
St. Neots
Biggleswade
Hitchin
Harpenden
Hemel Hempstead
Dunstable
Slough
Windsor
Reading
Maidenhead
Kingston
Croydon
Dartford
Tilbury
Gravesend
Rochester
Bishop's Stortford
Saffron Walden
Haverhill
The Wash
Hunstanton
Holbeach
Long Sutton
Melton Mowbray
Oakham
Corby
Oundle
Market Harborough
Rushden
Ampthill
Shefford
Royston
Buntingford
Stansted
Ware
Hatfield
Cheshunt
Epping
Billericay
Dagenham
Heathrow
Richmond
Staines
Esher
Sutton
Orpington
Epsom
Woking
Farnborough
Aldershot
Camberley
Bracknell
Wokingham
Tring
Berkhamsted
Amersham
Beaconsfield
Marlow
Potters Bar
Hoddesdon
Sawbridgeworth
Welwyn Garden City
Newport Pagnell
Bletchley
Woburn
Leighton Buzzard
Sandy
Potton
Eltisley
Godmanchester
St Ives
Ramsey
Chatteris
March
Whittlesey
Littleport
Soham
Downham Market
Crowland
Bourne
Donington
Sutterton
Guyhirn
Outwell
Thrapston
Higham Ferrers
Desborough
Rothwell
Weldon
Uppingham
Oadby
Husbands Bosworth
Bingham
West Bridgford
Swanley
Grays Thurrock
Benfleet
Great Dunmow
Finchingfield
Puckeridge
Baldock
Letchworth
Linslade
Buckingham
Henley-on-Thames
Rutland
Northampton
Bedford
Cambridge
Hertford
Buckingham
Surrey
England
Essex

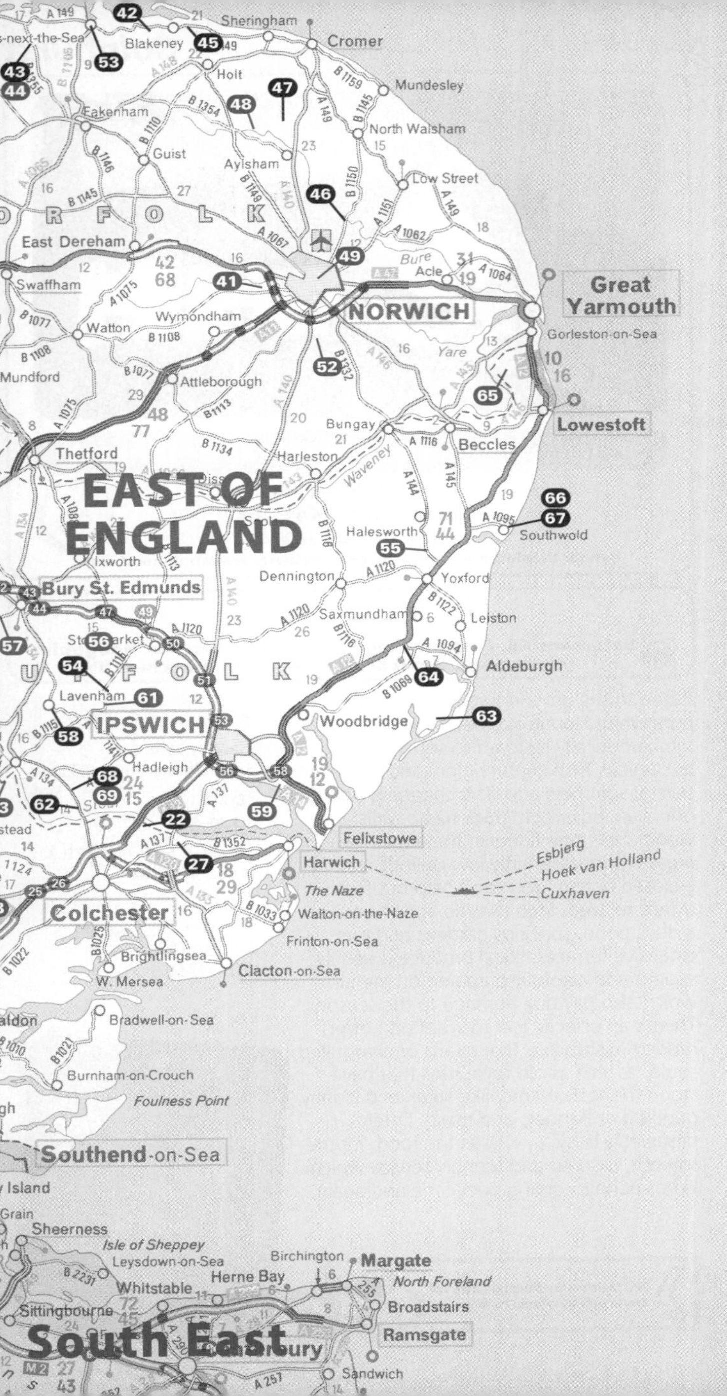
EAST OF ENGLAND
SOUTH EAST
NORFOLK
SUFFOLK
Sheringham
Cromer
Blakeney
Holt
Mundesley
North Walsham
Fakenham
Guist
Aylsham
Low Street
East Dereham
Swaffham
Acle
Great Yarmouth
NORWICH
Gorleston-on-Sea
Wymondham
Watton
Mundford
Attleborough
Bungay
Beccles
Lowestoft
Thetford
Harleston
Halesworth
Southwold
Ixworth
Bury St. Edmunds
Dennington
Yoxford
Saxmundham
Leiston
Aldeburgh
Lavenham
IPSWICH
Woodbridge
Hadleigh
Felixstowe
Harwich
Esbjerg
Hoek van Holland
Cuxhaven
The Naze
Colchester
Walton-on-the-Naze
Frinton-on-Sea
Brightlingsea
Clacton-on-Sea
W. Mersea
Bradwell-on-Sea
Burnham-on-Crouch
Foulness Point
Southend-on-Sea
Grain
Sheerness
Isle of Sheppey
Leysdown-on-Sea
Birchington
Margate
North Foreland
Herne Bay
Whitstable
Broadstairs
Sittingbourne
Ramsgate
Sandwich

001 The Plough at Bolnhurst

Kimbolton Rd,
Bolnhurst MK44 2EX
Tel.: 01234 376274
e-mail: theplough@bolnhurst.com - Website: www.bolnhurst.com

We most liked

    MC

Batemans XB, Potton Village Bike and 1 guest ale: Hobgoblin, Wychwood, Great Scot, Caledonian, Deuchars IPA

Razed to the ground two decades ago, the pure white Plough has been lovingly and sympathetically restored to something like its original 14th century glory and reopened several summers ago. The charming interior offers an inglenook, thick rustic walls and wood and stone floors in three main seating areas with reassuringly low ceilings and exposed beams. You can't help but feel utterly relaxed. Step outside and there's a duck pond, spacious gardens and two extensive terraces. Local produce is keenly sought and carefully prepared on menus which also pay due homage to the seasons. There's an eclectic feel to what's on offer: modern dishes like Thai salads or chargrilled squid, as well as old favourites that have stood the test of time, like steak and kidney pudding or bangers and mash. Often deservedly busy, as well as the food, it's the smooth, assured and friendly service which keeps people coming back time and again.

Food serving times

Tuesday-Saturday:
12pm-2pm, 6.30pm-9.30pm

Sunday:
12pm-2pm

Closed at New Year, first 2 weeks in January

Prices

Meals: 16.00 (3 course lunch) and a la carte 25.00/37.00

Typical Dishes

Yellow split pea broth
Char-grilled calves liver
Lemon tart

7mi North of Bedford by B660, on South side of village. Parking.

002 Knife and Cleaver

The Grove,
Houghton Conquest MK45 3LA
Tel.: (01234) 740387 - Fax: (01234) 740900
e-mail: info@knifeandcleaver.com - Website: www.knifeandcleaver.com

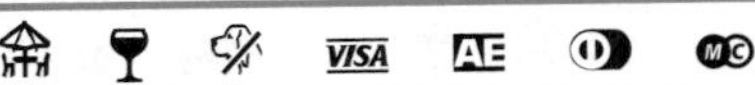

Batemans XB, Potton Village Bike

Personally and warmly run by long-established owners, the unusual-looking 17C Knife and Cleaver is a cut above the norm and great place to come for a meal. Situated opposite the medieval All Saints Church, it has a snug bar complete with squishy sofas and Jacobean oak panelling reputedly from nearby Houghton House, a small former darts room with a few tables at which you can munch on lighter snacks, plus a spacious, more formal conservatory overlooking the pretty rear garden. Seasonal, daily-changing menus present a wide selection of appealing dishes, with the emphasis firmly on fresh fish. Whole lobsters come flavoured according to this week's serving suggestion; you can indulge in a seafood platter, a classic Dover sole or sea bass fillet, and there are several meat and vegetarian options too. The converted stables house nine homely bedrooms, while the reasonable prices ensure that staying overnight won't break the bank.

Food serving times

Monday-Friday and Sunday: 12pm-2.30pm, 7pm-9.30pm

Saturday: 12pm-2.30pm (bar meals only), 7pm-9.30pm

Closed 27-30 December

Set price dinner Monday-Friday only; a la carte menu Monday-Saturday only

Prices

Meals: 16.95/24.00 (3 course lunch/dinner) and a la carte 21.15/37.40

9 rooms: 59.00/84.00

Typical Dishes

Rabbit and vegetable terrine

Tempura seabass fillets

Baked cheesecake

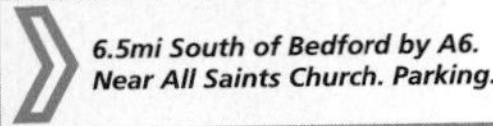

6.5mi South of Bedford by A6. Near All Saints Church. Parking.

003 The Red Lion

Toddington Rd, Milton Bryan MK17 9HS
Tel.: (01525) 210044
e-mail: paul@redlion-miltonbryan.co.uk
Website: www.redlion-miltonbryan.co.uk

Greene King IPA, Abbot Ale, Old Speckled Hen and 1 guest ale in summer

The Red Lion is not the sort of place you come across by chance, and even when you're looking for it, it can be difficult to find. But the search is worth it - and getting lost in and around Woburn or in the surrounding country lanes is no hardship either. Lunch can be eaten in the bar, with its country-style seating and stone floors, or in the larger restaurant area, and both the lunch and dinner menus contain lots of choice. All the old favourites are here; hearty and wholesome dishes such as lasagne, steak and chips and sausage and mash, plus popular puddings like spotted dick and sticky toffee pudding, all freshly prepared, and well-presented, with sandwiches and daily-changing fish specials also available at lunch. Hanging baskets bring a blaze of colour to the outside of this charming red-brick pub in summer, and on a hot day, it's a delight to eat to the sound of birdsong on the patio terrace or in the garden.

Food serving times

Monday-Saturday:
12pm-2.30pm, 7pm-9.30pm

Sunday:
12pm-2.30pm

Closed 25-26 December and 1 January

Closed Monday in winter

Prices

Meals: a la carte
17.95/30.00

Typical Dishes

Grilled Queen scallops
Chargrilled fillet steak
Toffee peach meringue

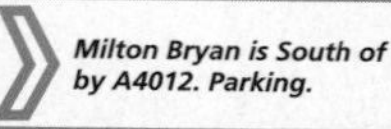
Milton Bryan is South of Woburn by A4012. Parking.

004 Hare & Hounds

The Village, Old Warden SG18 9HQ
Tel.: (01767) 627225 - Fax: (01767) 627588
e-mail: thehareandhounds@hotmail.co.uk
Website: www.hareandhoundsoldwarden.co.uk

   VISA 

Charles Wells Bombardier, Eagle IPA, Youngs

One of the highlights of this picture postcard village on the Shuttleworth estate, the Hare and Hounds has immense charm and style. Lounge in front of a blazing open fire in one of the squashy, leather seats in the bar, or laze the day away outside in the mature garden – you're welcome here for anything from a drink to a three course meal, but if you do pop in for a pint, you may well find yourself tempted to stay for food. The British menu has been compiled with care and understanding, and provides a good range of options to suit all tastes. Where possible, ingredients have been sourced locally and dishes change regularly to reflect what's fresh and in season. Choices might include Shuttleworth belly of pork, lemon sole or braised wild rabbit, and the chef even produces his own homemade range of goods including oils, chutneys and preserves. Service is attentive, and the atmosphere warm and friendly.

Food serving times

Tuesday-Saturday:
12pm-2pm, 6.30pm-9.30pm

Sunday:
12pm-3pm

Closed 26 December, 1 January, Monday except Bank Holiday Monday

Closed meals 25 December; closed dinner 31 December

Prices

Meals: a la carte
22.00/30.00

Typical Dishes

Rabbit & pistachio ravioli
Braised lamb shank
Bakewell tart

3.5mi West of Biggleswade by A6001 off B658. Parking and at Village Hall.

East of England • Bedfordshire

005 The Black Horse

Ireland,
Shefford SG17 5QL
Tel.: (01462) 811398 - Fax: (01462) 817238
Website: www.blackhorseireland.com

Greene King IPA, Fuller's London Pride, Village Bike - Potton Brewery

Situated in Ireland, - Ireland in Bedfordshire, not the Emerald Isle - The Black Horse is a traditional 17C village inn, boasting original feature fireplaces, polished wooden tables and comfy banquettes. The smart country style is in evidence in the beamed bar through to the adjacent dining area and the rear extension, while the attractive gardens have bench seating and a patio for use in good weather. When it comes to the food, plan ahead, since it's likely you'll only need two courses and you might not want to miss out on dessert. The seasonally-changing menus have a hearty base, with local suppliers very much in evidence, so dishes might include Bedfordshire pork and ale sausages or 31 day hung rib eye steak from the griddle. Fish often feature, and more unusual offerings might mean tucking into creole chicken, salmon and cod saltimbocca or lime leaves, aduki and borlotti croquettes.Two simple bedrooms are accessed from the garden.

Food serving times

Monday-Saturday:
12pm-2.30pm, 6.30pm-10pm

Sunday:
12pm-6pm

Closed 25-26 December and 1 January

Prices

Meals: 19.95/25.95 (3 course lunch/dinner) and a la carte 19.95/29.95

2 rooms: 55.00

Typical Dishes

Roast belly pork
Cornish lamb's liver
Coconut & lime pannacotta

1.75mi Northwest of Shefford by B658 and Ireland Rd. Parking.

006 The French Horn

Church End,
Steppingley MK45 5AU
Tel.: (01525) 712051 - Fax: (01717) 334305
e-mail: manager@thefrenchhorn.com - Website: www.thefrenchhorn.com

 **IPA and guest ale**

The pretty hamlet of Steppingley boasts this late 18th century pub that features a beautiful period restaurant from the 1950s that's metamorphosed via a super makeover. Original character remains in the front bar, where flag flooring and rustic beams are the order of the day. But it's the main dining room that's taken the regulars by pleasant surprise. There are stylish dark leather chairs, dark varnished solid wood tables, bright, modern oil paintings and contemporary lighting. The food is very well regarded. Menus change seasonally and skilfully combine a classic base with the chef's individual flair. Presentation is strong and flavours intense, raising the standard to above the pub norm. To build up a hunger before your visit, take a leisurely stroll through the glories of nearby Woburn Park.

Food serving times

Monday-Sunday:
12pm-2.30pm, 6pm-10pm

Booking essential

Prices

Meals: a la carte
30.00/50.00

Typical Dishes

Mille feuille of Cromer crab
Fillet of Welsh lamb
Poire Belle Hélène

4.5 miles from Woburn through The Park. Between junctions 12 and 13 of M1. Parking.

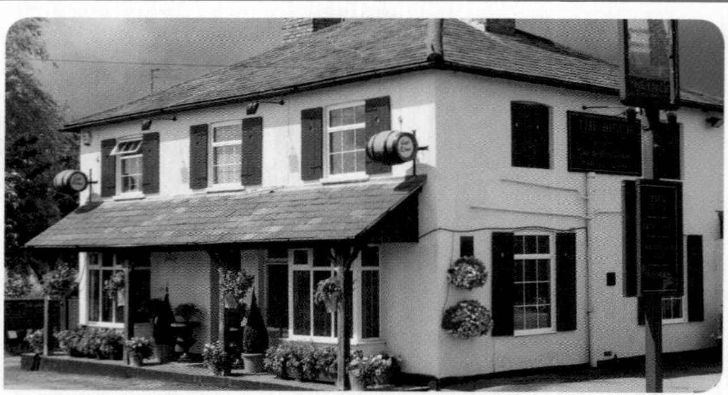

007 The Birch

20 Newport Rd,
Woburn MK17 9HX

Tel.: (01525) 290295 - Fax: (01525) 290899

e-mail: etaverns@aol.com - Website: www.birchwoburn.com

We most liked

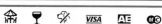

Fuller's London Pride, Adnams

If you've spent the day playing golf, exploring the Abbey, or having your wing mirrors stolen by the monkeys at the safari park, you'll probably be in need of refreshment come dinner time. Plenty of others will have had the same idea, however, so it would be wise to book ahead if you want a table at The Birch. It's a well-run establishment - and needs to be given the numbers it attracts – but you get the feeling the staff know exactly what they are doing. The small bar serves a decent selection of real ales and you can sit up high here on a stool or lie low on one of the cosy sofas. The main dining room contains well-spaced wooden tables, and the large conservatory is split onto two levels, with Tim Bulmer sketches on the walls. The extensive menu has a dish to suit every taste and appetite, but it is the grill which really impresses, serving fresh meat and fish ordered by the ounce and cooked to your idea of perfection.

Food serving times

Monday-Saturday:
12pm-2.30pm, 6.30pm-10pm

Sunday:
12pm-5pm

Closed 25-26 December and 1 January

Booking essential

Prices

Meals: a la carte
19.95/27.50

Typical Dishes

Portabella mushroom with brie

Lamb noisettes

Lemon crème brûlée

0.5mi North on A5130. Parking.

008 The Crown

Bridge Rd, Broughton PE28 3AY
Tel.: (01487) 824428 - Fax: (01487) 824912
e-mail: simon@thecrownbrougton.co.uk
Website: www.thecrownbroughton.co.uk

Greene King IPA, City of Cambridge Hobson's Choice, Elgood's Black Dog, Potton Shambles

It's not often that you find a pub which is actually owned by the village, but this is one such establishment; bought by forty-four of its inhabitants in order to stop their local from becoming a private house. In every other respect, though, this is a typical English pub; stood next to a typical village church in a typical pretty country village – the word 'typical' here carrying all its positive connotations, naturally. Not surprisingly, there's a real community feel amongst the locals in the bar, but visitors are also made to feel most welcome – a good thing, too, since its reputation continues to spread. Inside, it's rustic country-style throughout, with chunky wood tables, an open fire and a snug, cottagey feel. The seasonally-changing menu has a hearty, British base, with the odd Mediterranean and Asian touches and dishes make vibrant use of local ingredients. Events in the warmer months include hog roasts and live music.

Food serving times

Tuesday:
6.30pm-9pm

Wednesday-Saturday:
12pm-2pm, 6.30pm-9pm

Sunday:
12pm-2pm

Closed 1st week in January

Prices

Meals: 14.50 (3 course lunch) and a la carte 20.00/28.00

Typical Dishes

Irish black pudding
Confit Gressingham duck
Carrot cake

6mi Northeast of Huntingdon by B1514 off A141. Opposite the village church. Parking.

009 The Crown Inn

8 Duck St,
Elton PE8 6RQ
Tel.: (01832) 280232
e-mail: marcus@marcuslamb4.wanadoo.co.uk

Golden Crown Bitter, Greene King IPA and many guest ales (3 at a time)

Situated in a honey pot village overlooking the village green, the Crown could hardly nestle in a finer, more rewarding spot. This is a charming 17C thatched mellow stone inn: try and grab yourself a place at the small seven-tabled front terrace. It's an enviable place to sit and sup. Super keen owners add a friendly and cordial tone to the place: Mr Lamb is meticulous about his beers, and serves a wide range from all over the UK, not just Cambridgeshire. You can sample them in a beamed and thoroughly engaging bar boasting a feature log fire, or in the spacious rear conservatory. Daily-changing blackboard menus offer an interesting mix, including fresh seafood, underpinned by a strong traditional base. Printed menus at dinner highlight how seriously food is taken here – cooking is strong, tasty and fresh and might include steak and ale pie or a plate of locally reared lamb. Eagerly awaited bedrooms nearing completion.

Food serving times

Tuesday-Saturday:
12pm-2.15pm, 6.30pm-8.45pm

Sunday:
12pm-2.15pm

Closed 25 December, 2 weeks January

Booking essential for dinner

Prices

Meals: a la carte 13.00/25.00

Typical Dishes

Seafood and saffron broth
Cumberland sausages
Dark chocolate tart

6mi Southwest of Peterborough by A1139, A605 and minor road North. Parking and on village green opposite.

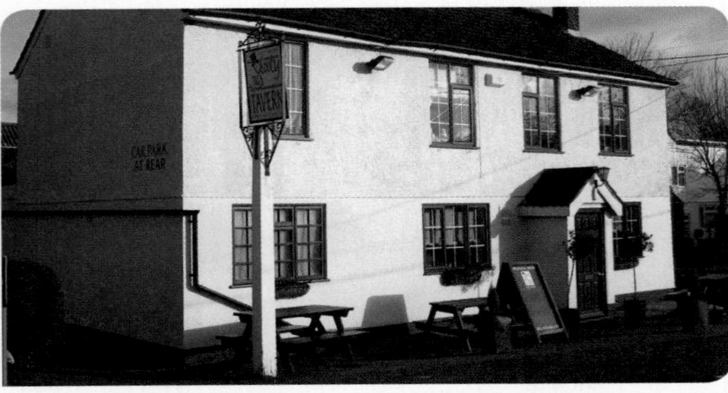

010 The Snooty Tavern

12 The Green,
Great Staughton PE19 5DG
Tel.: (01480) 860336
e-mail: snootytavern@btconnect.com - Website: www.snootyinns.co.uk

 **Timothy Taylor's Landlord, Village Bike, Fuller's London Pride, Elgoods Cambridge**

What used to be the Tavern on the Green has now gone all Snooty on us. Thankfully this snootiness doesn't refer to the customers who frequent this pub or the service therein; in fact the only thing they're particularly snooty about here is the quality of food they serve.Cuts of meat are on display in a chilled, glass-fronted cabinet, ready to be cut to the size you want, menus change daily and cooking has a strong seasonal base. The lunch menu offers sandwiches and a traditional 'pub grub' section, including dishes such as steak and chips or sausage and mash. The simple dinner menu is good value and might include dishes such as duck breast or pot roasted pork collar. Relax by the fire in the open main bar – the leather seats are the best - or at one of the solid dark wood tables in the more formal rear dining room. The ample rear garden has an intimate feel and is perfect for al fresco dining in summer.

Food serving times

Monday-Sunday:
12pm-2pm, 6pm-9.30pm

Closed dinner 25-26 December, dinner 1 January

Prices

Meals: 12.00/15.00 (3 course lunch/dinner) and a la carte 16.00/24.00

Typical Dishes

Carpaccio of Highland beef

Pork belly with clams

Chocolate caramel brownie

On A45 northwest of St Neots. Parking.

Hemingford Grey

011 The Cock

47 High St,
Hemingford Grey PE28 9BJ
Tel.: (01480) 463609 - Fax: (01480) 461747
e-mail: cock@cambscuisine.com - Website: www.cambscuisine.com

We most liked

Earl Soham Victoria Bitter, Woodforde's Wherry and guest ales: Milton, Wolf, Potbelly, Nethergate, England

The Cock cocks a snook at most other Huntingdon hostelries and is the place to come if you are after a relaxing meal in a country pub. Centrally located, this busy 17C pub serves local ales and has kept the feel of the village local, with a split-level bar specifically for drinkers on one side, and a spacious, L-shaped dining room on the other. Rustic in feel, it has polished wood floors and an open fire, and is brightened by oil paintings – available to take home with you for the right price. The menus provide plenty of choice, from a 2 course lunch menu to a full à la carte and daily-changing fish specials. Dishes range from Jerusalem artichoke and truffle risotto to sirloin steak, but the best choice would have to come from the sausage board; a kind of mix and match between differently flavoured homemade sausages and a similarly diverse choice of mashed potato and sauces.

Food serving times

Monday-Thursday:
12pm-2.30pm, 6.30pm-9pm

Friday-Saturday:
12pm-2.30pm, 6.30pm-9.30pm

Sunday:
12pm-2.30pm, 6.30pm-8.30pm

Prices

Meals: 12.95 (3 course lunch) and a la carte 20.00/35.00

Typical Dishes

Duck parcel
Roast lamb chump
Plum and almond tart

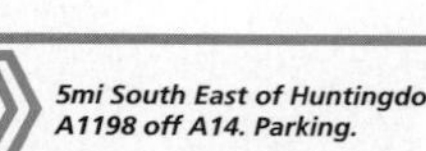

5mi South East of Huntingdon by A1198 off A14. Parking.

012 Crown and Punchbowl

High St,
Horningsea CB25 9JG
Tel.: (01223) 860643 - Fax: (01223) 441814
e-mail: info@the crownandpunchbowl.co.uk

 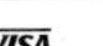  MC

 **City of Cambridge Brewery**

You won't find locals passing the time of day with a pint at the bar in the Crown and Punchbowl. Not because the locals don't patronize the place, but because there is no bar here - which makes it a weird kind of pub, if you think about it. What it does have is plenty of snug pubby charm, with rustic walls, wooden floors, open fires - and beamed ceilings low enough to present a danger to anyone over 5ft 5". Located next to a pretty church and graveyard, the pub is actually a blend of two buildings; one dating from the 17C, the other from the 19C, and inside, there are two main dining areas as well as a small private dining room for parties. Food is local, seasonal and appealing, with choices like steak and chips and confit duck leg on the à la carte, supplemented by fish specials and mix and match homemade sausage and mash, which are chalked up on blackboards. Five modern, spacious and relaxing bedrooms complete the picture.

Food serving times

Monday-Saturday:
12pm-2.30pm, 6.30pm-9.30pm

Sunday:
12pm-2.30pm

Prices

Meals: a la carte
12.95/35.00

5 rooms: 69.95/89.95

Typical Dishes

Asparagus in Parma ham
Confit duck leg
Rhubarb and ginger mousse

4mi Northeast of Cambridge by A1303 and B1047 on Horningsea rd. Parking.

013 The Pheasant

Village Loop Road,
Keyston PE28 0RE
Tel.: (01832) 710241
e-mail: thepheasant@cyberware.co.uk

Adnams Best and 2 guest ales

Hidden away in the sleepy hamlet of Keyston, this charming thatched inn is well worth searching out for a dining experience that reaches way above your average. Run by a husband and wife team; while he's cooking up dishes of distinction in the kitchen, she's heading the efficient, friendly team of servers out front. The building's full of character too: cosy up on the sofa by the fire in the timbered bar, or sit more formally in the dining room with its hunting print walls. The best seat in the house in the summer season would have to be in the delightful rear garden. The menus provide a huge choice of value for money dishes; these change on a weekly basis and are made with seasonal, local ingredients. A glossary of terms is provided for those who don't know their bresaola from their baba ganoush or their gremolata from their gnocchi, and the food is complemented by an excellent selection of wines by the glass.

Food serving times

Sunday-Friday:
12pm-2pm, 6.30pm-9.30pm

Saturday:
12-2pm, 6.30pm-8.30pm

Booking essential

Prices

Meals: 15.95 (set price lunch) and a la carte 20.00/33.00

Typical Dishes

Razor clams
Roast guinea fowl
Treacle tart

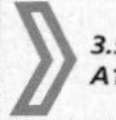

3.5mi Southeast of Thrapstone by A14 on B663. Parking.

014 The Hole in the Wall

2 High St,
Little Wilbraham CB21 5JY
Tel.: (01223) 812282
Website: www.the-holeinthewall.com

 Woodforde's Wherry, Nelson's Revenge, Elgood's Cambridge Bitter

This extended cottage is situated on a country road at the edge of a pretty village. The pub's nomenclature is of pleasing origin: when the ale house was first built in the 15th century, the local farm workers would pass their empty jugs through a hole in the wall on their way to work. These were then filled during the day and left in the hole for the workers to collect on their way home. The firmly traditional timbered qualities of 'The Hole' have rightly been left alone, with modernisation principally taking place where many might say is most important: in the kitchen. There's a small bar, two dining rooms in rustic style with exposed beams and, since there's no central heating, it's warmed solely by real fires. It's all about British food here; classically cooked using traceable, seasonal ingredients, the interesting and well-priced modern menu offering dishes such as local mackerel or 12 hour beef brisket with oxtail mash.

Food serving times

Tuesday-Saturday:
12pm-2pm, 7pm-9pm

Sunday and Bank Holiday Monday:
12pm-2pm

Closed 25 December, dinner 26 December, 2 weeks in January

Prices

Meals: a la carte
19.50/25.75

Typical Dishes

Warm ham hock salad
Sirloin steak with chips
Treacle tart

5mi East of Cambridge by A1303 and minor road South. Parking.

015 The Three Horseshoes

High St,
Madingley CB4 8SA
Tel.: (01954) 210221 - Fax: (01954) 212043

Adnams Bitter, Cambridge Boathouse, Timothy Taylor's Landlord

Swap the bustle of Cambridge City centre for the tranquillity of Madingley for a few hours and you'll not want to go back. Just a few miles out of town, this delightful thatched inn makes a picturesque location for lunch or dinner – get out of driving duties and you can also take advantage of the local ales or the superb selection of wines on offer. The same menu is served throughout, so you can be inspired by the food-themed pictures in the snug, fire-warmed bar or dine in a more formal fashion at one of the dressed tables in the conservatory / dining room. The weekly-changing à la carte offers seasonal Italian food made with the best of local produce; imaginative dishes and clean flavours run through from the bruschetta and the primi piatti to the dolce and the gelato. Set 2, 3 and 5 course menus are a good way to keep a firm hold on those purse-strings if you're on a budget. Professional, unobtrusive service completes the picture.

Food serving times

Monday-Friday:
12pm-2pm, 6.30pm-9.30pm

Saturday:
12pm-2.30pm, 6.30pm-9.30pm

Sunday:
12pm-2.30pm, 6pm-8pm

Prices

Meals: 15.95 (3 course lunch & dinner) and a la carte 15.95/35.00

Typical Dishes

Portland crab
Roast saddle of venison
Caramelised lemon tart

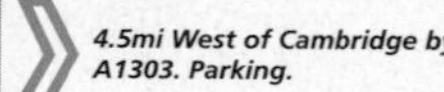

4.5mi West of Cambridge by A1303. Parking.

016 The George Inn

5 High St, Spaldwick PE28 0TD
Tel.: (01480) 890293 - Fax: (01480) 896847
e-mail: info@georgeofspaldwick.co.uk
Website: www.georgeofspaldwick.co.uk

 **Adnams Broadside, Greene King IPA, Youngs Special**

Contemporary meets old world charm at this distinctive, yellow-painted pub, its spacious, stylish interior balanced out by a host of traditional features, such as stone floors, thick walls and exposed ceiling timbers. Bag yourself a leather sofa in the roomy bar and get comfortable by one of the coffee tables; the blackboard informs you of what's on offer food-wise, and an eclectic bunch of dishes there are too. Hearty favourites like sausage and mash and shepherd's pie will put paid to the hunger pangs at lunch, while in the evening, you can choose between universally appealing dishes like coq au vin, roast guinea fowl and sirloin steak. Specials change daily, and the à la carte to match the season. The cosy front seats are a popular place to sit, while the two characterful dining areas situated in the original 15C area of the pub provide more formal dining for when the occasion demands it.

Food serving times
Monday-Sunday:
12pm-2.30pm, 6pm-9.30pm

Prices
Meals: a la carte
20.00/30.00

Typical Dishes
Crispy duck salad
Crispy pork belly
Sticky toffee pudding

7.5mi West of Huntingdon by A141 off A14. Parking.

East of England • Cambridgeshire

017 Village Bar (at Bell Inn)

Great North Rd,
Stilton PE7 3RA
Tel.: (01733) 241066 - Fax: (01733) 245173
e-mail: reception@thebellstilton.co.uk - Website: www.thebellstilton.co.uk

Greene King IPA, Fuller's London Pride, Abbot, JHB, Crop Circle and guest ales

Stilton? Mmmmm. That name rings a bell. Just two minutes from the busy A1, and yet a world away, this striking 16C stone building dominates the village in which it sits. With its solid stone floor, open fire and rough wooden tables, the charming bar is the hub of activity and, thanks to the village's reputation as the birthplace of Stilton, is filled with cheesy memorabilia including an ornamental cheese press. Although the bistro shares a menu with the bar, the latter is the more atmospheric place to sit – just make sure that you avoid the window seats, as you might get cheesed off with the draughts. Whilst there is the odd international influence, most dishes are hearty, filling and close to home, as pub dishes should be. The menu also offers several Stilton-based recipes, including soups and dressings, but if you're crackers about cheese, surely nothing can beat a mature hunk of the stuff all by itself.

Food serving times

Monday-Friday:
12pm-2pm, 7pm-9.30pm
Saturday: 12pm-2pm (bistro only), 7pm-9.30pm
Sunday: 12pm-2pm, 7pm-9pm (bistro only)
Closed dinner 25-26 December

Prices

Meals: 26.95 (3 course lunch & dinner) and a la carte 20.95/31.90

22 rooms: 72.50/99.50

Typical Dishes

Celery and Stilton soup
Yellow fin tuna steak
Hot rhubarb soufflé

4mi South of Peterborough by A15; in centre of village. Parking.

018 The Anchor Inn

Sutton Gault CB6 2BD

Tel.: (01353) 778537 - Fax: (01353) 776180

e-mail: anchorinn@popmail.bta.com

Website: www.anchor-inn-restaurant.co.uk

 **City of Cambridge Brewery: Hobson's Choice, Boathouse Bitter**

This charming inn, built on reclaimed marshland on the western edge of the Isle of Ely, was originally constructed in 1650 to house the workers who were digging up the Old and New Bedford Rivers. The previous chef and manager are now the owners, and have made some positive changes whilst retaining the essential character of the pub. There are three main rooms in which to dine, and scrubbed wooden tables and deep panelling reflect the flickering of candlelight in the evenings. An eclectic range of dishes is served, including old favourites such as lamb shank and supreme of chicken. East Anglian produce, such as venison from the Denham estate and Sutton sausages, is used wherever possible, and daily specials feature mainly fish. Sit out on the terrace and watch the beautiful sunset light up the sky, which seems to stretch forever over the fens, before retiring to one of the four comfortable bedrooms; the front-facing twin is the best.

Off B1381; follow signs to Sutton Gault from Sutton village. Pub is near the New Bedford River. Parking.

Food serving times

Monday-Friday:
12pm-2pm, 7pm-9pm

Saturday:
12pm-2pm, 6.30pm-9.30pm

Sunday:
12.30pm-3pm, 7pm-9pm

Prices

Meals: 10.95 (2 course meal) and a la carte 14.50/30.00

4 rooms: 59.50/155.00

Typical Dishes

Grilled dates in bacon
Loin of venison
Vanilla rice pudding brûlée

Blackmore

019 The Leather Bottle

The Green,
Blackmore CM4 0RL

Tel.: (01277) 823538

e-mail: leatherbottle@tiscali.co.uk - Website: www.theleatherbottle.net

 **Adnams Best and Broadside and 3-4 guest ales: Timothy Taylor's Landlord, Woodforde's Wherry, Ridley's Old Bob, Directors**

If you're anywhere near the picturesque village of Blackmore and are wanting a good meal, then the best advice would be to hit the bottle – the Leather Bottle. The pub dates from the 1750s and overlooks the village green - known as Horsefayre Green – where horse fairs used to be held when Blackmore was an old centre for the leather trade in the 19C. The pub is divided into two, with a bar on one side and a dining area and conservatory on the other. The flagstoned bar serves a selection of real ales and is cosy and relaxing, with an open fire, while the conservatory, with its wooden floor and stylish leather chairs, has an airy, natural feel and overlooks the rear garden. The all-encompassing seasonal menu has a traditional British base with European influences, and sometimes involves the odd Asian dish too. The set two-course lunch menus are particularly popular and a traditional roast is served on Sundays.

Food serving times

Monday-Saturday:
12pm-2pm, 7pm-9pm

Sunday:
12pm-4pm

Prices

Meals: 9.95 (2 course lunch) and a la carte 19.00/30.00

Typical Dishes

Chicken liver parfait
Lamb chump with jus
Chocolate & nutmeg pannacotta

2.75mi Southeast of High Ongar by A414. Parking in front of the pub.

020 The Alma

37 Arbour Lane,
Chelmsford CM1 7RG

Tel.: (01245) 256783 - Fax: (01245) 256793

e-mail: info@thealma.biz - Website: www.thealma.biz

Greene King IPA, Nethergate, Crouchvale Brewers Gold

Go into the suburbs of Chelmsford to find this very popular place. You can't miss it – it has an immaculately yellow painted façade, and you get to the entrance via a terrace of crazy paving. Its brightly lit windows are a welcoming sight in the dark. If you're here to drink, sit on a stool at the informal front bar; diners in this section have the benefit of high-backed black leather chairs. Everyone can make use of a flat-screen TV on the wall. The rear of The Alma, meanwhile, becomes something else again: a very smart formal restaurant, where the décor is stylish to a tee. Even the loos boast piped episodes of TV comedy programmes. Wide-ranging menus offer an accomplished a la carte of modern dishes on a classic base (restaurant and bar) or popular pubby favourites (bar only). Check them out for regular theme and quiz nights.

Food serving times

Monday-Saturday:
12pm-2.30pm, 6pm-9.30pm

Sunday:
12pm-8pm

Closed 25-26 December

Prices

Meals: 7.99/9.99 (2-course lunch / dinner) and a la carte 18.20/25.30

Typical Dishes

Confit of pork belly

Seabass with braised fennel

Dark chocolate fondant

East of town centre; off northside of Springfield Road (A1099). Parking.

021 The Cricketers

Clavering CB11 4QT
Tel.: (01799) 550442 - Fax: (01799) 550882
e-mail: cricketers@lineone.net
Website: www.thecricketers.co.uk

Adnams, Adnams Broadside, Greene King IPA

The hallowed ground where celebrity chef Jamie Oliver first learned to chop an onion, his parents have been here since 1976, and have quite a following of their own, especially among the locals. The 16C pub has a very traditional feel, with its low ceilings, beams and velour banquettes, and if you're staying the night there's a good selection of bedrooms to choose from - those in the pavilion are cottagey in style, while those in the courtyard are more modern. The separate bar and restaurant menus, plus the vast array of daily specials ensure that there's plenty of choice – and not a turkey twizzler in sight. The seasonal menu offers a refreshing mix of classic and more modern dishes, all homemade from quality, locally sourced produce. There's a strong Italian leaning, so you'll find plenty of pastas and risottos as well as choices such as slow braised wild rabbit, half a roasted local duck or even a spicy vegetable biriani. Pukka.

Food serving times

Monday-Sunday:
12pm-2pm, 7pm-9.30pm

Closed 25-26 December

Prices

Meals: 27.00 (3 course dinner) and a la carte 21.00/27.00

14 rooms: 75.00/110.00

Typical Dishes

Baked stuffed mushrooms

Pan-fried lambs' kidneys

Summer pudding

On B1038; Southwest of Saffron Walden. Parking.

022 The Sun Inn

High St,
Dedham CO7 6DF
Tel.: (01206) 323351
e-mail: info@thesuninndedham.com - Website: www.thesuninndedham.com

We most liked

Adnams Broadside, Brewers Gold

The Sun Inn is one of those rare, old-fashioned village locals where everyone knows everyone else, but if you're not a regular, don't let that put you off - they're a friendly bunch in this part of the world. While its exterior is painted a modern and fittingly sunny shade of yellow, this pub's characterful timbered interior is a reminder of its 15C origins. Open fires keep punters toasty, and photos of local history line the walls. The rustic, frequently-changing menu has a real Mediterranean base with strong leanings towards Italy, but there are also some more robust dishes for the more traditionally-minded. Locally grown fruit and vegetables are sold in the pub's own shop, 'Victoria's Plums,' and old-style country charm meets modernity in the comfortable bedrooms. Go for a stroll around the beautifully picturesque village or along the River Stour before sundown, and behold the views that so inspired Constable.

Food serving times

Monday-Friday:
12pm-2.30pm, 6.30pm-9.30pm

Saturday-Sunday:
12pm-3pm, 6.30pm-10pm

Closed 25-27 December

Prices

Meals: 15.50/18.00 (3 course lunch & dinner) and a la carte 15.00/25.00

5 rooms: 60.00/130.00

Typical Dishes

Seared pigeons' breasts
Grilled lamb chops
Four local cheeses

7mi North East of Colchester by A137 and minor road; in the centre of the village opposite the church. Parking.

Henny Swan

023 Henny Swan

Henny St,
Great Henny CO10 7LS
Tel.: (01787) 269238
e-mail: harry@hennyswan.com - Website: www.hennyswan.com

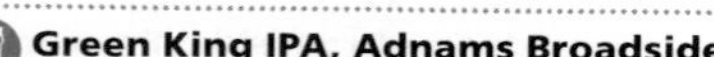

Green King IPA, Adnams Broadside

This converted barge house, now totally refurbished, is run by experienced ex-hoteliers and has a distinctive, contemporary feel to it. The L-shaped, beamed bar with its wood burning stove and modern artwork, is full of comfy sofas and armchairs, whilst the dining room is more bright and airy, with two sets of French windows leading out onto a large terrace. The best place to sit in fine weather is the lawn across the lane, from where you can watch the River Stour flow slowly past, while the willows sway gently from side to side in the breeze. Barbeques are unsurprisingly popular here in the summer, and the occasional band also fills the Essex evening air with the mellow sound of jazz. The diverse, fairly-priced menu has a Mediterranean base but offers something for everyone. Dishes range from grilled haloumi cheese to aubergine au gratin, but there are also choices such as steak, Thai-style fishcakes and lunchtime baguettes too.

Food serving times

Monday-Saturday:
12pm-2.30pm, 6.30pm-9.30pm

Sunday:
12pm-2.30pm

Prices

Meals: a la carte
17.70/25.40

Typical Dishes

Feta and tomato tart Tatin

Seared fillet of wild salmon

Fresh fruit Pavlova

2mi South of Sudbury by A131 South West and a minor road South. Parking.

024 **The Headley**

Great Warley CM13 3HS
Tel.: (01277) 216104
e-mail: reservations@theheadley.co.uk
Website: www.theheadley.co.uk

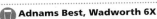

 **Adnams Best, Wadworth 6X**

The exterior of this vast building isn't necessarily the most attractive to behold, but inside it's spacious and split over two floors, containing comfy leather furniture, open fires and solid wooden tables, with a small terrace for al fresco dining too. The décor is perfectly pleasant but at the same time rather beside the point, since here it's all about the food. The oft-changing menus are a joy and include a mix of unusual snacks and sandwiches, from jellied eels to a venison 'bookmakers;' classical French bistro dishes such as cassoulet, beef bourguignon and ham and celeriac remoulade; plus some good old British favourites like bangers and mash. Dishes like roast mallard and Provençal fish stew are made for two to share and for afters, moreish puddings include the wonderfully-named icky sticky toffee pudding. Chef Scott is passionate about using locally produced, seasonal ingredients and his cooking is confident and flavoursome.

Food serving times
Monday-Sunday:
12pm-3pm, 6pm-9.30pm

Prices
Meals: a la carte
20.00/35.00

Typical Dishes
Salad of scallops
Herdwick mutton chop
Lemon and lime cheesecake

2mi South West of Brentwood by B186. Parking.

025 The Wheatsheaf

King St,
High Ongar CM5 9NS
Tel.: (01277) 822220

 **No real ales offered**

Not really a pub, but not quite a restaurant either, The Wheatsheaf would probably best be classed as a pestaurant, or perhaps a restapub. Whatever you want to call it, it's certainly a charming place and new, experienced owners are running a tight ship, with very friendly staff and efficient service. Three stylishly furnished dining areas have varnished wood floors, semi-panelled cream walls, banquette window seating and unique, kidney-shaped tables. There's a more intimate room at the rear, as well as a fully carpeted snug. You might have to ponder over the menus awhile, given the large choice they provide; traditional, seasonal dishes form the base, while influences come from all over and flavours are well-combined. When the sun decides to put in an appearance, seats in the spacious rear garden and terrace begin to look very appealing, but wherever you sit, word about The Wheatsheaf has got round, so booking is essential.

Food serving times

Tuesday-Saturday:
12pm-2pm, 6.30pm-9pm

Sunday:
12pm-2pm

Booking essential

Prices

Meals: a la carte
23.25/29.95

Typical Dishes

Crown mussels in white wine
Crispy duck confit
Lemon sponge pudding

2mi East by A414 on Blackmore rd. Parking.

026 The Bell

High Rd,
Horndon-on-the-Hill SS17 8LD

Tel.: (01375) 642463 - Fax: (01375) 361611
e-mail: joanne@bell-inn.co.uk - Website: www.bell-inn.co.uk

Greene King IPA, Bass, Crouchvale Brewers Gold, Shepherd Neame Spitfire, Tribute and Archers Golden

It has oft-times been heard tell / If thy hunger thy need quell / It would plainly do thee well / To get thee straight down to The Bell. The current owners' family have been behind the bar of this busy Essex pub now for nigh on 50 years; a long time in the world of pub ownership, but a mere drop in the ocean compared to how long the pub has been standing. Construction began in the 15C and its country-style décor reflects this with open fires flickering in the grate and original beams hanging overhead. The characterful décor also continues in the charming period bedrooms, named after famous mistresses such as Anne Boleyn and Lady Hamilton; their decoration and furnishings inspired by their famous names. The wide-ranging blackboard menu includes lots of daily specials and has something for everyone, from the more traditional sausage and mash / steak and chips combos to dishes such as tuna Niçoise.

Food serving times

Monday-Saturday:
12pm-1.45pm, 6.30pm-9.45pm

Sunday:
12pm-1.45pm, 7pm-9.45pm

Closed 25-26 December

Closed Bank Holiday Mondays

Prices

Meals: a la carte 22.00/30.00

15 rooms: 60.00/85.00

Typical Dishes

Ballotine of duck
Fillet of beef
Caramelised pannacotta

3mi Northeast of Grays by A1013 off A13. Parking.

027 The Mistley Thorn

High Street,
Mistley CO11 1HE
Tel.: (01206) 392821 - Fax: (01206) 390122
e-mail: info@mistleythorn.com - Website: www.mistleythorn.com

We most liked

Adnams, Mersea Island Brewery

This Georgian inn is reputedly the spot where Witchfinder General Matthew Hopkins lived and held his trials in the 17C. Happily, nowadays, you won't get thrown into the ornamental swan pond to see if you float, but you will get a warm, friendly welcome from the enthusiastic young staff, and a good value, quality meal to boot. The Californian owner knows her food and runs a cookery school called 'The Mistley Kitchen' when not hard at work at the Thorn. The first rule of good cooking is to use good produce, and that maxim certainly applies here. The daily-changing menus have an emphasis on fresh fish and seafood, and the well-sourced ingredients are seasonal, local and organic. A similar simplicity informs the décor here; with open fires, half-timbered walls and local art for sale on the walls, the feel of the place is contemporary, yet down to earth. Bedrooms are cosy and well-maintained, and two of them overlook the River Stour.

Food serving times

Monday-Sunday:
12pm-3pm, 6.30pm-9pm

Closed 25 December

Prices

Meals: 14.95 (3 course lunch/dinner) and a la carte 17.95/28.95

5 rooms: 65.00/105.00

Typical Dishes

Chargrilled calamari

Beer-battered local haddock

Chocolate amaretti torte

9mi North East of Colchester by A137 and B1352; not far from Mistley Towers. Parking.

028 The Compasses at Pattiswick

Compasses Rd, Pattiswick CM77 8BG
Tel.: (01376) 561322 - Fax: (01376) 564343
e-mail: info@thecompassesatpattiswick.co.uk
Website: www.thecompassesatpattiswick.co.uk

VISA MC

Adnams, Woodforde's Wherry, St Austell Tribute

Something of a hikers haven, this huge hulk of a pub – formerly two estate workers' cottages - has a modern interior with a country feel. Its delightful dining room is decorated by Hugo Fircks artwork, while the spacious, rustic bar boasts cosy leather sofas, a tiled floor and open fires. Hikers are hardly the only habitués of this hidden hideaway, however, and it's often deservedly busy. They like to look after their customers here; service from the young staff is very friendly and keen, whilst the owner's professionalism and hands on approach keeps things running just so. Appealing, seasonally-changing menus feature freshly-prepared, locally-sourced cooking and might include hearty favourites such as cottage pie or sausage and mash, as well as game shot locally on the Holifield estate, and lunchtime snacks like Croque Monsieur or a Ploughman's. Extensive gardens include a pleasant outdoor terrace - a great spot to eat in the summer.

Food serving times

Monday-Saturday:
12pm-2.45pm, 6pm-9.45pm

Sunday:
12pm-4pm

Prices

Meals: a la carte
17.00/25.00

Typical Dishes

Prawns with brown bread
Cottage pie
Winter berries

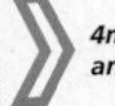

4mi West of Braintree by A120 and a minor road North. Parking.

029 The Woodmans Arms

Rayleigh Rd,
Thundersley SS7 3TA
Tel.: (01268) 775 799 - Fax: (01268) 590 689
e-mail: thewoodman@hotmail.co.uk

Charles Wells Bombardier, Courage Directors, Courage Best, Old Speckled Hen

The Woodmans Arms is something of a desert oasis. In an area crying out for a stylish venue to eat and drink, it ticks a lot of the right boxes. Set on a busy main road – admittedly not the most attractive location – it's a Victorian stalwart that's been modernised to a good standard, with etched and frosted bay windows and smart, wood-furnished al fresco terraces. A snazzy little lounge bar with squashy brown leather sofas and low tables is reserved for drinkers. The remainder of the pub is given over to diners, and locals are making the most of the stylish modern surroundings: each area is separated by screens and highlighted by warm modern colours. There are some old photos of the pub as it was in its former days. Good-sized menus have an international flavour, with, typically, Thai and French dishes mingling alongside the British selection. These are supplemented by simpler daily specials, prepared to a good standard.

Food serving times

Monday-Sunday:
12pm-3pm, 6pm-9.30pm

Prices

Meals: a la carte
18.00/27.00

Typical Dishes

Smoked salmon and crab
Calves liver and bacon
Mango crème brûlée

Between Basildon and Southend-on-Sea off A127. Parking.

030 The Bull of Cottered

Cottered SG9 9QP
Tel.: (01763) 281243
e-mail: cordell39@btinternet.com

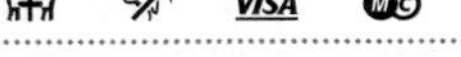

Greene King IPA and Abbot Ale

In a pretty village blighted by a busy A road, you need somewhere to keep your spirits up. The Bull is that place: a well looked-after and neighbourhood pub in the old tradition that's genuinely eager to please and worth a visit for its understated friendliness and recently extended and refurbished to provide a more stylish and comfortable dining environment. If you're stopping by at lunchtime, expect anything from homemade burgers, ploughman's or jacket potatoes to full meals – good "beer-friendly" pub meals, in other words. Dinner, though, sees the addition of tasty and sustaining seasonal British dishes like steak, calves' livers with Roquefort cheese or rack of lamb, plus a couple of daily specials.

Food serving times
Monday-Sunday:
12pm-2pm, 6.30pm-9.30pm

Prices
Meals: a la carte
16.90/31.00

Typical Dishes
Seared scallops
Fillet of seabass
Bread and butter pudding

6mi South East of Baldock by A507; in the centre of the village. Parking at the front of the pub.

031 The Bricklayers Arms

Hogpits Bottom, Flaunden HP3 0PH
Tel.: (01442) 833322 - Fax: (01442) 834841
e-mail: goodfood@bricklayersarms.com
Website: www.bricklayersarms.com

VISA AE MC

Tring Sack o' Legs, Fuller's London Pride, Timothy Taylor's Landlord, Greene King IPA, Old Speckled Hen

Take a map with you on your trip to The Bricklayers Arms, or you may well end up getting lost among the leafy lanes of Hertfordshire. Situated in the enchantingly named, 'Hogpits Bottom,' this charming, brick built 18C pub used to be three cottages, and original features include the slate roof, wooden beams and low ceilings. The spacious main bar is the best place to sit, with its exposed brick walls, country-style prints and well-spaced tables, but there is also a slightly more formal dining room too. The French chef is passionate about the freshness of his food, and the team here grow a lot of their vegetables and soft fruit on their own north London smallholding. Unsurprisingly, the menu is grounded in French classics, so you might find foie gras and snails on the menu alongside more English dishes such as steak and kidney pie as well as home-smoked fish and meats. Book ahead to avoid disappointment, especially at weekends.

Food serving times

Monday-Saturday:
12pm-2.30pm, 6.30pm-9.30pm

Sunday:
12pm-4pm, 6.30pm-8.30pm

Closed restaurant 25 December

Prices

Meals: a la carte 25.00/35.00

Typical Dishes

Duck breast
Rack of Chiltern lamb
Cointreau cream crêpe

4mi North of Rickmansworth by A404 and a minor road North. Parking.

032 The Alford Arms

Frithsden HP1 3DD
Tel.: (01442) 864480 - Fax: (01442) 876893
e-mail: inn@alfordarmsfrithsden.co.uk
Website: www.alfordarmsfrithsden.co.uk

  VISA AE 

Marstons Pedigree, Brakspear, Flowers Original, Marlow Rebellion IPA

When you are searching for a seat on the front terrace on a summer's afternoon, it might seem to you as if the whole of Hertfordshire has heard about this pub. Certainly, its reputation for good food has spread further than the quiet hamlet in which it is situated and you'll need to arrive early, book a table or preferably both if you want to guarantee yourself a space in the car park as well as a meal. Although there is also a more formal rear dining room, it's best to eat at one of the chunky wooden tables in the front bar, with its wooden and tiled floor and small open fire. Bubbly, casually-attired young staff serve a real mix of diners, from local businesspeople to walkers and cyclists, as well as those simply popping in for a pint of local ale. Moroccan bean tagine, pigeon and calamari might be included on the frequently changing menu; portions suit particularly healthy appetites so a main course may be all you really need.

Food serving times

Monday-Saturday:
12pm-2.30pm, 7pm-10pm

Sunday:
12pm-4pm, 7pm-10pm

Closed 25-26 December

Prices

Meals: a la carte
18.50/28.25

Typical Dishes

Bubble and squeak

Crispy spiced pork belly

Elderflower crème brûlée

4.5mi Northwest of Hemel Hempstead by A4146. By the village green. Parking.

033 The Fox

469 Luton Rd,
Kinsbourne Green, Harpenden AL5 3QE
Tel.: (01582) 713817
Website: www.thefoxharpenden.co.uk

  VISA AE MC

 **Timothy Taylor's Landlord**

Situated away from the town, The Fox is a smart, comfy and characterful place to be, made up of various rooms that impress equally with thick chunky beams, country styling and interesting ornaments of wood and stone. A spacious sitting room boasts an open fire and comfy leather sofas; elsewhere, diners are catered for at heavy wood tables and chairs giving the whole place a robust, rustic ambience, and the decked terrace is popular in good weather. An appealingly eclectic menu offers something for everyone with a mix of styles and cooking: the menu offers salads, fired pizzas and pasta; plates to share include tapas and mezze and the rotisserie is a very popular choice here. Brisk, attentive service from conspicuously-attired waiting staff used to being on their toes.

Food serving times
Monday-Sunday :
12pm-2.30pm, 6pm-10pm

Prices
Meals: a la carte
25.00/30.00

Typical Dishes
Crab cakes
Ribeye steak
Sticky ginger toffee pudding

5mi North of St Albans by A1081. Parking.

034 The Three Horseshoes

136 East Common,
Harpenden AL5 1AW
Tel.: (01582) 713953
e-mail: threehorseshoes@spiceinns.co.uk - Website: www.3horseshoes.net

 **Greene King IPA**

Locals will know where to find the Three Horseshoes, but anyone from outside the Harpenden postcode may need to check directions to the wooded environs of East Common. This smart-looking pub has had a stylish and tasteful conversion, but there are reminders that it dates back 400 years; for instance, a large inglenook dominates the small sofa furnished, low-ceilinged bar dedicated for drinkers. Not that too many customers hang around this area for long – after making the effort to get here, most punters have built up a decent hunger. The lovely rustic interior is certainly conducive to good dining, and the extensive à la carte menu is more restaurant than pub oriented; service is renowned for being pacy and attentive. The versatile range of modern European dishes – from steak to green Thai monkfish curry or rare grilled ostrich - benefit from a herb garden, which is handily placed right outside the kitchen.

Food serving times

Monday-Saturday:
12pm-2.30pm, 6pm-9.30pm

Sunday:
12pm-2.30pm

Prices

Meals: a la carte
26.70/33.45

Typical Dishes

Crayfish and onion risotto
Pan-fried wild seabass
Banana & cinnamon crumble

5mi North of St Albans by A1081.
Parking.

035 The White Horse

Hatching Green,
Harpenden AL5 2JW
Tel.: (01582) 469290
e-mail: info@atouchofnovelli.com - Website: www.atouchofnovelli.com

Part owned by TV's very own Jean Christophe Novelli, The White Horse has some pretty ambitious foody aspirations on show. Set in an immaculately whitewashed pub with 17C origins, the past soon gives way to a sleek modernity, typified by modern art and brash 21C décor. You can have a drink in the pub part of the building, where there's a wood-topped bar and some original beams, but most people come here for the cuisine, served in the large dining room with its A-framed beamed ceiling and open kitchen. Jean Christophe has a major input on the menus; these are most definitely not of the traditional type. In fact, the original dishes are quite complicated and ambitious, with French influences overlaying the well-used local ingredients. Friendly, organised service completes the picture. This is a very busy destination pub: remember to book well in advance.

Food serving times

Monday-Saturday:
12pm-2.30pm, 6pm-9.30pm

Sunday:
12pm-5pm

Closed 24-25 December

Prices

Meals: 21.50 (3 course lunch) and a la carte 29.00/36.00

Typical Dishes

Wild mushroom gratin
Roast veal sweetbreads
Baba au rum

5mi North of St Albans by A1081. Parking.

036 The Hillside

45 Port Hill,
Bengeo, Hertford SG14 3EP
Tel.: (01992) 554556 - Fax: (01992) 583709
e-mail: justin624@hotmail.com - Website: www.thehillside.co.uk

A suburb of Hertford would not perhaps be one's immediate first port of call when searching for a quality pub in which to eat, but you could do far worse than to stop off at this smart establishment, situated - funnily enough - on the side of a hill. Built in the 17C, it has a charming interior, with the original thick wooden floors, an intimate beamed bar and a large, very comfy leather sofa in which to sink. The raised dining room is light and airy and contains smart leather banquette seating and scrubbed wooden tables. He cooks, she serves and the combination patently works well here. Daily changing menus have a heavy seasonal leaning with lots of appeal. A classic British base leans towards France, but encompasses global influences, so you might have pressed terrine of local wild rabbit, wood pigeon and duck to start, followed by fillet of monkfish, leek and pumpkin risotto or Szechuan spiced lamb.

Food serving times
Monday-Saturday:
12pm-2pm, 6.30pm-9.30pm
Sunday:
12pm-2pm

Prices
Meals: a la carte
30.00/45.00

Typical Dishes
Foie gras
Rack of Welsh lamb
Pecorino basilischi

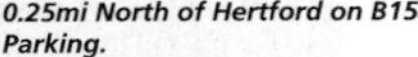
0.25mi North of Hertford on B158.
Parking.

037 Fox and Hounds

2 High St, Hunsdon SG12 8NH
Tel.: (01279) 843999 - Fax: (01279) 841092
e-mail: info@foxandhounds-hunsdon.co.uk
Website: www.foxandhounds-hunsdon.co.uk

 **Adnams Bitter and Broadside, Red Squirrel Brewery Organic blonde**

300 years old in parts, this is a village pub with a great rural ambience not too many miles from the teeming streets of north London. Outside is a spacious garden and paved patio for summer solipsism. Inside, it's basically one long room with a beamed bar counter in the centre, a crackling log fire with sofa seating at one end and a cosy dining area at the other. A smart dining room sits to the rear. Books, guides and magazines are dotted around too. The earnestly rustic character isn't above its cheeky side: loos are accessed through false bookcases. There's nothing fake about the food. Seasonality and simplicity reign and accomplished, classically based, robust cooking encompasses a global range, broad enough to take in dishes such as grilled squid and pepperonata, Spanish charcuterie and olives and saddleback pork sausages, mash and onion gravy. The well-priced two course early evening set menus are worth investigating.

Food serving times

Tuesday-Saturday:
12pm-3pm, 6.30pm-9.30pm

Sunday and Bank Holiday Monday:
12pm-3pm

Prices

Meals: 11.00/13.00 (2 course lunch / dinner) and a la carte 22.00/40.00

Typical Dishes

Grilled squid
Home cured ham
Bitter chocolate tart

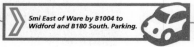

5mi East of Ware by B1004 to Widford and B180 South. Parking.

038 The Cabinet at Reed

High St,
Reed SG8 8AH
Tel.: (01763) 848366 - Fax: (01763) 849407
e-mail: thecabinet@btconnect.com - Website: www.thecabinetatreed.co.uk

We most liked

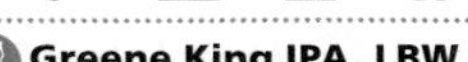
Greene King IPA, LBW

This white, clapperboard-clad building has stood eminently by the village green since the 16C. Much more than just another village pub, it is, however, not actually responsible for controlling the government; a shame really, because you get the feeling ministers might make better decisions after eating a good meal here. In reality, this pub's name refers to a small room, and the linen laid restaurant with its smart / casual dress code is certainly formal enough, and the staff attentive enough, for a prime ministerial visit. A wide choice of dishes is available on the British-based menus, but the Chancellor would probably advise on the set daily menu, as carefree ordering from the à la carte could really push the bill up. The cosy bar has a welcoming open fire and shotguns mounted on the walls, while the delightful snug with its original brick floor and chunky wooden furniture has to be the best seat in the house.

Food serving times

Monday-Saturday:
12.30pm-2.30pm, 7pm-9.30pm

Sunday:
12.30pm-2.30pm

Prices

Meals: 18.50/24.50 (3 course lunch/dinner) and a la carte 27.00/35.00

Typical Dishes

Oysters on crushed ice
Rack of lamb
Cappuccino crème brûlée

3mi South of Royston, just off the A10 London to Cambridge road. Parking.

039 Jacoby's

Churchgate House,
15 West St, Ware SG12 9EE
Tel.: (01920) 469181 - Fax: (01920) 469182
e-mail: info@jacobys.co.uk - Website: www.jacobys.co.uk

 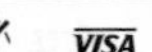  

 **No real ales offered**

Delightfully situated close to St. Mary's Church in the centre of town, Ware's second oldest building boasts the sort of character you'd expect from a late 15C, timber framed, Grade II listed edifice. Inside, its been carefully renovated to give a modern, stylish feel; there's a large bar with comfortable, low level leather seats in which to sink, as well as spacious up and downstairs dining rooms and a continental style pavement terrace. It's professionally run and busy, with a buzzing atmosphere, so if it's peace and quiet you're after, it's best to head upstairs. You won't find any funny fusion flavours here - the chef's classical background means that there's something on the frequently-changing menu to suit all tastes. Appealingly straightforward dishes might include half a Barbury duck, grilled calves liver and bacon or char-grilled tuna, while the fixed price lunch menu offers good value for money.

Food serving times

Tuesday-Saturday:
12pm-3pm, 6pm-10.30pm

Sunday:
12pm-3pm

Prices

Meals: 9.95 (3 course lunch) and a la carte 20.00/35.00

Typical Dishes

Crispy tiger prawns
Fillet steak
Hot chocolate mousse

In the town centre, just off the High St. Public car park in High St.

040 The Fox

Willian SG6 2AE
Tel.: (01462) 480233 - Fax: (01462) 676966
e-mail: info@foxatwillian.co.uk - Website: www.foxatwillian.co.uk

Adnams Best, Woodeforde's Wherry and Bitter, Fuller's London Pride, Timothy Taylor's Landlord, Potton Brewery Village Bike

Pretty Willian had two of the three boxes ticked: a church to the rear and a pond to the front. To complete the 'archetypal English village' equation, its pub – set between the two – was gutted in 2004 and then refurbished with an extension to the rear, a spacious restaurant whose attractive pitched ceiling windows gave it the feel of a conservatory. With third tick firmly in place, locals now swarm to the rejuvenated Fox to sample its delights. Summer dining is enhanced by a pretty little terrace which can be completely covered with an extendable awning. The airy modern bar area comes complete with its own substantial dedicated menu – and a conspicuous plasma TV to share it with, should the feeling take you. For more serious diners, there's an interestingly extensive restaurant menu with an emphasis on fish and shellfish imported from Norfolk.

Food serving times

Monday-Friday:
12pm-2pm, 6.45pm-9.15pm

Saturday:
12pm-2pm, 6.30pm-9.30pm

Sunday:
12pm-3pm

Prices

Meals: a la carte
20.00/27.00

Typical Dishes

Pavé of smoked salmon
Noisettes of lamb
Glazed cinnamon rice pudding

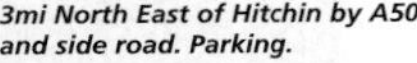
3mi North East of Hitchin by A505 and side road. Parking.

041 Kings Head

Harts Lane, Bawburgh NR9 3LS
Tel.: (01603) 744977 - Fax: (01603) 744990
e-mail: jandncatering@hotmail.co.uk
Website: www.kingshead-bawburgh.co.uk

   VISA 

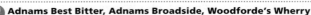

 **Adnams Best Bitter, Adnams Broadside, Woodforde's Wherry**

Only a short drive out of Norwich but already well into the countryside, this traditional place has plumped for Edward VII as its royal figurehead, the under-represented pub monarch perhaps getting the nod here for his generous appetite and his Sandringham connections. The old bon vivant would be baffled by the fruit machines, but drawn instinctively to the casual but comfortable dining room leading off from one side of the main bar. The daily changing menu blends modern European with traditional dishes: an equal mix of traditional and modern recipes might offer anything from ½ pint of prawns or sweet chilli chicken ciabatta to saffron, pea and mint risotto, homemade steak and mushroom pudding or seared red snapper. Once the woodburning stove is fired up on winter afternoons, it's also pleasant enough for a quiet pint.

Food serving times

Monday-Sunday:
12pm-2pm, 7pm-9pm

Closed 25 December, dinner 26 December, dinner 1 January

Prices

Meals: 15.00/18.00 (3 course lunch Mon-Sat/ dinner Mon-Thurs) and a la carte 23.00/34.50

Typical Dishes

Pan seared scallops
Confit of pork belly
White chocolate cheesecake

5mi Northwest of Norwich by B1108. Parking.

042 White Horse

4 High St, Blakeney NR25 7AL
Tel.: (01263) 740574 - Fax: (01263) 741303
e-mail: info@blakeneywhitehorse.co.uk
Website: www.blakeneywhitehorse.co.uk

Yetmans, Woodforde's Wherry, Adnams Southwold, Adnams Broadside

Estuary, saltings, quayside, and a gaggle of tourists from the Capital make up much of the character of 21C Blakeney. It's further defined by this popular part-17C pub of flint-and-brick which draws in the locals and weekenders a-plenty. They gather round a split-level bar and sup good real ale at wooden tables, chairs and banquettes – an appealing conservatory provides a smart alternative. Go to the rear, to the former stables, to eat: the food is proudly local in nature and naturally enough, seafood is the staple here. For those not climbing back into their 4X4s, there's the option of small, cosy bedrooms.

Food serving times

Tuesday-Saturday:
12pm-2.15pm, 7pm-9pm

Sunday-Monday:
12pm-2.15pm, 7pm-9pm
(bar meals only)

Closed 25 December

Prices

Meals: 25.95 (3 course dinner) and a la carte 17.50/30.00

9 rooms: 70.00/150.00

Typical Dishes

Smoked duck breast salad

Roast skate wing

Lemon polenta cake

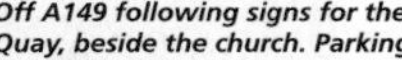

Off A149 following signs for the Quay, beside the church. Parking.

Burnham Market

043 The Hoste Arms

The Green,
Burnham Market PE31 8HD
Tel.: (01328) 738777 - Fax: (01328) 730103
e-mail: reception@hostearms.co.uk - Website: www.hostearms.co.uk

We most liked

   VISA 

Abbot Ale, Adnam's, Woodforde's Wherry, Nelson

The popularity of this coaching inn has almost come to define the charming north Norfolk town of Burnham Market: set on the picturesque Green, its 17C quirks have been fully restored; in startling contrast, there's an intriguing wing decorated in Zulu style, and a Moroccan garden terrace. The bar is an invariably bustling place, and the sound of champagne corks popping is not uncommon; you'll find similar levels of volume and bonhomie in the restaurant. The staff respond well to being busy, and are invariably attentive and friendly, with good attention to detail. Fairly-priced menus offer a mix of global styles, with much local produce in evidence; dishes might include braised pork belly, caramelised escalope of foie gras, roast quail or homemade steamed steak and kidney pudding. There's an excellent wine selection featuring 180 bins.

Food serving times
Monday-Sunday:
12pm-2pm, 7pm-9pm
Booking essential

Prices
Meals: a la carte
23.45/43.70
36 rooms:
90.00/188.00

Typical Dishes
Roast breast of pigeon
Seared fillets of black bream
Milk chocolate fondant

 *Overlooking the green. Parking.* 

044 The Lord Nelson

Walsingham Rd,
Burnham Thorpe PE31 8HL
Tel.: (01328) 738241 - Fax: (01328) 738241
e-mail: enquiries@nelsonslocal.co.uk - Website: www.nelsonslocal.co.uk

 **Greene King IPA, Abbot, Woodforde's Wherry, Ruddles County, Old Speckled Hen**

Named in honour of Burnham Thorpe's most illustrious son, and perhaps Britain's first modern celebrity, this 17C inn honours the Victor of the Nile with just enough in the way of pictures and memorabilia: too much swashbuckling nauticalia would clutter up this shipshape little place. Three low-ceilinged parlours, one with a Battle of Trafalgar mural, lead off from a firelit taproom with a tiny cubby-hole of a bar: the landlord opens up the timbered barn, with chunky pine tables and benches, if the pub itself starts to feel overcrowded. Simple, fresh, good-value dishes, both classic and modern, could include steak and kidney pudding, veal kidneys in a Dijonnaise sauce or swordfish with crab, cream and vodka sauce.

Food serving times

Monday-Saturday:
12pm-2pm, 7pm-9pm

Sunday:
12pm-2pm

Closed Monday except Bank Holidays, school holidays and half term holidays

Prices

Meals: 19.95 (3 course dinner) and a la carte 21.25/28.70

Typical Dishes

Scallops and black pudding
Supreme of turbot
Sticky toffee pudding

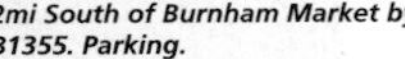

2mi South of Burnham Market by B1355. Parking.

045 The George

High St, Cley-next-the-Sea NR25 7RN
Tel.: (01263) 740652 - Fax: (01263) 741275
e-mail: thegeorge@cleynextthesea.com
Website: www.thegeorgehotelcley.com

 **Greene King IPA, Abbot, Yetmans (Holt) and guest ale - Adnam's Explorer**

There are two imposing buildings in Cley: the famous windmill which can be viewed from miles around, and the rather grand-looking George, its red-brick Victorian/ Edwardian façade providing a solid security to this charming little coastal village. Etched frosted windows and plenty of hanging baskets add lustre to the ornate exterior. Inside, there's an individual style to the place. Three rooms are divided into a bar and two dining areas, decorated in warm coloured wallpapers, and enhanced by wood-burning stoves. A large book on a brass pulpit records bird sightings from the nearby bar: whether these are influenced by pints consumed, you decide! Weighty menus make great use of local mussels and oysters, while the village smokehouse supplies other seafood. Rustic modern British cooking is tasty and accomplished. Bedrooms come in various configurations: the superior version, on the top floor, has finer views over the marshes.

Food serving times
Monday-Sunday:
12pm-2.15pm, 6.30pm-9pm
Closed 25 December

Prices
Meals: a la carte
22.00/30.00
12 rooms:
65.00/130.00

Typical Dishes
Cley smokehouse platter
Peppered salmon fillet
Selection of local cheeses

12mi West of Cromer by A149.
Parking.

046 King's Head

26 Wroxham Rd,
Coltishall NR12 7EA
Tel.: (01603) 737426 - Fax: (01603) 266113

Adnams Best, Fuller's London Pride, Marstons Pedigree, Courage Directors

One of the nicest things about this rather ordinary looking pub in deepest Norfolk is its attractive setting – diners with window tables can look out onto the meandering River Bure. Elsewhere within, a relaxed air pervades. Open fires crackle beneath solid timbers and pieces of fishing and boating memorabilia hang from the ceiling, lending a particularly atmospheric air at night: meals can be ordered in the bar as well as the dining room. Seafood specialities take pride of place with the Norfolk catch freshly served each day or, as an alternative to fish, chef's special meat dishes.

Food serving times

Monday-Sunday:
12pm-2pm, 7pm-9pm

Closed 25 December (dinner), 26 December, 1 January

Prices

Meals: 9.95 (3 course lunch) and a la carte 18.95/31.50

4 rooms: 29.50/59.00

Typical Dishes

Scallops wrapped in bacon

Fillet of seabass

Glazed lemon tart

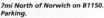

7mi North of Norwich on B1150.
Parking.

047 The Saracen's Head

Wolterton, Erpingham NR11 7LX
Tel.: (01263) 768909 - Fax: (01263) 768993
e-mail: saracenshead@wolterton.freeserve.co.uk
Website: www.saracenshead-norfolk.co.uk

 VISA 

Adnams Best Bitter, Woodforde's Wherry

Charmingly faded and quirky by turns, this individualistic 19C former coaching inn is in the middle of nowhere and loses nothing by its isolation. It contains an impressive walled garden and courtyard set back from two busy, bustling bar rooms and a boldly red-painted parlour filled with odd pictures, bric-a-brac and little wooden tables and chairs with plastic tablecloths. Traditional dishes come dressed in local ingredients such as mussels from Morston and crab from Cromer: unpretentious, country dishes that draw in regular shoals of satisfied customers from miles around. Bright, modest bedrooms nevertheless share the long-standing owner's mild and endearing eccentricity.

Food serving times

Monday-Sunday:
12.30pm-2pm, 7.30pm-9pm

Closed 25 December, dinner 26 December

Prices

Meals: 8.00 (2 course lunch) and a la carte 21.50/27.15

6 rooms: 50.00/90.00

Typical Dishes

Grilled goat's cheese
Medallions of Gunton venison
Treacle tart

West 1.5mi on Wolterton Hall rd. Parking.

048 The Walpole Arms

The Common,
Itteringham NR11 7AR
Tel.: (01263) 587258 - Fax: (01263) 587074
e-mail: goodfood@thewalpolearms.co.uk - Website: www.thewalpolearms.

 **Adnams Bitter, Adnams Broadside, Woodforde's Wherry, Walpole Ale**

Blickling Hall sets an awesome architectural benchmark in this part of Norfolk; in its more modest way, the nearby part-18C Walpole Arms reaches out in empathy. It's hugely characterful and inviting, with a warm ambience, roaring fires, exposed brick walls and heavy timbers marking out the bar as a great place for modern dining. New, varied menus are devised daily; the accomplished kitchen interweaves Italian and Spanish ideas. Extensive use is made of local and seasonal ingredients; the owners heartily take on board recommendations from their fishmonger and game supplier. There's a more formal restaurant beyond the bar, but no let-up on the character front, with linen-clad tables and exposed roof trusses lending it an appealing air. Wednesday night is quiz night.

Food serving times

Monday-Saturday:
12pm-2pm, 7pm-9pm

Sunday:
12pm-2pm

Closed 25 December

Prices

Meals: a la carte
21.00/25.00

Typical Dishes

Moroccan broad bean salad

Gurnard fillet wrapped in ham

Apple and sultana compote

5mi Northwest of Aylsham by B1354. Signed The Common. Parking.

049 1 Up at the Mad Moose Arms

2 Warwick St, Norwich NR2 3LD
Tel.: (01603) 627687
e-mail: madmoose@animalinns.co.uk
Website: www.themadmoosearms.co.uk

Adnams Broadside, Deuchars IPA, Wolf Brewery

The moose is a shy creature, found tucked away in a residential area, and it can be hard to get close to it, (due to lack of free parking). Downstairs is the pub, popular with students – all flat-screen TVs, moose-themed cartoons and loud music - but it's the upper room that you want to head to for – via a back staircase - if you are after flavourful, modern food in more formal surroundings. Having undergone a refurbishment, the elegant 1 Up must certainly be feeling a sense of one-upmanship over other pubs in the area; light and open plan with ornate chandeliers and cream and silver colour schemes, it has a stylish, modern feel. There's lots of choice on the menu and some interesting touches; starters might include grilled green figs, mizuna, marscarpone, pomegranate and crisp Parma ham, while mains might mean pan fried black bream or roast breast of Norfolk pheasant. With well-organised service to boot, you can't elk but like it here.

Food serving times

Monday-Saturday:
7pm-10pm

Sunday:
12pm-3pm

Closed 25 December

Bar meals only Saturday lunch and Sunday dinner

Prices

Meals: 21.00 (3 course dinner) and a la carte 17.00/26.00

Typical Dishes

Seared scallops
Loin of Norfolk venison
Sticky ginger cake

In residential area West of city centre. Designated parking bays lunchtime, street parking in the evening.

050 The Gin Trap Inn

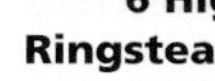

6 High St,
Ringstead PE36 5JU
Tel.: (01485) 525264
e-mail: thegintrap@hotmail.co.uk - Website: www.gintrapinn.co.uk

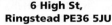

 **Adnams, Woodforde's Wherry and guest ales - Abbot**

A vast sycamore tree stands right outside, and two old iron ploughs crown the modest doorway of this whitewashed inn, which dates back to 1667. In all those years it can rarely have looked and felt so inviting: a proper country pub, warm and comfortable, with a real fire stoked up in the stove on frosty winter evenings. There's a bar, with glossy wood-topped tables, a smartly set dining room and also a new wooden floored conservatory overlooking the garden. The blackboard menu offers favourites like fish and chips and sausage and mash while the à la carte might boast delights such as glazed clam and cockle tagliatelle with chive and caviar fish cream, braised beef bourguignon or pan-fried skate wing. Bedrooms are a very tasteful blend of subtle country patterns, and two bathrooms have luxurious roll-top baths. Think the owner looks vaguely familiar? He used to be an actor, working on shows such as The Bill and EastEnders.

Food serving times
Moday-Sunday:
12pm-2pm, 6pm-9pm

Prices
Meals: a la carte
16.00/25.00

3 rooms: 45.00/140.00

Typical Dishes
Moules marinières
Beef Bourguignon
Chocolate & orange marquise

3,25 miles East of Hunstanton by A149. Parking.

051 The Rose and Crown

Old Church Rd, Snettisham PE31 7NE
Tel.: (01485) 541382 - Fax: (01485) 543172
e-mail: info@roseandcrownsnettisham.co.uk
Website: www.roseandcrownsnettisham.co.uk

Adnams Bitter, Adnams Broadside, Woodforde's Wherry and guest ales

A buzzing, convivial place at its best, though first-time guests may struggle to get their bearings in a maze of cosy, rustic bars and brightly styled rooms, where quirky decorative details and bric-a-brac give just a hint of well-composed muddle. Whatever you do, don't plan on a quick dinner – for all its good intentions, the service can start to unravel on busy evenings, leaving some diners feeling slightly lost – but go prepared to flag down waitresses and allow time for a drink and a chat between courses. The menu is a conversation piece in itself. Modern European dishes mix with the out-and-out traditional, with dishes ranging from Mediterranean vegetable pasta to braised knuckle of lamb or beef stew and dumplings. There is a well-priced lunch menu and good choice on the à la carte. Tidy, interestingly appointed bedrooms, in a colourful style you'll recognise from downstairs, and good breakfasts.

Food serving times

Monday-Thursday:
12pm-2pm, 6.30pm-9pm

Friday:
12pm-2pm, 6.30pm-9.30pm

Saturday-Sunday:
12pm-2.30pm, 6.30pm-9.30pm (9pm Sunday)

Prices

Meals: a la carte
16.00/25.00

16 rooms:
70.00/110.00

Typical Dishes

Ham hock salad
Prime Holkham beefburger
Banana bread cake

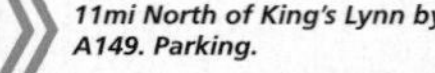
11mi North of King's Lynn by A149. Parking.

052 Wildebeest Arms

82-86 Norwich Rd,
Stoke Holy Cross NR14 8QJ

Tel.: (01508) 492497 - Fax: (01508) 494946
e-mail: wildebeestl@animalinns.co.uk - Website: www.thewildebeestarms.

We most liked

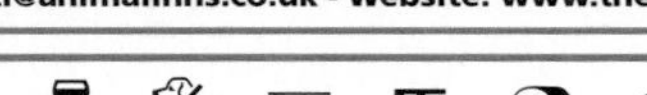

Adnams Best Bitter

With a name like the Wildebeest Arms, you know that this is not going to be just another run-of the-mill pub. Yes, it has the rustic beams and the wood floors, but the deep yellow-coloured walls, African carvings and tree-trunk tables mean that at heart it's more savannah than tequila slammer. An open-plan space with a central bar and an open kitchen, it still manages to feel extremely cosy, there are picnic tables in the garden, and service is bright and attentive. The set lunch and dinner menus offer ample choice and great value for money, while the contemporary and inventive à la carte proposes tasty, well-presented, restaurant-style dishes, which vary according to what's in season. Busy both with locals and visitors, booking here is essential – but if you can't get a table, the owner does own two more eateries in the area. Refurbishment is imminent, so, if all goes according to plan, this beast will soon be looking as good as a gnu.

Food serving times

Monday-Sunday:
12pm-2pm, 7pm-10pm

Closed 25-26 December

Booking essential

Prices

Meals: 15.50/18.50 (3 course lunch/dinner) and a la carte 25.00/32.00

Typical Dishes

Lowestoft smoked salmon

Braised shin of Anglian beef

Treacle tart

5.75 mi South of Norwich by A140. Parking.

053 The Globe Inn

The Buttlands,
Wells-next-the-Sea NR23 1EU
Tel.: (01328) 710206 - Fax: (01328) 713249
e-mail: globe@holkham.co.uk - Website: www.globeatwells.co.uk

  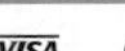 MC

 **Woodforde's Wherry, Adnams Best, Adnams Broadside**

Just a five-minute stroll from the harbour - where fishermen set out for inshore crab, whelk, sea trout and bass – this renovated inn boasts its own charming position, overlooking the town's leafy Georgian square. Sun-filled courtyards surround its whitewashed exterior, and birds drift by along the breezes of the north Norfolk coast. Inside, all is neat, tidy and spruce. 'Front of house' is the more characterful part of the pub, where a log-burning stove churns out winter warmth, and brick faced walls add rustic flavour to wood tables and chairs. Beyond, the airy, neutral dining area is enlivened by excellent, blown up local photos on the walls. Everywhere you go, daily papers lie around for you to pick up and peruse. Menus are a mixture of modern British and classic pub dishes, washed down by local Adnams and Woodfordes beers. Bedrooms, too, charmingly merge the contemporary with the past.

Food serving times
Monday-Sunday:
12pm-2.30pm, 7pm-9pm

Prices
Meals: a la carte
17.25/22.00

7 rooms: 65.00/125.00

Typical Dishes
Chicken Caesar salad
Chargrilled tuna steak
Bread and butter pudding

18mi East of Hunstanton by A149. Parking restrictions around the Buttlands.

054 The Bildeston Crown

104 High Street, Bildeston IP7 7EB
Tel.: (01449) 740510 - Fax: (01449) 741843
e-mail: info@thebildestoncrown.co.uk
Website: www.thebildestoncrown.co.uk

VISA AE MC

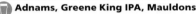

Adnams, Greene King IPA, Mauldons

15C origins, a part-timber frontage and a smart yellow finish announce this extremely popular hostelry in the heart of Suffolk. Smart modern styling mixes well with the traditional appeal of the exterior, as exemplified by the bar area, where delightful inglenook, beams and heavy wood furniture evolve into comfy sofas in an adjacent room. The old and the new also rub shoulders in the dining room – the whole pub boasts a well-integrated feel. Locals enjoy a drink in the popular bar, and if you choose, you can eat here as well as sup. Good-sized menus are of two types: the Crown Classic, which is mainly traditional, or the dinner menu, which offers more elaborate temptations. Overnighters have made a sound choice: bedrooms are very strong here: individually styled, they merge pleasant traditional features with up-to-date facilities like Wi-Fi.

Food serving times
Monday-Sunday:
12pm-3pm, 7pm-10pm

Prices
Meals: 20.00 (3 course lunch/dinner) and a la carte 22.00/37.00

10 rooms:
70.00/170.00

Typical Dishes
Calves' sweetbreads
Fillet of turbot
Pear and ginger ravioli

9mi Northeast of Sudbury by B1115. Parking.

055 Queen's Head

**The Street,
Bramfield IP19 9HT**
Tel.: (01986) 784214
e-mail: qhbfield@aol.com - Website: www.queensheadbramfield.co.uk

Adnams Bitter, Adnams Broadside

In the heart of the village of Bramfield, near the edge of the Suffolk coast, lies this well-run, cream-washed roadside pub. In winter, take a seat in the high-raftered main room and warm yourself by the huge log fireplace. In summer, sit in the conservatory or in the beautiful terraced gardens and enjoy one of the homemade ice creams on offer. These and other delicious puddings are by no means the only homemade food to be had here; on the contrary. An eclectic menu draws on locally sourced food and organic farm produce, including rare-breed meats, and it is not unusual to see on the menu the name of the farm from which the principle ingredients of a dish have come. The beamed interior with its wood and flagstone flooring reflects the age of this long-standing pub. After you've eaten, a wander around the equally historic thatched church next door with its unusual detached round tower is a must.

Food serving times

Monday-Friday:
12pm-2pm, 6.30pm-9pm

Saturday:
12pm-2pm, 6.30pm-10pm

Sunday:
12pm-2pm, 7pm-9pm

Closed 26 December

Prices

Meals: a la carte
16.00/25.00

Typical Dishes

Grilled dates with bacon

Braised beef in red wine

Pavlova with cream

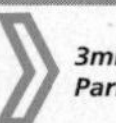

*3mi South of Halesworth on A144.
Parking.*

056 The Buxhall Crown

Mill Road, Buxhall IP14 3DW
Tel.: (01449) 736521
e-mail: trevor@thebuxhallcrown.co.uk
Website: www.thebuxhallcrown.co.uk

 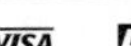 

 **Greene King IPA, Woodforde's Wherry, Cox & Holbrook 'Old Mill'**

Two buildings join to make this pub; one of them dates from 17C, the other's birth date nobody knows – but what is known is that at one time it housed both a butcher and a piggery. You might well feel a compulsion to piggery yourself when you peruse the menu at The Buxhall Crown. Dishes might range from mussels or prawns to venison casserole or lambs hearts stuffed with sausage meat, the quality of the cooking helped by the use of superior local produce, including some sumptuous beef, which makes the steak a good choice for a main course. You can eat in either side of the pub, or outside at wooden tables on the impressively lit, heated and sheltered terrace. The left side is the more cosy and characterful, with wattle and daub walls, heavy wood beams and an inglenook fireplace, while the right hand side, where photos of the village and the pub line the walls, is lighter and more contemporary in style.

Food serving times

Tuesday-Saturday:
12pm-2pm, 6.30pm-9pm

Sunday:
12pm-2pm

Closed 25-26 December

Prices

Meals: a la carte
25.00/45.00

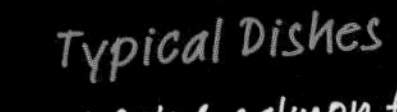

Typical Dishes

Monkfish & salmon fish cakes

Plaice fillets with prawns

Lemon tart

3 3/4mi West of Stowmarket by B1115; follow the road to Buxhall across Rattlesden Junction. Parking.

057 The Beehive

The Street,
Horringer IP29 5SN
Tel.: (01284) 735260 - Fax: (01284) 735532

 **Greene King IPA, Abbot, Old Speckled Hen**

Staggeringly rich and deeply eccentric, even by the standards of the Regency gentry, the 4th Earl of Bristol spared no expense on Ickworth House and its Italianate gardens, now owned by the National Trust. His ideal local would probably have been a neoclassical gastro-folly, but The Beehive, just down the road, brings us back down to earth in the very best sense. An attractive, traditional brick and flint house, its old timbers and flagstones set off nicely with a bright, modern décor, it always seems to have one last inviting corner waiting and an old wooden table free. A good-sized blackboard menu, with its share of lighter dishes, combines predominantly British themes with a subtle taste for the modern and the exotic – perhaps His Lordship would have approved after all. Well run by long-standing landlords.

Food serving times

Monday-Saturday:
12pm-2pm, 7pm-9.30pm

Sunday:
12pm-2pm

Closed 25-26 December

Prices

Meals: a la carte
19.40/26.85

Typical Dishes

Cured meats
Roast belly of pork
Meringue floating island

3.5mi South West of Bury St Edmunds by A143. Parking.

058 The Angel

Market Pl,
Lavenham CO10 9QZ
Tel.: (01787) 247388 - Fax: (01787) 248344
e-mail: angellav@aol.com - Website: www.theangelhotel.com

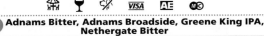

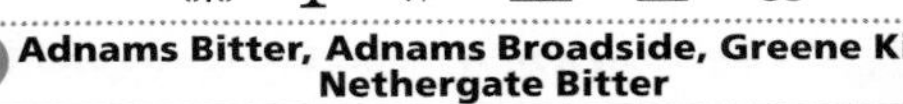
Adnams Bitter, Adnams Broadside, Greene King IPA, Nethergate Bitter

History's timbered face appears at every turn in the gorgeous old town of Lavenham, and the Angel wears one of its more delightful countenances. This charming inn has stood in the market square since 1420 and receives a never-ending stream of curious tourists and relaxed locals. There's a pubby bar with several dining areas including lots of timbers, simple wooden tables and a log fire. On the first floor is the Solar, which contains a rare fully pargetted ceiling constructed in the early 1600s, featuring the remains of early wall paintings on some of its beams. This has great views of the Guildhall and Church and is now a residents' sitting room. Hearty, varied menus employ seasonal, local produce, while well-kept bedrooms provide effortlessly comfortable accommodation.

Food serving times

Monday-Sunday:
12pm-2.15pm, 6.45pm-9.15pm

Closed 25-26 December

Prices

Meals: a la carte 17.00/30.00

8 rooms: 60.00/110.00

Typical Dishes

Smoked salmon with fennel

Roast loin of lamb

Steamed syrup pudding

6mi North of Sudbury by B1115 and B1071; in town centre. Parking.

059 The Ship Inn

Church Lane,
Levington IP10 0LQ
Tel.: (01473) 659573

 **Greene King IPA, Adnams Broadside and Best**

In an age of rebranding, some pub names still go deeper. The salt of the Suffolk marshes is in the very timbers of this part 14C thatched inn, which stands in sight of the estuary. Though built from the broken-up hulks on the coast and full of seafaring pictures, curiosities and keepsakes, it now feels just too neat and cosy ever to have been a smugglers' haunt, but read the old newspaper cutting on the wall and you'll find the atmosphere of excisemen and contraband hangs about you a little more thickly. Relaxed, smiling and attentive service recalls you to the present for an appetizing menu with a good balance tilted in favour of the traditional: seafood includes Cromer crab and fresh griddled plaice with crispy salad. Save a space for homemade puddings like apple and rosemary crumble with custard.

Food serving times

Monday-Sunday:
12am-2pm, 6.30pm-9.30pm

Closed 25-26 December, dinner 31 December, dinner 1 January

Prices

Meals: a la carte
17.00/25.00

Typical Dishes

Baked goat's cheese
Roast fillet of cod
Poached meringue & compote

 *6mi Southeast of Ipswich by A14. Parking.* 

060 The Star Inn

The Street,
Lidgate CB8 9PP
Tel.: (01638) 500275 - Fax: (01638) 500275

 **Greene King IPA, Abbot Ales and Ruddles**

This part 16C village inn may just prove the point: any fusion of traditions will work if you understand both well enough. Its three intimate rooms and snugs are full of restful, old-English charm, braced with ancient beams worn smooth and warmed by drowsy inglenooks. Absolutely the last place, in fact, that you would expect to find sparklingly fresh Iberian cooking. The day's menu comes on blackboards that offer a good variety of simply stated Spanish and Mediterranean dishes. Even locally sourced wild boar and venison are prepared to authentic recipes: at once hearty, piquant and satisfyingly different. Suffolk summers seldom feel properly continental: even so, the terraced garden is very pleasant once the weather finally gets it right.

Food serving times

Monday-Saturday:
12pm-2.30pm, 7pm-10pm

Sunday:
12pm-2.30pm

Closed 25-26 December and 1 January

Spanish

Prices

Meals: 12.50 (2 course lunch) and a la carte 25.00/30.00

Typical Dishes

Carpaccio of venison
Wild boar with strawberries
Banoffe pie

7mi southeast of Newmarket on B1063. Parking.

061 The Swan

The Street,
Monks Eleigh IP7 7AU
Tel.: (01449) 741391
e-mail: swan@monkseleigh.com - Website: www.monkseleigh.com

Adnams Best and Broadside

Heading, perhaps, for the Tudor delights of Lavenham, there's every chance you'll come across this attractive little 16C roadside pub with its thatched roof and honey yellow façade. Stop off and step inside. The interior is as fresh as the country air, with rustic olive tones and shiny wooden floors. It's a charming mix of the old and the new, undertaken with understated style. You won't be let down by the food, either. The chef and landlord specialises in innovative menus that treat local ingredients with the utmost respect: fish, for instance, is the day's catch from the coast. Early dinners come at bargain prices – a great time to sample the homemade seasonal game dishes. When you've left the pub, remember to look round the quaint little streets of Monks Eleigh itself.

Food serving times

Wednesday-Sunday:
12pm-2pm, 7pm-9.30pm

Closed 25-26 December, 1 January

Prices

Meals: a la carte
15.00/35.00

Typical Dishes

Pan-fried scallops
Roast duck breast
Poached pear in red wine

3.5mi Southeast of Lavenham on A1141. Parking.

062 The White Hart Inn

11 High St,
Nayland CO6 4JF
Tel.: (01206) 263382 - Fax: (01206) 263638
e-mail: nayhart@aol.com - Website: www.whitehart-nayland.co.uk

We most liked

No real ales offered

It's more about dining than drinking at this whitewashed former coaching inn, situated on the high street of a typically charming Suffolk village. The front door opens straight into an area where the tables are dressed for dinner; if you're after an aperitif, head beyond these to the sofas and the bar, and if you suffer from vertigo, it's best to avoid the tables over the wine cellar as the floor tiles here are made of glass. The atmosphere and service here are formal, as is the food; modern European dishes demonstrate the chef's pedigree and are well-presented without being over-embellished. Choose between classics such as crispy pork belly or roasted rump of lamb and dishes with a touch of La France or Italia. Six well-furnished bedrooms are creaky but very comfortable; before you shoot off in the morning, have a peek behind the corner hedge in the car park; there's a beautiful stretch of riverbank you'd never even know was there.

Food serving times

Monday-Sunday:
12pm-2pm, 7pm-9pm

Closed 2 weeks after New Year

Prices

Meals: 17.90 (3 course lunch) and a la carte 23.00/37.00

6 rooms: 66.00/129.00

Typical Dishes

Potted rillette of rabbit
Coq au vin
Cappuccino chocolate mousse

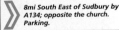

8mi South East of Sudbury by A134; opposite the church. Parking.

Kings Head Inn

063 King's Head Inn

Front Street,
Orford IP12 2LW
Tel.: (01394) 450271
Website: www.kingshead-orford-suffolk.co.uk

Adnams Bitter, Adnams Broadside

The King's Head Inn is a proper, honest English pub, with no pretence to be anything but. Decked out in heraldic prints and banners and kingly furnishings fitting to its name, it boasts 16C origins and a history of smuggling. The bar is traditional in décor, with wooden tables and an open fired stove, but the best place to sit if you're eating is in the large dining room. A proper pub needs proper pub food and the King's Head Inn doesn't disappoint. Fit for a pauper rather than a king – but in the nicest possible sense - the cooking is down to earth but still eminently worthy, so ham and eggs means local cured ham and free range eggs, the scampi is real, whole and home battered, and sandwiches are 'doorstops.' Puddings are also commendably classic, and choices might include rice pudding, apple crumble or treacle tart; all washed down with a good selection of real ales and wines. Spacious bedrooms are well furnished and comfortable.

Food serving times

Monday-Sunday:
12pm-2.30pm, 6.30pm-8.30pm

Prices

Meals: a la carte 17.00/23.00

4 rooms: 70.00/90.00

Typical Dishes

Orford smoked mackerel
Whole home-battered scampi
Hot treacle tart

12mi East of Woodbridge by A1152 and B1084. Parking.

064 The Crown Inn

Bridge Rd,
Snape IP17 1SL
Tel.: (01728) 688324

Adnams Broadside, Adnams Old Ale, Oyster, Mayday

This gem of a Suffolk pub, with its origins firmly entrenched in the 15C, draws in visitors from upmarket Aldeburgh and The Maltings. They come for the Suffolk ale, the pubby atmosphere enhanced enormously by standing timbers and rafters, old brick flooring and horseshoe-shaped high-backed settles around a grand brick inglenook, and the heart-warming popular dishes served from the blackboard menu. These have a sharp emphasis on fresh fish, game and organic vegetables supplied by local producers. Quaint bedrooms continue the aged theme, complete with sloping floors, beams and some low, low doorways.

Food serving times

Monday-Sunday:
12pm-2pm, 7pm-9pm

Closed 25 December, dinner 26 December

Prices

Meals: a la carte
19.40/27.50

3 rooms: 70.00/80.00

Typical Dishes

King prawns tempura
Seared scallops
Chocolate soufflé torte

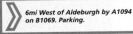

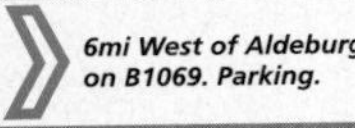

6mi West of Aldeburgh by A1094 on B1069. Parking.

065 The Duke's Head

Slugg's Lane,
Somerleyton NR32 5QR
Tel.: (01502) 730281
e-mail: dukeshead@somerleyton.co.uk - Website: www.somerleyton.co.uk

Greene King, Adnams, Oulton Ales, Green Jack, Woodforde's, Crouch Vale

Up the coast and inland a bit from Lowestoft stands one of Suffolk's finest stately homes, Somerleyton Hall, and its watering hole has a friendly and welcoming feel about it. Located in the unfortunate sounding Slugg's Lane, it's not the prettiest of pubs, but its setting, down by the river, and its super sun-drenched terrace, enhance the feeling that all is not lost. The characterful interior is thronged with locals and visitors to the Hall, and there are regular live music evenings as well as 'big screen' events. A spacious, simply furnished restaurant stands by the bar, and this is home to some appetising grub at very digestible prices. Simply prepared, well executed dishes are full of tasty, fresh ingredients originating from, or around, the estate, with Cromer crab and brown shrimps a couple of tasty possibilities.

Food serving times

Monday-Sunday:
12pm-3pm, 6.30pm-10pm

Bar snacks all day

Prices

Meals: a la carte
25.00/40.00

Typical Dishes

Warm goat's cheese croute
Grilled Lowestoft cod
Lemon posset

6mi Northwest of Lowestoft by B1074. Parking.

066 The Crown

90 High St,
Southwold IP18 6DP
Tel.: (01502) 722275 - Fax: (01502) 727263
e-mail: crown.hotel@adnams.co.uk - Website: www.adnamshotels.co.uk

VISA

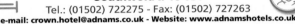

 **Adnams: Bitter, Broadside, Explorer and seasonal varieties**

The sophisticated elegance of The Crown sits easily within the beguiling surrounds of delightful Southwold. Its mellow yellow tones have graced the high street for many a year, standing proudly adjacent to the Adnams Sole Bay brewery. This smart, intimate old coaching inn is the ideal stopping-off point for a pint with the Suffolk locals in the compact oak-panelled rear bar where, not surprisingly, a nautical edge permeates. Get to the front bar early if you want to bag a seat for dining: it can get packed in there. Or choose a more formal option in the intimate, linen-clad restaurant. The same daily changing menu is served throughout: a well-established and well-prepared mix of modern and more classical dishes, which find favour with East Anglians and the metropolitan influx alike. Individually styled bedrooms.

Food serving times
Monday-Sunday:
12pm-2pm, 6.30pm-9pm

Prices
Meals: a la carte
20.75/32.95

14 rooms:
83.00/146.00

Typical Dishes
Gratin of Devon crab
Seared Suffolk lamb's liver
Honey & thyme roast figs

In the town centre. Parking.

067 The Randolph

41 Wangford Rd,
Reydon, Southwold IP18 6PZ
Tel.: (01502) 723603 - Fax: (01502) 722194
e-mail: reception@therandolph.co.uk - Website: www.therandolph.co.uk

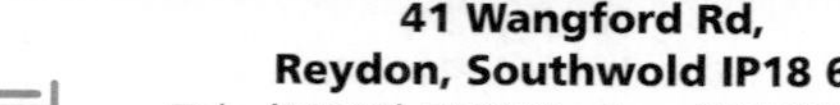

Adnams: Bitter, Broadside, Explorer and seasonal ales

Following a bracing walk along the beach at the charming town of Southwold, you might want to head inland slightly to the equally charming but quieter village of Reydon. All that sea air will have given you an appetite, so what better than a meal at The Randolph? Named after the father of Sir Winston Churchill, its Victorian façade is suitably grand, while the interior has been renovated in a bright, contemporary style. Take a seat in the garden or settle into one of the comfy sofas in the light, airy bar area for a pre-dinner drink courtesy of the local Adnams brewery, before moving into the larger dining area to tuck into the hearty yet modern food, ranging from sandwiches through to steaks with plenty of fresh fish in between. If you're staying the night in one of the spacious, well-kept rooms, the knowledge that you've got good value for money is bound to help you sleep particularly well.

Food serving times
Monday-Sunday:
12pm-2pm, 6.30pm-9pm

Prices
Meals: a la carte
16.00/21.00

10 rooms:
50.00/120.00

Typical Dishes
Terrine of braised ham hock
Fillet of seabass
Chocolate crème brûlée

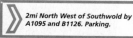

2mi North West of Southwold by A1095 and B1126. Parking.

068 The Angel Inn

Polstead St,
Stoke-by-Nayland CO6 4SA
Tel.: (01206) 263245 - Fax: (01206) 263373
e-mail: the.angel@tiscali.co.uk

Greene King IPA, Adnams Best and Broadside

Parts of this 16C inn in the heart of Constable country creak with age: not surprisingly, a traditional air is worn with pride. It's heavily beamed and timbered, with exposed brickwork and roaring fires, and a cheerily informal bar that leads through to a sitting room where you can recline in deep sofas. Dine in the main bar or repair to the Well Room, which contains the house's original well and a superb beamed ceiling. Menus here are the same as elsewhere, but the pervading atmosphere is a touch more tranquil and formal. Seasonally influenced dishes abound with locally sourced meat, fish and game prepared in a modern British style. It's the kind of place you might not want to leave, so stay on in one of the traditionally and individually styled bedrooms.

Food serving times
Monday-Saturday:
12pm-2pm, 6pm-9.30pm

Prices
Meals: a la carte
17.00/28.00

7 rooms: 60.00/95.00

Typical Dishes
Smoked duck
Baked cod
Bakewell tart

8mi South East of Sudbury by A134 and B1068. Parking.

Stoke-by-Nayland

069 The Crown

Stoke-by-Nayland CO6 4SE
Tel.: (01206) 262001 - Fax: (01206) 264026
e-mail: thecrown@eoinns.co.uk - Website: www.eoinns.co.uk

  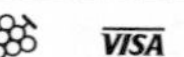 

Adnams, Greene King IPA, Pitfield Eko Warrior, Humpty Dumpty Reedcutter, Brewers Gold

"1530" is stamped on the outside of this promising-looking pub, but its comfortable and stylish interior – with a mis-match of sofas, leather armchairs and farmhouse chairs at broad tables – owes much to a recent sympathetic refit. Such is its local reputation that several spacious dining rooms soon fill with a mix of couples, friends and families, particularly for long lunches at weekends and holidays, so booking really is a must. With a new menu every fortnight, the hearty cooking keeps pace with the seasons and brings a regional touch to a couple of daily specials – plus a catch of the day – and a wider range of surefire gastropub classics: a handful of these come in either starter or main portions. The Crown is owned by a firm of wholesale vintners, and its wine shop sells an interesting selection, as well as local homemade chocolates.

Food serving times

Monday-Thursday:
12pm-2.30pm, 6pm-9.30pm

Friday-Saturday:
12pm-2.30pm, 6pm-10pm

Sunday:
12pm-9pm

Closed 25-26 December

Booking essential

Prices

Meals: a la carte
18.45/34.90

Typical Dishes

Palourde clams with bacon

Roasted Quail

Chocolate & pistachio mousse

Village centre at the junction of B1068 and B1087. Parking.

It's Britain's cultural centre, a business superpower and a fashionista's paradise, but where do you go to find the heart of London itself? Amid the money and the power of Westminster and the City, the mini-Manhattan of Canary Wharf or the bars and studios of Shoreditch and Hoxton in between? Down by Tate Modern and The Globe on rejuvenated Bankside, in the Thames meadows of Richmond and Kew or at the top of the London Eye? The boutiques on New Bond Street or the market stalls of Borough and Billingsgate? Dreaming in the Pavilion End at Lord's or paddling on the Serpentine? In leafy Greenwich, chic Kensington and Chelsea or the glitzy streets of Soho? Wherever you start within this changing patchwork of neighbourhoods, somewhere between The Mall and Metroland, the capital's pubs are moving with the times. Away from the bright lights, brassy Victorian gin-palaces, quiet mews bars and old local boozers are being restored and reborn as London's newest gastronomic gems, bringing good-value informal dining closer to home…

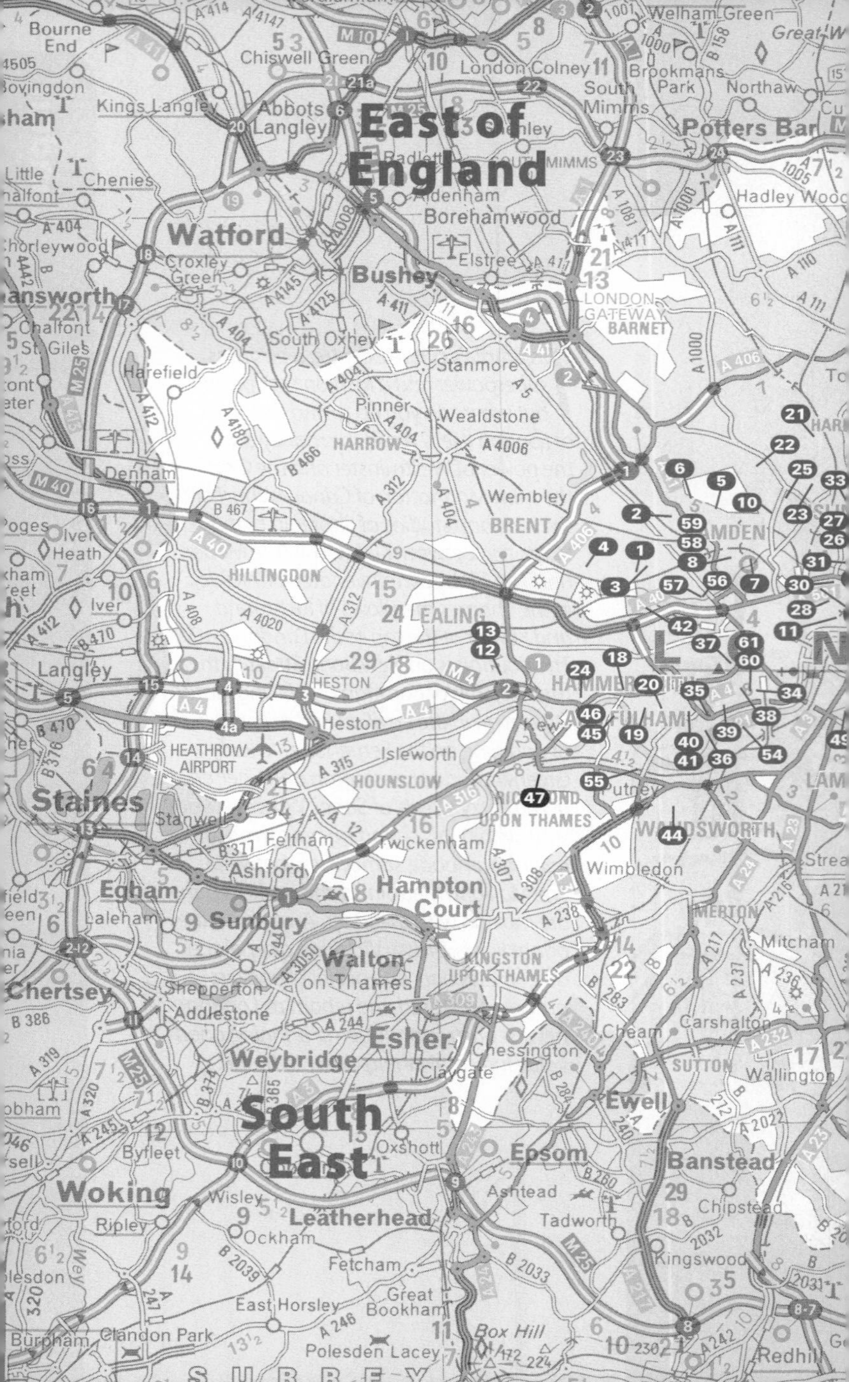
East of England
South East
Watford
Staines
Woking
Leatherhead
Esher
Epsom
Banstead
Hampton Court
Weybridge
SURREY

East of England
London
South East
Cheshunt
Epping
Waltham Abbey
Loughton
Chigwell
Abridge
Theydon Bois
N. Weald Bassett
Fyfield
High Ongar
Blackmore
Fryerning
Ingatestone
Pilgrims Hatch
Brentwood
Ingrave
Stapleford Abbotts
Hornchurch
Upminster
Ilford
Bulphan
South Ockendon
Aveley
Beckton
Woolwich
Blackwall Tunnel
Erith
Dartford Crossing
Grays Thurrock
Tilbury
Northfleet
Dartford
Swanscombe
Sydenham
Sidcup
Wilmington
Darenth
Istead Rise
Longfield
Swanley
Hartley
Farningham
Meopham
Orpington
Eynsford
Ash
West Wickham
New Addington
West Kingsdown
Biggin Hill
Otford
Wrotham
Warlingham
Woldingham
Ightham
Borough Green
Sevenoaks
Sundridge
Knole
Westerham
Ightham Mote
Mereworth
Shipbourne
Limpsfield
Chartwell
Oxted
Crockham
Waltham
Redbridge
Hackney
Tower Hamlets
Newham
Barking and Dagenham
Havering
Greenwich
Bexley
Thurrock
Lewisham
Bromley
Langdon
Downs
North

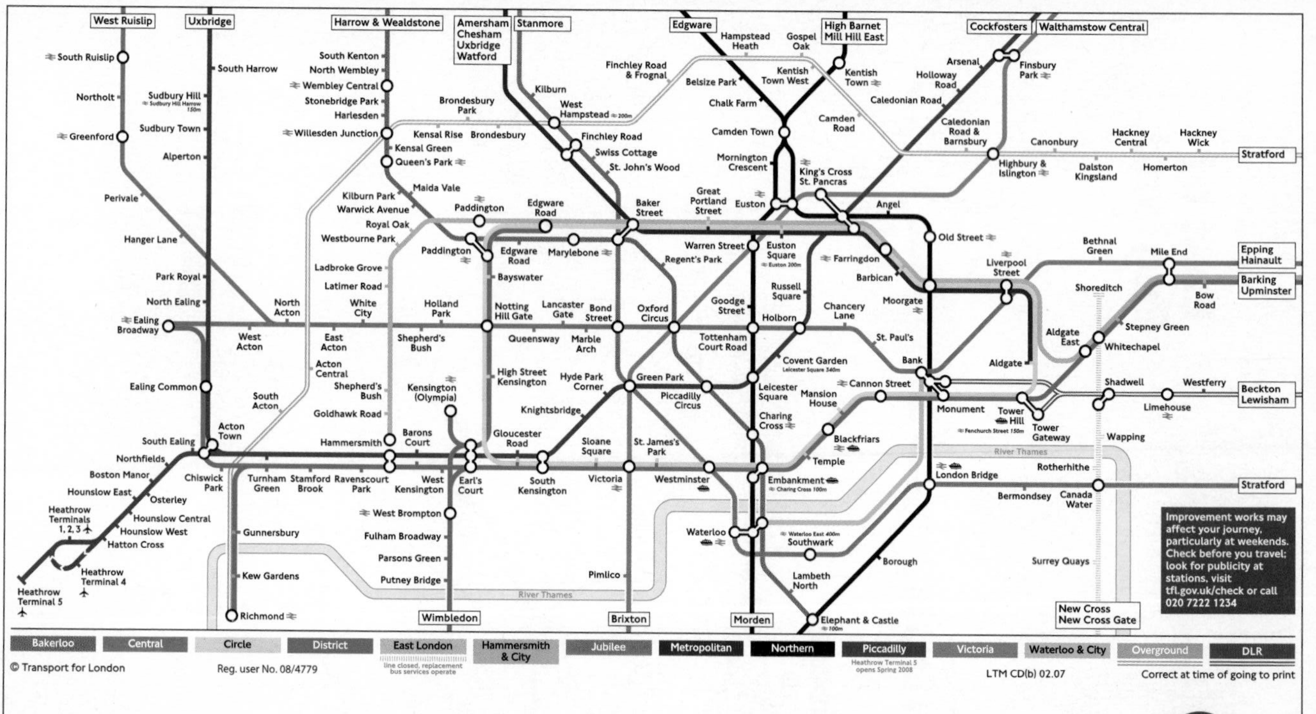

Registered User No 08/477

001 The Greyhound

64-66 Chamberlayne Road,
Kensal Rise NW10 3JJ
Tel.: (020) 8969 8080 - Fax: (020) 8969 8081
e-mail: thegreyhound@needtoeat.co.uk

 **Adnams Bitter**

On the left you have the bar, decorated with assorted sporting memorabilia and black and white photos of everyone from Samuel Beckett to Ronnie Wood. There's a blackboard menu on the wall which is served throughout the place, including the slightly more formally dressed dining room which occupies the right side room. This has an almost Edwardian feel with its green walls, mirrors, leather seating, mounted animals and old adverts. The flowers on each table brighten it all up and there's a pleasant enclosed terrace at the back. The menu covers all points, from the burger, steak or haddock in an Adnam's beer batter to dishes where a lighter touch is required such as sea bass with lentils. Pâtés are robust and come with homemade piccalilli, the chicken is free range, fish comes daily from Cornwall and vegetarians are looked after (if they can avert their eyes from the taxidermy). There are over a dozen wines available by the glass.

Food serving times

Tuesday-Thursday:
12.30pm-3pm, 6.30pm-10.30pm

Monday:
5pm-10.30pm

Prices

Meals: a la carte
18.00/25.00

Typical Dishes

Greyhound Welsh rarebit

Fisherman's pie

Rhubarb & apple crumble

 ⊖ *Kensal Green.* 

002 North London Tavern

375 Kilburn High Rd,
Kilburn NW6 7QB
Tel.: (020) 7625 6634 - Fax: (020) 7625 6635
e-mail: northlondontavern@realpubs.co.uk - Website: www.realpubs.co.uk

Timothy Taylor's Landlord, Grand Union, Harvey's Sussex Bitter, Adnams, IPA

Its Johnny-Cash-black exterior is a clue that here's an imposing former railway inn that's been given the makeover. The large bar, with its enormous blood red ceiling and original Victorian features, pulls in the punters while the dining room at the back is half separated by glass panelling and operates at a somewhat gentler pace. Here old church seats, large candles, glass chandeliers and high ceilings add a hint of Gothic. Kilburn Through the Ages comes courtesy of the black and white photos lining the walls.The cooking is satisfyingly full-bodied. Crusty bread is brought to the table and dishes come fully dressed so there is none of that side-dish paraphernalia. Along with the robust stuff like rib-eye, duck and tagines you'll find some Iberian influences which suit the pub environment well. This is also the sort of place where you find puddings rather than desserts and these come in man-size portions but diminutive prices.

Food serving times

Monday-Friday:
12pm-3.30pm, 6pm-10.30pm

Saturday-Sunday:
12pm-3.30pm, 6pm-10.30pm

Bar lunch Monday-Friday

Prices

Meals: a la carte
19.75/24.00

Typical Dishes

Parmesan & spinach tart

Calves' liver and chorizo

Plum and apple crumble

⊖ *Kilburn.*

003 The Salusbury

50-52 Salusbury Road,
Queen's Park NW6 6NN
Tel.: (020) 7328 3286
e-mail: thesalusbury@london.com

  VISA MC

 **Adnam's Broadside, Adnam's Bitter**

Salusbury Road is becoming quite a foodie quarter. There's a Sunday farmers' market up the road, plenty of local cafés and The Salusbury Pub & Dining Room whose success is evident by the presence of their own food store a couple of doors down. Two large aubergine coloured canopies highlight the location with one emblazoned with "pub" the other with "dining room" although you have to pass through the permanently busy former to get to the equally popular latter. Mirrors and large tables make the room seem bigger but the style is pleasantly higgledy and the occasional shared table contributes to the general bonhomie. The cooking, though, is more restaurant than pub and the menu has a distinct Italian accent. Good quality bread and olive oil set things off and the assorted pasta dishes come as either starters or mains. Flavours are pronounced, ingredients good and portions generous. It's also well worth leaving trouser space for dessert.

Food serving times

Monday:
7pm-10.15pm

Tuesday-Sunday:
12.30pm-3.30pm, 7pm-10.15pm

Prices

Meals: a la carte
24.00/32.00

Typical Dishes

Spinach and ricotta ravioli

Rack of lamb with mint

Chocolate fondant

⊖ *Queen's Park.*

004 The Green

110 Walm Lane,
Willesden Green NW2 4RS
Tel.: (020) 8452 0171 - Fax: (020) 8452 0774
e-mail: info@thegreennw2.com - Website: www.thegreennw2.com

Everything about The Green says gastropub, everything except the fact that this was never actually a pub in the first place - it was the snooker room of the local Conservative Club which, presumably, never got close to ever being this busy or, indeed, this much fun. Laudably, The Green has a healthy and involved relationship with the local community and the atmosphere is always relaxed and welcoming. The larger front section is the bar which offers a simple and appealing menu that might include jerk chicken or tiger prawns. The dining room at the rear comes in bold red, with high ceilings and an open hatch into the kitchen. That kitchen sends forth dishes that are both robust in flavour and generous in size, whether that's a bowl of mussels, a vegetarian risotto or more sophisticated restaurant-style food like foie gras terrine. The wine list is concise but inexpensive and there's an equally satisfying brunch menu available at weekends.

Food serving times

Monday-Sunday: 11am-10pm

Closed 25 December, 1 January

Prices

Meals: 18.00 (3 course lunch & dinner) and a la carte 16.00/28.00

Typical Dishes

Foie gras terrine
Pan-fried monkfish
Chocolate tart

005 The Magdala

2A South Hill Park,
Hampstead NW3 2SB
Tel.: (020) 7435 2503 - Fax: (020) 7435 6167
e-mail: themagdala@hotmail.co.uk

 **Greene King IPA, Fuller's London Pride**

Hampstead Heath covers nearly 800 acres of north London, so it is hardly surprising that there are a few strategically placed pubs for those seeking sustenance. Whether it was a stroll, an amble or a full scale hike, The Magdala is just the sort of place we'd all want to come across after physical exertion and is usefully placed just off South End Green. There are two bars, both with a hassle-free and welcoming atmosphere and the open-plan kitchen dispenses your typical modern gastro-fare which uses influences from around Europe but is also not afraid of dropping in the occasional Asian note. Those who prefer to dine in slightly more formal surroundings should head upstairs to the dining room which is used primarily at the end of the week and at weekends. Finally, all great pubs should have a secret and The Magdala was where Ruth Ellis, the last woman to be hanged in Britain, shot her lover in 1955.

Food serving times

Monday-Friday:
12pm-2.30pm, 6pm-10pm

Saturday:
12pm-10pm

Sunday:
12pm-9.30pm

Prices

Meals: a la carte
17.25/26.50

Typical Dishes

Tempura green lipped mussels

Oxtail and butterbean stew

Orange & Grand Marnier tart

⊖ Belsize Park/Hampstead Heath (rail). Pay and display street parking outside or 5min walk to Hampstead Heath car park.

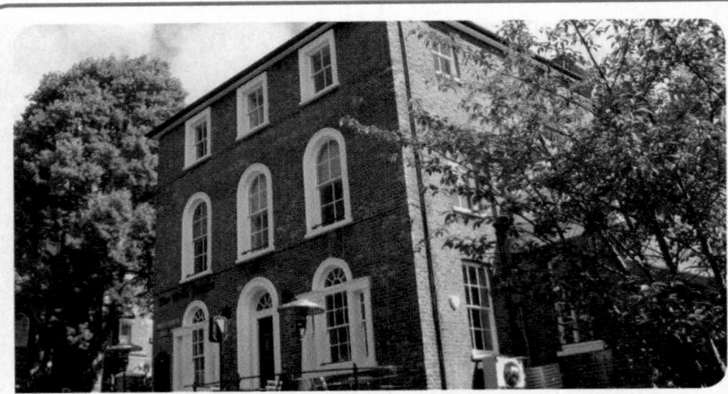

006 The Wells

30 Well Walk, Hampstead NW3 1BX
Tel.: (020) 7794 3785 - Fax: (020) 7794 6817
e-mail: info@thewellshampstead.co.uk
Website: www.thewellshampstead.co.uk

 **Adnams Broadside, Black Sheep Best Bitter**

Owned by Beth Coventry, the sister of restaurant critic Fay Maschler, The Wells is somewhere in between a restaurant and a pub. But whatever you consider it to be, one thing for sure is that it's in a grand old spot and adds to the mystery of why there are not more places to eat in Hampstead. It's equi-distant from the Heath and the High Street so whether you've been walking or shopping The Wells makes an ideal stopping-off point and the villagey atmosphere makes you feel that you're miles from London. The ground floor is the pubbier part, with a well chosen menu of dishes that go well with beer, but it can be a bit of a bun-fight, especially in summer and at weekends. Upstairs is an altogether more composed affair but one that still has considerable charm. Muscular gastropub staples like lamb shank or calf's liver with onion gravy sit alongside dishes whose flavours are more Asian in origin while others exhibit Italian roots.

Food serving times

Monday-Friday:
12pm-3pm, 7pm-10pm

Saturday-Sunday:
12pm-4pm, 7pm-10pm

Closed 1 January

Prices

Meals: a la carte
20.00/30.00

Typical Dishes

Pan-fried scallops
Seabass fillet
Passionfruit cheesecake

⊖ Hampstead. Limited metered parking on Christchurch Hill.

007 The Engineer

65 Gloucester Ave,
Primrose Hill NW1 8JH

Tel.: (020) 7722 0950 - Fax: (020) 7483 0592
e-mail: info@the-engineer.com - Website: www.the-engineer.com

 **Charles Wells Bombardier**

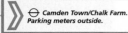

Über cool staff in T-shirts and jeans provide enthusiastic service in this pleasant part of town and a convivial, relaxing ambience prevails. The striking, part-stuccoed building is rumoured to have been built by Isambard Kingdom Brunel, and inside, the décor is contemporary and relaxing. The open bar has a light, airy feel to it, with tables not too closely spaced. The menu's the same whether you're in the bar, in the arty dining room or outside in the popular, plant-filled terrace, and it's an all day affair, with people coming in for breakfast, lunch and dinner. Food is well-sourced and boldly flavoured, with eclectic influences from Europe to the Pacific Rim, and choices might include salt and pepper tofu or tequila cured organic salmon. The chefs are well-established and take pride in their work - and it shows. People come in especially for the organic cheeseburger and the fabulous baker fries.

Food serving times

Monday-Sunday:
9am-12pm, 12pm-4pm, 7pm-12pm

Closed 3 days at Christmas

Prices

Meals: a la carte
18.00/45.00

Typical Dishes

Tequila cured salmon blinis

Miso marinated cod

Chocolate pot

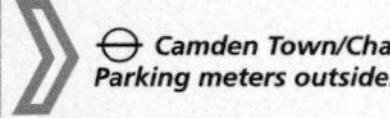

Camden Town/Chalk Farm.
Parking meters outside.

008 The Queens

49 Regent's Park Rd, Primrose Hill NW1 8XD
Tel.: (020) 7586 0408 - Fax: (020) 7586 5677
e-mail: thequeens@geronimo-inns.co.uk
Website: www.geronimo-inns.co.uk

Youngs Tied House, Youngs Best, Youngs Special, Bombardier, Waggledance

The Queens will have a place in the annals of gastropub history, as it was one of the pioneers in bringing decent food into an environment hitherto resistant to change and proved that a local pub with good food was not an oxymoron. Its location on Primrose Hill's main drag and alongside the grassy knoll is clearly another attraction and the balcony terrace is a sought after summer spot. The whole place was stripped down and done up in 2006 but the narrow ground floor bar remains an established local meeting point, with the footie on the TV in the corner. Head upstairs and you'll find a warm and welcoming dining room, prettily decorated in green. More importantly, the food is just the sort you'd want to find in a pub. Cassoulet, pork belly, pies of the shepherd or fish variety are all there in generous portions and dishes come with an interesting selection of sides. Wine prices are kept low and there's plenty on offer by the glass.

Food serving times

Monday-Friday:
10am-3pm, 7pm-10pm

Saturday:
10am-6pm, 7pm-10.30pm

Sunday:
10am-6pm

Closed 25 December

Prices

Meals: a la carte
15.00/25.00

Typical Dishes

Broad bean and feta salad
Queens fish pie
Eton mess

⊖ Chalk Farm. Parking meters in High Street; free parking after 6pm and at weekends.

009 Norfolk Arms

28 Leigh Street,
St Pancras WC1H 9EP
Tel.: (020) 7388 3937
e-mail: info@norfolkarms.co.uk - Website: www.norfolkarms.co.uk

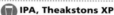

IPA, Theakstons XP

A onetime drinkers' paradise, the transformation of The Norfolk Arms to a North London gastropub has been as welcome as it has been absolute. The bench-strewn exterior is beautifully tiled and the inside is just as charming, with ornate ceiling squares, raw plaster walls and tables neatly laid with teacloth napkins. Dried peppers, chillies and strings of onions hang from the walls and light fittings, and the cured hams and salami that decorate the bar can be sized to order by the chef. On the menu you will find some British dishes, but it's heavily influenced by the Mediterranean and particularly Spain, and dominated by tapas. Quirky touches include food served in ceramic dishes (they say it retains the flavour), and the lack of traditional course divisions on the menu. Wines are taken seriously here and have their own blackboard to prove it. The private room upstairs is great for candle-lit tapas-sharing parties.

Food serving times

Monday-Sunday: 12.30pm-3pm, 6.30pm-10.15pm

Closed 25 December

Prices

Meals: 14.50 (3 course lunch) and a la carte 17.50/24.50

Typical Dishes

Buffalo mozzarella & fennel
Whole mackerel
Chocolate tart

⊖ Russell Square. Parking meters in the street.

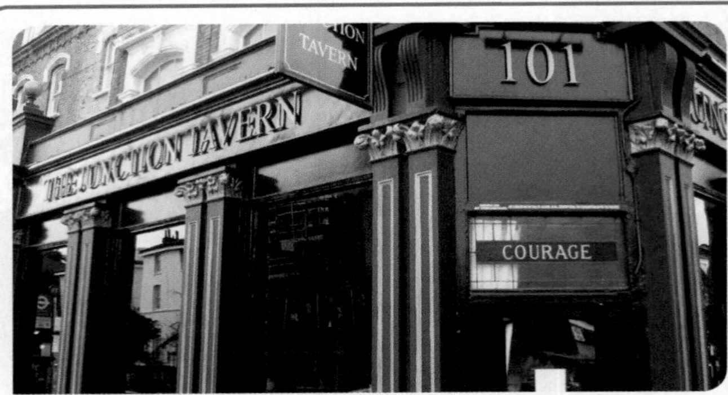

010 Junction Tavern

101 Fortess Rd,
Tufnell Park NW5 1AG
Tel.: (020) 7485 9400 - Fax: (020) 7485 9401
Website: www.junctiontavern.co.uk

Cask ales from regional breweries changing weekly

An immense pub a short walk from Tufnell Park Tube; with its brass cock glinting in the sun, you can't miss The Junction, and nor would you want to. Inside, it's just as impressive; painted ox blood red, with rich wood panelling, large windows and high ceilings. With a conservatory, dining room and terrace as well as the bar, there's plenty of space to accommodate the young crowds who gather here, and service is relaxed and efficient. The choice on the daily-changing menu is as eclectic as the range of cookbooks propped up at one end of the open kitchen. Wholesome and bold, choices might include wild mushroom and spinach crepes or dukkah crusted tofu - and the chunky chips deserve a special mention. An ale pub at heart, the weekly-changing selection here boasts a menu all of its own. Ale lovers also congregate several times a year for a beer festival, when pints are poured straight from the mass of barrels lined up inside.

Food serving times

Monday-Sunday:
12pm-3pm, 6.30pm-10.30pm

Closed 24-26 December and 1 January

Prices

Meals: a la carte 20.00/28.00

Typical Dishes

Spatchcock quail
Chilli crab linguine
Bramley apple strudel

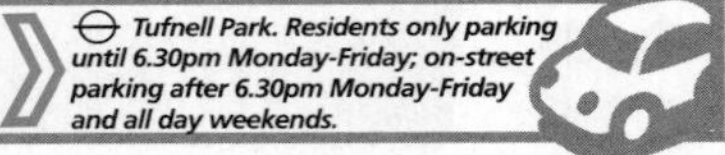

Tufnell Park. Residents only parking until 6.30pm Monday-Friday; on-street parking after 6.30pm Monday-Friday and all day weekends.

011 The White Swan

108 Fetter Lane, City of London EC4A 1ES
Tel.: (020) 7242 9696 - Fax: (020) 7404 2250
e-mail: info@thewhiteswanlondon.com
Website: www.thewhiteswanlondon.com

 **Fuller's London Pride, Adnams Broadside, Adnams Bitter**

Just off Fleet Street, the old Mucky Duck has completed an elegant transformation. A lively, free-spending after-work crowd can make the ground floor a busy press of suits and pints, but the vast mirror, reflecting the white sweep of the mezzanine and the big blackboards, makes this handsome, part-panelled bar feel bigger than it really is. In the quieter dining room upstairs, a long mirrored ceiling again gives a sense of space, while elegant, close-set tables and low-backed leather chairs lend a smart brasserie atmosphere. The bar menu with pub classics and a few earthier Old English dishes – pheasant pie, pork cheeks on mash and pints of prawns – makes way for a European and British daily repertoire that might include monkfish fricassee or lamb with gnocchi and root veg. Tidy if rather formal service. Good value for The City.

Food serving times

Monday-Friday:
12pm-3pm, 6pm-10pm

Closed at Christmas and Bank Holidays

Prices

Meals: 27.00 (3 course lunch) and a la carte 26.00/32.50

Typical Dishes

Seared scallops
Roast loin of venison
Pecan pie

Chancery Lane. NCP car park in Shoe Lane or free on street parking after 6pm.

012 The Bollo

13-15 Bollo Lane,
Acton Green W4 5LR
Tel.: (020) 8994 6037
e-mail: thebollohousel@btconnect.com - Website: www.thebollohouse.co.uk

 VISA AE 

Adnams Best Bitter

Already a popular neighbourhood meeting-place, this handsome redbrick tavern is at its best on bright summer days, when a buoyant crowd of drinkers and diners fill the spacious bar and make themselves at home on the terrace. There's a slightly smarter rear dining room – its wood panelling, burgundy walls and tan leather banquettes rather suit the pub's Victorian dimensions – but the full menu is served throughout. A core of suitably generous gastropub favourites needs no introduction, but the daily changing menu finds room for more eclectic and original dishes in the same forthright, full-flavoured style: their tasty, medium-rare tuna with braised peas, chorizo and celery is worth looking out for.

Food serving times
Monday-Sunday:
12pm-11pm
Closed 25 December

Prices
Meals: a la carte
20.00/45.00

Typical Dishes
Asian vegetable spring rolls
Honey grilled spring poussin
Home-made chocolate torte

Chiswick Park. Parking meters outside.

013 The Ealing Park Tavern

222 South Ealing Rd,
South Ealing W5 4RL
Tel.: (020) 8758 1879 - Fax: (020) 8560 5269

 **IPS, Old Speckled Hen, Timothy Taylor, Grand Union Wheat**

This impressive Arts and Crafts property was built in 1886 and extended in 1939, when the cavernous 'hall' area was added. Now used for dining, light streams into the hall through large windows and were it not for the open plan kitchen spanning the back walls, with its high ceilings and wood panelling, this could well be a schoolroom. Fittingly, the daily-changing menu is written on a huge blackboard above the kitchen, although how they actually get up there to do the scribbling is a question you could spend your entire meal pondering. No nonsense dishes made with quality ingredients are mainly British, with some French and Italian influences. Portions are generous and good value for money. Some tapas type dishes are also available in the bar, although this is primarily a space for drinkers. At lunchtimes businessmen from nearby office blocks come in to eat, but the buzzy atmosphere in the evening is down to the locals.

Food serving times

Monday:
6pm-10pm

Tuesday-Sunday:
12pm-3pm, 6pm-10pm

Closed 25-26 December, 1 January

Prices

Meals: a la carte
23.50/28.00

Typical Dishes

Whole roast quail
Barbary duck breast
Prune & amaretto crème brûlée

 *⊖ South Ealing. On street parking.* 

014 Cat & Mutton

76 Broadway Market,
Hackney E8 4QJ
Tel.: 020 7254 5599
e-mail: catandmutton@yahoo.co.uk - Website: www.catandmutton.co.uk

Adnams, Greene King IPA, Old Speckled Hen

In Broadway Market's trendier moments, Hackney's old drinking habits feel a world away and, to most of the Cat and Mutton's regulars, the names of Carrington and Toby, etched on its windows, must seem about as up-to-date as medieval stained glass. It still looks like a Victorian corner pub on first sight, but inside it's one large space: the plain, clean lines of the counter, the brick walls, the open kitchen, and the retro school chairs are lit up by those massive windows. A slate board announces the day's menu: snackier at lunchtime, with rarebit or hot sandwiches next to more substantial dishes. All in all, the cooking is robustly tasty; produce from the Saturday farmers' market is worked in well, and anyone showing up for a late, late Sunday lunch, deep into the afternoon, could find themselves staying for the live DJ in the evening.

Food serving times

Monday: 6.30pm-10.30pm

Tuesday-Saturday: 12pm-3pm, 6.30pm-10.30pm

Sunday:
12pm-3pm

Closed 25-26 December, 1 January

Prices

Meals: 15.00 (3 course dinner Monday) and a la carte 23.00/30.00

Typical Dishes

Sautéed duck livers
Braised pork cheeks
Bitter chocolate tart

Cambridge Heath/London Fields (rail). Parking Pay and Display in Broadway Market.

015 The Empress of India

130 Lauriston Road, Victoria Park, Hackney E9 7LH
Tel.: (020) 8533 5123 - Fax: (020) 7404 2250
e-mail: info@theempressofindia.com
Website: www.theempressofindia.com

 **Fuller's London Pride, Adnams Broadside, Timothy Taylor's Landlord**

Fancy a cup of tea? No, not a cuppa from the greasy spoon, but an aromatic infusion from the excellent afternoon tea menu at the eminently named Empress, just around the corner from Victoria Park. The building dates from the 1880s and pays homage to said title-bearer, Queen Victoria and her era, but has enjoyed various past incarnations as a nightclub, a print works, and a floristry training school. Now a smart, open plan pub with the emphasis firmly on dining, it's brightly lit with high ceilings, mosaic flooring, red leather banquettes and eye-catching murals picturing Indian scenes. Smart young serving staff wearing delicate pink bow-ties complete the look. The seasonally-evolving menu is classically based with some Mediterranean influences, and blends the robust with the more refined. The patrons use rare breeds for their meats and poultry, and these can often be temptingly seen and smelt cooking on the rotisserie.

Food serving times
Monday-Sunday:
12pm-3pm, 6pm-10.30pm
Closed 25 December

Prices
Meals: a la carte
23.50/35.00

Typical Dishes
Smoked and soused mackerel
Old spot pork belly
Chocolate fondant

⊖ Mile End/Cambridge Heath (rail). Parking in neighbouring side streets.

016 The Fox

28 Paul St, Shoreditch EC2A 4LB

Tel.: (020) 7729 5708

e-mail: thefoxpublichouse@thefoxpublichouse.com

Website: www.thefoxpublichouse.com

Charles Wells Bombardier and guest beers including Wye Valley Pale Ale, Sharp's Cornish Coaster, Hopback Summer Lightning

The Fox changed hands towards the end of 2006 but the new owners have wisely not interfered too much with the winning formula. For one thing, it still has that relaxed and lived-in feel despite the fresh coat of paint and the upstairs dining room continues to boast a sense of Victorian decorum in contrast to the animated bar downstairs. Now, though, the menu is slightly longer and is available throughout both floors, although the upstairs is still the best place to eat in – even the terrace is spoiled somewhat by the presence of an extractor fan. The kitchen knows its way around an animal and much of the cooking is red blooded – quite literally so if you order the onglet or ox heart. Many of the dishes come with a satisfyingly rustic edge and this no-nonsense approach married with seasonal pertinence keeps the flavours honest and to the fore. The service comes nicely paced and reassuringly knowledgeable.

Food serving times

Monday-Friday:
12pm-3pm, 6pm-10pm

Saturday:
6pm-10pm

Sunday:
12pm-4.30pm

Prices

Meals: a la carte
23.00/26.00

Typical Dishes

Smoked cod's roe
Braised rabbit
Rhubarb granita

⊖ *Old Street, Moorgate.*

017 The Princess

76-78 Paul St,
Shoreditch EC2A 4NE
Tel.: (020) 7729 9270
e-mail: theeaston@btconnect.com

Timothy Taylor's Landlord, Fuller's London Pride

A traditional Victorian pub which has travelled the modernist path of others within this trendy postcode, The Princess announces its gastro credentials atop an iron staircase within an eye-catchingly stylish first floor setting. Here you'll find bold wallpaper, oil paintings, sash windows and very comfortable leather cushioned chairs arranged at dark wooden tables. Rather than a lengthy list of dishes, chef concentrates on a concise menu, and the choice is invariably interesting and original. And well priced, to boot. The style is international, with Mediterranean combinations particularly to the fore. Waiters are friendly and efficient, and obviously used to being busy. This is a well-run pub that's strong in every aspect, and great to visit after a trip to nearby Spitalfields Market or Columbia Road flower market.

Food serving times

Sunday-Friday:
12.30pm-3pm, 6.30pm-10pm

Closed 24 December to 8 January

Prices

Meals: a la carte
22.00/27.00

Typical Dishes

Cuttlefish with fennel
Pata negra pork cheeks
Chocolate fondant

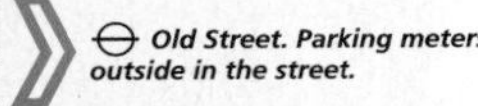

Old Street. Parking meters outside in the street.

018 The Farm

18 Farm Lane,
Fulham SW6 1PP
Tel.: (020) 7381 3331
e-mail: info@thefarmfulham.co.uk - Website: www.thefarmfulham.co.uk

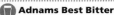

 **Adnams Best Bitter**

Don't misjudge The Farm by its offer of a football lunch menu, served before match-days at nearby Stamford Bridge: The Farm sums up the "nouveau" pub as much as Chelsea stand for "nouveau" football. Lustrous dark wood, dark-chocolate leather and subtle, sidelong lighting give the bar and dining room an ultra-stylish look, particularly at the back where smartly set tables aspire to the height of chic. Confident and flavoursome cooking introduces a French and Italian tone to a steady Modern British style; service is efficient, and its element of restaurant poise hardly feels out of place. It's just what the locals wanted: a good-spirited pub-full of them can always be found doing justice to the well-composed cocktail list, enjoying a few bar snacks or meeting up for dinner.

Food serving times

Monday-Sunday:
12pm-11pm

Closed 25 December

Prices

Meals: 24.95/28.95 (3 course lunch) and a la carte 20.00/45.00

Typical Dishes

Cornish lump crab meat
Poached skate wing
Crème brûlée

⊖ Fulham Broadway. Parking meters in the street.

019 Anglesea Arms

35 Wingate Rd,
Hammersmith W6 0UR
Tel.: (020) 8749 1291 - Fax: (020) 8749 1254

   MC

Timothy Taylor's Landlord, Fuller's London Pride, Old Speckled Hen, Hook Norton Bitter, Hop Back Brewery Summer Lightning

The best thing about the Anglesea Arms is that it's a proper pub. Granted, it was one of the pioneers of the gastropub movement, but it has managed to retain the looks, feel and atmosphere of a corner local and is all the more popular for that. This popularity does have a downside: if you have come to eat then take note that reservations for tables are not taken, so be prepared to wait. Fortunately the bar is a welcoming spot at which to pass the time. Another reason for the pub's continuing prosperity is the standard of the food. The open kitchen offers a decent selection of satisfying and full flavoured fare and they are not afraid of serving the type of dish more usually seen on the menu of an ambitious restaurant. Service makes up in endeavour what it lacks in alacrity and the wine list offers quite a choice if you're prepared to spend a few pounds, although the prices by the glass are far friendlier.

Food serving times

Monday-Saturday:
12.30pm-2.45pm, 7pm-10pm

Sunday:
12.30pm-3.30pm, 7pm-10pm

Closed Christmas week

Bookings not accepted

Prices

Meals: a la carte 24.00/35.00

Typical Dishes

Foie gras and duck terrine

Wild seabass

Apple tarte Tatin

⊖ Ravenscourt Park/Goldhawk Road. Pay and display parking Monday-Friday, 9am-5pm; after 5pm and weekend free.

020 The Havelock Tavern

57 Masbro Rd, Brook Green, Shepherd's Bush W14 0LS

Tel.: (020) 7603 5374

e-mail: info@thehavelocktavern.co.uk

Website: www.thehavenlocktavern.co.uk

Flowers Original cask, Fuller's London Pride, Marston's Pedigree

The Havelock Tavern has stuck firmly to its roots as a 'proper' pub, just one that happens to do decent food. Refitted and re-launched in 2006 following a serious fire, the place still looks quite imposing on the corner, and inside it remains not a million miles away from paid up membership of the spit-and-sawdust brigade. Don't bother booking: it is all done on a strictly first-come-first-served basis and you can leave your plastic at home – they only take the readies, although irritatingly that means paying at the bar with each order. However, it's all about the food which is good enough and well-priced enough to overlook these inconveniences. The daily changing blackboard menu lobs up a selection of balanced, hearty dishes, in portions so generous you'll be hard pressed to manage the full three courses. The influences range across the board from modern European to the occasional touch of Thailand.

Food serving times

Monday-Saturday:
12.30pm-2.30pm, 7pm-10pm

Sunday:
12.30pm-3pm, 7pm-9.30pm

Closed 22-26 December, Easter Sunday, second Monday in August

Bookings not accepted

Prices

Meals: a la carte 19.00/25.00

Typical Dishes

Hot 'n' sour steamed mussels

Pan-fried skate wing

Orange & amaretti cheesecake

Kensington Olympia. Pay and display parking Monday-Friday 9am-5pm, free after 5pm and at weekends.

021 The Queens Pub and Dining Room

26 Broadway Parade,
Crouch End N8 9DE
Tel.: (020) 8340 2031
e-mail: queens@foodandfuel.co.uk

 **Charles Wells Bombardier**

This classic Victorian pub was once known more for the fighting than the food but the 2006 makeover ensures that the closest thing now to an episode of EastEnders is the occasional presence of a cast member or two. The young owners have kept the eye-catching Victoriana, from the mahogany panelling and ornate plasterwork to the stained glass windows and wrought iron but the presence of a separate dining room shows where the emphasis now lies. The menu changes daily and food is served all day. It's a confident kitchen, offering a mix of modern British with plenty of Mediterranean influence so the sausages that come with the mash may include Toulouse as well as wild boar, and apple crumble might arrive with pistachio ice cream. There's a cocktail of the week and an accessible wine list with plenty available by the glass or carafe; non-drinkers are not ignored – there's home-made lemonade to stir childhood memories in many.

Food serving times

Monday-Saturday:
12pm-10.30pm

Sunday:
12pm-9pm

Prices

Meals: a la carte
20.00/32.00

Typical Dishes

Sautéed new season artichokes

Fillet of John Dory escabeche

Espresso pannacotta

Archway / Finsbury Park / Turnpike Lane. On street parking.

022 The Bull

13 North Hill,
Highgate N6 4AB
Tel.: (0845) 456 5033 - Fax: (0845) 456 5034
e-mail: info@inthebull.biz - Website: www.inthebull.biz

VISA AE MC

 **Weekly changing guest ales**

Since the spring of 2005, denizens of one of London's most sought-after areas have been flocking to this smart Grade II listed pub standing proudly on North Hill. The building dates only from 1906 but the earliest recorded date for a pub here is 1765. There is dining on both floors; upstairs, together with the small bar, there are striking floor to ceiling windows, a real fire and a relaxed style of décor; the art on the walls is for sale. Downstairs you eat at banquette seats in a smart, spacious area with good views of the chefs at work in the open kitchen. Menus are very appealing: simple European dishes, mostly English with a strong Gallic undercurrent, all home-made using top quality seasonal ingredients.

Food serving times

Monday:
6pm-10.30pm

Tuesday-Sunday:
12pm-2.30pm, 6pm-10.30pm

Prices

Meals: a la carte
30.00/45.00

Typical Dishes

Foie gras parfait
Chargrilled rib of beef
Apple tart

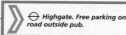

Highgate. Free parking on road outside pub.

023 The Old Dairy

1-3 Crouch Hill,
Stroud Green N4 4AP

Tel.: (020) 7263 3337 - Fax: (020) 7561 1851
e-mail: theolddairy@realpubs.co.uk - Website: www.realpubs.co.uk

No real ales offered

Of all the new pub conversions around, there can be few as characterful as The Old Dairy. Dating from 1890, the picture panels among the original red bricks and steel girders illustrate the listed building's former use when owned by Friern Manor Dairy Company. Despite the renovation and the locale's increasing gentrification, the pub has kept itself at the heart of the community by investing as much effort in the bar – which occupies quite a space – as it has in the dining room and the period photos of the area on the walls also help. The locals have certainly taken to the place and any background music is soon drowned out by the sound of contented customers. The cooking is bold and honest and how nice it is that dishes arrive exactly as described on the menu. It's modern British with a hint of Europe. The crisp sourdough gets you started and the portions are well judged and confidently flavoured. Weekend brunches are a real hit.

Food serving times

Monday-Saturday:
6.30pm-10.30pm

Sunday:
all day

Closed 25 December

Bar snacks all day

Prices

Meals: a la carte
19.00/24.75

Typical Dishes

Scallops & black pudding

Free range Chicken breast

Zabaglione & poached pear

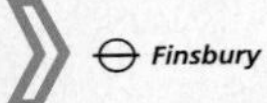

⊖ *Finsbury Park / Archway.*

024 The Devonshire House

126 Devonshire Rd, Chiswick W4 2JJ
Tel.: (020) 8987 2626 - Fax: (020) 8995 0152
e-mail: info@thedevonshirehouse.co.uk
Website: www.thedevonshirehouse.co.uk

 **Fuller's London Pride**

When a pub changes its name from Manor Tavern to The Devonshire House you can be pretty sure it has also turned itself into a gastropub. Strolling from the high street, past all the pretty terrace houses of Devonshire Road, and just when you're wondering if anything is down here, you'll come across The Devonshire, with its tell-tale modern sign and lettering. The interior has retained a sense of its Victorian heritage but with the addition of up to date leather furniture and a general feeling of openness. The daily changing menu is refreshingly concise and balanced, hints at the Mediterranean and proves that the owners here know their onions. They also know their hams, their olives and what goes with what. Those who prefer their food to be a little burlier are also catered for. Lunch is a simpler, less structured affair but still with sufficient choice. The shaded garden terrace provides a very pleasant little spot in the summer.

Food serving times

Tuesday-Friday:
12pm-2.30pm, 7pm-10.30pm

Saturday-Sunday:
12pm-3pm, 7pm-10.30pm

Closed 23 December to 3 January

Prices

Meals: 13.95/18.95 (2/3 course lunch) and a la carte 19.85/26.85

Typical Dishes

Deep fried brown shrimps
Irish lamb stew
Baked vanilla cream pudding

⊖ Turnham Green. Free parking in side street from noon to 4pm and 6.30pm to 8am.

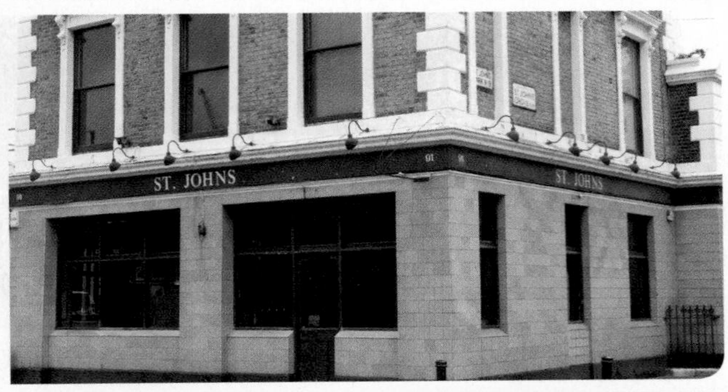

025 St John's

91 Junction Rd,
Archway N19 5QU
Tel.: (020) 7272 1587
e-mail: st.johns@virgin.net

Black Sheep, Abbot Ale, Grand Union, Summer Lightning, Cornish Coaster, Leffe, Hoegarden, Amstel, Guinness

If anywhere represents what can be achieved with imagination, enthusiasm and an eye for the bigger picture it is surely St John's. Not many years ago this was a dodgy old Archway boozer into which only the big and the brave would venture. It still looks pretty scruffy from the outside but inside it is a lively and very successful gastropub, whose fans include writers and actors from the smarter houses up the hill in Dartmouth Park. The front half is a busy bar but go through to the back (which was once the snooker hall) and you'll discover a vast and quite theatrical dining room, with a blackboard menu at both ends and one of the walls covered with pictures. The atmosphere is animated and bustling, helped along by the young staff who are chatty and obliging. The kitchen keeps the flavours to the fore, with dishes that are satisfyingly warming and gutsy in winter and lighter and more Mediterranean in the summer months.

Food serving times

Friday-Sunday:
12pm-4pm, 6.30pm-11pm

Monday-Thursday:
6.30pm-11pm

Closed 25-26 December, 1 January

Prices

Meals: a la carte
20.00/32.00

Typical Dishes

Beetroot & horseradish soup

Lamb ragout

Blackberry Bakewell tart

Archway. Street parking free after 6.30pm.

026 The House

63-69 Canonbury Rd,
Canonbury N1 2DG
Tel.: (020) 7704 7410 - Fax: (020) 7704 9388
e-mail: info@inthehouse.biz - Website: www.inthehouse.biz

 VISA AE MC

 **Adnams ales**

The House is a coolly sophisticated pub, tucked away in a residential part of Islington. It effortlessly combines a laid back vibe at the bar, which adjoins a triangular shaped terrace at the front, with a more urbane atmosphere found in the nattily attired dining room. Just reading the menu provides evidence that The House has loftier culinary ambitions than many a gastropub. Indeed, a number of the kitchen's carefully composed dishes would not look out of place in restaurants sporting a higher brow and a more prosperous postcode. But it also remembers it is a pub so alongside dishes such as saddle of venison with pomegranate or sea bass with braised fennel you'll find the good old ploughman's lunch (although ploughmen are rarely seen in Islington these days) and Shepherd's Pie (ditto). Weekend breakfasts are proving a hit and are undertaken in conjunction with the local farmers' market. Check out their other pub in Highgate, The Bull.

Food serving times

Monday:
6pm-10.30pm

Tuesday-Saturday:
12pm-2.30pm (3.30pm Sat),
6pm-10.30pm

Sunday:
12pm-3.30pm, 6pm-9.30pm

Closed 24-26 December

Prices

Meals: a la carte
30.00/45.00

Typical Dishes

Salt and pepper squid
Smoked haddock
Warm chocolate pudding

Highbury and Islington. Parking meters outside or free after 6.30pm.

027 The Marquess Tavern

32 Canonbury Street,
Canonbury N1 2TB
Tel.: 020 7354 2975
e-mail: info@marquesstavern.co.uk - Website: www.marquesstavern.co.uk

VISA AE 

 **Young's Bitter, Young's Special, Charles Wells Bombardier**

This Marquess is a handsome fellow standing proudly in his cosy corner spot. The Victorian character is still there but it's all been sympathetically updated for our age. Refreshingly, the owners' haven't just focused on the food and wine – beer and whisky enjoy equal billing with the former the perfect accompaniment to the offerings at the bar, like cheese sandwiches or pork pie and pickles and there's even mead and Pomona on offer. The dining room is at the far end, with high ceilings and a period feel, although the blackboard menu can be enjoyed anywhere. The cooking is resolutely and laudably British and suits the place perfectly. Sourcing and traceability are taken seriously, with small, independent suppliers used where possible. The cooking is satisfying and hearty, with some of the meat dishes such as lamb shoulder designed for sharing. The wine list continues the British theme by offering some bottles from Cornwall and Kent.

Food serving times
Monday-Sunday:
12pm-11pm
Closed 25 December

Prices
Meals: 15.00 (3 course lunch) and a la carte 22.00/30.00

Typical Dishes
Chicken livers
Forerib of Yorkshire beef
Spotted Dick

 ⊖ *Highbury and Islington.* 

028 The Coach & Horses

26-28 Ray St, Clerkenwell EC1R 3DJ
Tel.: (020) 7278 8990 - Fax: (020) 7278 1478
e-mail: info@thecoachandhorses.com
Website: www.thecoachandhorses.com

Adnams, Fuller's London Pride, Timothy Taylor's Landlord

Tucked away off the Farringdon Road, this is an establishment that delights in its self-confidence. Its ornate brick exterior is clothed in red and cream, and a cheeky sign might entice followers of Cinderella. Located off the 'main drag', it tends not to get as busy as most – the unaware are missing out on a certain element of eccentricity, not least from the chef who's called Scott Welsh and hails from Ireland! His dishes are fiercely seasonal and carefully compiled from painstakingly sourced suppliers. There aren't too many ingredients or unnecessary garnishes; you might even detect an influence from the nearby St John oozing from the rustic fare - for example: snipped pig's ear on split pea soup. No shortage of bare tables and chairs to sit at in the down-to-earth interior; in good weather, head for the sunny 'Back Room' terrace.

Food serving times

Monday-Friday:
12pm-3pm, 6pm-10pm

Saturday:
6pm-10pm

Sunday:
12pm-3pm

Closed 24-27 December

Prices

Meals: a la carte
19.00/26.50

Typical Dishes

Broccoli & boiled duck egg
Glo'ster Old Spot Hock
Chocolate and hazlenut cake

⊖ Faringdon. Parking meters across the road.

029 The Peasant

240 St John St,
Finsbury EC1V 4PH
Tel.: (020) 7336 7726 - Fax: (020) 7490 1089
e-mail: gapsbairs@aol.com - Website: www.thepeasant.co.uk

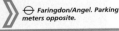

Sharp's, Skinners, Dark Star, Black Sheep, Crouch Vale, Czech Budvar, Leffe, de Konick Ale

As a senior member of the London gastropub scene, The Peasant continues to set the standard for others to follow and one of its greatest strengths is that it is still very much a 'real' pub. Bursting with character and atmosphere, the Victorian origins are there for all to see with its arched windows, high ceilings, mosaic floor and tiles showing St George slaying the dragon. In the bar, the light bites and tapas served provide the perfect accompaniment to the range of beers on offer. Those looking for a more structured dining experience and a less frenetic vibe should head for the upstairs restaurant, decorated with fairground-themed artwork. Here, the words 'pub' and 'traditional' seem less relevant as the cooking is decidedly original and far removed from the usual gastropub staples. The kitchen is not afraid of trying unusual combinations and flavours could be from India one moment, South America the next.

Food serving times

Monday-Sunday:
12pm-3pm, 6pm-10.30pm

Closed 25 December to 3 January

Booking essential

Prices

Meals: 14.00/18.00 (2 / 3 course lunch) and a la carte 30.00/35.00

Typical Dishes

Seared scallops
Denham Estate venison
Hazlenut profiteroles

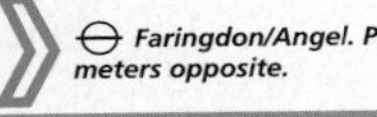

⊖ Faringdon/Angel. Parking meters opposite.

030 The Well

180 St John St,
Finsbury EC1V 4JY

Tel.: (020) 7251 9363 - Fax: (020) 7253 9683
e-mail: drink@downthewell.co.uk - Website: www.downthewell.co.uk

No real ales offered

Finsbury locals may not glance twice as they pass this predictable looking pub-on-a-corner in a trendy part of St John Street not unacquainted with food-and-drink destinations. But regulars in The Well know they're on to a good thing here. Big blue canopies hang out over the pavement providing shelter for drinkers at al fresco benches next to slide-open screen windows. Inside, it's small, busy and buzzing: all around is the ambience of the metropolitan gastropub with wooden floorboards, exposed brickwork and mismatched wood furniture. It's the food that lifts it above the average, with everything from the 'pie of the week' to sophisticated, accomplished dishes in the modern British vein: all the fish and shellfish is from Billingsgate down the road. Downstairs a sexy lounge with fish tanks and brown sofas draws a more louche crowd.

Food serving times

Monday-Sunday:
12pm-3pm, 6pm-10.30pm

Closed 25 December

Prices

Meals: a la carte
21.60/29.45

Typical Dishes

Grilled mackerel fillets
Boeuf bourguignon pie
Rhubarb crumble

Farringdon / Barbican / Angel. NCP in Clerkenwell Rd; free parking after 6.30pm in street outside.

031 The Barnsbury

209-211 Liverpool Rd,
Islington N1 1LX
Tel.: (020) 7607 5519 - Fax: (020) 7607 3256
e-mail: info@thebarnsbury.co.uk - Website: www.thebarnsbury.co.uk

     MC

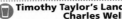

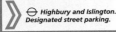

 **Timothy Taylor's Landlord, Fuller's London Pride, Charles Wells Bombardier**

It may have been spruced up a few years back but The Barnsbury is still your proper local. Hence, you'll find it on down-to-earth Liverpool Road rather than glossier Upper Street which runs parallel. The more traditional features of restored wood panelling and a large central counter contrast with contemporary touches, such as the chandeliers made from crystal wine glasses and the regularly changing local artwork. It's all very relaxed and the young staff helpful and competent. The owner, an acolyte of the Conran empire, clearly knows what he is doing. The menu will satisfy the appetites of both those who like to see recognisable British ingredients, as well as diners who prefer to see European influences on the plate. You'll find plenty of pasta, some Spanish charcuterie, Greek salads and cheeses from feta to Roquefort. British and Italian favourites feature in the desserts which come in man-size portions.

Food serving times

Monday-Sunday:
12pm-3pm, 6.30pm-10pm

Closed 25-26 December, 1 January

Prices

Meals: a la carte
22.50/33.00

Typical Dishes

Cornish crab cocktail
Roast breast of chicken
Rhubarb & apple crumble

⊖ Highbury and Islington.
Designated street parking.

032 The Drapers Arms

44 Barnsbury St,
Islington N1 1ER

Tel.: (020) 7619 0348 - Fax: (020) 7619 0413
e-mail: info@thedrapersarms.co.uk - Website: www.thedrapersarms.co.uk

    MC

 **Courage Best, Old Speckled Hen and 1 monthly guest ale**

An impressive and substantial stone façade announces this proud looking Georgian pub tucked away in one of fashionable Islington's quiet side streets. It was once a ramshackle boozer, but in the last few years has undergone something of a "gastropub" rebirth: rough wooden floors, plenty of space to air-kiss, shiny leather sofas, tables and booths sited along walls made over with a contemporary palette. A delightful rear courtyard terrace is great for summer smooching, and food comes with the guarantee of a light, precise touch: white gazpacho with chilli tiger prawns; gnocchi with Gorgonzola; salmon and cod fishcake with spinach and tartare sauce.

Food serving times

Monday-Saturday:
12pm-3pm, 7pm-10pm

Sunday:
12pm-3pm, 6pm-9.30pm

Closed 24-27 December, sometimes 31 December

Prices

Meals: a la carte
23.00/30.00

Typical Dishes

Squid & chorizo salad
Fish & chips
Lemon Tart

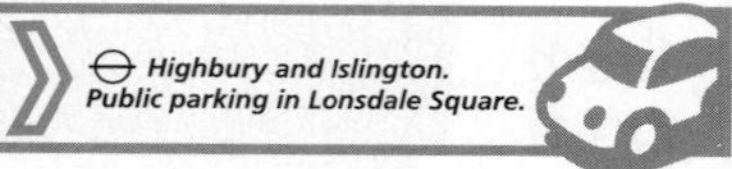
Highbury and Islington.
Public parking in Lonsdale Square.

033 The Northgate

113 Southgate Rd,
Islington N1 3JS
Tel.: (020) 7359 7392

 **Fuller's London Pride, Deuchars IPA and 1 regularly changing guest beer**

The Northgate is a large, square Victorian pub located on a corner of, rather confusingly, Southgate Road. It may look fairly unremarkable from the outside but this was one of the first of many Islington pubs to blossom into a gastro variety. However, there remains an honesty about this place which engenders a relaxed and welcoming vibe, even when it is full-on busy - which appears to be most evenings. The front section comes decked out with the gastropub uniform of mismatched furniture and modern art, with a large central bar. There's a separate dining room at the back with a skylight and the terrace is a big draw when the sun has got his hat on. From the blackboard menu comes liberally sized plates of satisfying wholesome gastropub staples mixed with others of more ambitious provenance. Care is taken to correspond with the seasons, fish is handled particularly dextrously and all appetites are guaranteed to be sated.

Food serving times

Tuesday-Saturday:
12pm-4pm, 6.30pm-10.30pm

Sunday:
12pm-4pm, 6.30pm-9.30pm

Monday:
6.30pm-9.30pm

Closed 25-26 December, 1 January

Prices

Meals: a la carte 18.50/30.00

Typical Dishes

Seared scallops
Pan roast venison rump
Chocolate soufflé

⊖ Essex Road/Canonbury (rail). Unrestricted street parking Sunday, after 6.30pm Monday-Saturday.

034 Builders Arms

13 Britten St, Chelsea SW3 3TY

Tel.: (020) 7349 9040

e-mail: buildersarms@geronimo-inns.co.uk

Website: www.geronimo-inns.co.uk

 VISA AE MC

Fuller's London Pride, St Austell Tribute, Sharp's Doombar, Adnams Best Bitter

Discreetly tucked away in a residential area of Chelsea, it can be hard to park near The Builders Arms before 6.30 p.m., by which time the bar is packed to bursting with well-heeled locals. It's advisable to arrive early for dinner, anyway, since they don't take bookings; and orders are only taken at 7.15 p.m. on the dot, at which point the service swings into action like a minor military operation. Once you understand all of these unwritten rules, however, you'll find service polite and helpful. Beyond the bar, swarms congregate noisily on sofas, while diners tend to head for the stripped pine tables on the other side. Slightly less frenetic is the glass-roofed area at the back. Food here mixes gutsy, classic pub food with contemporary European dishes, and pies and fish and chips sit happily on the menu alongside salt and pepper squid with chilli dip, or steak with marrow.

Food serving times

Monday-Wednesday:
12pm-2.30pm, 7pm-10pm

Thursday-Friday:
12pm-2.30pm, 7pm-11pm

Saturday-Sunday:
12pm-4pm, 7pm-11pm
(9pm Sunday)

Closed 25-26 December

Bookings not accepted

Prices

Meals: a la carte
20.00/35.00

Typical Dishes

Asparagus Toastie Box
Fish and chips
Sticky date pudding

South Kensington. Parking meters available on adjacent roads.

035 Chelsea Ram

32 Burnaby St,
Chelsea SW10 0PL
Tel.: (020) 7351 4008
e-mail: bookings@chelsearam.co.uk

 **Youngs Bitter, Youngs Special, Charles Wells Bombardier**

Standing out like a hardy reminder of old London near the rather soulless enclaves of Chelsea Harbour, this solid citizen of a dining pub draws in the punters like a magnet: it's on a corner so it's hard to miss it. Walk in and a feeling of good cheer is instantly awakened. This could be something to do with the bright, airy interior with warm yellow hued walls, or the light that pours in through the etched glass windows. Maybe it's just the knowledge that good beer is on handpump and interesting menus lurk round the back in intimate dining alcoves - an internationally influenced choice of dishes is up for grabs: start off, maybe, with Thai duck salad and follow it up with smoked haddock, black pudding and crushed potato. The shelves of old books might serve to remind you that in a past incarnation this was a junk shop.

Food serving times
Monday-Saturday:
12pm-3pm, 6.30pm-10.30pm
Sunday:
12pm-3pm, 6.30pm-9.30pm

Prices
Meals: a la carte
17.50/24.00

Typical Dishes
Pan-fried squid
Confit of duck leg
Rhubarb & apple crumble

⊖ West Brompton. Parking meters available nearby; single yellow lines after 6.30pm.

036 Lots Road Pub & Dining Room

114 Lots Rd,
Chelsea SW10 0RJ

Tel.: (020) 7352 6645 - Fax: (020) 7376 4975
e-mail: lotsroad@foodandfuel.co.uk - Website: www.lotsroadpub.com

  AE MC

Fuller's London Pride, Adnams, Hook Norton, Charles Wells Bombardier

If you make a decision not to pay a visit to this place based on the premise that the more people you can see through the windows, the better the pub, you'll be making a grave mistake. The high windows of this corner building give the impression that it is empty; in reality, the reverse is true. The local thirty and fortysomethings who frequent it might prefer you to think otherwise, however; that way they could keep it for themselves. What keeps them coming back time and again are the earthy pub dishes such as tasty hamburgers, lamb shanks and belly pork offered on a daily-changing menu, plus the heart-warming puddings just like Mamma used to make. The sign reads, 'You haven't lived until you've tried our sticky toffee pud,' and its popularity bears witness. Diligent and friendly young staff stay on the move between table and open kitchen. Thursday evenings see regular wine tastings, with bar snacks laid on.

Food serving times
Monday-Sunday:
12pm-5.30pm, 6pm-10pm

Prices
Meals: a la carte
35.00/60.00

Typical Dishes
Crab and avocado salad
Lincolnshire sausages
Sticky toffee pudding

West Brompton. On street parking meters.

037 Swag and Tails

10-11 Fairholt St,
Knightsbridge, Chelsea SW7 1EG
Tel.: (020) 7584 6926 - Fax: (020) 7581 9935
e-mail: theswag@swagandtails.com - Website: www.swagandtails.com

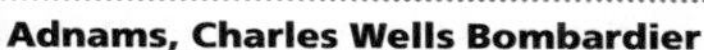

Adnams, Charles Wells Bombardier

The Swag and Tails is found in a quiet mews close to Harrods and is one of the prettier pubs around, with its charming display of hanging baskets. It is also one that has that welcoming atmosphere which comes from being privately owned. At the front you'll find the bar, with a log fire, panelling and those swaged and tailed drapes, while the dining area is at the rear with a conservatory extension. The kitchen clearly knows its customers and gives them a balanced selection, combining modern, Mediterranean-influenced cooking while still satisfying those who just want a decent steak sandwich. There's also a degree of sophistication in that the liver comes with pancetta and the duck is accompanied by pistachios; they also throw in the occasional Asian twist in the form of duck pancakes or spring rolls. Plates of charcuterie or Caesar salads are there for those with lighter appetites. Most of the wine comes in around £20 a bottle.

Food serving times

Monday (except Bank Holidays) to Friday: 12pm-3pm, 6pm-10pm

Closed from Christmas to New Year

Prices

Meals: a la carte 22.00/33.00

Typical Dishes

Pan-seared foie gras
Medallions of pork
Warm chocolate mud cake

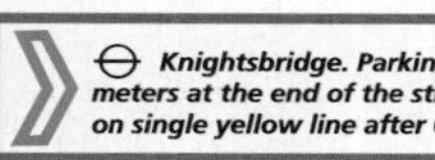

Knightsbridge. Parking meters at the end of the street, or on single yellow line after 6.30pm.

038 The Admiral Codrington

17 Mossop St, Chelsea SW3 2LY

Tel.: (020) 7581 4005 - Fax: (020) 7589 2452

e-mail: admiral-codrington@333holdingsltd.com

Website: www.theadmiralcodrington.co.uk

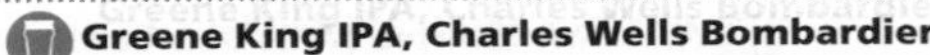

Greene King IPA, Charles Wells Bombardier

'The Cod' was perhaps best known in the 1980's when it became the unofficial common room of the Sloane Ranger. Twenty years later the pearls and Barbours have long gone and the pub has reinvented itself as a stylish gastro-pub. The bar is now a relaxed, easy-going spot for a drink with a short but well chosen menu. The separate long narrow dining room has been transformed into a comfortable and sophisticated space and comes with a clever retractable roof for summer days. The menu is an appealing balance of erudite restaurant sophistication balanced with dishes of a more comforting and familiar nature. So you'll find foie gras with a Muscat jelly alongside haddock fishcakes and rump of lamb next to baked lemon sole. There's also a healthy Mediterranean influence to a number of the dishes as well as a choice of homemade pastas available as starters or mains. Good old Blighty provides a few of the desserts.

Food serving times

Monday-Saturday:
12pm-2.30pm, 6.30pm-11pm

Sunday:
12pm-4pm, 7pm-10pm

Closed 24-27 December

Prices

Meals: a la carte
23.75/31.20

Typical Dishes

Salt & pepper crispy squid

Oxfordshire sirloin steak

Chocolate doughnuts

South Kensington.

039 The Cross Keys

1 Lawrence St,
Chelsea SW3 5NB
Tel.: (020) 7349 9111 - Fax: (020) 7349 9333
e-mail: xkeys.nicole@hotmail.co.uk - Website: www.thexkeys.co.uk

Courage Best, Directors (no guest ales)

The clue is in the façade. This may be a pub with a history dating back well over 200 years, but the interior owes more to today's sense of irony and fun. The bar offers plenty of elbow room and its own menu but, beyond, one finds the glass roofed dining room. This is the centre of things and comes complete with little statues, its own tree and an eye-catching frieze of garden implements. The kitchen is more conventional in its approach that the surroundings would suggest, with food that is modern in style but robust in flavour and influences are kept largely within old Europe. So expect to find alluring sounding dishes like smoked duck with glazed figs, wild mushroom tart with pesto, lamb cutlets, coq au vin and poached pear in red wine. There are also blackboard specials to supplement the menus. The two private dining areas, in the gallery above the bar and on the top floor, come with their own eccentric touches.

Food serving times
Monday-Friday:
12pm-3pm, 6pm-11pm
Saturday-Sunday:
12pm-4pm, 6pm-11pm
Closed Bank Holidays

Prices
Meals: a la carte
20.60/30.00

Typical Dishes
Bayonne ham
King scallops
Triple toffee Bavarois

⊖ Sloane Square. Parking in Oakley Street or in Battersea Park / Albert Bridge car park.

040 The Phoenix

23 Smith St, Chelsea SW3 4EE
Tel.: 020 7730 9182
e-mail: thephoenix@geronimo-inns.co.uk
Website: www.geronimo-inns.co.uk

Adnams Best Bitter, Sharp's Doombar

Even the most "comfortable" of London neighbourhoods has need of a superior kind of local, and the Phoenix gets the full approval of a friendly young crowd, all shopped-out from an afternoon on the King's Road or just kicking back on a balmy weekend evening. A retro tweak or two stops the stylish bar from feeling too uncongenially modern: only in Chelsea could this be thought of as 'shabby chic', but suede, stripped-back floorboards and some suitably clunky old wooden chairs give it a nicely lived-in feel. It's never less than pleasantly busy and, unlikely as it seems, the street-side seats have become one of the area's alternative "destinations". Extensive Modern British menus and a few specials serve their public well. Service is polite, friendly and never off-hand.

Food serving times
Monday-Sunday:
12pm-2.45pm, 7pm-9.45pm

Prices
Meals: a la carte
22.00/28.00

Typical Dishes
Boston style crab cakes
Pan-fried seabass fillet
Pear, chocolate & almond tart

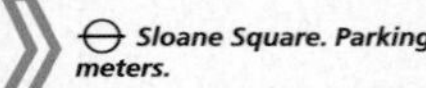
⊖ Sloane Square. Parking meters.

041 The Pig's Ear

35 Old Church St,
Chelsea SW3 5BS

Tel.: 020 7352 2908 - Fax: 020 7352 9321
e-mail: thepigsear@hotmail.co.uk - Website: www.thepigsear.co.uk

    MC

 **Uley Brewery 'Pigs Ear', Deuchars Caledonian IPA**

Around the corner from the King's Road, the lightly refurbished Pig's Ear still mixes in plenty of traditional style in a likeable ground-floor bar, with the odd pig-themed picture and ornament here and there. They're also represented on the menu – pigs' ears are not unknown as a starter, and are one of the more extreme examples of a taste for slightly uncommon but properly used ingredients. The bar menu works equally well if you want a set lunch or just a main course, though be warned that it can get very busy in here: you may need a little luck or determination to grab a space. If the panelled first-floor dining room offers more peace and quiet, and a more structured menu, the style of cooking carries over – hearty cuisine with a rustic edge.

Food serving times

Monday-Saturday:
12.30pm-3pm, 7pm-10.30pm

Sunday:
12.30pm-3pm, 7pm-10pm

Closed 25-26 December, 31 December, 1 January

A la carte menu Saturday-Sunday only

Prices

Meals: a la carte 25.00/30.00

Typical Dishes

Cured salmon & potato pancake

Crackled Tamworth pork belly

Caramelised banana tart

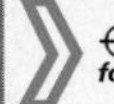 *⊖ Sloane Square (25 mins. on foot).* 

042 The Fat Badger

310 Portobello Road,
North Kensington W10 5TA
Tel.: (020) 8969 4500 - Fax: (020) 8969 6714
e-mail: info@thefatbadger.com - Website: www.thefatbadger.com

Fuller's London Pride, Charles Wells Bombardier

There's an inevitability about pubs around Portobello Road getting the full makeover treatment and, sure enough, The Fat Badger – named after one of the owner's with a stripy barnet – is the new moniker for that old haunt, The Caernarvon Castle. It appears to be the usual set-up inside with old sofas, church seats and wood floors but those chandeliers and that intriguing wallpaper hint at something different. Sure enough, one glance at the menu reveals that there is nothing gastropub-formulaic about the cooking. The chef's philosophy is British and seasonal, with a waste-not-want-not approach to butchery. Whole beasts are delivered to the kitchen and they are not afraid of offering unfamiliar cuts; the menu is constantly changing to reflect what the suppliers deem worthy and vegetables reflect what's in season. This is real and earthy cooking. Breakfast and brunch menus also reveal that this is a kitchen with imagination and integrity.

Food serving times

Monday-Friday:
12pm-3pm, 6pm-10pm

Saturday:
12pm-5pm, 6pm-11pm

Sunday:
12pm-5pm, 6pm-10pm

Closed 25-26 December

Prices

Meals: a la carte
20.00/28.00

Typical Dishes

Smoked eel
Roast haunch of English veal
Lemon posset

⊖ Ladbroke Grove. Parking meters in street; free parking after 6.30pm.

The Dartmouth Arms

043 The Dartmouth Arms

7 Dartmouth Road, Forest Hill SE23 3HN
Tel.: (020) 8488 3117 - Fax: (020) 7771 7230
e-mail: info@thedartmoutharms.com
Website: www.thedartmoutharms.com

 **Fuller's London Pride, Old Speckled Hen, Brakspear's Bitter**

The Dartmouth Arms' position opposite Forest Hill train station meant that this was once the sort of pub whose main selling point was as somewhere to dive into for a swift one on the way home. Since its makeover in 2004 it is now the sort of place in which to spend the evening. The original double doors now open into a friendly environment with art for sale on the walls, the usual hotchpotch of furniture and an open plan kitchen. The couple running the show know what their customers want and the menu offers an appealing mix of dishes from the single sheet of A4. Many have more of a restaurant pedigree than your average pub grub but there's commendable Britishness in evidence here, as well as a healthy regard for seasonality. So expect to see Barnsley chops, asparagus, samphire and Jersey Royals at certain times. There's also some invention so you'll find the black pudding in a risotto and crab in beignets with chilli jam.

Food serving times

Monday-Saturday:
12pm-3.30pm, 6.30pm-10pm

Sunday:
12pm-9pm

Closed 25-26 December, 1 January

Prices

Meals: 17.50 (3 course lunch) and a la carte 21.00/28.00

Typical Dishes

Smoked eel
Barnsley chop
Lemon posset

Forest Hill (rail). Parking.

044 The Fire Stables

27-29 Church Rd,
Wimbledon SW19 5DQ
Tel.: (020) 8946 3197 - Fax: (020) 8946 1101
e-mail: thefirestables@youngs.co.uk

 **Youngs Bitter**

'Gastropub' is a somewhat nebulous term to describe anywhere serving decent food in fairly casual surroundings and The Fire Stables proves that not all gastropubs were once old boozers. This may have originally been where the horses to pull the old fire engines were stabled but nowadays it calls itself a 'pub and dining room' and is modish in style without being threateningly trendy. It is also the nearest place to eat when leaving the well-known local tennis courts. Whatever it is, it seems to work. You'll find a separate bar area with its own snackier menu and a long dining room at the back overlooking the garden. Lunch times appear popular with mothers with young children, while noise levels become more boisterously adult in the evenings. The menu covers all bases, from Caesar salads and burgers to more adventurous choices such as game in season and rack of lamb. Puddings are full-bodied and satisfying.

Food serving times

Monday-Saturday:
12pm-4pm, 6pm-10.30pm

Sunday:
12pm-4pm, 6pm-10pm

Set price dinner Sunday only

Prices

Meals: 15.50/19.50 (3 course lunch/dinner) and a la carte 25.00/32.00

Typical Dishes

Foie gras & liver parfait
Saddle of venison
Sticky toffee pudding

 ⊖ *Wimbledon. Parking meters.* 

045 The Bridge

204 Castelnau Road, Barnes SW13 9DW
Tel.: (020) 8563 9811
e-mail: thebridgeinbarnes@btinternet.com
Website: www.thebridgeinbarnes.co.uk

 **Adnam's Broadside, Charles Wells Bombardier, Ruddles Best**

A short stroll from Hammersmith (and not Barnes) Bridge will bring you to the Bridge at Barnes. Got that? However you arrive, you'll find an attractively refitted Victorian pub. They have managed to retain much of the character and the front bar is a real delight and offers semi-private booth seating. Go through the second bar and you'll reach the surprisingly smart and neatly laid dining room that fortunately never gets too formal and opens out onto the modern decked terrace. The menu is all encompassing, from classic pub fare through to some pretty sophisticated creations. There are plenty of salads, both big and small, on offer which is something you don't often see in a pub and there are also dishes such as plates of charcuterie which are designed for sharing – an activity that should be positively encouraged in all pubs. There's a weekend brunch and a good value menu for those who like to dine early evening before the rush

Food serving times

Monday-Sunday:
12pm-3pm, 5.30pm-10.30pm

Closed 25 December

Prices

Meals: a la carte
25.00/40.00

Typical Dishes

Seafood pancake

Moroccan spiced rump of lamb

Banana bread

⊖ Hammersmith. Near Hammersmith Bridge, opposite Lonsdale Road. Parking in Arundel Terrace adjacent.

046 The Brown Dog

28 Cross Street,
Barnes SW13 0AP
Tel.: (020) 8392 2200 - Fax: (020) 8392 2200
Website: www.thebrowndog.co.uk

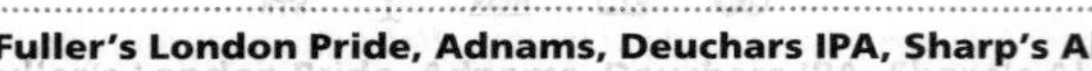
Fuller's London Pride, Adnams, Deuchars IPA, Sharp's Ales

Tucked away down a veritable labyrinth of residential streets, you almost feel you might need a ball of string to help you find your way back from The Brown Dog, and are unlikely to stumble across it in passing. Locals should count themselves lucky. Décor is charmingly stylish with cast iron fireplaces and antique furniture, eclectic artwork, and bulbous space age lamps. Set around a horseshoe bar, seating is split into snug lounge and separate dining area, and a relaxed atmosphere reigns. The daily-changing, seasonal menu takes a modern slant on traditional dishes and, although concise, is well-balanced. Good value food is popular in these parts, so make sure you book in advance; and if you're driving, factor in some time to park. Why the Brown Dog? Well, when a Geordie claims, "I'm taking the dog for a walk," what he really means is, "I'm off down the pub for a bottle of Newcastle Brown Ale." And not a lot of people know that.

Food serving times

Monday-Sunday:
12pm-4pm, 7pm-10.30pm
Closed 25-26 December, 1 January

Prices

Meals: 12.50 (3 course lunch) and a la carte 20.00/30.00

Typical Dishes

Ham hock & parsley terrine
Roast Barbary duck breast
Rhubarb fool

 ⊖ ***Barnes Bridge (rail). On street parking.***

047 The Victoria

10 West Temple Sheen,
East Sheen SW14 7RT

Tel.: (020) 8876 4238 - Fax: (020) 8878 3464
e-mail: reservations@thevictoria.net - Website: www.thevictoria.net

Old Speckled Hen

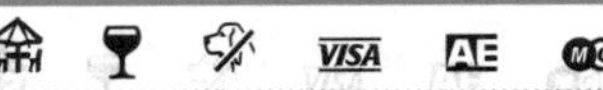

The Victoria is squirreled away in a leafy residential street but is also just moments away from the vast, regal expanse of Richmond Park, where over 600 deer roam free. Venison may not be on the menu but what will be is fresh, seasonal produce and a mix of British cooking alongside splashes of continental colour from the more southerly parts of Europe. Helpful menu notes are a lesson for all those chefs who try to bamboozle their diners with the muddled lexicon of modern cookery. So, expect a bit of pasta, fish soup, sweetbreads or sardines and the best UK produce such as asparagus, Jersey royals and samphire. The wines come in largely under £30 a bottle and are also accompanied by informative text. It's a sizeable place, with a roomy bar and a terrific conservatory. Children are positively encouraged, by virtue of the play area and the coffee-and-cake mornings which have proved a hit with local mothers.

Food serving times

Monday-Friday:
12pm-2.30pm, 7pm-10pm
Saturday:
12pm-3pm, 7pm-10pm
Sunday:
12pm-4pm, 7pm-9pm
Closed 24-27 December

Prices

Meals: a la carte
19.00/25.00
7 rooms: 108.50

Typical Dishes

Foie gras & Yorkshire rhubarb
Ossobuco alla Milanese
Seville orange tart

Mortlake/North Sheen (rail).
Parking.

048 **The Hartley**

64 Tower Bridge Road,
Bermondsey SE1 4TR

Tel.: (020) 7394 7023

e-mail: enquiries@thehartley.com - Website: www.thehartley.com

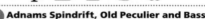

 **Adnams Spindrift, Old Peculier and Bass**

Local competition in this part of town may be a little thin on the ground but The Hartley still makes a valiant effort in flying the local gastropub flag. This red-bricked Victorian pub is also doing its bit to remember the diminishing local heritage by honouring, in name and decoration, the Hartley Jam Factory which once stood opposite and is now, predictably, a residential development. There are original posters, black and white photos and even jars of jam scattered around the place. The cooking also has a certain zesty appeal. Appetite-satisfying is the order of the day, with a refreshingly concise menu supplemented by daily-changing blackboard specials. Terrines, fishcakes and pies sit happily alongside more adventurous pork belly or swordfish dishes. The wine list is also kept quite short but is also kept affordable, with an adequate choice available by the glass. Service is relaxed and cool headed.

Food serving times

Monday-Saturday:
12pm-3pm, 6pm-10pm

Sunday:
12pm-3pm

Closed 25-26 December,
1 January

Prices

Meals: a la carte
16.00/28.00

Typical Dishes

Smoked duck breast carpaccio

Honey-glazed pork belly

Toffee and pecan cheesecake

⊖ Borough. On street parking (meters).

049 The Anchor & Hope

36 The Cut,
Southwark SE1 8LP
Tel.: (020) 7928 9898 - Fax: (020) 7928 4595
e-mail: anchorandhope@btconnect.com

Charles Wells Bombardier, Young's Ordinary

The Anchor & Hope is always and understandably busy, due to some degree to its proximity to both Vic theatres but mostly because of his culinary reputation. The fact that they don't take reservations means that it's worth getting here early - in fact very early – to secure a table although if you're willing to share you'll be seated sooner. The owners are of the sleeve-rolled-up school and take charge of the cooking, the delivery of the dishes and the serving of drinks. The general buzz creates a noisy but highly convivial atmosphere. From the tiny kitchen they produce immensely satisfying dishes, in a rustic and earthy style, drawing on influences from St John restaurant in Islington, but at prices which make the queuing worth it. Menu descriptions are understated but infinitely appealing: crab on toast, grilled razor clams, rare roast venison with duck fat potato cake, beef on dripping toast…

Food serving times

Monday-Saturday:
12pm-2.30pm, 6pm-10.30pm

Sunday: lunch at 2pm

Closed 25 December to 1 January, Easter weekend, last 2 weeks in August

Closed Bank Holiday Mondays

Prices

Meals: 30.00 (3 course Sunday lunch) and a la carte 20.00/37.80

Typical Dishes

Snail & bacon salad
Middle white pork
Pear & almond tart

Southwark. Parking in The Cut after 6.30pm.

050 The Morgan Arms

43 Morgan St, Bow E3 5AA

Tel.: (020) 8980 6389

e-mail: themorgan@geronimo-inns.co.uk

Website: www.geronimo-inns.co.uk

 **Timothy Taylor's Landlord, Adnams Best Bitter**

Within the sound of the Bow Bells stands this Cockney gastro-rub-a-dub; far removed from its previous life as a spit and sawdust battlecruiser. Inside, it's now all informal, shabby chic, with Chesterfields and banquettes and warm rugs on the floor. Snacks are served in the bar, but it's often noisily busy with locals, builders, students and whistles all having a tiddly, so your best bet if you're eating is to head for a Cain and Abel in the dining room. Take a butchers at the concise but constantly evolving menu; food is robust and hearty and will certainly fill your Auntie Nelly. Some dishes contain unusual ingredients and a glossary of terms is helpfully provided on a blackboard. Get yer Hampsteads around some braised pigs cheeks, devilled whitebait or oxtail ravioli. It won't matter if you don't have much sausage and mash in your sky rocket; you'll find starters for under an Ayrton and main courses for less than a Dudley.

Food serving times

Monday-Saturday:
12pm-3pm, 7pm-10pm

Sunday:
12pm-4pm

Closed 25-26 December, 1 January

Bookings not accepted

Prices

Meals: a la carte
22.00/35.00

Typical Dishes

Oxtail ravioli
Seared scallops
Assiette of chocolate

⊖ Bow Road. Before 6.30pm parking meters in Tredegar Square; after 6.30pm oustide.

051 The Gun

27 Coldharbour,
Canary Wharf E14 9NS
Tel.: (020) 7515 5222
e-mail: info@thegundocklands.com - Website: www.thegundocklands.com

Fuller's London Pride, Adnams Broadside

Restored after a fire, The Gun might have played more on an authentic naval heritage that begins in the era of the Blackwall cannon-foundry, the India Docks and that most saleable of maritime heroes, Lord Nelson. Thank goodness it didn't. The "Horatio" and "Emma" signs on the toilets are a small price to pay: relaid oak, polished black bar panels and white walls, and a print of a magnificent Dreadnought-era destroyer at full steam give it all the maritime London look it needs. Even the charming terrace keeps it real with a view of the Dome and the cement works. Blackboard specials make the most of nearby Billingsgate market, a great local source of fresh fish, and the modern cooking on a classic French base strikes a good balance between finesse and bold pub style. Keen service is neat and well-timed.

Food serving times

Monday-Sunday:
12pm-3pm, 6pm-10.30pm

Closed 25 December

Prices

Meals: a la carte
27.00/32.00

Typical Dishes

Salmon & oyster beignets
Braised daube of beef
Sticky toffee pudding

⊖ Blackwall (DLR). Street parking.

052 The Narrow

Narrow Street,
Limehouse E14 8DP
Tel.: (020) 7592 7950 - Fax: (020) 7592 1603
e-mail: thenarrow@gordonramsay.com - Website: www.gordonramsay.com

VISA AE  MC

 **Fuller's London Pride, Deuchar's IPA**

Gordon Ramsay's world or, at the very least, London domination, continues with his first foray into the world of the gastropub - and it appears he's cracked it already. For a start, he's found a handsome pub in a grand spot: a Grade II listed former dockmaster's house on the river. He may have sympathetically restyled it, but this still feels like the genuine article, albeit one with seating in the main dining room for only 32, so getting a table is going to be the trickiest part. But the real skill and experience is there to see on the menu; expect British classics alongside dishes that will stir childhood memories for many. You'll find potted crabs, sardines on toast, salt beef, monkfish and chips; and proper puddings, not fancy desserts. As you would expect, the kitchen knows what it's doing, and what's more, the prices are competitive, although too many of the tempting but individually priced side dishes can push up the final bill.

Food serving times

Monday-Sunday:
11.30am-3pm, 6pm-10.30pm

Booking essential

Prices

Meals: a la carte 17.00/25.75

Typical Dishes

Potted Cromer crab
Braised Gloucester pig cheeks
Gypsy tart

⊖ Limehouse (DLR). West side of inlet into Limehouse Basin. Parking.

053 L'Oasis

237 Mile End Rd,
Mile End E1 4AA

Tel.: (020) 7702 7051 - Fax: (020) 7265 9850
e-mail: info@loasisstepney.co.uk - Website: www.loasisstepney.co.uk

   VISA MC

 **Adnams Best Bitter, Timothy Taylor's Landlord**

Fully confident in his chef's abilities, the owner of the-pub-formerly-known-as-The-Three-Crowns decided that the new name L'Oasis would perfectly reflect its role in the culinary desert that is Stepney Green. The question is: does this watering hole refresh the parts that others do not reach? The answer would have to be yes. Although it doesn't look much like a modern dining pub - more like a narrow bar with slightly dubious neighbours – the inside is cavernous and brightly lit, with wooden furniture and floors, and original features including a delightful ornamental Victorian ceiling and decorative glazed tiles. Upstairs, a bright yellow function room copes with any overflow, service is friendly and efficient and food delivery is prompt even when they are busy. Concise menus offer hearty, rustic cooking with influences from all over the world, and what dishes may lack in finesse, they more than make up for in flavour and size.

Food serving times

Tuesday-Sunday:
12pm-9.30pm

Closed 25 December to 1st Monday in the New Year, 2 weeks in August

Prices

Meals: a la carte
25.00/37.50

Typical Dishes

Rock oysters
Wild seabass
Chocolate cheesecake

⊖ Stepney Green. Parking in main road and side street.

054 The Greyhound at Battersea

136 Battersea High St,
Battersea SW11 3JR

Tel.: (020) 7978 7021 - Fax: (020) 7978 0599

e-mail: sam@sampubs.com - Website: www.thegreyhoundatbattersea.co.uk

 **No real ales offered**

The owner's knowledge and experience, gained as a sommelier, is given full rein in The Greyhound's superb wine list, but its concise contemporary menu deserves to be at least as well known in this corner of South West London. Behind its neat, tile-and-glass frontage in navy and gun-metal grey, the comfortably remodelled pub divides into a stylish bar and a cosy, nicely lit dining room which opens on to a courtyard: great to have up your sleeve in summer. Even if you're not eating, there's an understated buzz out front, not to mention some interesting beers, but with such a well-priced set lunch on offer, plenty of people take them up on the deal. As in the evening, dishes make use of carefully selected, largely organic produce.

Food serving times

Tuesday-Saturday:
12pm-3pm, 7pm-10pm
Sunday:
12pm-3pm
Closed 24 December to 2 January

Prices

Meals: 31.00 (3 course dinner) and a la carte 16.00/30.00

Typical Dishes

Grilled octopus
Herdwick mutton loin
Chocolate tortellini

Clapham Junction (rail). Parking in Simpson Street or Battersea High Street.

055 The Spencer Arms

237 Lower Richmond Road,
Putney SW15 1HJ

Tel.: (020) 8788 0640 - Fax: (020) 8780 2216
e-mail: info@thespencerarms.co.uk - Website: www.thespencerarms.co.uk

VISA MC

 **Fuller's London Pride, Adnams Broadside, Hogs Back TEA**

If you're not drinking, you can go for a stroll on adjacent Putney Common. If you're not strolling, you can take in the more sedentary charms of this attractive Victorian corner pub, which, on a warm day, offers visitors smart pavement seating and a pint of Fuller's London Pride. Inside, the dining pub transformation is total. Left of the main entrance is an enticing 'library' area with leather sofas – lose yourself here amongst a plethora of books and games - a fireplace and plasma TV. Over the other side, the hungry are catered for in a rustic bar-cum-restaurant: scrubbed tables and mix-and-match chairs exert an old church/old school charm. Blackboard menus are concise - six starters, six mains, three puds the max - ranging from the likes of home-made soups to duck pie to Dundee cake with rhubarb compote…maybe the stroll should wait till this point.

Food serving times

Monday-Friday:
12pm-2.30pm, 6.30pm-10pm
Saturday:
12pm-3pm, 6.30pm-10pm
Sunday:
12pm-4pm, 6.30pm-9.30pm
Closed 25 December, 1 January

Prices

Meals: a la carte 22.50/29.00

Typical Dishes

Grilled foie gras
Mini rack of organic pork
Gingerbread & stewed rhubarb

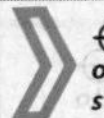

East Putney. Parking at top of Putney Common and in nearby streets.

056 Prince Alfred & Formosa Dining Room

5A Formosa St,
Bayswater and Maida Vale W9 1EE
Tel.: (020) 7286 3287
e-mail: princealfred@youngs.co.uk

 **Young's, Charles Wells Bombardier**

It is possible, if you're approaching from Warrington Crescent, to find yourself seated in the Formosa Dining Room and be virtually unaware of the pub to which it is attached. This would be a crying shame as the Prince Alfred is a magnificent Grade II listed pub which dates back to 1863. Its most striking feature, along with the etched glass, is the partitions creating individual private booths. Architectural purists may shudder at the more contemporary, almost semi-industrial, dining room which has been attached but local diners seemingly have little regard for such sensibilities and just enjoy the space. The very open open-kitchen produces satisfyingly robust gastro-pub staples of a mostly European nature. Typically, you could expect grilled sardines with rocket, followed by fillet of pork with apple and finished with a rich chocolate brownie. The wine list commendably features over thirty choices available by the glass.

Food serving times

Monday-Saturday:
12pm-3pm, 6.30pm-10.30pm

Sunday:
12pm-4pm, 6.30pm-10pm

Prices

Meals: 10.00 (3 course lunch Monday-Friday) and a la carte 21.00/31.00

Typical Dishes

Foie gras parfait
Roast lamb rump
Double chocolate truffle

 Warwick Avenue.

057 The Waterway

54 Formosa St,
Bayswater and Maida Vale W9 2JU
Tel.: (020) 7266 3557 - Fax: (020) 7266 3547
e-mail: info@thewaterway.co.uk - Website: www.thewaterway.co.uk

   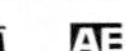 

 **Fuller's London Pride, Adnams Broadside**

A glimpse of sun and we're all outside, so praise be for places like The Waterway. Not only does it have a large terrace but its pleasing vista takes in the canal, barges and the church spire beyond, although you have to be quick off the mark to get a spot. This is as far as from the spit and sawdust pub as it is possible to get. You'll have to fight through the throng of drinkers in the stylish bar to get through to the restaurant which is quite a swanky affair - all wood and leather, with the staff dressed all in black. The kitchen balances the tradition with the contemporary to the clear satisfaction of its customers. So, the 'classics' section on the menu may include moules or burgers and there are barbecues and Sunday roasts but you'll also find more restaurant kind of dishes involving sea bass, belly pork or lamb. Puds are quite delicate little things and it's nice to see that cheese is taken seriously.

Food serving times

Monday-Friday:
12pm-3.30pm, 6.30pm-10.30pm

Saturday:
12pm-4pm, 6.30pm-10.30pm

Sunday:
12pm-4pm, 6.30pm-10pm

Prices

Meals: a la carte
28.00/38.00

Typical Dishes

Lobster ravioli
Roast rump of lamb
Valhrona chocolate tart

Warwick Avenue. Parking.

058 Queen's Head & Artichoke

30-32 Albany St,
Regent's Park and Marylebone NW1 4EA
Tel.: (020) 7916 6206
e-mail: info@theartichoke.net - Website: www.theartichoke.net

VISA AE MC

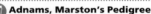

 **Adnams, Marston's Pedigree**

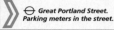

The location may be just about spot-on: bordering the park to catch the strollers and close enough to the Euston Road to get the office bods. The formula too looks like it hits the spot: modern European influenced food mixed with a large selection of 'tapas' in its loosest form. Either way, the place is always jumping, with the restaurant in an upstairs room decorated in a whimsical non-theme. The pub's history includes time as a royal hunting lodge, demolition and relocation but the licence can be traced back to good Queen Bess and apparently she loved a bit of artichoke. Today's customers can all enjoy completely differing culinary experiences. One might be having pâté followed by roast lamb while their partner has chicken satay followed by red duck curry. Tapas is the nebulous term for a huge and appealing mix of small dishes where the influences take in North Africa, the Middle East as well as Europe and is offered all day.

Food serving times

Monday-Sunday:
12.30pm-3pm, 6.30pm-10.15pm

Closed 24 December to 2 January

Prices

Meals: a la carte 19.00/25.00

Typical Dishes

Grilled calamari
Grilled poussin
Cape gooseberry tart

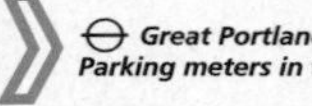

Great Portland Street.
Parking meters in the street.

059 The Salt House

63 Abbey Road,
St John's Wood, Regent's Park and Marylebone NW8 0AE
Tel.: (020) 7328 6626
e-mail: salthousemail@majol.co.uk - Website: www.thesalthouse.co.uk

 **Adnams Best Bitter**

First it was The Salt House, then The Abbey Road, then it changed back again to The Salt House. But whatever the name it has remained a reliable and inviting neighbourhood pub, with cooking that has a sunny, country feel and comes in man-size portions. The dining room's a few steps down from the bar, where the large picture windows overlook the pleasant semi-enclosed outside terrace and its style is of the relaxed, higgledy-piggledy school, with posters and lamps; some tables are dressed with tablecloths, others are nude. There's an upstairs for the weekend overflow and a snackier menu available in the bar. The bill can tot up without you noticing but there's plenty of interest in the menu, whether that's the sea bass cartoccio, the rack of lamb with sweet potatoes or the top-notch quality Scottish beef. There are always assorted pasta dishes available and more unusual offerings like rabbit casserole or honey-glazed poussin.

Food serving times
Monday-Sunday:
12pm-11pm

Prices
Meals: a la carte
20.00/45.00

Typical Dishes
Goat's cheese salad
Home-made tagliatelle
Home-made tiramisu

⊖ *St John's Wood/Maida Vale.*
Parking meters.

060 The Ebury

11 Pimlico Rd,
Victoria SW1W 8NA

Tel.: (020) 7730 6784 - Fax: (020) 7730 6149
e-mail: info@theebury.co.uk - Website: www.theebury.co.uk

 **Fuller's London Pride**

The Ebury has become an established feature in this part of town and has done so by successfully offering both satisfyingly hearty food and by providing its customers with the choice of two different dining options. On the ground floor one finds the busy and lively brasserie/pub with floor to ceiling windows and a thrusting young crowd, with a bar that is equally adept at satisfying their demands. Ascend the oak staircase and you come upon altogether more tranquil and restful surroundings, where the added formality and pretty decorative touches help create a very soothing ambience. There's a crustacean bar, ideal for those who wish to share their food, while the main menu reads like a manifesto for modern European cooking: there's everything from foie gras, pork belly and rump of lamb to other less artery-bothering offerings like roast cod with Puy lentils and guinea fowl with root vegetables. Desserts will be hard to resist.

Food serving times

Monday-Friday:
12pm-3.30pm, 6pm-10.30pm

Saturday:
12pm-4pm, 6pm-10.30pm

Sunday:
12pm-4pm, 6pm-10pm

Closed 25-26 December

Prices

Meals: a la carte
25.00/30.00

Typical Dishes

Pumpkin risotto
Salmon & sauerkraut
Roast pineapple

⊖ Sloane Square. On street parking after 6.30pm.

061 The Thomas Cubitt

44 Elizabeth Street, Victoria SW1W 9PA
Tel.: (020) 7730 6060 - Fax: (020) 7730 6055
e-mail: reservations@thethomascubitt.co.uk
Website: www.thethomascubitt.co.uk

VISA  AE MC

 **Adnam's Ale, Greene King IPA, Reverend James, Abbott Ale**

This sizable Georgian pub has been converted and renamed after the famous master builder, who would have approved of its elegant and well-furnished style. There's a split personality here: downstairs is where the drinkers gather and where those wanting pie of the day can repair to rustic tables at the back. Upstairs, however, it's a different story. The dining room is divided into three, with fine period detail at every turn, including edging to the ceilings, marble fireplaces, wooden laid floor, huge floral arrangements and chic grey painted walls. For the sheer sake of a talking point, wall pictures are hung upside down! Unobtrusive service is nevertheless warm and friendly. Time is spent sourcing suppliers, and the modern British dishes are appealingly seasonal.

Food serving times

Monday-Sunday:
12pm-3pm, 6pm-9.30pm

Closed 24 December to 1 January

Prices

Meals: 24.50 (3 course lunch) and a la carte 23.00/40.00

Typical Dishes

Poached crayfish salad
Crisp Norfolk pork belly
Poached pears

⊖ Sloane Square. Pay and display parking in Elizabeth Street and adjoining streets.

Strengthened by the iconic BALTIC Centre, the Millennium Bridge and the Angel of the North, the sense of identity which binds Newcastle, Gateshead and the region around them has made northeastern unity a modern reality. In the days of the mighty border fiefdom, Northumbria's independent spirit took shape in the castles of Bamburgh and Alnwick and the splendour of Durham Cathedral, though the most celebrated symbols of the region date back still further. The ruins of Lindisfarne Priory and lonely Inner Farne, just off the beautiful Northumberland coast, recall the austerity and learning of the first monastic settlers, and from Housesteads to Wallsend, Hadrian's Wall is the cornerstone of Northern history. But the North East doesn't stop here – to the surprise of many visitors from further south! Some of England's most impressive working countryside can be found in the vast man-made pinewoods of Kielder Forest and the rolling line of the Cheviots: these weathered volcanic slopes are renowned for flavourful Cheviot lamb, while Kielder is known for its venison. Other specialities include fresh and smoked fish and, of course, Newcastle's famous Brown Ale, the national beverage of the "Geordie Nation"!

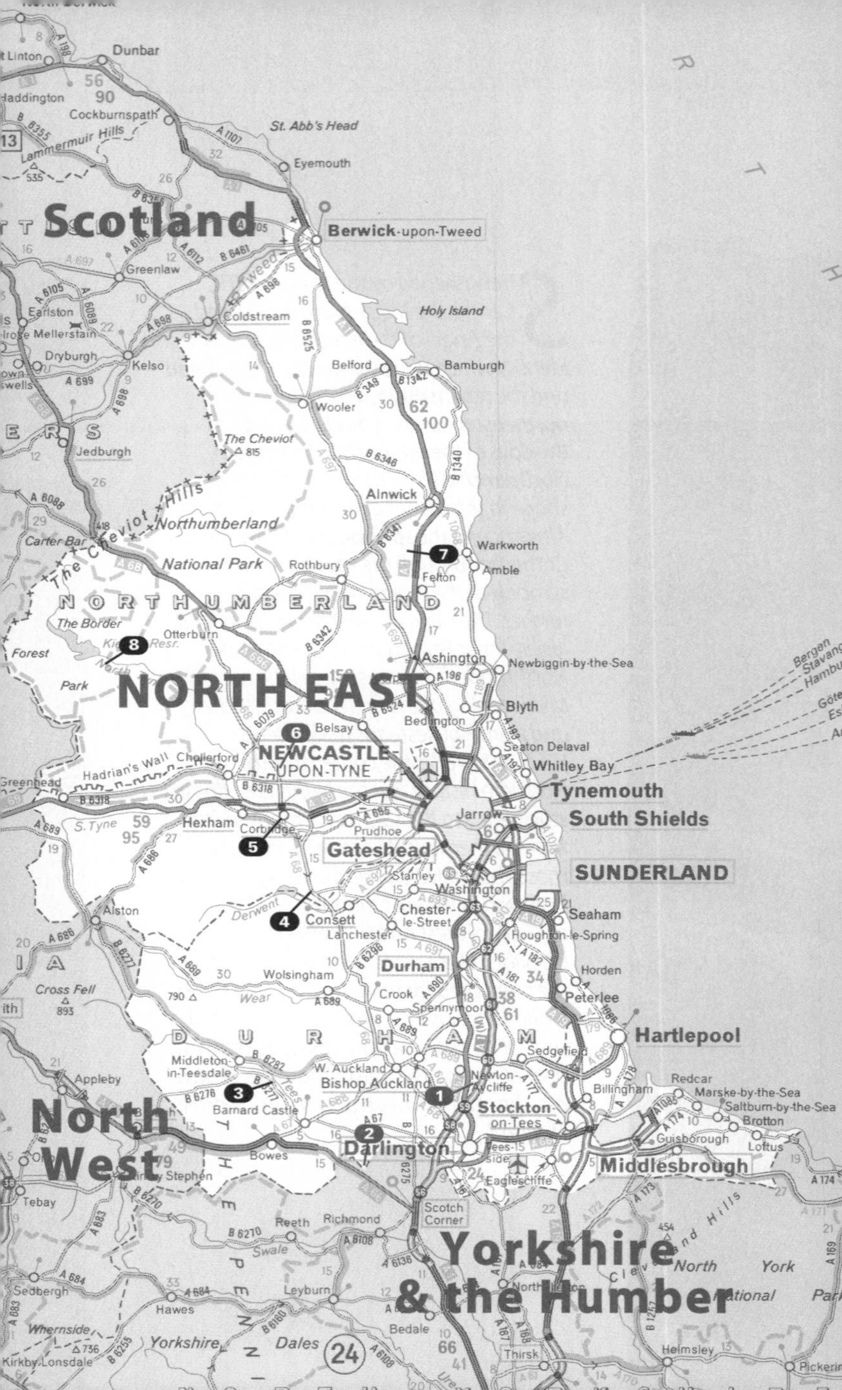

Scotland
NORTH EAST
North West
Yorkshire & the Humber
NORTHUMBERLAND
DURHAM
Dunbar
Haddington
Cockburnspath
St. Abb's Head
Lammermuir Hills
Eyemouth
Berwick-upon-Tweed
Greenlaw
Earlston
Mellerstain
Coldstream
Holy Island
Dryburgh
Kelso
Belford
Bamburgh
Wooler
Jedburgh
The Cheviot
Alnwick
The Cheviot Hills
Northumberland National Park
Carter Bar
Warkworth
Amble
Rothbury
Felton
The Border Forest Park
Otterburn
Kielder Resr.
Ashington
Newbiggin-by-the-Sea
Blyth
Bedlington
Belsay
Seaton Delaval
Whitley Bay
NEWCASTLE-UPON-TYNE
Hadrian's Wall
Chollerford
Greenhead
Tynemouth
South Shields
Jarrow
Hexham
Corbridge
Prudhoe
Gateshead
SUNDERLAND
Stanley
Washington
Consett
Chester-le-Street
Lanchester
Seaham
Houghton-le-Spring
Alston
Durham
Horden
Peterlee
Wolsingham
Crook
Cross Fell
Spennymoor
Hartlepool
Sedgefield
Middleton-in-Teesdale
W. Auckland
Bishop Auckland
Newton Aycliffe
Appleby
Barnard Castle
Stockton-on-Tees
Billingham
Redcar
Marske-by-the-Sea
Saltburn-by-the-Sea
Brotton
Guisborough
Loftus
Darlington
Bowes
Middlesbrough
Teesside
Eaglescliffe
Kirkby Stephen
Tebay
Scotch Corner
Reeth
Richmond
Swale
Cleveland Hills
North York Moors National Park
Sedbergh
Hawes
Leyburn
Northallerton
Bedale
Whernside
Yorkshire Dales
Kirkby Lonsdale
Thirsk
Helmsley
Pickering
Bergen
Stavanger
Hamburg

001 The County

13 The Green,
Aycliffe DL5 6LX
Tel.: (01325) 312273

Charles Wells Bombardier, Theakstons XB, Village Brewer Old Raby

Chef Andrew Brown was the first person to win a Raymond Blanc scholarship in 1995, and is certainly making up for a late start to the profession. Thanks to owning a pub in Tony Blair's constituency, he can count presidents and prime ministers among his previous customers. Perhaps they had heard about the friendly, informal atmosphere to be found here and wanted to experience it for themselves. They certainly must have heard about the quality of the robust, modern, seasonally-inspired cooking, the efficient service from uniformed staff, and the fact that the pub overlooks the pretty village green. Inside, they would have found four different rooms to choose from, each smart and modern, with wood floors, heavy wooden furniture and framed posters and awards on the walls. Rest assured; whether you're a politician or a civilian, a visitor or a local, you'll find the welcome extended here is always just as warm.

Food serving times

Monday-Saturday:
12pm-2pm, 6pm-9pm

Sunday:
12pm-2pm

Closed 25-26 December

Booking essential

Prices

Meals: 17.95 (Sunday lunch) and a la carte 26.00/32.00

Typical Dishes

Saffron risotto
Poached halibut
Rhubarb tart

5.5mi North of Darlington off A167. Parking.

Hutton Magna

002 The Oak Tree Inn

Hutton Magna DL11 7HH
Tel.: (01833) 627371
Website: www.elevation-it.co.uk/oaktree

Black Sheep Best Bitter, Timothy Taylor's Landlord, Charles Wells Bombardier

If you are privy to the fact that owner/chef Alastair spent many years perfecting his craft at various upmarket London establishments, you'll be expecting a lot from a meal at this part-18C whitewashed inn and, the good news is, you won't be disappointed. This unpretentious dining pub serves good value, modern pub dishes made with locally sourced, seasonal ingredients, and wife Claire supplies a friendly welcome and polite service. Rural life in this small, unspoilt village is about as far from the frenetic pace of the city as it is possible to get, so relax and sip an aperitif by the fire, flick through the eclectic collection of reading matter provided or simply admire the beams and stone walls of the simply-furnished, old-fashioned, homely bar. Once ready to eat, move through to the dining area with its plain décor, heavy wood tables, leather chairs and food-themed prints.

Food serving times

Tuesday-Sunday:
6.30pm-8.30pm

Closed 25-26 and 31 December, 1 January

Dinner only. Booking essential.

Prices

Meals: a la carte
24.25/30.25

Typical Dishes

Roast saddle of hare
Roast fillet of wild seabass
Hot chocolate fondant

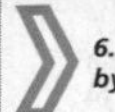

6.5mi Southeast of Barnard Castle by B6277 off A66. Parking.

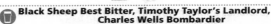

003 Rose and Crown

Romaldkirk DL12 9EB
Tel.: (01833) 650213 - Fax: (01833) 650828
e-mail: hotel@rose-and-crown.co.uk
Website: www.rose-and-crown.co.uk

 **Theakstons Best, Black Sheep Bitter, Emmerdale Bitter**

With the warmth of the welcome, the service and the décor, plus the heat from the open fires, you'll be feeling positively balmy after a visit to this ivy-clad former coaching inn, a previous pub of the year winner. Built in 1733, the village green it overlooks is still home to antiquated stocks and an aged water pump, and inside, the various dining areas come accompanied with large dollops of rustic charm. The well-stocked, wood-fitted bar is central to proceedings and its rough stone walls are hung with various brasses and etchings. The panelled, linen-laid restaurant is similarly decorated with ornaments, cartoons, wine labels and other such paraphernalia. Good-sized menus offer classically-based meals of a superior quality, local serving staff are polite and efficient, and comfortable, individually-appointed bedrooms further illustrate the owners' commitment to providing those all-important extra touches.

Food serving times

Monday-Sunday:
12pm-1.30pm, 7.30pm-9pm

Closed 24-26 December

Set price lunch Sunday only

Prices

Meals: 17.25/28.00 (3 course lunch/dinner) and a la carte 15.00/28.00

12 rooms:
80.00/215.00

Typical Dishes

Smoked haddock soufflé

Pan-fried pink woodpigeon

Hot bread and butter pudding

3.5mi Southeast of Middleton-in-Teesdale on B6277. On the village green, next to the church. Parking.

North East • Durham

004 Manor House Inn

Carterway Heads DH8 9LX
Tel.: (01207) 255268
Website: www.manorhouse@68.co.uk

 VISA AE MC

Theakstons Best, Charles Wells Bombardier, Courage Directors and changing guest ales

A personally owned and run pub with a growing reputation for good, honest homecooked food: a separate dining room overlooking the countryside allows you to forget the inn's on a busy road, but you'll find more of a local atmosphere in the trim little wood-fitted bar – good for a pint and a game of darts with the locals if you're feeling confident; a characterful lounge with comfy banquettes and views over the fields has the best of both worlds. Amiable staff serve a mix of popular pub dishes and robust British classics. Pleasant, conveniently appointed bedrooms make a handy stopover if you're heading on north of the border, while a deli shop at one end of the restaurant sells local farm produce and home-made goodies. A short drive west takes you to Derwent Reservoir, with lakeside walks through rolling moorland and pine forest.

Food serving times

Monday-Saturday:
12pm-2.30pm, 7pm-9.30pm

Sunday:
12pm-9pm

Closed dinner 25 December

Prices

Meals: a la carte
20.00/30.00

4 rooms: 45.00/75.00

Typical Dishes

Pan-fried scallops
Braised lamb shank
Sticky toffee pudding

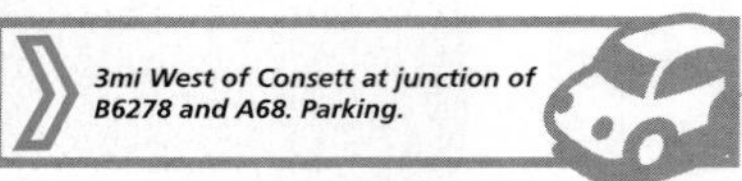

3mi West of Consett at junction of B6278 and A68. Parking.

005 The Angel of Corbridge

Main St,
Corbridge NE45 5LA
Tel.: (01434) 632119 - Fax: (01434) 633796

Timothy Taylor's Landlord, Deuchar's IPA, Nell's Best, Auld Hemp, Farne Island, Magus

This 18C coaching inn took on a new lease of life when it was refurbished in the not-too-distant past. It's now the focal point of a pretty, riverside village and quite rightly so. At the entrance, the warm, wood-panelled lounge is furnished with leather Chesterfield and comfy chairs and would be a nice place to settle into, if it weren't for counter claims in other parts of the establishment. A rather charming bar has coil flooring, whitewashed walls, beams and open fires - in other words, a winning mix of rustic and contemporary – while a modern, split-level restaurant sources elaborate weekend meals. During the week, like the bar, it proffers good-sized menus, classical in style with modern twists, on which Northumbrian produce is proudly served at good value prices. Stay overnight in rooms whose taste harmonises with the age of the inn; those at the front boast Tyne Valley views.

Food serving times

Monday-Saturday:
12pm-3pm, 6pm-9pm

Sunday:
12pm-3pm

Prices

Meals: a la carte
16.00/35.00

5 rooms: 60.00/85.00

Typical Dishes

Seared King scallops
Duck breast & roasted peppers
Warm spiced apple cake

In the town centre. Parking.

Great Whittington

006 Queens Head Inn

Great Whittington NE19 2HP
Tel.: (01434) 672267 - Fax: (01434) 672267

High House Farm Brewery Matfen - Nels Best and guest ales Auld Hemp, Red Shep

Take one charmingly sleepy, rural village near Hadrian's Wall, only half an hour's drive from Newcastle city centre. Add a traditional stone built 17C coaching inn with long-standing owner, an accomplished chef and a pinch of classic, regionally-influenced cooking with dishes involving black pudding, local lamb, fresh fish and reassuring hotpots and casseroles. Blend with delicious desserts, good sized menus and a warm welcome. Combine a small characterful timbered bar and seating area with a large dining area with cloth-laid tables. Mix with open fires and stone walls and furnish with wooden chairs and pews. Sprinkle with ornaments, pictures, and assorted knick-knacks. Garnish with polite, friendly, aproned staff, add a dash of relaxed, informal atmosphere, marinate in beautiful, rolling wooded countryside for several years and serve. The perfect recipe to protect against the stressful pace of modern life.

Food serving times

Monday-Thursday:
12pm-2pm, 5.30pm-9pm

Friday-Saturday:
12pm-2pm, 5.30pm-9.30pm

Sunday:
12pm-8pm

Closed 25 December

Prices

Meals: a la carte
17.00/29.50

Typical Dishes

Pan-seared scallops
Rump of new season local lamb
Prune and almond tart

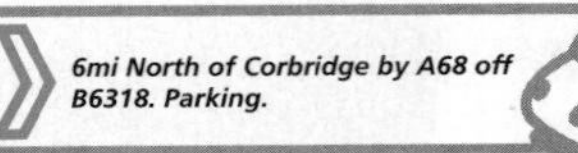

6mi North of Corbridge by A68 off B6318. Parking.

007 The Cook and Barker Inn

Newton on the Moor NE65 9JY

Tel.: (01665) 575234 - Fax: (01665) 575234

Website: www.cookandbarkerinn.co.uk

Black Sheep, Timothy Taylor's Landlord, Theakstons XB

There's a bit of everything on the extensive menu at the Cook and Barker: seafood features quite heavily, reminding us of their proximity to the coast, but there are also roasts, grills and even some Asian influences at work. You'll also find an eclectic bunch of people here too; locals pop in for a pint and a snack, businesspeople arrive fresh from the airport, weary travellers stop in on their way to or from Scotland and stay in the smart, modern bedrooms, and tourists stop in for food after visiting sites such as the famous Alnwick Castle, a television and film set for everything from Harry Potter to Blackadder. Run by the same team for nearly twenty years, this stone built inn is attractive inside and out. There are various cosy rooms and snugs furnished in a period style, with pictures and ornaments decoratively arranged, a more formal, linen laid dining room and an outside terrace too.

Food serving times

Monday-Sunday:
12pm-2pm, 7pm-9pm

Prices

Meals: 10.00/25.00 (3 course lunch/dinner Monday-Tuesday) and a la carte 30.00/40.00

18 rooms: 47.00/75.00

Typical Dishes

Slow cooked crispy belly pork

Slow roasted organic lamb

Steamed syrup sponge

5mi South of Alnwick by A1.
Parking.

North East • Northumberland

008 The Pheasant Inn

Falstone, Stannersburn by Kielder Water NE48 1DD
Tel.: (01434) 240382 - Fax: (01434) 240382
e-mail: enquiries@thepheasantinn.com
Website: www.thepheasantinn.com

 **Wylam Brewery 'Whistle Stop' and Goblin HA, Timothy Taylor's Landlord**

If you've been admiring any of the modern visual art and architecture dotted about the Kielder landscape, you'll find it contrasts sharply with the traditional setting of The Pheasant Inn. Here, framed prints, photos and cartoons of the local community in times gone by hang on the stone walls alongside old farm implements, brass jugs and pans. Take a seat next to the log fire in the low-beamed bar of this old, ivy-clad 17C farmhouse, and you'll find yourself transported back to a time when life went by at a slower pace. Family run for over twenty years, service is friendly and polite and the changing blackboard menu offers hearty homemade pub classics made with local ingredients. Stay in one of the comfy, cottage-style rooms set around a pretty courtyard; a great base from which to take advantage of the cycling, fishing and riding to be enjoyed in the beautiful surroundings of the Northumberland National Park.

Food serving times

Monday-Sunday:
12pm-2.30pm, 7pm-9pm

Closed 25-26 December, Monday-Tuesday November to mid-March

Bar lunch Monday-Saturday

Prices

Meals: a la carte
15.00/23.50

8 rooms: 45.00/85.00

Typical Dishes

Sweet pickled herring

Roast Northumberland lamb

Lemon and lime cheesecake

0.5mi Northeast crossing North Tyne river. Parking at front and rear.

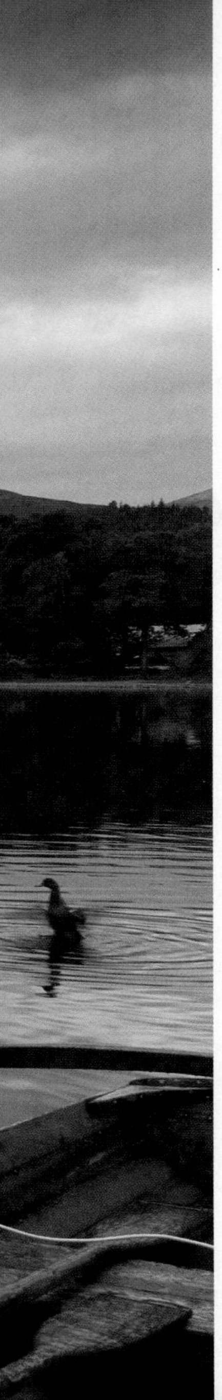

Stretching from the Cheshire plains to the Solway Firth, this region defies all easy definitions. Roman Chester, the busy Pennine market towns and the peaceful and scenic West Cumbrian coast are North-West England at its most traditionally picturesque, though there's a very different history to be traced in the decline and renewal of Liverpool's Albert Dock and in the shimmering modern metal of Salford Quays. Lancashire's towns, built for industry and "King Cotton", are now at least as well-known for their cross-Pennine rivalries in football, rugby and the Roses Match as for Lowry's busy cityscapes. Most famous by far, though, is Cumbria's Lake District which, at its best and quietest, remains both a challenging wilderness and a picture of serenity. Bikes, boats, trains, bridle paths and hiking trails will all get you closer to the beauty of Derwentwater and Buttermere and the bleak grandeur of Striding Edge. Local specialities like hot pot, black pudding, Morecambe shrimps, Cumberland sausage, Cumberland sauce and air-dried ham, sticky toffee pudding and Cheshire cheese have all spread well beyond the bounds of the region, but taste as good as ever after all that fresh North Country air…

Scotland
North East
NORTH
Yorkshire & the Humber
CUMBRIA
Dumfries
Carlisle
Workington
Whitehaven
Barrow-in-Furness
Morecambe
NEWCASTLE UPON TYNE
New Galloway
Cairnryan
Newton Stewart
Glenluce
Gatehouse of Fleet
Castle Douglas
Ringford
Kirkcudbright
Auchencairn
Dalbeattie
New Abbey
Wigtown
Port William
Whithorn
Isle of Whithorn
Drummore
Luce Bay
Wigtown Bay
Burrow Head
Mull of Galloway
Solway Firth
Lockerbie
Annan
Gretna
Canonbie
Longtown
Brampton
Greenhead
Hadrian's Wall
Chollerford
Hexham
Corbridge
Belsay
Consett
Alston
Wolsingham
Bowness-on-Solway
Silloth
Abbey Town
Wigton
Thursby
Aspatria
Bothel
Maryport
Cockermouth
Skiddaw
Keswick
Derwent water
Buttermere
Frizington
Egremont
St. Bees Head
Gosforth
Lake District
Cumbrian Mountains
Scafell Pikes
Rosthwaite
Grasmere
Ambleside
Coniston
Bowness
Windermere
Ullswater
Patterdale
Penrith
Cross Fell
Appleby
Brough
Kirkby Stephen
Orton
Tebay
Kendal
Sedbergh
Broughton-in-Furness
Greenodd
Ulverston
Dalton
Millom
Grange-over-Sands
Carnforth
Ingleton
Whernside
Hawes
Leyburn
Reeth
Bowes
Barnard Castle
Middleton-in-Teesdale
Yorkshire Dales
Threshfield
Point of Ayre
ISLE OF MAN
Ramsey
Ballaugh
Snaefell
Peel
Douglas
Port Erin
Port St. Mary
Castletown
Ronaldsway
Belfast

IRISH SEA
LANCASHIRE
BLACKPOOL
Fleetwood
Cleveleys
Lytham St. Anne's
Preston
Southport
LIVERPOOL
Liverpool Bay
WEST
Blackburn
Bolton
Wigan
Burnley
Halifax
BRADFORD
Keighley
Nelson
Clitheroe
Accrington
Rochdale
Oldham
MANCHESTER
Stockport
East Midlands
Warrington
St. Helens
Birkenhead
Wallasey
Chester
Wrexham/ Wrecsam
CHESHIRE
Macclesfield
Congleton
Crewe
Newcastle-under-Lyme
STOKE-ON-TRENT
West Midlands
Wales
Rhyl
Colwyn Bay/ Bae Colwyn
Llandudno
Conwy
Bangor
Caernarfon
Caernarfon Bay
ANGLESEY
Isle of Anglesey
Holyhead/ Caergybi
Holy Island
Great Ormes Head
Snowdonia
Snowdon
GWYNEDD
Llŷn Peninsula
Llangollen
Oswestry
Bala
Belfast
Dublin
Larne
Mostyn

Alderley Edge

001 The Wizard

Macclesfield Rd,
Alderley Edge SK10 4UB
Tel.: (01625) 584000 - Fax: (01625) 585105

 **Golden Glory, Tanglefoot, 1st Gold Champion**

The National Trust has a good presence in these parts in the shape of Hare Hill and the local watermill. The Wizard – named after a children's book called "Wizard of Alderley Edge" – has proved an institution worth preserving in its own right. It's a 200 year-old pub which, these days, has restaurant sensibilities. Standing on the edge of a woodland park with superb walks clsoeby, it earns a tick in the box on most rustic counts: beamed, flagged and wood floors, with heavy wooden tables and chairs located everywhere. The menu - good value lunches and evening à la carte - is wide ranging and eclectic; the cooking's interesting and precise. Try grilled black pudding on mash with poached egg and mustard cream, cod with buttered spinach and salsa verde, or sea bass with red chard, avocado salad, lemongrass and coriander.

Food serving times

Tuesday-Saturday:
12pm-2pm, 7pm-9.30pm

Sunday:
12pm-2pm

Closed Christmas to New Year

Prices

Meals: 10.00/15.00 (2/3 course lunch/dinner) and a la carte 22.00/37.00

Typical Dishes

Marinated King prawns
Roast canon of lamb
Chocolate and orange tart

1.25mi Southeast on B5087.
Parking.

002 The Grosvenor Arms

Chester Rd, Aldford CH3 6HJ
Tel.: (01244) 620228 - Fax: (01224) 620247
e-mail: grosvenor-arms@brunningandprice.co.uk
Website: www.grosvenorarms-aldford.co.uk

 **Weetwood Eastgate, Deuchars IPA, Thwaites**

This striking, 19C, red brick pub, designed by the locally celebrated architect, John Douglas, can be found in the pretty, rural village of Alford, not too far from the Welsh border. There's plenty of elbow-room both inside and out, with several spacious interior rooms, including one lined with bookshelves, and a conservatory, terrace and rear lawned gardens that come into their own on mild summer evenings. Solid stone and tiled floors, open fires and chunky wooden tables provide plenty of rustic charm and the crowds who frequent this place are a testament to its enduring popularity with locals and visitors alike. Daily changing, wide-ranging menus offer something for everyone, with a large selection of modern, seasonal dishes that see pub favourites and local specialities set alongside food with a Mediterranean flavour. Sandwiches are available for those who want a snack, the service is slick and the atmosphere warm.

Food serving times

Monday-Saturday:
12pm-10pm

Sunday:
12pm-9pm

Prices

Meals: a la carte
15.70/32.35

Typical Dishes

Chicken liver parfait
Steakburger
Warm apricot tart

3.5mi South of Chester by B5130.
On the main village road. Parking.

003 Dysart Arms

Bowes Gate Rd, Bunbury CW6 9PH
Tel.: (01829) 260183 - Fax: (01829) 261286
e-mail: dysart-arms@brunningandprice.co.uk
Website: www.dysartarms-bunbury.co.uk

  VISA

Thwaites Original, Weetwood Eastgate, Rudgate Special, Phoenix Arizona

Next to the impressive part-14C parish church, this trim, redbrick house, standing four-square by a little lane, is handsome enough in itself, particularly when floodlit at night. Away from the central bar, Victorian portraits, engravings and memorabilia line the white walls and polished wood, Persian rugs and floor-to-ceiling bookshelves give the place a spacious, country feel: broad French windows flood the back room with sunlight on bright days and lead out to benches and tables on the lawn. Fresh, tasty cooking ranges from pie and ploughmans to dishes with a more modern edge, including sweet potato and pepper tarte Tatin and seafood casserole. Though busy with eaters and drinkers in the early evening, it's usually a little quieter after 8.30.

Food serving times
Monday-Saturday:
12pm-9.30pm
Sunday:
12pm-9pm

Prices
Meals: a la carte
17.75/30.95

Typical Dishes
Savoury goat's cheese brûlée
Cider glazed ham
Apple and cinnamon crumble

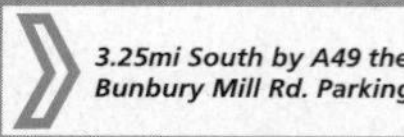
3.25mi South by A49 then take Bunbury Mill Rd. Parking.

004 The Combermere Arms

Burleydam SY13 4AT

Tel.: (01948) 871223 - Fax: (01948) 661371

e-mail: combermere.arms@brunningandprice.co.uk

Website: www.combermerearms-burleydam.co.uk

Flowers Original, Black Sheep Best, Weetwood Cheshire Cat, Woodlands Oak Beauty, Green King IPA, Country Brewery Ale

A clever merging of styles allows the old and the new to link stylistic arms here. There are old beams on view as you step inside, but beyond them the adjoining rooms have been opened up around the central bar, and skylights added, so that everything's open and airy, although you can still find a snug spot if that's what you're after. Walls are covered in pictures of every style and hue. There's an informal menu, and you can eat anywhere you like: lots of choice right across the board means a good selection from sandwiches to more substantial dishes; the wine list is worthy of note, too. This is the ideal dining spot for bigger parties, as some truly cavernous tables are up for grabs. Service is efficient from staff who are used to being busy.

Food serving times

Monday-Sunday:
all day

Prices

Meals: a la carte
18.20/27.40

Typical Dishes

Slow roast duck terrine

Grilled Cajun swordfish

Blackberry cheesecake

4.25mi East of Whitchurch on A525. Parking.

005 Old Harkers Arms

1 Russell St, Chester CH3 5AL

Tel.: (01244) 344525 - Fax: (01244) 344814

e-mail: harkers.arms@brunningandprice.co.uk

Website: www.brunningandprice.co.uk

Timothy Taylor's Landlord, Weetwood Cheshire Cat, Thwaites, Flowers Original and guest ales

Tucked away outside the historic city centre, just a few minutes walk from the station, proudly stands this converted canalside warehouse; transformed by its owners from a derelict shell into a buzzing modern boozer. Friendly staff serve an appealingly wide range of wholesome, traditional English dishes such as fish and chips, sausage and mash or Ploughman's, plus a range of 'light bites' and sandwiches from the blackboard menu, and there are also a good selection of local ales and wines by the glass. The interior décor is rustically styled, with wooden floors and scrubbed wooden tables, whilst the walls are lined with bookshelves, prints, photographs and a miscellany of other odds and ends. The L- shaped bar and adjoining seating area are spacious and light, and a busy yet relaxed atmosphere prevails, with everyone from students to businessmen enjoying the informal vibe to be had here.

Food serving times

Monday-Saturday:
12pm-9.30pm

Sunday:
12pm-9pm

Closed 25-26 December

Prices

Meals: a la carte
19.00/25.00

Typical Dishes

Harkers gammon & apple pie

Free range chicken

Local cheeses

Between A51 and the canal. Limited parking in City Rd; NCP car park round the corner.

006 Fox and Barrel

Forrest Road,
Cotebrook CW6 9DZ
Tel.: (01829) 760529 - Fax: (01829) 760192

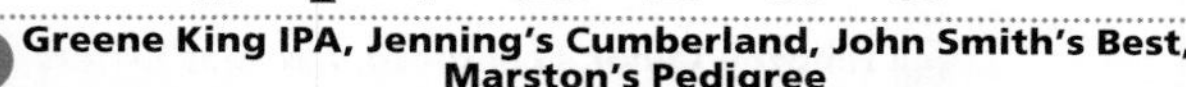

Greene King IPA, Jenning's Cumberland, John Smith's Best, Marston's Pedigree

If it's a traditional English pub with an open fire you're after, then look no further; sit yourself down at one of the tables in the cosy bar area and have a chat with the locals over a leisurely Sunday lunch and a pint. Maybe they'll tell you the story of the hunted fox, who gave the pub its name when a former landlord let it hide in his cellar, or perhaps they'll let you in on the secret of the tender care to be found here; one of the owners was formerly a nurse. Things go from local to global on the seasonally-changing menu, as hearty English dishes like pie and steak share space with more worldly offerings such as Thai curry and Tandoori chicken. You can dine al fresco out on the terraced patio, and special events such as menu and wine tasting evenings and live music on the first and second Monday of every month also help contribute to a more international feel. Country and Western or jazz anyone?

Food serving times

Sunday-Friday:
12pm-5pm, 6pm-9pm

Saturday:
12pm-5pm, 6pm-10pm

Prices

Meals: a la carte
20.00/35.00

Typical Dishes

Fan of melon
Barbary duck breast
Belgian waffle stack

1.5mi Northeast of Tarporley by A49. Parking.

007 Netherton Hall

Chester Road,
Frodsham WA6 6UL
Tel.: (01928) 732342 - Fax: (01928) 739140
Website: www.nethertonhall.com

 **Timothy Taylor's Landlord, J W Lees Bitters**

Hiding under its all-enveloping greenery, Netherton Hall is a large Georgian farmhouse, its interior now converted into three relaxing and pleasantly busy dining areas. Books and knick-knacks line the walls throughout and a collection of mix and match wooden tables seem to add the warm homely atmosphere; the personal hand of the patron is everywhere in evidence. It's also worth knowing that there's plenty of room to eat in the spacious garden. Food is definitely the focus here, with an unusually large choice written up on the blackboards: it's all freshly prepared, and the list can change twice a day. A freely ranging mix of traditional and European ideas guarantees plenty of good, sustaining cooking. The steady, well-run atmosphere of the place is most noticeable in the service, which is invariably alert and smooth.

Food serving times
Monday-Sunday:
12pm-2.30pm, 6pm-9.30pm

Prices
Meals: a la carte
18.50/30.00

Typical Dishes
Wild rabbit terrine
Fillet of halibut
Chocolate chip cookie stack

0.75 miles Southwest of Frodsham on A56. Parking.

008 The Pheasant Inn

Higher Burwardsley CH3 9PF
Tel.: (01829) 770434 - Fax: (01829) 771097
e-mail: info@thepheasantinn.co.uk
Website: www.thepheasantinn.co.uk

Weetwood Best, Weetwood Eastgate, Weetwood Old Dog and guest ale by Firkin

The exertions of a day's hiking will seem worthwhile when you reach this secluded spot with its stunning views over the Cheshire plains. All that walking will have worked up an appetite, so tuck into a traditional, hearty meal such as sausage and mash or lambs liver from the 'Home Comforts' section of the menu, or be adventurous and try one of the more modern, elaborate dishes on offer. You can eat in the main bar, in one of the two dining rooms or make the most of your position atop the Peckforton Hills by sitting outside in the pleasant garden; wherever you choose to sit, the young staff are friendly and efficient. The young owner's enthusiasm means that this three hundred year old brick built pub has been smartened up without losing any of its relaxed, rural charm and character, and you'll find that the stylishness also extends to the modern bedrooms, found in the converted sandstone barn.

Food serving times

Monday-Thursday:
12pm-9.30pm

Friday-Saturday:
12pm-10pm

Sunday:
12pm-8.30pm

Prices

Meals: a la carte
20.00/28.00

12 rooms:
65.00/130.00

Typical Dishes

Goosnargh Chicken liver pâté

Suckling pig

The Pheasant Eton mess

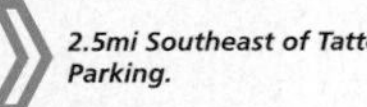

2.5mi Southeast of Tattenhall.
Parking.

009 Duke of Portland

Penny's Lane,
Lach Dennis CW9 7SY
Tel.: (01606) 46264 - Fax: (01606) 41724
e-mail: info@dukeofportland.com - Website: www.dukeofportland.com

 **Banks Original, Pedigree and at least 4 changing guest ales**

The Belle Epoque in Knutsford is not an oxymoron: it's a restaurant that's been a renowned local stalwart for 30 years, and its long-standing owners have built up a solid reputation. Good reason, then, for a visit to the rurally set Duke of Portland, seven miles away, now overseen by those same owners, the Mooney family. There's a nice rustic feeling of space inside, accentuated by two airy lounges where low-level sofas are a good place to peruse the menus. Adjacent dining areas feature natty wooden balustrades; in summer months, visitors often prefer to tuck in on the smart outdoor terrace or in the garden. Frequently changing menus offer a very well priced and eclectic mix of modern and traditional dishes: local favourites are the delicious homemade burgers or hotpot. Drinkers are well catered for with an impressive range of real ales and wines by the glass.

Food serving times

Monday-Sunday:
12pm-2.30pm, 5.30pm-9.30pm

Prices

Meals: 4.95/10.00 (2/3 course lunch/dinner) and a la carte 18.20/24.50

Typical Dishes

Black pudding

Confit of Lune Valley lamb

Chocolate semi-freddo

3.5mi West of Northwich by B5082. Parking.

010 The Foxcote

Station Lane,
Little Barrow CH3 7JN
Tel.: (01244) 301343 - Fax: (01244) 303287

No real ales offered

From the outside, this traditional looking inn certainly gives the impression of being somewhere to sink a pint. Wrong! This is now a dining pub, pure and simple, though the courteous, friendly staff and relaxed atmosphere certainly create a very gentle, local feel. The Foxcote is in a tiny Cheshire village off the beaten track, its interior given over to dining tables with gingham cloths; seafood and country prints line the walls; fine view of the Cheshire countryside from the side room. A vast number of blackboards greet you upon arrival: they mostly list seafood dishes featuring a broad variety of ingredients prepared in an accomplished, modern manner. Vegetarians and meat eaters are not forgotten, though, and are well catered for on the blackboards.

Food serving times

Monday-Friday:
12pm-2.15pm, 6pm-9.30pm

Sunday:
12pm-2.15pm

- Seafood -

Prices

Meals: 9.50/15.00 (2 course lunch/dinner) and a la carte 15.00/25.00

Typical Dishes

Thai style fillet of beef

Monkfish stuffed and wrapped

Sticky toffee pudding

6.5mi Northeast of Chester by A56 on B5132. Parking.

Lower Whitley

011 Chetwode Arms

Street Lane,
Lower Whitley WA4 4EN
Tel.: (01925) 730203 - Fax: (01925) 730203
e-mail: claudia.d@btinternet.com - Website: www.chetwodearms.com

Shepherd Neame Spitfire, Jennings Cumberland, Adnams Broadside

Popularity is clearly nothing new to this neighbourhood favourite, where a brisk, personally led team are well used to a full house of contented diners. The 17C brick-built former coaching inn still welcomes its regulars for a pint, and there are few better places for it than the inviting front bar: old framed prints, real fires, even the Victorian style tiled floor all add to the unassuming charm. The three bedrooms are equipped in the same homely style. Find a simply set table in one of the three former bar-parlours and choose from a blackboard menu which lists a few dishes reflecting the patrons' links with South Africa as well as Bury black pudding with mustard mash or liver and onions: honest, unfussy and full of appetising Northern flavour. If ever there were cooking tailor-made for a decent local ale, this is it.

Food serving times

Monday-Sunday:
12pm-3pm, 5.30pm-10pm

Closed 25 December, 1 January

Prices

Meals: a la carte 20.00/40.00

3 rooms: 50.00/70.00

Typical Dishes

Black pudding
Game pie
Sticky gingerbread pudding

6.5mi Northwest of Northwich by A533 off A49. Parking.

012 Drunken Duck Inn

Barngates,
Ambleside LA22 0NG
Tel.: (01539) 436347 - Fax: (01539) 436781
e-mail: info@drunkenduckinn.co.uk - Website: www.drunkenduckinn.co.uk

We most liked

  AE MC

 **Barngates Brewery - Tag Lag, Catnap, Cracker, Chesters**

A handsome inn that takes its name from a story involving a 19C landlady, a leaky barrel and a gaggle of unsteady ducks, this trusty Lakeland landmark still marks the old crossroads, in the midst of stunning fell and high peak scenery. Its bar with open fire is a haven for walkers, particularly those who like real ale, as The Duck has an on-site micro-brewery producing four beers on handpump. Beers can be enjoyed in one of the cosy, beamed rooms which radiate from the bar, but this is a dining destination at heart, with meals served in two pleasant dining rooms: lunch offers dishes such as cold poached asparagus or scallops, while the modern style evening à la carte has an ambitious edge with dishes such as Westmorland gold brined Anjou pigeon and salt and peppered foie gras. Bedrooms are of fine quality; they all boast the excellent view and cream tea greets you on arrival. Booking is essential, as this place can get very busy.

Food serving times

Monday-Sunday:
12pm-2.30pm, 6pm-9.30pm

Booking essential

Prices

Meals: a la carte
30.00/60.00

16 rooms:
20.00/235.00

Typical Dishes

Maldon cured foie gras

Fillet of beef on the bone

English Stilton cheesecake

3mi Southwest of Ambleside by A593 and B5286 on Tarn Hows road. By the crossroads at the top of Duck Hill. Parking.

013 The Wheatsheaf

Brigsteer LA8 8AN

Tel.: (015395) 68254 - Fax: (015395) 68948

e-mail: wheatsheaf@brigsteer.gb.com

Website: www.brigsteer.gb.com

VISA AE

Hawkshead, Hesket Newmarket

No longer hidden deep underneath Artex and thick carpets, The Wheatsheaf's inner beauty has once again been allowed to shine through. Total refurbishment means that the 18C pub is now light and airy, with tiled and wooden floors, and contemporary furnishings in each of its three rooms. The menu is proudly seasonal, Cumbrian and traceable, so you know that your smoked salmon came from Cartmel Valley and the shrimps were netted in Morecombe Bay, while wild garlic, flat mushrooms and damsons are sourced from even closer to home; the bank just outside the inn. Dishes on the à la carte might include carved loin of organic roe deer, roast crown of wild mallard, rabbit and leek stew or grilled whole local trout – all fairly priced and prepared with the greatest of care by a young, ambitious and disciplined team. Word is spreading fast, so it's a good idea to book. Three classically styled bedrooms come with pine furniture.

Food serving times

Monday-Sunday:
12pm-2pm, 5.45pm-9pm

Booking essential Monday in winter

Prices

Meals: a la carte 16.00/23.00

3 rooms: 70.00/85.00

Typical Dishes

Grilled local wood pigeon

Local roe deer loin

Hazelnut praline parfait

3 3/4mi South West of Kendal by All Hallows Lane. Parking.

014 The Weary at Castle Carrock

Castle Carrock CA8 9LU

Tel.: (01228) 670230 - Fax: (01228) 670089

e-mail: relax@theweary.com - Website: www.theweary.com

Parson's Pledge Cask, Worthington Cask

Formerly known as the Weary Sportsman, the original sign still hangs above the door of this pub, but it's the newer sign alongside which hints at its modern interior. The candlelit bar area with its comfy seating and relaxed ambience is the most popular area in which to eat, but there is also an outside terrace, a conservatory and a room known as 'The Square.' Whilst the bar menu serves traditional dishes such as chunky fish pie and lasagne, the à la carte also incorporates more international flavours, with Thai dishes a particular bent. Steak nights on Tuesdays are popular, and the servers' friendliness and good cheer compensate for any slippages in service during busy periods. Superior, strikingly contemporary bedrooms are equipped with the latest technology, including televisions in the bathroom tiles so you watch while you wash. Stay overnight and you will conclude that it must be really rarely that the weary leave The Weary weary.

Food serving times

Monday-Friday:
7pm-9pm

Saturday-Sunday and Bank Holidays:
12pm-2pm, 6pm-9pm

Closed 25-26 December, 1 January

Monday residents only

Prices

Meals: a la carte 14.50/35.00

5 rooms: 79.00/145.00

Typical Dishes

Black pudding stack

Snapper with crab mash

Assiette of today's desserts

4mi south of Brampton on B6413. Parking.

015 The Punch Bowl Inn

Crosthwaite LA8 8HR

Tel.: (01539) 568237 - Fax: (01539) 568875

e-mail: info@the-punchbowl.co.uk

Website: www.the-punchbowl.co.uk

 **Barngates Brewery: Tag Lag, Westmorland Gold, Cat Nap**

Seasonal ingredients and a traditional base define the menu in this part 17C Cumbrian inn. The fine balanced cuisine draws out robust, pronounced flavours from classic combinations - at good value prices - and among the best are a satisfyingly meaty pea and ham soup, crisp, juicy beetroot tart with goat's cheese, honey and mustard chicken and chocolate and ginger tart served with honey ice cream. Framed menus from around the world decorate three dining areas, including a raised gallery, and the friendly, efficient service would be worthy of a restaurant, but the Punch Bowl is still recognisibly a neighbourhood pub, with locals propping up the front bar. In the fells and banks of the Lake District, there's no shortage of after-lunch walks in the area, and the road running west leads on to Windermere. The bedrooms have modern facilities and each is individually designed.

Food serving times

Monday-Sunday:
12pm-3pm, 6pm-9pm

Prices

Meals: a la carte
18.00/32.50

9 rooms: 85.00/280.00

Typical Dishes

Cumbrian cheese soufflé

Rack of lamb

Chocolate fondant

5.25 West of Kendal by A11
Hallows Lane. Next to the church.
Parking.

016 The Highwayman

Nether Burrow LA6 2RJ
Tel.: (01524) 826888
e-mail: enquiries@highwaymaninn.co.uk
Website: www.highwaymaninn.co.uk

 **Thwaites Wainwrights, Lancaster Bomber and Original**

(With apologies to Alfred Noyes) The meat's from the Forest of Bowland among the gusty trees, / The fish it comes from Fleetwood, tossed upon cloudy seas, / The asparagus comes from Formby, over the purple moor, / The suppliers are on the menu – menu - menu, / and the customers they come riding, up to the old inn door. Having undergone a million pound refurbishment, and with owners passionate about local, traceable food, The Highwayman is certainly delivering the goods - from all over Lancashire, Cumbria and Yorkshire - and so serious are they here about sourcing their ingredients locally, they even have framed pictures of their suppliers decorating the walls. Friendly and efficient service from the smartly attired staff oils the wheels of the dining experience, and the spacious inn with its numerous open fires, banquette seating and pleasant stone terrace makes an agreeable environment in which to enjoy the flavoursome food.

Food serving times

Monday-Friday:
12pm-2pm, 6pm-9pm

Saturday:
12pm-2pm, 5.30pm-9pm

Sunday:
12pm-8.30pm

Closed 25 December

Prices

Meals: a la carte
16.50/23.50

Typical Dishes

Kipper fillet
Herdwick mutton pudding
Lancashire Curd tart

2mi South of Kirkby Lonsdale by A65 and A683. Parking.

017 The Strickland Arms

Sizergh LA8 8DZ
Tel.: (01539) 561010 - Fax: (01539) 561067
e-mail: the_strickland_arms@hotmail.com
Website: www.strick@ainscoughs.co.uk

Thwaites Original, Lancaster Bomber, Coniston Bluebird, Hawkshead, Hesket Newmarket

This imposing grey building is owned – like next door Sizergh castle - by the National Trust and, having been cleverly restored to its former glory, is now attracting locals and tourists, walkers, dogs and children in large numbers. Huge portions of hearty, traditional home-cooking, with the hiker obviously in mind, ensure that no one leaves this historic hostelry hungry and the good selection of real ales and wines by the glass help refresh the parts that food cannot reach. Extremely friendly service is a bonus. The interior is simply and stylishly decorated with period furniture, fixtures and fittings and there is a strong feel of the country here, with stone and bare wooden floorboards and dark wood dining tables. Inside, there is plenty of space over two floors but if the kids still need somewhere to burn off any extra energy, there is also a large garden with pretty apple trees along one side of the pub.

Food serving times

Monday-Friday:
12pm-2pm, 6pm-9pm

Saturday:
12pm-2.30pm, 6pm-9pm

Sunday:
12pm-8.30pm

Closed 25 December

Prices

Meals: a la carte
18.00/25.00

Typical Dishes

Cumbrian potted beef
Strickland steak & ale pie
Bread and butter pudding

3mi South West of Kendal by A391. Parking.

018 The Queen's Head

Troutbeck LA23 1PW

Tel.: (01539) 432174 - Fax: (01539) 431398

e-mail: feast@queensheadhotel.com

Website: www.queensheadhotel.com

Coniston Bluebird, Black Sheep, Hawkshead Red, Boddingtons, Tirrel

Not many pub bars are built around superbly carved Elizabethan four-poster beds. In fact, this 400 year old posting inn boasts probably the only one in the country. The place has charm and character to spare. You might get lost in the warren of beamed and panelled rooms, in which cobwebbed musical instruments hang, and beribboned stuffed beasts gaze. You'll come across old cushioned settles, stone walls and a roaring open fireplace. The upstairs dining room has capacious windows for even bigger views over valley and moor. Settle down at scrubbed oak tables and extinguish countryside appetites with imaginative, well-cooked, tasty Northern food with traditional and modern options, served by staff eager to please. You might want to stay the night: bedrooms boast antique furnishings and terrific views.

Food serving times

Monday-Sunday:
12pm-2.30pm, 5pm-9pm

Closed 25 December

Prices

Meals: 18.50 (3 course lunch/dinner) and a la carte 22.15/29.70

15 rooms:
67.50/120.00

Typical Dishes

Seared scallops
Whole roast Cheshire poussin
Hot chocolate pudding

4mi North of Ambleside by A592.
Parking.

019 The Bay Horse

Canal Foot, Ulverston LA12 9EL
Tel.: (01229) 583972 - Fax: (01229) 580502
e-mail: reservations@thebayhorsehotel.co.uk
Website: www.thebayhorsehotel.co.uk

VISA AE MC

Pendle Witches Brew, Cocker Hoop, Cumberland, Moorhouses

Commanding views of the Lancashire and Cumbria Fells are just one reason to recommend this well-established little inn by Ulverston Sands. The bar area, well known for its capacious horse's head of stone, has a smart ambience, afforded by plush built-in wall banquettes, stylish wooden armchairs, beams and open fire. An adjacent conservatory houses a more formal linen-clad restaurant, which boasts fine views over Morecambe Bay. Tasty, effectively prepared cooking finds favour with appreciative diners, who have long admired the flavourful, seasonal menus, typified by roast fillet of halibut, or Cumberland sausage with date chutney, cranberry and apple sauce. Bedrooms - snug and with a host of extras - have the enviable coastal view.

Food serving times

Monday:
at 7.30pm

Tuesday-Sunday:
12pm-2pm, at 7.30pm

One sitting for dinner
7.30pm for 8pm

Prices

Meals: a la carte
20.00/40.00

9 rooms: 80.00/122.50

Typical Dishes

Pork and pheasant terrine
Irish corned beef
Malva pudding

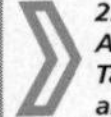

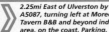

2.25mi East of Ulverston by A5087, turning left at Morecambe Tavern B&B and beyond industrial area, on the coast. Parking.

020 Brackenrigg Inn

Watermillock CA11 0LP

Tel.: (017684) 86206 - Fax: (017684) 86945

e-mail: enquiries@brackenrigginn.co.uk

Website: www.brackenrigginn.co.uk

  VISA 

Coniston Bluebird, Skipton Brewery Copper Dragon, Tirril Old Faithful, Theakstons Best Bitter

Commanding fine views of the lakes and mountains, the Brackenrigg Inn is sure to appeal to Lakeland pub lovers, for many reasons. Its open main bar has changed a little since it welcomed the post coach in the 18C, but its comfy seats, dartboard and promising line of bar taps still sends the right message to the tired traveller. Meals are also served in two more formal adjoining rooms and the appealing, full-flavoured cooking casts its net surprisingly wide. They aim to offer something for everyone, serving potato, chorizo and trout salad or salmon with basil and asparagus alongside well-known favourites, snacks and daily specials. Well marshalled service directed by the experienced patrons – still as keen and amiable as ever – binds the whole place together.

Food serving times

Monday-Sunday:
12pm-3pm (bar meals),
6pm-9pm

Prices

Meals: a la carte
17.00/25.00

17 rooms: 38.00/90.00

Typical Dishes

Spicy fish soup
Fillet with oxtail croquette
Sticky toffee pudding

On A592 besides Ullswater.
Parking.

021 Brown Horse Inn

Winster LA23 3NR

Tel.: (01539) 443443

e-mail: steve@thebrownhorseinn.co.uk

Website: www.thebrownhorseinn.co.uk

VISA MC

Theakstons, Timothy Taylor's Landlord, Coniston Bluebird

Nestled in the countryside of the Winster valley, not too far from Lake Windermere, sits this traditional 1850s coaching inn. Previously an Italian restaurant, the new owners said arrivederci to pizza and welcomed back the locals with the lure of log fires and a dartboard, plus seasonal, flavoursome food made with locally sourced ingredients. Brown horse paintings and dried hops decorate the green walls, and diners sit at candlelit tables. The lunch menu offers soup, sandwiches, salads and jacket potatoes, plus favourites such as sausage and mash and fish and chips. Blackboard specials add to the choice, with local lamb always a feature. The dinner menu offers robust, tasty food, classically prepared with prime produce, with dishes such as steak and chunky chips or deep fried squid salad – but book ahead at weekends, as this place is making a name for itself. Bedrooms are light and modern, simply decorated yet comfortable.

Food serving times

Monday-Sunday:
12pm-2pm, 6pm-9.30pm

Prices

Meals: a la carte
18.00/25.00

9 rooms: 70.00/90.00

Typical Dishes

Seared scallops

Brown Horse rack of lamb

Banoffee parfait

4mi South of Windermere by A5074. Parking.

022 The Yanwath Gate Inn

Yanwath CA10 2LF

Tel.: (01768) 862386 - Fax: (01768) 899892

e-mail: enquiries@yanwathgate.com - Website: www.yanwathgate.com

 VISA  MC

No real ales offered

This charming drovers' inn, built back in 1683, takes its name from the tollgate which once stood outside, and hanging above the door, a miniature gate now reads, 'This gate hangs well and hinders none, refresh and pay and travel on.' If you're unfortunate enough to be caught by a Lakeland downpour, or find yourself cold and lunchless on the hills, this is the kind of place you dream of finding. The old taproom, in the light of candles and an open fire, looks wonderfully inviting, with scrubbed wooden tables and thoughtful, welcoming service from behind the bar, but the panelled dining room beyond is no less pleasant – the friendly owner willingly takes a hand in both to keep things going according to plan. Seasonal cooking made with locally sourced ingredients displays care and finesse and portions are never less than generous. Good value pub food with a sound slice of local character - and local ales on tap to boot.

Food serving times

Monday-Sunday:
12pm-2.30pm, 6pm-9pm

Prices

Meals: a la carte
27.65/43.40

Typical Dishes

Galloway bresaola

Ulverston salt marsh lamb

Irish mist cheesecake

2mi South West of Penrith by A6 on B5320. Parking.

023 Marmalade

60 Beech Road,
Chorlton-cum-Hardy M21 9EG

Tel.: (0161) 862 9665 - Fax: (0161) 861 7788
e-mail: jqmarmalade@tiscali.co.uk - Website: www.mymarmalade.co.uk

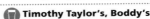

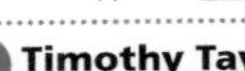 **Timothy Taylor's, Boddy's**

Don't get the impression that this neighbourhood hostelry deals only in charming knickknacks. Yes, there are things like silver three-tier cake stands, wall-hung antique suitcases and framed replicas of Manchester buses. You can even buy a jar of the eponymous sticky stuff which gives the pub its name. All of which could sidetrack you from the fact that, most of all, John the owner wants you to enjoy the serious food served here. Seasonally changing menus have a strong British accent, from the cracking Lancashire hotpot to mouth-watering mussels and lobster from Wales. Mature ribs of local beef are hung for 42 days and served with home-made chips; everything is freshly cooked on the premises, and the result is well-executed, tasty fare, eaten at simple wooden tables.

Food serving times

Monday-Friday:
5.30pm-9.30pm

Saturday-Sunday:
11am-3pm, 5.30pm-9.30pm

Prices

Meals: 12.00/14.00 (2/3 course dinner) and a la carte 20.00/26.50

Typical Dishes

Welsh mussel harvest
Tatton Park loin of venison
Bread and butter pudding

3mi South of Manchester by A5103 and minor road west. Parking in the road.

024 The Ox

71 Liverpool Rd,
Castlefield, Manchester M3 4NQ
Tel.: (0161) 839 7740/60
e-mail: gmtheox@baabar.co.uk - Website: www.theox.co.uk

 **Boddington's Cask, Deuchars IPA, Holts Bitter, Timothy Taylor's Landlord**

The pub's proximity to Castlefield Heritage Park, the Science Museum and the local Granada studios provides a steady flow of drinkers and diners to The Ox, as well as incognito appearances by a few television celebrities. Apart from the massive, block-bold "OX" monogram, stamped like a cattle-brand between the eaves and glowering in at the windows, it's an understated corner pub, more pleasant and homely than the logo suggests. An open though still intimate-feeling bar room leads on to a traditionally styled dining area, and this is where The Ox sets itself apart from its neighbours: the menu has an unmistakeably eclectic touch, with a number of lightly fusion-influenced dishes in among the more familiar favourites. Fresh and popular food served unpretentiously.

Food serving times

Monday-Sunday:
12pm-3pm, 5.30pm-9pm

Closed 25 December, 1 January

Breakfast not provided

Prices

Meals: 13.95 (3 course Sunday lunch) and a la carte 18.00/27.00

9 rooms: 54.95/74.95

Typical Dishes
Seared scallops
Roast rump of lamb
Chocolate fondant

City centre. Pay and display in neighbouring streets.

025 The White Hart Inn

51 Stockport Rd,
Lydgate, Oldham OL4 4JJ
Tel.: (01457) 872566 - Fax: (01457) 875190
e-mail: bookings@thewhitehart.co.uk - Website: www.thewhitehart.co.uk

We most liked

Timothy Taylor's Landlord, JW Lees, Tetleys, Copper Dragon

Rurally set, overlooking Saddleworth Moor, The White Hart Inn presents you with several choices. Firstly, where to eat: will you dine near the open log fire in the cosy, beamed brasserie or more formally, in the modern, linen-clad restaurant? The library is the choice for more private dining, while the smart Oak Room is also available for functions. Once you are settled, more choice comes in the form of the seasonally changing menus. Will you opt for the sensibly-priced set menu, perhaps the 2-4-1 dinner menu or the à la carte? Dishes range from soups, sandwiches and smoked sardines through to roast rabbit leg or rib eyed steak. The sumptuous selection of homemade Saddleworth sausages and differently flavoured mashed potatoes are particularly popular, while a fish menu is also available on Tuesdays. Staying the night? Twelve comfortable bedrooms, named after local dignitaries, are housed in the original building, built in 1788.

Food serving times

Monday-Sunday:
12pm-2.30pm, 6pm-9.30pm

Booking essential

Prices

Meals: 16.00/40.00 (3 course lunch/dinner) and a la carte 24.00/32.00

12 rooms:
90.00/140.00

Typical Dishes

Goosnargh chicken terrine

Roast fillet of beef

Raspberry & orange Savarin

3mi East of Oldham by A669 on A6050. Parking.

Fence Gate Inn

026 Fence Gate Inn

Wheatley Lane Road,
Fence BB12 9EE

Tel.: (01282) 618101 - Fax: (01282) 615432
e-mail: info@fencegate.co.uk - Website: www.fencegate.co.uk

Theakstons Best Bitter and Directors, Caledonian Deuchars IPA and guest ales: Bowland Brewery, Moorhouses, Copper

Owner Kevin Berkins has been at The Fence Gate Inn for over a quarter of a century. A former master butcher, he is committed to serving locally sourced food, so your lamb might come from Pendle, your beef from Bowland, and your pork from Samlesbury. If bangers and mash is your thing, then you're in for a treat, as he produces a fine selection of speciality sausages on the premises. Perched high on the moorland, this huge 17C pub offers a wide selection of dishes, with the traditional bar serving simpler offerings like cod and chips, burgers and pies, whilst the more contemporary Topiary brasserie serves more elaborate creations, ranging from classical dishes like Lancashire tart through to dishes with an international influence, such as crispy duck and pancakes. Eight daily specials on top means that it could take you a while to order, but when you do finally decide, you'll find the local staff friendly, with a good sense of humour.

Food serving times

Monday-Saturday:
12pm-2.30pm, 6.30pm-9.30pm

Sunday:
12pm-2.30pm, 6pm-8.30pm

Prices

Meals: a la carte
22.50/27.50

Typical Dishes

Taste of Lancashire
Roast chump of Pendle lamb
Chocolate fondant pudding

2mi South West of Junction 13 on M65 by A6068. Parking.

027 The Forest Inn

Cuckstool Lane,
Fence BB12 9PA
Tel.: (01282) 613641 - Fax: (01282) 698140
Website: www.theforestinn.co.uk

 **Moorhouses, Thwaites,**

Fresh-tasting and seasonal in character, the food at the Forest Inn has plenty of generous country flavour to it. Lighter, simpler lunches and more substantial dinners, most with a hearty, traditional base, are prepared with equal care, and it's no surprise that word has reached well beyond the little Lancashire village. If the setting of fields and trees comes as a relief after the madness of the M65, the plain-fronted inn looks respectable but nondescript. A contemporary interior, however, complete with comfortable leather chairs, blond wood dining tables, modern art and hushed, neutral colours feels much less stark than it sounds and the service lends real warmth to the place: a dedicated local team is never short on friendliness or effort when helping out the family owners.

Food serving times

Tuesday-Sunday:
5.30pm-9pm

Prices

Meals: 9.95 (3 course dinner) and a la carte 9.95/27.00

Typical Dishes

Thai fish cakes
Slow cooked lamb shank
Frostys Frozen Finale

3mi Northeast of Padiham by A6068, then 0.5miles Southwest by A6248. Parking.

028 The Bay Horse Inn

Bay Horse Lane,
Forton LA2 0HR

Tel.: (01524) 791204 - Fax: (01524) 791204
e-mail: bayhorseinfo@aol.com - Website: www.bayhorseinn.com

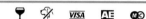

 **Black Sheep, Adnams Broadside, Moorhouse Blond Witch, Robinson's Double Hop, Pendle Witches Brew**

The photos hanging among the quirky bibelots in the bar of the Bay Horse Inn display the local Lancashire landscape with an almost tangible sense of pride; and it is this Lancastrian pride that is also palpable in the provenance of the produce on the menu. Shrimps are fresh from Morecambe Bay, duckling and chicken have travelled only as far as Swainson Farm, venison is from Grizedale and beef from Bowland. Tasty choices conjured up by self-taught chef Craig might include classics such as Lancashire hot pot or fish pie as well as more modern dishes such as smoked duck Caesar salad. The welcome here is a warm one and the inn is a delightful spot for a meal – choose between the dining room and the rustic bar with its open fire. Two new bedrooms, located in a converted corn mill opposite the pub, are beautifully appointed with bespoke bathrooms – but book well in advance as they are proving very popular.

Food serving times

Wednesday-Saturday:
12pm-1.45pm, 7pm-9.30pm

Sunday:
12pm-3pm, 6pm-8pm

Closed 25-26 December, 1 January, day following a Bank Holiday

Prices

Meals: 16.00 (3 course lunch) and a la carte 18.00/35.00

3 rooms: 75.00/95.00

Typical Dishes

Roast west coast scallops
Braised rabbit
Sherry cheesecake

1.25mi North by A6 on Quernmore Rd. Parking.

029 Feilden's Arms

Whalley Rd,
Mellor Brook BB2 7PR
Tel.: (01254) 769010
Website: www.fielden-arms.co.uk

   MC

 **Jennings Cumberland**

This pub had lost its identity somewhat over the years, until along came its saviour in the form of chef Stephen Midgley; returning to his roots and armed with cooking utensils and a new menu. Locals still partake of a pint or two of real ale and a game of pool in the spacious bar, while others gather to chat in the lounge with its low, comfy seating, but the conservatory-style dining room, furnished with simple wooden tables and decorated with pictures of wine, is where most of the culinary action is centred. Food is home cooked, with vibrant use of local ingredients and produce, and at the heart of the establishment are the dual goals of simplicity and regionality. The menu is full of all the old favourites - think Lancashire hotpot, black pudding, potted prawns, or steak and chips – but remember of course that these are chips of the homemade variety. Four bright, modern rooms have recently undergone refurbishment.

Food serving times
Monday-Saturday:
12pm-9pm
Sunday:
12pm-5pm

Prices
Meals: a la carte
14.00/22.00
4 rooms: 45.00/55.00

Typical Dishes
Duck leg
Braised belly pork
Baked egg custard

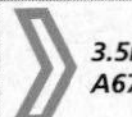
3.5mi Northwest of Blackburn by A677. Parking.

030 The Three Fishes

Mitton Road,
Mitton BB7 9PQ
Tel.: (01254) 826888 - Fax: (01254) 826026
Website: www.thethreefishes.com

  VISA  MC

 **Thwaites Original, Thwaites Bomber, Bowland Brewery Chipping Steamer**

Pies and hotpots, platters of tongue and brisket, black pudding and potted Morecambe shrimps – a look at the Three Fishes menu is the stuff of northern dreams. It's rare to find cuisine so thoroughly rooted in a region, but the richly savoury and heartening Lancastrian recipes are given pride of place here, prepared in a kitchen which is stocked by a host of hand-picked local suppliers, and served in a very spacious, modern pub. There is a special menu for children but the dairy specials are for all. Find a table then order at the bar – this is such beer-friendly food that it's worth trying a north-western cask ale to go with it. This updated and professionally run pub has come a long way since it served passengers from the river Ribble ferry, but its change of tack has been a definite success, so be warned: it gets very busy.

Food serving times

Monday-Friday:
12pm-2pm, 6pm-9pm

Saturday:
12pm-2pm, 5.30pm-9pm

Sunday:
12pm-8.30pm

Closed 25 December

Bookings not accepted

Prices

Meals: a la carte
15.50/22.00

Typical Dishes

Lancashire curd crumpet
Shoulder of mutton
10 Lancashire cheeses

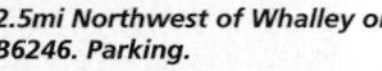

2.5mi Northwest of Whalley on B6246. Parking.

031 The White Bull

Church Street, Ribchester PR3 3XP
Tel.: (01254) 878303
e-mail: enquiries@whitebullribchester.co.uk
Website: www.whitebullribchester.co.uk

Black Sheep Best Bitter, Copper Dragon, Moorhouses

The chef may have an international C.V., but there's nothing fancy or pretentious about the food served at The White Bull in Ribchester. This is unfussy, British cooking at its best, with proper hearty pub dishes such as fish pie, bangers and mash and pork chops. All are homemade using the best produce available; traceability and seasonality are of paramount importance and the menus and specials change often. Proper pub food needs a proper village pub, and The White Bull fits the bill very nicely. With a 1707 birth date, pillars which some say have their roots in Roman times, and the remains of the Roman bath visible from the beer garden, the pub has a suitably ancient history; the open fire in the bar creates a warm, welcoming feel, and three charming bedrooms complete the picture.

Food serving times

Monday-Sunday:
12pm-2pm, 6pm-9pm

Closed Monday in winter

Prices

Meals: a la carte
14.00/23.00

3 rooms: 55.00/70.00

Typical Dishes

Black pudding fritters
White Bull fish pie
Steamed chocolate pudding

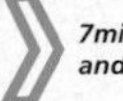

7mi North of Blackburn by A666 and B6245. Parking.

032 The Lunesdale Arms

Tunstall LA6 2QN

Tel.: (01524) 274203 - Fax: (01524) 274229

e-mail: info@thelunesdale.co.uk - Website: www.thelunesdale.co.uk

 **Dent Brewery Aviator, Black Sheep**

This rural dining pub with Cumbria to the north and Yorkshire to the east is making friends across the board, and across the borders. What was probably once a licensed room of the old village hall now feels pleasantly, deliberately modern; uncluttered and bright with chunky tables and chairs dotted around, squashy sofas facing a vast fireplace and a combined family and games room for post-lunch pool or table football. Eat – or drink – where you like: a blackboard menu changes as seasons and local suppliers dictate, but sharp, simple, flavourful dishes like spinach, pea and mint soup with homemade bread, goujons of cod, or broccoli, mustard and cheese tart make good, nourishing lunches, while a larger dinner selection could take in chicken with pesto or herb-crusted fennel with garlic butter.

Food serving times

Tuesday-Friday:
12pm-2pm, 6pm-9pm

Saturday-Sunday:
12pm-2.30pm, 6pm-9pm

Closed 25-26 December

Prices

Meals: a la carte
19.00/24.50

Typical Dishes

Goat's cheese soufflé
Slow-roast leg of lamb
Damson crème brûlée

4mi South of Kirkby Lonsdale on A683. Parking.

033 The Inn at Whitewell

Whitewell BB7 3AT
Tel.: (01200) 448222 - Fax: (01200) 448298
e-mail: reception@innatwhitewell.com
Website: www.innatwhitewell.com

Bowland Brewery Hen Harrier, Skipton Brewery Copper Dragon, Timothy Taylor's Landlord

A delightful location in a river valley in the Forest of Bowland means that a visit is always going to be special. The pub itself is an extended 14C cottage which once served as a coaching inn; nowadays it's very personally run with a endearing eccentricity which surfaces at the unlikeliest moments! It has considerable charm downstairs with a lovely faded bar full of eyecatching curios, a reception-cum-shop and an intimate restaurant overlooking the River Hodder and Trough of Bowland. Dishes have a traditional base and make good use of sound Lancastrian produce: just pull up a chair in the bar for a hearty meal or ask for a table in the restaurant for a more formal occasion. The large, comfortable bedrooms, whether traditional or modern, boast plenty of style, with good views and, in some cases, real peat fires. All have CD players and fittings that touch on the highest inn standards.

Food serving times

Monday-Sunday:
12pm-2pm, 7.30pm-9.30pm

Prices

Meals: a la carte
19.50/35.00

23 rooms: 74.00/98.00

Typical Dishes

Pan-fried chicken livers

Roast loin of Bowland lamb

Local hand-made cheeses

6mi Northwest of Clitheroe by B6243. Parking.

034 The Mulberry Tree

Wrightington Bar WN6 9SE
Tel.: (01257) 451400 - Fax: (01257) 451400
e-mail: mulberrytree@btconnect.com

 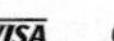 

Seasonal and according to demand

Not a pub for the traditionally-minded lover of beams and foaming ale. Nevertheless, what it lacks in traditional character, it makes up for in ample size and ultimately in the quality of the food. The rather cavernous open plan interior has a spacious bar with simple tables and chairs occupying one end, and a large, more formal, and slightly more expensive, linen-clad restaurant at the other. Both share a warm, buzzy atmosphere as well as the same range of specials, and this is where the pub comes into its own: the satisfying modern cooking demonstrates sound experience and culinary know-how and portions are, by any standards, generous. Local, seasonal ingredients are to the fore in the quality cuisine which pays due homage to global influences. Keenly-priced menu with a strong Lancashire base and plenty of choice.

Food serving times

Monday-Friday:
12pm-2.30pm, 6pm-9.30pm

Saturday-Sunday:
12pm-9.30pm

Bar snacks available all day Saturday-Sunday

Prices

Meals: 12.75/16.75
(2 course bar/restaurant lunch/dinner) and a la carte 22.00/31.00

Typical Dishes

Cox apple & black pudding
Slow roast belly of pork
Vanilla pannacotta

3.5mi Northwest of Standish by A5209 on B5250. Parking.

Not content with seven historic counties, the South East has always looked further for inspiration. This, after all, is the region that gave the world a prince's Indian pavilion facing the Brighton seafront, the pretty redbrick streets of Sandwich, bridging the Channel to Holland and Germany, and Waddesdon Manor, a perfect Loire Chateau just off the A41. Yet these are as much an image of "Englishness" as the domes and spires of Oxford or Kent's white-capped oasthouses amid the hop-poles and apple orchards of the Weald. Here in the South East you'll find the start of the Cotswolds and the freedom of the South Downs Path, the ancient vantage point White Horse Hill and the rural calm of Royal Berkshire's riverside villages, while Canterbury and Winchester, Blenheim, Chartwell and Windsor all have their special place in British history. For a change of pace, fast or slow, the quiet countryside or the colourful cultural life of Brighton are both within an hour of the capital. The South East is also a place to dine well: Whitstable oysters, delicately flavoured Romney Marsh lamb and Aylesbury duck, not to mention a long brewing tradition, are just some of its specialities.

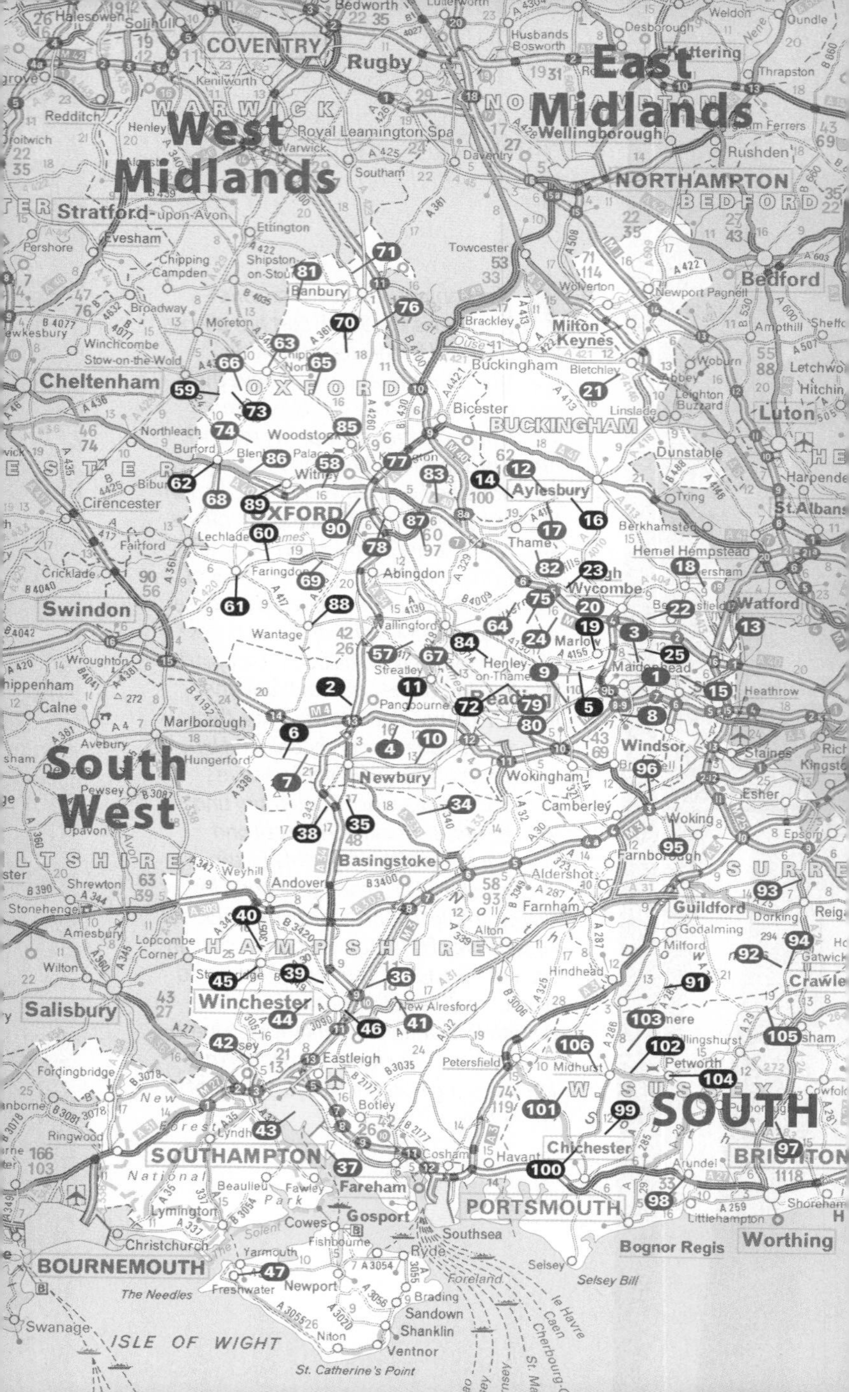
West Midlands
East Midlands
South West
SOUTH
COVENTRY
Rugby
NORTHAMPTON
BEDFORD
Bedford
Stratford-upon-Avon
Cheltenham
OXFORD
Aylesbury
Milton Keynes
Swindon
Newbury
Basingstoke
Reading
Windsor
Watford
Luton
Winchester
Salisbury
SOUTHAMPTON
PORTSMOUTH
BOURNEMOUTH
BRIGHTON
Worthing
Chichester
Guildford
ISLE OF WIGHT

East of England
London
EAST
Cambridge
Ipswich
Colchester
Chelmsford
Southend-on-Sea
Maidstone
Canterbury
Dover
Folkestone
Hastings
Eastbourne
Boulogne

Bray-on-Thames

001 The Hinds Head

High St,
Bray-on-Thames SL6 2AD
Tel.: (01628) 626151 - Fax: (01628) 623394
e-mail: info@thehindshead.co.uk - Website: www.thehindshead.co.uk

We most liked

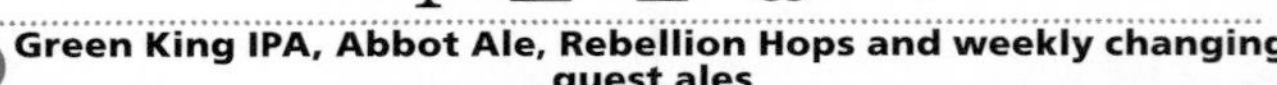

Green King IPA, Abbot Ale, Rebellion Hops and weekly changing guest ales

Cross Heston Blumenthal's dedication with the warm, true-grained charm of the English pub and you have a recipe for success. The ground-breaking modern cuisine of the Fat Duck, four doors away, is little reflected in the pub's menu, but the team at the Hind's Head do share the owner's fascination with the lost glories of English cookery: try a glass of pear cider or a sip of mead with satisfying and full-flavoured dishes that include pies and puddings, syllabubs and trifles. The most imaginative choices are based on favourites from the old royal kitchens downriver at Hampton Court. The pub itself has its origins in the 1600s – with its beams, panelled walls and real fire, it feels wonderfully inviting – but it's more used to keeping up with 21C demand, so arrive early.

Food serving times

Monday-Saturday:
12pm-2.30pm, 6.30pm-9.30pm

Sunday:
12pm-4pm

Closed 25-26 December

Closed dinner Bank Holiday Monday

Prices

Meals: a la carte
24.00/35.00

Typical Dishes

Hind Head tea smoked salmon
Lancashire hotpot
Treacle tart

1mi South of Maidenhead by A308. Parking in 2 village car parks outside the pub.

002 The Crab at Chieveley

Wantage Rd,
Chieveley RG20 8UE
Tel.: (01635) 247550 - Fax: (01635) 248440
e-mail: info@crabatchieveley.com - Website: www.crabatchieveley.com

 **Fuller's London Pride, Timothy Taylor's Landlord, West Berkshire Brewery**

Down a country road, surrounded by waving fields of wheat and well-ordered countryside, The Crab doesn't look like the kind of place to rock the boat, but country pub preconceptions are best forgotten here. The old fishing nets give you a clue to the menu – an extensive choice of seafood served in the more casual bistro and a surprisingly formal dining room. The real surprise, though, is reserved for diners who decide to stay the night. Ten bedrooms in the modern annex eclipse the average inn for originality and luxury. Decorated in the style of famous hotels from Raffles to Sandy Lane in Barbados and La Mamounia in Marrakesh, each one is equipped with DVD players and other delightful extras: ground floor rooms have their own private terrace with a hot tub!

Food serving times

Monday-Sunday:
12pm-2.30pm, 6pm-10pm

- Seafood -

Prices

Meals: 15.00/29.50 (3 course lunch/dinner) and a la carte 25.00/40.00

15 rooms:
80.00/210.00

Typical Dishes

Butter poached lobster
Fillets of John Dory
Assiette of desserts

2.5mi West of Chieveley by School Road on B4494. Parking.

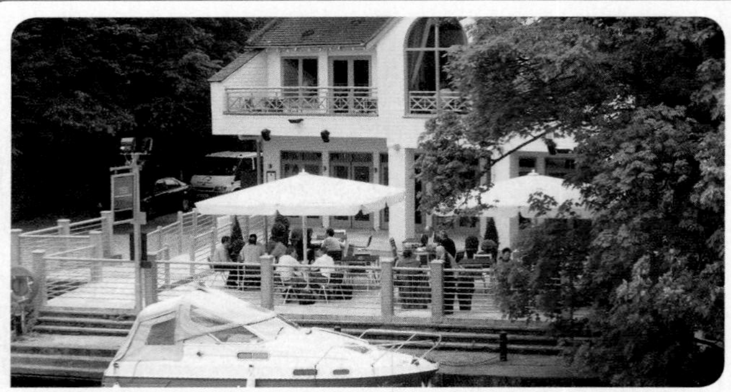

003 The Ferry

Sutton Rd,
Cookham SL6 9SN
Tel.: (01628) 525123
Website: www.theferry.co.uk

  VISA AE MC

Timothy Taylor's Landlord, Fuller's London Pride

In terms of location, it's hard to imagine a pub more enviably situated than The Ferry, which stands alongside the meandering Thames overlooking Cookham Bridge. It even has its own landing stage for those who like to arrive in a bit of style. Some don't even make it inside, but are tempted to linger on the lovely wood furnished dining terrace, but those who do venture through the front doors are hardly short-changed. The pub boasts a part-14th century interior, and its recent restoration offers modernised, rustic charm. There's a smart snug with leather seats, a bar with sofas to snuggle into, and a restaurant with good views over the river. Appealing menus wander through the gastro universe, from sharing plates and snacks to pasta and pizza, and on to rotisserie and grill, all of which can be walked off afterwards with a nice stroll along the Thames Path.

Food serving times

Monday-Saturday:
12pm-2.30pm, 6pm-9.30pm

Sunday:
12pm-7pm

Prices

Meals: 25.00 (3 course lunch & dinner) and a la carte 21.00/30.00

Typical Dishes

Grilled asparagus
Spit chicken with aioli
Mango Pavlova fool

By the river 2 mins walk from the centre of the village. Parking.

004 The Pot Kiln

Frilsham RG18 0XX

Tel.: (01635) 201366

e-mail: info@potkiln.co.uk - Website: www.potkiln.co.uk

VISA AE MC

Brick Kiln, Mr Chubbs, Magg's Mild (West Berkshire Brewery) and changing guest ales

Hard to believe that dull roar you hear in the background is the M4. This 350 year-old brick built house – a former brick makers' - transports you to a quieter age. Run by TV chef Mike Robinson, you enter into a tiny, wonderfully characterful front bar that's wood floored with benches unchanged for over a century. You might be tempted to eat here, but most prefer the dining area through a door, complete with chunky pine tables and chairs. "Locally caught" is the absolute principle here. Game is from the nearby Berkshire countryside, wild mushrooms come from the woods, and herbs and salad leaves travel all the way from the back garden. Filled roll or roasted game dish, you're sure of a good mouthful, washed down by wine from the excellent list, or a pint from the West Berkshire Brewery – it's based at the bottom of the garden!

Food serving times

Monday-Sunday:
12pm-2pm, 6pm-9pm

Closed 25 December

Bar meals only Sunday evening

Prices

Meals: a la carte
25.00/30.00

Typical Dishes

Warm salad of wood pigeon

Pavé of venison

Sticky toffee pudding

6mi North East of Newbury by B4009 to Hermitage and minor road. Parking.

005 Black Boys Inn

Henley Rd,
Hurley SL6 5NQ
Tel.: (01628) 824212
e-mail: info@blackboysinn.co.uk - Website: www.blackboysinn.co.uk

 **Brakspears**

This part-16C inn shows the benefits of a thorough renovation: it's intimate, relaxing, and obviously run with real pub know-how. True to form, the gently helpful, conversational service strikes just the right note: the friendly team are justifiably proud of their good food and will talk you through the daily specials. Dishes might include grilled halibut fillet, slowly cooked lamb rump or burgundy braised snail and seasonal mushrooms. The concern for fine ingredients is typical of a pub which even draws its water from its own well, but the result is the sort of flavourful, well-prepared, original cooking which is very easy to enjoy, complemented by a fine selection of wines by the glass. Comfortable and pleasantly furnished modern bedrooms, situated in converted outbuildings, really stand out for value.

Food serving times

Tuesday-Saturday:
12pm-2pm, 7pm-9pm

Sunday:
12pm-2pm

Closed 2 weeks at Christmas, 2 weeks in August

Prices

Meals: a la carte
25.00/30.00

7 rooms: 75.00/85.00

Typical Dishes

Blue fin tuna tartare

Caramelized veal sweetbread

Rhubarb & marzipan fritter

4mi East of Henley-on-Thames by A4130. Parking.

006 The Dundas Arms

Station Rd,
Kintbury RG17 9UT
Tel.: (01488) 658263
e-mail: info@dundasarms.co.uk

Ramsbury Brewery Gold, Adnams Best Bitter, West Berks Brewery 'Good Old Boy', Young's Special

After supplying Kintbury with sustaining dinners and its daily pint for over four decades, the long-standing landlord knows he's among friends in the bar. Never ones to pass up a good thing, the locals arrive on the dot for filling dishes like steak and chips or roast duck breast and a friendly, familiar atmosphere prevails. If it gets a bit busy for your taste, the trick is to ask if they're opening the rear restaurant, usually reserved for more formal dinners; enjoy dishes such as pan-fried pigeon breasts or rump of lamb here, with views over the canal. On a summer afternoon, there's only one place to be, however. A lovely double terrace borders the edge of the Kennet and the canal: watch the narrowboats passing the lock as the stopping trains roll away to Bedwyn and the Wessex Downs. Five neat, light bedrooms face the river.

Food serving times

Monday:
12pm-2pm

Tuesday-Saturday:
12pm-2pm, 7pm-9pm

Closed 25-26 December,
1 January

Prices

Meals: a la carte
20.00/30.00

5 rooms: 80.00/95.00

Typical Dishes

Crab au gratin
Steak and kidney pie
Raspberry brûlée

3.5mi East of Hungerford by A4.
Parking.

Marsh Benham

007 The Red House

Marsh Benham RG20 8LY
Tel.: (01635) 582017 - Fax: (01635) 581621
e-mail: enquiries@redhousemarshbenham.co.uk
Website: www.redhousemarshbenham.co.uk

 **6X, Good Old Boy**

Once inside this well cared-for thatched, 18C red brick inn, there's a choice to be made. To the front, the more casual bar with its wooden floors: grab one of several tables by the old bay windows, if you can. To the back, pleasant countryside views, courteous, attentive service and smartly set dining tables, and outside, a terrace for al fresco dining when the weather holds up. A classical French influence comes through in rather delicate, carefully presented dishes. Starters might include Provençale fish soup, roasted quail or goat's cheese tart, while mains might take the form of crayfish, mussel and tiger prawn risotto, Cornish seabass or pan-fried guinea fowl.

Food serving times

Monday-Saturday:
12pm-2.15pm, 7pm-9.30pm

Sunday:
12pm-2.15pm

Closed 26 and 31 December, 1 January

Prices

Meals: 13.95/15.95 (3 course lunch & dinner) and a la carte 21.45/30.85

Typical Dishes

Provençale fish soup
Pan-fried Guinea fowl
Apple tart Tatin

Off the A4 between Newbury and Hungerford. Parking.

008 The Royal Oak

Paley Street SL6 3JN
Tel.: (01628) 620541
Website: www.theroyaloakpaleystreet.com

VISA AE MC

Fuller's London Pride

A pleasant, proudly preserved village pub, but with a difference: framed photos of the owner's father, chatshow legend Michael Parkinson, and his showbiz friends beam affably from the wattle and timber walls. Attentive staff share Parky's talent for putting guests at their ease and serve up classically tasty, no-nonsense cooking with proper seasonal character: dishes could include calf's sweetbreads with celeriac purée and braised lettuce, butternut squash risotto or fricassee of duck hearts with bacon and onions, followed by bread and butter pudding or apple and rhubarb crumble. A smart yet cosy bar, complete with dedicated regulars, offers a fine selection of wines and real ales and a quietly convivial atmosphere, or you can dine at laid tables to the rear. Regular music nights are held on Mondays – some famous names putting in the odd appearance.

Food serving times

Monday-Sunday:
12pm-3pm, 6pm-10pm

Closed dinner Sunday September-April

Prices

Meals: a la carte 20.00/30.00

Typical Dishes

Potted rabbit
Angus rib of beef
Cambridge burnt cream

3.5 mi Southwest of Bray-on-Thames by A308, A330 on B3024. Parking.

009 St George & Dragon

High Street,
Wargrave RG10 8HY
Tel.: (0118) 940 5021
e-mail: pubs@simon-king.co.uk - Website: www.stgeorgeanddragon.co.uk

Timothy Taylor's Landlord, Fuller's London Pride

Set on the edge of the historical, Thames-side village of Wargrave, this pub has a prime location. A position on its raised decked terrace will grant you excellent views of the ducks and swans meandering down the river on a sunny afternoon, but arrive early to ensure a seat as everyone's sure to have had the same idea. Inside, despite its conversion into a contemporary gastropub, this place has still managed to retain plenty of character with its open kitchen, stone-fired oven, log burning fires and beams. Discerning locals mix with those from further afield and a friendly, informal atmosphere prevails. Like the interior, the menu also contains a pleasing blend of styles, with a choice of favourites such as pizza and pasta or the more adventurous crispy duck, tapas or crab cakes. Unlike St. George, you probably won't get the opportunity to rescue a beautiful princess, but rest assured that you can at least slay your hunger.

Food serving times

Monday-Sunday:
12pm-2.30pm, 6pm-9.30pm

Closed 25-26 December

Prices

Meals: a la carte
15.00/30.50

Typical Dishes

Baked Camembert
Pork fillet & blue cheese
Grilled fruit & yoghurt

Moorings on the River Thames, at the end of the garden. Parking.

010 **The Angel**

Bath Rd,
Woolhampton RG7 5RT
Tel.: (0118) 971 3301
e-mail: mail@thea4angel.com - Website: www.thea4angel.com

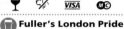

Conveniently situated for motorists, off the A4 between Newbury and Reading, the Angel sits in the heart of the village of Woolhampton, providing passers-by and locals alike with tasty, satisfying food. First impressions – green window frames in a curtain of ivy – offer no hint of the distinctive design inside; tropical plants, flowers, hops and yet more ivy set off a series of intimate, candlelit rooms in burgundy, green and ochre, with wooden floors, log fires burning in the grate and rows of wine bottles glinting between the beams. You can still pop in here for a pint, but food is where the main emphasis now lies – as illustrated by the self-applied 'gastro' tag, and while the lunchtime menu offers sandwiches, the à la carte is more adventurous, with dishes ranging from a simple steak and chips to mussels steamed in a Thai broth, slow roast belly of pork or tiger prawns with linguini.

Food serving times
Monday-Sunday:
12pm-3pm, 6pm-11pm

Prices
Meals: a la carte
15.50/30.00

Typical Dishes
Black pudding & sausage salad
Welsh beef fillet
Warm chocolate fondant

On A4 between Reading and Newbury. Parking.

011 The Royal Oak

The Square, Yattendon RG18 0UG
Tel.: (01635) 201325 - Fax: (01635) 201926
e-mail: info@royaloakyattendon.com
Website: www.royaloakyattendon.com

West Berkshire Brewery Good Old Boy and Mr Chubbs

Though not a million miles from the roaring intensity of the M4, this very pleasant redbrick former coaching inn could inhabit another age. Sympathetically set in a picture postcard village, its well-appointed lounge with real fire sets the scene, evoking English country house style at its more comfortable and unassuming. The beamed bar, where local drinkers mix with diners, is the centre of the action; take a seat at the front and watch village life go by out of the window. For a more formal meal at weekends, try the smartly dressed restaurant. Menus, invariably with plenty of choice, never stray far from a confidently executed classic base with distinctly modern overtones, their influences stretching globally. Dishes might include braised octopus or roast suprême of duck, with desserts such as apple and sultana crumble or poached pear with Amaretto cookies. Comfortable, pretty bedrooms, with a rather chintzy quality, beckon upstairs.

Food serving times

Monday-Sunday:
12pm-2.30pm, 7.30pm-9.30pm

Closed 1 January

Prices

Meals: 15.00 (3 course lunch weekdays only) and a la carte 26.00/35.00

5 rooms:
110.00/130.00

Typical Dishes

Artichoke heart & mushrooms
Calves kidney
Beignet soufflé

6mi North East of Newbury by B4009 and minor road; in the village centre. Parking.

012 The Crown

Aylesbury Rd, Cuddington HP18 0BB
Tel.: (01844) 292222
e-mail: david@thecrowncuddington.co.uk
Website: www.thecrowncuddington.co.uk

 VISA AE MC

Fuller's London Pride, Adnams ESB

There are many attractive thatched properties in pretty Cuddington, but, even so, this 16C pub still seems to stand out. From the outside, it looks appealingly like a traditional village pub - and what you see is exactly what you get. No gastropub modernisation here, thank you very much. It's got the carpets, the low beamed ceilings, the quarry tiled floors and the burgundy walls. Bric-à-brac and horse brasses abound and the gents has a surprisingly large collection of Victorian nudes. Two huge inglenook fireplaces featuring beehive chimneys add to the sense of history, although neither of them is actually used. Still very much a drinkers pub, there's plenty of room at the bar, but the food also attracts many a hungry punter. Enjoy tasty, modern dishes made with an eclectic range of ingredients; dishes might include fillet of red mullet with Spanish rice and saffron sauce or warm duck and bacon salad with raspberry vinaigrette.

Food serving times

Monday-Saturday:
12pm-2pm, 6.30pm-9.30pm

Sunday:
12pm-2pm

Prices

Meals: 16.50 (3 course lunch/dinner weekdays only) and a la carte 21.50/28.00

Typical Dishes

Black pudding bhaji
Corn-fed chicken
Tarte au citron

West of Aylesbury by A418. Some parking spaces available.

013 The Swan Inn

Village Rd,
Denham UB9 5BH

Tel.: (01895) 832085 - Fax: (01895) 835516
e-mail: info@swaninndenham.co.uk - Website: www.swaninndenham.co.uk

 VISA 

 **Courage Best, Wadworth 6X, Marlow Rebellion IPA**

You can hear the muted rumble of the M25 and the A40 in the distance - or maybe it's your empty stomach complaining - but this unspoiled village is nevertheless an attractive spot for this wisteria clad pub. The open plan bar has a relaxed feel to it, happily harbouring both drinkers and diners, as does the large garden and terrace, whilst 'The room behind the bar' is used for private parties of up to ten. The contemporary à la carte menu evolves with the seasons and, along with the specials board, offers ample choice. Among the 'small plates,' you might try the baked thyme-studded brie, which comes with sticky red cabbage and melba toast, or the twice-baked crab soufflé, accompanied by saffron and grain mustard syrup. The interesting flavours continue with the mains, so wasabi tempura seabass might come on Asian salad with hoi sin dressing, and a confit duck leg on sage gnocchi with fig and sherry cream sauce. Booking is recommended.

Food serving times

Monday-Saturday:
12pm-2.30pm, 7pm-10pm

Sunday:
12pm-4pm, 7pm-10pm

Closed 25-26 December

Booking essential

Prices

Meals: a la carte
18.75/29.00

Typical Dishes

Seared scallops
Buckinghamshire beef parcel
Rice pudding brûlée

6mi North East of Slough by A412; in the centre of the village. Small car park.

014 Mole & Chicken

The Terrace,
Easington HP18 9EY
Tel.: (01844) 208387 - Fax: (01844) 208250
Website: www.moleandchicken.co.uk

  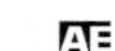 

Greene King IPA, Old Speckled Hen

This attractive creeper-clad inn is to be found in the quiet hamlet of Easington, through the back roads of Buckinghamshire. On a seasonally suitable day, a seat on the multi-levelled terrace is a must for the scenic southerly views. In snow and showers, snuggle up on a leather sofa next to the fire. Furniture is chunky pine, floors are flagged, and the country style décor is dimly lit. The serving staff are friendly and the atmosphere is relaxed and chatty. You'd be advised to book ahead though, because this place gets deservedly busy, especially at weekends. An interesting blackboard menu above the fire offers an eclectic range of modern, international dishes served in generous portions, and popular social events throughout the year see everything from haggis to hog roasts consumed here. Two terraced cottages next door provide simple rooms, where you can be soothed to sleep by the sound of snoring sheep.

Food serving times

Monday-Sunday:
12pm-2pm, 7pm-9pm

Closed 25 December

Booking essential

Prices

Meals: a la carte
22.00/28.00

5 rooms: 50.00/65.00

Typical Dishes

Creamed chilli mussels
Duck and bacon salad
Baileys crème brûlée

2.5mi Northwest of Thame by B4011. Parking.

The King of Prussia

015 The King of Prussia

Blackpond Lane,
Farnham Royal SL2 3EG
Tel.: (01753) 643006
e-mail: gm@tkop.co.uk - Website: www.thekingofprussia.com

  **VISA**  MC

Marlow Brewery, Fuller's London Pride

Perched between the M4 and the M40, not far 'up' from Windsor and just 'down' from Burnham Beeches, Farnham Royal is a smart village that now boasts an equally smart country dining pub. It may be a little hard to locate, but once you've arrived, you'll see that TKOP (as it's known) presents a shiny, cream-washed appearance to visitors and its part 17C credentials lose nothing by the bright lick of exterior paint. The impressive interior is rich in character, exemplified by beamed ceilings, polished wood floors and panels. Take your choice from three dining areas: either around or off the bar, or in a formal but wonderfully welcoming barn conversion with rafters – or alternatively, grab a seat on the decking in the rear garden. The modern cooking is constantly evolving and benefits from an unfussy approach. Top English produce is used to fine effect, and effortless service – keen and organised – completes a smooth picture.

Food serving times

Monday-Saturday:
12pm-2.15pm, 6.30pm-9.30pm

Sunday:
12pm-2.15pm

Closed 1 January

Prices

Meals: 10.00 (2 course dinner Monday-Wednesday) and a la carte 20.00/31.00

Typical Dishes

Pan roast fishcake
Steak and kidney pudding
Tarte Tatin

3/4mi Northwest of Farnham Royal by A355 (off Cherry Tree Road). Parking.

016 The Dinton Hermit

Water Lane,
Ford HP17 8XH
Tel.: (01296) 747473 - Fax: (01296) 748819
e-mail: dintonhermit@btconnect.com - Website: www.dinton-hermit.com

VISA AE MC

Batemans, Brakspears

This intriguingly titled 16C inn was named after John Bigg, a native of the parish who, after the execution of Charles I in 1649, reputedly lived in a cave until his own death more than forty years later, only ever venturing out in order to go for a pint in the inn. That last bit about the pint is actually made up, but the rest is true; and his picture now hangs in the bar to prove it. Lunch here is a simple affair, with choices including fish and chips, salads and sandwiches, while the concise à la carte dinner menu offers dishes such as sea bass or duck. Warm yourself by the vast inglenook fireplace as you eat in the cosy bar or sit at a linen-laid table in one of the dining rooms. If you are staying over, the choices continue; two King Charles rooms above the bar boast four poster beds, the five Regency rooms in an adjoining cottage are furnished in dark wood, while the six barn rooms have a more modern, minimalist style.

Food serving times

Monday-Saturday:
12pm-2pm, 7pm-9pm

Sunday:
12pm-4pm

Closed 25-31 December

Prices

Meals: a la carte
23.30/33.25

13 rooms:
80.00/125.00

Typical Dishes

Crispy seabass salad Niçoise
Grilled red mullet
Sticky toffee pudding

5.5mi Southwest of Aylesbury by A418. Parking.

017 The Green Dragon

8 Churchway,
Haddenham HP17 8AA
Tel.: (01844) 291403 - Fax: (01844) 299532
e-mail: sue@eatatthedragon.co.uk - Website: www.eatatthedragon.co.uk

We most liked

 **IPA, Deuchars, Wadworth 6X and local guest ale Wychert**

Situated in what is reputed to be the largest village in England, it is perhaps no surprise that this pub can, on occasion, be a little tricky to find. If in doubt, the advice from those in the know is: look for the church tower. Once you enter the dragon, you'll find a typically traditional little pub which still warmly welcomes drinkers. It is 350 years old, with pictures of those eponymous winged creatures on the walls, a slate tiled roof and exposed brick and stonework. Friendly staff look after you attentively and the food is tasty as well as kind on the pocket, with choices ranging from the more traditional steak and kidney pudding or fish and chips to dishes such as duck breast with bak choy, or ballottine of salmon for those after something lighter. Special event nights are hosted regularly throughout the year by the pub's down to earth owners, but whatever the night, it can get busy, so booking is recommended.

Food serving times

Monday-Saturday:
12pm-2pm, 6.30pm-9.30pm

Sunday:
12pm-2pm

Closed 25 December

Booking essential

Prices

Meals: a la carte
24.00/32.00

Typical Dishes

Salmon and prawn fishcake

Seared fillet of seabass

Vanilla pannacotta

6mi South West of Aylesbury by A418 and minor road; by the Green and St Mary's Church. Parking.

The Sugar Loaf Inn

018 The Sugar Loaf Inn

Station Road,
Little Chalfont HP7 9PN
Tel.: (01494) 765579
e-mail: info@thesugarloafinn.com - Website: www.thesugarloafinn.com

Adnams Bitter, Adnams Broadside, Timothy Taylor's Landlord

This inn was originally a motel, built by the local railway company in the 1930s to serve travellers arriving at the nearby station. Typical of its period, its exterior is not exactly prepossessing, but venture inside and you'll be impressed by the restored oak panelling and wooden floors. Simple, contemporary décor is enhanced by the Jack Vettriano prints for sale on the walls. The central bar serves two areas; one with sofas and tables for drinkers, and the other exclusively for diners. There is also a pleasant conservatory and a rather modest rear garden and decked terrace. Lunch and dinner menus offer value-for-money pub classics, as well as more modern dishes with a European flavour. No one seems to know the origins of the pub's sweet-sounding name but suggestions range from the shape in which refined sugar used to be exported, to a type of pineapple, via a breed of horse and a 1970s pop band. Answers on a postcard, please.

Food serving times

Monday-Friday:
12pm-3pm, 5pm-10.30pm

Saturday:
12pm-4pm, 5pm-10.30pm

Sunday:
12pm-4pm, 5pm-10pm

Closed 26 December,
1 January

Prices

Meals: a la carte
19.95/35.00

Typical Dishes

Grilled asparagus
Gressingham duck
Chocolate & raspberry pudding

2mi East of Amersham by A404.
Parking.

019 The Hand and Flowers

126 West St,
Marlow SL7 2BP
Tel.: (01628) 482277
Website: www.thehandandflowers.co.uk

 **Abbot Ale, Green King IPA**

The Hand and Flowers was originally a pretty row of period cottages, dating back at least to the 1800s by the look of their black and white timbered facades. A necessary modicum of modernisation inside has left it feeling nice and unspoilt, with beams, exposed brick and flint walls and chunky wooden tables. It also comes divided into three areas; the most animated part being the central section facing the bar, but throughout it still feels very much like a real pub. The chef-owner has a fine pedigree, and the classically based cuisine is well-balanced, excellent in sourcing and preparation and full of richly appealing, sophisticated flavours. Dishes might include potted Dorset crab, oysters or foie gras parfait with orange chutney followed by pigeon en croûte with girolles, halibut with mussels or belly of pork with broad beans. An informal ambience and professional but decidedly unstuffy service help the enjoyment no end.

Food serving times

Closed 23 (dinner), 24-26, 30 (dinner) and 31 (lunch) December and 1 January (dinner)

Prices

Meals: a la carte 25.00/38.00

4 rooms: 140.00/190.00

Typical Dishes

Smoked haddock omelette

Highland canon of lamb

Vanilla crème brûlée

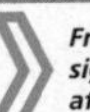

From town centre follow Henley signs West on A4155. Pub on right after 350metres. Parking.

020 The Royal Oak

Frieth Rd,
Bovingdon Green, Marlow SL7 2JF
Tel.: (01628) 488611 - Fax: (01628) 478680
e-mail: info@royaloakmarlow.co.uk - Website: www.royaloakmarlow.co.uk

Brakspear, Marlow, Fuller's London Pride, Rebellion IPA

Travel to the outskirts of historic Marlow and, on a busy country lane just past the woods, you will light upon The Royal Oak. Its name splashed boldly across its front, this pub is contemporary in style; open plan, with a large bar and a light and airy conservatory. Parts of the pub date from 17C – so for a taste of its rustic character, head for the cosy beamed area on the left behind the bar, with its mismatch of furniture, wood burning stove and flagged floors. Out front you are greeted by the scent of rosemary, and the pub's sizeable lawned garden – complete with petanque piste - makes for a very pleasant spot to dine on a summer's evening. Well-run by an enthusiastic team, service is friendly and a relaxed atmosphere prevails throughout. The modern menu is supplemented with blackboard specials, and dishes on offer might range from creamy Italian bean cassoulet to steak and fat chips, with plenty of fresh fish and local game.

Food serving times

Monday-Saturday:
12pm-2.30pm, 7pm-10pm

Sunday:
12pm-4pm, 7pm-10pm

Closed 25-26 December

Prices

Meals: a la carte
18.75/28.50

Typical Dishes

Devilled lambs kidneys
Classic fish pie
Warm chocolate Brownie

From Marlow town centre head towards Bovingdon Green; pub is on the left as you leave the woods. Parking.

021 The Crooked Billet

2 Westbrook End,
Newton Longville MK17 0DF
Tel.: (01908) 373936
e-mail: john@thebillet.co.uk - Website: www.thebillet.co.uk

We most liked

   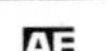 

Abbot Ale, H & H Olde Trip, Hobgoblin, Batemans XXXB, Everards Tiger

You can't help feeling that this attractive, 17C thatched pub would be better suited to life in a picturesque little countryside village than on the outskirts of MK, but everything else about it feels exactly right, thanks to the formidable team that is John and Emma Gilchrist. As illustrated by the way the suppliers are credited on the menu, the couple are serious about food - even the people of the village get a mention for growing the vegetables and herbs – and Emma cooks well-balanced, modern dishes. Menus range from sandwiches, wraps and pasta at lunchtime through to a six course gourmet menu, and there is a rather interesting cheeseboard too. John's former life as a sommelier is evident in the remarkable wine list, with over 300 bins to choose from - and the vast majority of them available by the glass. Locals still gather solely for a drink, and the pub's low ceilinged, firelit bar makes this an atmospheric place for a pint.

Food serving times

Monday:
7pm-10pm

Tuesday-Saturday:
12pm-2pm, 7pm-10pm

Sunday:
12.30pm-3pm

Closed 25 December

Prices

Meals: a la carte
19.00/30.00

Typical Dishes

Scallops
Crispy roast pork belly
Selection of British cheeses

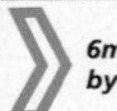

6mi Southwest of Milton Keynes by A421. Parking.

The Old Queens Head

022 The Old Queen's Head

Hammersley Lane, Penn HP10 8EY
Tel.: (01494) 813371 - Fax: (01494) 816145
e-mail: info@oldqueensheadpenn.co.uk
Website: www.oldqueensheadpenn.co.uk

Greene King IPA, Morlands Original

In the same year that the Great Fire of London was destroying large parts of the capital city, not too far away, in a tile-making village in leafy Buckinghamshire, the original part of the Old Queens Head was being constructed. Nowadays, it's an attractive, modern dining pub but it still retains charmingly rustic reminders of its ancient vintage, like its flagged floors now decorated with rugs, low ceiling rafters and beams, brick fireplaces and roughly plastered walls. There are a number of adjoining rooms but the oldest and most characterful is the more formal dining room, built over two levels and containing a hotchpotch of old wooden furniture. A small rear garden with picnic tables extends the pub's relaxed atmosphere outside. The menu offers an eclectic mix of traditional and more modern dishes, seasonally changing and served in generous portions, while specials are chalked up on a blackboard.

Food serving times

Monday-Saturday:
12pm-2.30pm, 7pm-10pm

Sunday:
12pm-4pm, 7pm-10pm

Closed 25-26 December

Prices

Meals: a la carte
18.75/27.50

Typical Dishes

Wild garlic & sorrel gnocchi

Braised shin of beef

Pineapple & ginger sponge

4mi North of A40, Junction 2, via Beaconsfield by B474. Parking.

023 The Three Horseshoes Inn

Bennett End, Radnage HP14 4EB

Tel.: (01494) 483273

e-mail: threehorseshoes@btconnect.com

Website: www.thethreehorseshoes.net

 **Rebellion Brewery, Marlow**

In the heart of the Buckinghamshire countryside stands the Three Horseshoes Inn; an attractive red brick pub dating from 1745. Its tiny front bar with its unusual inglenook fireplace, flagged floor and settles gets busy with locals at the weekends and although you can eat here, most people tend to dine at the linen-laid tables in the rear restaurant area. In the laid-back summer months you can eat tapas on the terrace while enjoying views out over fields and the garden – including the duck pond with its strangely submerged red telephone box. Numerous plates by the bar detail the owner / chef's fine pedigree, and the good value, modern British cooking he serves up here has a noteworthy precision and quality. Meals are well-presented, and ingredients are carefully sourced - locally wherever possible. Modern, comfortable bedrooms are individually decorated - Molières is the nicest - with character beds and modern bathrooms.

Food serving times

Tuesday-Saturday and Bank Holiday Monday:
12pm-2.30pm, 7pm-9.30pm

Sunday:
12pm-2.30pm

Closed Tuesday following Bank Holiday Monday

Prices

Meals: 17.50 (3 course lunch) and a la carte 22.50/30.00

6 rooms: 75.00/145.00

Typical Dishes

Scottish salmon rillette

Panfried fillet of seabass

Hot chocolate fondant

5mi West of High Wycombe by A40 and minor road North. Parking.

024 The Bull & Butcher

Turville RG9 6QU
Tel.: (01491) 638283 - Fax: (01491) 638836
e-mail: info@thebullandbutcher.com
Website: www.thebullandbutcher.com

 **Brakspear's Bitter, Special and Brewers Selection, Hooky Dark**

This whitewashed, 16C, Grade II listed pub is situated in the middle of the charming village of Turville; a location which may well give you a sense of déja vu, having been immortalised in various television programmes and films including The Vicar of Dibley and Goodnight Mr. Tom. Seek out a seat at the well table, built around a well in the middle of one of the rooms or sit in the garden facing north, and you'll see a beautiful white windmill on the hill, which was part of the set from Chitty Chitty Bang Bang. The atmosphere here is one of cosy comfort; local photos line the walls and there are wood beams, quarry tiles, log fires and scrubbed pine tables. The Bull room – a small converted barn - is used for private parties. Tried and tested pub favourites are to be found on the menu here, - steak and Dibley pudding, anyone? - but for more modern, Truly Scrumptious dishes, plump for one of the specials chalked up on the blackboard.

Food serving times

Monday-Saturday:
12pm-2.30pm, 6.30pm-9.30pm

Sunday and Bank Holiday:
12pm-4pm, 7pm-9pm

Prices

Meals: a la carte
20.00/27.00

Typical Dishes

Crayfish cocktail
Smoked haddock
Selection of British cheeses

5mi North of Henley-on-Thames by A4130 off B480. Parking.

025 Chequers Inn

Kiln Lane,
Wooburn Common HP10 0JQ
Tel.: (01628) 529575 - Fax: (01628) 850125
e-mail: info@chequers-inn.com - Website: www.chequers-inn.com

   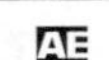  

Greene King IPA, Abbot Ale, Old Speckled Hen, Marlow Brewery Smuggler

Run by the same family for more than thirty years, this attractive red brick 17C inn has had time to build itself a reputation and, although seemingly situated on a country lane in the middle of nowhere, it does get surprisingly busy. The beamed bar with its open fire is as charming as it is small and makes a cosy place for a meal from the blackboard bar menu with its choice of old favourites, whereas the spacious, stylish lounge with its comfy sofas and coffee tables is more popular with the ladies who lunch. The à la carte menu is served in the formal restaurant housed in the extension, and might include pork or pigeon, beef or bream, and a table d'hôte and a two course 45 minute menu are also available for those counting either the pennies or the clock. Good-sized modern bedrooms also housed in the extension have views over the surrounding fields; room 17 has a four poster and is the most comfortable.

Food serving times

Monday-Friday:
12pm-3pm, 7pm-10pm

Saturday-Sunday:
12pm-10pm

Closed dinner 25 December, dinner 1 January

Prices

Meals: 19.95 (3 course lunch menu) and a la carte 26.65/40.65

17 rooms:
82.50/107.50

Typical Dishes

Baked mozzarella tuille
Saddle of rabbit
Berry crème brûlée

3.5mi Southwest of Beaconsfield by A40. Parking.

026 The George Inn

High St, Alfriston BN26 5SY
Tel.: (01323) 870319
e-mail: info@thegeorge-alfriston.com
Website: www.thegeorge-alfriston.com

 VISA  MC

 **Greene King IPA, Abbot Ale, Old Speckled Hen**

The most charming sight on Alfriston's pretty High Street, the overhanging front of the listed, brick-and-timber-built George Inn looks the picture of a good, old-fashioned English pub, and first impressions are confirmed in the front bar, with its strings of hops and its flickering fire. There's even some original 15C art on the walls. A relaxed landlord succeeds in making everyone feel properly at home, from the South Downs walkers who come for pints and ploughmans to a good crowd of locals – many pub cricket club and panto society members among them. Tasty dishes with an international or Asian touch offer plenty of choice and put their faith in the local greengrocer and butcher. The refurbished bedrooms have antique furniture but modern facilties; at the front, the sound of traffic to and fro on a weekday is noticeable, but no more than that.

Food serving times

Sunday-Thursday:
12pm-2.30pm, 7pm-9pm

Friday-Saturday:
12pm-2.30pm, 7pm-10pm

Closed 25-26 December

Prices

Meals: a la carte
20.00/26.00

6 rooms: 60.00/130.00

Typical Dishes

Goats cheese stack
Fillet steak
Spiced pears in red wine

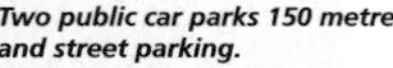

Two public car parks 150 metres and street parking.

027 The Curlew

Junction Rd, Bodiam TN32 5UY
Tel.: (01580) 861394
e-mail: enquiries@thecurlewatbodiam.co.uk
Website: www.thecurlewatbodiam.co.uk

Badger First Gold, Old Speckled Hen, Charles Wells Bombardier, Timothy Taylor's Landlord

The Curlew is indeed that rare bird; a traditional Sussex pub serving a choice of snacks as well as ambitious restaurant food, plus a notable list of fine wines featuring more than two hundred bins. The wide-ranging, if slightly complex, menu contains a mix of mostly Mediterranean and British dishes and if you're wanting a treat for afters, try a plate of miniature desserts, made just for sharing. Situated at the Bodiam castle crossroads, this white weather-boarded inn dates from the 17C and is Grade II listed. Inside, the traditional beamed interior gives the pub a rural feel, and there are two spacious restaurants with elegantly dressed tables, and a homely main bar in which to sit. If at any point, however, you find that the swirly-patterned carpets inside are starting to give you a headache, then a seat in the pretty ornamental garden with pond might make a pleasing alternative.

Food serving times

Tuesday-Saturday:
12pm-2pm, 7pm-9pm

Monday:
12pm-2pm

Prices

Meals: 20.00 (3 course lunch/dinner) and a la carte 25.00/32.50

Typical Dishes

Marinated tuna carpaccio

Local rump of lamb

Rhubarb and fig pudding

On B2244 Hawkhurst to Sedlescombe road, by the Bodiam Castle crossroads. Parking.

028 Coach & Horses

School Lane,
Danehill RH17 7JF
Tel.: (01825) 740369 - Fax: (01825) 740369
e-mail: coachandhorses@danehill.biz

Harveys Best and 2 guest ales changing weekly

In trying to appeal to a greater range of people, some pubs forget those living on their doorstep, but not The Coach and Horses. There's a formally laid area for dining, converted from the original stables, but at the hub of this characterful stone pub is its charming bar, seemingly unchanged since the pub's creation in 1847, and where locals still chew the fat. The bar can't take all the credit for the relaxed, unpretentious atmosphere here, though - the friendly, informal service also plays its part, and on sunny days the pretty garden positively encourages somnolence. Modern menus offer a range of dishes made with quality ingredients; locally sourced wherever possible and with prices that won't leave you counting pennies. Snacks and sandwiches are available at lunchtimes, specials are chalked up on blackboards and you can purchase handmade chutneys, jams, mustards and the like at the bar under the curious name of 'Ladypots.'

Food serving times

Monday-Saturday:
12pm-2pm, 7pm-9pm

Sunday:
12pm-2pm

Closed dinner 25 December, 26 December, dinner 1 January

Prices

Meals: a la carte
20.15/26.15

Typical Dishes

Jerusalem artichoke soup

Pan-fried Ashdown venison

Pain d'épice au chocolat

0.75mi North East on Chelwood Common Rd. Parking.

029 The Jolly Sportsman

Chapel Lane, East Chiltington BN7 3BA
Tel.: (01273) 890400 - Fax: (01273) 890400
e-mail: info@thejollysportsman.com
Website: www.thejollysportsman.com

 **Dark Star Hophead and regularly changing micro brewery beers**

Meandering through the winding lanes of Sussex, even the journey to this pub feels like a jolly japer; staff are jolly and they serve jolly good food too. With a raised rear garden looking towards the South Downs and a paved patio terrace area, this creeper-clad, candlelit pub is very popular during the summer months, but a seat by the fire in the sage green bar, or admiring the artwork in the smart country-style dining room is just as pleasant any month of the year. The owner's hands-on approach helps this place run like proverbial clockwork and regulars and visitors alike enjoy its relaxed, friendly atmosphere. This is a confident kitchen, whose cooking delivers the promise of the menu, and lets the quality of the ingredients shine through. There is a subtle Mediterranean influence with fish a particular strength, but all dishes display a vitality that comes from knowing which flavours go well together.

Food serving times

Tuesday-Thursday: 12.30pm-2.15pm, 7pm-9pm

Friday-Saturday: 12.30pm-2.15pm, 7pm-10pm

Sunday and Bank Holiday Monday: 12.30pm-3pm

Closed 4 days at Christmas, 1 January

Prices

Meals: 15.75 (3 course lunch) and a la carte 19.50/29.00

Typical Dishes

Roast quail
Rump of Ditchling lamb
Date and almond tart

5.5mi Northwest of Lewes by A275 and B2116 off Novington Lane. Parking.

030 The Griffin Inn

Fletching TN22 3SS
Tel.: (01825) 722890 - Fax: (01825) 722810
e-mail: info@thegriffininn.co.uk
Website: www.thegriffininn.co.uk

 **Harveys Best Bitter, Horsham Best, Iron Horse**

This red and white brick 16C coaching inn is the kind of pub everyone would like to have in their village. Well-established and run by the same family for thirty years, it's got the beamed bar, packed with locals, the open fires, plus a linen-laid candlelit dining area. It also has a terrace and a large garden looking out over the surrounding countryside, which makes it the ideal spot for summer barbeques. The buzzing atmosphere more than makes up for any slippage in service and the food here is fresh and homemade, using local produce wherever possible. The daily-changing restaurant menu offers modern British cooking with some Mediterranean influences, while a lighter blackboard menu – with dishes such as squid salad, Thai curry and moules frites - is served in the bar. For guests, a choice of individually decorated rooms is available; each comfortable, and some with four posters and roll top baths.

Food serving times

Monday-Sunday:
12pm-2.30pm, 7pm-9.30pm

Closed 25 December

Restaurant closed dinner Sunday

Prices

Meals: 30.00 (3 course Sunday lunch) and a la carte 20.00/35.00

13 rooms: 70.00/130.00

Typical Dishes

Goat's cheese bruschetta

Rye Bay fish pie

Chocolate & ginger cheesecake

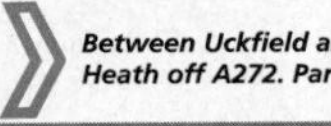

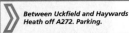

Between Uckfield and Haywards Heath off A272. Parking.

031 The Ginger Pig

3 Hove Street,
Hove BN3 2TR
Tel.: (01273) 736123
Website: www.gingermanrestaurants.com

 **Harveys, Theakstons and a guest ale**

Located just off the seafront in up and coming Hove actually, The Ginger Pig is the third of the Gingerman group's ventures in the Brighton area and is proving just as popular as its siblings. Entry into this striking, part-gabled building – a former smugglers' haunt - is through equally striking revolving doors. Once inside, chill out with a drink on low sofas in the contemporary bar or venture up the steps to the spacious, open plan dining area with its mix of leather banquettes and dark wood chairs and tables, beyond which lies the sun-trap of a terrace. Like the décor and the bold art hanging on the walls, the cooking here is modern and fresh, and the concise European menu offers tasty, refined dishes, all homemade using local produce, and served in filling portions. Specials are chalked up on a blackboard menu and keen, young servers form a well-drilled team – but bookings are not accepted, so those in the know arrive early.

Food serving times

Monday-Sunday:
12pm-2pm, 6.30pm-10pm

Bookings not accepted

Prices

Meals: a la carte
18.00/24.50

Typical Dishes

Crab and celeriac remoulade

Pork belly

Vanilla and lemon pannacotta

Off north side of shore road, Kingsway, A259. Parking meters (2 hours maximum during day).

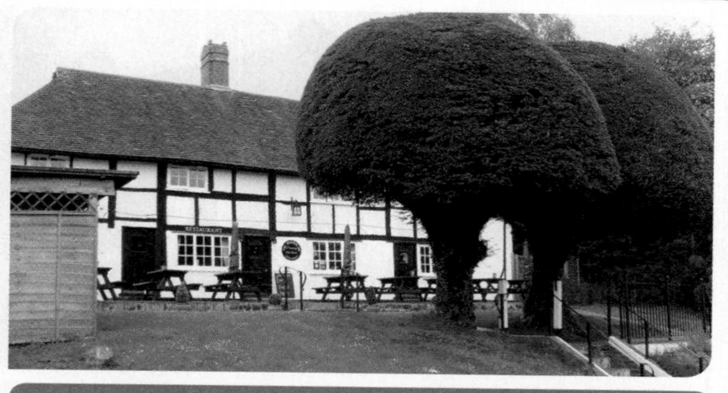

032 The Peacock Inn

Shortbridge,
Piltdown TN22 3XA
Tel.: (01825) 762463
e-mail: matthewarnold@aol.com - Website: www.peacock-inn.co.uk

Harveys Best, Fuller's London Pride, Abbot Ale

A quintessentially English pub in the heart of the Sussex countryside, its 16C black and white timbered exterior enhanced by two very neatly trimmed yew trees at the entrance. There are benches at the front, too, and a sign with a brightly painted peacock in full plumage. The rear has a children's play area and large paved terrace, where they sometimes host barbecues in summer. Inside are spacious bar rooms, full of character: log fire, dark beams, brass ornaments and an old framed peacock tapestry in pride of place. A variety of photos cover the walls: those of the owner with celebrity guests testify to the Peacock's enduring popularity and warm atmosphere. Menus are traditional and unpretentious, complemented by chef's blackboard specials, with fresh ingredients from mainly local suppliers. The home-made desserts are warmly recommended.

Food serving times

Monday-Sunday:
12pm-2.30pm, 6pm-9.30pm

Closed 25-26 December

Booking advisable at weekends

Prices

Meals: a la carte
18.00/30.00

Typical Dishes

Baked Camembert
Grilled seabass fillets
Baileys crème brûlée

8mi East of Haywards Heath by A272 and Shortbridge Lane. Parking.

033 The Lamb Inn

Wartling Rd,
Wartling BN27 1RY

Tel.: (01323) 832116 - Fax: (01323) 832637

e-mail: alison.farncombe@virgin.net - Website: www.lambinnwartling.co.uk

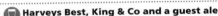

 **Harveys Best, King & Co and a guest ale**

With its traditional whitewashed appearance and attractive rear courtyard, it is perhaps easy to see that this elevated roadside inn began life as a pair of cottages, and its characterful interior, with its flag floors and beamed ceilings further vouches for its early 16C origins. Quality and traceability are the bywords here when it comes to food; they bake their own bread, whilst seafood comes from Hastings and Newhaven and most of the meat hails from neighbouring Chilley Farm, who specialise in traditionally-farmed stock with no additives, and slow-reared rare breeds such as Gloucester Old Spot pork and extra mature Sussex beef. Homemade dishes might include anything from robust pies to cassoulet of duck, and mutton, enjoying something of a renaissance, also appears. Eat in the bar or in the more formal restaurant; the welcome is friendly and this place is clearly a hit with the locals, with themed evenings particularly popular.

Food serving times

Monday-Saturday:
11.45am-2.15pm, 6.45pm-9pm

Sunday:
11.45am-2.15pm

Prices

Meals: a la carte
17.50/29.50

Typical Dishes

Baked egg Florentine
Shoulder of lamb
Chocolate praline

3.75miles Southeast of Herstmonceaux by A271 and Wartling Rd. Parking.

The Wellington Arms

034 The Wellington Arms

Baughurst Rd, Baughurst RG26 5LP
Tel.: (0118) 982 0110
e-mail: info@thewellingtonarms.com
Website: www.thewellingtonarms.com

 **Wadworth 6X**

Cluttered and characterful, this former hunting lodge of the Duke of Wellington is 'one to watch'. Remodelled as a dining pub, it's a very cosy, atmospheric place with original terracotta tile floors and lots of impressive wood décor and beams. The clutter is a pleasing amalgam of ornaments, books, rustic pictures and knickknacks, never quite enough of a diversion to keep punters away from the well-stocked bar and adjacent wine rack. Chickens are kept in a pen in the rear paddock; by way of contrast, teas are imported from Australia! There are only eight tables for dining, so booking is essential. Modern British cooking takes centre stage, but worldwide influences are always simmering near the surface. Lunches are simpler, and very good value; it's all backed up by polite but chatty service.

Food serving times

Wednesday-Saturday:
12pm-2.30pm, 6.30pm-9.30pm

Sunday:
12pm-2.30pm

Tuesday:
6.30pm-9.30pm

Prices

Meals: 15.00/18.00 (2/3 course lunch) and a la carte 22.00/33.00

Typical Dishes

Goat's cheese soufflé

Roast rack of local pork

Vanilla sponge pudding

8mi North of Basingstoke by A339 and minor road through Ramsdell and Pound Green; On the Kingsclere / Newbury road. Parking.

Burghclere

035 Carnarvon Arms

Winchester Rd,
Whitway, Burghclere RG20 9LE
Tel.: (01635) 278222 - Fax: (01635) 278444
e-mail: carnarvon@merchant-inns.com - Website: www.carnarvonarms.com

   MC

Weekly changing guest ales - Timothy Taylor's Landlord, Fuller's London Pride

Named after Lord Carnarvon – the man who discovered Tutankhamen's tomb - the very smart looking exterior of this north Hampshire establishment gives no clue to its origins: the 1850s. Refurbishment has gone on apace inside too: a particularly spacious main bar and lounge area is enhanced by temptingly comfortable low-back leather sofas. While away the time browsing through handily placed newspapers and magazines. A good selection of real ales is complemented with an admirably eclectic mix of wines by the glass. Dining takes place in two rooms: the open, L-shaped main restaurant, or the anteroom for private parties. Menus are the same wherever you may be. If you're feeling adventurous, try dishes with an interesting range of modern combinations; if your taste is more conventional, then the classics section includes fish and chips or sausage and mash. At day's end, The Carnarvon Arms boasts comfy, modern bedrooms.

Food serving times

Monday-Sunday:
12pm-2.30pm, 6.30pm-9pm

Prices

Meals: 9.95/14.95 (2/3 course lunch) and a la carte 20.00/32.00

23 rooms: 79.95/89.95

Typical Dishes

Pan-roasted wood pigeon

Berkshire Black pork cutlet

Warm chocolate fondant

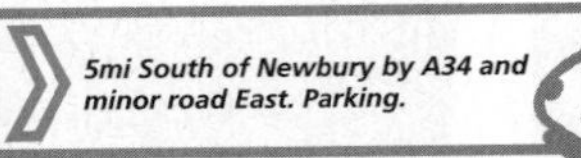

5mi South of Newbury by A34 and minor road East. Parking.

036 The Chestnut Horse

Easton SO21 1EG
Tel.: (01962) 779257 - Fax: (01962) 779037

 **Badger, Sussex, Hopping Hare**

A colourful pub, in more ways than one, despite being not a million miles from Winchester or the M3, the Chestnut Horse is still set in a pleasantly rural village and its pretty rear terrace spills over with vibrant floral blooms. If it's an intimate atmosphere you're after of an evening, take a seat next to the log fire in the romantic red room, where you can gaze lovingly at your partner over candlelight. The green room is the natural choice for lunch, but be aware that reservations are essential at weekends if you want to eat in either room. The building dates from 1564, and the characterful timbered bar, where tankards and jugs hang from the beams, is a monument to old times. Pub favourites rub alongside more modern dishes on the extensive menu; supplemented with an interesting list of daily specials chalked up on the blackboard. Pleasant staff are on hand, and are happy to deal with any special requests.

Food serving times

Monday-Sunday:
12pm-2.30pm, 6pm-9.30pm

Prices

Meals: 15.95 (3 course lunch/dinner) and a la carte 21.00/32.00

Typical Dishes

Dorset crab & crayfish tian
Seared scallops
Iced nougat parfait

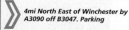

4mi North East of Winchester by A3090 off B3047. Parking

037 The Bugle

High St,
Hamble SO31 4AH

Tel.: (02380) 453000 - Fax: (02380) 453051
e-mail: manager@buglehamble.co.uk - Website: www.buglehamble.co.uk

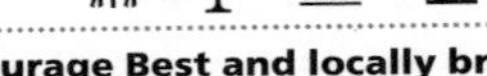

Courage Best and locally brewed beers in rotation

The chaps at the White Horse have set their sights five miles down-water and come up with another winner. Nicely located amongst the craft on Southampton Water, The Bugle is a part 12C inn that's been carefully restored with much original charm remaining intact: to wit, a 15C footstep, exposed beams, wattle walls, stone and oak floors and an open fire stove with brick lining. On the ground floor the 16C dining room is intimately cosy and dotted with chunky wooden tables; upstairs, there's a lovely, snug private dining room with a tempting enticement: when you book, you get the key to the glass door of your own wine cellar. There's nothing fancy about the dishes on offer, just good, honest traditional favourites, all freshly prepared and ideal after messing about in a boat. Come along at lunchtime and you'll find some very good value menus up for grabs.

Food serving times

Monday-Thursday:
12pm-2.30pm, 6pm-9.30pm

Friday:
12pm-3pm, 6pm-10pm

Saturday-Sunday:
12pm-10pm (9pm Sunday)

Prices

Meals: a la carte
15.00/25.00

Typical Dishes

Home-made fish cake
Pot roasted chicken
Apple tart Tatin

7mi South East of Southampton by A3024 or A3025 and B3397. Public car park next to pub.

038 The Yew Tree

Hollington Cross,
Andover Road, Highclere RG20 9SE
Tel.: (01635) 253360 - Fax: (01635) 255035
e-mail: info@theyewtree.net - Website: www.yewtree.tableset.com

Adnams Broadside, Timothy Taylor's Landlord

Marco Pierre White's name writ large on the front wall of the pub kind of gives away his involvement in this venture, but if you remained in any way doubtful, further evidence comes in the shape of the extensive menus, which contain a mixture of pub and restaurant food, and where herrings come à la Baltique, fillet of cod is served à la Viennoise and other choices might include chou farci à l'ancienne or rillettes de canard. For those who prefer their culinary influences closer to home, the menus also include some quintessentially British dishes such as fish pie, boiled beef and dumplings or omelette Arnold Bennett, plus delicious old school desserts like bread and butter pudding, sherry trifle or strawberries and cream.The rustic bar with low beams, scrubbed wooden tables and vast open fireplaces provides a charmingly characterful setting in which to enjoy your meal, whilst the linen-clad dining room is the more formal alternative.

Food serving times
Monday-Sunday:
12pm-2.30pm, 6pm-9.30pm

Prices
Meals: 17.50 (3 course lunch/dinner before 7.30pm) and a la carte 27.50/41.50

6 rooms: 80.00

Typical Dishes
Fresh sardines on toast
Confit of lamb
Sherry trifle Wally Lad

5mi South of Newbury by A343. Parking.

039 The Running Horse

88 Main Road, Littleton SO22 6QS

Tel.: (01962) 880218 - Fax: (01962) 886596

e-mail: runninghorseinn@btconnect.com

Website: www.runninghorseinn.co.uk

 **Ringwood, Itchen Valley**

This smart yellow building houses a contemporary bar, with white walls, wood floors and a cosy fireplace, as well as a stylish rear restaurant extension with stone floor and wicker-backed chairs. Lighter meals are served in the bar at lunchtime, with a more sophisticated, frequently-changing, seasonal menu available in the evenings. Dine on dishes such as steak and ale pie, fish and chips and fillet of sea bass - there's plenty of real ale on tap with which to wash your food down. When the sun comes out, the rush is on for a seat either on the front terrace or in the back garden. Staff are organised and friendly, and if you're planning on making a weekend of it, there are nine simply-styled bedrooms situated in a courtyard behind the pub. This horse looks set to run and run.

Food serving times

Tuesday-Saturday:
12pm-2pm, 6.30pm-9.30pm

Sunday:
12pm-2pm, 6.30pm-8.30pm

Closed 25 December

Prices

Meals: a la carte
19.95/30.00

9 rooms: 65.00/75.00

Typical Dishes

Grilled goats' cheese
Braised lamb shank
Bête noir

2.5mi North West from Winchester by B3049. Parking.

040 The Peat Spade Inn

Village Street,
Longstock SO20 6DR
Tel.: (01264) 810612 - Fax: (01264) 811078
e-mail: info@peatspadeinn.co.uk - Website: www.peatspadeinn.co.uk

  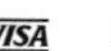

Ringwood Best, Ringwood 49er, King Alfred's, Hopback

The 19C Peat Spade Inn is the ultimate shooting and fishing pub, and therefore often teems with anglers here for the rivers, and hunters here for the game. Locals certainly don't lose out though – and even have tables reserved especially for them. The country pursuits theme is reflected in the delightful décor, and main dining room's relaxed country-life ambience is enhanced by the fine framed photos on the walls and the soft glow of candlelight in the evenings. The patrons are very experienced, with city C.V.s and while he runs a tight ship in the kitchen, she's in charge of the friendly team out front. The food here is proper, proud pub cooking sourced locally, featuring classics such as shepherds pie, fish and chips and sausage and mash. Bedrooms are modern and stylish, with everything just so; from the plump beds to the jet showers and fluffy towels. The residents lounge has an honesty bar and is stacked with DVDs.

Food serving times

Monday-Saturday:
12pm-2pm, 7pm-9pm

Sunday:
12pm-4pm

Closed 25-26 December,
1 January

Booking essential

Prices

Meals: a la carte
23.00/35.00

2 rooms: 110.00

Typical Dishes

Chicken liver parfait
Donald Russel rib-eye steak
Pineapple tarte Tatin

1.5mi North of Stockbridge on A3057. Parking.

041 The Bush Inn

Ovington SO24 0RE
Tel.: (01962) 732764 - Fax: (01962) 735130
e-mail: thebushinn@wadworth.co.uk

VISA AE MC

Wadworths 6X, Henrys IPA, JCB, Malt and Hops, Summersault, Bishop's Tipple, Old Timer and regular guest ales

Well-hidden down a winding country road, near the banks of the river Itchen, the 17C Bush Inn has all the understated friendliness you would hope to find in a family-run pub. Over the years it's accumulated an interesting collection of framed photographs and country memorabilia, and the feeling in the four little rooms, mostly for dining, is an easy and very natural one. Choose a table and pick from the blackboard: with a genuinely appetising range of wholesome, well-made dishes, including daily specials, this could be harder than you'd expect. Friendly service deserves a mention too, but the real bonus here is a lovely garden with plenty of seating: add some sun, and it's just perfect.

Food serving times

Monday-Saturday:
12pm-2.30pm, 6pm-9pm

Sunday:
12pm-4pm, 7pm-8.30pm

Closed 25 December

Prices

Meals: 10.00/15.00 (3 course lunch/dinner weekdays only) and a la carte 19.00/30.00

Typical Dishes

Smoked trout mousse
Steak and mushroom pie
Plum and port tart

5.75 mi East of Winchester by B3404 and A31. Parking.

042 The Three Tuns

58 Middlebridge St,
Romsey SO51 8HL
Tel.: (01794) 512639

VISA AE MC

Ringwood Best Bitter, Ringwood 49er, Romsey Pride, Timothy Taylor's Landlord

Romsey town centre has seen various changes over the years, but The Three Tuns remains an engaging constant. It's been in Middlebridge Street for 300 years and the perennial log fire and timbers help it retain its period feel, much to the contentment of a large group of regulars. A facelift, though, is evident in the slate flooring and understated décor. The fairly large bar with vast wooden tables inhabits one side of the pub; a restaurant the other – this has a haphazard, rustic appeal with bare tables of various shapes and sizes alongside mismatched chairs. Relaxed but helpful service will ease you into a modern menu which you'll find characterised by capable, well-judged cooking using first-rate ingredients, not least game from the nearby Broadlands Estate, with lighter dishes available at lunchtime. Expect changes under the new owners.

Food serving times

Tuesday-Sunday:
12pm-2.30pm, 6.30pm-10pm

Monday:
6.30pm-10pm

Prices

Meals: 12.00/15.00
(2/3 course Sunday lunch)
and a la carte 15.00/23.00

Typical Dishes

Seared scallops
Slow roast Romsey lamb shank
Warm fudge Brownie

Towards the western end of the town, off the by-pass. Parking.

043 White Star Tavern and Dining Rooms

28 Oxford Street, Southampton SO14 3DJ
Tel.: (02380) 821990 - Fax: (02380) 369274
e-mail: manager@whitestartavern.co.uk
Website: www.whitestartavern.co.uk

 **Fuller's London Pride**

Naming their new venture after the Titanic's ill-fated shipping line was a brave move but, a few years on, it's full steam ahead for the team behind the White Star, who are making their London experience count in Southampton's wining and dining district. Neatly redesigned, the former chain pub is now split into an intimate lounge bar - complete with chill-out leather armchairs - and a comfortable dining room, spacious, understated and stylishly functional: all the old tables can be extended if a few more friends show up for dessert. A British/ eclectic menu with a pleasantly familiar ring to it goes more free-form at lunch, with no distinction between "starters" and "mains".

Food serving times

Monday-Thursday: 12pm-2.30pm, 6.30pm-9.30pm

Friday-Saturday: 12pm-3pm, 6.30pm-10.30pm

Sunday: 12pm-9pm

Closed 25-26 December, 1 January

Prices

Meals: a la carte 20.00/30.00

Typical Dishes

Pressed ham hock terrine

Roast monkfish tail

Treacle tart

Southeast of West Quay shopping centre, off Bernard Street. Parking meters directly outside and public car park 2 mins walk.

044 Plough Inn

Main Road,
Sparsholt SO21 2NW
Tel.: (01962) 776353 - Fax: (01962) 776400

Wadworth 6X, Henry's IPA, Bishop's Tipple

Proving that people really will go the extra mile for a good pub lunch, the friendly Plough Inn is often packed, even in midweek, so booking is a must. Even at its busiest, though, the atmosphere in the softly lit bars and lounges remains relaxed and warm, and in fine weather, a good-hearted crowd from the village and beyond are only too happy to spread out onto the front terrace and cottage garden, or take a seat on the benches in the field at the back, where the pub's donkeys crop the pasture with Eeyore-ish reserve. Back inside, big blackboard menus of wholesome country cooking offer some subtle variation: after a range of tasty starters, the mains diverge, with lighter pub fare on the one hand and more elaborate entrées on the other.

Food serving times

Monday-Sunday:
12pm-2pm, 6pm-9pm

Closed 25 December

Booking essential

Prices

Meals: a la carte
20.00/30.00

Typical Dishes

Sautéed kidneys
Fillet of Black bream
Banana bread

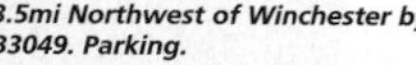
3.5mi Northwest of Winchester by B3049. Parking.

045 The Greyhound

31 High St,
Stockbridge SO20 6EY
Tel.: (01264) 810833
e-mail: thegreyhouse-inn@hotmail.com

Butcombe Traditional Bitter, Deuchars Caledonian IPA

You've perused the antique shops and art galleries in this elegant market town, and now you want to escape from the bustle for something to eat. Follow the ducks down the hill as they waddle along by the babbling brook, for there is fine dining to be found behind the yellow brick façade of this high street pub. The chef makes very good use of seasonal produce, has a keen eye for detail and produces refined, inventive dishes with a contemporary slant on some of the old classics. Unwind in a leather seat by the fire or sit at one of the aged wooden tables in the smart, low-beamed dining room and enjoy the relaxed, rustic feel to be found here, and which also extends to the airy, comfortable country-style bedrooms. If you're still feeling energetic, a postprandial perambulation by the riverside may be in order, or alternatively, take a seat out in the garden and watch J. R. Hartley and chums doing a spot of fly fishing on the Test.

Food serving times

Tuesday-Saturday:
12pm-2pm, 7pm-9pm

Sunday:
12pm-2pm

Closed 25-26 and 31 December, 1 January

Prices

Meals: 21.50 (3 course lunch) and a la carte 25.00/40.00

8 rooms: 90.00/120.00

Typical Dishes

Greyhound fishcake

Braised noisette of lamb

Vanilla pannacotta

15mi East of Salisbury by A30.
Parking.

046 The Wykeham Arms

75 Kingsgate St, Winchester SO23 9PE
Tel.: (01962) 853834 - Fax: (01962) 854411
e-mail: wykehamarms@accommodating-inns.co.uk
Website: www.accommodating-inns.co.uk

 **Butser, HSB, Chiswick, Fuller's London Pride and one guest ale**

On a quiet street between the Cathedral and the College stands Winchester's third great institution, the Wykeham Arms. Founded back in the 1700s, it continues to draw a loyal local following but should be first on any visitor's itinerary too: intimate and charming, its comfortable snugs contain an intriguing collection of prints, flags, rackets, straw boaters and other sporting and school memorabilia, as well as old oak desks from the nearby classrooms. Well-informed young staff serve with enthusiasm and a good sense of timing; fresh, appetising cuisine – a modern-classic blend with nicely weighted flavours – puts the region's seasonal produce at the top of the list. Bedrooms are split between the main house – rich colour scheme and historical prints – and the annex across the road; the oak-panelled breakfast room is on the first floor.

Food serving times

Monday-Saturday:
12pm-2.30pm, 6.30pm-9pm

Sunday:
12pm-2.30pm

Closed 25 December

Prices

Meals: 15.50 (3 course meal Sunday) and a la carte 19.15/30.95

14 rooms:
62.00/150.00

Typical Dishes

Sesame prawn toast
Grilled fillet of seabass
Raspberry pannacotta

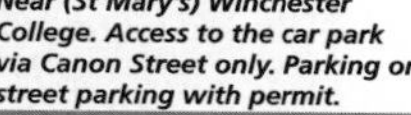

Near (St Mary's) Winchester College. Access to the car park via Canon Street only. Parking or street parking with permit.

South East • Hampshire

047 The Red Lion

Church Pl,
Freshwater, (i.o.w.) PO40 9BP
Tel.: (01983) 754925 - Fax: (01983) 754483
e-mail: info@redlion-wight.co.uk - Website: www.redlion-wight.co.uk

  VISA MC

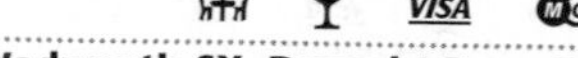
Wadworth 6X, Draught Bass, Flowers Original, Goddards Best Bitter

A handsome, part 14C building with little bay windows, this is as traditionally English a pub as any you might find on the slightly larger island across the water, and the characterful country style continues in its rustic interior. Run with a mix of enthusiastic quirkiness and good old fashioned hard work, it continues to do a thriving trade, with the focus squarely on a blackboard menu with daily variations – mostly traditional in its essentials, the pub's cuisine makes good use of its fresh ingredients, including newly-landed Channel fish. On busy days, your best chance of a seat may be in the garden or under the mini-marquee: a fixture since 2000, "the Dome" gets rather more use than the Greenwich version, but is generally reserved for private parties.

Food serving times

Monday-Saturday:
12pm-2pm, 6.30pm-9pm

Sunday:
12pm-2pm, 7pm-9pm

Closed restaurant 25 December

Prices

Meals: a la carte
20.00/27.50

Typical Dishes

Warm chicken & bacon salad
Halibut steak
Citrus cheesecake

By the saltings of the River Yar.
Parking.

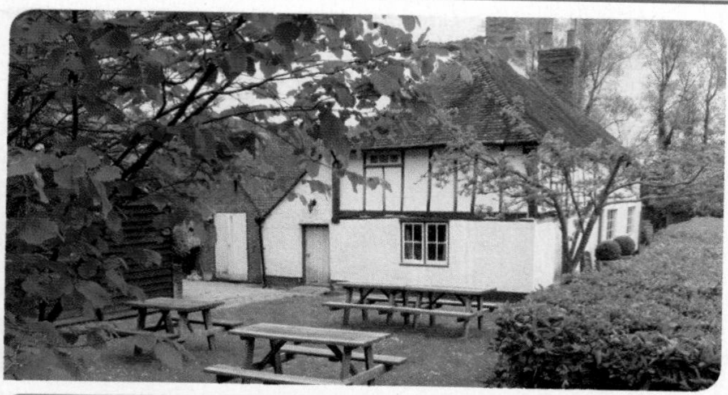

048 The Three Chimneys

Hareplain Road,
Biddenden TN27 8LW
Tel.: (01580) 291472

 **Adnams Best, Shepherd Neame Kent Best, Youngs Special**

Here's a pub full of Kentish character: it's only down the road from Sissinghurst, so make a day of it and combine a visit to both. The Three Chimneys has been around since about 1420, and its lovely old exterior has a rough thick cream coat. The attractive terrace is packed in summer; at other times, don't miss the definitively rustic bar: yellowing walls, dried hops, absurdly characterful (and original) beams, little burner fire, lots of rough furniture. The restaurant, at the back, is smarter, in a palette of chocolate brown, with leather chairs, sealed wooden floors, painted wood-panelled walls and spacious tables; what's more, it faces the garden (where only Ploughman's are served). Dishes change regularly, from substantial salads to fish and steaks. Puddings are all homemade, in keeping with the warm, genuine feel that pervades here.

Food serving times

Monday-Sunday:
12pm-2pm, 6.30pm-9.30pm

Closed 25 December,
31 December

Prices

Meals: a la carte
22.00/32.50

Typical Dishes

Warm crab tart

Pan-roasted smoked haddock

Strawberry crème brûlée

 *West 1.5mi off A262. Parking.* 

Froggies at the Timber Batts

049 Froggies at the Timber Batts

School Lane,
Bodsham TN25 5JQ

Tel.: (01223) 750237 - Fax: (01223) 750176
e-mail: post@thetimberbatts.co.uk - Website: www.thetimberbatts.co.uk

Fuller's London Pride, Adnam's Southwold, Woodforde's Wherry

A little piece of "la France profonde" in a lovely, creeper-clad, early Tudor pub. This unlikely success story is all down to the charming, French-born landlord who provides gentle bar-room bonhomie, superintends the spit-roast at the summer barbecues and teams up with his son in the kitchen to produce light bar lunches and unfussy and authentic Gallic classics from the regional cookbook. Fine fish and game are sourced locally, but the cheeseboard and the wine list – including a few vintages from a cousin's vineyard by the Loire – are proudly continental. Care and appreciation are obvious, and echoed in the service: staff are genuinely happy to recommend, explain, or provide enthusiastic translations. Frog ornaments decorate the brick pillars and window sills, and a welcoming, cosy feeling prevails.

Food serving times

Tuesday-Saturday:
12pm-2.30pm, 7pm-9.30pm

Sunday:
12pm-2.30pm

Closed 25-26 December, 1 January, Tuesday following Bank Holiday Monday

- French -

Prices

Meals: 26.00 (3 course lunch) and a la carte 24.00/36.00

Typical Dishes

Stuffed mussels
Confit of duck
Tarte Tatin

Off B2068 between Canterbury and Hythe; close to Wye. Parking.

050 The Fitzwalter Arms

The Street,
Goodnestone CT3 1PJ
Tel.: (01304) 840303

 **Masterbrew, Earlybird, Late Red**

About as far from your typical-looking boozer as it's possible to get, this striking brick building, with its castellated exterior and mullioned windows may well owe something to the fact that, before it served as a hostelry, it was reputedly the keep for Goodnestone Park, manor house of the Fitzwalter estate - famous for the beautiful country gardens where Jane Austen regularly used to take a turn. With such a history, you might think this place would have since been turned into a fancy dining pub, but thankfully, no – it has very much kept the feel of the village local, with people playing darts or bar billiards, or simply shooting the breeze by the open fire in the characterful, beamed bar. Eat in the small dining area overlooking the headstones in the churchyard, where the daily-changing blackboard menu might offer dishes such as coq au vin, faggots or John Dory. The large beer garden comes into its own in the summer months.

Food serving times

Monday-Saturday:
12pm-2pm, 7pm-9pm

Sunday:
12pm-2.30pm

Closed restaurant
25 December

Prices

Meals: a la carte
16.00/24.00

Typical Dishes

Mulligatawny soup
Roast and jugged hare
Rhubarb fool

7mi West of Sandwich by A257, B2046 and minor road. Parking on road in front of pub.

051 Harrow Inn

Common Rd,
Igtham Common TN15 9EB
Tel.: (01732) 885912 - Fax: (01732) 885912

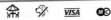

Greene King IPA, Abbot Ale

Don't be misled by the Harrow Inn's location, down a sleepy little lane in a Kentish hamlet – you'll have to get here pretty early to be sure of securing a seat in this pretty, part 17C stone and brick pub. An open fire divides the lovely, pleasingly traditional bar, although you might also find a free table in the back dining room and conservatory extension, where a printed menu replicates the list on the blackboard. With its share of more inventive recipes, there's a little more to this good, honest country cooking than you might expect: enjoy a tasty light lunch before a trip to nearby Knowle or the Tudor castle at Ightham Mote. Cheerful service.

Food serving times

Tuesday-Saturday:
12pm-2pm, 6pm-9pm

Sunday:
12pm-2pm

Closed 26 December, 1 January, Bank Holiday Monday

Prices

Meals: a la carte 20.00/34.00

Typical Dishes

Chicken, pork & duck pâté
Pan-fried calves' liver
Rhubarb crumble

5mi South East of Sevenoaks by A25 on Common Road. Parking.

052 The Granville

Street End,
Lower Hardres CT4 7AL
Tel.: (01227) 700402 - Fax: (01227) 700925

 **Masterbrew and Shepherd Neame seasonal ale**

Though big and open-plan in design, The Granville couldn't be more different from the chain-run drinking hangars of Britain's town centres. Light, well-kept and comfortable, its split into nicely airy sections which still share the good overall buzz of the place, and the service, though wonderfully laid-back, remains personal and helpful. The varied, interesting selection of dishes, frequently changing, is chalked up on the blackboard and delivers all the liveliness, piquancy and balance it promises. A serious regard for ingredients makes for distinct, resonant flavours: greens taste a fresh, chlorophyll green, and the excellent fish, much of it from the Kent coast, is always worth a try. Devotees of The Sportsman, Seasalter, will notice a strong family resemblance.

Food serving times

Tuesday-Saturday:
12pm-2pm, 7pm-9pm

Sunday:
12pm-2pm

Closed 25 December

Prices

Meals: a la carte
21.40/32.00

Typical Dishes

Pear and Roquefort salad

Grilled best end of lamb

Flourless chocolate cake

3mi South of Canterbury on B2068. Parking.

053 The Dering Arms

Station Rd,
Pluckley TN27 0RR
Tel.: (01233) 840371 - Fax: (01233) 840498
e-mail: jim@deringarms.com - Website: www.deringarms.com

Goachers, Dering Ale, Gold Star, Old Ale

Step through the heavy, original doors of this mid-19C Dutch-gabled former hunting lodge and experience the genuine feel of a 'local'. A pleasant rural atmosphere is evoked from blazing log fires, reclaimed tables and chairs, farming implements and bars festooned with hops. Emphasis is on the hefty seafood menus. You might find salmon fishcakes with sorrel sauce; monkfish with bacon, orange and cream; or skate wing with capers and black butter. If you're not in the mood for fish, then opt for the likes of confit of duck or the pie of the day. Afterwards, order a pint of real farm cider – the Dering specialises in them - and flop into a leather armchair in the cosy lounge.

Food serving times

Tuesday-Saturday:
12pm-2pm, 7pm-9.30pm

Sunday:
12pm-2pm

Closed 25-29 December, 1 January

Prices

Meals: a la carte
20.00/35.00

Typical Dishes

Soft herring roes
Fillet of seabass
Chocolate fudge cake

1.5mi Southeast of Bethersden rd. Beside the Railway Station. Parking.

054 The Sportsman

Faversham Rd,
Seasalter CT5 4BP
Tel.: (01227) 273370
Website: www.thesportsmanseasalter.co.uk

   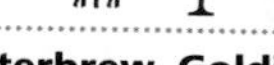

Masterbrew, Goldings, Late Red, Porter

Travelling along the coastal road, you spot The Sportsman from far off, sandwiched between sea and marsh. Inside the owners have refrained from going gastro, and instead have their own blend of shabby chic, with open fires, worn wood flooring and scrubbed pine tables - but the décor's irrelevant anyway, since here, it's all about the food. Self-taught chef Stephen is seriously passionate about his job and an advocate of 'terroir' – that is, cooking that is rooted in its locality - so his ingredients come from local farms, he makes his own salt from the sea in order to cure his own hams, he makes butter from unpasteurised cream and, where possible, picks his vegetables the very day they are to be served up on the plate. Not surprisingly, his cooking is confident, unfussy and fantastically flavoursome, but this does mean that, despite its isolated position, this place is often deservedly busy, and you'd be advised to book in advance.

Food serving times

Tuesday-Saturday:
12pm-2pm, 7pm-9pm

Sunday:
12pm-2pm

Closed 25-26 December

Prices

Meals: a la carte
19.00/29.00

Typical Dishes

Crab risotto
Roast farm chicken
Rhubarb sorbet

2mi Southwest of Whitstable and then 2mi Southwest following coast road. Parking.

055 George & Dragon

Speldhurst Hill, Speldhurst TN3 0NN
Tel.: (01892) 863125 - Fax: (01892) 863216
e-mail: julian@leefe-griffiths.freeserve.co.uk
Website: www.speldhurst.com

 **Harvey's Best, Chiddingstone Larkins, Harvey's Hadlow**

An ideal blend of North London pub style and deep-rooted Kentish loyalty, a sentiment fully returned by the regulars, who stop to read the parish news pinned up inside the door. Its interior is increasingly trendy but still fits perfectly and hasn't upset the welcomingly mellow but busy mood. Arty black-and-white shots of the owners' favourite pheasant shooters, chicken rearers and all-England cheesemakers – imagine Mario Testino and Lord Snowdon at the farmers' market – are a tribute to the primacy of fine ingredients. Here, "imported" food comes from the other side of the Medway and the chef regularly sends suppliers gleaning, foraging and rummaging round the county to unearth produce in the wild. Vigorously tasty dishes – combining culinary finesse with flavour in the raw – offers diners a real scope of seasonal originality.

Food serving times

Monday-Saturday:
12pm-2.45pm, 7pm-9.30pm

Sunday:
12pm-5pm

Prices

Meals: a la carte
20.00/30.00

Typical Dishes

Local pigeon breast
Slow roast belly of pork
Valrhona chocolate cake

3,5 mi North of Royal Tunbridge Wells by A26. Parking.

056 The Swan on the Green

West Peckham ME18 5JW
Tel.: (01622) 812271 - Fax: (0870) 056 0556
e-mail: info@swan-on-the-green.co.uk
Website: www.swan-on-the-green.co.uk

On-site microbrewery

Pub settings rarely come more attractively old English than this – the Swan's redbrick and ornate gabled exterior sits idyllically by the green, right next to the village's Saxon church. There's no pub garden, but benches perch along the terrace at the front. Inside, a framed history puts the inn's origins at 1526, but it's been given a pleasing modern makeover with pale wood throughout: the dried hops and real fire add a rustic twist. At the back is a micro-brewery, so a selection of unique ales are chalked up on the board behind the bar. There's a loyal local following and menus, featuring an interesting eclectic à la carte, change weekly. Try to visit in summer, when the owners provide blankets for you to eat on the green.

Food serving times

Tuesday-Saturday:
12pm-2.30pm, 7pm-9pm

Sunday-Monday:
12pm-2pm

Prices

Meals: a la carte
21.50/28.50

Typical Dishes

Cold duck breast
Salmon & seabass
Lemon curd syllabub

7.75mi South West of Maidstone by A26 and B2016. Follow sign to church and green. Parking.

057 The Sweet Olive at The Chequers Inn

Baker St,
Aston Tirrold OX11 9DD
Tel.: (01235) 851272
Website: www.sweet-olive.com

 **Hooky Bitter, Deuchars IPA**

You can't get much more English than the ancient Ridgeway path or the rolling Chiltern Hills, both of which lie close to this solid, red-brick Victorian hostelry. French, though, is the prevailing culture here, with frequent cries of "Bonjour" and "Bon Appétit" renting the refined Oxfordshire air. That's because Stephane and Olivier, the owners, have brought their Gallic influence to bear and The Sweet Olive is reaping rich dividends. There's a drinkers' side to the pub, repaired to frequently by the locals, and a cosy, red tile floored dining room: you can lift knife and fork in either. Blackboard menus evolve constantly, and daily specials are verbally explained. French country cooking takes precedence, but classic British dishes are also available. Local produce is used in season, and cordial service is a byword. Incidentally, the French connection extends to décor, which includes wine box ends from renowned chateaux and growers.

Food serving times

Monday-Tuesday and Thursday-Sunday: 12pm-2pm, 7pm-9pm

Closed February

Closed dinner Sunday October-April

Prices

Meals: a la carte 20.95/30.75

Typical Dishes

Tiger prawns in tempura

Escalope of venison

Treacle sponge

4mi South West of Wallingford by minor road through South Moreton. Parking.

058 The Boot Inn

Barnard Gate OX29 6XE
Tel.: (01865) 881231
e-mail: info@theboot-inn.com - Website: www.theboot-inn.com

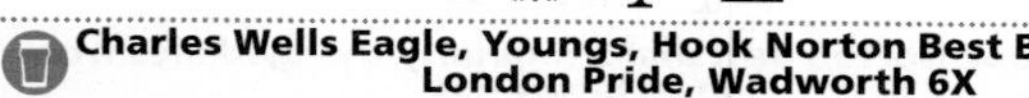

Charles Wells Eagle, Youngs, Hook Norton Best Bitter, Fuller's London Pride, Wadworth 6X

Foot fetishists take note: a fascinating collection of celebrity footwear is displayed on the walls at The Boot Inn, ranging from the Bee Gees' shoes to a flipper from Michael Heseltine and a football boot from George Best, along with signed photos and letters; all obtained by the pub's owners in exchange for a donation to each celebrity's favourite charity. Aside from its bootylicious collection, this is very much a traditional inn; with flagged floors, beamed ceilings, a central bar and an open fire. A perfect stopping off point for anyone who happens to be pootling along the A40, light lunches on offer might include salmon, steak, salads and sandwiches, while more substantial dinner dishes could include beef fillet, roast duck breast or monkfish brochettes – with daily specials expanding your choice further. Jazz nights in winter are just the thing to get your fingers clicking and your boots tapping.

Food serving times

Monday-Thursday:
12pm-2.30pm, 7pm-9.30pm

Friday-Saturday:
12pm-2.30pm, 7pm-10pm

Sunday:
12pm-3pm, 7pm-9pm

Booking essential

Prices

Meals: a la carte
20.00/30.00

Typical Dishes

Salmon rillette
Fish and chips
Cheesecake

3.25mi East of Witney by B4022 off A40. Parking.

059 The Kings Head Inn

The Green,
Bledington OX7 6XQ
Tel.: (01608) 658365 - Fax: (01608) 658902
e-mail: kingshead@orr-ewing.com - Website: www.kingsheadinn.net

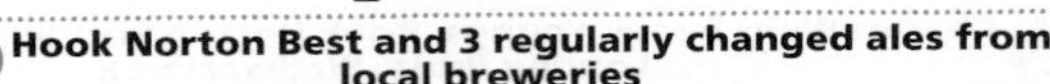
Hook Norton Best and 3 regularly changed ales from local breweries

A charming Cotswold setting and a warmly welcoming pub: what could be more idyllic on a perfect summer's day? The Kings Head traces its origins back to the 15C, and in all that time it can rarely have looked more inviting: it certainly entices the Morris dancers who happily congregate each summer on the green outside to perform the Bledington Dances. The place oozes style, with stone and wood floors, real fires and an archetypal modern country pub feel. Printed evening menus identify a solid traditional base, with good use of local produce: meat is bought from a renowned Cotswold butcher, fresh Cornish fish arrives daily, and vegetables are from nearby Evesham Vale. Bedrooms hold the promise of comfy country repose: a low-beamed stairway leads the way.

Food serving times

Monday-Sunday:
12pm-2pm, 7pm-9pm

Closed 25-26 December

Prices

Meals: a la carte
18.25/28.75

12 rooms:
50.00/125.00

Typical Dishes

Devilled lamb's kidneys
Smoked haddock & crayfish pie
Chocolate caramel brownie

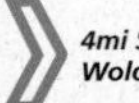
4mi Southeast of Stow-on-the-Wold by A436 on B4450. Parking.

060 The Lamb at Buckland

Lamb Lane, Buckland SN7 8QN
Tel.: (01367) 870484 - Fax: (01367) 870675
e-mail: enquiries@thelambatbuckland.co.uk
Website: www.thelambatbuckland.co.uk

 **Hooky Norton, Tribute, Brakspears**

Thankfully The Lamb is well signposted, for you'd never find it otherwise. Once inside, there's no doubting you're in the right pub though, thanks to the veritable flock of ovine-inspired items to be found here – in the form of cuddly toys, paintings, curios, life-sized models and even lamb motif carpets. This 17C stone-built building has a bar in which you can eat, a linen-laid restaurant in the heavily beamed oldest part of the building, plus a rear garden with a little sunken terrace for al fresco dining in the summer. Tasty, traditional British food is chalked on the large blackboard menu above the open fireplace, and the same food is served throughout. In quiet months, they also offer a good value fixed price menu. Family owned for a number of years, the atmosphere is one of cosy familiarity, so even if you're not a local, there's no need to feel sheepish. Altogether now; 'Four legs good, two legs baaad…'

Food serving times

Tuesday-Thursday: 12pm-2.30pm, 6.30pm-9.30pm

Friday-Saturday: 12pm-2.30pm, 6.30pm-10pm

Sunday:12pm-2.30pm

Closed 24 December to 8 January

Prices

Meals: a la carte 17.00/35.95

1 room: 95.00/145.00

Typical Dishes

Seared fillet of beef
Whole baked seabass
Raspberry brûlée

Between Faringdon and Kingston Bagpuize off A420. Parking.

Buckland Marsh

061 The Trout at Tadpole Bridge

Buckland Marsh SN7 8RF
Tel.: (01367) 870382 - Fax: (01367) 870912
e-mail: info@troutinn.co.uk - Website: www.troutinn.co.uk

Ramsbury Bitter, Young's Bitter, Old Hooky, Brakspear Organic Blonde, Barbus Barbus, Arkells Moonlight, Burford Best Bitter

Its location by the River Thames makes this pretty stone-built pub, and more specifically its garden, the place to be in summer months, and since it has its own moorings, it's particularly popular with boat users. Its experienced owners have breathed new life into the old Trout, and it offers quality cooking made with fresh, local produce at sensible prices. The open plan bar, where locals gather for their evening pint, has space for dining on either side; log burners glow enticingly and the large table by the dartboard is a sought-after spot for anyone after a little privacy. For those who prefer to sit away from the bar, a light, modern room is available at the rear – but if you're here for an evening meal or Sunday lunch, wherever you sit, booking is essential. Superior bedrooms – six in the main house, three in a ground floor extension – are comfortable and well-furnished in light, pastel shades.

Food serving times

Monday-Sunday:
12pm-2pm, 7pm-9pm

Closed 25 December, 31 December, 1 January

Closed dinner Sunday October-April

Prices

Meals: a la carte 23.00/32.00

6 rooms: 80.00/110.00

Typical Dishes

Sautéed King scallops
Slow roast suckling pig
Lemon posset

4.5mi Northeast of Faringdon by A417, A420 on Brampton road. Parking.

062 The Lamb Inn

Sheep St, Burford OX18 4LR
Tel.: (01993) 823155 - Fax: (01993) 822228
e-mail: info@lambinn-burford.co.uk
Website: www.cotswold-inns-hotels.co.uk

 **Hook Norton, Brakspear,**

This attractive Cotswold stone inn lies in a quiet spot on Sheep Street; not a coincidence, but a reminder that this town was historically the site of sheep fairs and famous for its wool. Upon entering, the delicious smell of wood smoke wafts by your nostrils, but watch out for the uneven flag floors, for this inn has all the charming features you would expect from one with its origins in the 14C. Open fires blaze in front of deep sofas in the lounges, and you can eat from the bar menu here or at one of the simple wood tables in the characterful bar. For a much more formal dining experience, the restaurant, with its glass skylight, burgundy walls and dressed tables has a separate, fixed price menu, offering dishes such as roasted squab pigeon, roast mallard or confit pork belly. Bedrooms named after flowers have a cosy, warm feel. Choose 'Rosie,' which has its own private garden,
or 'Allium;' the most luxurious.

Food serving times

Monday-Sunday:
12pm-2.30pm, 7pm-9.30pm

Prices

Meals: 32.50 (3 course dinner) and a la carte 20.00/32.50

17 rooms:
145.00/165.00

Typical Dishes

Fried lamb sweetbreads
Fillet steak with oxtail
Chocolate torte

In town centre. Parking on the street or care of the Bay Tree Hotel.

063 The Masons Arms

Banbury Rd,
Swerford, Chipping Norton OX7 4AP
Tel.: (01608) 683212 - Fax: (01608) 683105
e-mail: themasonschef@hotmail.com - Website: www.masonsarms.com

VISA AE MC

 **Hook Norton Best, Brakspear Special**

A roadside stone built Cotswold inn, raised above the norm by the keenness of a husband and wife team, whose hospitable approach seems to have spread to the rest of the helpful young staff. Dating back to the 1800s, its origins are rather mysterious – quite appropriate for a former Freemason's lodge – but apart from a nod to its Masonic past near the entrance, and the odd beam and inglenook, the interior resonates with bright, 21C country style: more rattan chairs and polished floors than horse brasses and swirly carpets. Menus offer precise, flavourful English dishes, cooked using local produce, such as duck and pistachio terrine, char-grilled 21 day hung rib eye steak or pan-fried lambs' liver with bubble and squeak; the set lunch and dinner menus offering particularly good value for money. Lovely westerly views from picnic benches in the neat lawned garden.

Food serving times

Monday-Sunday:
12pm-2.15pm, 7pm-9.15pm

Closed 25-26 December

Prices

Meals: 11.25/15.95 (3 course lunch/dinner) and a la carte 20.00/27.00

Typical Dishes

Pan fried soft herring roes

Oxford Down lamb

Belgian chocolate cup

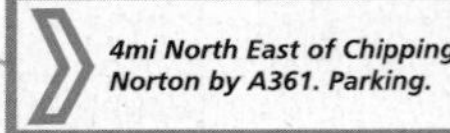

4mi North East of Chipping Norton by A361. Parking.

064 The Fox and Hounds

Christmas Common OX49 5HL
Tel.: (01491) 612599
e-mail: kiran.daniels@btconnect.com

 **Brakspear Bitter, Brakspear Seasonal and guest ale**

Set on the outskirts of a traditional village, this pretty 17C pub and barn conversion is ideally placed for hungry ramblers and mountain bikers fresh from the Chiltern Hills. The owner certainly obeyed the mantra to chuck out the chintz and has now gone in totally the other direction; with modern prints in the bar, and white walls and lime washed tables and chairs in the large restaurant giving the place a contemporary, minimalist feel. Thankfully, the neutral décor is far from replicated in the food. Whilst he runs the place fairly casually, the chef is passionate about his craft, and uses fresh, seasonal ingredients sourced from carefully chosen local suppliers to create daily changing menus with a range of cooking styles. Watch him prepare your meal in the kitchen, which opens onto the main dining room or take a seat in the herby garden to see if you can spot any rare red kites hovering overhead.

Food serving times
Monday-Saturday:
12pm-2.30pm, 7pm-10pm

Prices
Meals: 10.00/15.00 (3 course lunch/dinner) and a la carte 22.50/37.50

Typical Dishes
Griddled asparagus
Scottish venison fillet
Hot chocolate fondant

South East of Watlington, near Shotridge Wood. Parking.

065 The Crown Inn

Mill Lane,
Church Enstone OX7 4NN
Tel.: (01608) 677262 - Fax: (01608) 677394
Website: www.crowninnenstone.co.uk

  VISA

Hook Norton Bitter, Spitfire, Timothy Taylor's Landlord, Wychwood Brewery Hobgoblin, Cotswold Lager

A pretty inn built with Cotswold stone, situated in a picturesque village, The Crown Inn has the feel of a true dining pub, where drinkers and diners gladly mix. Well-kept and well-run, with a homely feel, regulars sit on stools at the bar, close to the open fire, while the light and airy conservatory overlooking the picnic tables outside makes a particularly pleasant place to eat. In the entrance hall, you'll find a large display of locally handcrafted walking sticks for sale and the many accolades displayed on the wall of the pub testify to the success of the owner chef's signature dish, steak pie. Food here is unfussy, honest and well-prepared, with ingredients sourced from local farms and a nod to the chef's Northern roots. The large menu is chalked up on blackboards and might offer a simple steak and Hooky pie or crispy duck salad at lunch, and maybe sea bass, steak and chips or breast of pheasant in the evening.

Food serving times

Monday (bar meals only):
12pm-2pm, 7pm-9pm

Tuesday-Saturday:
12pm-2pm, 7pm-9pm

Sunday:
12pm-2pm

Closed 25-26 December, 1 January

Prices

Meals: a la carte
17.00/25.00

Typical Dishes

Mixed fish pâté
Slow roast belly pork
Warm chocolate pudding

3.5mi Southeast of Chipping Norton by A44. Parking.

066 The Chequers

Church Rd,
Churchill OX7 6NJ
Tel.: (01608) 659393

Old Hookey, Marston's Pedigree, Hook Norton, Abbot Ale, Timothy Taylor, Bass, Deuchars

If popularity with the locals is the test of a good pub, then The Chequers passes with flying colours, its big bar providing ample space for all the regulars to assemble on their stools. The rest of the pub is open plan, and has charm aplenty in the form of its flagstone floors, exposed Cotswold stone walls and inglenook fireplace. If you are eating here during the week then the best seats are in the large high-ceilinged extension at the rear, but at weekends – when it can get very busy and is a good idea to book ahead - the rooms on the mezzanine above the bar are your best bet for a little peace and quiet. Even during hectic periods, the experienced owners run a tight ship, and the overall ambience is warm and welcoming. Set menus are available at both lunch and dinner, while the à la carte offers quite traditional dishes, such as rack of lamb, sea bass, guinea fowl or fisherman's pie - and Thursday nights are roasted half duck night.

Food serving times

Monday-Sunday:
12pm-2pm, 7pm-9.30pm

Closed 25 December

Prices

Meals: 20.00/26.00 (3 course lunch/dinner) and a la carte 18.50/23.00

Typical Dishes

Smoked haddock kedgeree

Baked ham

Chocolate Bavarois

South West of Chipping Norton by B4450. Parking.

067 The White Lion

Goring Rd, Goring Heath, Cray's Pond RG8 7SH
Tel.: (01491) 680471 - Fax: (01491) 684254
e-mail: reservations@whitelioncrayspond.com
Website: www.whitelioncrayspond.com

 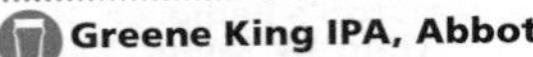 **Greene King IPA, Abbot**

The walls are filled with menus from renowned restaurants around Great Britain; a sign perhaps of the dizzy heights to which the team at The White Lion aspire. Their dinner menus - a small à la carte plus a set menu – certainly contain their own culinary contenders, such as breast of partridge or swordfish steak, while their lunch menus contain good old pub favourites like steak or sausage and mash – all well-presented and served in ample portions. Local drinkers gather near the open fire in the characterful bar, while diners have a choice between wooden tables and paper napkins in the dining area or tablecloths and a garden view in the conservatory. The atmosphere throughout is warm and friendly, but take heed; the pub was built in 1756 and has the low beams to prove it – and while helpful signs warn you to 'duck or grouse,' some thoughtfully-placed cushions make any bumps that are incurred that little bit less traumatic.

Food serving times

Tuesday-Saturday:
12pm-3pm, 6.15pm-9.30pm

Sunday:
12pm-3pm

Closed 25-26 December

Prices

Meals: a la carte
23.90/33.40

Typical Dishes

Carpaccio of aged beef
Herb fried red mullet
Pear and marzipan strudel

2mi East of Goring on B4526.
Parking.

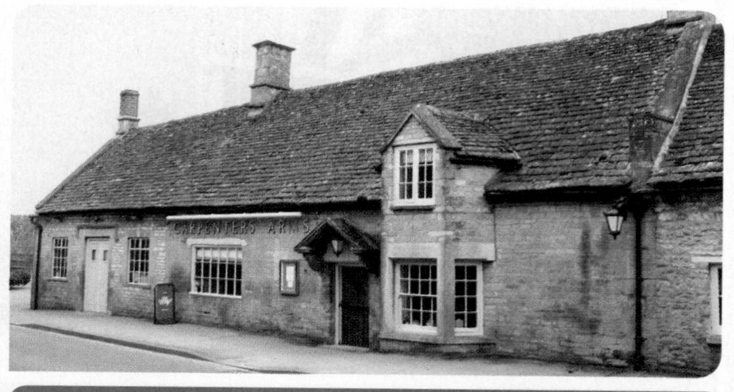

068 The Carpenter's Arms

Fulbrook Hill,
Fulbrook OX18 4BH
Tel.: (01993) 823 275
Website: www.thecarpentersarmsfulbrook.co.uk

VISA AE MC

 **Abbot, IPA, Bellhaven**

Just outside the charming town of Burford, known as the southern gateway to the Cotswolds, sits this long, narrow and rather unprepossessing pub. Do not be fooled by its commonplace appearance, however, for inside you will find character and charm galore in the form of flagged floors, beamed ceilings and chunky mismatched furniture, as well as a stylish sprinkling of modern touches, like a pair of matching wood burners, a selection of contemporary art, and a conservatory, which leads out into the rear garden. Simple, carefully-presented cooking casts its net surprisingly wide, with choices such as gravadlax, coq au vin, bonito sashimi or osso bucco risotto Milanese featuring on the menus alongside plenty of fresh fish landed at Looe, Newlyn or Brixham. Desserts might include rhubarb crumble or a choice of ice creams, and bright, friendly service is the other key ingredient in a pleasant, unhurried lunch or evening out.

Food serving times

Tuesday-Saturday:
12pm-2.30pm, 6.30pm-9.30pm

Sunday:
12pm-2.30pm

Prices

Meals: 12.50 (2 course lunch) and a la carte 22.00/30.00

Typical Dishes

Potted shrimps
Fillet of wild bass
Vanilla pannacotta

1mi North of Fulbrook by A361.
Parking.

069 The White Hart

Main Road,
Fyfield OX13 5LW
Tel.: (01865) 390585
e-mail: info@whitehart-fyfield.com - Website: www.whitehart-fyfield.com

We most liked

 VISA 

Regularly changing ales including White Horse Village Idiot, Hook Norton Best, Marston's Pedigree, Timothy Taylor's Landlord

Hurtling along the A420, on your way up to Oxford or down to Swindon? Take the turning for Fyfield, head for The White Hart and allow yourself to get into another gear entirely. Found it yet? Its white exterior is appealing enough, but gives no hint of the character that lies within, or the fascinating history that lies behind, and it's only once you're inside that you can truly appreciate the historic structure of this 15C former chantry house, complete with huge timbered arch, minstrels' gallery and cellar room. The set lunch menu is a prudent option, but you might well find yourself drawn to the large choice available on the globally influenced à la carte, whose sharing boards – antipasti, mezze or fish – are great to go halves on as a starter. Local sources are listed and food is fresh and flavoursome. The uplit terrace and large garden are popular in the summer; your meal oiled by smooth service from a polite, friendly young crew.

Food serving times

Monday-Friday:
12pm-2.30pm, 6pm-9.30pm

Saturday:
12pm-3pm, 6pm-9.30pm

Sunday:
12pm-4pm

Prices

Meals: 16.95 (3 course lunch) and a la carte 22.00/35.00

Typical Dishes

Japanese cured local beef
Fillet of seabass
Spiced apple strudel

10mi South West of Oxford by A420. Parking.

070 Falkland Arms

Great Tew OX7 4DB

Tel.: (01608) 683653 - Fax: (01608) 683656

e-mail: sjcourage@btconnect.com

Website: www.falklandarms.org.uk

Wadworth IPA, 6X, Pint Size Mild, Shepherd Neame Early Bird, Exmoor Wild Cat, Nethergate Barley Special

Charming village full of chocolate box cottages? Check. Fire flickering gently in the grate? Check. Locals gathered at the bar? Check. If it's a traditional country inn you're looking for, look no further, for this is the real deal, to the extent that as you enter The Falkland Arms, you get a sense that time seems to have stood still. Real ales are still dispensed from antique pot hand pumps, hundreds of jugs and cups hang from the low beams and the walls are crowded with adverts from years gone by. Folk groups play here on Sunday evenings and five comfortable, traditionally furnished bedrooms – two with four poster beds - are located up a steep spiral staircase. Lunch here can be a simple affair, with baguettes, jacket potatoes and casseroles, while the short, seasonally-changing à la carte dinner menu offers traditional dishes like lamb shank and poached haddock. No bookings are taken at lunch, but booking for dinner is imperative.

Food serving times

Monday-Saturday:
12pm-2pm, 7pm-8pm

Sunday:
12pm-2pm

Booking essential for dinner - not accepted for lunch

Prices

Meals: a la carte
15.00/30.00

5 rooms:
110.00/115.00

Typical Dishes

Rabbit & apple terrine

Baked smoked haddock

Warm apple tart

6.5mi East of Chipping Norton by A361 and B4022. Parking in village car park.

071 Moon and Sixpence

Main St, Hanwell OX17 1HW
Tel.: (01295) 730544
e-mail: moonand.sixpence@virgin.net
Website: www.moonandsixpencehanwell.com

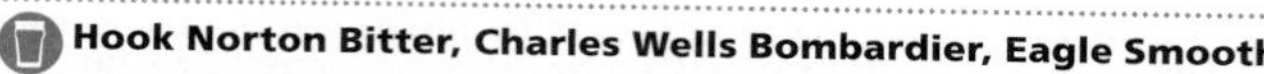

Hook Norton Bitter, Charles Wells Bombardier, Eagle Smooth

Interesting times at this quiet village's thatched inn, owned and run by two brothers who were determined to give the Moon and Sixpence more than just a quick spit and polish. Even after the most well-meaning makeovers, a new lease of community spirit is never guaranteed, but Hanwell has really taken to its new-look pub. It's kept the best of its traditional features, like the wood panelled walls said to come from the castle, the shotguns on the door handles and the horse brasses on the beams, while the TV and slot machine keep the locals happy. An appealing, wide-ranging menu certainly helps, offering everything from dependable pub classics to more contemporary recipes, all soundly prepared and very fairly priced. A barbecue at the back, with a little terrace next to it, gets plenty of use in the summer if the weather plays its part. The real-ale enthusiasts have no complaints either, and its modern bar is as popular as ever.

Food serving times

Monday:
6pm-9pm

Tuesday-Saturday:
12pm-2pm, 6pm-9pm

Sunday:
6pm-8pm

Closed 26 December

Prices

Meals: 7.50 (3 course lunch & dinner) and a la carte 7.50/30.00

Typical Dishes

Seared scallops
Fillet of red mullet
Apple tart Tatin

3.5mi northwest of Banbury by A422 and B4100. Parking.

072 The New Inn

Chalkhouse Green Rd,
Kidmore End RG4 9AU

Tel.: (0118) 972 3115 - Fax: (0118) 972 4733
e-mail: thenewinn@4cinns.co.uk - Website: www.thenewinnrestaurant.co.uk

  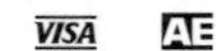 

The hustle and bustle of Reading is only five miles away but you wouldn't realise it from the sleepy charms of this Oxfordshire hamlet and the comfy enticements of its focal point, The New Inn, which, though smartened up outside, still proudly bears its 16C hallmarks within. The cosy, atmospheric bar's rough floorboards, beams and open fires are all you'd expect from a proper pub of the era, and this is a fine spot to lay your hat and sup a pint. Most diners, meanwhile, head to the snazzy restaurant, where a few original beams merge tastefully with the smart wood tables and crisp white walls. Here, there's a nicely balanced menu ranging from pub favourites to more adventurous fare; you can also eat in the bar or delightful canopied terrace. A treat awaits overnighters: six bedrooms, some with balconies, which are stylish, modern, very comfy and well equipped.

Food serving times

Monday:
6.30pm-9.30pm

Tuesday-Saturday:
12pm-2.30pm, 6.30pm-9.30pm

Sunday:
12pm-2.30pm

Prices

Meals: a la carte
15.00/29.00

6 rooms: 65.00/220.00

Typical Dishes

Chicken liver parfait
Kidmore End roast pork
Sticky toffee pudding

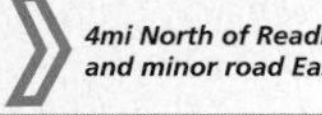

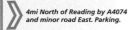

4mi North of Reading by A4074 and minor road East. Parking.

The Tollgate Inn

073 The Tollgate Inn

Church St,
Kingham OX7 6YA
Tel.: (01608) 658389
e-mail: info@thetollgate.com - Website: www.thetollgate.com

 VISA AE MC

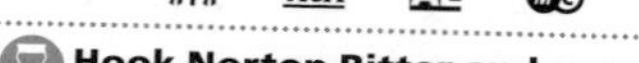

Hook Norton Bitter and guest ales

At the northwest corner of Oxfordshire stands this 17C Grade II listed former farmhouse built of local stone. It's situated in a typically attractive Cotswold village within striking distance of Stow and Moreton-in-Marsh, and has been sympathetically modernised with oak floors and bright colours. Plenty of original charm remains in place courtesy of rafters and wood-burning stove, and the well-populated front bar is a buzzing mix of locals and tourists. You can choose to eat here, or repair to a rear dining area, where smartly laid tables and comfortable high-back chairs lend it a slightly more formal air. Lunch here is a simple affair of sandwiches or compact blackboard menu. Dinner takes on a more serious tone, with restaurant style dishes encompassing a global range, underpinned by good Cotswold ingredients. Pleasantly appointed bedrooms await the weary tourist.

Food serving times

Tuesday-Saturday:
12pm-2.30pm, 7pm-9.30pm

Sunday:
12pm-2.30pm

Closed 1 week in early January

Prices

Meals: 15.95 (3 course Sunday lunch) and a la carte 20.00/30.00

9 rooms: 60.00/80.00

Typical Dishes

Scallop & asparagus salad
Braised belly of pork
Raspberry crème brûlée

3mi South West of Chipping Norton by B4450 to Churchill and minor road West. Parking.

074 The Navy Oak

Lower End,
Leafield OX29 9QQ
Tel.: (01993) 878496
e-mail: thenavyoak@aol.com - Website: www.thenavyoak.webeden.co.uk

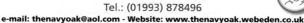

We most liked

  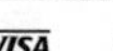 

Cotswold Boy, Brakspear, Hook Norton

For five years this solid stone pub lay barren in its leafy environs on the eastern edge of the Cotswolds, awaiting the kiss of life. Along came Alastair and Sarah with a warm and personal style, and refurbishment ideas that would kick-start the Navy Oak into a stylish new existence. A glowing fire, cosy seating and warm, modern colours tick all the right boxes on a chilly day when the wind blows in from the hills. There are two main dining areas exuding a fine rustic air. Though not close to the sea, this is a pub with the bracing smell of seafood in its nostrils: Alastair worked for Rick Stein, and the menu reflects his time there. Good value, appealing, daily-changing menus are supplemented by a more formal dining experience on Fridays and Saturdays. Special events like fish or Indian evenings are held regularly, as well as barbeques in the summer.

Food serving times

Tuesday-Saturday:
12.30pm-2.30pm, 7pm-9.30pm

Sunday:
12.30pm-2.30pm

Closed 1st week in January

Prices

Meals: a la carte
18.50/27.50

Typical Dishes

Air-dried Cumbrian ham

Braised pork belly and cheek

Pannacotta with raspberries

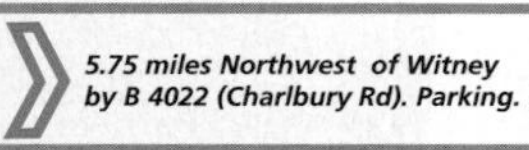

5.75 miles Northwest of Witney by B 4022 (Charlbury Rd). Parking.

075 The Five Horseshoes

Maidensgrove RG9 6EX
Tel.: (01491) 641282 - Fax: (01491) 641086
e-mail: admin@thefivehorseshoes.co.uk
Website: www.thefivehorseshoes.co.uk

Brakspears Bitter, Special and seasonal

Line up your muddy boots outside, sit in one of the snug, beamed, burgundy bars, or enjoy the fine southerly views over the Chilterns from the suntrap conservatory. The food served here includes homely lunchtime classics such as pork pie or bangers and mash plus mains like grilled sea trout or rump of Chiltern lamb. Dare you attempt to devour a 'Doorstep of the Day'; so bulky it comes with its own breadboard? Still very much a locals' pub, bar games like bagatelle and dominoes are positively encouraged here, and the value for money Friday 'Pie and a pint' evenings and first Sunday of the month hog roasts attract many takers. It is in the summer months when this pub really comes to life though, with busy weekend barbeques in the gardens, and Pimms and Mojitos the drinks du jour. If you ask for a glass of Chablis in a loud voice, be aware that the owner's dog might well come running. Classier than a daughter called Chardonnay, anyday.

Food serving times

Monday-Friday:
12pm-2.30pm, 6.30pm-9.30pm

Saturday:
12pm-3pm, 6.30pm-9.30pm

Sunday:
12pm-4pm

Prices

Meals: a la carte
17.00/27.00

Typical Dishes

Barbary duck terrine
Field Farm roast beef sirloin
Banana crème brûlée

Near Stonor Park. North of Henley by A4130 on B480, then 0.75mi West. Parking.

076 The Black Boy Inn

Milton OX15 4HH

Tel.: (01295) 722111

e-mail: info@blackboyinn.com - Website: www.blackboyinn.com

Adnams, Greene King IPA, Old Speckled Hen

This 16C inn could have been named after its previous incarnation as a tobacconist – which were then known as 'Black Boys' - or might equally have been named after swarthy Charles II; but even to its owners, its history is a bit of a mystery. There's no mystery when it comes to its popularity as a dining destination, however; traceability is all important, the enthusiastic, confident kitchen sources ingredients from local farms, and its modern menu, although it has a French edge, does not overlook the pub classics. Service is old fashioned in the nicest sense of the word – the keen, experienced staff are caring without being overbearing and make guests' enjoyment the priority; candles and fresh flowers decorate the tables, and diners haven't been allowed to usurp the drinkers, so the locals can still be found enjoying a tipple or two in the bar. The conservatory is a pleasant spot for dining – but booking is essential at weekends.

Food serving times

Monday-Sunday:
12pm-2.30pm, 6pm-9.30pm

Prices

Meals: 20.00 (3 course Sunday lunch) and a la carte 21.95/29.40

Typical Dishes

Crab, lime and chilli cakes

Cotswold shoulder of lamb

Warm dark chocolate fondant

4mi South of Banbury by A4260 and a minor road West via Adderbury. Parking.

077 The Nut Tree

Murcott OX5 2RE
Tel.: (01865) 331253

 **Hook Norton Hooky Bitter, Wadworth 6X, Oxfordshire Ales Marshmellow**

Near Oxford? Nuts about food? Get down to the Nut Tree Inn, where the accomplished chef makes vibrant, confident use of quality ingredients to produce attractive, flavoursome dishes. Light lunches might include good old British classics like shepherd's pie or sausage and mash, while the à la carte features more modern, restaurant-style dishes. Portions sizes are spot on and the set menu a very reasonable choice if you're short on resources. The 16C origins of this delightfully characterful thatched inn are evident in the low ceilings, heavy beams and partially flagged floors, and the famous nursery rhyme with its similarly ancient beginnings is displayed on the sign outside. Though overly formal in places, with its Chesterfield suite and linen-clad tables, the welcome here is effusive, the service enthusiastic, and it's the kind of pub where the locals still gather for a drink and to play a traditional game of Aunt Sally in the garden.

Food serving times

Tuesday-Saturday:
12pm-2.30pm, 7pm-9.30pm

Sunday:
12pm-2.30pm

Prices

Meals: 15.00 (3 course lunch & dinner) and a la carte 26.00/36.00

Typical Dishes

Grilled scallops
Slow roast belly of pork
Sticky toffee pudding

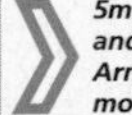

5mi from Bicester by A41 East and a minor road South via the Arncotts; at T-junction beyond the motorway turn right. Parking.

078 The Fishes

North Hinksey OX2 0NA
Tel.: (01865) 249796
e-mail: fishes@peachpubs.com - Website: www.fishesoxford.co.uk

 **Greene King IPA and 1 guest beer**

First impressions of this red brick pub, with its wood flooring, low leather seating and lively atmosphere might be of a modern wine bar - but there's much more to it than that. The pretty gardens are an idyllic spot for riverside picnics in the summer; order at the bar, before picking your spread up from the kitchen hatch, complete with cutlery, crockery and even a blanket on which to sit. Inside, colourful abstract artwork mixes with traditional features like stuffed fish in display cases; the best place to sit being the conservatory-style extension. In keeping with the company's ethos, local suppliers and producers are well-used, and the resulting robust dishes get the thumbs up from all comers. Tapas-style deli boards made for sharing are a popular feature, and the wine list is small but well-chosen, with a decent selection by the glass. Servers in T-shirts are friendly, polite, well-organised and obviously used to being busy.

Food serving times

Monday-Saturday:
12pm-2.30pm, 6.30pm-10pm

Sunday:
12pm-4pm, 6.30pm-9.30pm

Closed 25 December

Prices

Meals: a la carte 20.00/28.00

Typical Dishes

Pork and chicken paté
Panfried seabass
Bakewell tart

3mi west of Oxford city centre by A420 and minor road south on east side of A34. Parking.

079 The Greyhound

Gallowstree Rd, Rotherfield Peppard RG9 5HT
Tel.: (01189) 722227 - Fax: (01189) 242975
e-mail: greyhound@awtrestaurants.com
Website: www.awtrestaurants.co.uk

 **Fuller's London Pride, Marlow Rebellion, Hoppit**

This attractive, timbered 17C pub is situated on the edge of a picturesque village. There is a small bar for regular drinkers and several more formal areas for dining, including a clapperboard-clad barn extension with exposed timbers and banquette seating, where boar and deer heads stare down at you from the walls. The sizeable front garden has a Petanque pitch for anyone who fancies their chances at the Gallic game, plenty of seating and a classic Italian car won by Antony Worrall Thompson in a celebrity rally a few years ago. There's plenty of choice here, with a light lunch menu, two or three course set menus, salads, side orders and specialities. Dishes from the recent past such as prawn cocktail and beef Stroganoff make a cheery comeback, but the menu is dominated by meat. 'Well bred, well fed, well hung' is Worrall Thompson's motto, and the aged Aberdeen Angus steak and Middle White suckling pig are pretty good too.

Food serving times

Monday-Thursday:
12pm-2.30pm, 6pm-9.30pm

Friday-Saturday:
12pm-2.30pm, 6pm-10.30pm

Sunday:
12pm-9pm

Booking essential

Prices

Meals: a la carte 20.45/38.90

Typical Dishes

Hot cheesy filo parcels
Fillet steak au poivre
Triple chocolate plate

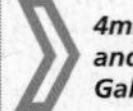

4mi South of Nettlebed by B481 and minor road ~West towards Gallowstree Common. Parking.

080 The Lamb

Satwell RG9 4QZ
Tel.: (01491) 628482 - Fax: (01491) 628257
e-mail: thelamb@awtrestaurants.com - Website: www.awtonline.co.uk

VISA MC

Loddon Hoppit, Rebellion IPA, Fuller's London Pride

If you've previously avoided The Lamb, suspicious that a celebrity chef at the helm might equal fiddly, overpriced food, then take heart; this unpretentious pub serves simple, heart warming classics, representing good value for money. The menu is split into distinctive sections, including 'Fodder for a fiver' and 'World in a stew;' with generous portions making side orders seem somewhat surplus to requirements. 'Soup and a couple of hunks' might sound particularly tempting…but, regrettably, Antony Worrall Thompson's not in everyday. The interior of this tiny 17C pub is full of cosy character, with its low beamed ceilings, quarry tiled floors and inglenook fire. Old photos hang on the walls and candlelight casts spectral shadows on the walls; or is it just George, the resident ghost, making an appearance? Bookings are not accepted here and it can get very busy, tending to quieten down somewhat later in the evenings.

Food serving times

Monday-Friday:
12pm-2.30pm, 6pm-9.30pm (10.30pm Friday)

Saturday:
12pm-4pm, 6pm-10.30pm

Sunday:
all day (bar snacks only)

Closed dinner 25-26 December, dinner 1 January

Bookings not accepted

Prices

Meals: a la carte 16.50/25.40

Typical Dishes

Tapas platter
Hungarian goulash
Chocolate mousse

3mi South of Nettlebed by B481. Parking.

081 The Wykham Arms

Temple Mill Road,
Sibford Gower OX15 5RX
Tel.: (01295) 788808 - Fax: (01295) 788806
e-mail: info@wykhamarms.co.uk - Website: www.wykhamarms.co.uk

   MC

Hook Norton Bitter, Fuller's London Pride, Adnams, St Austell Tribute, Wizard Ales

The thatched 17C Wykham Arms is one of the highlights of this picturesque, narrow-laned village situated on the county border; another being the Manor house opposite, whose blue plaque tells us was once home to Frank Lascelles (1875-1934) pageant master, writer, painter and sculptor. Pageants involving hundreds or thousands of people were the fashion of the day and the grandiose Lascelles made his name directing them. Although the interior of the pub has been modernised, history is writ large within its rural character, typified by the exposed beams and flag floor, and also evident in the glass-covered well in the floor. The bar menu offers classic dishes such as beef pie and spaghetti, while the sensibly-priced evening à la carte, though small, provides a more varied selection, including dishes such as sautéed chicken livers, trout or sea bass. All dishes are freshly prepared and local suppliers are listed on the blackboard.

Food serving times

Tuesday-Saturday:
12pm-3pm, 7pm-9.45pm

Sunday:
12pm-3pm

Closed 1 January

Prices

Meals: a la carte
15.00/30.00

Typical Dishes

Wood pigeon terrine
Gloster Old Spot pork chop
Brioche and butter pudding

8mi West of Banbury by B4035.
Parking.

082 Sir Charles Napier

Sprigg's Alley OX39 4BX

Tel.: (01494) 483011 - Fax: (01494) 485311

e-mail: info@sircharlesnapier.co.uk - Website: www.sircharlesnapier.co.uk

Wadworth IPA and 6X

Reputedly the first gastropub in the UK, the Sir Charles Napier has been run by the same family since 1975 and the mother and daughter team are as serious about food now as they ever were. The modern British menus are heavily seasoned with French flavourings, so dishes are as likely to include roast partridge with bubble and squeak or omelette 'Arnold Bennett', as they are bouillabaisse or French onion soup. Hardly your typical pub grub – and with an international wine list to match, it's no wonder the Sir Charles Napier is so well-regarded. Situated in a small hillside hamlet, this early 18C inn seems to charm all who eat in her. Sofas occupy the quarry-tiled bar area and a hotchpotch of wooden tables provides rustic appeal in the two beamed dining rooms, while the beautiful rear gardens and vine-covered terrace come alive in the warmer months. Sculptures inside and out are by Michael Cooper, a family friend – and all are for sale.

Food serving times

Tuesday-Saturday:
12pm-2.30pm, 6.30pm-10pm

Sunday:
12pm-3.30pm

Closed 25-26 December, 1 other day over Christmas

Prices

Meals: 15.50/16.50 (2 course lunch/dinner) and a la carte 31.00/40.00

Typical Dishes

Scallops with celeriac purée

Roast partridge

Hot chocolate fondant

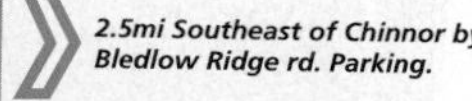

2.5mi Southeast of Chinnor by Bledlow Ridge rd. Parking.

Stanton St John

083 The Talkhouse

Wheatley Rd,
Stanton St John OX33 1EX
Tel.: (01865) 351648 - Fax: (01865) 351085
e-mail: talkhouse@fullers.co.uk - Website: www.talkhouse@foyers.co.uk

We most liked

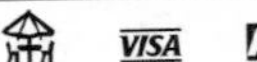

 **Fuller's London Pride, Discovery, ESB**

The meaning of the carved stone flag in the bar room reading, 'Home of the Wind and Bottom Club,' at first seems sure to be scatological, but actually stems from an alliterative tale involving buxom barmaid Betty Bottom, her absent husband and his rival suitor, Lord Wind, whose ghost is now rumoured to haunt this pub. Situated on the outskirts of Oxford, the partly thatched building dates from the 1660s and has been sympathetically modernised in order to keep its charming character. The walls are lined with artwork, flag floors gleam, open fires crackle, and heavy beams hang over the open plan interior. Refurbished bedrooms look onto the summer terrace; a suntrap perfect for lazy summer lunches. The modern pub menu features classics, which come in generous portions, including pies of the shepherd and fish variety as well as more adventurous dishes involving oysters or lobster, foie gras or maybe duck.

Food serving times

Monday-Friday:
12pm-3pm, 6pm-9.30pm

Saturday:
12pm-9.30pm

Sunday:
12pm-9pm

Prices

Meals: 15.50 (2 course lunch and dinner) and a la carte 20.00/28.00

Typical Dishes

Pea soup
Honey roast pork
Vanilla pannacotta

5mi East of Oxford via Headington and minor road North East from roundabout on A40 bypass. Parking.

084 The Cherry Tree Inn

Stoke Row RG9 5QA
Tel.: (01491) 680430
e-mail: info@thecherrytreeinn.com
Website: www.thecherrytreeinn.com

 **Brakspears Bitter and Special**

An attractive 400 year old, Grade II listed building, this pub is set right in the heart of Stoke Row, a village famous for the Maharajah's well and the making of tent pegs during World War II. Contemporary in style and decor, it still retains its rustic charm in the shape of bare scrubbed floorboards, flagged stone floors and low beamed ceilings. Originally made up of four cottages, there are now numerous rooms in which to dine. Food is an interesting mix of good value, modern European dishes, such as moules marinière, roast guinea fowl or belly of pork with mash. Drinkers are still welcomed too and recommended beers are printed next to individual dishes on the menu. Should conversation dry up after dinner, there's a cupboard of board games thoughtfully provided. Bedrooms in a converted barn annex are modern and spacious and, like the pub itself, are named after fruit-bearing trees.

Food serving times

Monday-Saturday:
12pm-4pm, 7pm-10.30pm

Sunday:
12pm-5pm

Closed 25-26 December,
1 January

Prices

Meals: a la carte
25.00/35.00

4 rooms: 95.00

Typical Dishes

Haddock fish cakes
Slow roast belly of pork
Chocolate & raspberry pudding

Between Henley-on-Thames and Goring off B481. Parking.

085 The White Horse

The Ridings,
Stonesfield OX29 8EA
Tel.: (01993) 891063
e-mail: info@thewhitehorse.uk.com - Website: www.thewhitehorse.uk.com

 **Hooky Bitter, Hooky Dark**

It's the only pub in the village, but doesn't really look like one, save for the small red and white sign swaying in the breeze.
So far, so unremarkable. Venture inside, however, and you'll see that this pub is actually more of a dark horse than a white horse, and having lain derelict for four years, has undergone a vast transformation into a modern dining pub. Admire the abstract landscapes on the walls whilst eating in the smart, oak-floored dining room, or lounge in a leather sofa or comfy chair next to the open fire. Locals make the most of the real ales on offer, whilst people travel to taste the snacks and salads on the lunch menu, as well as the more modern dishes on the evening à la carte. Choices range from the simple - cassoulet, steak, salmon, soup - to the more ambitious, including some curious combinations, such as wood pigeon and chocolate pithivier or slow roasted belly pork with sage and onion ice cream.

Food serving times

Tuesday-Saturday and Bank Holiday Monday:
12pm-2.30pm, 6.30pm-10pm

Sunday:
12pm-4pm

Prices

Meals: 10.00/12.95 (2/3 course lunch Tuesday-Saturday) and a la carte 21.00/34.00

Typical Dishes

Foie gras terrine
Fillet of seabass
Farmhouse cheeses

8mi South of Chipping Norton by B4026, B4437 and minor road South. Parking.

086 The Swan Inn

Swinbrook OX18 4DY
Tel.: (01993) 823339
e-mail: swanninnswinbrook@btconnect.com
Website: www.swanninnswinbrook.co.uk

 **Hook Norton, 6X, local micro**

Situated on a little country lane next to a bridge over the River Windrush sits The Swan Inn. The pub is owned by the Dowager Duchess of Devonshire, the last of the Mitford sisters, who spent her childhood in the area, and black and white photos of family and friends from her own private collection decorate the walls, having been transposed onto canvasses, and labelled by the great lady herself. Wisteria climbs the pub's 400 year old walls, while the partly-modernised interior manages to simultaneously feel cosy and spacious. Sit in one of several small, white-painted rooms or in the green oak conservatory with its huge glass wall. Modern British cooking graces the menus, with choices such as calamari or sweetbreads to start, followed by sautéed calves liver or steak and ale pie. Much of the produce is sourced within 5 miles of the pub, including beef from the leasee's uncle and game from the neighbouring Barrington estate.

Food serving times

Monday-Sunday:
12pm-2pm, 7pm-9pm

Closed 25 December

Closed dinner Sunday in winter

Prices

Meals: a la carte
20.00/30.00

Typical Dishes

Mackerel salad
Sautéed calves' liver
Warm lemon pudding

3mi North East of Burford by A40 and minor road North. Parking.

087 The Mole Inn

Toot Baldon OX44 9NG
Tel.: (01865) 340001 - Fax: (01865) 343011
e-mail: info@themoleinn.com
Website: www.themoleinn.com

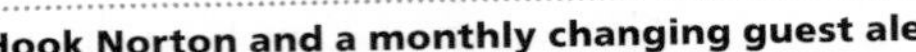

Hook Norton and a monthly changing guest ale

You can see from this pub's neat, well-kept exterior that it's something out of the ordinary and on stepping inside, first impressions are thoroughly confirmed. It's an old building but has clearly had the full treatment, with no stone, brick or beam left unturned; the ceilings are timber-filled, floors are wooden or tiled and brickwork exposed. There are plenty of places to sit to match your mood; maybe on a sofa in the lounge, at a chunky wooden table in the Victorian-style conservatory or out on the charming landscaped terrace. Their lunch menus offer traditional pub dishes, but your best bet is to choose from the more modern à la carte or daily specials, where dishes like sautéed baby squid with hot peanut sauce and chop of Old Spot pork reside. Cooking is tasty and assured and well-priced portions are princely enough to render side orders redundant. Friendly staff add to an all round delightful dining experience.

Food serving times

Monday-Saturday:
12pm-2.30pm, 7pm-9.30pm

Sunday:
12pm-4pm, 6pm-9pm

Closed 25 December

Prices

Meals: a la carte
20.00/30.00

Typical Dishes

Wild mushroom on toast
Seafood risotto
Lemongrass brûlée

6mi Southeast of Oxford; between B480 and A4074. Parking.

088 The Boar's Head

Church St, Ardington, Wantage OX12 8QA
Tel.: (01235) 833254
e-mail: info@boarsheadardington.co.uk
Website: www.boarsheadardington.co.uk

Hook Norton, Butts Barbus Barbus, White Horse Brewery, Dragon Hill

This pretty, part-timbered pub is the 18C centrepiece of unspoiled Ardington, a Victorian model village built by local benefactor Lord Wantage in the Vale of the White Horse. A teetotaller, he decided that the pub profits would be best put to use paying for the lighting in the village. The pub has three rooms which surround the bar, with beams and bunches of dried hops providing a sense of the building's rustic past. Family run, by real foodies, the few snacks and sandwiches chalked up above the bar are the only pub grub in sight here. The regularly-changing à la carte menu offers a small selection of competently cooked modern British dishes, with fish a speciality, and presentation is exacting. If you're after a quick meal at lunchtime, the 'Menu Rapide' will promptly deliver. Three large, stylish, modern bedrooms provide more than you would expect from a pub. Room number 3 is your best bet - and perfect for a family.

Food serving times

Monday-Sunday:
12pm-2.15pm, 7pm-9.30pm

Prices

Meals: 22.50 (3 course Sunday lunch) and a la carte 23.50/45.00

3 rooms: 75.00/130.00

Typical Dishes

Scottish langoustines
Poached fillet of venison
Assiette of chocolates

2.25mi East of Wantage by A417. Next to the church. Parking.

089 The Fleece

11 Church Green,
Witney OX28 4AZ
Tel.: (01993) 892270
e-mail: thefleece@peachpubs.com - Website: www.fleecewitney.co.uk

    MC

 **Greene King IPA, Old Speckled Hen, Morland**

One of the things that makes The Fleece special is its staff; polite and bubbly, they take pride in recognising their regulars and provide keen yet informal service, efficient even when busy – and with its all-age appeal and ability to attract a wide range of people, The Fleece does often get busy. Its modernised interior consists of a front room with polished wood tables, leather suites and newspapers, and an open plan rear restaurant decorated in warm shades of brown, cream and burgundy, where mirrors create a feeling of space and black and white photos hang on the walls. The British-based menu uses freshly prepared, seasonal ingredients and local produce to create flavourful dishes; daily specials, written on the mirrors, include sausage and risotto of the week, and the deli boards make for a very social way to eat. Ten comfortable bedrooms boast individual, eye-catching décor – the ones at the front overlook the village green.

Food serving times

Monday-Sunday:
12pm-2.30pm, 6.30pm-9.45pm

Closed 25 December

Prices

Meals: a la carte 17.50/18.50

10 rooms: 80.00/90.00

Typical Dishes

Hot smoked salmon
Slow roast pork belly
Baked cheesecake

11mi West of Oxford by A40.
Parking.

090 The White Hart

Wytham OX2 8QA

Tel.: (01865) 244372 - Fax: (01865) 248595
e-mail: enquiries@thewhitehartoxford.co.uk
Website: www.thewhitehartoxford.co.uk

 **Hook Norton, Timothy Taylor's Landlord**

Located in a charming village, just out of earshot of the A34, this pretty, ivy-clad, stone building is just as characterful on the inside as it is on the out. Four distinct rooms are designed to give a different dining experience; choose from the romantic Red Room, with its mellow lighting and elm floorboards, the French-style Parlour with its scrubbed pine tables, the comfy Vine Room with its wood burner, or the cosy bar with open fire and flagstone floor. On sunny summer days, the courtyard terrace is an added delight. Erring towards being a restaurant rather than a pub, people now come to this popular place primarily to eat. The food is modern gastrofare, with a seasonal European menu which mixes the classic with the contemporary. Supplemented by daily specials, the menu should also please any vegetarians in your group. The service manages to be at once laid back and efficient and the atmosphere is warm and welcoming.

Food serving times

Monday-Friday:
12pm-3pm, 6.30pm-10pm

Saturday:
12pm-10pm

Sunday:
12pm-9pm

Closed dinner 25 December

Prices

Meals: 10.00/12.50 (2/3 course lunch/dinner Monday-Thursday) and a la carte 20.00/30.00

Typical Dishes

Carpaccio of tarragon tuna
Wild fillet of venison
Vanilla pannacotta

3.25mil North West of Oxford by A420 off A 34 (northbound). Parking.

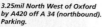

091 The Swan Inn

Petworth Rd,
Chiddingfold GU8 4TY

Tel.: (01428) 682073 - Fax: (01428) 683259
e-mail: enquiries@theswaninn.biz - Website: www.theswaninn.biz

Fuller's London Pride, Hogback TEA

The handsomely mature exterior of this 14C Surrey redbrick village pub belies the extensive and stylish refurbishment which took place here in 2004. Despite the modern makeover, there remains a determinedly rustic atmosphere in most of the dining areas, with their bare wood tables. However, a formal dining room is available with white linen and elegant porcelain, while expansive terraced gardens beckon the summer visitor - dishes remain constant to all eating areas. Chic, understatedly-stylish bedrooms with air-conditioning and marble bathrooms await those staying overnight; their high-tech features, including plasma televisions, DVD players and broadband internet access will appeal to gadget-lovers.

Food serving times

Monday-Sunday:
12pm-2.30pm, 6.30pm-10pm

Prices

Meals: a la carte
18.50/34.00

11 rooms: 70.00/95.00

Typical Dishes

Crayfish & smoked salmon
Whole stuffed seabass
Chocolate & hazelnut Brownie

On East side of the A283. Parking opposite.

Parrot Inn

092 Parrot Inn

Forest Green RH5 5RZ

Tel.: (01306) 621339

e-mail: drinks@the parrot.co.uk - Website: www.the parrot.co.uk

Ringwood Best, Youngs Bitter and 3 regularly changing ales

When you find out that, tucked in between its bar and restaurant, a pub has its own shop selling meat from the owners' nearby farm, as well as homemade sausages, home–baked bread and pies, pickles, preserves and charcuterie, you know that it is probably a safe bet for a quality meal. And you'd be right: lunchtime sees a mouth-watering array of Ploughman's and meat platters with hearty homemade soups, while the concise and seasonal à la carte reflects what's freshest in from the farm. Cooking is wholesome, and the robust dishes are served in sizeable portions, whilst service is assured and friendly. Overlooking the green in a picturesque village in the 'Hills' area of Surrey, this attractive, part 17C inn is an appealing place to dine, with a series of semi-private seating areas and a vast inglenook fireplace in the low beamed, flag-floored bar, and a formally-laid out restaurant furnished with old church chairs.

Food serving times

Monday-Sunday:
12pm-3pm, 6pm-10pm

Prices

Meals: a la carte
18.00/25.00

Typical Dishes

Pork and pistachio terrine
Shoulder of mutton
Banana tarte Tatin

8mi South of Dorking by A24, A29 and B2126 West. Parking.

093 The King William IV

Byttom Hill,
Mickleham RH5 6EL
Tel.: (01372) 372590
e-mail: iduke@another.com

Hogsback TEA, Badger First Gold, Adnams, Sharp's Doombar

Overhung with trailing creepers, this very traditional, part-tiled pub stands a little way above the hamlet itself, its pretty terrace commanding views of the gentle hills. Where the workers from Lord Beaverbrook's estate once propped up the little taproom bar, you're now more likely to find weekend walkers and locals from round about, drawn by the promise of wholesome, dependable English cooking. Look for the list of modern seafood dishes up on a large blackboard. Personally run by a good-natured team, this is just the kind of unfussy place that would have got the approval of the bluff Sailor King, or his contemporary, the cleric and wit Sidney Smith, nicknamed "The Bishop of Mickleham" for his many visits of the village.

Food serving times

Monday-Saturday:
12pm-2.30pm, 7pm-9.30pm

Sunday:
12pm-5pm

Prices

Meals: a la carte
13.20/26.40

Typical Dishes

Salmon mousse
Pan-fried calves liver
Treacle tart

0.5mi North of Mickleham by A24.
Difficult off-road parking nearby.
Public car park at the bottom of Byttom Hill.

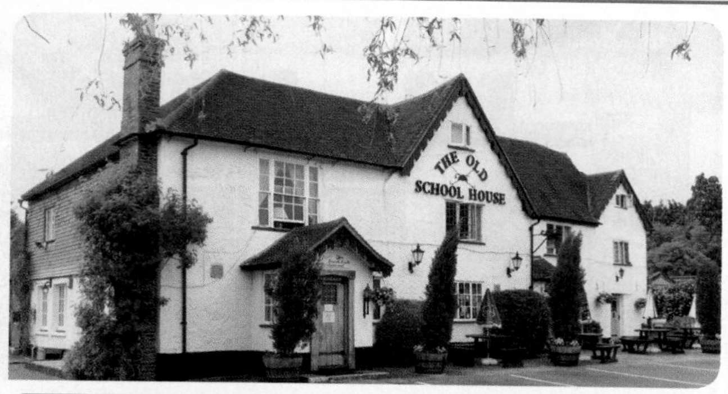

094 Bryce's

Old School House,
Stane St, Ockley RH5 5TH
Tel.: (01306) 627430 - Fax: (01306) 628274
e-mail: bryces.fish@virgin.net - Website: www.bryces.co.uk

Fuller's London Pride, Young's IPA

Just a short walk from the lovely green stands the former village school, now a traditional, personally run pub with a sound reputation in this quietly well-to-do part of Surrey. The spacious if low-beamed bar is the place to go for fresh fish and chips, langoustines and lighter meals, though for something closer to restaurant dining, the more formal room to one side is the better bet. Besides a few meat dishes, it concentrates on fresh seafood, introducing some more adventurous choices on the specials board, like red mullet with spinach and pesto or a puff pastry galette of devilled crab, without dispensing with the classics: there would be an outcry if they tried, albeit a very polite one. As it is, a rather reserved regular clientele soon warm to the friendly and attentive service from a smartly dressed team.

Food serving times

Monday-Sunday:
12pm-2.30pm, 7pm-9.30pm

Closed 25-26 December; dinner Sunday November, January and February

- Seafood -

Prices

Meals: 29.00 (3 course lunch/dinner) and a la carte 29.00/35.00

Typical Dishes

Loch Fyne queenie scallops
Pan-fried fillets of seabass
Orange & stem ginger pudding

8mi South of Dorking by A24 and A29. Parking.

The Inn @ West End

095 The Inn @ West End

42 Guildford Road,
West End GU24 9PW

Tel.: (01276) 858652

e-mail: greatfood@the-inn.co.uk - Website: www.the-inn.co.uk

VISA AE MC

Fuller's London Pride and guest beers including Hogsback TEA, Young's Ordinary, Shepherd Neame Spitfire, Courage Best

A busy roadside pub where the personable owners really lead from the front, energetically organising everything from themed suppers and wine tastings to just-for-fun boules tournaments in the pleasant garden out back. Even on an ordinary day you're likely to find the place busy, with a few knots of chatting regulars in the neatly overhauled modern bar and most of the diners in the conservatory or the dining room to the left; it's smarter than you might expect from the easy, informal tone of the place. A carefully prepared Modern British à la carte menu and their two or three-course lunch menus stand out as particularly good value: it's worth double-checking first, all the same.

Food serving times

Monday-Sunday:
12pm-2.30pm, 6pm-9.30pm

Prices

Meals: 11.95/18.95 (2 course lunch/dinner) and a la carte 25.00/30.00

Typical Dishes

Mushroom with rarebit topping
Seabass in Parma ham
Chocolate sponge

2.5mi South East of Junction 3 on M3 by A322. Parking (40 spaces).

096 The Brickmakers

Chertsey Rd,
Windlesham GU20 6HT
Tel.: (01276) 472267
e-mail: thebrickmakers@4cinns.co.uk - Website: www.brickmakers.co.uk

  AE MC

 **Courage Best Bitter, Fuller's London Pride, Youngs**

The very picture of a trim, Home Counties pub, built in Southern brick – naturally – and hung with baskets of flowers in summer. A simply styled room at the front, dominated by its big bar island, leads into a formal but still relaxed restaurant and adjoining conservatory. Sound, well-prepared cuisine weighs modern and traditional approaches to British cuisine and seems to have struck the right balance for its affluent clientele. A polite young team approach the job in hand with cheery enthusiasm. A short drive away is Chobham Common, a rolling heathland nature reserve; sometimes bleak, but a rare piece of quiet wilderness so close to the capital.

Food serving times

Monday-Sunday:
12pm-2.30pm, 6.30pm-10pm

Prices

Meals: 25.95 (3 course dinner) and a la carte 20.00/26.00

Typical Dishes

Filo parcel
Slow roast pork belly
Almond mille feuilles

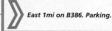

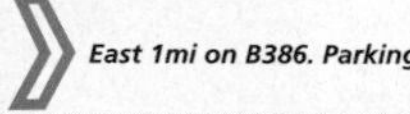
East 1mi on B386. Parking.

097 The Fountain Inn

Ashurst BN44 3AP
Tel.: (01403) 710219

 **Harvey's Sussex Best, Fuller's London Pride; also seasonal ales and weekly local guest ales**

This whitewashed, tiled former farmhouse, dating from 1572, draws in locals like flies to a trap: Paul McCartney's even been in. It's not hard to see what attracts so many here, apart from the obvious charms of the South Downs. An alluring garden and decked area by a pond is instantly relaxing, a skittle alley at the front fosters a bit of healthy local competition and the scents of the pleasant kitchen garden carry gently on the breeze. It's no less charming inside: the low-ceilinged bar has beams galore and leads into a series of characterful rooms where fires and flagged floors set the tone. Flavourful traditional cooking.

Food serving times

Monday-Friday:
11.30am-2pm, 6pm-9.30pm

Saturday:
all day

Sunday:
12pm-3pm, 6pm-8.30pm

Prices

Meals: a la carte
16.00/32.00

Typical Dishes

Soup of the day
Home-made burger
Home-made cheesecake

3.5mi North of Steyning on B2135. Parking.

098 George and Dragon

Main St,
Burpham BN18 9RR
Tel.: (01903) 883131 - Fax: (01903) 883341
Website: www.georgeanddragonburpham.com

VISA  MC

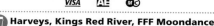

Harveys, Kings Red River, FFF Moondance

This splendid old pub of mellow stone is set in a South Downs valley with sweeping views across to Arundel Castle on the skyline. Not surprisingly, it's prime walking country, so be prepared to share a pint with someone wearing big muddy boots. There's a large area at the front for outside dining in the sunny months, but at other times you'll want to get inside to sample the beamed bar, scrubbed pine tables and frothing real ale. It's where the regulars like to eat: steaks, pies and the like are on offer. To the left more diners settle into the small but irresistibly formed restaurant, which features an inglenook, full linen on antique tables and appealing mix of polished wood chairs. Menus are balanced, interesting and contemporary, using local produce and prepared with care and no little skill.

Food serving times
Monday-Sunday:
12pm-2pm, 7pm-9pm
Closed 25 December

Prices
Meals: a la carte
22.00/32.00

Typical Dishes
Vegetable tart
Fillet steak
Sticky toffee pudding

3mi Northeast of Arundel by A27.
Parking.

099 The Fox Goes Free

Charlton PO18 0HU
Tel.: (01243) 811461 - Fax: (01243) 811712
e-mail: thefoxgoesfree-always@virgin.net
Website: www.thefoxgoesfree.com

 **Arundel Castle, Ballards Best**

Arriving through the pretty village or off the hills, you can't miss this charming brick and flint pub, which is well-loved by its locals and gives them plenty back in return. Music nights, pub quizzes and themed dinners make it more than just a village meeting-place; fresh and hearty pub cooking, from sandwiches and bar favourites up to full meals, mixes contemporary and traditional ideas, and service is very warm and helpful. The dining room, cosy snug, big main bar and garden room have been carefully modernised but are still rich in originality and down-to-earth character, while the picnic tables, out in the sun or under the boughs of the trees, look far out over the start of the South Downs. Well-kept ensuite bedrooms, two reached from behind the bar, are well above pub average.

Food serving times

Monday-Friday:
12pm-2.30pm, 6.30pm-10pm

Saturday:
12pm-10.30pm

Sunday:
12pm-10pm

Closed 25 December

Prices

Meals: a la carte
20.00/28.00

5 rooms: 55.00/140.00

Typical Dishes

Crispy confit duck leg salad

Grilled fillet of seabass

Chocolate torte

6,75 mi North of Chichester by A286. Parking.

100 The Royal Oak Inn

Pook Lane,
East Lavant PO18 0AX
Tel.: (01243) 527434
e-mail: ro@thesussexpub.co.uk - Website: www.thesussexpub.co.uk

We most liked

 **Arundel, Ballards, Sussex Best, Badgers**

This elegant but relaxed Georgian pub, within a turbo blast of Goodwood Motor Circuit and close to the Channel and the South Downs, adds up to more than the sum of its parts. It contains not just an exceptionally busy inn with rustic walls of red brick and rafters, but also a barn and cottage – all with tastefully decorated and well-equipped bedrooms – set cosily round a charming courtyard. The pub cuisine is well-renowned in the Chichester area. There's an interesting à la carte choice with south European influence, and the specials board features perennial country pub favourites alongside modern dishes.

Food serving times

Monday-Sunday:
12pm-2.30pm, 6pm-9.30pm

Prices

Meals: a la carte
19.50/30.00

5 rooms: 65.00/120.00

Typical Dishes

Yellow fin tuna
Fish and chips
Sticky toffee apple pudding

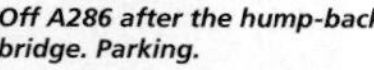

Off A286 after the hump-back bridge. Parking.

101 Three Horseshoes

Elsted GU29 0JY
Tel.: (01730) 825746

 **Ballards Best, Fuller's London Pride, Bowman Ales**

From Uppark House to the Iron Age trails around Beacon Hill, the high, open downlands of East Sussex can make for exhilarating walking, and there are few more satisfying feelings than the stroll down from the scarp path to this welcoming 16C former drovers' inn, where you can enjoy more far-reaching countryside views from the garden or clink well-earned pints by the warmth of the wood burners. A delightful beamed bar where the beers are racked up in casks fills up quickly at the weekend, when it's as well to get your reservation in early; locals and even one or two escaping Londoners enjoy modern dishes from the blackboard or tuck into homemade pies, puddings and other hearty British favourites. Cordial and kindly service.

Food serving times

Monday-Sunday:
12pm-2pm, 6.30pm-9pm

Prices

Meals: a la carte
20.00/25.00

Typical Dishes

Smoked duck & red pepper
Steak & kidney pie
Raspberry & hazelnut meringue

5mi Southwest of Midhurst by A272 on Elsted rd. Parking.

102 The Halfway Bridge Inn

Halfway Bridge GU28 9BP
Tel.: (01798) 861281
e-mail: enquiries@halfwaybridge.co.uk

Betty Stoggs Cornish Bitter, Ballard's Best Bitter, Ringwood Best Bitter

An easy-going, eat-where-you-like policy makes it all the more tempting to drop in and grab a table, but you may not always find your favourite corner free. A bustling crowd know a good thing when they see one, and come in numbers for seasonal cooking at a competitive price: winter dishes, for instance, could include black pudding salad with bacon and mushrooms or duck confit with honey and thyme, but tasty fish and game also make the specials board. To the back of the 17C pub itself – cosy and rustic with its stripped pine floors and log fires – you'll find the old barn, a reminder of the days when this was a coaching halt. Now smartly converted and facing a courtyard garden, it's split into thoughtfully appointed rooms, with vaulted ceilings, a few pieces of antique pine furniture and particularly impressive bathrooms.

Food serving times

Monday-Sunday:
12pm-2.30pm, 6.30pm-9.15pm

Closed 25 December

Prices

Meals: a la carte
11.50/25.00

6 rooms: 65.00/130.00

Typical Dishes

Goats' cheese tart
Rack of lamb
Warm chocolate fondant

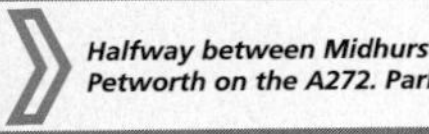

Halfway between Midhurst and Petworth on the A272. Parking.

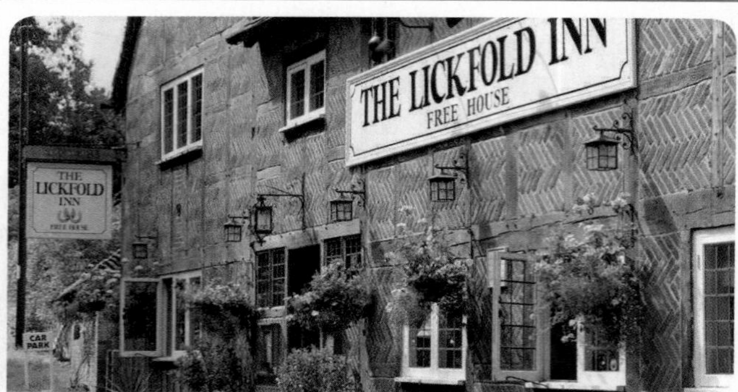

103 The Lickfold Inn

Lickfold GU28 9EY
Tel.: (01798) 861285
e-mail: thelickfoldinn@aol.com - Website: www.thelickfoldinn.co.uk

 **Young's Best Bitter, TEA (Traditional English Ale)**

Follow the narrow country road as it winds through the gentle Sussex countryside and eventually you'll catch a glimpse of the Lickfold Inn, a pretty, tile-hung pub dating back to the 1400s. The smart rear terrace, backing on to a mature garden, and the trimly kept bar, with its stone floor, open fires and scrubbed pine tables, are rather less formal than the dining room upstairs, but the same enjoyable modern cooking is available everywhere. Even on a weekday lunchtime you may find the place busy, but it doesn't dilute the informal charm and service is only a little stretched. Concise menu and specials board; ask about their popular summer barbecues.

Food serving times

Tuesday-Saturday:
12pm-2.30pm, 7pm-9.30pm

Sunday and Bank Holiday Monday:
12pm-2.30pm

Closed 25-26 December

Prices

Meals: 12.00/15.00 (2/3 course lunch) and a la carte 22.00/33.00

Typical Dishes

King prawn & crayfish risotto
Baked fillet of venison
Classic lemon tart

6mi Northwest of Petworth by A272. Parking.

104 Badgers

Coultershaw Bridge,
Petworth GU28 0JF
Tel.: (01798) 342651

 **Badger's Gold Bitter, King & Barnes Sussex Bitter and seasonal guest ales**

With its sash windows and River Rother location (it's just past the bridge), this smart white-painted former railway tavern is an ideal destination in pretty Petworth. Its eye-catching garden boasts weeping willows, and next door is the unique, Michelin Red Guide recommended Old Railway Station guesthouse. Badgers' interior is most pleasant: a beautiful oak-panelled bar has carvings with a 'badger and honey' theme, and lots of old photos depict its former Railway Inn-carnation. Jack Vettriano fans will find two of his sexy pictures, The Assessment and Game On, in a single-table alcove that gives a new twist to the word 'intimate'. Menus offer plenty of choice, a robust and wholesome mix of classic British dishes with global influences. There are fresh fish specials and homemade puddings too. South Downs ramblers staying on have the choice of three comfy, spacious rooms a cut above normal pub accommodation.

Food serving times

Monday-Sunday:
12pm-2pm, 6.30pm-9pm

Closed 25 December

Closed dinner Sunday October-April

Prices

Meals: a la carte 23.00/34.00

3 rooms: 80.00

Typical Dishes

Seafood tapas

Peppered honey duck breast

White chocolate torte

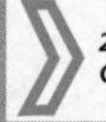 *2mi South of Petworth by A285 at Coultershaw Bridge. Parking.* 

105 The Chequers Inn

Rowhook RH12 3PY

Tel.: (01403) 790480

e-mail: thechequers1@aol.com - Website: nealsrestaurants.biz

 **Harveys, Youngs, Fuller's London Pride, Black Sheep**

Duck is not only the name of a bird on the menu at The Chequers Inn, but also the word your friends will shout at you as you go through the doorways. Annoying maybe, but along with its log fires and relaxed atmosphere, its low ceilings are part of this delightful 18C inn's charm and character. Travel up a few stairs and you'll enter into another rustic seating area, where farming implements and pictures of the rural hamlet of Rowhook through the ages hang on the walls. On the other side is what at first glance appears to be a corrugated metal shed but is in actual fact Neal's restaurant, the more formally laid part of the establishment; but since the same menu is served throughout, the bar would have to be your choice for a seat every time. Far from typical pub nosh, the menu offers aspirational cooking which showcases local produce, with dishes such as belly pork, foie gras and sea bass, as well as fresh homemade puddings.

Food serving times

Monday-Saturday:
12pm-2pm, 7pm-9pm

Sunday:
12pm-2pm

Prices

Meals: a la carte
27.50/32.50

Typical Dishes

Seared scallops
Tasting of lamb
Tonka bean pannacotta

3mi West of Horsham by A281. Parking.

106 Nava Thai at The Hamilton Arms

School Lane,
Stedham GU29 0NZ

Tel.: (01730) 812555 - Fax: (01730) 817459

e-mail: hamiltonarms@hotmail.com - Website: www.thehamiltonarms.co.uk

VISA AE MC

Ballard's Best, Fuller's London Pride

Happily situated in the rolling South Downs, this whitewashed inn boasts an authentic Asian ambience barely a couple of miles from the attractive and quintessentially homespun appeals of Midhurst. The bar area at the front is brimming with Thai artefacts set around polished tables – during the week, this is where lunch is usually served. Adjacent: a homely, comfortable restaurant with a similar interior gets you in the mood for excellently prepared, tasty Thai dishes, monosodium glutamate and additive free. Enjoyment is enhanced by polite service from traditionally attired Thai waiters.

Food serving times

Tuesday-Sunday:
12pm-2.30pm, 6pm-10.15pm

Bank Holiday Monday:
12pm-2.30pm

Closed 1 week from 1 January

- Thai -

Prices

Meals: 19.50 (3 course lunch/dinner) and a la carte 20.00/35.00

Typical Dishes

Stuffed chicken wings
King tiger prawns
Thai egg custard

2mi West of Midhurst by A272.
Parking.

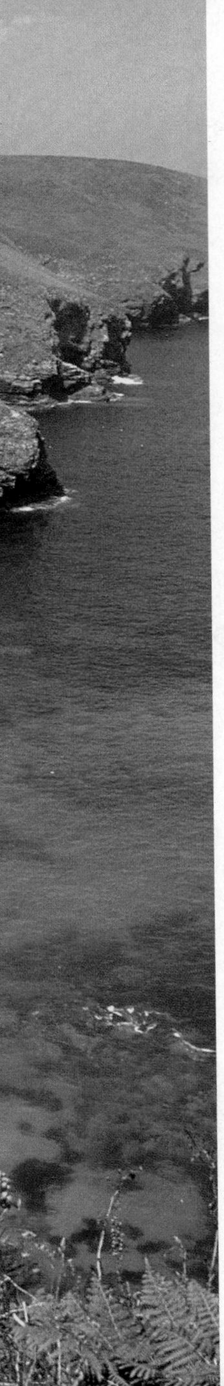

As anyone west of the Avon will tell you, the historic West Country has been many countries in its time: the ancient land of Celtic saints and Arthurian legend, Drake's home port and the Old England of Hardy's Wessex are rediscovered every year by countless visitors, drawn by sun and surf and the West's astonishing variety. Where else can you find untamed moorland next to semi-tropical fantasy gardens? Which other region combines the magnificent Elizabethan Longleat House with the mysterious standing sarsens at Stonehenge, the genius of Brunel's grand designs and the exquisite style of Georgian Bath, not to mention the ultra-modern Eden Project? Add to this the seaside villages, sandy beaches and hundreds of miles of breathtaking clifftop trails and you have a glimpse of this amazing region, but for a real flavour of the place, get down to the dairy, the quay and the orchard. Come harvest time, Pippins, Dabinetts and Somerset Redstreaks are ripened for slow-matured dry ciders, "real" Cheddar and Blue Vinney cheeses are in every farmers' market and Brixham and Newlyn's fresh and cured seafood appear on the specials boards. But there's much more to West Country cooking than these three famous exports, as you'll soon discover…

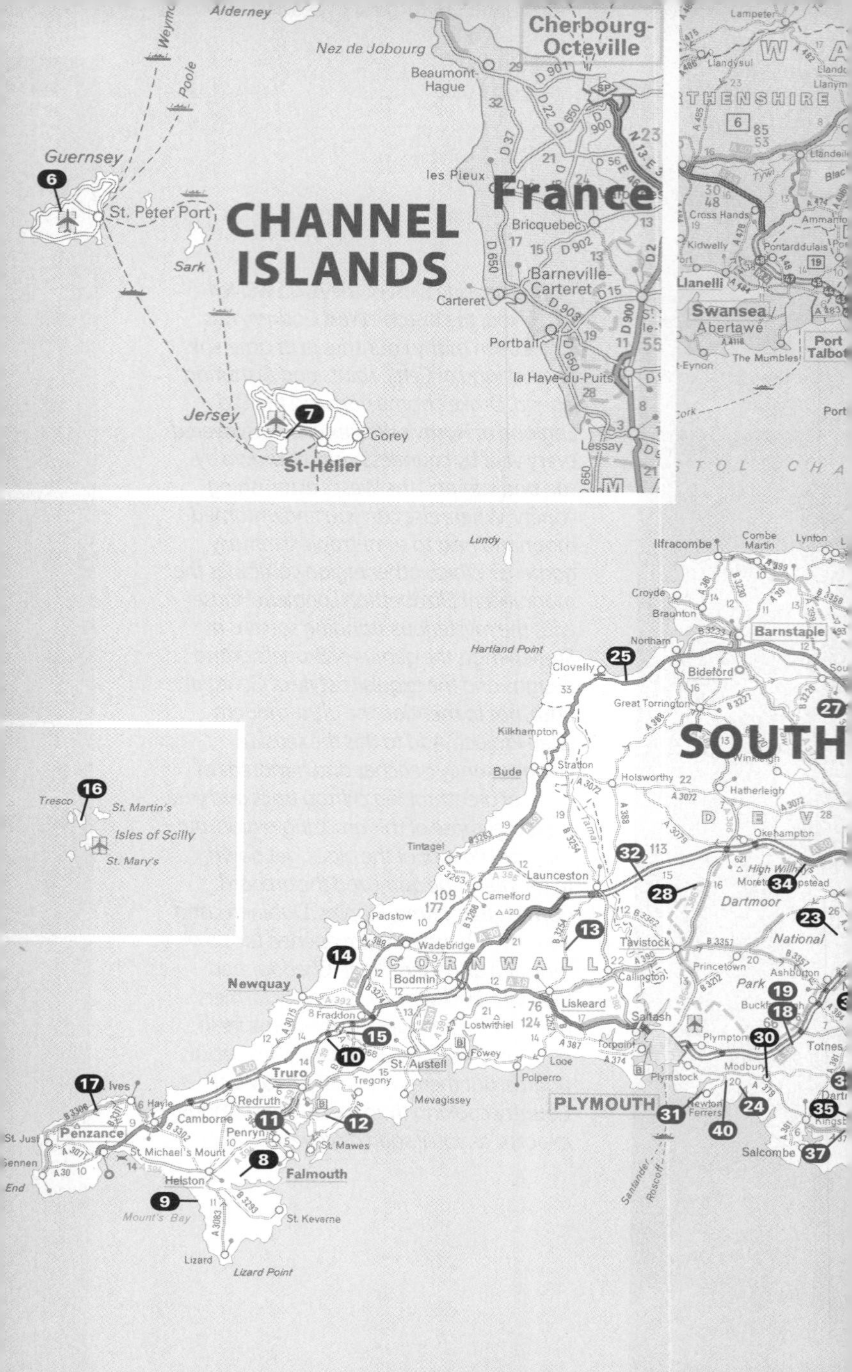

Alderney
Nez de Jobourg
Cherbourg-Octeville
Beaumont-Hague
Guernsey
St. Peter Port
Sark
CHANNEL ISLANDS
France
les Pieux
Bricquebec
Barneville-Carteret
Carteret
Portbail
la Haye-du-Puits
Lessay
Jersey
Gorey
St-Hélier
Lampeter
Llandysul
CARMARTHENSHIRE
Cross Hands
Kidwelly
Pontarddulais
Ammanford
Llanelli
Swansea
Abertawe
The Mumbles
Port Talbot
Cork
Lundy
Ilfracombe
Combe Martin
Lynton
Croyde
Braunton
Northam
Barnstaple
Hartland Point
Clovelly
Bideford
Great Torrington
Kilkhampton
SOUTH
Winkleigh
Bude
Stratton
Holsworthy
Hatherleigh
DEVON
Okehampton
Tresco
St. Martin's
Isles of Scilly
St. Mary's
Tintagel
Launceston
Camelford
Dartmoor
National
Park
Padstow
Wadebridge
CORNWALL
Tavistock
Princetown
Ashburton
Newquay
Bodmin
Callington
Liskeard
Saltash
Fraddon
Lostwithiel
Fowey
Torpoint
Plympton
Totnes
Truro
St. Austell
Looe
Polperro
Modbury
Ives
Hayle
Redruth
Tregony
Mevagissey
PLYMOUTH
Plymstock
Newton Ferrers
Penzance
Camborne
Penryn
St. Just
Sennen
St. Michael's Mount
St. Mawes
Salcombe
Helston
Falmouth
Mount's Bay
St. Keverne
Santander
Roscoff
Lizard
Lizard Point

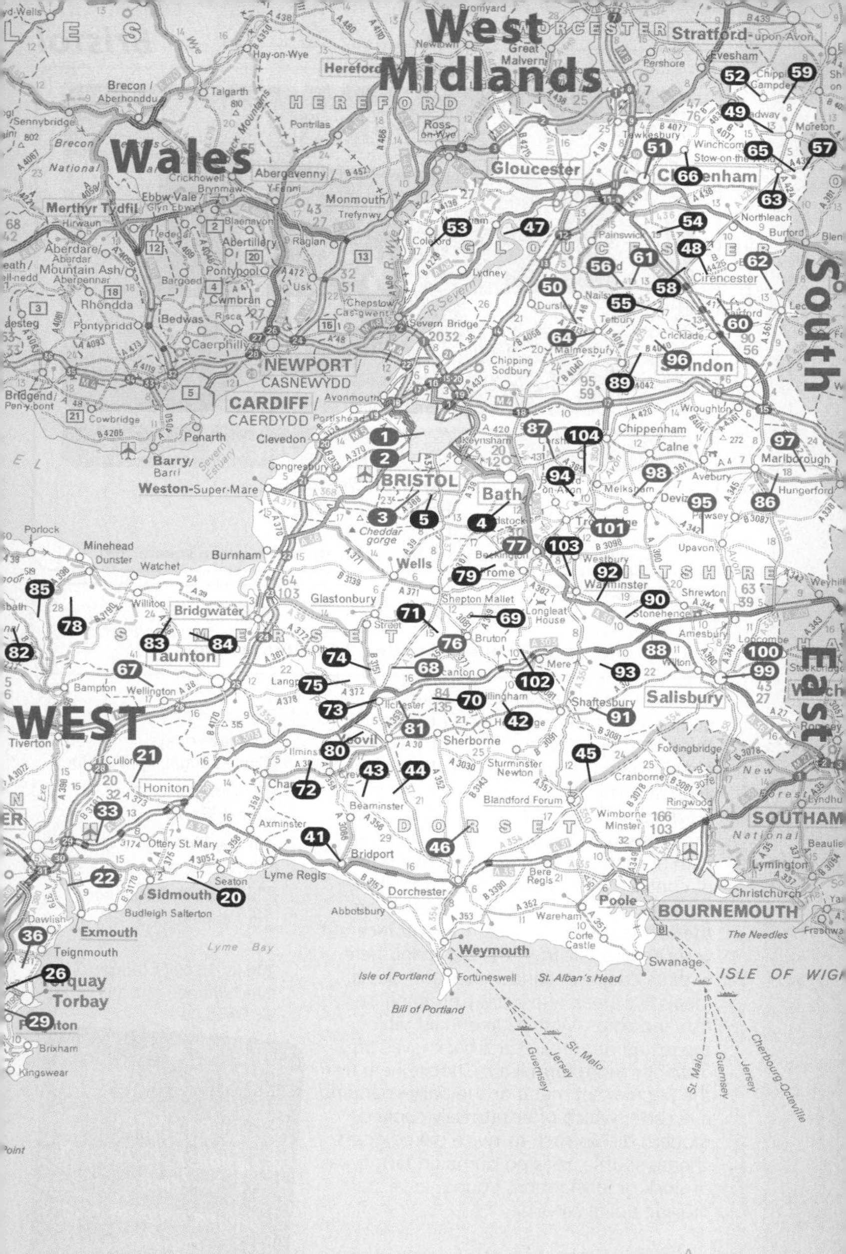
West Midlands
Wales
South East
WEST
BRISTOL
Bath
Gloucester
Swindon
Salisbury
Taunton
Bridgwater
Yeovil
Weymouth
Poole
BOURNEMOUTH
NEWPORT
CARDIFF
Lyme Bay
ISLE OF WIGHT

001 Queen Square

63 Queen Square,
Bristol BS1 4JZ
Tel.: (0117) 929 0700
e-mail: info@queen-square.com - Website: www.queen-square.com

 **Fuller's London Pride, Butcombe**

It's easy to while away a few hours people-watching as you dine outside this bar, set just off the corner of the redeveloped Georgian square. Inside, the vibe's a contemporary one; bright abstract art decorates the open plan space, while the noise from the open kitchen mingles with modern music and the gentle hum of contented customers to create a lively atmosphere. Drinkers tend to gather on the soft leather sofas near the entrance but you can also eat from the bar menu here, with its choice of sandwiches and classic meals like steak and kidney pudding or fish and chips. With its linen-laid tables, the restaurant area at the back gives off a distinctly more formal air. Choose here from the popular set menu or the daily-changing à la carte, which offer precisely cooked, modern dishes such as twice baked goats cheese soufflé, roasted pumpkin tart, breast of duck or local rabbit. Young, local staff provide polite service.

Food serving times

Tuesday-Friday:
12pm-2.30pm, 6pm-9.30pm

Saturday:
6pm-9.30pm

Sunday-Monday:
12pm-2.30pm

Closed 25-30 December, 1-6 January

Prices

Meals: 16.00 (3 course lunch/dinner) and a la carte 20.00/28.00

Typical Dishes

Cod cheeks

Slow roast shoulder of lamb

Chilled coconut rice pudding

In city centre in the bend of the Floating Harbour, North side. Parking meters in Queen Square.

002 **The Albion**

Boyces Avenue,
Clifton Village, Bristol BS8 4AA
Tel.: (0117) 973 3522 - Fax: (0117) 973 9768
e-mail: info@thealbionclifton.co.uk - Website: www.thealbionclifton.co.uk

 **Sharp's Doombar, Butcombe, Wye Valley, Barnstormer**

Charming Clifton is not all showy attractions like the bridge and the boutique shops; some treats take a little bit of finding, and to say The Albion was hidden away would be an understatement. Armed with a local map, search out this Grade II listed 17C inn hiding in a mews in the heart of the village. At the front is a terrace fronting a seemingly cosy little hostelry. Inside, though, things are more spacious than you'd expect. There's an open plan kitchen, reclaimed wood floors, flagstones, and plenty of space to relax in front of the fires, stand at the big bar or eat at one of the numerous chunky wood tables. Settles and benches line the walls, but if they're all taken, then try upstairs. Menus are concise but read well. They're firmly British, with plenty of locally sourced ingredients and good, down-to-earth West Country dishes.

Food serving times

Tuesday-Saturday:
12pm-3pm, 7pm-10pm

Sunday:
12pm-3pm

Closed 25-26 December,
1 January

Booking essential. Sunday evening barbecue in summer.

Prices

Meals: a la carte
24.00/34.00

Typical Dishes

Bath chaps
Baked hake
Valrhona chocolate fondant

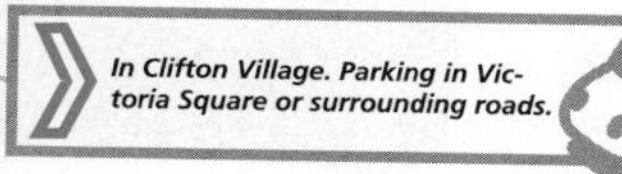

In Clifton Village. Parking in Victoria Square or surrounding roads.

003 Bear & Swan

South Parade,
Chew Magna BS40 8SL

Tel.: (01275) 331100 - Fax: (01275) 331204
e-mail: enquiries@bearandswan.co.uk - Website: www.bearandswan.co.uk

Butcombe Bitter, Courage Best, Cheddar Best

A sturdy homage to Victoriana in the heart of a small, pretty but truly bustling village. The exterior is of sturdy stone and the 'proper' bar at one end has the same sterling qualities. Here you can enjoy a pint or a tasty snack at chunky rustic tables- mind you- only at lunchtime. In the evenings, the main blackboard menu takes centre stage. This can also be enjoyed in the main dining area at the other end of the bar where a hotchpotch of antique tables and chairs, reclaimed floor boards, and exposed stone work give a pleasant feel. You can watch the chefs at work in their open-plan kitchen as they prepare an ample, modern, eclectic range of dishes that draw diners from far and wide, attracted by locally renowned menus full of tasty West Country produce on daily changing menus.

Food serving times

Monday-Saturday:
12pm-2pm, 7pm-9.45pm

Sunday:
12pm-2pm

Prices

Meals: 8.95 (2 course lunch) and a la carte 25.00/30.00

Typical Dishes

Tiger prawns & chorizo
Supreme of Bombay duck
Crème brûlée

8.25mi South of Bristol via A37 on B3130. Parking.

004 The Wheatsheaf

Combe Hay BA2 7EF
Tel.: (01225) 833504 - Fax: (01225) 836123
e-mail: info@wheatsheafcombehay.com
Website: www.wheatsheafcombehay.com

VISA AE MC

Butcombe Bitter, Butcombe Brunel, Itchiban, Oranjeboom

Order a drink, bag yourself a seat in one of the comfy fireside sofas by the entrance and grab yourself a magazine to flick through. When you're ready, you can move to one of the starkly modern dining rooms, stripped back to a stylish minimum, where artwork decorates the walls, the atmosphere is chatty and informal, and Northern soul plays quietly in the background. This is pub dining, The Wheatsheaf style, and it's a world away from your traditional spit and sawdust pub of yesteryear. You won't find any classic pub dishes on the menu here. Instead, there's a choice of amuse bouches pre- and petits fours post-, with appealing, modern dishes in between. Cooked using local produce, choices might include quail and watercress soup, Thai beef salad or belly pork. Perched on the side of a hill in a wooded valley, the lawned garden is the perfect spot for al fresco dining. Three smart bedrooms are situated in converted outbuildings.

Food serving times

Tuesday-Saturday:
12pm-2.30pm, 6.30pm-9.30pm

Sunday:
12pm-2.30pm

Closed 25 December

Prices

Meals: a la carte
22.00/45.00

3 rooms: 95.00/120.00

Typical Dishes

Scottish King scallops
Fillet of Buccleuch beef
Coconut baked Alaska

4mi South of Bath by A367 and minor road South. Parking.

005 Carpenters Arms

Stanton Wick BS39 4BX
Tel.: (01761) 490202 - Fax: (01761) 490763
e-mail: carpenters@buccaneer.co.uk
Website: www.the-carpenters-arms.co.uk

 **Wadworth 6X, Butcombe, Courage Best**

The Carpenters Arms is actually a group of 300-year old converted miners' cottages. Now it glows with a pubby contentment, typified by dark wooden furniture, candles in wine bottles, built-in wall seats and, of course, the original exposed stone walls. A big log fire roars in winter. Its long, low exterior is offset with hanging baskets, bright flowers and the tranquility of the surrounding countryside. For diners, a snug inner "parlour" awaits with fresh flowers on the tables and beams above. Modern cooking prevails, proof of popularity confirmed by the number of tables taken. Upstairs: sizable, pine furnished bedrooms in subtle floral patterns and modern bathrooms.

Food serving times

Monday-Saturday:
12pm-2pm, 7pm-10pm

Sunday:
12pm-2.30pm, 7pm-9pm

Closed dinner 25-26 December

Prices

Meals: a la carte 20.00/29.00

12 rooms: 67.00/95.00

Typical Dishes

Stir-fried chicken
Herb-crusted fillet of salmon
Sticky toffee slice

9mi South of Bristol (just off the A37) signed off A368. Parking.

006 Fleur du Jardin

Castel,
Kings Mills (Guernsey) GY5 7JT
Tel.: (01481) 257996 - Fax: (01481) 256834
e-mail: info@fleurdujardin.com - Website: www.fleurdujardin.com

Fuller's London Pride, Guernsey Sunbeam, Old Speckled Hen

This attractive stone built inn stands in its elevated position as it has done for centuries, surrounded by neat lawned gardens and looking out over countryside and sea. With its hanging baskets and colourful borders, it's aptly named, and the heated terrace adds a stylish touch to the exterior. One of the bar areas has recently been refurbished, waving goodbye to cottage-style chintz and saying hello to a new, cosmopolitan look befitting the 21C; three adjoining dining areas await a similar makeover. Extensive à la carte menus offer big portions, from rump of lamb or steak to Thai curry; supplemented by seafood specials and making use of local produce in the form of Guernsey crab, scallops and veal sausages. Service is charming and the Fleur's reputation among both locals and tourists ensures it's often busy. Four contemporary new bedrooms offer superior comfort, while plans to refurbish the remainder are in the pipeline.

Food serving times
Monday-Sunday:
12pm-2pm, 6pm-9pm

Prices
Meals: 12.95 (3 course lunch) and a la carte 25.00/30.00

17 rooms:
50.00/125.00

Typical Dishes
Timbale of Guernsey crab
Rump of lamb
Seasonal fruit crumble

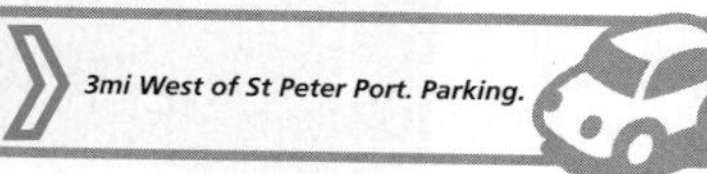

3mi West of St Peter Port. Parking.

007 Old Court House Inn

St Aubin's Harbour, Saint Aubin (Jersey) JE3 8AB
Tel.: (01534) 746433 - Fax: (01534) 745103
e-mail: info@oldcourthousejersey.com
Website: www.oldcourthousejersey.com

   VISA   

 **Marston's Pedigree and Bass**

The owners of this whitewashed quayside inn have long been on the right tack, hence its favourable local reputation. Dating from 1450, it has been witness over the years to judicial comings and goings, as well as being a onetime storehouse for seafarers' illegal booty. There's something for everyone on the extensive menus, including daily seafood specials chosen from the wettest and freshest on offer that day. Thus, local lobster and crab sit alongside more traditional dishes like steak and lasagne, while the dessert menu includes old favourites such as sticky toffee pudding. You'll also be spoilt for choice when it comes to where to sit; the conservatory or the rustic bar are good choices for a lunchtime snack, whilst a seat on the decked terrace affords scenic views across the harbour; and if you feel like pushing the boat out, head for one of the more formal dining rooms, one of which is built in the shape of a galleon.

Food serving times

Monday-Sunday:
12.30pm-2.30pm, 7pm-10pm

Closed 25 December

Prices

Meals: 12.50/23.00 (3 course lunch/dinner) and a la carte 30.00/50.00

9 rooms: 40.00/120.00

Typical Dishes

Moules marinières
Lamb cutlets
Toffee pudding

4mi West of St Helier. Public car park opposite and parking in street.

008 Trengilly Wartha Inn

Nancenoy,
Constantine TR11 5RP
Tel.: (01326) 340332 - Fax: (01326) 340332
e-mail: reception@trengilly.co.uk - Website: www.trengilly.co.uk

Lizard Ales (Halford River, Lizard, Frenchman's Creek, Helligan Honey, St Perrans), Skinners Keel Over, Betty Stoggs

Out in the pretty, lesser spotted Cornwall countryside lies this, literally translated, 'settlement above the trees.' Its slightly ramshackle appearance lends it a charming air, and the interior is just as characterful, with several atmospheric rooms and a bar decorated with beer mats; a helpful reminder that there are plenty of real ales here for you to try. You can eat either in the bar, choosing from dishes such as beef Stroganoff or lasagne, or have dinner in the more formal modern restaurant, with its waitress service and set menu. Starters might include Thai crab soup, mussels or oysters, while main courses, cooked using local produce, might include steak, butternut squash gratin or monkfish cheeks. Six well-kept, cottage style bedrooms are available, with a couple of larger rooms also situated in a separate annex overlooking the lake and garden. The residents lounge offers a cosy place to relax.

Food serving times

Monday-Sunday:
12pm-2.15pm, 7pm-9.30pm

Prices

Meals: 29.00 (3 course dinner) and a la carte 16.00/30.00

8 rooms: 50.00/96.00

Typical Dishes

Thai fish cake
Locally smoked pollock
Chocolate cheesecake

1.5mi South by Fore St off Port Navas rd. Parking.

009 The Halzephron Inn

Gunwalloe TR12 7QB
Tel.: (01326) 240406 - Fax: (01326) 241442
e-mail: halzephroninn@gunwalloe1.fsnet.co.uk
Website: www.halzephron-inn.co.uk

 **Sharp's Doombar, Wills Resolve, St Austell Tribute, Halzephron Gold (organic ale)**

A visit to this extreme south-westerly corner of Cornwall wouldn't be complete without a visit to the Halzephron, staring out imperturbably across Mount's Bay. It knows its place: it's been here 500 years, and is wonderfully snug and rustic. The low ceiling boasts fine old timbers; gleaming copper and original paintings adorn the walls. Knick-knacks, curios and higgledy-piggledy décor enrich four adjoining dining rooms: food's a serious business here, and wide-ranging menus are fiercely Cornish in produce and style. Portions are of the hearty variety; an impressive selection of local real ales is an ideal way to wash down lunch or dinner, followed by a walk on the nearby South West Coast Path. Two neat, cosy bedrooms await.

Food serving times

Monday-Sunday:
12pm-2pm, 7pm-9pm

Closed 25 December

Prices

Meals: a la carte
18.00/27.00

2 rooms: 50.00/86.00

Typical Dishes

Smoked duck
Gressingham duck breast
Chocolate & amaretto torte

3.5mi South of Helston by A3083.
Parking.

010 The Plume of Feathers

Mitchell TR8 5AX

 Tel.: (01872) 510387 - Fax: (01872) 511124

Courage Best, Sharp's Doombar, Directors, Abbot Ale, Eden Ale

As good a break as you'll find from the drone of the A30, this smartly refurbished part 16C dining pub, away from the visitors' hotspots, comes into its own as an escape from the tourist influx of a Cornish summer, but you'll find a reassuringly good turnout - families and couples, groups of friends - on most days of the year. Set aside from an airy, sympathetically restored bar, several connecting lounges serve as the restaurant, although service is just as alert and organised at the bar. The cooking itself is steady as she goes - there is a sound, classic menu with blackboard specials - but the real draw is the relaxed, everyday atmosphere of the place: they have plenty of regulars, but are always happy to take on a few more. Large, bright bedrooms in the restored barns and stable. A well provides ample pure drinking water and water for the baths and showers.

Food serving times

Monday-Sunday:
12pm-10pm

Prices

Meals: a la carte
16.20/25.00

8 rooms: 46.25/80.00

Typical Dishes

Salmon & cod fishcake
Char-grilled Angus burger
Cheesecake

Near the junction of A30 and A3076. Parking.

Mylor Bridge

011 Pandora Inn

Restronguet Creek,
Mylor Bridge TR11 5ST
Tel.: (01326) 372678 - Fax: (01326) 378958
Website: www.pandorainn.co.uk

 **Tinners, Tribute, Hicks Special Draught (HSD), Bass, Duchy**

Sail up Mylor Creek, moor at the pontoon, and you'll have taken the scenic route to this stunningly located pub, which dates back to the 13C. Its charming interior comes courtesy of timbered ceilings for the vertically challenged, shiny stone floors, cosy corners, open fire and seaside pot pourri. Food can be eaten at the bar or at the slightly more formal Andrew Miller restaurant upstairs: hearty pub menus take in a wide range of favourites, but are quite rightly dominated by fresh seafood off the blackboard, so be patient with service. Crab bucket and bait are available at the bar or work off your meal with a relaxed walk along the creekside paths.

Food serving times

Monday-Thursday:
12pm-3pm, 6.30pm-9pm

Friday-Saturday:
12pm-3pm, 6.30pm-9.30pm

Closed meals 25 December

Prices

Meals: a la carte
18.95/26.95

Typical Dishes

Pan-fried scallops
Grilled seabass fillets
Coconut, lemon & treacle tart

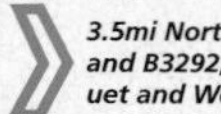
3.5mi North of Falmouth by A39 and B3292; fork left via Restronguet and Weir rd for 1mi. Parking.

012 Roseland Inn

Philleigh TR2 5NB
Tel.: (01872) 580254

Skinner's Betty Stoggs, Sharp's Doombar and summer guest beer - Adnam's Best

You know you're edging into rural heaven when you come by ferry to this out-of-the-way family-run Cornish pub – the church's next-door neighbour for the last 500 years – and step inside from the rose-covered courtyard. Just look around and admire the charming rustic surrounds: exposed black beams, open fires, rugged stone floors and scattered knick-knacks. A fine selection of real ales is on hand – a pint or two will go down exceptionally well with a dish or two from the traditional and unpretentious menus, which owe much of their hearty character to Cornish produce.

Food serving times
Monday-Sunday:
12pm-2.30pm, 6pm-9.30pm

Prices
Meals: a la carte
21.00/31.00

Typical Dishes
Whole baked Camembert
Home farm ribeye steak
Chocolate fudge cake

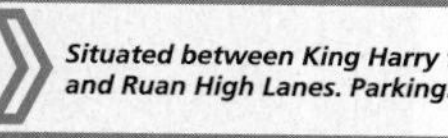
Situated between King Harry ferry and Ruan High Lanes. Parking.

013 The Manor House Inn

Rilla Mill PL17 7NT
Tel.: (01579) 362354

 VISA 

Sharp's Own, Sharp's Special, Charles Wells Bombardier, Marston's Pedigree, Fuller's London Pride, Adnams Broadside

Chancing upon the somnolent village of Rilla Mill near the grand bleakness of Bodmin Moor, you'd be forgiven for not expecting anything too special down at the local. Wrong. An eye-catching makeover of the 360 year-old Manor House hits you as soon as you walk in. Homely touches light up all corners, from the very pleasant bar to the neat curtains, perfectly shelved books and colourful stack of board games. "No cheap peanuts here," says the landlord. He's good to his word: proper handmade crisps are for sale, and fresh walnuts with nut-crackers adorn each table. Exotic cocktails (you read it right) are also prominent here, courtesy of a blackboard selection called 'The Inn Thing'. Dining areas are neat and thoughtfully decorated, with local artwork for sale. Dinner itself is not to be taken lightly, with very seasonal, local produce to the fore, exemplified by suppliers taking pride of place on the blackboard.

Food serving times
Monday-Sunday:
12pm-2pm, 6pm-9pm

Prices
Meals: a la carte
13.00/26.00

Typical Dishes
Grilled goat's cheese
Marinated duck breast
Baileys crème brûlée

5mi North of Liskeard by B3254 to Upton Cross and side road East. Parking.

014 The Falcon Inn

St Mawgan TR8 4EP
Tel.: (01637) 860225 - Fax: (01637) 860884
e-mail: enquiries@thefalconinn-newquay.co.uk
Website: www.thefalconinn-newquay.co.uk

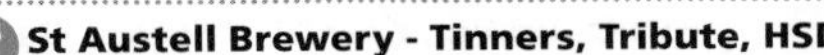
St Austell Brewery - Tinners, Tribute, HSD

Set just inland from the delights of Newquay, in the splendid Vale of Mawgan, this 16C wisteria-clad hostelry rejoices in a totally unspoilt character and a quaint surrounding of antique shops. The bar is cosiness itself: roaring log fire, comfy settles, large antique prints and, naturally enough, pictures of falcons on the walls; you can sit at homely farmhouse tables and chairs. Eat either here, in the French-windowed restaurant, or at a delicious cobbled courtyard in the front. Dishes are based around freshly-caught seafood which arrives on the plate from the nearby beaches at Newlyn; classic dishes also make a solid appearance.

Food serving times
Monday-Sunday:
12pm-2pm, 6pm-9pm
Closed 25 December

Prices
Meals: a la carte 8.95/18.00
3 rooms: 44.00/84.00

Typical Dishes
Home-made vegetable tartlet
Steak and mushroom pie
Falcon orange & treacle tart

Follow signs for the airport on A3059 between Newquay and St Colomb Major; the pub is down the hill. Parking.

015 Viners

Carvynick,
Summercourt TR8 5AF
Tel.: (01872) 510544 - Fax: (01872) 510468
Website: www.vinersrestaurant.co.uk

 **Sharp's Doombar, Cornish Knocker, Betty Stoggs**

This charming stone-built cottage, with origins stretching back to the 17C, can claim to have been here long before the landscaped encampments of mobile homes or the golf course next door, but it's a much more recent change which has really captured the local imagination. The bar near the entrance remains a good place for beer, nuts and pub chat, and drinkers are positively encouraged, though most will stay for one and head straight for the elegant new restaurant. Pale-toned walls, slate floors and high-backed velvet chairs strike a sophisticated note, taken up in a creative but affordable menu that shows sound culinary understanding: for an example of this generosity and balance, try grilled oysters in lime and chilli or sole in parsley butter with bean salad.

Food serving times

Monday-Sunday:
12.30pm-3pm, 6.30pm-9.30pm

Closed 4 weeks in winter

Closed dinner Sunday end October to Whitsun; also dinner Monday mid September to mid July

Prices

Meals: 16.95 (3 course Sunday lunch) and a la carte 25.00/33.50

Typical Dishes

Twice baked cheese soufflé
Shoulder of Cornish lamb
Baileys chocolate temptation

At Carvynick Golf and Country Club, 1.5mi North West of the junction of A30 and A3058. Parking.

016 New Inn

Tresco (Scilly Isles) TR24 0QQ

Tel.: (01720) 423006 - Fax: (01720) 423200
e-mail: newinn@tresco.co.uk
Website: www.tresco.co.uk

 **Ales of Scilly - Natural Beauty**

An hospitable stopping off point on your way, perhaps, to the Old Blockhouse or Tresco Abbey Gardens, this stone built former inn may prove difficult to leave. It has a charming terrace garden - with plenty of seating - and views that extend across the beautiful island. In keeping with its surroundings, the traditional bar is packed with nautical memorabilia; other lounges have a friendly, bustling ambience – it's where the locals congregate. Back outside, a large semi-decked sun lounge is a good place to tuck into an extensive "snacky" menu or indulge in blackboard seafood specials. The dining room (remember to book first) is a striking bistro-style restaurant serving traditional favourites. If, indeed, you haven't moved on, bedrooms are simple, well-kept and comfortable.

Food serving times

Monday-Sunday:
12pm-2.30pm (3pm March-October), 6pm-9pm (7pm November-February)

Booking essential to non-residents

Prices

Meals: a la carte 18.50/32.00

16 rooms: 70.00/105.00

Typical Dishes

Salmon fishcakes
Whole baked Cornish brill
Steamed treacle sponge

Near Tresco Stores. Parking at Penzance heliport (no cars on Tresco).

017 The Gurnard's Head

Treen,
Zennor TR26 3DE
Tel.: (01736) 796928
e-mail: enquiries@gurnardshead.co.uk - Website: www.gurnardshead.co.uk

VISA 

Skinners Heligan Honey, St Austell Tribute, Skinners Betty Stoggs

If you're arriving by helicopter you'll have no problem locating this pub, thanks to the large sign boldly painted on its roof. Perfectly situated for St. Ives, Penzance and St. Just, The Gurnard's Head overlooks the rocky headland after which it is named, with its ancient hill fort, abandoned tin mines and hidden coves. Eat in either the main bar or the restaurant, surrounded by paperbacks, stacks of newspapers and colourful art. The menu offers confident cooking, with clever, carefully balanced combinations and an innovative edge, and the wine list is pleasingly unpretentious. Service is laid back, and at Sunday lunch you may be asked to share a large table with other guests. If you've stayed overnight in one of the comfortable rooms, breakfast is a treat with big pots of homemade jam, freshly squeezed orange juice and toast just like it should be. A walk along the coastal path will blow away any remaining cobwebs.

Food serving times
Monday-Sunday:
12.30pm-2.30pm, 6pm-9.30pm

Prices
Meals: a la carte
20.00/28.00

7 rooms: 50.00/92.50

Typical Dishes
Smoked mackerel paté
Grey mullet
Walnut frangipane tart

6mi West of St Ives by B3306.
Parking.

018 The Avon Inn

Avonwick TQ10 9NB
Tel.: (01364) 73475
e-mail: rosec@beeb.net - Website: www.eatoutdevon.co.uk

Sharps Doombar, Teignworthy Spring Tide

If you're in this area of South Devon, there's a good chance you've been wandering on Dartmoor, in which case, thoughts turning to sustenance, the Avon Inn is a sure-fire bet. There's nothing too fancy about the pub itself: hanging floral baskets and a small side garden without, a few exposed beams and hop bines within. It's the food that takes centre stage here. The pleasant owners make everyone feel at home, and they take a great pride in the menus on offer. These are wide-ranging with a classical Gallic base (husband Dominique is French). A daily changing blackboard menu incorporates everything from light lunches to full-on dishes featuring plenty of local seafood and fish. The mats are local too, made of the local slate.

Food serving times

Tuesday-Sunday:
12pm-2pm, 6pm-9pm

Monday:
6pm-9pm

Closed lunch Monday and dinner Sunday

Prices

Meals: a la carte
14.00/28.00

Typical Dishes

Terrine of foie gras

Seabass & red mullet fillets

Raspberry & almond sponge

1.5mi South of South Brent by minor road. Parking.

019 The Turtley Corn Mill

Avonwick TQ10 9ES

Tel.: (01364) 646100 - Fax: (01364) 646101

e-mail: mill@avonwick.net - Website: www.avonwick.net

Tamar, Jail Ale, Dartmoor IPA, Otter Bright, St Austell Tribute

Driving down to Cornwall? You could do a lot worse than take a minute's detour off the A38 to locate this refurbished 18C establishment named after one of its former owners. Smart oak and slate floors, local prints and slender bookcases, thoughtfully allied to beams and pillars from the original structure, give the place a clean, light and airy style, spacious enough to seat about 120. It's in an enviable setting, with a duck pond (including info on different breeds) and six acres of grounds bordered by the river Glazebrook. The wheel's been renovated too, though if you think you see it turning you've had too much to drink. There's a good selection of local ales, and the menu offers an ample selection for tired drivers, everything from pub classics to more up-to-date concoctions.

Food serving times

Monday-Saturday:
12pm-9.30pm

Sunday:
12pm-9pm

Closed 25 December

Prices

Meals: a la carte
22.00/30.00

Typical Dishes

Trio of fish

Pork & pepper sausages

West Country cheeses

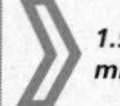

1.5mi South of South Brent by minor road. Parking.

020 Masons Arms

Branscombe EX12 3DJ
Tel.: (01297) 680300 - Fax: (01297) 680500
e-mail: reception@masonsarms.co.uk
Website: www.masonsarms.co.uk

Otter Bitter, Masons Ale, Branoc, Tribute, Teignworthy Spring Tide

The picturesque village of Branscombe is one of the joys of the East Devon coast, nestling peacefully in a deep valley right next to the sea. At its heart lies this 14C creeper-clad inn, visible to anyone up in the hills. It has a wonderfully bustling atmosphere, built around the unspoilt bar where hotel guests and locals mingle with a pint. The hearty ambience is enhanced with the surrounding ancient ships' beams, slate floors, and stone walls; a huge central fireplace is regularly used to spit-roast joints of meat at lunchtime and in the evening: modern British menus are highlighted by crab and lobster landed on Branscombe's beach. Bedrooms - some of them large and luxurious - are divided between inn and cottages opposite.

Food serving times

Monday-Sunday:
12pm-2pm, 7pm-9pm

Bar lunch

Prices

Meals: 27.50 (3 course dinner) and a la carte 16.20/25.95

22 rooms:
85.00/165.00

Typical Dishes

Carpaccio of tuna

Confit of aromatic duck leg

Cinnamon & mascarpone risotto

Between Seaton and Sidmouth; South of A3052; in the village centre. Parking.

Broadhembury

021 The Drewe Arms

Broadhembury EX14 3NF
Tel.: (01404) 841267

 **Otter Bitter, Otter Ale, Otter Bright**

Situated next to the church in the heart of a historic and picturesque cob and thatch village, this pub should be the first port of call in East Devon for any confirmed lover of fish. No typical pub grub here; instead you'll find prime local fish, simply prepared with quality ingredients to produce flavourful dishes. Open sandwiches are available, there's the occasional meat dish and you might also see a few Swedish classics on the menu thanks to the owner's heritage. Family run for years and seen by the residents of the village as their local, this popular pub also attracts outsiders so you'd be advised to book in advance. The slightly casual, if pleasant, service seems to become slicker during busy periods. The snug bar area is strictly for drinkers so grab a seat by the log fire in one of the rustically characterful dining areas, soak up the relaxed atmosphere and marvel at the unusual décor with its marine theme.

Food serving times

Monday-Saturday:
12pm-2pm, 7pm-9pm

Sunday:
12pm-2pm

Closed 25 December

Booking essential - Seafood

Prices

Meals: a la carte
20.00/50.00

Typical Dishes

Crab thermidor
Dover sole
St Emilion chocolate

5mi Northwest of Honiton by A373. Parking.

022 The Puffing Billy

Station Rd,
Exton EX3 0PR
Tel.: (01392) 877888
Website: www.eatoutdevon.com

 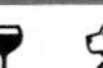  

 **Otter Bitter, Cotleigh, Doombar, Reel Ale**

If only all railway pubs were so inviting. Round the corner from Exton station and along the path beside the water, you come upon this smart, white pub. The open plan interior is decorated with original artwork: wood burner and leather sofas in the bar, banquettes in the dining room or halogen lights and exposed beams in the big airy extension. Wherever you decide to eat, the menu is a broad one, covering lunchtime sandwiches, traditional pub dishes on the blackboard, fine-dining classics and more 'informal' dishes, many of which are available in either starter or main size. If you're interested in seeing how it all happens, a few tables face the open kitchen. Your meal may even be spiced up by gunfire from the Royal Marines' barracks next door.

Food serving times

Monday-Sunday:
12pm-2.15pm, 6.30pm-9.30pm

Closed 25 December to early January

Prices

Meals: a la carte
19.15/29.40

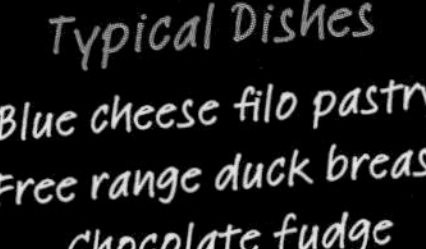

Typical Dishes

Blue cheese filo pastry
Free range duck breast
Chocolate fudge pudding

Brown tourist sign off A376 to Exmouth, 3mi from junction 30 M5. Parking.

023 The Rock Inn

Haytor Vale TQ13 9XP
Tel.: (01364) 661305 - Fax: (01364) 661242
e-mail: cg@rock-inn.co.uk - Website: www.rock-inn.co.uk

  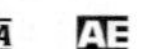  

 **Dartmoor Best, Old Speckled Hen**

Having built up an appetite walking on Dartmoor, eat to the sound of birdsong in the quintessentially English garden of this 18C coaching inn, tucked away in amongst a row of cottages in a tiny, very picturesque, rural village. From salads and sandwiches to steak and chips, the simple bar menu is a good choice for lunch; although a more elaborate restaurant menu is also available for dinner. The interior is bursting with rustic character, with several log fires, wood beams, oak furniture and flag floors. The bedrooms, quirkily named after past winners of the Grand National, are set on different levels and the sloping floors simply add to the charm. Once frequented by the quarrymen who transported granite along the railway, this pub is still popular with locals. It has been run by the same family for many years, and the green, white and black flag flying out front is a fitting symbol of the Devonshire pride to be found here.

Food serving times
Monday-Sunday:
12pm-2pm, 7pm-9.30pm
Closed 25-26 December

Prices
Meals: 20.00 (3 course dinner) and a la carte 19.00/30.00
9 rooms: 65.95/106.95

Typical Dishes
River Teign mussels
Pan-fried John Dory
Brandy snap basket

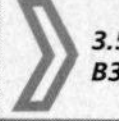

3.5mi West of Bovey Tracey by B3387. Parking.

024 The Dartmoor Union

Fore St,
Holbeton PL8 1NE
Tel.: (01752) 830288 - Fax: (01752) 830296
e-mail: info@dartmoorunion.co.uk - Website: www.dartmoorunion.co.uk

  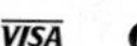

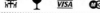

 **Union Pride, Union Jacks, Otter, Dartmoor Bitter**

Once a Victorian workhouse and later a cider press-house, the Dartmoor Union seems to have found its true vocation at last - maintaining the tradition of pulling pints brewed in its own microbrewery. For all the activity inside, the pub can be hard to spot, as there's only a discreet brass plaque on its stone façade. Its bar is spacious and smartly furnished, hung with pictures of old Holbeton: gold inscriptions on the walls – including "manners maketh man" – may or may not inspire a more philosophical tone of pub debate. The dining room to one side offers a large, seasonal selection of modern and traditional dishes including a good value set lunch. The flower-filled terrace is lovely in summer, and so are Coastguards beach and its cliff walks, a short drive away.

Food serving times
Monday-Sunday:
12pm-2pm, 6.30pm-9pm

Prices
Meals: 13.95 (3 course lunch/dinner) and a la carte 21.50/35.50

Typical Dishes
Foie gras ballotine
Fillet of wild seabass
Pears poached in red wine

10mi Southeast of Plymouth by A379 via Yealmpton (signpost). Parking.

025 The Hoops Inn

Horn's Cross EX39 5DL
Tel.: (01237) 451222 - Fax: (01237) 451247
e-mail: sales@hoopsinn.co.uk
Website: www.hoopsinn.co.uk

 VISA 

Hoops Ale, Hoops Best, Golden Pig, Sharp's Doombar

An old wayside inn since the Middle Ages, this sizeable thatched pub still has plenty to offer the passer-by, including those who need a bed for the night – four rooms in the main house are particularly comfortable, but there are a further eight "standard" ones at the back. Its handsome bar preserves its wooden settles, bowed ceiling beams, cups, tankards and porcelains, not to mention traces of the well which once supplied water for home-brewed ales. A wide-ranging menu covers everything from lunchtime ploughman's and bar favourites, through to tasty modern dishes from the à la carte, eaten in the rustic restaurant. A pretty terrace looks out over the water garden- and don't be surprised if you see a golden eagle merrily perched in the garden – the pub sometimes hold falconry days.

Food serving times
Monday-Sunday:
12pm-3pm, 7pm-9.30pm

Prices
Meals: 25.00 (3 course dinner) and a la carte 25.00/35.00

13 rooms: 65.00/95.00

Typical Dishes
Moules marinières
Roast rack of lamb
Hoops pavlova

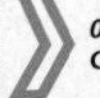

0.5mi West on A39 going to Clovelly. Parking.

026 Bickley Mill

Stoneycombe,
Kingskerswell TQ12 5LN
Tel.: (01803) 873201 - Fax: (01803) 875129
e-mail: info@bickleymill.co.uk - Website: www.bickleymill.co.uk

VISA AE MC

Otter Ale and 1 Teignworthy Ale (Spring Tide, Old Moggie, Reel Ale)

Hidden away in the sleepy village of Stoneycombe lies this converted flour mill dating back to the 13th century. A Free House since 1971, when it was adapted to allow for guest bedrooms, as much thought has been given to the outside of this establishment as the inside. The first thing that strikes you on arrival is the pleasant garden with its large decked terrace; a delightful area in which to soak up the sun on a summer's day. This is a pub for all seasons, however, and there are numerous cosy areas inside ideal in which to dine when dark wintry nights draw in. Although this pub has been modernised and has contemporary art hanging on the walls, it still manages to retain its rustic charm and character with features such as its open fire, stone walls and exposed beams. Pub staples have also been given a makeover here; the mash with your sausages might contain cheddar and chives or your salmon might be cured with beetroot.

Food serving times

Monday-Thursday:
12pm-2pm, 6.30pm-9pm

Friday-Saturday:
12pm-2pm, 6.30pm-9.30pm

Sunday: 12pm-8pm

Closed 25 and 27-28 December

Prices

Meals: 10.00 (2 course lunch) and a la carte 18.00/26.00

9 rooms: 55.00/70.00

Typical Dishes

Devilled kidneys

Smoked haddock fishcakes

Espresso pannacotta

3mi South of Newton Abbot by A380 and minor road east. Parking.

027 The Masons Arms Inn

Knowstone EX36 4RY
Tel.: (01398) 341231
e-mail: dodsonmasonsarms@aol.com
Website: www.masonsarmsdevon.co.uk

 **Cotleigh 'Tawny' Bitter**

In the years following his celebrated stint as head chef at The Waterside Inn, country life beckoned for Mark Dodson and his family, and the residents of this secluded Devon village in the foothills of Exmoor have had reason to thank their lucky stars ever since. Dine beneath a beautiful ceiling mural, on food that is clearly both sophisticated and precise. Dishes come attractively presented but never over-wrought and the flavours are pronounced and assured. The excellent quality of the food is further complemented by the charming service. Not surprisingly, booking is essential. Built in the 13th century by the masons who also constructed the village church, the small interior of this pretty, yellow-washed, thatched inn is as full of character as its exterior. There's a tiny beamed bar with inglenook fireplace where the locals gather to drink, a lounge with comfy sofas in which to recline and a rear dining room.

Food serving times

Tuesday-Saturday:
12pm-2pm, 7pm-9pm

Sunday:
12pm-2pm

Booking essential

Prices

Meals: 29.50 (3 course lunch Sunday only) and a la carte 25.00/36.00

Typical Dishes

Risotto of smoked haddock
Roulade of pork belly
Amaretto parfait

7mi Southeast of South Molton by A361. Opposite the village church. Parking.

028 The Dartmoor Inn

Moorside,
Lydford EX20 4AY
Tel.: (01822) 820221 - Fax: (01822) 820494
e-mail: info@dartmoorinn.com - Website: www.dartmoorinn.com

Otter Ale, Dartmoor Best Bitter

There's something refreshingly different about a pub which politely asks its customers to turn off the modern menace that is their mobile phone, and although not necessarily the most picturesque of buildings on the outside, this roadside dining pub on the edges of Dartmoor certainly provides an experience above the average when you venture in out of the cold. Gently rustic, with an intimate fireside bar, there are also several dining rooms with linen-laid tables and prints on the walls, and a sheltered terrace to the rear. Keenly run, the seasonal menu serves modern dishes with a Mediterranean influence, whilst a cheaper, more informal 'Easy Dining' menu is also served in both of the bars. After eating, browse in the boutique for a memento of your visit. If you are staying over, three large and stylish bedrooms with modern colour schemes and distinctive beds provide a good night's sleep.

Food serving times

Tuesday-Saturday:
12pm-2.30pm, 6pm-9.30pm

Sunday:
12pm-2.30pm

Prices

Meals: a la carte
18.00/35.00

3 rooms:
115.00/125.00

Typical Dishes

Home-cured corned beef
Roast Aylesbury duck
Steamed ginger pudding

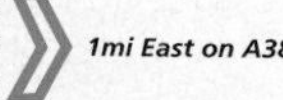
1mi East on A386. Parking.

029 Church House Inn

Village Rd,
Marldon TQ3 1SL
Tel.: (01803) 558279 - Fax: (01803) 664185

 **Dartmoor Best, Otter Ale, Fuller's London Pride, Bass**

Visitors to Torbay might like to make an excursion from the delights of Torquay and Paignton to this nearby, attractive inn by the church in Marldon: the pub itself is well sign-posted. It's a listed, whitewashed Georgian structure of 14C origins, and its characterful aspect continues inside with beams, rough stone walls and flagstone floors. There's a large central bar with adjoining rooms which tend to be used for dining but you can eat anywhere: you'll find plenty of drinkers mingling with diners. The bustling atmosphere doesn't faze the waiting staff: there's an invariably friendly service. Blackboard menus offer plenty of choice from the traditional to the more modern, with a guarantee that the vegetables have come from the village's allotment. Dishes on offer might include pan-fried king prawns in Indian spiced butter, slow cooked shoulder of lamb, or roast monkfish on sautéed leeks with a saffron and mussel sauce.

Food serving times
Monday-Sunday:
12pm-2pm, 6.30pm-9.30pm

Prices
Meals: a la carte
22.00/30.00

Typical Dishes
Venison sausage
Pan-fried duck breast
White chocolate fondant

Off A380 between Torquay and Paignton - well signed. Parking.

030 **The White Hart**

Church St,
Modbury PL21 0QW
Tel.: (01548) 831561
e-mail: info@whitehart-inn.co.uk

Bass, Otter (local beer)

This traditional black-and-white fronted pub leaves behind all traces of its coaching inn heritage once you step through the front door. This is most definitely a modern dining pub, but one where the locals happily fit in clutching a pint at the bar, especially in winter with the log fire burning brightly and ladies relaxing in the deep leather Chesterfields. The rest of the pub is given over to the enjoyment of food. Smart linen napkins on large wooden tables herald innovative dishes listed on a vast A3 sheet. The wide choice has a modern bistro/brasserie feel – particularly impressive is the great value fixed price lunch and early evening menu. Parties are catered for in the first floor Assembly Rooms. Word of warning: watch out for the well if you find yourself over-refreshed. It's covered with glass but might still surprise the unwary! Simply furnished bedrooms have modern facilities.

Food serving times

Tuesday-Sunday: 12pm-3.30pm, 6.30pm-9.30pm

Closed 25 December, 1 January

Prices

Meals: 12.95 (3 course lunch) and a la carte 21.00/29.85

5 rooms: 35.00/50.00

Typical Dishes

Crab and crayfish tian
Duo of Wilkinson lamb
Chocolate truffle cake

On A379 between Kingsbridge and Yealmpton. Public car park at rear.

031 The Ship Inn

Noss Mayo PL8 1EW

Tel.: (01752) 872387 - Fax: (01752) 873294

e-mail: ship@nossmayo.com - Website: www.nossmayo.com

 **Summerskills Tamar, Princetown Jail Ale, St Austell Tribute, Butcombe Blonde**

Time and tide wait for no man, so get yourself down to The Ship Inn, pronto, but be careful. Arguably one of the most picturesque, peaceful spots in South Devon, those foolhardy souls who park on the beach, or 'Noss Hard', of the Yealm estuary at Noss Mayo might later choke on their calamari as they catch sight of their car floating past at high tide. Floating vehicles aside, the upside to this location is, of course, the wonderful waterside views, and the large outside patio and first floor decked terrace are both perfect for idling away the hours boat and people-watching. The oldest part of this beamed pub dates from the 1700s, and the interior is full of character, with wooden floors, open fires and a large collection of local knick-knacks and pictures lining the walls. Friendly staff serve a wide range of dishes including local seafood and fresh fish from a daily-changing menu.

Food serving times

Monday-Sunday:
12pm-9.30pm

Prices

Meals: a la carte
20.00/30.00

Typical Dishes

Goat's cheese & apple tart
Pan-fried duck
Chocolate & raspberry tart

Signed off A379 10.5mi South-east of Plymouth; turn right into B3186. Restricted parking, particularly at high tide.

032 The Harris Arms

Portgate EX20 4PZ
Tel.: (01566) 783331 - Fax: (01566) 783359
e-mail: whiteman@powernet.co.uk - Website: www.theharrisarms.co.uk

 **Sharp's Doombar, Exe Valley Dobbs Best Bitter**

Much more than just a stopping off point on the way down to Cornwall, The Harris Arms' reputation attracts 'locals' from Okehampton to Tavistock, Launceston to Bodmin. The owners of this traditional 16C pub offer a very friendly welcome and have helped create a warm, relaxed ambience with their hands-on style. Award-winning winemakers previously based in New Zealand and France, it stands to reason that their wine list is excellent, with bottles personally selected and fairly priced. It's not only the wine that impresses here though. The aroma of home cooking and spices fills the air and robust, hearty, confidently flavoured food shows off the chefs' artistic talent. The owners pride themselves on local and seasonal cooking and have a regularly changing specials board, whilst puddings are proudly homemade. Sit in the front bar or in the back extension overlooking the decked terrace, and keep an eye out for Reg the cat.

Food serving times

Tuesday-Saturday:
12pm-2pm, 6.30pm-9pm

Sunday:
12pm-2pm, 7pm-9pm

Closed 26 December, 1 January

Closed dinner Sunday in winter

Prices

Meals: 15.00 (3 course lunch Tuesday-Saturday) and a la carte 18.95/25.00

Typical Dishes

Home-cured gravadlax
Roast breast of Devon chicken
Sticky toffee pudding

3mi East of Launceston by A388 and side road. Parking.

033 Jack in the Green Inn

London Rd,
Rockbeare EX5 2EE
Tel.: (01404) 822240 - Fax: (01404) 823540
e-mail: info@jackinthegreen.uk.com - Website: www.jackinthegreen.uk.com

We most liked

Otter Ale, Cotleigh 'Tawny' Bitter, Yellow Hammer, Butcombe

Don't let the unremarkable outside appearance of this pub put you off; the real reason for coming here is the food. In the traditional main bar, with its carpets and beams, you'll find proper, value-for-money pub favourites like steak and chips or sausage and mash chalked up on blackboards, and there's plenty of space in the extension to serve the hordes who have heard about the hearty home-cooking to be had here. In the older, low-ceilinged restaurant you can savour more sophisticated, modern dishes from the à la carte menu, rubbing shoulders with the local businessmen who lunch at the linen-laid tables before catching a flight at nearby Exeter airport. Food obviously matters to the owners of this efficiently-run pub; ingredients are sourced from local suppliers, menus are dictated by the seasons, every dish is well-presented and they even produce monthly recipe cards so that regulars can reproduce their favourite dishes at home.

Food serving times

Monday-Saturday:
12pm-2pm, 6pm-9.30pm

Sunday:
12pm-9pm

Closed 25 December to 6 January

Prices

Meals: 25.00 (3 course lunch/dinner) and a la carte 24.00/39.50

Typical Dishes

Caramelised belly pork
Roast rump of lamb
Rhubarb crumble

6.25mi East of Exeter by A30.
Parking at the back.

034 The Sandy Park Inn

Sandypark TQ13 8JW
Tel.: (01647) 433267
e-mail: enquiries@sandyparkinn.co.uk
Website: www.sandyparkinn.co.uk

Otter, St Austell Tribute, O'Hanlon's Yellow Hammer and 1 guest beer

They say that good things come in small packages and could well have been talking about The Sandy Park Inn. Situated on the edge of Dartmoor, five minutes drive from Castle Drogo, this 17C thatched inn is full of character, with flagged floors, open fires and heavy beams. Its three rooms are on the small side, however, and in winter you can expect to be shoulder to shoulder with your fellow pub-goers, keeping one another warm. In summer, the lawned hillside garden is a delight. Modern, sophisticated dishes are made with ingredients sourced from local suppliers and the blackboard menu is displayed above the fireplace. Lighter snacks, sandwiches and soups are also available at lunchtimes. Bedrooms here are small and cosy and you may or may not think they've got their priorities right, depending on your sensibilities; some rooms do not have ensuites, yet they all have flat screen TVs.

Food serving times
Monday-Saturday:
11am-11pm
Sunday:
12pm-10.30pm

Prices
Meals: a la carte
20.00/26.00
5 rooms: 60.00/98.00

Typical Dishes
Home-made soup
Braised lamb shank
Local cheeses

5mi South of A30 from roundabout at Whiddon Down by A382. Parking.

035 The Tower Inn

Church Rd,
Slapton TQ7 2PN

Tel.: (01548) 580216
e-mail: towerinn@slapton.org - Website: www.thetowerinn.com

Butcombe Bitter, St Austell Tribute, Badger Tanglefoot

Luckily this pub is signposted because, tucked away up a narrow lane in a corner of the quaint little village, you might otherwise miss it. Built in 1347 as cottages for the men who were working on the chantry, much of the tower still overlooks its rear walled garden. The interior is everything you would expect to find in a proper English pub; several cosy adjoining rooms with stone walls, beams, flag floors and, for people of height, dangerously low ceilings. Separate dinner and lunch menus offer wholesome, hearty food including daily specials and an appealing array of traditional puddings. This pub is a great base from which to explore the local area and its history, so stay in one of the simple annex bedrooms and explore the Slapton Ley nature reserve and the misleadingly-named Slapton Sands (they're covered in pebbles), where American troops practised for the D-Day landings in 1944 in the ill-fated Exercise Tiger.

Food serving times

Monday-Saturday:
12pm-2pm, 7pm-9pm

Sunday:
12pm-2pm

Closed Monday in winter

Prices

Meals: a la carte
20.00/30.00

3 rooms: 45.00/75.00

Typical Dishes

Locally smoked prawns
Pheasant breasts
Apple and rhubarb crumble

6mi Southwest of Dartmouth by A379; signed between Dartmouth and Kingsbridge. Parking with exceptionally narrow access.

036 **The Chasers**

Stoke Road,
Stokeinteignhead TQ12 4QS
Tel.: (01626) 873 670 - Fax: (01626) 873 670
e-mail: enquiries@thechasers.co.uk - Website: www.thechasers.co.uk

We most liked

 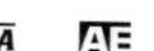 

Teignworthy - Spring Tide and other varieties, Bass, Flowers IPA

This traditional, thatched 16C inn is found in the tiny, remote village of Stokeinteignhead, nestled in a quiet valley between the holiday resort of Torquay and the market town of Newton Abbott. The contemporary pub sign outside hints at a modern makeover – and inside you'll find that the original floors have been sanded down, and that modern sofas in creams and chocolates sit waiting to be lounged in. Peruse the menu in the warm, homely glow of the fire before being shown to your table. The young owners are an experienced couple with a reputation for providing quality food, and local suppliers are proudly listed. Menus here offer great flexibility, with 'The Light List' provided at lunch, and some dishes at dinner available in both starter and main sized portions. Try roasted monkfish with lentils and bacon or roasted baby artichokes and pepper salad with goats' cheese. Weekends tend to be busy, so book ahead.

Food serving times

Tuesday-Thursday:
12pm-2pm, 7pm-9pm

Friday-Saturday and Bank Holiday Monday:
12pm-2.30pm, 7pm-9.30pm

Sunday: 12pm-2.30pm

Closed 26 December and last 2 weeks of February

Prices

Meals: 15.95 (3 course lunch) and a la carte 22.00/29.50

Typical Dishes

Potted Crediton duck
Brixham day-boat seabass
Honey pannacotta

5.5mi North of Torquay by A379.
Parking.

037 The Tradesman's Arms

Stokenham TQ7 2SZ
Tel.: (01548) 580313 - Fax: (01548) 580657
e-mail: nick@thetradesmansarms.com
Website: www.thetradesmansarms.com

Local breweries - Eddystone, Devon Pride; also Brakspear Bitter and 3 guest ales

The owners of this pretty 14C part thatched pub learned the tricks of their trade in Buckinghamshire before migrating to this little village in the beautiful South Hams area of Devon, close to the coast and to the famous freshwater ley nature reserve. The sea air must suit them, because they've now made their mark here too, and the pub is popular with locals, tourists and passing tradesmen alike. You can sit in the main beamed bar with its paisley carpets and stone fireplace or in the redecorated, linen-clad dining area, but on sunny days, the seat of choice is at a picnic table in the terrace garden, overlooking the village field and its resident sheep. Service may not necessarily always come with a smile, but the menu offers good, filling pub favourites like steak and kidney pie or sausage and mash, plus specials of meat and locally caught fish. It can get busy, so booking is advised.

Food serving times

Monday-Sunday:
12pm-2.30pm, 6.45pm-9.30pm

Booking essential

Prices

Meals: a la carte
17.95/25.00

Typical Dishes

Mackerel paté
Roast duck breast
Chocolate & hazelnut brownie

On A379 between Kingsbridge and Dartmouth. Parking.

038 The Kings Arms

Dartmouth Rd,
Strete TQ6 0RW
Tel.: (01803) 770377
Website: www.kingsarms-dartmouth.co.uk

Adnams, Fuller's London Pride, Otter Ale

From being slightly rundown – to put it kindly – The Kings Arms has picked itself up in fine style. A white-painted roadside pub with a distinctive balcony, it's easy to spot as you drive up, but this is not its best side, and anyone who has spent a slow, sunny lunchtime in the garden or the pleasant rear terrace is sure to agree. The bar itself, decorated with old local pictures, is fine but small; it's worth going for the extra comforts of the dining room. Two window tables are the prime spots, but bare beams and seats in nautical blue give the whole place a nice, fresh feel. Lunches are slightly lighter but, even here, fish and chips with mushy peas is the odd one out in a menu of modern classics. Dinners make even more use of local, seasonal ingredients, including Devon seafood, meats and cheeses. Fresh, unfussy flavours.

Food serving times

Monday-Sunday:
12pm-2pm, 6.30pm-9pm

Closed Monday December-February

Prices

Meals: a la carte
23.25/33.00

Typical Dishes

Seared Beesands scallops
Roast fillet of cod
Chilli chocolate tart

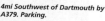

4mi Southwest of Dartmouth by A379. Parking.

039 The Steam Packet Inn

St Peter's Quay, Totnes TQ9 5EW
Tel.: (01803) 863880 - Fax: (01803) 862754
e-mail: steampacket@buccaneer.co.uk
Website: www.steampacketinn-totnes.co.uk

VISA AE MC

Otter Bright, Courage Best, Butcombe, Jail Ale

There's been a pub here since the turn of the 19th Century, delightfully sited on the quay in the centre of Totnes, where boats still tie up and bobble on the gentle tides. Much original charm is retained in the cosy, rustic bar with its rafters and wood floors; peer deep and you'll find locals hidden away in the nooks and crannies. But it's the large conservatory overlooking the River Dart and its huge terrace that people come for. This is an idyllic spot to tuck into something off the versatile menu that offers simple pub dishes as well as more adventurous and interesting modern alternatives. Ingredients are as local as the herbs from chef's kitchen garden. There are four bedrooms where relaxing river views go hand-in-hand with clean, fresh designs.

Food serving times

Monday-Sunday:
12pm-2.30pm, 6pm-9.30pm

Prices

Meals: a la carte
16.00/24.00

4 rooms: 59.50/79.50

Typical Dishes

Buffalo mozzarella
Thai green curried monkfish
Banoffee Knickerbocker Glory

At the bottom of the hill by the river. Parking.

040 Rose & Crown

Market St,
Yealmpton PL8 2EB
Tel.: (01752) 880223 - Fax: (01752) 881058
e-mail: info@theroseandcrown.co.uk

 **Sharp's Doombar, Fuller's London Pride, Courage Best, Otter Ale, IPA, 6X**

It's easy to whiz through South Hams villages on your way to the delights of Noss Mayo, Newton Ferrers or Burgh Island. But put the brakes on in Yealmpton, and check out this neat, modernised pub on a corner, not least for its attractive rear walled terrace with canopies and water feature. Inside, enclosed by rough stone walls, is a big central bar and a spacious, open plan design that allows for casual seating areas with family-sized leather sofas, and places to eat with large benches and tables or a more formal dining space. Here you can tuck into modern 'restaurant' dishes with a Pacific Rim edge, along with a good value fixed priced lunch menu, washed down by Devon ales or something off the accessible wine list. If your taste is for something a bit more fishy, then you can step outside the pub to the Seafood Restaurant where a good range of shellfish is on offer.

Food serving times
Monday-Sunday:
12pm-2pm, 6.30pm-9pm

Prices
Meals: 9.95 (3 course lunch) and a la carte 18.00/27.00

Typical Dishes
Oriental marinated duck
North Atlantic monkfish tails
Chocolate parfait

7mi Southeast of Plymouth by A379. Parking.

Dave Young 2006

041 The Bull

34 East St,
Bridport DT6 3LF

Tel.: (01308) 422878 - Fax: (01308) 426872
e-mail: info@thebullhotel.co.uk - Website: www.thebullhotel.co.uk

Otter Ales

From the moment you spot its striking blue façade, it is apparent that the owners have taken the 16C, Grade II listed Bull by the horns and given it a 21C facelift. Sumptuous bedrooms are decorated in highly individual styles, with signature wallpaper and antique furniture, some of it sourced from Parisian flea markets. Add top quality bathrooms, and organic toiletries and you can see why the owners like to refer to it now as a boutique hotel. They've certainly hit the bull's eye with the cooking. The Bull serves a simple, regularly-changing menu sourced from local produce, and cooking is confident without being over-fussy. Breakfast is an impressive affair, whilst Saturday market brunch is a more laid-back occasion. Sit at individually-designed, locally-made tables, each topped with a different wood. The large front window overlooks Bridport's main street, whilst the booth at the back is more secluded.

Food serving times
Monday-Sunday:
12.30pm-3pm, 6.30pm-9pm

Prices
Meals: a la carte
15.95/28.00

13 rooms:
50.00/180.00

Typical Dishes
Fresh Cornish sardines
Chargrilled sirloin steak
Fresh lemon mousse cake

In town centre on South side of main street. Parking.

042 The Stapleton Arms

Church Hill,
Buckhorn Weston SP8 5HS
Tel.: (01963) 370396 - Fax: (01963) 370396
e-mail: relax@thestapletonarms.com - Website: www.thestapletonarms.com

  VISA AE MC

Timothy Taylor's Landlord, Butcombe Bitter and 3 guest ales

If you are carrying on down the A303 towards Devon and Cornwall having admired the engineering feat that is Stonehenge, you might do well to stop off for a meal in The Stapleton Arms. It's situated in pretty Buckhorn Weston, a village with its own historical claim to fame: a mention in the Magna Carta. There's nothing ancient about the interior of this pub though- it's up-to date, smart and stylish with an elegant dining room. This modernity hasn't scared off the locals though-and you'll find your muddy boots, dogs and children are all similarly welcome. On a sunny day, sit out the front on the terrace or in the rear garden. With a wide-ranging menu, this pub serves some traditional food although you may have to look for it amongst other dishes with more of a Mediterranean influence. Comfortable contemporary rooms with good facilities are available, with underfloor heating a nice touch for cold feet on wintry mornings.

Food serving times

Monday-Sunday:
12pm-3pm, 6pm-10pm

Prices

Meals: a la carte
18.50/25.50

4 rooms: 72.00/120.00

Typical Dishes

Baked buffalo mozzarella

Seared black bream fillets

Vanilla pannacotta

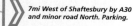

7mi West of Shaftesbury by A30 and minor road North. Parking.

Corscombe

043 The Fox Inn

Corscombe DT2 0NS

Tel.: (01935) 891330 - Fax: (01935) 891330

Website: www.thefoxinn.co.uk

 **Exmoor Ale, Butcombe Bitter and occasional guest ales - Taunton Ale, Youngs**

Sticky soot, built up over time, lies ingrained on the walls above the fireplaces here. It's one of many endearing features of this mightily charming thatched 17C pub, which boasts several fascinating areas. Two stone floored main bar rooms are intimate and dripping with rural ambience, typified by pews, slate-clad bar and scrubbed pine furniture. Country style imbues the extremely characterful breakfast room, where the first meal of the day is cooked on the Aga; look out for the dog that rests there. A mellow old conservatory has a large table constructed from one strip of oak felled in the 1987 storms. And the food? Dine on well-judged traditional dishes using the best seasonal produce, including well-renowned blackboard fish specials, washed down with something from the reasonably-priced wine list. There are cosy bedrooms, too, endowed with homely charm.

Food serving times

Monday-Sunday:
12pm-2pm, 7pm-9pm

Prices

Meals: a la carte 20.00/27.00

4 rooms: 55.00/100.00

Typical Dishes

Panfried wood pigeon breast

Spiced English duck breast

Home-made lemon treacle tart

3.5mi Northeast of Beaminster. Parking.

044 Acorn Inn

28 Fore St,
Evershot DT2 0JW
Tel.: (01935) 83228 - Fax: (01935) 83707
e-mail: stay@acorn-inn.co.uk - Website: www.acorn-inn.co.uk

  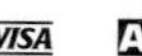 

 **Draymans, Port Stout, Abbot Ale, Fuller's London Pride**

This neat 16C inn in sleepy Evershot still feels like a proper village local, with friendly neighbourhood rivalries kindled at the skittle alley and cooled off with pints of Devon guest ales and ciders, but the oak-panelled main bar, warmed by an open fire in winter, also attracts diners from further afield. Two further rooms in pale wood are just for dining. British pub favourites appear alongside classic dishes with a light modern touch and plenty of local produce; a blackboard menu lists daily changing seafood specials. Recently refurbished bedrooms with designer touches including plasma televisions and separate breakfast room with country style feel.

Food serving times
Monday-Sunday:
12pm-2pm, 7pm-9.30pm

Prices
Meals: a la carte
24.00/34.00

10 rooms:
155.00/170.00

Typical Dishes
Roasted aubergine
Rump of Dorset lamb
Honey & pistachio burnt cream

7mi Northeast of Beaminster by B3163. Parking.

045 The Museum Inn

Farnham DT11 8DE

Tel.: (01725) 516261 - Fax: (01725) 516988
e-mail: enquiries@museuminn.co.uk
Website: www.museuminn.co.uk

Ringwood Best, Timothy Taylor's Landlord, Hop Back, Summer Lightning

Standing at the main crossroads of the village, the original, part-thatched Museum Inn has long since received an addition here and an extension there, but the pub as it stands today seems not only smart, bright and well-tended, but seamlessly characterful too. Diners have the choice of four dining rooms, furnished with antique dressers and scrubbed tables and decorated with curiosities from old paintings to stags' heads, but as they don't take bookings here, you may be asked to take a seat in the bar first before heading through for classic-contemporary dishes like chicken parfait, duck confit and haddock and mustard risotto. Spacious, quite luxuriously styled bedrooms really are a cut above the average inn; if you don't feel quite ready for bed, the residents lounge might tempt you with a cosy fire and plenty of reading matter.

Food serving times

Monday-Sunday:
12pm-2pm, 7pm-9.30pm

Closed 25 December, dinner 31 December, 1 January

Prices

Meals: a la carte 28.00/31.00

8 rooms: 85.00/150.00

Typical Dishes

Goat's cheese ravioli

Pan-fried John Dory fillets

Baked banoffee cheesecake

7.5mi Northeast of Blandford Forum by A354. Parking.

046 The Brace of Pheasants

Plush DT2 7RQ
Tel.: (01300) 348357 - Fax: (01300) 348959
e-mail: bennett.family@btinternet.com
Website: www.braceofpheasants.co.uk

  VISA 

Butcombe Traditional, Ringwood Best, Otter Bitter, Sharp's Doom-bar and Eden Ale, Palmers Copper Ale, Weymouth Bitter

The Giant of Cerne Abbas is not much more than a (giant's) stone-throw from this gloriously secluded 16C thatched inn, which revels in a pleasant rural setting midway between Dorchester and Blandford Forum. In keeping with the surroundings and exterior, the pub – formerly two thatched cottages and a smithy - has a cosy, characterful interior, dominated by the large bar where locals gather to sup pints or partake of the robust, tasty cooking, which has earned a solid local reputation. The same is served in a slightly more formal parlour, or dining area for families. There's a pretty rear garden for summer use, with the woods and bridleways of the Piddle valley beyond.

Food serving times

Monday-Sunday:
12.30pm-2.30pm, 7.30pm-9.30pm

Closed 25 December

Prices

Meals: a la carte
20.00/30.00

Typical Dishes
Warm chicken liver salad
Herb-roast loin of red deer
Almond tart & raspberries

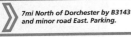

7mi North of Dorchester by B3143 and minor road East. Parking.

047 The Old Passage Inn

Passage Rd, Arlingham GL2 7JR
Tel.: (01452) 740547 - Fax: (01452) 741871
e-mail: oldpassage@ukonline.co.uk
Website: www.fishattheoldpassageinn.co.uk

VISA AE MC

Wickwar Severn Bore

Originality is the keyword to this bright green painted family-run establishment, perched in an isolated spot where the Severn starts to twist and turn. Any resemblance to a cosy, small-town country inn ends at the dining room, where gastronomic ambitions spiral off on a modern tangent. All efforts go into an accomplished seafood menu; cooking is bold, generous and suitably rustic. A small private dining area at the front can be booked for special occasions. The three bedrooms are funky. They're called Red Mullet, Yellow Finned Tuna and Green Lipped Mussel, and they're all strikingly modern, bright, hi-tec and highly individual and with a kingsize bed. Views of the Severn from the restaurant and rooms.

Food serving times

Tuesday-Saturday:
12pm-2pm, 6.30pm-9pm

Sunday:
12pm-2pm

Closed 24-30 December

Prices

Meals: a la carte
22.50/32.50

3 rooms: 65.00/110.00

Typical Dishes

Diver scallops
Roast John Dory fillet
Single Gloucester cheese

2.5mi Northwest of Frampton on Severn; on the banks of the River Severn. Parking.

048 Village Pub

Barnsley GL7 5EE
Tel.: (01285) 740421 - Fax: (01285) 740925
e-mail: info@thevillagepub.co.uk
Website: www.thevillagepub.co.uk

 **Wadworth 6X, Hook Norton 'Hooky', Donnington 'BB'**

Set in the charming Cotswold village of Barnsley, this part 17C pub is appealingly relaxing, with its stone walls and cosy open fire-warmed interior. The five connecting rooms, with their oak and flagstone floors are furnished with period pieces, and the specialist painting effects on the walls adds a spark of individuality. The rear terrace is a great place to while away a sunny summer afternoon. Regularly changing menus are a cut above your typical pub grub, with dishes involving pigeon, quail, squid or rabbit, lording it alongside the ubiquitous steak and chips or chicken breast. Homemade bread accompanies all dishes, and meats are local and organic where possible, with suppliers listed on the menus. Prices remain attractively low and service is efficient. If you plan to stay overnight, slumber stylishly in one of six elegant, beamed bedrooms containing either a four poster or a Victorian iron bedstead.

Food serving times

Monday-Thursday: 12pm-2.30pm, 7pm-9.30pm

Friday-Saturday: 12pm-2.30pm (3pm Sat), 7pm-10pm

Sunday: 12pm-3pm, 7pm-9.30pm

Room rates include continental breakfast

Prices

Meals: a la carte 20.00/29.00

7 rooms: 75.00/150.00

Typical Dishes

White bean soup
Roast hake fillet
Selection of cheeses

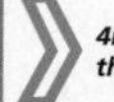

4mi North East of Cirencester, on the B4425. Parking.

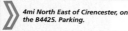

Bourton-on-the-Hill

049 Horse & Groom

Bourton-on-the-Hill GL56 9AQ
Tel.: (01386) 700413 - Fax: (01386) 700413
e-mail: greenstocks@horseandgroom.info
Website: www.horseandgroom.info

Regularly changing selection including - Everard's, Hook Norton, Greene King, Purity Brewing

Be careful getting to the Horse and Groom. It's on a busy main road (especially in the summer) adjacent to a dangerous corner. That said, and precautions taken, this is a lovely 18C former coaching inn built of attractively yellowing Cotswold stone, with a neat little terraced garden to the rear that has a veg and fruit patch on view. Inside, you'll feel instantly at home in a big, welcoming bar that shows its age with pride in the form of weathered beams and exposed stone. Tables are scattered hither and thither, and a friendly team is on hand to take care of your order: the owners know all about what makes a good pub – their parents run the delightful Howard Arms in Ilmington. Blackboard menus at the Horse and Groom change constantly, sometimes twice a day. Expect to see proper English cooking with good Cotswold produce setting the pace. It's a busy place, so book in advance. Evolving bedrooms are being upgraded and modernised.

Food serving times

Monday:
7pm-9pm

Tuesday-Saturday:
12pm-2pm, 7pm-9pm
(9.30pm Friday & Saturday)

Sunday: 12pm-2pm

Closed 25 December

Prices

Meals: a la carte
18.00/28.00

5 rooms: 70.00/125.00

Typical Dishes

Home-made ravioli
Dexter beef pastie
Vanilla pannacotta

1mi West of Moreton in the Marsh by A44. Parking.

050 The Gumstool Inn

Calcot GL8 8YJ
Tel.: (01666) 890391 - Fax: (01666) 890394
e-mail: reception@calcotmanor.co.uk
Website: www.calcotmanor.co.uk

Cotswold Way, Butcombe Blonde, Sharp's IPA, Wickwar Long John Silver

Following refurbishment, The Gumstool Inn has a new, contemporary look. Art decorates the walls, cosy leather armchairs come in chocolate and orange to match the comforting décor, and the log fires, dark wood furniture and flag flooring help retain a country pub feel. An attractive stone building set within the grounds of the Calcot Manor Hotel, the pub is served by the same kitchen as the Conservatory restaurant, hence the advice to book ahead. Choice is the byword here; seasonal monthly menus blending British classics with more international flavours offer more variety than most, there is an excellent selection of wine by the glass and even a choice of portion sizes. Equally, you can dine inside or out - the pleasant outdoor dining area is particularly popular with families. A gumstool, in case you were wondering, was a middle age instrument of torture, used to duck rude, loudmouthed people into the pond. You have been warned.

Food serving times

Monday-Sunday:
12pm-2pm, 7pm-9pm

Booking essential

Prices

Meals: a la carte
20.00/50.00

Typical Dishes

Welsh Rarebit cheese soufflé

Venison steaks 'au poivre'

Italian walnut tart

3.5mi West of Tetbury on A4135, in grounds of Calcot Manor Hotel. Parking.

South West • Gloucestershire

051 The Beehive

1-3 Montpellier Villas,
Cheltenham GL50 2XE
Tel.: (01242) 702270 - Fax: (01242) 269330
e-mail: beehive@slak.co.uk - Website: www.slak.co.uk

VISA AE

 **Goffs Jouster, Pedigree, Butcombe; also Black Rat cider**

The quiet, residential Georgian Montpelier area of Cheltenham may not be the first place you'd think of for locating a down-to-earth pub, especially one tucked away on a corner, but it's worth going that extra mile to check out the Beehive. Though expanded, its original cosy green and frosted glass façade is still present. Not a lot has changed inside, either: rough wooden floorboards, a bar and various settles, benches and large wood tables, along with a wood burner and even a slot machine, give it a genuine unaffected 'proper' pub feel. There's a separate snug, above which is a former Masonic lodge hall, where more dining tables are set. Locally renowned, the cooking here is good and honest, not really traditional pub fare, but in the up-to-date restaurant league.

Food serving times

Monday-Tuesday:
12pm-2.30pm, 6pm-9pm

Wednesday-Saturday:
12pm-2.30pm, 6pm-10pm

Sunday:
12pm-3.30pm

Closed 25 December

Prices

Meals: 15.00 (3 course Sunday lunch) and a la carte 20.00/27.50

Typical Dishes

Steak tartare with toast
Confit of duck
Chocolate & raspberry tart

South of town centre; off south-side of Montpellier Terrace. Some on road parking or the Bath Road car park.

052 Eight Bells Inn

Church St, Chipping Campden GL55 6JG

Tel.: (01386) 840371 - Fax: (01386) 841669

e-mail: neilhargreaves@bellinn.fsnet.co.uk

Website: www.eightbellsinn.co.uk

  VISA 

Hook Norton Best Bitter, Goffs Jouster, Purity Brewery Co Ubu, Wye Valley

Situated in the old wool merchants' town of Chipping Campden, with its historic high street, this pub is a great base from which to explore the Cotswolds. Dating from the 14th century when it accommodated the stonemasons building the nearby St. James' church, it gets its name from the fact that it was used to store the bells for the church tower, and even has a 'priest hole' rumoured to lead underground to the church. The pub was redecorated in 2006 after a fire, but has lost none of its charm, with a beamed bar area and stone fireplaces. The menu offers an appealing blend of contemporary dishes, with a choice of specials chalked up on a board. If you're saving yourself for an evening meal, and you want a lighter bite for lunch, a sandwich and a pint will go down just as well in the terraced garden. If you're staying over, you'll find the bedrooms simply decorated and well looked after.

Food serving times

Monday-Thursday:
12pm-2pm, 6.30pm-9pm

Friday-Sunday:
12pm-2.30pm, 6.30pm-9.30pm

Closed 25 December

Prices

Meals: a la carte 20.00/30.00

7 rooms: 55.00/95.00

Typical Dishes

Grilled sardines

Stuffed English pork fillet

Summer pudding

In centre of town. Unlimited parking on road.

053 The Wyndham Arms

Clearwell GL16 8JT

Tel.: (01594) 833666 - Fax: (01594) 836450

e-mail: res@thewyndhamhotel.co.uk

Website: www.thewyndhamhotel.co.uk

 **Freeminer Fair Trade, Wyndham Brew**

Visitors are spoiled for choice in this part of the Forest of Dean: the Clearwell Caves and medieval Castle are close at hand, while the Perrygrove Railway is just up the road. Paying a visit to this attractive village inn with 13C origins fits in seamlessly on the tourist trail. A pleasant outside terrace is a good spot for summer relaxing; inside, there's much character to admire, particularly in the bar, which proudly boasts flagstones, bare white walls, rafters, chimney, old bread baking oven in a corner, and paintings for sale on the walls. Hearty, well-cooked, keenly priced dishes keep locals and tourists alike happy and might include local game and pistachio nut terrine, faggots or fish and chips; with suppliers proudly listed on the menu. Six bedrooms in the original inn provide characterful accommodation and there are twelve further rooms in the nearby annexe.

Food serving times

Monday-Sunday:
12pm-2pm, 6.30pm-9pm

Closed 1st week in January

Prices

Meals: 15.00 (3 course lunch) and a la carte 15.00/25.00

18 rooms: 50.00/115.00

Typical Dishes

Chicken liver parfait

Roast stuffed pork loin

Sticky toffee & date pudding

By the Cross in the village.
Parking.

054 The Green Dragon Inn

Cockleford GL53 9NW

Tel.: (01242) 870271 - Fax: (01242) 870171
e-mail: green-dragon@buccaneer.co.uk
Website: www.green-dragon-inn.co.uk

VISA AE

Hook Norton, Courage Directors, Butcombe

There can't be many pubs in which you can say the mice are part of the furniture - but here they literally are. Many of the seasoned oak furnishings, including tables, the bars and even the lynch gate in the car park, are made by Robert 'Mouseman' Thompson, and his distinctive hand carved mouse hallmark scampers merrily along each one. As you watch the burning embers reflecting off beamed ceilings and bare wooden floorboards, you'll agree that the furniture is far from the only characterful thing about this 17C Cotswold stone pub, however. Fancy a game of skittles? Masquerading as a function room, the skittle alley opens out onto the peaceful patio garden, and comfortable, modern bedrooms named after famous racehorses can be found in an annexed block. Alongside British staples come other dishes with more of a colourful Mediterranean pedigree, and lighter meals also available for lunch. Book ahead to avoid disappointment.

Food serving times

Monday-Friday:
12pm-2.30pm, 6pm-10pm

Saturday:
12pm-3pm, 6pm-10pm

Sunday:
12pm-3.30pm, 6pm-9pm

Closed dinner 25-26 December, dinner 1 January

Prices

Meals: a la carte
22.00/28.00

9 rooms: 65.00/85.00

Typical Dishes

Potted organic salmon
Seared local venison steak
Selection of regional cheeses

5mi South of Cheltenham by A435. Parking.

055 The Wild Duck Inn

Drake's Island,
Ewen GL7 6BY
Tel.: (01285) 770310 - Fax: (01285) 770924
e-mail: wduckinn@aol.com - Website: www.thewildduckinn.co.uk

Theakstons Old Peculier, Theakstons Best, Duck Pond, Ruddles Best, Charles Wells Bombardier, Abbot Ale, Archers Golden

Forget the warning never to judge a book by its cover; if you're impressed by the exterior of this part 16C former mill, you'll be just as bowled over by its equally rustic interior, bursting with Cotswold character and charm. There are several open rooms and little alcoves, with oak floors and some exposed stonework, while dried hops hang throughout from wooden beams. Low ceilings and a huge fire create an intimate atmosphere and the distinctive dining room is deep-red in colour and hung with portraits. Sit at stripped wood tables inside or, on a warm day, dine al fresco on the terrace. The menu is hard to pin down - there are grilled dishes, with meat from nearby Highgrove, for the traditionalists, but the culinary influences on the main menu are from far and wide, with some dishes proving more successful than others. Service can be a little laid back. Four-poster beds in the rooms provide a regal night's rest.

Food serving times

Monday-Friday:
12pm-2pm, 6.30pm-10pm

Saturday-Sunday:
12pm-10pm

Prices

Meals: a la carte
20.00/35.00

12 rooms:
70.00/120.00

Typical Dishes

Baked Camembert in Parma ham
Seared scallops
Apple & blueberry tart

3.25mi Southwest of Cirencester by A429. Parking.

056 The White Horse

Cirencester Rd, Frampton Mansell GL6 8HZ
Tel.: (01285) 760960
e-mail: emmawhitehorse@aol.com
Website: www.cotswoldwhitehorse.com

Hook Norton Best Bitter, Uley Best Bitter, Arkell's Summer Ale (in season)

More cheerful-looking inside than you would ever guess from its slightly drab-looking, roadside exterior, the White Horse is enjoying an ever-growing reputation as a dining destination. Personally and professionally run, it keeps both drinkers and diners happy with its cosy, relaxed bar and its colourful, formally-laid dining room. Art lovers are also sure to be delighted with its regularly-changing collection of original artwork. Fairly priced dishes blend bold, contemporary flavours with a streak of originality and might include pressed pork terrine with an apple, cashew nut and balsamic salad, noisettes of lamb stuffed with apricots, or grilled lemon sole with a caper, anchovy and black olive butter; and lobsters, crabs and oysters are a speciality in season. Friendly, responsive service adds to the overall experience.

Food serving times

Monday-Saturday:
12pm-2.30pm, 7pm-9.45pm

Sunday:
12pm-3pm

Closed 24-26 December, 1 January, 1st Monday-Thursday in January

Prices

Meals: 16.95 (3 course lunch/dinner Monday-Thursday) and a la carte 23.50/30.00

Typical Dishes

Seared Cornish scallops
Pan-fried calves liver
Chocolate and coconut terrine

7mi West of Cirencester by A419. Parking.

South West • Gloucestershire

Lower Oddington

057 The Fox Inn

Lower Oddington GL56 0UR
Tel.: (01451) 870555 - Fax: (01451) 870669
e-mail: info@foxinn.net - Website: www.foxinn.net

Hook Norton Best, Abbot Ale, Wickwar's Old Bob

Finding yourself in Lower Oddington, you may wish to study the medieval wall painting of the seven deadly sins depicted within scenes of the Last Judgement at the local 11C church of St. Nicholas. And whilst the avaricious are spending their money in Stow-on-the-Wold's many antique shops, gluttons should head to the nearby ivy-clad Fox Inn where they can indulge to their hearts' content in classic, hearty British food. Popular with both locals and visitors, this pub can become busy, so if you're prone to anger, it's best to book ahead. Rustically romantic, with its flag floors, wooden beams and open fires, the red-painted dining room is perfect place for the lustful to enjoy a candlelit meal.Feeling slothful after you've eaten?
Stay the night in one of the sumptuously furnished bedrooms. The envy of others who just can't compete, the team at The Fox must feel justifiably proud of their charming village inn.

Food serving times

Monday-Saturday:
12pm-2pm, 6.30pm-10pm

Sunday:
12pm-3.30pm, 7pm-9.30pm

Closed 25 December

Prices

Meals: a la carte
18.45/29.80

3 rooms: 95.00

Typical Dishes

Wild mushroom risotto
Casserole of rabbit
Ginger poached pears

3mi East of Stow-on-the-Wold by A436. Parking.

058 **The Bathurst Arms**

North Cerney GL7 7BZ
Tel.: (01285) 831 281
e-mail: james@bathurstarms.com
Website: www.bathurstarms.com

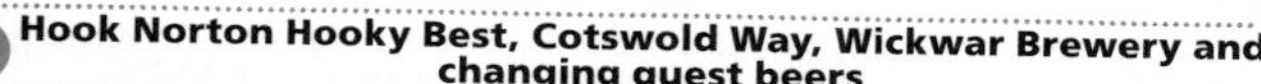

Hook Norton Hooky Best, Cotswold Way, Wickwar Brewery and changing guest beers

Pretty in pink, though often cloaked in a coat of ivy, The Bathurst Arms stands in the village of North Cerney, with the River Churn running alongside. The 17C beamed bar is often busy with locals, while the former stables now house the dining area, with its exposed stone walls, animal art and leather sofas. Starters like hot and sour baby squid salad and foie gras and rabbit terrine hint at the style of things to come, with generously-sized mains including dishes such as loin of monkfish or fresh pancakes, plus favourites like the infamous Bathurst burger. An accompanying bottle of wine is unusually not chosen from a list - instead you'll need to pick a bottle off the shelves for yourself. Six simple but comfortable bedrooms – one with a four poster - are available, and if you know your Reykjavik from your Rome and your Darwin from your Dickens, you might want to make sure your visit coincides with one of the regular quiz nights.

Food serving times
Monday-Sunday:
12pm-2pm, 6pm-9pm

Prices
Meals: a la carte
20.00/28.00
6 rooms: 55.00/85.00

Typical Dishes
Duck & vegetable spring roll
Twice cooked pork belly
Ginger and syrup sponge

3mi North of Cirencester by A435.
Parking.

059 Churchill Arms

Paxford GL55 6XH
Tel.: (01386) 594000 - Fax: (01386) 594005
e-mail: mail@thechurchillarms.com
Website: www.thechurchillarms.com

We most liked

Hook Norton, Ansells Moonlight and 1 guest ale usually from North Cotswold Brewery or Wye Valley

The Churchill Arms is a proper village pub. Set in picturesque surroundings, it has the wooden beams, the oak floors and the open fire, with a relaxed atmosphere to boot. But the food's the thing here: good quality, reasonably priced cooking made from locally sourced ingredients, and it's popular with locals and visitors alike. Be sure to arrive early though; bookings aren't accepted and when you've made your choice from the chalked up menu, you'll need to order at the bar. With such great food to choose from, it's a shame that the service sometimes lacks a little enthusiasm, but happily, this doesn't affect the atmosphere. Already an integral part of village life, this pub has gone one step further and provides a take-away menu that's a real hit with the locals. Take the opportunity to feel like a local yourself by staying over in one of the stylish, tidy bedrooms and waking up to views across the Cotswold countryside.

Food serving times

Monday-Sunday:
12pm-2pm, 7pm-9pm

Bookings not accepted

Prices

Meals: a la carte
17.00/30.00

4 rooms: 40.00/70.00

Typical Dishes

English asparagus
Fillet of hake
Soft almond meringue roulade

3mi East of Chipping Campden by B4035. On street parking.

060 The Falcon Inn

London Rd, Poulton GL7 5HN
Tel.: (01285) 850844 - Fax: (01285) 850844
e-mail: thefalconpoulton@hotmail.co.uk
Website: www.thefalconpoulton.co.uk

Wickwar Brewery Cotswold Way or Old Bob, Hook Norton Brewery - changing regularly

Keenly run by its young owner/chef, The Falcon is certainly in fine feather. A country pub at heart, but with an attractive, modernised interior, its easy-going atmosphere makes this a popular choice for the locals, who are often to be found propping up the central bar. Warm yourself up by the fire or get a bird's eye view through the window of your food being prepared in the kitchen when you sit down to eat at a pine table in one of two comfortable dining rooms. The à la carte menu offers a range of food to suit any appetite; from a quick snack or a sandwich for lunch through to a three course meal for dinner. Choose from a mix of traditional pub favourites like steak and kidney pie or steak and chips and more contemporary dishes such as slow roasted belly of pork and pigeon breast. Lunch menus change daily, dinner menus monthly and both make good use of fresh ingredients from local suppliers.

Food serving times

Tuesday-Saturday:
12pm-3pm, 5pm-11pm

Sunday:
12pm-6pm

Prices

Meals: 12.00 (3 course lunch) and a la carte 12.00/32.00

Typical Dishes

Torbay crab cakes
Pan-fried duck breast
Sticky toffee pudding

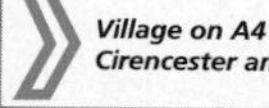

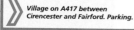

Village on A417 between Cirencester and Fairford. Parking.

061 The Bell

Sapperton GL7 6LE
Tel.: (01285) 760298 - Fax: (01285) 760761
e-mail: thebell@sapperton66.freeserve.co.uk
Website: www.foodatthebell.co.uk

 **Uley Old Spot, Bath Ales Spa, Butcombe Bitter, Wickwar Cotswold Way**

The Bell is a personally-run, much-loved local institution: spotless, stylish, uncluttered and wonderfully comfortable, with local ales on offer at the bar and the warm glow of Cotswold stone inside and out. Numerous rooms encircle the central bar, all well-furnished, cosy and attractive. A well thought-out menu finds room for popular pub favourites as well as appetising modern dishes – all homemade with locally sourced, seasonal ingredients: choose from dishes such as cottage pie, steak and kidney pudding or grazing boards at lunch, and pan-fried chicken livers or crispy Gloucester Old Spot pork belly in the evenings, plus daily specials often featuring seafood. There are some invigorating walks through woods and meadows, and a log fire and a big wood-burning range to welcome you back, or tables in the Mediterranean-style courtyard if the sun is shining.

Food serving times

Monday-Sunday:
12pm-2pm, 7pm-9.30pm

Closed 25 December

Prices

Meals: a la carte
21.00/32.00

Typical Dishes

Smoked Scottish venison
Home-made Burger
Ginger bavarois with rhubarb

5mi West of Cirencester by A419.
Parking.

062 The Swan

Southrop GL7 3NU
Tel.: (01367) 850205 - Fax: (01367) 850479
e-mail: grazzer@gmail.com
Website: www.theswanatsouthrop.co.uk

 Hook Norton, Wadworth 6X, Fuller's London Pride

Looking little changed by the centuries, this creeper-clad inn has kept its characterful beamed ceiling, its log fire and its busy public bar. It still has a room dedicated to drinkers, but the main room is laid for informal eating, and features interesting modern art, available for sale. Here, the manager and chef bring their experience from London's Bibendum restaurant to a contemporary menu with a subtle Mediterranean flavour and a touch of West End sophistication, serving precise dishes such as ragout of hare with pappardelle, fish soup with rouille, gruyère and croutons, or fillet of sea bass, and there's a very good value fixed price set menu too. To round off the evening with some healthy competition, they even have a skittle alley for hire: try finding one of those in Fulham!

Food serving times

Monday-Sunday:
12pm-2.30pm, 7pm-10pm

Prices

Meals: 16.50 (3 course lunch) and a la carte 18.95/46.95

Typical Dishes

Steak Tartare
Pink sea bream
Pear tart Tatin

Village signed off A417 to the North of Lechlade. Parking on road.

063 Eagle & Child

Digbeth St,
Stow-on-the-Wold GL54 1BN
Tel.: (01451) 830670 - Fax: (01451) 870048
e-mail: stay@theroyalisthotel.co.uk - Website: www.theroyalisthotel.co.uk

Hook Norton, Goffs, Donnington, Cheltenham SPA, Battledown

An erstwhile hospice to shelter lepers, where once it would have repelled, it now attracts, and is popular with both locals and tourists alike. One of several inns claiming to be the oldest in England, at over a thousand years of age, it certainly boasts an impressive history, and if you ask a native nicely, you'll be able to learn about everything from witch marks and tunnels to ducks swimming in blood. The interior of this stone pub is everything you would expect from such a veteran; a snug, beamed dining room with flagged floor, low ceiling and tons of rustic character - and nowadays, it comes with added light from the sunny conservatory and tiny courtyard attached. When it comes to the food, there's plenty of choice, with traditional, robust pub favourites such as steak and kidney pudding served alongside more modern, Mediterranean-influenced dishes. Like its surroundings, some might even be inclined to describe it as historic.

Food serving times

Monday-Saturday:
11am-2.30pm, 6pm-9.30pm

Sunday:
11am-3pm, 6pm-9.30pm

Prices

Meals: a la carte
22.00/27.00

14 rooms:
70.00/130.00

Typical Dishes

Salad of local crayfish
Bread-crumbed local trout
Apple rice pudding

At the Royalist Hotel. Parking.

064 The Trouble House

Cirencester Rd,
Tetbury GL8 8SG
Tel.: (01666) 502206
e-mail: enquiries@troublehouse.co.uk - Website: www.troublehouse.co.uk

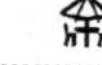  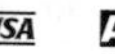  MC

Wadworth's Henry's IPA, Wadworth's 6X

Going by its outer appearance and proximity to a noisy road, you would be forgiven for thinking that there was not much of any consequence to be found within the walls of this pub. But you'd be wrong. Very wrong. Negotiate past the speeding cars and in through the door and you'll find a country haven awaits; beamed rooms with low ceilings, simply decorated, and with open fires and chunky mismatched tables and chairs. With a big city chef at the helm, you might also expect food to be over-priced and pretentious. On the contrary. Excellent quality, full-flavoured, modern classics are made using local produce and the service is friendly and unimposing. All those well-to-do locals must make for a slightly chilly atmosphere though, surely? Wrong again. The welcome here is warm and the ambience delightfully cosy and relaxed. And this is all guaranteed? Afraid not - the word on the street suggests changes are afoot.

Food serving times

Tuesday-Saturday:
12pm-2pm, 7pm-9.30pm

Sunday:
12pm-2pm

Closed Christmas-New Year period

Prices

Meals: a la carte
28.00/37.00

Typical Dishes

Roasted scallops & Parma ham

Braised oxcheeks in red wine

Trouble House dessert plate

2mi Northeast on the A433.
Parking.

065 Horse & Groom Village Inn

Upper Oddington GL56 0XH
Tel.: (01451) 830584
e-mail: info@horseandgroom.uk.com
Website: www.horseandgroom.uk.com

   VISA MC

Wye Valley Best, Hereford Pale Ale, Wickwar Bob, Archers Best, Wye Valley Butty Bach

Modernised into a spacious, fairly open plan pub with a large rear terrace, original features still abound in this 16C former coaching inn. With a pretty Cotswold stone exterior, inside it charms with wooden floors, exposed beams and blazing log fires. Although orientated towards diners, this inn has still managed to retain its pub atmosphere, and locals catch up over a pint as they relax in armchairs in the small lounge. The experienced owners run a tight ship and as a consequence this place can become busy. They serve modern, pub food from a regularly changing, seasonal menu, and fruit and vegetables are often supplied from organic gardens within the village, including the pub's own. There is an excellent selection of wines by the glass, but after a few drinks, beware the sloped ceilings and beams in the well-appointed bedrooms. A peaceful walk through the open Cotswold countryside will help clear your head.

Food serving times

Monday-Sunday:
12pm-2pm, 6.30pm-9pm

Closed 2 weeks in January

Prices

Meals: a la carte
19.00/30.00

8 rooms: 70.00/98.00

Typical Dishes

Prawn, crab & avocado tian

Moroccan spiced chicken

Steamed marmalade sponge

2mi East of Stow-on-the-Wold by A436. Parking (50 spaces).

066 The White Hart Inn

High St,
Winchcombe GL54 5LJ
Tel.: (01242) 602359 - Fax: (01242) 602703
e-mail: info@wineandsausage.com - Website: www.wineandsausage.com

St Austell Tribute, Donnington BB, Hook Norton Old Hooky, Cotswold Whiskers

Refurbished and re-launched as Winchcombe Wine and Sausage, this 16C former coaching inn does what it says on the tin, plus a bit more. You want wine? A well-stocked, decently-priced wine shop contains the owner's top 100 wines from around the world – take your pick, pay £5 corkage and enjoy with dinner in the pub; the top 25 each week are also available by the glass. You want sausages? They have their own menu here – choose from flavours such as lamb, mint and apricot or Gloucester Old Spot. You want somewhere to eat? Try the atmospheric and aptly named Eating Room, complete with picture of comedy pig. And the bit more? Well, they don't just serve wine and sausages. And you don't have to eat in The Eating Room. Real ales, cider, whisky et al; a large selection of hearty homemade dishes, a characterful bar, a rustic dining room and chatty, friendly service; all this plus eight comfortable bedrooms in which to sleep off your excesses.

Food serving times

Sunday-Thursday:
12pm-3pm, 6.30pm-9.30pm

Friday-Saturday:
12pm-3pm, 6.30pm-10pm

Prices

Meals: a la carte
17.50/26.50

8 rooms: 75.00/115.00

Typical Dishes

Chick liver parfait
Toad in the hole
Apple crumble

8mi North East of Cheltenham by B4632; in town centre. Parking.

067 The Globe Inn

Appley TA21 0HJ
Tel.: (01823) 672327
Website: www.theglobeinnappley.co.uk

VISA MC

Masters Brewery Appley Ale, Exmoor Ales, Cotleigh 25, Sharp's Doombar, Butcombe Bitter

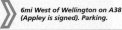

Cosy and traditional, even pleasantly old-fashioned in some ways, the inn's welcoming interior shows the influence of a genial man who clearly sees himself as custodian of the Globe as well as its chef and long-standing landlord. The building itself has origins in the 1400s, but there's nautical history too, in the pictures, prints and photos of the Titanic decorating one wall, and a touch of nostalgia in the display case of die-cast Dinky and Corgi cars and vans. Hard to fault for generosity, the tasty, substantial pub cooking often has a subtle international touch; service is well-organised and invariably polite. If the sun's out, lounge with lunch and beers in the garden before setting off on a walk near the Devon border; if it's not, you could always ask to book the skittle alley.

Food serving times

Tuesday-Saturday and Bank Holiday Monday:
12pm-2pm, 7pm-9.30pm

Sunday:
12pm-2pm, 7pm-9pm

Closed 25-26 December

Bar measl dinner Sunday

Prices

Meals: a la carte
18.00/30.00

Typical Dishes

Fish soup
Game pie
Sticky toffee pudding

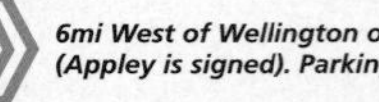
6mi West of Wellington on A38 (Appley is signed). Parking.

068 The Red Lion Inn

Babcary TA11 7ED

Tel.: (01458) 223230 - Fax: (01458) 224510

   MC

 **Teignworthy Spring Tide, Otter Ales Otter Bright, Bath Ales Gem**

Set to one side, the bar of the Red Lion Inn- complete with bar skittles- cedes pride of place to two spacious, airy lounges. One's more particularly given over to eating, but they share a contemporary country style: oriental rugs, neatly set, rustic wooden tables and framed paintings and Red Lion posters on the walls. It's not over-formal, and this clearly suits a lively crowd of lunchers, from local families to passers-by who were lucky enough to drop in on spec.; service might slow a fraction on the busiest days, but a young team stays positive and polite. Exciting menus and regularly changing blackboards feature contemporary combinations and locally reared Somerset beef.

Food serving times

Monday-Saturday:
12pm-2.30pm, 7pm-9.30pm

Sunday:
12pm-2.30pm

Closed 25 December

Prices

Meals: a la carte
19.00/26.45

Typical Dishes

Scallop & crab pastry
Marinated poussin
Lemon treacle tart

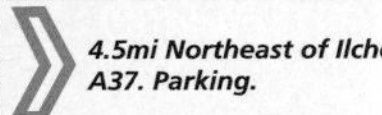

4.5mi Northeast of Ilchester by A37. Parking.

069 The Three Horseshoes Inn

Batcombe BA4 6HE

Tel.: (01749) 850359 - Fax: (01749) 850615

Website: www.thethreehorseshoesbatcombe.co.uk

 **Blind Man's Brewery - Bats in the Belfry, Butcombe Bitter, Adnams Broadside; also draught Somerset ciders**

There's nothing like knowing exactly where your food comes from and, as you enter this pub through its neat little garden, you might spot some of the sprouting seasonal vegetables, or at least get a glance at the wonderfully silky egg-providers as they root around amongst the fish pond and the summer furniture. Inside, the long low-beamed bar with its window seating, inglenook fireplace and wood burning stoves cultivates a cluttered feel; its peach walls covered in old photos of village life, plates, hanging pewter mugs and old beer bottles. The smaller snug off the main bar is the place to head if you're after a more intimate setting, but for a more formal feel, try the restaurant. Local, organic produce features highly on the menu, in the form of dishes such as shoulder of lamb or sausages and mash, but there are other lighter dishes too, and a more extensive choice in the evenings. Bedrooms are neat and simply decorated.

Food serving times

Tuesday-Saturday:
12pm-2pm, 7pm-9pm

Sunday:
12pm-2pm

Prices

Meals: a la carte
25.00/35.00

3 rooms: 50.00/75.00

Typical Dishes

Home-smoked chicken salad

Poached Cornish haddock

Treacle sponge pudding

Signed off the A359, midway between Castle Carey and Frome. Tucked away behind the church. Parking.

070 The Queen's Arms

Corton Denham DT9 4LR
Tel.: (01963) 220317
e-mail: relax@thequeens-arms.com
Website: www.thequeens-arms.com

 **Butcombe, Timothy Taylor, Otter Bitter and 1 weekly changing guest ale**

Tucked away in a quiet village between the lovely town of Sherborne and the roaring A303 stands this pleasant 18th century stone built pub, personally run by young owners. Appearances can deceive: the traditional façade here hides an interior where the 'usual' rustic pubby staples have been pretty much jettisoned for a relaxed, contemporary, informal feel, typified by armchairs and sofas you can sink into while sipping your real ale or bottled beer, of which there is a fine worldwide range. British dishes using fine local produce form the backbone of the menus: you can eat in the bar or book for the smart adjacent dining room. There's a delightful rear terrace, too. Bedrooms are more than a cut above the pub norm, offering individually styled luxury with superb bathrooms.

Food serving times

Monday-Saturday:
12pm-3pm, 6pm-10pm

Sunday:
12pm-3pm, 6pm-9.30pm

Prices

Meals: a la carte
18.00/26.00

5 rooms: 60.00/120.00

Typical Dishes

Potted rabbit
Honey glazed pork belly
Molten chocolate pudding

3mi North of Sherborne by B3145 and minor road West. Parking.

071 The Manor House Inn

Ditcheat BA4 6RB
Tel.: (01749) 860276
e-mail: info@manorhouseinn.co.uk
Website: www.manorhouseinn.co.uk

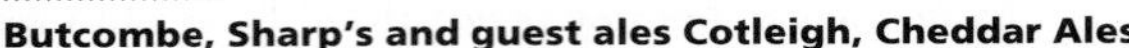

Butcombe, Sharp's and guest ales Cotleigh, Cheddar Ales

Fans of the turf are well catered for – in both senses - at this characterful part 17C ex-coaching inn near Glastonbury. Not only can they tuck into the Manor House's locally renowned rustic fare, they can also sit by the windows of the bar or restaurant and watch a regular procession of horses and jockeys making its way to the local gallops. In the recently opened Sports Bar, framed silks hang proudly: Ditcheat is home to one of racing's top trainers Paul Nichols. Diners can take their pick of places to eat: apart from the flagged bar with hatch and similarly traditional dining room, there's a lawned garden for fine weather. Food covers a pretty eclectic range, from classic British staples to more modern European influenced offerings. There are pleasantly refurbished bedrooms, and an enviable setting next to the village's pretty St.Mary's church.

Food serving times

Monday-Saturday:
12pm-2pm, 7pm-9.30pm

Sunday:
12pm-2pm

Closed meals 25 December

Prices

Meals: 16.95 (Sunday lunch) and a la carte 16.00/29.00

3 rooms: 50.00/90.00

Typical Dishes

Stilton & wild mushroom tart
Roasted belly pork
Maryland local cheese

4mi South of Shepton Mallet by A37 and minor road left. Parking.

Lord Poulett Arms

072 Lord Poulett Arms

High St, Hinton St George TA17 8SE
Tel.: (01460) 73149
e-mail: steveandmichelle@lordpoulettarms.com
Website: www.lordpoulettarms.com

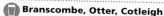

VISA MC

 **Branscombe, Otter, Cotleigh**

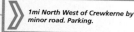

A delightful village, full of thatched period houses, with a delightful village pub at its centre. The 17C Lord Poulett Arms – family motto; Keep the Faith – really does lie at the heart of the community of Hinton-St-George, and you'll find locals, having popped over for a pint before dinner, propping up the bar, while their dogs reacquaint themselves down below. The welcome is warm, as is the atmosphere, and the three main dining rooms are full of character, with open fires, exposed brickwork and solid stone and bare wood floors. The menu offers seasonal cooking made with best local ingredients and dishes might, for example, involve mackerel or scallops from Dorset and pork or lamb from Somerset, with herbs from the pub's own garden. A great selection of real ales and chatty service from local staff complete the picture, unless you are also staying the night, in which case, you'll find the bedrooms are luxurious.

Food serving times
Monday-Sunday:
12pm-2pm, 7pm-9pm

Prices
Meals: a la carte
18.00/28.00

4 rooms: 59.00/88.00

Typical Dishes
Dorset mackerel
Somerset pork shoulder
Rhubarb cheesecake

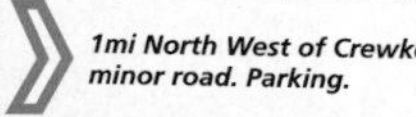

1mi North West of Crewkerne by minor road. Parking.

073 Ilchester Arms

The Square,
Ilchester BA22 8LN
Tel.: (01935) 840220 - Fax: (01935) 841353
Website: www.ilchesterarms.com

Fuller's London Pride

First licensed in 1686, this impressive looking Somerset pub shows its age with appropriate dignity, the profusion of ivy on its exterior just adds a little more rural charm. It stands proudly in the village centre, a relaxing oasis from the hustle and bustle of nearby Yeovil. Public areas are relaxing and intimate, typified by two small lounges and an airy, wood decorated bar - like being down at the local, which many of the customers are. A bistro continues this informal theme, its daily changing blackboard menus have a hearty and familiar ring. At any given time you might try rich, rosemary scented lamb casserole with spring vegetables, confit of duck with garlic crust and cassoulet beans or seared calves liver with onions, bacon and mash. Sizable bedrooms have a good range of facilities.

Food serving times

Monday-Saturday:
12pm-2.30pm, 7pm-9.30pm

Sunday:
12pm-2.30pm

Closed 26 December

Bar lunch

Prices

Meals: a la carte
17.50/26.50

7 rooms: 60.00/75.00

Typical Dishes

Crab spring rolls
Medallions of pork tenderloin
Chocolate truffle cake

6mi North of Yeovil by A37; in town centre. Parking.

074 **Kingsdon Inn**

Kingsdon TA11 7LG
Tel.: (01935) 840543
e-mail: enquiries@kingsdoninn.co.uk
Website: www.kingsdoninn.co.uk

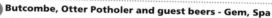

Butcombe, Otter Potholer and guest beers - Gem, Spa

This part 17C thatched inn knows how to pack 'em in. The best advice is: "Get here early!" Punters are drawn by the unadulterated charm of the place, as well as its rather handy position just off the A303 in a picturesque village near the attractive town of Somerton. It possesses bags of character: low bowed ceiling, wood burning stove, stripped pine built-in wall seat, scatter cushions and stone floors. Four snug, adjoining rooms provide dining options; there's a pleasant garden too. Traditional, popular dishes – and lots of them – show up on a busy looking blackboard menu: everything from whitebait to lambs liver to goats' cheese salad.

Food serving times
Monday-Sunday:
12pm-2pm, 6.30pm-9pm
Closed meals 25 December

Prices
Meals: 13.95 (3 course Sunday lunch/dinner) and a la carte 12.00/23.00
2 rooms: 50.00/70.00

Typical Dishes
Somerset goat's cheese salad
Braised oxtail
Sticky ginger pudding

2.5 mi South East of Somerton on B3151. Parking.

Long Sutton

075 The Devonshire Arms

Long Sutton TA10 9LP
Tel.: (01458) 241271 - Fax: (01458) 241037
e-mail: mail@thedevonshirearms.com
Website: www.thedevonshirearms.com

Teignmouth Reel Ale, Bath Spa Ales, Hopback Crop Circle

In a lovely little spot overlooking the village green stands this creeper-clad 17C former hunting lodge. Inside, save for the fireplaces, all vestiges of period character are gone, and in their place is contemporary dining pub styling; all wooden floors, deep brown leather sofas and chunky wood tables. The large walled garden and terrace is a sun trap in the warmer months, so arrive early to stake your claim to a table - bookings are not accepted. Eating here at lunchtime can be a simple affair with a light sandwich, a salad or a ploughman's; or a reliably satisfying classic such as steak and chips or bangers and mash from the bar menu. The daily-changing à la carte dinner menu offers more refined dishes such as foie gras or crab crème brûlée, as well as locally sourced meats and fish. Nine large, luxurious bedrooms have bold, modern colour schemes and artwork as well as up-to-date facilities.

Food serving times

Monday-Sunday:
12pm-2.30pm, 7pm-9.30pm

Closed 25 December

Closed dinner Sunday October-May

Bookings not accepted

Prices

Meals: 14.95 (3 course lunch) and a la carte 22.00/33.00

9 rooms: 65.00/120.00

Typical Dishes

Squid with Le Puy lentils

Duck confit

Passion fruit crème brûlée

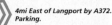

4mi East of Langport by A372. Parking.

076 The Pilgrims at Lovington

Lovington BA7 7PT
Tel.: (01963) 240597
Website: www.thepilgrimsatlovington.co.uk

 **Cottage Brewing Champflower**

You'd probably not stop here at first sight: Pilgrims doesn't look anything special from the outside. But its slogan – 'the pub that thinks it's a restaurant' – gives a hint of what to expect inside. Beyond the front door, there's a transformation. It does, indeed, have a smart, pleasant restaurant style: deep burgundy and exposed stone walls, coir mat flooring and bright, cheerful watercolours mostly by a local village artist. The bar isn't forgotten; it's traditional in character, with flag floors and low beams. Cookery books are piled on a piano and matchboxes from around the world decorate the walls. Menus, in the modern style, revel in interesting variations.

Food serving times
Monday-Sunday:
12pm-3pm, 7pm-9pm
Closed October

Prices
Meals: a la carte
15.00/33.00

Typical Dishes
Goat's cheese in filo pastry
Roast pheasant breast
Somerset apple crumble

4mi South West of Castle Cary by B3153 signposted Somerton and A371 on B3153. Parking.

Lower Vobster

077 The Vobster Inn

Lower Vobster BA3 5RJ
Tel.: (01373) 812920 - Fax: (01373) 812920
e-mail: info@vobsterinn.co.uk - Website: www.vobsterinn.co.uk

 **Butcombe Ale, Butcombe Blonde**

Very much the centre of its tiny Somerset village, the Vobster Inn, run by a husband and wife team, takes its duty seriously and does its best to keep everyone happy, from young families and older couples, out enjoying the sun at the terrace tables, to the unhurried neighbours enjoying a slow pint inside. Adjoining the bar, a long lounge serves as the restaurant, its walls painted with grapes and lined with posters, labels, wine racks and even old wine cases. Sensibly allowing room for market-fresh specials, fish and seafood are always on the menu and there's always a good selection of hand-crafted West Country cheeses on offer.

Food serving times

Monday-Saturday:
12pm-3pm, 6.30pm-9pm

Sunday:
12pm-3pm

Closed 25-26 December,
1 week in February

- Seafood -

Prices

Meals: a la carte
18.00/25.00

Typical Dishes

Seared scallops in the shell

Braised feather blade of beef

Coffee liqueur pannacotta

From Frome head northwest to Radstock on the A362. Vobster is signposted approx 5.5mi off the A362. Parking.

078 The Royal Oak Inn of Luxborough

Exmoor National Park, Luxborough TA23 0SH

Tel.: (01984) 640319 - Fax: (01984) 641561

e-mail: info@theroyaloakinnluxborough.co.uk

Website: www.theroyaloakinnluxborough.co.uk

Cotleigh Tawny, Cotleigh Snowy, Exmoor Gold, Palmers IPA and Palmers 200

In a fold of the rolling Brendon Hills, surrounded by picture postcard cottages, the Royal Oak is in the most idyllic position possible. Once you've located the pub among the many lanes of the area, step into a low beamed and log fired bar featuring an impishly accurate cartoon of one of the regulars (who may well be sitting there with dog and pint). Invitingly furnished dining rooms in deep olive tones lead off from here; another rustic bar keeps them company and the atmosphere carries over from here. Suppliers knock at the front door with their produce, so there's no shortage of local inspiration: chicken with bacon lardons, cider, cream and local apple brandy is a satisfying blend of West Country flavours. There are a dozen en-suite bedrooms for those wishing to stay on.

Food serving times

Monday-Sunday:
12pm-2pm, 7pm-9pm

Closed 25 December

Prices

Meals: a la carte
15.00/30.00

11 rooms: 55.00/95.00

Typical Dishes

Smoked haddock & poached egg

Seared breasts of pigeon

Bread and butter pudding

Luxborough is signed off A39 East of Minehead or off B3224 Exford to Taunton road. Parking

079 The Talbot Inn

Selwood St,
Mells BA11 3PN

Tel.: (01373) 812254 - Fax: (01373) 813599
e-mail: enquiries@talbotinn.com - Website: www.talbotinn.com

 **Butcombe Bitter and guest ale Fuller's London Pride**

This utterly charming 15C stone-built coaching inn boasts an immediate impact with its cobbled courtyard and walled garden with pétanque piste and vine-covered pergola. The effect continues in a pleasant, intimate main bar, where dried hops cling to the beams and green candles flicker in old wine bottles. Here, indulge in hearty, traditional bar meals with daily changing blackboard dishes or a more serious dinner menu with fish specials from Brixham. You can also drink in a large tythe barn, its ancient character recently enhanced by a mural depicting life in Mells through the ages. Bright, pretty, individually appointed bedrooms make a night's stopover worthwhile.

Food serving times

Monday-Sunday:
12pm-2.30pm, 6.45pm-10.30pm

Closed 25 December

Prices

Meals: a la carte 25.00/30.00

8 rooms: 75.00/145.00

Typical Dishes

Cornish mussels in white wine

Grilled Brixham lemon sole

Mango cheesecake

 *4mi West of Frome. Parking.* 

080 Phelips Arms

The Borough,
Montacute TA15 6XB

Tel.: (01935) 822557
e-mail: info@phelips.co.uk - Website: www.phelipsarms.co.uk

 **Palmers IPA, Palmers Gold and Palmers Copper Ales**

Montacute derives most of its fame from historic Montacute House, owned by the National Trust (100 yards down the road), but this attractive part-17C sand coloured inn provides another reason to turn off the A303. It's a good, traditional pub but very small - there are only 11 tables. Bright lights and swirly carpet are offset with dark wood tables and chairs given a modern lift by bright red and blue curtains and cushions with the owner's own photos and paintings displayed on the walls. The contemporary touches carry over to the cooking, which boasts some interesting, eclectic choices which are cooked to perfection and well presented. Long back garden with benches.

Food serving times

Monday-Saturday:
12pm-2pm, 7pm-9pm

Sunday:
12pm-2pm

Prices

Meals: a la carte
15.00/25.00

4 rooms: 55.00/75.00

Typical Dishes

Prawns with chilli & garlic

Roast guinea fowl

Sunken chocolate pudding

5mi Northwest of Yeovil by A3088 (Montacute is signed). Public parking in the square in front of the pub.

South West • Somerset

081 The Camelot

Chapel Rd,
South Cadbury BA22 7EX
Tel.: (01963) 440448
e-mail: enquiries@thecamelot.co.uk - Website: www.thecamelot.co.uk

 **Several guest beers**

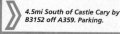

This creeper-clad village pub is so named because a hill in Cadbury is allegedly the original site of King Arthur's Camelot. It may be true, it may not, but one thing's for sure…good food here is no myth. Okay, so you might not be eating at a round table, and you may not feel any mystical vibes, but there are plenty of hearty dishes to choose from. The bar menu offers traditional British favourites like steak and ale pie, lamb hotpot or cod and chips, while on the à la carte, you can take your pick from dishes such as cassoulet, mussels, salmon, duck or steak; all precisely cooked, using locally sourced produce. There's a light, airy, uncluttered ambience about the place, enhanced by stylish local artwork on the walls, and while modish wood tables are dotted about and laid for eating, there's still plenty of space for locals and walkers who've stopped off en route to enjoy a pint of real ale.

Food serving times

Monday-Sunday:
12pm-2.30pm, 7pm-9pm

Prices

Meals: a la carte
22.50/35.90

Typical Dishes

Mussels steamed with ginger
Linguine with lobster
Icecream lime posset

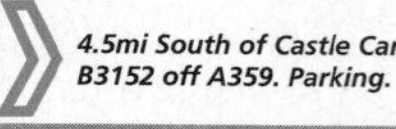

4.5mi South of Castle Cary by B3152 off A359. Parking.

082 Tarr Farm Inn

Tarr Steps TA22 9PY
Tel.: (01643) 851507 - Fax: (01643) 851111
e-mail: enquiries@tarrfarm.co.uk
Website: www.tarrfarm.co.uk

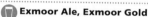

Exmoor Ale, Exmoor Gold

The old clapper bridge at Tarr Steps has crossed the River Barle since time immemorial, and Tarr Farm has had privileged access to this unchanging tranquillity since the Elizabethan age. In the heart of Exmoor, it's one of the more gloriously remote inns of the West Country, and its neat garden is a fine spot to absorb the peaceful surroundings. Your rapture may well continue when you step inside…there's a hugely characterful and cosy beamed bar serving Exmoor ales. Typical pubby lunchtime dishes give way to a comprehensive evening menu of accomplished, interesting dishes featuring a wealth of fine local produce, served in the bar or intimate restaurant. Bedrooms here are special, too. Comfy, spacious and furnished in an eye-catching way, they offer every conceivable luxury, while, for the more adventurous, a host of Exmoor outdoor pursuits are on the doorstep, and can be arranged by the hosts.

Food serving times

Monday-Sunday:
12pm-3pm, 6.30pm-9.30pm

Closed 1-9 February

Bar lunch

Prices

Meals: a la carte
16.00/38.00

9 rooms: 90.00/150.00

Typical Dishes

Char-grilled venison

Pork stuffed sea bream

Apple and cinnamon tart Tatin

Signed off B3223 Dulverton to Exford road. Parking.

South West • Somerset

083 The Blue Ball Inn

Triscombe TA4 3HE
Tel.: (01984) 618242 - Fax: (01984) 618371
e-mail: info@blueballinn.co.uk
Website: www.blueballinn.co.uk

Cotleigh's Tawny and 2 other beers including Cotleigh, Exmoor, Otter, St Austell

A walk in the gorgeous Quantocks requires sustenance along the way, so arm yourself with a map and pitch up at the Blue Ball in good time for lunch. It's a wonderfully inviting place: you can't go far wrong with a 15C thatched and stone-built former stables. There are exposed roof timbers, wooden floors and a large picture window with beautiful views over the surrounding countryside. The menus are imaginative, wide ranging and full of local ingredients. Hungry ramblers can get chunky baguettes at lunchtime; more serious diners can feast on modern and traditional British pub classics. Two modern, stylish and open-plan bedrooms with luxury bathrooms are set in what was the original pub next door.

Food serving times

Monday-Sunday:
12pm-2.30pm, 7pm-9.30pm

Restaurant closed
25 December

Booking essential

Prices

Meals: a la carte
22.50/25.00

2 rooms: 40.00/85.00

Typical Dishes

Crayfish risotto
Whole baked bream
Vanilla cheesecake

4.5mi North of Bishops Lydeard by A358. Parking.

084 The Rising Sun Inn

West Bagborough TA4 3EF
Tel.: (01823) 432575
e-mail: jon@brinkmancatering.co.uk
Website: www.therisingsun.info

Butcombe, John Smith's, Guinness and 2 guest ales changed every 2 weeks

Grab a pint, sit for a while on one of the outside benches hard up against the front of this pretty stone pub, and take in the invigorating air of one of Somerset's most elevated and delightfully located pubs: indeed, it feels like the whole village is on the verge of dropping off the side of the Quantocks. The Rising Sun has 16th century origins, but was rebuilt a few years ago after a fire that lit up the surrounding hillside. There's oak in the beams and slate on the floors, but a modern feel prevails. It's not a big place, and you'll find locals at the bar in close proximity to diners from far afield. A smart upstairs room has exposed trusses, local artwork and a wonderful rural view from big windows. Light, traditional pub lunches give way in the evening to more interesting modern dishes with fresh Somerset ingredients. Wake up to a stylish bedroom with exposed beams.

Food serving times
Monday-Sunday:
12pm-2pm, 6pm-10pm

Prices
Meals: a la carte
14.50/21.00

2 rooms: 55.00/85.00

Typical Dishes
White onion soup
Roast rack of lamb
Caramelised rhubarb & custard

10.5mi North West of Taunton off A358. Parking in the road.

085 The Royal Oak Inn

Exmoor National Park, Winsford TA24 7JE
Tel.: (01643) 851455 - Fax: (01643) 851009
e-mail: enquiries@royaloak-somerset.co.uk
Website: www.royaloak-somerset.co.uk

 **Exmoor Ale, Exmoor Gold, Exmoor Beast**

Facing the shaded green and its trim cottages, the old Royal Oak, its thatched roof turned and folded, stands at the heart of Winsford, a charming village best known for its little interlacing streams and its old packhorse bridge across the River Exe. Inside the pub, one cosy lounge leads into another, their original rural style proudly preserved, to the delight of visitors from out of town; cushioned benches are grouped to form intimate little booths. Out-and-out English cooking seems right at home here, and a no-nonsense menu sticks to the classics, from lunchtime pies and sandwiches in the bar to generous plates of steak and kidney pudding with tasty rhubarb crumble and cream to follow. After lunch, Exmoor beckons, with mile upon mile of heather upland and wooded valleys to be explored.

Food serving times

Monday-Sunday:
12pm-2.30pm, 7.30pm-9pm

Bar lunch

Prices

Meals: a la carte
19.75/25.00

12 rooms:
65.00/136.00

Typical Dishes

Smoked salmon

Chicken with mustard mash

Chocolate mousse

5mi North of Dulverston by B3223. Opposite the village green. Parking.

086 The Red Lion Inn

Axford SN8 2HA

Tel.: (01672) 520271

e-mail: info@redlionaxford.com - Website: www.redlionaxford.com

 **Axford Ale, Ramsbury Gold and guest beer - Cornerstone (Keystone Brewery)**

This brick-and-flint inn of 17C pedigree immediately impresses as a warm and welcoming place. The top area is a lovely lounge bar with roaring fire and a gaggle of contented smokers, and there are fresh flowers on the main bar. Throughout the remainder of the inn a wide range of pictures by local artists is on sale. The blackboard choice of dishes is split into starters, mains and fish and is, largely speaking, from a traditional base. They're served in either the neatly kept dining room, full of old and new silver and china jostling for attention, or conservatory, where tankards and water jugs hang beseechingly from the ceiling. There's one more blackboard, announcing wines by the glass, and when the scoffing and quaffing are done, diners are invited to fill in a card and be kept informed on future menus and events.

Food serving times

Monday-Sunday:
12pm-2pm, 7pm-9pm

Closed 25 December, dinner 26 December, dinner 1 January

Prices

Meals: a la carte 24.00/29.00

Typical Dishes

Seared goose breast
Grilled Brixham brill
Chocolate Pecan pie

4mi East of Marlborough; follow signs for Axford. Parking.

087 The Northey

Bath Road,
Box SN13 8AE
Tel.: (01225) 742333
e-mail: office@ohhcompany.co.uk - Website: www.ohhcompany.co.uk

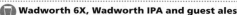

Wadworth 6X, Wadworth IPA and guest ales

There's not really anything remarkable about this roadside pub, at least, not from the outside. It's worth pulling over all the same, though. A thorough makeover has worked wonders on the old, slightly charmless interior and, while the bar remains, with a few sofas, much of the space is given over to simply set dining tables. It's less of a drinking "local" than it was before, but you can hardly blame the friendly team at The Northey for sticking to what they do best: well-weighed flavours are a constant theme in their appetising, well-judged dishes, which are served with tidy efficiency, and all for a very fair price. You could just have a sandwich but, with good modern cooking for the asking, you might feel you were missing out.

Food serving times

Monday-Sunday:
11.30am-2.30pm, 6.30pm-9.30pm

Closed 25-26 December

Prices

Meals: a la carte
21.00/29.00

Typical Dishes

Salmon & crayfish terrine
Stuffed veal escalope
Chocolate & hazelnut terrine

4,75 mi from Bath on A4. Parking.

088 The Ship Inn

Burcombe Lane,
Burcombe SP2 0EJ
Tel.: (01722) 743182
e-mail: theshipburcombe@mail.com - Website: www.theshipburcombe.co.uk

 VISA 

Wadworth 6X, Courage Best, Flowers IPA

Looking traditional and well cared-for, the trim, part 17C Ship Inn lives up to expectations on the inside. Pass under the model of a man o' war in full sail, fixed in a gabled niche above the door, and into a nicely modernised open-plan bar: old exposed timbers and open fires are still in place, and so too is the rural atmosphere you'd expect. Diners and drinkers take their seats where they like and a fresh and tasty seasonal menu with a modern touch, together with traditional classics and a blackboard full of specials, offers plenty of choice: regular themed dinners and summer barbecues lend further variety. But one of the nicest things about the Ship is its lovely rear garden which runs down to a tributary of the river Nadder – find a table in the sun and make yourself comfortable.

Food serving times

Monday-Sunday:
12pm-2.30pm, 6.30pm-9pm

Closed first 2 weeks in January

Prices

Meals: a la carte
20.00/32.00

Typical Dishes

Seared scallops
Char-grilled lamb gigot
Vanilla fudge cheesecake

5,25 mi West of Salisbury by the A36 off A30. Parking.

089 The Horse & Groom Inn

The Street, Charlton SN16 9DL
Tel.: (01666) 823904
e-mail: info@horseandgroominn.com
Website: www.info@horseandgroominn.com

VISA MC

Archers Village, Wadworth 6X and regularly changing guest beers

After a 21C makeover, this pretty Grade II listed, 16C coaching inn fast secured a firm toehold in the country dining league, and now attracts locals and visitors in equal numbers. It boasts a small rustic bar with stone floor and open fire to one side, and a larger dining room, with dark wood floors and country pursuit cartoons, on the other. The lawned garden boasts the only outside bar in Wiltshire – very handy for lazy summer dining. The Horse and Groom's alliterative motto is to offer the warmest welcome in Wiltshire and, although it's a difficult thing to measure, the consensus is that they certainly can't be far off. Cooking ranges from classic bar snacks and sandwiches to more imaginative, contemporary dishes, and the constantly evolving menus show that this is a kitchen happy to experiment, while keeping the winning combination of affordable prices and flavourful, well-judged British cooking, based on quality, local produce.

Food serving times

Monday-Thursday:
12pm-2.30pm, 6.30pm-9pm

Friday-Saturday:
12pm-2.30pm, 6.30pm-9.30pm

Sunday:
12pm-2.30pm

Prices

Meals: 20.00 (3 course lunch) and a la carte 18.00/25.00

5 rooms: 79.95/89.95

Typical Dishes

Roast scallop salad
Cotswold shoulder of lamb
Dark chocolate fondant

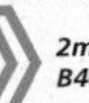

2mi North of Malmesbury by B4040. Parking.

090 The George

High St,
Codford St Mary BA12 0NG
Tel.: (01985) 850270
Website: www.thegeorgecodford.co.uk

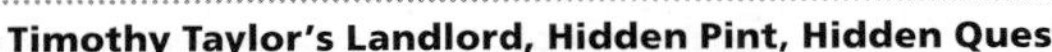

Timothy Taylor's Landlord, Hidden Pint, Hidden Quest

The wild expanse of Salisbury Plain stretches away from this whitewashed 18C pub-hotel in a pretty village. Culture prevails in the Woolstone Theatre opposite; The George, meanwhile, makes a successful appeal to other senses. Although not the place for a cosy meal à deux - there are no beams or cosy decor - the strength of this place lies in the food. The experienced chef-patron uses seasonally changing, locally-sourced ingredients with daily specials appearing on a blackboard. Lunch menus are simpler in style and give way to a concise, regularly changing evening menu. Whet the appetite first by relaxing with a drink and a magazine in the comfortable lounge. If thoughts of the dark Plain are too much to contemplate at night, stay in one of their clean, simple bedrooms.

Food serving times

Wednesday-Monday:
12pm-2pm, 7pm-9pm

Closed dinner Sunday in winter

Prices

Meals: a la carte
18.00/35.00

3 rooms: 45.00/70.00

Typical Dishes

Smoked salmon and crab tian

Breast of Barbary duck

Apple tart

8mi South East of Warminster or 13mi North West of Salisbury by A36. Parking.

Donhead St Andrew

091 Forester Inn

Lower Street,
Donhead St Andrew SP7 9EE
Tel.: (01747) 828038 - Fax: (01747) 828038
e-mail: possums1@btinternet.com

 **Ringwood, Butcombe, Keystone**

If you've a penchant for stone-built, thatched pubs with 13th century origins, then this most definitely is the place for you. The Forester is tucked away in a quaint village on the Dorset/Wiltshire border, and its beguiling exterior is enhanced by a small garden and lovely terraced area that surrounds one of its sides. All that's missing is the sea… The main bar is just like you'd expect: beamed, exposed stone walls, large inglenooks; with an attractive extension which resembles the interior of a barn: a big space with exposed roof trusses and doors and windows out onto the terrace. Menus here offer ample choice, and locally sourced ingredients make a plentiful showing; cooking is firmly in the modern bracket. Upstairs, the spacious bedrooms are done out in a pleasant contemporary style – a surprising juxtaposition to the pub's more rustic charms.

Food serving times

Monday-Sunday:
12pm-3pm, 6.30pm-9.30pm

Prices

Meals: a la carte
15.00/25.00

Typical Dishes

Sauté herring roes
Cornish monkfish
Hot Morello cherry soufflé

5 mi East of Shaftesbury by A30. Parking.

092 The Angel Inn

High St,
Heytesbury BA12 0ED
Tel.: (01985) 840330
Website: www.theangelheytesbury.co.uk

VISA MC

 **Greene King IPA and 1 guest beer changing weekly**

In a pretty village on the edge of Salisbury Plain stands this attractive roadside 17C inn. There's a delightful courtyard terrace and stylish, refurbished ground floor, boasting a cosy lounge with soft leather tub seats, roaring fire, and, further along, a snug though spacious bar. To one side, an elegant, contemporary restaurant completes the picture. Modern pub classics go down well at lunch, as you would expect but, in the evening, things move on with a particularly interesting à la carte that's well prepared and cooked with precision with steak a speciality. Staying overnight is a wise move here. Cosy, well-appointed bedrooms.

Food serving times

Monday-Sunday:
12pm-2.30pm, 7pm-9.30pm

Closed meals 25 December

Prices

Meals: 18.00 (3 course lunch) and a la carte 25.00/35.00

8 rooms: 60.00/75.00

Typical Dishes

Warm smoked mackerel
Roast rump of beef
Coffee crème brûlée

On A36 4 mi Southwest of Warminster by B3414, or off A303. Parking.

093 The Lamb Inn

High St,
Hindon SP3 6DP

Tel.: (01747) 820573 - Fax: (01747) 820605
e-mail: info@lambathindon.co.uk

Charles Wells Bombardier, Young's Bitter, Young's Special

The Lamb has a substantial reputation for feeding travellers as it used to be a much-frequented coaching inn. The 21st century sees it adequately keeping up the tradition: its attractive creeper-clad façade is the destination for a steady stream of hungry diners, many of them passing nearby on their way to the West Country. Conveniently set just off the A303, it has a most beguiling interior of deep burgundy walls, wood and flagged floors, rafters, a gallery's worth of pictures, and higgledy-piggledy tables and chairs filling every conceivable space. A large blackboard menu forms the core of the dishes offered: expect game and traditional English fare, peppered with lighter and more traditional pub favourites. As befits an inn, there are 14 bedrooms pleasantly furnished and not without some character…especially their tartan carpets.

Food serving times
Monday-Sunday:
12pm-2.30pm, 6.30pm-9.30pm

Prices
Meals: a la carte
20.00/25.00

14 rooms:
70.00/135.00

Typical Dishes
Dunkeld smoked salmon
Dorset sirloin steak
Home-made vanilla cheesecake

12mi West of Wilton by A30 and B3089. Parking.

094 The Tollgate Inn

Ham Green,
Holt BA14 6PX

Tel.: (01225) 782326 - Fax: (01225) 782805
e-mail: alison@tollgateholt.co.uk - Website: www.tollgateholt.co.uk

Sharp's Doombar, RCH Pitchfork, Hopback Summer Lightning and others

Despite its rather noisy location at a busy road junction, the locals of Holt have made this hearty old pub of Bath stone a wonderfully friendly place to be. Conviviality stretches across all areas, aided and abetted by strategically placed sofas and a log-burning stove. No one seems in a rush as they linger over newspapers and magazines. If and when you decide to eat you have a choice of two venues. A cosy room adjacent to the bar offers a traditional feel, while upstairs, in a former chapel, is a more formal restaurant with original chapel windows and lofty timbers. Local ingredients are proudly advertised on the menus, and dishes exhibit distinctly modern overtures. Bedrooms have a more traditional outlook, but are cosy and comfortable.

Food serving times

Tuesday-Saturday:
12pm-2pm, 7pm-9pm

Sunday:
12pm-2pm

Closed 25-26 December,
1 January

Prices

Meals: 13.95 (3 course lunch) and a la carte 24.00/35.00

4 rooms: 50.00/95.00

Typical Dishes

Foie gras terrine
Panfried seabass & gurnard
Assiette of chocolate

On B3107 midway between Bradford-on-Avon and Melksham. Parking.

095 The Millstream

Marden SN10 3RH

Tel.: (01380) 848308 - Fax: (01380) 848337

e-mail: info@the-millstream.net - Website: www.the-millstream.net

Wadworths 6X, Henry's IPA and seasonal ales - Summersault, Bishop's Tipple

The motto at The Millstream is 'live a little, drink a little, laugh a lot,' and to this might well be added 'eat a little or a lot, but eat well.' Food here is freshly prepared, using quality, local ingredients, including herbs from the pub's own garden. The orthographically-suspect 'Lite bites' include sandwiches and ploughman's, while more substantial meals might include pot roast poussin, tangine of venison or tempura vegetables, Basmati rice and a sweet and sour red pepper coulis. The regularly-changing blackboard menu also lists seasonal specialities. Eat al fresco in the delightful garden overlooking the river Avon, or get comfy at an antique table in the snug. Much of the pub's original character remains, in the form of pale beams and thick wattle walls, and vertical beams act as dividers for the different dining areas. Log burners provide comfort on dark winter evenings.

Food serving times

Tuesday-Saturday:
12pm-3pm, 6.30pm-9.30pm

Sunday:
12pm-4pm

Bank Holiday Monday:
10.30am-6pm

Closed 25 December

Prices

Meals: 14.95 (3 course lunch/dinner) and a la carte 25.00/36.00

Typical Dishes

Seared mackerel fillet

Local venison Wellington

Rhubarb crumble tart

6.5mi Southeast of Devizes by A342 and minor road North. Parking.

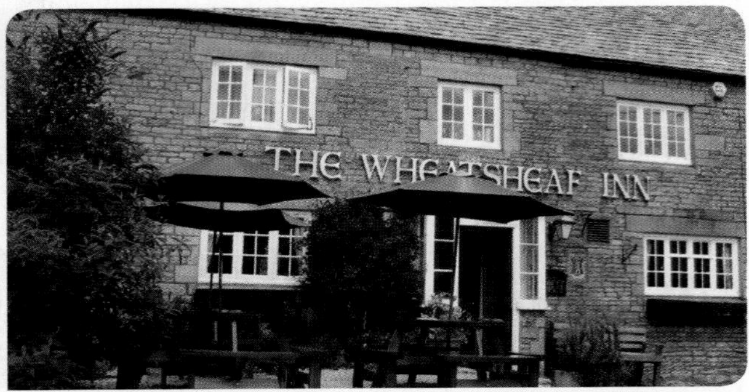

096 The Wheatsheaf at Oaksey

Wheatsheaf Lane,
Oaksey SN16 9TB
Tel.: (01666) 577348

 **Hook Norton Best Bitter, Bath Gem, Sharp's Doombar**

Neatly flanked by the attractive trio of Malmesbury, Tetbury and Cirencester, this charming little inn reflects the minimalist appeal of the gloriously rural village from which it takes its name. There's lots of pubby character here: the original bar in situ, solid beams, wood floor, and exposed walls of stone decorated with farming implements above an inglenook fire. Rubbing shoulders with locals having a pint, you can eat at the simple tables or repair for a touch more comfort to the rear of the bar where a hint of modernisation has taken place. A tiny front terrace is popular in clement weather. Food is important here. Menus offer a concise choice of simple lunch fare to far more ambitious modern British dishes cooked with care and accomplished assurance. For the athletic, there's a skittle alley across the road!

Food serving times

Tuesday-Saturday:
12pm-2pm, 6.30pm-9.30pm

Sunday:
12pm-2pm

Prices

Meals: a la carte
16.00/25.00

Typical Dishes

Vegetable tart

Shoulder of English lamb

Apple & Calvados cheesecake

5.5mi North of Malmesbury; signed from A429. Parking.

097 The Bell

The Square, Ramsbury SN8 2PE
Tel.: (01672) 520230
e-mail: bookings@thebellramsbury.com
Website: www.thebellramsbury.com

 **Ramsbury Gold, Bell Bitter**

Last year saw this Victorian veteran taken over by new owners and a revamp begun; and the locals seem well and truly won over by its new menus and friendly atmosphere. This black and white pub has two distinct sides to it; the bar with its open fire, country scene prints and soft sofas, and the long dining room with its polished wood tables and eye-catching abstract artwork. The bar is the busier side of the establishment, and although you can dine here – or out on the small cobbled terrace - most people choose to eat in the dining room. Lunchtime sandwiches and bar bites are available, whilst the British-themed à la carte provides enough choice to render its side orders all but redundant. Cooking makes good use of local produce and while classical dishes might include homemade sausages or fish cakes, other mains could include sea trout, lamb or venison. The young staff are polite - but a little more enthusiasm would not go amiss.

Food serving times

Monday-Saturday:
12pm-2.30pm, 7pm-9pm

Sunday:
12pm-2.30pm

Prices

Meals: a la carte
17.85/32.85

Typical Dishes

Fresh potato gnocchi
Roast salmon
Rhubarb & apple crumble

4mi Northwest of Hungerford by B4192 and minor road West. Parking.

098 The George & Dragon

High Street, Rowde SN10 2PN
Tel.: (01380) 723053
e-mail: thegandd@tiscali.co.uk
Website: www.thegeorgeanddragonrowde.co.uk

Butcombe Bitter, Nicks

The lazy waters of the nearby Kennet and Avon Canal create the ideal mood for a visit to this divinely characterful pub in the Vale of Pewsey. Its epicentre is a gorgeous stone fireplace crackling heartily in the darker months. The low timbered ceiling just adds to the feeling of rich warmth; outside, summer sunshine can be enjoyed in a smart little garden. There are two small areas in which to dine - adjacent to the fire or in the dining room - but either way, you can't go wrong, but be sure to book as it gets very busy. Keenly-priced menus place the emphasis on plenty of daily changing specials, and the cooking is simple, robust and classic, with the emphasis on seafood specialities. As well as good value menus, you can also rely on polite, friendly service from the young owners.

Food serving times

Tuesday-Friday:
12pm-3pm, 7pm-10pm

Saturday:
12pm-4pm, 6.30pm-10pm

Sunday:
12pm-4pm

Closed 1-8 January

Booking essential

Prices

Meals: 15.50 (3 course lunch) and a la carte 28.00/35.00

Typical Dishes

Baked fig
Wild seabass
Eton mess

Just North of Devizes on A342.
Parking.

099 The Gastrobistro at the Pheasant Inn

19 Salt Lane,
Salisbury SP1 1DT
Tel.: (01722) 414 926
e-mail: gastrobistro@aol.com - Website: www.gastrobistro.co.uk

Hopback Summer Lightning, Courage Best

It's hard to know why good places to eat have been so thin on the ground in Salisbury but it's steadily improving and now the locals and the many tourists have another place to try, however odd the name of that place may be. The owner is an anglophile Frenchmen who has made the Cathedral City his home over the last few years, so you are just as likely to find steak and chips or smoked pheasant on the menu as you are duck confit or bouillabaisse - all freshly made and served with a hefty dollop of Gallic charm. The plaque on the wall dates the black and white timbered building back to 1638, but it has the air of one even older, and its rough quarry tiled floors, inglenook fireplaces and ancient beams all add to its distinctive character. The copper-topped bar, with accompanying sofas still attracts its fair share of drinkers, but most people come here to dine, with the set menus and weekend brunch proving particularly popular.

Food serving times

Monday-Sunday:
12pm-2.30pm, 6pm-9.30pm

Closed 26 December,
1 January

Prices

Meals: 7.00 (2 course lunch & dinner) and a la carte 100.00/25.00

Typical Dishes

Crab ravioli
Pressed belly pork
Passion fruit tart

In city centre North of the cathedral. Salt Lane car park 1 minute's walk.

100 The Haunch of Venison

1 Minster St,
Salisbury SP1 1TB
Tel.: (01722) 411313 - Fax: (01722) 341774
e-mail: oneminsterst@aol.com - Website: www.haunchofvenison.co.uk

Courage Best, Summer Lightning, Greene King IPA, Charles Wells Bombardier

Most people come to Salisbury to visit the Cathedral; locals stay in the city to frequent The Haunch – they've been doing it since the 14th century when its first recorded use was to house craftsmen working on the spire. It's an immensely charming and characterful place. Its huge oak beams pre-date even the building itself and are believed to originate from early sailing vessels. Half way up the stairs is 'The House of Lords', once used to accommodate higher clergy, now a snug for private parties, where an old bread oven, with iron gate, keeps guard of a mummified hand! The ground floor bar has its own charms: unique floor with former Choristers tiles and bar top completely made of pewter. The main dining room, 'One Minster Street', on the first floor, has bags of individuality including original wobbly ceilings. Menus are eclectic, drawn from past and modern eras, served on lovely polished wooden tables.

Food serving times

Thursday-Saturday:
12pm-2.30pm, 6pm-10pm

Thesday-Wednesday:
12pm-2.30pm, 6pm-9.30pm

Closed dinner 25 December

Prices

Meals: 9.90/9.90 (3 course lunch/dinner) and a la carte 9.90/25.00

Typical Dishes

Asparagus with Parma ham

Haunch of venison

Sloe gin and pannacotta

In the city centre; south of the bus station. Parking next to pub in Market Square or in Sainsbury's car park

101 The Lamb on the Strand

99 The Strand,
Semington BA14 6LL
Tel.: (01380) 870263 - Fax: (01380) 871203
e-mail: philip@cbcc.fsworld.co.uk

Ringwood Best, Butcombe Bitter, Black Sheep Emmerdale, Palmers IPA

This ivy clad, red brick inn is a rather diverting attraction on the busy road out of Trowbridge. It has a characterful feel, its 18C origins typified by the low beams; a woodburner and log fire adds to the pleasing ambience. A series of pleasantly furnished rooms affords lots of space to relax with a pint of real ale or a glass of wine from the landlord's carefully selected list. If the weather's good, eat outside in the attractive walled garden. Menus are traditional and extensive; consistently fresh food is served with abundant use of local produce: the mouth-watering cheese pudding is a sure-fire hit. Service at this family-run establishment is invariably efficient, friendly and helpful.

Food serving times

Monday-Saturday:
12pm-2pm, 6.30pm-9pm

Sunday:
12pm-2pm

Closed 25-26 December, 1 January

Booking essential

Prices

Meals: a la carte
16.75/20.30

Typical Dishes

Game terrine

Spicy fillet of beef tortilla

Chocolate & walnut fudge tart

Between Trowbridge and Devizes on A361 near Semington village. Parking.

102 The Spread Eagle Inn

Church Lawn,
Stourton BA12 6QE
Tel.: (01747) 840587 - Fax: (01747) 840954
e-mail: enquiries@spreadeagleinn.com - Website: www.spreadeagleinn.com

 **Kilmington, Butcombe, Dorset Gold**

Stourhead House is a superb National Trust property and its gardens are rightly acknowledged as amongst the best in England. Not so well known is this attractive 18C inn tucked away in a charming courtyard at the end of the invigorating circular walk round the grounds. There are three rooms to settle into: one at the front with a bar, and two to the rear, larger and pleasantly appointed with rough wooden tables and chairs and typical 18C styling, set off by deep burgundy coir floor coverings and even a few sofas. It all gets very busy at lunchtimes as visitors to the gardens arrive for sustenance, and simple menus reflect this; evenings take on a more serious aspect, with a la carte menus of locally sourced ingredients. The five bedrooms offer simple comforts – they're a great idea for those who want to enjoy the estate at a less hurried pace!

Food serving times

Monday-Sunday:
12pm-3pm, 7pm-9pm

Prices

Meals: 16.95 (3 course Sunday lunch) and a la carte 20.00/25.00

5 rooms: 70.00/110.00

Typical Dishes

Chicken tarragon terrine
Cornish fish pie
Sticky toffee pudding

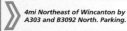

4mi Northeast of Wincanton by A303 and B3092 North. Parking.

103 The Angel Inn

Upton Scudamore BA12 0AG
Tel.: (01985) 213225 - Fax: (01985) 218182
e-mail: mail@theangelinn.co.uk
Website: www.theangelinn.co.uk

Wadworth 6X, Butcombe Gold, Charles Wells Bombardier, Bass

To the east the vast expanses of Salisbury Plain offer a rather forbidding prospect, but in this cosy 16C inn all is relaxed and cheerful. The patrons see to that, running the Angel in their own personalised and dedicated way; the warm character of the establishment all adds to the experience. There's a lovely, sunny rear terrace with barbeque for summer days, but the interior's no less inviting, rustic charm seamlessly linked to rural setting. Scrubbed wooden floors, original artwork and candlelight will make you want to linger. Fine cooking will have much the same effect. Appealing, modern dishes are supplemented by blackboard fish specials: try, perhaps, roast scallops with chilli jam followed by roast monkfish with spinach and new potatoes. The comfortable rooms are invariably spotless.

Food serving times

Monday-Sunday:
12pm-2pm, 7pm-9.30pm

Closed 25-26 December,
1 January

Prices

Meals: a la carte
20.00/30.00

10 rooms: 75.00/85.00

Typical Dishes

Asparagus in smoked salmon
Rack of Wiltshire lamb
Dark chocolate marquise

Village signed off A350 to the north of Warminster. Parking.

104 The Pear Tree Inn

Top Lane, Whitley SN12 8QX
Tel.: (01225) 709131 - Fax: (01225) 702276
e-mail: enquiries@thepeartreeinn.com
Website: www.thepeartreeinn.com

Stonehenge Ales - Pigswill, Spire; The Hidden Brewery - Hidden Pint, Quest; Sharp's Brewery - Doombar, Cornish Coaster

Though not far from Bath, visitors to this attractive Cotswold stone inn may be tempted to stay put once they've indulged what's on offer here. A pleasant front garden leads in to what can best be described as a stylish country dining pub and restaurant. Owners are keen to stress the amount of home produced food that goes into their menus: soups, sausages, bread, sorbets and ice cream are all made on the premises and Wiltshire suppliers provide game and meat. End results are a pleasing amalgam of traditional and modern dishes with a European accent. Staying overnight is a pleasure: bedrooms drip with contemporary style. There's impressive use of beautiful local oak and re-claimed barn doors; you'll also find top quality linen, the very best toiletries, and super-smart chrome fittings.

Food serving times

Monday-Sunday:
12pm-2.30pm, 7pm-9.30pm

Closed 25-26 December, 1 January

Prices

Meals: 16.00 (3 course lunch) and a la carte 25.00/30.00

8 rooms: 75.00/105.00

Typical Dishes

Brixham scallops
Braised beef Jacobs Ladder
White chocolate cheesecake

Northwest of Melksham; Whitley is signed off A365. Parking.

In recent years, the restored Jewellery Quarter, Brindleyplace and Centenary Square, not to mention the shops and bars of Mailbox and the new Bullring, have brought revival and recognition to ever-evolving Birmingham. But not far from Britain's hard-wrought second city, Coalbrookdale, picturesque Ironbridge and the towns of The Potteries and The Black Country offer poignant reminders of the industries that made them and shaped their working way of life. Further afield, and further back in time, Warwick and world-famous Stratford span the centuries, while the reflections of Viking and Celtic art at Kilpeck Church look back to a more ancient past. Explore prosperous period towns like Ludlow and Lichfield, visit the cathedral cities of Hereford and Worcester or take in some of England's most captivating countryside, from the upper Wye to the lower Peaks, by way of Elgar's beloved Malverns and Housman's "blue remembered hills". The discoveries continue in the region's pubs and inns, with cider and orchard fruits from the Vale of Evesham, Herefordshire beef, Gloucester's well-known cheeses and, most famously of all, the Burton beers which transformed the great British pint over 200 years ago.

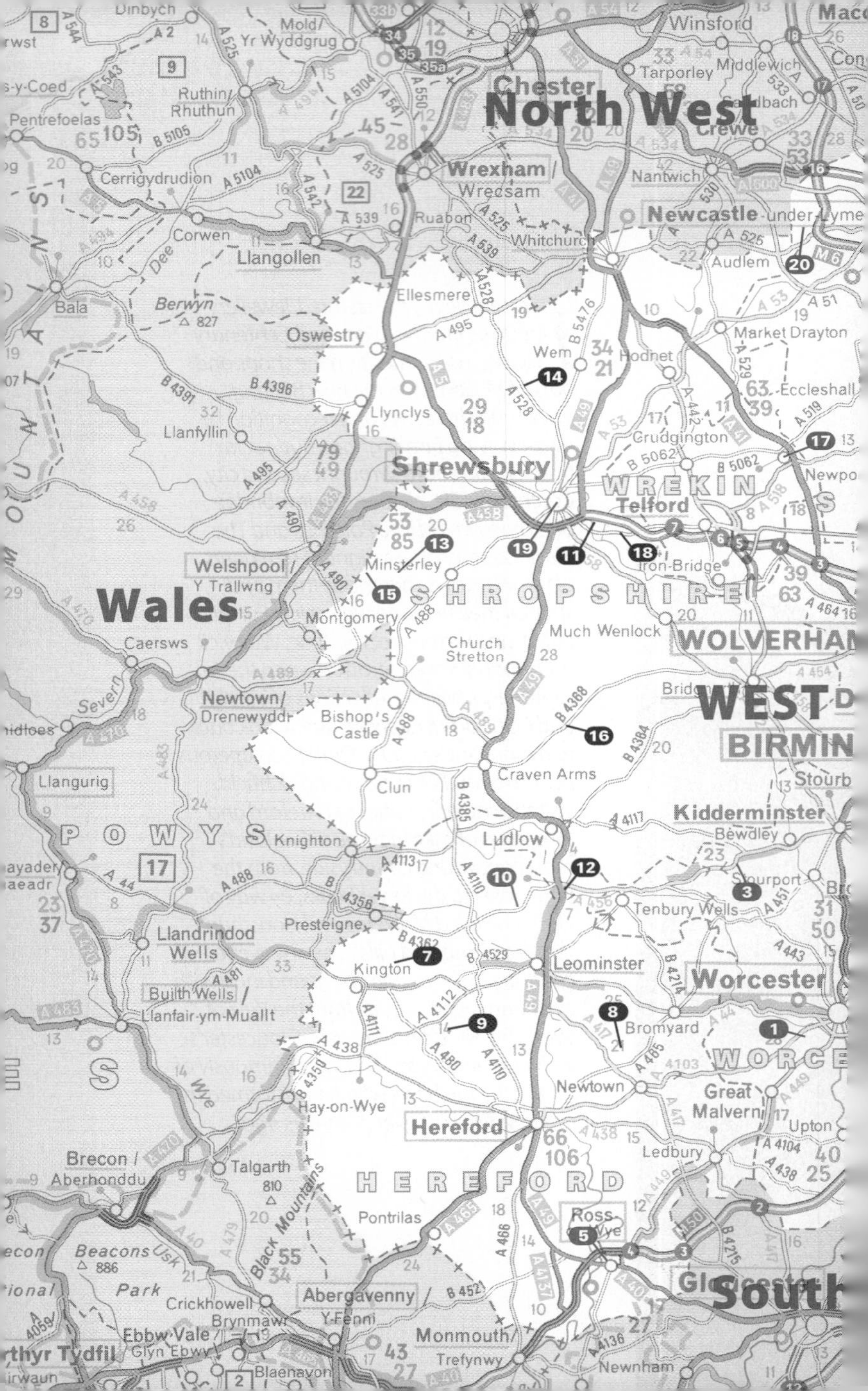

North West
Wales
West
Chester
Winsford
Tarporley
Middlewich
Sandbach
Crewe
Nantwich
Newcastle-under-Lyme
Audlem
Market Drayton
Eccleshall
Mold/ Yr Wyddgrug
Ruthin/ Rhuthun
Pentrefoelas
Cerrigydrudion
Corwen
Llangollen
Wrexham / Wrecsam
Ruabon
Whitchurch
Ellesmere
Oswestry
Llynclys
Wem
Hodnet
Crudgington
Bala
Berwyn
Dee
Llanfyllin
Shrewsbury
WREKIN
Telford
Iron-Bridge
Welshpool / Y Trallwng
Minsterley
SHROPSHIRE
Montgomery
Much Wenlock
Church Stretton
WOLVERHAM
Caersws
Newtown/ Drenewydd
Bishop's Castle
Severn
Bridg
BIRMIN
Llangurig
Clun
Craven Arms
Stourb
Kidderminster
Bewdley
POWYS
Knighton
Ludlow
Stourport
Tenbury Wells
Presteigne
Llandrindod Wells
Kington
Leominster
Worcester
Builth Wells / Llanfair-ym-Muallt
Bromyard
WORCE
Newtown
Great Malvern
Upton
Hay-on-Wye
Hereford
Wye
Ledbury
Brecon / Aberhonddu
Talgarth
HEREFORD
Pontrilas
Ross-on-Wye
Black Mountains
Beacons
Usk
Park
Crickhowell
Abergavenny / Y Fenni
Brynmawr
Ebbw Vale / Glyn Ebwy
Monmouth / Trefynwy
Blaenavon
Newnham
South

Baslow
Chesterfield
Bakewell
Chatsworth House
Park
Little Moreton Hall
Hardwick Hall
Tuxford
Ollerton
Kidsgrove
Clay Cross
Leek
Matlock
Alfreton
Mansfield
Sutton-in-Ashfield
DERBY
Ripley
Heanor
Southwell
Ashbourne
Belper
Hucknall
R. Trent
STOKE-ON-TRENT
NOTTINGHAM
Stone
Ilkeston
Derby
Uttoxeter
Binghan
Sudbury
West Bridgford
Long Eaton
Stafford
Abbots Bromley
Burton-upon-Trent
Rempstone
Rugeley
East Midlands
Swadlincote
Loughborough
Cannock
Ashby de la Zouch
Brownhills
Lichfield
Coalville
LEICESTER
Walsall
Tamworth
Sutton Coldfield
Oadby
Atherstone
Hinckley
MIDLANDS
Upping
Nuneaton
Market Harborough
Bedworth
Lutterworth
Halesowen
Solihull
COVENTRY
Husbands Bosworth
Rugby
Rothwell
Kenilworth
WARWICK
NORTHAM
Henley
Royal Leamington Spa
Wellingborou
Warwick
Daventry
Southam
Stratford-upon-Avon
Ettington
Pershore
Chipping Campden
Shipston-on-Stour
Towcester
Banbury
Wolverton
Broadway
Moreton
Brackley
Milton Keynes
Winchcombe
Chipping Norton
Stow-on-the-Wold
Buckingham
Bletchley
West
South East
OXFORD
Bicester
Northleach
Woodstock
BUCKINGHAM

001 Bear and Ragged Staff

Station Rd,
Bransford WR6 5JH
Tel.: (01886) 833399 - Fax: (01886) 833106
e-mail: mail@bear.uk.com - Website: www.bear.uk.com

 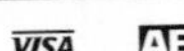  

St George's Best Bitter, Shepherd Neame Spitfire

Satisfyingly familiar pub classics and more formal restaurant recipes run side by side on the Bear and Ragged Staff's huge blackboards; add to this the occasional fish specials and there's sure to be something that appeals. What's more, even with such a big choice, it's safe to assume the cooking will be tasty and prepared with sound culinary know-how. In fact, it would be easy to take this country pub for granted: unremarkable on the outside, comfortable and traditional within, it seems almost too pleasant and unassuming for its own good, but fortunately the locals know a good thing when they see it. Service is friendly with no standing on ceremony: though the pub is divided into a classically styled dining room and bar, you can order what you like and eat it where you choose.

Food serving times

Monday-Saturday:
12pm-2pm, 7pm-9pm

Sunday:
12pm-2pm, 7pm-8.30pm

Closed dinner 25 December and dinner 1 January

Prices

Meals: a la carte
19.00/35.00

Typical Dishes

Stuffed boned quail
Best end of lamb
Lemon & treacle sponge

4.5mi Southwest of Worcester by A44 and A4103; from Bransford follow signs to Powick. Parking.

002 Bell & Cross

Holy Cross,
Clent DY9 9QL
Tel.: (01562) 730319
Website: www.bellandcrossclent.co.uk

 **Timothy Taylor's Gonville Ale, Wadworth 6X**

Every inch of wall space seems to be filled with framed photos at this friendly little pub – little being the operative word, given the cosy feel in each of its rooms. Traditional-looking both outside and in, with its tiled floors, wheelback chairs and wooden tables; one of its snugs is a great place to settle down in for the evening – while the terrace and pretty garden are the natural choice on sunny days - and the servers are attentive wherever you sit. Cooking is tasty, balanced and well executed and you'll find that classic dishes such as lamb chops and roasted chicken share the menu with more modern and international offerings such as Peking duck rolls or veal Schnitzel Carbonara. Desserts will definitely take you back a few years with old favourites such as knickerbocker glory, rice pudding and trifle on the menu, and who can resist the temptation of treacle tart, when it's listed as being served with Granny's thick custard?

Food serving times

Monday-Saturday:
12pm-2pm, 6.30pm-9.15pm

Sunday:
12pm-2.30pm, 6.30pm-9.15pm

Closed 25 December, dinner 26 and 31 December, dinner 1 January

Prices

Meals: a la carte 15.00/25.00

Typical Dishes

Onion and cider soup
Collar of pork
Peach Melba pavlova

Between Stourbridge and Bromsgrove; off Northbound A491; the pub is on the left hand side in Holy Cross. Parking.

003 The Colliers Arms

Tenbury Road,
Clows Top DY14 9HA
Tel.: (01299) 832242
e-mail: thecolliersarms@aol.com - Website: www.colliersarms.com

  AE MC

 **Hobson's Best, Hobson's Town Crier, Wyre Valley Butty Bach**

A young new owner may have taken over at the helm of The Colliers Arms but the pub is still very popular with the older generation, who obviously appreciate good quality, homecooked food. Several rooms offer differing atmospheres in which to dine; there's a snug little bar with a traditional feel to it, an open main bar with a log fire, furnished with polished wooden tables and decorated with some decidedly fishy wall paper, plus – the best place to sit - an airy dining room at the rear of the pub, with pleasant views of the garden. There's no danger of finding fashionable fusion dishes here: instead you'll find all the old favourites on the menu; traditional hearty British dishes like steak and chips, sausage and mash and steak and kidney pudding, as well as sandwiches and lighter snacks at lunch. The choice of food on the menu is dictated by the seasons and everything is fresh and homemade.

Food serving times

Monday-Saturday:
12pm-2pm, 6.30pm-9pm

Sunday:
12pm-3pm

Closed 27-29 December

Prices

Meals: a la carte
19.50/26.50

Typical Dishes

Marinated goats' cheese

Rack of lamb

Raspberry mille feuilles

9mi West of Kidderminster by A456. Parking.

004 **The Chequers**

Kidderminster Rd,
Cutnall Green WR9 0PJ
Tel.: (01299) 851292 - Fax: (01299) 851744
Website: www.chequerscutnallgreen.co.uk

 **Enville Ale, Wadworth 6X, Timothy Taylor's Landlord**

Don't be put off by this roadside pub's unremarkable exterior: it's obviously just a cover to stop the masses thronging here in their droves. Inside it's a different story - extremely characterful, with rustic style aplenty in the form of sandblasted beams, exposed brickwork and wood and tiled floors. There's a lounge bar with sofas and armchairs in which to make yourself comfortable and a restaurant with chunky dark wood tables, whilst the patio and garden area are popular in the spring and summer months. The large à la carte dinner menu offers modern dishes and is supplemented by daily specials. Cooking is flavoursome, with international leanings, so your chicken might come Yuk Sung style, your sea bream might be made into a Goan curry, and your chicken breast might come served with kumara potato and chorizo. The lunchtime menu offers lighter bites; from sandwiches and salads to pasta and panini.

Food serving times

Monday-Sunday:
12pm-2pm, 6.30pm-9.15pm

Closed 25 December, dinner 26 December, 1 January

Prices

Meals: a la carte
17.50/25.00

Typical Dishes

Sweet 'n' sour king prawns
Grilled calves liver
Poached strawberries

3mi North of Droitwich Spa on A442. Parking.

005 The Lough Pool at Sellack

Sellack,
Ross-on-Wye HR9 6LX
Tel.: (01989) 730236 - Fax: (01989) 730548
e-mail: david@loughpool.co.uk - Website: www.loughpoolinn.co.uk

Wye Valley Best, ABV, Butty Bach (Little Friend), John Smith's Cask ABV, Old Speckled Hen, Spitfire

This 16C black and white timbered inn is in a wonderfully rural spot tucked away among the country lanes of Herefordshire - an ideal location for garden and terrace dining in the summer months. It's a solid traditional establishment with exposed stone, flag flooring and lots of space to wander around with a pint of local ale. No trouble in spotting the dining areas: they're painted bright yellow with red cedar-stained pine flooring. Menus change frequently, depending on ingredients. The Lough Pool serves excellent modern style cooking where good local produce is unerringly to the fore: look out for the blackboard specials.

Food serving times

Monday-Sunday:
12pm-2pm, 7pm-9pm

Closed 2 January-February, Monday and dinner Sunday October-November

Prices

Meals: a la carte
21.00/30.00

Typical Dishes

Goat's cheese brûlée
Rib eye steak
Apple and frangipane slice

3.25mi Northwest of Ross-on-Wye; turn right off A49 (Hereford) and follow signs for Hoarwithy. Parking.

006 Epic

68 Hanbury Rd,
Stoke Prior B60 4DN
Tel.: (01527) 871929
e-mail: epic.bromsgrove@virgin.net - Website: www.epicbrasseries.co.uk

Timothy Taylor's Landlord, Black Sheep, Ludlow Gold

The only remnants here of its days as a roadside pub are the tiled floor and odd rafter. Otherwise this stylish establishment has benefited greatly from a major facelift and extensions. At the centre, a large modern bar with comfy sofa lounge area. All around, an airy dining space with lots of glass, brick and wood, which has been cleverly worked into the modern design. The overall feel is one of effortless style, accentuated by comfortable seating at smart wood tables with good accessories. Menus are large and dominated by popular modern classics at reasonable prices. Service is efficient from staff who are used to being busy.

Food serving times

Tuesday-Saturday:
12pm-2.30pm, 6.30pm-9.30pm

Sunday:
12pm-2.30pm

Prices

Meals: 12.95 (3 course lunch) and a la carte 25.00/30.00

Typical Dishes

Mediterranean fish soup
Soy & ginger blackened salmon
Coconut & dark rum ice cream

2.25mi Southwest of Bromsgrove by A38 and B4091; pub is on the right after traffic lights. Parking.

The Stagg Inn

007 The Stagg Inn

Titley HR5 3RL
Tel.: (01544) 230221
e-mail: reservations@thestagg.co.uk
Website: www.thestagg.co.uk

Hobson's Best Bitter, Hobson's Town Crier, Brains Reverend James, Timothy Taylor's Landlord

In the delightful surroundings of the Welsh Marches stands this nationally renowned whitewashed landmark. A carefully cultivated network of local suppliers, a real regard for quality and exemplary belief in value for money have all contributed to its singular success. You can eat in three different areas: the cosy bar, the dining room with chunky wooden tables, or, assuming the weather is clement, the rear garden. Menus change every five or six weeks, but the cooking itself, assured and original with a hint of classic French flair, is a model of consistency, allowing fresh, natural flavours to shine through. Comfortable, softly lit surroundings and pleasant, intelligent service, contribute to a really memorable meal. If you wish to prolong the Stagg experience, there are two rooms above the pub, and more in the quieter part-Georgian vicarage down the road.

Food serving times

Tuesday-Saturday:
12pm-2pm, 6.30pm-9pm

Sunday:
12pm-2pm

Closed 25-26 December, 1 January, 1 week in February, 1 week in November

Prices

Meals: a la carte
20.00/29.00

6 rooms: 60.00/120.00

Typical Dishes

Scallops on cauliflower purée
Fillet of Herefordshire beef
Crème brûlée trio

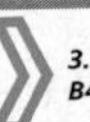

3.5mi Northeast of Kington on B4355. Parking.

008 Three Crowns Inn

Bleak Acre,
Ullingswick HR1 3JQ
Tel.: (01432) 820279 - Fax: (08700) 515338
e-mail: info@threecrownsinn.com - Website: www.threecrownsinn.com

We most liked

   VISA 

Wye Valley Butty Bach, Timothy Taylor's Landlord, Black Sheep, Hobsons Best

A hallmark of this rural, family-run pub is its unfussy cooking: the chef-owner takes the finest of local ingredients and gives them Three Crowns treatment, producing robust, tasty dishes which are easy on the eye as well as on the pocket. The set blackboard lunchtime menu, located above the fire, offers classic dishes such as moules and frites, while the daily-changing à la carte might tempt you with starters such as roast woodcock with risotto of its liver, followed by confit duck or peppered sirloin of Herefordshire beef. Service is chatty and polite and the atmosphere is relaxed. Hops hang from low beams and there are seats both for drinkers and diners - the most popular being those by the open fire - while the more modern extension is used for dining during busier periods. A bedroom also housed in the extension is smart, with contemporary styling; the owners hope to add more soon.

Food serving times

Tuesday-Sunday:
12pm-2.30pm, 7pm-9.30pm

Closed 25-26 December, Bank Holidays

Prices

Meals: 12.95/14.95 (2/3 course lunch) and a la carte 14.95/25.00

1 room :75.00/95.00

Typical Dishes

Home-smoked goose salad

Shortwood Farm pork belly

Tarte al `Coloche

1.25mi East of the village on unsigned country lane. Parking.

009 The Salutation Inn

Market Pitch, Weobley HR4 8SJ
Tel.: (01544) 318443 - Fax: (01544) 318216
e-mail: salutationinn@btinternet.com
Website: www.thesalutationinn.co.uk

 **Goff's Jouster, Wye Valley Butty Bach, Dorothy Goodbody**

A old country pub through and through, this 16C cider house, in the heart of this pretty Herefordshire village, truly looks and feels the part: crooked timbers are hung with jugs, hop-bines and horse-brasses, blue and white china plates are ranged along the mantelpiece. The traditional partition of lounge and public bar is still in evidence too: one pleasant corner of the pub is set as a formal dining room, with candles and neat, white tablecloths, although the same menu is served throughout. The sound and classically based cooking seems in tune with the atmosphere of the place. Tidily kept bedrooms, some in traditional floral patterns, are kept in good order.

Food serving times

Monday-Saturday: 6.30pm-9.15pm

Closed 25 December, 2 weeks after New Year

Closed Monday January-April

Prices

Meals: a la carte 15.00/30.00

3 rooms: 50.00/90.00

Typical Dishes

Scallops with Mornay sauce
Herefordshire beef
Sweet risotto

8mi Southwest of Leominster by A44 and B4230. Parking.

010 The Bell Inn

Green Lane,
Yarpole HR6 0BD
Tel.: (01568) 780359
Website: www.thebellinnyarpole.co.uk

Hooky Bitter, Hereford Pale Ale, Timothy Taylor's Landlord

Temptingly set between Leominster and Ludlow, the black-and-white timbered Bell Inn, first mentioned in the Domesday Book, promises delightful rustic ambience and it does not disappoint. The Bell does not try to be a gastropub but operates in traditional style. An impressive interior takes its cue from heavy beams, horse brasses, open fires and rural ornaments and pictures. Adjoining is a very characterful converted barn dining room boasting high, raftered ceilings, heavy wood tables and original stone cider press. Drinkers are catered for in a separate bar and snug. Well-paced, friendly service is a given here. Sizable menus feature British pub classics, while French influences and modern styles slide easily into the mix. Seasonal Herefordshire ingredients are to the fore; cooking is hearty and robust. You'd expect nothing less!

Food serving times

Tuesday-Sunday and Bank Holiday Monday:
12pm-2.30pm, 6.30pm-9.30pm

Prices

Meals: 14.50 (3 course lunch) and a la carte 16.95/24.95

Typical Dishes

Classic prawn cocktail
Toulouse cassoulet
Sherry trifle

4mi North of Leominster by B4361 and minor road West. Parking.

011 The Mytton and Mermaid

Atcham SY5 6QG

Tel.: (01743) 761220 - Fax: (01743) 761292
e-mail: reception@myttonandmermaid.co.uk
Website: www.myttonandmermaid.co.uk

Wood's Shropshire Gold, Wood's Shropshire Lad

Dating from the 18C, this impressive, ivy-clad Georgian inn is located opposite Attingham Park on the banks of the river Severn and, with its neat lawns and terraces, is a great spot for a summer afternoon meal. It's far from being just a fair weather pub, however; inside you'll find several formal dining areas as well as the rustically modern Mad Jack's Bar with its log fire, strategically placed sofas and interesting history. The bar menu contains traditional dishes such as mussels or steak and chips, alongside more modern treats such as asparagus and goats cheese terrine, or crayfish Caesar salad. The seasonal restaurant menu contains local Shropshire meats as well as dishes such as guinea fowl and foie gras, or Jerusalem artichoke mousse with beetroot crisps. Bedrooms are split between the main house and the stable block annex – those in the former being the more luxurious, although all are well kept and comfortable.

Food serving times

Monday-Sunday:
12pm-2.30pm, 7pm-10pm

Closed 25 December

Prices

Meals: a la carte
19.95/35.00

16 rooms:
80.00/160.00

Typical Dishes

Seafood assiette

Fillet of Shropshire pork

Apple and vanilla parfait

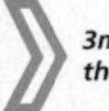

3mi Southeast of Shrewsbury on the B4380 Ironbridge rd. Parking.

012 The Roebuck Inn

Brimfield SY8 4NE
Tel.: (01584) 711230
e-mail: info@theroebuckinn.co.uk
Website: www.theroebuckinn.com

 **No real ales offered**

The Roebuck Inn has seen several changes in owner in recent years, its fortunes rising up and down accordingly, but with new French chef-owner Olivier Bossut in charge, its star is once again on the up. It comes as no surprise to find dishes such as gateaux of crab in a saffron beurre blanc, terrine of piglet and foie gras, millefeuille of green asparagus or cassoulet Toulousain on the menu, but French or otherwise, dishes are freshly cooked, seasonal and full of flavour. Meat comes from a butcher in nearby Ludlow, and ingredients are sourced locally. Located right in the middle of the village, and dating back to the 15C, this inn is every inch the classic country pub, with friendly staff and a relaxed, informal feel, and you can eat in either the stylishly furnished dining room or in the bar. If you want to stay a while and discover the Ludlow area, three bedrooms have a homely feel.

Food serving times

Monday-Saturday:
12pm-2.30pm, 6.30pm-9.30pm

Sunday:
12pm-2.30pm

Prices

Meals: a la carte 22.50/28.00

3 rooms: 55.00/78.50

Typical Dishes

Brie and smoked salmon parcel
Coq au vin
Vanilla cheesecake

4.5mi South of Ludlow; signed off A49. Parking.

013 The Feathers at Brockton

Brockton TF13 6JR

Tel.: (01746) 785202 - Fax: (01746) 785202

e-mail: kayiatou@hotmail.com - Website: www.feathersatbrockton.co.uk

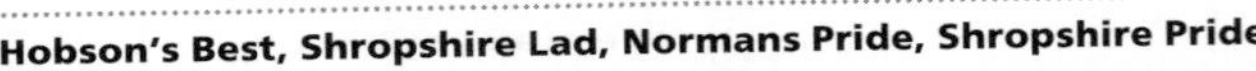

Hobson's Best, Shropshire Lad, Normans Pride, Shropshire Pride

Wenlock Edge, in the heart of the Shropshire countryside, is a popular spot for walkers, and word-of-mouth has contributed to this attractive part 16th century pub becoming one of their more favoured watering holes. The owner/chef cut his teeth in well-thought-of London establishments and dining is to the fore here, with the constantly changing blackboard menus providing interesting modern English dishes underpinned by local produce, such as Shropshire partridge or beef. Ambience is ideal: the characterful interior boasts a tiled floor, white washed stone walls, beams, and vast inglenooks with wood-burning stoves. Lots of little areas surround the central bar so a cosy feel snuggles within the rusticity. If anyone feels like splashing out, there are various examples of local artwork for sale lining the walls.

Food serving times

Tuesday-Sunday and Bank Holiday Monday: 12pm-2.30pm, 6.30pm-9.30pm

Closed 26-28 December

Prices

Meals: 14.95 (3 course lunch/dinner) and a la carte 18.50/30.00

Typical Dishes

Garlic king prawns
Slow cooked pork belly
Bread and butter pudding

5mi Southwest of Much Wenlock on B4378. Parking.

014 The Burlton Inn

Burlton SY4 5TB

Tel.: (01939) 270284

e-mail: robertlesterrc@yahoo.co.uk

 **Robinsons Best, Double Hop, Old Stockport, Dark Horse**

Midway between Shrewsbury and Ellesmere, lies the village of Burlton and its traditional beamed, 18C inn. Inside it's a contemporary look which greets you, and the fire-lit ambience is informal and friendly. Join the regulars for a drink at the bar before choosing a seat, or head outside instead to have your meal on the patio, made pretty with hanging baskets that spill over with flowers. There's no reinventing of the wheel happening on the menu here – cooking focuses on traditional British dishes such as steak, kidney and beer pie, sausage and mash and cod and chips, while more unusual offerings include dishes like a tapas platter of olives, chorizo and crusty bread, goats' cheese, sun-dried tomato, mozzarella and black olive panzotti, or chicken jalfrezi. Six comfortable, modern bedrooms are situated in a separate annex; en suites are well-kept, and breakfast is definitely worth getting up for.

Food serving times

Monday-Friday:
12pm-2pm, 6.30pm-9.45pm

Saturday-Sunday:
12pm-3pm, 6.30pm-9.45pm

Closed 25 December and 1 January

Closed dinner Sunday January-February

Prices

Meals: a la carte 18.00/30.00

6 rooms: 60.00/90.00

Typical Dishes

Seared scallops

Roast lamb rump

Lemon meringue roulade

8mi North of Shrewsbury on A528. Parking.

015 The Sun Inn

Marton SY21 8JP
Tel.: (01938) 561211
e-mail: info@suninn.biz - Website: www.suninn.biz

 **Hobson's and guest beers from Six Bells Brewery and other local breweries**

The simply styled Sun with its neat and tidy stone facade is a credit to this quiet Marches village on the English-Welsh border. The owners previously ran a restaurant in the New Forest and their cooking experience shows to good effect, even down to tasty home-made bread. Light snacks are available all day in the rather spartan little front bar while dinner is served in the recently refurbished dining room, now resplendent in pine. The chef makes a point of using local ingredients and the well-prepared cooking, nourishing and enjoyable, has a real flavour of the season to it. Genial service from the experienced young owners helps things along nicely, as do the extensive selection of wines by the glass and real ales. An ever-increasing number of regulars and visitors who've picked up on the Sun - often by word of mouth - are proof positive of its widening appeal.

Food serving times

Tuesday:
7pm-9.30pm

Monday and Wednesday-Saturday:
12pm-2.30pm, 7pm-9.30pm

Sunday:
12pm-2.30pm

Booking essential

Prices

Meals: 15.95 (3 course Sunday lunch) and a la carte 18.00/30.00

Typical Dishes

Pickled fish in Cointreau

Venison steak

Iced rhubarb & ginger parfait

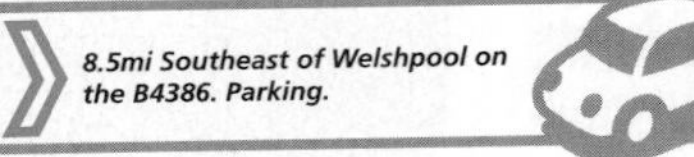
8.5mi Southeast of Welshpool on the B4386. Parking.

016 The Crown Country Inn

Munslow SY7 9ET

Tel.: (01584) 841205 - Fax: (01584) 841255
e-mail: info@crowncountry-inn.co.uk
Website: www.crowncountry-inn.co.uk

Holdens Golden Glow and Black Country, Three Tuns Clerics' Cure and Hobson's and Wood's beers

Quite how old the Crown really is, no-one really knows, but it was already long-established when it served as a "hundred house" for travelling magistrates. Warm and characterful, it certainly has all the hallmarks of a charming old rural inn, with stout beams propping up its cosy taproom, a well-stoked fire and trains of hops dangling from the woodwork. Its cuisine is not bound by tradition, though: light but still substantial modern dishes are served in the bar at lunch, while the evening menu is planned and prepared with a dash of imagination. Local vegetables, rare-breed meats, a fine English cheeseboard and even local spring water demonstrate a taste for regional produce. The large garden and terrace are popular with walkers from nearby Wenlock Edge.

Food serving times

Tuesday-Saturday:
12pm-1.45pm, 6.45pm-8.45pm

Sunday:
12pm-1.45pm

Closed at Christmas

Prices

Meals: 17.00 (3 course lunch/dinner) and a la carte 22.00/30.00

3 rooms: 50.00/75.00

Typical Dishes

Black pudding fondue crostini

Roast rump of Sibdon lamb

Vanilla crème brûlée

On B4378 between Much Wenlock and Craven Arms. Parking.

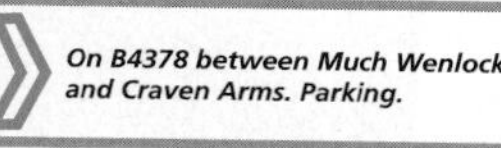

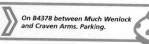

017 The Fox

Pave Lane,
Chetwynd Aston, Newport TF10 9LQ
Tel.: (01952) 815940 - Fax: (01952) 815941
e-mail: fox@brunningandprice.co.uk - Website: www.fox-newport.co.uk

Thwaites Original, Timothy Taylor's Landlord, Shropshire Lad, JHB, Black Sheep, Summer Lightning

Bright and uncluttered, the Fox has a welcoming feel to it. The old pattern of nooks, parlours and lounges has been opened up and the well-chosen furnishings, though mostly restored or reclaimed, fit this more modern layout very well. A collection of framed fashion-plates and cigarette cards, rural scenes and period caricatures run the length of the walls and into the more intimate rooms off to the sides. It's nearly always possible to find a quieter corner somewhere, but the Fox really excels at the big get-together. Long dining tables are perfect for eating out in eights and tens: family brunches on a Sunday or an evening catching up with friends. A sizeable menu of modern classics is delivered with friendly efficiency. Big rear terrace and garden.

Food serving times

Monday-Saturday:
12pm-10pm

Sunday:
12pm-9.30pm

Closed 26 December

Prices

Meals: a la carte
17.70/27.15

Typical Dishes

Thai crab cakes

Steak and kidney pudding

Bara Brith & butter pudding

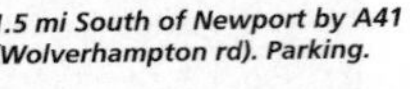

1.5 mi South of Newport by A41 (Wolverhampton rd). Parking.

018 Hundred House

Bridgnorth Rd, Norton TF11 9EE
Tel.: (01952) 730353 - Fax: (01952) 730355
e-mail: reservations@hundredhouse.co.uk
Website: www.hundredhouse.co.uk

 **Heritage, Saddlers, Dark Mild**

Run for over twenty years by two generations of the Phillips family, this inn has a quirky style all of its own. History seems deeply ingrained into its web of rooms, with their tiled floors, open fires and oak panelling, and the dried herbs and hops hanging from ceilings add to the rustic flavour. Hearty food on the menus includes classics such as steak and kidney pie, venison casserole and sausage and mash, as well as dishes which take their influences from further afield, such as tapas, Thai green curry and Greek salad. Ingredients are sourced from local suppliers – and none more so than the inn's own beautiful herb and flower garden.
The country style bedrooms offer comfort as well as character with features such as half testers and four posters; and if you enjoy swinging then you've come to the right place - thanks to the velvet covered seats artfully suspended from the beams in some of the rooms.

Food serving times
Monday-Sunday:
12pm-2.30pm, 6pm-9.30pm

Prices
Meals: a la carte
22.00/35.00

10 rooms:
59.00/135.00

Typical Dishes
Seared scallops
Panfried duck breast
Double chocolate mousse

7 mi. South of Telford on A 442.
Parking.

019 The Armoury

Victoria Quay, Welsh Bridge, Shrewsbury SY1 1HH

Tel.: (01743) 340525

e-mail: armoury@brunningandprice.co.uk
Website: www.brunningandprice.co.uk

 **Armoury Pale Ale, Outlaw, Shropshire Lad, Flavers Original and 8 rotating ales**

This 18C former warehouse has a fascinating history: built for military use, it's done service as a bakery and a World War II convalescent home, and even been moved brick by brick to this spot in sight of the old bridge, where it cries out for a bankside terrace to enjoy the summer sunshine. Inside, gilt-framed mirrors, engravings and Edwardiana cover the brick walls, yard upon yard of old books are rivalled only by row upon rows of malts and liqueurs behind the bar, and a huge ceiling and tall arched windows make the open-plan room feel light and spacious. Lots of big tables, with a hotch-potch of second-hand chairs, make it ideal for a big get-together: its great popularity means there's usually a buzzy atmosphere, and the daily changing menu of modern favourites offers something for everyone.

Food serving times

Monday-Saturday:
12pm-9.30pm

Sunday:
12pm-9pm

Closed 25 December and dinner 1 January

Prices

Meals: a la carte
20.00/30.00

Typical Dishes

Crayfish & prawn cocktail

Rump steak

Chocolate and hazelnut tart

By the Welsh Bridge. Frankwell car park over Welsh Bridge.

020 The Hand and Trumpet

Main Road,
Wrinehill CW3 9BJ
Tel.: (01270) 820048 - Fax: (01270) 821911
Website: www.hand and trumpet-wrinehill.co.uk

Thwaites Original, Timothy Taylor's Landlord, Deuchar's IPA, Woodland's Oak Beauty, Enville's Nail Makers Mild

The ancient village of Wrinehill (mentioned in the Domesday Book) has made a smooth transition into the 21C with this handsomely refurbished and sizable country pub. You're immediately struck by the delightful decked terrace, overlooking duck pond and gardens. On a warm day, you might just fancy plonking yourself down here and admiring the view, but then you'd be doing the stylish interior a disservice. The well-stocked bar has a shiny tiled floor with kilims lending a rather exotic touch, and the classy feel continues into the main dining area, where book shelves and rustic prints create just the right mood of relaxation to enjoy a leisurely lunch or dinner. Menus cover a tried-and-tested country route, with traditional dishes very much to the fore. There's a wide range of wines by the glass and draught real ales to wash it all down with. Incidentally, don't miss the pub's website, complete with a superb history of the area.

Food serving times

Monday-Saturday:
12pm-10pm

Sunday:
12pm-9.30pm

Closed 25 December

Prices

Meals: a la carte
25.00/35.00

Typical Dishes

Shredded salt beef
Rabbit pie
Spotted Dick and custard

6mi West of Newcastle-under-Lyme by A525 and A531. Parking.

021 The Baraset Barn

1 Pimlico Lane,
Alveston CV37 7RF

Tel.: (01789) 295510 - Fax: (01789) 292961
e-mail: barasetbarn@lovelypubs.co.uk - Website: www.lovelypubs.co.uk

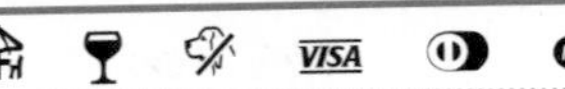

 **Purity UBU**

The historic structure of the old barn is still apparent in the lofty ceilings and rich, golden beams, but the main impression of this very contemporary pub is of one stylish setting after another: a smart lilac-and-white lounge conservatory, a main dining area in brick, pewter, oak and crushed velvet, an intimate rear mezzanine, and a dark, moody cigar bar for savouring an after-dinner drink and clustering round the log burner. A modern British and Mediterranean menu changes a couple of times a year: favourite signature dishes, grills, steaks, and their popular lobster and chips remain ever-present and sum up the bold, fresh culinary style. Bright, prompt service is the other key ingredient in a pleasant, unhurried lunch or evening out.

Food serving times

Monday -Saturday:
12pm-2.30pm, 6.30pm-9.30pm

Sunday:
12pm-2.30pm

Closed 25 December

Prices

Meals: 10.00/20.00 (3 course lunch) and a la carte 25.00/45.00

Typical Dishes

Asparagus with duck's egg
Spit-roast chicken
Hot chocolate fondant

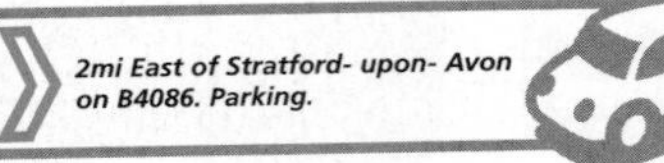

2mi East of Stratford- upon- Avon on B4086. Parking.

022 The Golden Cross

Wixford Road,
Ardens Grafton B50 4LG
Tel.: (01789) 772420 - Fax: (01798) 491358
e-mail: pat@thegoldencross.net - Website: www.thegoldencross.net

Charles Wells Bombardier, Young's Bitter, Purity UBU and Gold

This remote, 18C pub began life as three cottages and its uneven flag floors, wooden beams and local photos give a nod to its past. With its affable atmosphere, and contented mix of drinkers and diners of all ages, you get a real sense that this pub is close to the heart of the local community - and little touches like the glossy magazines on the tables and the fact that you can buy champagne by the glass demonstrate that this is a place which really looks after its customers. The busy, confident kitchen cooks traditional British classics like fisherman's pie, toad in hole and steak and kidney pudding, whilst the oft-changing fish specials might well tempt you to opt for something from the blackboard instead. Eat well – in the bar, the more formal restaurant or out on the patio or in the garden - happy in the knowledge that everything that can be is homemade, including the chips and some particularly mouth-watering desserts.

Food serving times

Monday-Saturday:
12pm-2.30pm, 5.30pm-9.30pm

Sunday:
12pm-8pm

Prices

Meals: 12.95 (3 course Sunday lunch) and a la carte 20.00/25.00

Typical Dishes

Devilled tiger prawn tails
Roast breast of duck
Poached pears

5mi Southwest of Stratford-upon-Avon by A46. Parking.

023 The Fox & Goose Inn

Front St,
Armscote CV37 8DD

Tel.: (01608) 682293 - Fax: (01608) 682293
e-mail: email@foxandgoose.co.uk - Website: www.foxandgoose.co.uk

 **Hook Norton, Shepherd Neame Spitfire, Cotswold Brewery**

Happily situated just north of Shipston on Stour, in the peaceful hamlet of Armscote, this creeper-clad, red brick inn has a more modern, slightly quirkier interior than its traditional outer appearance might suggest. A bright, open plan bar and dining room boast a log burner at their centre, candles sit in wrought iron holders on each table and cushions are scattered around, as are papers and magazines. A stuffed fox chases a goose along the mantelpiece, stencil drawings of animals from encyclopaedias decorate the walls, and the bright and buzzy service from T-shirted staff fits the atmosphere perfectly. Modern cooking has a delicate touch, with refined flavours and a clever combination of well-priced dishes. Four compact and fun bedrooms are decorated on a Cluedo theme, with bold colour schemes of scarlet, mustard, plum and blue, while claw foot baths with candles bring a touch of luxury to proceedings.

Food serving times

Monday-Sunday:
12pm-2.30pm, 7pm-9.30pm

Prices

Meals: 10.00/15.00 (3 course lunch/dinner) and a la carte 23.50/35.00

4 rooms: 49.00/120.00

Typical Dishes

Goats' cheese parcel
Fillet of Scottish beef
Petit pot au chocolat

2.5 mi North of Shipston-on-Stour by A3400. Parking.

024 **The King's Head**

21 Bearley Rd,
Aston Cantlow B95 6HY
Tel.: (01789) 488242 - Fax: (01789) 488137
e-mail: info@thekh.co.uk - Website: www.thekh.co.uk

Brew XI, Greene King, Abbot, Purity Gold

People purportedly travel to this pretty pub from quite a distance to enjoy the now revived duck suppers for which the pub was formerly famous. They are not its only claim to fame, however, since in 1557, Shakespeare's parents reputedly held their wedding reception here. Would the wedding banquet have involved the wild venison casserole, the pheasant or the saddle of rabbit? We can only speculate; although it's probably safe to say that they would not have feasted on the pork Yuk Sung or tomato risotto now also on offer. The abstract art hanging on the walls brings a contemporary touch to the restaurant, while the tables and cushion-clad chairs would not look out of place in a French farmhouse. With its low, heavily beamed ceiling, flag stoned floors and large stone fireplaces, the main lounge bar is equally as charming, while if it's privacy you're after, there are also several smaller nooks in which to make yourself cosy.

Food serving times

Monday-Saturday:
12pm-2.30pm, 6.30pm-9.30pm

Sunday:
12.30pm-3pm

Closed 25 December

Prices

Meals: 15.00 (3 course lunch/dinner) and a la carte 20.00/25.00

Typical Dishes

King prawn and crab satay

Rack of Welsh lamb

Apple and cinnamon pie

3mi South of Henley-in-Arden, off B4089. Parking.

025 The Fox & Hounds Inn

Great Wolford CV36 5NQ
Tel.: (01608) 674220
e-mail: info@thefoxandhoundsinn.com
Website: www.thefoxandhoundsinn.com

VISA 

 **Hook Norton Best, Purity UBU, Teme Valley**

It takes something special to catch the eye in an area as rich in delights as the Cotswolds, but this 16C inn passes the test with flying colours. It's located in the heart of a delightful village, its honey coloured exterior luring the visitor into a series of hugely characterful rooms with bags of period appeal, typified by exposed beams with hop bines, an ancient bread oven, lovely open log fire and solid stone floor. Select from a good array of wines and local real ales and dine at candlelit tables; there's a daily changing blackboard menu of well executed, hearty, fresh fare, that puts many local ingredients to good use. In warmer months, make for the summer terrace. Stay overnight in cosy, well-kept bedrooms.

Food serving times

Tuesday-Saturday:
12pm-2pm, 6pm-9pm

Sunday:
12pm-2pm

Closed 2nd week in January

Prices

Meals: a la carte
17.50/35.00

3 rooms: 60.00/90.00

Typical Dishes

Innesbutton Goats' cheese
Hereford fillet steak
Fig and almond tart

4 mi Northeast of Moreton-in-Marsh by A44. Parking.

026 The Howard Arms

Lower Green,
Ilmington CV36 4LT
Tel.: (01608) 682226 - Fax: (01608) 682226
e-mail: info@howardarms.com - Website: www.howardarms.com

Everards Tiger, Hook Norton Gold and guest beers including Timothy Taylor's Landlord, Purity UBU

Set on the village green in peaceful Ilmington, this picture perfect golden stone inn is the very epitome of the English country pub. The highly polished flag floors gleam, the embers in the log fires glow, and previous generations of the owners' family look nobly down from the old photos and portraits that hang on the walls. With prime seasonal and local ingredients to the fore, the modern menu has an international edge, and dishes such as fresh mussel tart, and beef, ale and mustard pie are served in good sized portions, while 'mrs g's toffee meringue' is quite a favourite on the dessert menu. Wine is Mr Greenwood's passion and is given special attention by the glass; there's a decent choice of real ales available; and if you're driving, there's no need to sulk since there's a great choice of soft drinks too. Cosy bedrooms are furnished with antique furniture and designer fabrics, and the breakfast choice is a real treat.

Food serving times

Monday-Thursday:
12pm-2pm, 7pm-9pm

Friday-Saturday:
12pm-2pm, 7pm-9.30pm

Sunday: 12pm-2.30pm, 6.30pm-8.30pm

Closed 25 December, dinner 31 December

Prices

Meals: 23.50 (3 course Sunday lunch) and a la carte 25.00/32.50

3 rooms: 87.50/145.00

Typical Dishes

Dolcelatte fritters
Seared pigeon breasts
Mrs G's toffee meringue

4 mi Northwest of Shipston-on-Stour. Located in the centre of the village. Parking.

Long Compton

027 The Red Lion

Long Compton CV36 5JS
Tel.: (01608) 684221 - Fax: (01608) 684968
e-mail: info@redlion-longcompton.co.uk
Website: www.redlion-longcompton.co.uk

 **Hooky Bitter, Adnam's Broadside, Bass, Hooky Gold**

Fine oak tables, log fires, lantern style lamps and flag flooring help to create a richness and charm at the 18C, Grade II listed Red Lion, where original art decorates the walls and the tastefully made-over rooms feel cosy and intimate. Live acoustic music every fortnight attracts a local crowd, and the games room and rear terrace and garden provide extra space should the bar become too crowded. The seasonal menu offers mostly British favourites from the tried-and-tested school of cooking, so you'll find mains such as homemade steak and Hook Norton pie, savoury herb pancakes or rack of lamb, plus classic desserts such as apple crumble or chocolate mousse. Service is spot-on and smiley, creating a friendly atmosphere, and Cocoa the chocolate Labrador also makes sure you feel at home when he plonks his nose in your lap and looks up at you with doleful eyes. Comfortable bedrooms are stylishly furnished in cool linen shades.

Food serving times
Monday-Thursday:
12pm-2.30pm, 6pm-9pm
Friday-Sunday:
12pm-9.30pm

Prices
Meals: 11.50 (3 course lunch/dinner until 7pm) and a la carte 17.50/29.50
5 rooms: 50.00/80.00

Typical Dishes
Stilton and fig tart
Cod fillet in batter
Lime and ginger parfait

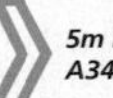
5m North of Chipping Norton by A3400. Parking.

028 The College Arms

Lower Quinton CV37 8SG
Tel.: (01789) 720342 - Fax: (01789) 720392
e-mail: mail@collegearms.co.uk
Website: www.collegearms.co.uk

Purity Ales Pure Gold, Greene King IPA

Henry VIII once owned this place, so current incumbents Mr and Mrs Love inherited an establishment where feasting was hardly a new concept. England's portliest monarch would have approved, because food's still considered mighty important here, with two restaurants and one private dining room taking pride of place. A mix of modern and traditional dishes offers much choice and flexibility in surroundings with bags of character, tailor-made for relaxation: exposed beams, crackling fire, solid stone floors and solid part-16C walls. The pub is set on the northern edge of the Cotswolds and visitors don't need much temptation to stay overnight: four bedrooms, recently refurbished, are smart and cosy.

Food serving times

Tuesday-Saturday:
12pm-2pm, 7pm-9.30pm

Sunday:
12pm-2pm

Closed 1st week in January

Prices

Meals: a la carte
20.00/45.00

4 rooms: 75.00

Typical Dishes

Grilled goats' cheese
Braised gammon & poached egg
Poached pear Belle Hélène

5mi South of Stratford-upon-Avon by A3400, B4632 and minor road east. Parking.

Preston Bagot

029 The Crabmill

Preston Bagot, Claverdon, B95 5EE
Tel.: (01926) 843342 - Fax: (01926) 843989
e-mail: thecrabmill@lovelypubs.co.uk
Website: www.lovelypubs.co.uk

 **Ubu, Abbot Ale, Tetleys**

A delightful rural hideaway, but one which doesn't quite leave its urbane smartness behind: a surprisingly spacious contemporary interior mixes smooth blond wood with ancient cross-beams and wattle walls, the warmth of a real fire and squishy tan leather sofas, so comfortable they demand a real battle of wills for a trip to the bar. A touch of brasserie style comes across in the competent cooking, with dishes like roast pigeon breast and mash, or pepper sirloin and chips, but it's the kind of food you can linger over, and you may find that hearty ramble up and down the Warwickshire hills being put back by another round. The staff look almost as nonchalant as the customers – the emblemed T-shirts are the clue – but provide prompt and conversational service with that noticeable bit extra. Justifiably popular, so consider booking.

Food serving times

Monday-Friday:
12pm-2.30pm, 6.30pm-9.30pm

Saturday:
12pm-2pm, 6.30pm-9.30pm

Sunday:
12.30pm-3.30pm

Closed 25 December

Booking essential

Prices

Meals: a la carte
20.00/28.00

Typical Dishes

Bubble and squeak
Chicken Kiev
Baked raspberry cheesecake

1mi East of Henley-in-Arden on A4189. Parking.

030 The Bell Inn

The Green, Tanworth-in-Arden B94 5AL

Tel.: (01564) 742212

e-mail: thebell@realcoolbars.com

Website: www.thebellattanworthinarden.co.uk

Timothy Taylor's Landlord, Black Sheep Bitter

With its squashy sofas and leather bar stools, The Bell's much modernised, stylish interior has a cool and relaxed feel to it. Its open log fire and rich wood furniture and panelling help it to retain an essence of homeliness, however, and the Morris dancers occasionally seen shaking their hankies and sticks on the village green opposite add to the authentic villagey feel of the place. The food on offer here is not your typical pub grub, but its diversity, bold flavours and generous portions should please both traditionalist and the more adventurous customer. The chef's Middle Eastern experience is evident in the regularly-changing menus and dishes range from coq au vin to Algerian lamb tagine, with daily fish specials on offer too. Overnight stays here are popular with those visiting the NEC. Opt for a front-facing, newer bedroom; all are individually decorated, with sleek, minimal styling and modern furniture.

Food serving times

Monday-Saturday:
12pm-2pm, 6.30pm-9pm

Sunday:
12pm-2pm

Prices

Meals: 10.50 (3 course lunch) and a la carte 15.00/25.00

9 rooms: 55.00/115.00

Typical Dishes

Stilton & port mushrooms

Marinated Moroccan chicken

Crème brûlée

4.5mi Northwest from Henley-in-Arden by A3400 and Tanworth Road. Close to church. Parking.

031 The Bell Inn

Binton Rd,
Welford-on-Avon CV37 8EB
Tel.: (01789) 750353 - Fax: (01789) 750893
e-mail: info@thebellwelford.co.uk - Website: www.thebellwelford.co.uk

Purity Gold, Purity UBU, Hood Norton Hooky Bitter, Hobsons Best, Flowers Original OB

Visitors fanning out from Stratford strike lucky when they come across this part 17C redbrick inn. If it's the summer months, they can flop down at The Bell's enticingly attractive wood-furnished outside terrace with its array of hanging baskets. Or step inside, any time of year, and admire the flagged and beamed bar, glowing fire and rustic knick-knacks. Various other rooms mean there's space to breathe in here, with a range of tables, chairs and pews to stretch out at: the recently refurbished glass roofed dining room is maybe the most stylish place to eat. Local produce is very much to the fore, with local suppliers' names printed on the back of the menus. These offer a good balance of modern British and classic cuisine. They change a couple of times a year, and are supplemented by an extensive range of daily specials.

Food serving times

Monday-Thursday:
11.45am-2.30pm, 6.45pm-9.30pm

Friday-Saturday:
11.45am-2.30pm,
6pm-10pm

Sunday:
12pm-9.30pm

Prices

Meals: a la carte
19.75/27.95

Typical Dishes

Breaded goujons of chicken

Beef and tomato casserole

Sticky toffee pudding

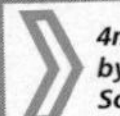

4mi West of Stratford-upon-Avon by B439 and a lefthand turn South. Parking.

032 The White Horse

Kenilworth Road, Balsall Common CV7 7DT
Tel.: (01676) 533207 - Fax: (01676) 532827
e-mail: info@thewhitehorseatbc.co.uk
Website: www.thewhitehorseatbc.co.uk

Greene King IPA, Adnams, Directors, Abbott Ale, Otter Ale, Young's Waggledance, Young's Special

Modernity strikes the Midlands in the form of this monumental pub – part of the Metro Group – which, having undergone refurbishment, now boasts a spacious bar lounge with low-backed leather tub chairs, art-adorned walls and a distinctive feel. The L-shaped dining area is as good as divided in three; the conservatory part being the best in which to sit, unless the British weather is uncharacteristically fine, in which case head for either the decked front terrace or the rear paved one. The menu has a universal appeal, as attested to by the pub's popularity, and dishes are freshly prepared, with care and understanding. Meat comes from the Midland's finest; Aubrey Allen, with spit roast chickens from the pub's rotisserie particularly worth a go. Old favourites like fish pie and toad in the hole are here, as is the odd European flavour, with dishes such as lamb koftas or spaghetti. Portions are generous so two courses should suffice.

Food serving times
Monday-Sunday:
12pm-10pm

Prices
Meals: a la carte
16.40/28.35

Typical Dishes
Thai spiced fishcakes
Beer battered fish and chips
Warm cherry Bakewell tart

5mi Northwest of Kenilworth by A452. Parking.

033 The Malt Shovel

Barston Lane,
Barston B92 0JP

Tel.: (01675) 443223 - Fax: (01675) 443223
Website: www.themaltshovelatbarston.com

 **Old Speckled Hen, St Austell Tribute, Brew XI**

The Malt Shovel is not that far from either Solihull or the M42 but, as you dine al fresco at one of the picnic tables in its lawned garden, surrounded by shrubs and hanging baskets, you certainly get the feeling that you are right out in the middle of the countryside. Not that sitting outside is the only attractive option. This cream-painted dining pub boasts a bright, modern interior with music to match; tiled floors, open fireplaces and wooden tables, chairs and banquettes all set out around a central bar, with the kitchen partly on show at one end. For more formal dining, there's also a separate restaurant in the stylish barn annex. The modern, seasonally-led menus boast a real range of dishes to suit all tastes, from toasted crumpet or cod and chips to Moroccan spiced pork, or sweet potato and red onion Korma. Food arrives well-presented and puts many local ingredients to good use.

Food serving times

Monday-Saturday:
12pm-2.30pm, 7pm-9.30pm

Sunday:
12pm-4pm

Closed 25 December

Lunch bookings not accepted

Prices

Meals: 25.00 (3 course lunch & dinner) and a la carte 18.40/31.40

Typical Dishes

Mexican spiced beef pattie
Veal noisettes
Kirsch blinis

Off the A452 just South of Hampton-in-Arden: follow signs for Barston village. Parking.

034 The Orange Tree

Warwick Road,
Chadwick End B93 0BN
Tel.: (01564) 785364 - Fax: (01564) 782988
Website: www.theorangetree.co.uk

Greene King IPA, Tetleys, Purity Brewery UBU

Enjoy the relaxed and informal atmosphere at this contemporarily stylish, cream-washed dining pub, where the young staff serve up a friendly welcome to go with their efficient service. Open plan and airy, with beams and wooden floors, the interior runs over different levels and there's plenty of comfy seating to choose from. You can eat anywhere, so get a friend to grab a sofa while you order the drinks from the central bar - or if the weather takes a turn for the better, head for the large gardens instead. The simple menu won't win any prizes for innovation, but this is the place to come if you're after hearty modern food, cooked with neatness and precision, and at prices that won't clean out your piggy bank. The menu has an Italian base, and reads along the lines of pizza, pasta, and grilled meats and fish, but also contains a smattering of far flung flavours in the form of dishes such as Thai crab cakes and crispy duck salad.

Food serving times

Monday-Saturday:
12pm-2.30pm, 6pm-10pm

Sunday:
12pm-4.30pm

Closed 25 December

Booking essential

Prices

Meals: a la carte
18.00/35.00

Typical Dishes

Grilled gambas
Pork escalope
Chestnut praline crème brûlée

On A4141 midway between Solihull and Warwick. Parking.

035 The Boot Inn

Old Warwick Rd,
Lapworth B94 6JU

Tel.: (01564) 782464 - Fax: (01564) 784989
e-mail: bootinn@hotmail.com - Website: www.thebootatlapworth.co.uk

Old Speckled Hen, Hobgoblin

Make sure you book ahead if you want to eat at the Boot; it gets deservedly busy despite – or even perhaps because of - its village location, close to the junction of the Grand Union and Stratford-upon-Avon canals. The front pub area, with its central bar and surrounding warren of little nooks and crannies, has a cosy, rustic feel to it, whilst the large main dining room, with its wooden floor and stylish décor, is on a different level, both literally and metaphorically. On sunny days, the favoured seats are those in the garden, but wherever you sit, the welcome is a warm one, and the service from t-shirted staff is friendly and attentive. The modern menus contain a mix of classics that take you on a gastronomical tour around Europe and beyond, so you'll find plates of a Baltic or Iberian flavour to share, and dishes such as pie of the day or steak alongside pot au feu or crispy oriental duck salad.

Food serving times

Monday-Sunday:
12pm-3pm, 6.30pm-10pm

Closed 25 December and 1 January

Booking essential

Prices

Meals: a la carte
18.00/25.00

Typical Dishes

Kidneys with black pudding
Spit roast pig
Blueberry cheesecake

2mi Southeast of Hockley Heath on B4439; on the left hand side just before the village. Parking.

036 The Cock Inn

Bulls Lane,
Wishaw, Sutton Coldfield B76 9QL
Tel.: (0121) 313 3960
Website: www.cockinnwishaw.co.uk

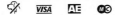

  VISA AE MC

Adnams, Timothy Taylor's

Although it looks every inch the village pub from the outside, the Cock Inn is a modern dining pub through and through; all comfy seating, wood floors and chunky wooden tables. Logs smouldering in the fires add to the relaxing ambience in the stylish bar, and the inn is plenty spacious enough to house the hungry hordes, with the decked terrace coming into its own these days from about April onwards, thanks to global warming. The à la carte menu is modern and fairly simple, split into sections including pizzas, pasta and salads and starches and greens. Sharing plates sees ingredients such as hummus, stuffed peppers, olives and roasted vegetables to fight over, and the grills might include fish such as tuna and swordfish as well as various steaks. Service, like the general vibe here, is informal, and the surrounding countryside and the nearby Belfry Golf course make this a great spot for a post-prandial stroll.

Food serving times

Monday-Saturday:
12pm-2.30pm, 6pm-9.30pm

Sunday:
12pm-7pm

Prices

Meals: a la carte
18.00/32.00

Typical Dishes

Smoked salmon
Slow roasted lamb shank
Chocolate fondant

7mi East of Sutton Coldfield just off A446 following signs over M6 toll road to Wishaw and Grove End. Parking.

Yorkshire, for many, means the countryside: a mind's-eye landscape of fells and fields spreading out from the Pennines, neat Dales villages above the Wharfe and the Swale, and Aysgarth Falls and Hardraw Force in all their secluded beauty. But the Ridings also lay claim to the genteel charm of Harrogate and Ripon, the striking ruins of Fountains Abbey and Rievaux and the unexpected brilliance of Vanburgh's Castle Howard, to say nothing of York, its medieval walled town and its awe-inspiring Minster. Industrial change has left its mark in the pit towns and the Steel City of Sheffield, but also in Leeds' rejuvenated centre and at Saltaire, the 19C mill village where Bradford-born David Hockney's gallery is housed. The counties' pubs range from the proudly classic to the ceaselessly inventive, each striking its own balance with the famous local love of tradition: roast beef and Yorkshire pudding may have been adopted by the rest of Britain, but this is still the place to go for Wensleydale cheese, York ham, moorland game and parkin, the rich spiced oatmeal cake baked specially for Bonfire Night!

North East
DURHAM
Middleton-in-Teesdale
Bishop Auckland
Spennymoor
Sedgefield
Newton Aycliffe
Stockton-on-Tees
Barnard Castle
Appleby
Brough
Bowes
Darlington
Tees-side
Eaglescliffe
Ullswater
Patterdale
Shap
Orton
Kirkby Stephen
Tebay
Windermere
Ambleside
Scotch Corner
Richmond
Reeth
Swale
Kendal
Sedbergh
Hawes
Leyburn
Bedale
Northallerton
Thirsk
Whernside
Yorkshire
Dales
Kirkby Lonsdale
Lune
Ingleton
Clapham
National
Wharfe
Ure
NORTH YORK
PENNINES
Ripon
Pateley Bridge
Threshfield
Fountains Abbey
Settle
Lancaster
Knaresborough
Boroughbridge
Park
North West
Long Preston
Gisburn
Skipton
YORKSHIRE
Ilkley
Otley
Harewood
Wetherby
Tadcaster
LANCASHIRE
Ribble
Clitheroe
Colne
Keighley
Bingley
Blackburn
Padiham
Nelson
Burnley
BRADFORD
LEEDS
Accrington
Halifax
Garforth
Castleford
Leyland
Darwen
Rawtenstall
Todmorden
Brighouse
Chorley
Rochdale
Bury
Dewsbury
Pontefract
Wakefield
Bolton
Huddersfield
Oldham
Holmfirth
Barnsley
Wigan
Leigh
MANCHESTER
Ashton-under-Lyne
St Helens
Glossop
Stocksbridge
Conisbrough
Altrincham
Hyde
Peak District
Rotherham
Widnes
Stockport
SHEFFIELD
High Peak
Knutsford
Wilmslow
Whaley Bridge
Castleton
Northwich
Chapel-en-le-Frith
Dronfield
CHESHIRE
National
Staveley
Winsford
Macclesfield
Buxton
Baslow
Chesterfield
Tarporley
Middlewich
Congleton
Bakewell
Chatsworth House
Sandbach
Park
Little Moreton Hall
Clay Cross

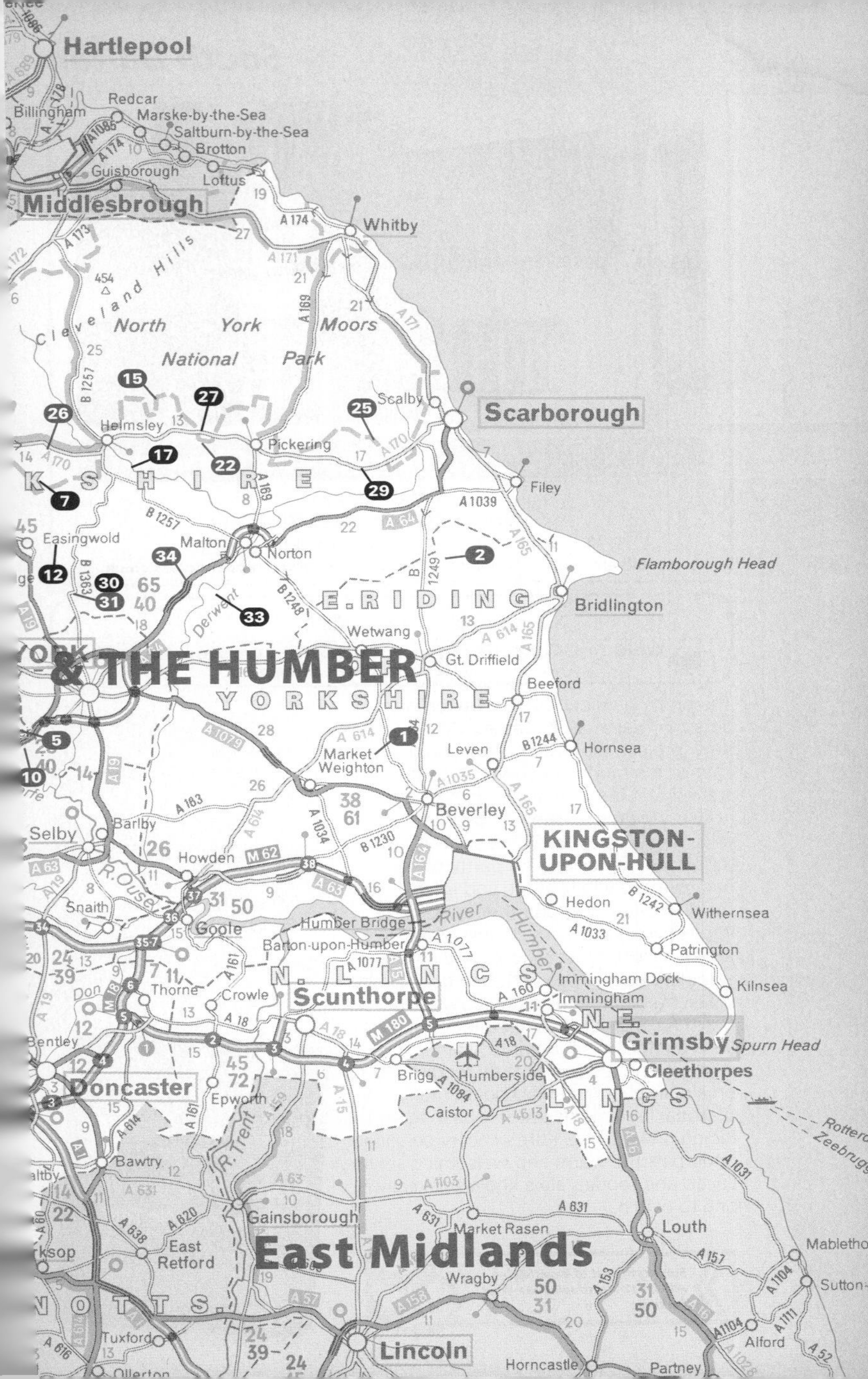

Hartlepool
Redcar
Billingham
Marske-by-the-Sea
Saltburn-by-the-Sea
Brotton
Guisborough
Loftus
Middlesbrough
Whitby
Cleveland Hills
North York Moors National Park
Scalby
Scarborough
Helmsley
Pickering
Filey
Easingwold
Malton
Norton
Flamborough Head
E. RIDING
Bridlington
Wetwang
Gt. Driffield
YORKSHIRE & THE HUMBER
Beeford
Market Weighton
Leven
Hornsea
Beverley
KINGSTON-UPON-HULL
Selby
Barlby
Howden
R. Ouse
Snaith
Goole
Hedon
Withernsea
Humber Bridge
River Humber
Barton-upon-Humber
Patrington
N. LINCS
Immingham Dock
Immingham
Kilnsea
Thorne
Crowle
Scunthorpe
N.E. LINCS
Grimsby
Spurn Head
Bentley
Doncaster
Brigg
Humberside
Cleethorpes
Epworth
Caistor
R. Trent
Rotterdam
Zeebrugge
Bawtry
Gainsborough
Market Rasen
Louth
East Retford
East Midlands
Mablethorpe
Wragby
NOTTS.
Tuxford
Lincoln
Alford
Horncastle
Partney
Ollerton

001 The Pipe and Glass Inn

West End,
South Dalton HU17 7PN
Tel.: (01430) 810246 - Fax: (01430) 810246
e-mail: email@pipeandglass.co.uk - Website: www.pipeandglass.co.uk

Wold Top, Copper Dragon, John Smith's, Cropton, Daleside, Garton, Black Sheep

The pretty hamlet of South Dalton was abuzz in March 2006: James McKenzie's new 'project' was up-and-running. Ex-head chef of the much-heralded, Michelin-starred Star Inn at Harome, James was now bringing his talents to bear at this once neglected pub. Optimism was not misplaced. James and his partner Kate had invested a lot of time and effort into the Pipe and Glass, and the results were impressive: hand made chunky wooden tables, stripped wood floors and coir carpets, sleek lounge with low-back leather sofas, framed menus on rustic walls. So much for the décor. What about the food? Served either in snug bar or dining room, it's a well-honed mix of tasty modish dishes on a daily changing blackboard menu, the seasonal ingredients proudly bearing an East Riding provenance. Kate's cheery persona underpins the warm and welcoming service. Locals and foodies alike know this really is one to watch.

Food serving times

Tuesday-Saturday:
12pm-2pm, 6.30pm-9.30pm

Sunday:
12pm-4pm

Closed 2 weeks in January

Prices

Meals: a la carte
21.00/28.00

Typical Dishes

Hare, ham & foie gras terrine

Braised Harpham lamb

Warm treacle tart

5mi Northwest of Beverley by A164, B1248 and side road West. Parking.

002 The Falling Stone

Main St,
Thwing YO25 3DS
Tel.: (01262) 470403

Falling Stone, Wold Gold, Wold Top, Mars Magic, Wolds Way and one guest beer changing weekly

Named after a meteorite which dropped from the skies here many years ago, The Falling Stone is the life-and-soul of this sleepy East Riding hamlet. A warm atmosphere extends from the greeting bestowed by Fudge, a delightfully friendly mastiff, to the blissfully informal and snug sitting areas with their range of low-level leather sofas, tea lights and open fire. This is a pub that takes its beer seriously: there's a fine selection of local ales from the Wold Brewery. Things are a little more formal in the linen-clad dining room, though rustic décor reminds you that this is the heart of the country and not a chic part of town. Menus change daily and start from a classical French base; they're ordered from a blackboard above the crackling fire.

Food serving times

Monday-Sunday:
12pm-3pm, 6pm-9pm

Prices

Meals: a la carte
18.00/30.00

Typical Dishes

Grilled rabbit salad
Mustard & hazelnut lamb
Mascarpone & raspberry tart

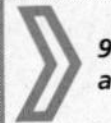
9mi West of Bridlington by B1253 and minor road North. Parking.

003 Crab and Lobster

Dishforth Rd,
Asenby YO7 3QL
Tel.: (01845) 577286 - Fax: (01845) 577109
Website: www.crabandlobster.com

 **Theakston's XB, Skipton Ale 1816**

The Crab and Lobster's thatched exterior may fool you into assuming it's just like any other long-established pub, but venture inside and you'll realise that this inn is one of a kind, thanks to the eclectic mix of memorabilia, ornaments, knick-knacks and pictures which clutter the rooms. There are three distinctive dining areas; a low-ceilinged bar with matted flooring, a more formal restaurant, just the place for a candlelit meal, and an airy conservatory-style extension, known as the pavilion. Outside, a cobbled terrace boasts wrought iron furniture. The Crab hasn't got a marine moniker for nothing – the emphasis here is on fresh seafood landed as locally as possible. Feast on fishcakes, fish pie, fillet of wild sea bass or Tandooried monkfish; the same extensive menu is served throughout, supplemented by daily specials chalked on blackboards, and service is polite, friendly and efficient.

Food serving times

Sunday-Friday:
12pm-2pm, 7pm-9pm

Saturday:
12pm-2pm, 6pm-9.30pm

- Seafood -

Prices

Meals: 14.75 (3 course lunch) and a la carte 20.00/35.00

14 rooms: 150.00

Typical Dishes

Seared king scallops
Whole seabass with fennel
Chocolate fondant

5.25 mi Southwest of Thirsk by A168. Parking.

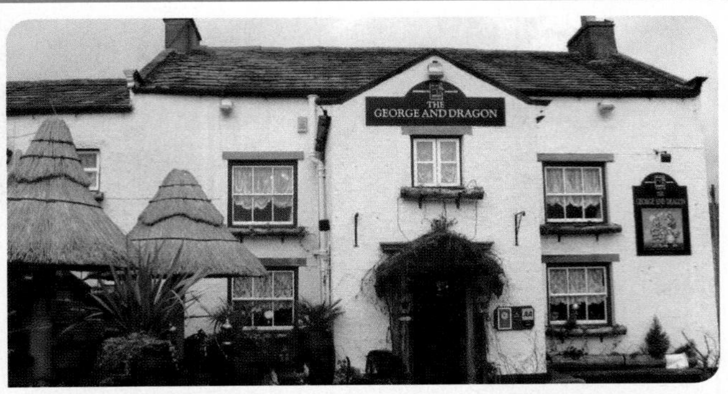

004 George and Dragon Inn

Aysgarth DL8 3AD

Tel.: (01969) 663358 - Fax: (01969) 663773
e-mail: info@georgeanddragonaysgarth.co.uk
Website: www.georgeanddragonaysgarth.co.uk

 **2 Black Sheep, John Smith's Cask, Theakstons Best Bitter, Herriott Country Ale**

With its proximity to the impressive Aysgarth Falls and the Dales Countryside Museum at Hawes, as well as its setting in the heart of Wensleydale, this traditional family pub packs an instant punch. There's a pleasant terrace with thatched umbrellas, and, inside, a snug little bar highlighted by a crackling fire and fine array of Yorkshire ales. The feel for local produce extends to lunchtime sandwiches with, typically, Nidderdale salmon and Swalesdale cheddar. More substantial old favourites like Wensleydale park sausages and mash or fish and chips make a reassuring appearance alongside more ambitious fare: tuck into this lot in either the airy Victorian styled dining room, or the open dining area with its display of wine knickknacks on the walls. There are seven comfy bedrooms; remember to book in advance – with its lovely scenery and superb walks, this is a popular spring and summer destination.

Food serving times

Monday-Sunday:
12pm-2pm, 5.30m-9pm

Closed 2 weeks in January

Prices

Meals: 13.95/16.95 (lunch & dinner) and a la carte 20.00/35.00

7 rooms: 40.00/99.00

Typical Dishes

Smoked Salmon
Sirloin steak
Crème brûlée

7mi West of Leyburn by A684.
Parking.

005 The Three Hares Country Inn

Main St,
Bilbrough YO23 3PH
Tel.: (01937) 832128 - Fax: (01937) 834626
e-mail: info@thethreehares.co.uk - Website: www.thethreehares.co.uk

   AE

Timothy Taylor's, Bradfield Farmer's Blonde, Black Sheep and 1 guest ale

This immaculately whitewashed village pub feels miles away from the eager crowds of summer visitors to York; it's a great escape, certainly, but serves Bilbrough itself well enough, too. Traditional on the outside, the ambience inside is modern and fresh. The small bar area has rafters and exposed brickwork and is great for a cosy, informal lunch of sandwiches and salads. Two other rooms provide something of a contrast for those evening visitors with heartier appetites: here is a neat and tidy, linen-clad restaurant. Bar and dining room menus vary quite considerably: if you've chosen the latter, you'll have more ambitious options to choose from. Either way, service is smooth and polite.

Food serving times
Tuesday-Sunday:
12pm-2.30pm, 7pm-9.30pm

Prices
Meals: 15.00 (3 course Sunday lunch) and a la carte 21.00/30.00

Typical Dishes
Chicken liver parfait
Pan-fried seabass fillets
Apple and pear tart Tatin

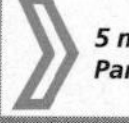
5 mi Southwest of York off A64.
Parking.

006 The Red Lion

Burnsall BD23 6BU

Tel.: (01756) 720204 - Fax: (01756) 720292

e-mail: redlion@daelnet.co.uk - Website: www.redlion.co.uk

Timothy Taylor's, XB, Theakstons and changing guest beers in summer

At the heart of the small rural community of Burnsall, on the banks of the River Wharfe, lies this stone built, ivy-clad inn; a historical haven for diners, fresh from fishing, walking, hunting, touring or business. With reputedly haunted cellars dating from the 12C, and a panelled bar – formerly a Ferryman's inn dating from the 16C - there's certainly plenty of character imprinted in this inn's creaking beams. Two comfortable lounge areas are perfect for relaxing or for a spot of lunch, while the traditionally furnished restaurant is perfect for dinner. Lunchtimes might see sandwiches, meatballs and chickpea fritters on offer while an evening menu might include locally shot game casserole or free range calves liver. Bedrooms come in various shapes and sizes but the original rooms have the most character, with beams, sloping floors, uneven walls and antique furniture. The newer rooms, though less individual, also have good facilities.

Food serving times

Monday-Sunday:
12pm-2.30pm, 7pm-9.30pm

Prices

Meals: a la carte
25.00/40.00

31 rooms:
63.75/210.00

Typical Dishes

Queenie scallops

Wharfedale lamb confit

Lemon torte

3mi Southeast of Grassington by B6265 West and B6160 South. Parking.

Byland Abbey

007 The Abbey Inn

Byland Abbey YO61 4BD
Tel.: (01347) 868204 - Fax: (01347) 868678
e-mail: abbeyinn@english-heritage.org.uk
Website: www.bylandabbeyinn.com

 **Black Sheep and home-brewed Byland Brew**

The cowl may not make the monk, but you can trust that the interior of this part 17C inn fulfils the promises made by its charming, ivy-clad exterior. Spacious, yet atmospheric, its small bar and three dining rooms are full of character, and their old beams, flagged floors and stonework are complemented by tapestries, ornaments, statues, Jacobean style chairs and heavy wood tables. Situated at the foot of the Hambleton Hills and overlooking Byland Abbey, the inn is a great place for a meal pre or post a tour of the ruins. Menus offer a pleasing mix of hearty rustic cooking and more contemporary dishes, with choices changing according to what's in season, and local ladies provide polite, efficient service. If your trip to the inn is an extended one, you'll find that bedrooms are modern, comfortable; individual in style and with good facilities; and two out of three enjoy views of the Abbey.

Food serving times

Monday:
6.30pm-9pm

Tuesday-Saturday:
12pm-2pm, 6.30pm-9pm

Sunday:
12pm-2pm

Prices

Meals: a la carte
21.00/28.00

3 rooms: 155.00

Typical Dishes

Bleiker's smoked salmon

Holme Farm venison steak

Steamed plum sponge pudding

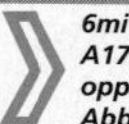

6mi Southwest of Helmsley by A170 and minor road South; opposite the ruins of Byland Abbey. Parking.

008 Foresters Arms

Carlton-in-Coverdale DL8 4BB
Tel.: (01969) 640272 - Fax: (01969) 640272
e-mail: chambersmic@hotmail.co.uk
Website: www.forestersarms-carlton.co.uk

John Smith's Cask, Black Sheep, Timothy Taylor

Whether you've built up an appetite walking, grouse shooting or having fun fighting folly at the Forbidden Corner, the Foresters Arms will provide welcome sustenance and an open fire by which to warm yourself. Situated at the entrance of the rural village of Carlton, this small, stone-built pub has two characterful, picture-filled, flag-floored rooms in which to eat, plus a formal beamed dining room which is open in the evenings, and seats outside for sunny afternoons. The welcome and the service are friendly, and the keen owners have put the emphasis here firmly onto the food, with traditional home-cooked dishes, made wherever possible with locally sourced ingredients. Specials are chalked up on the blackboard by the bar and you can choose between dishes such as Roe deer steak, pheasant breast or seafood parcel. Three rooms offer a comfortable bed for the night; décor ranges from cottage-style to modern.

Food serving times

Tuesday-Saturday:
12pm-2pm, 6.30pm-8.30pm

Sunday:
6.30pm-8.30pm

Closed lunch Tuesday-Thursday, November-April

Prices

Meals: 14.95 (3 course Sunday lunch) and a la carte 20.00/26.00

3 rooms: 65.00/79.00

Typical Dishes

Warm bacon & mushroom salad

Roe deer steak

Home-made chocolate brownies

4.5 mi Southwest of Middleham by Coverdale rd. Parking next to pub in village car park.

009 Fox and Hounds

Carthorpe DL8 2LG
Tel.: (01845) 567433 - Fax: (01845) 567155
e-mail: helenst36@btinternet.com
Website: www.foxandhoundscarthorpe.co.uk

 **Black Sheep, Worthington**

This pub has been in the same family for more than 25 years and its walls and shelves are stacked with ornaments, plates, photos and old farm equipment attesting to its recent past. Its sense of history goes back further than this, however, and the forge and water pump in the restaurant bear witness to its time as the village smithy. Situated close to the A1 in a small rural village, this pretty, ivy-clad pub serves up locally-sourced produce in a selection of classic, homemade pub dishes, with specials chalked up on the blackboard menu. You can eat in the bar or at an old wooden table in the beamed dining room and service is friendly and polite. Can't decide on a dessert? Then try tasting them all in the 'Fox and Hounds Special.' There's also a cabinet containing homemade meringues, jams, chutneys and the like to take away, so you can thrill your taste buds further in the privacy of your own home.

Food serving times

Tuesday-Sunday:
12pm-3pm, 7pm-11pm

Closed 25 and 31 December, 1 week January

Prices

Meals: 16.95 (3 course lunch & dinner) and a la carte 22.95/30.00

Typical Dishes

Honey roast ham hock terrine
Pan-fried fillet steak
Poached pear

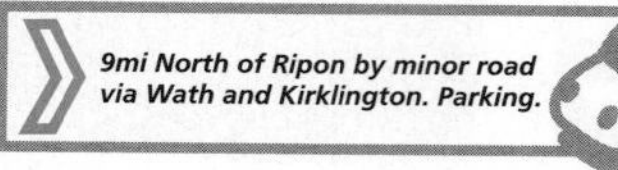

9mi North of Ripon by minor road via Wath and Kirklington. Parking.

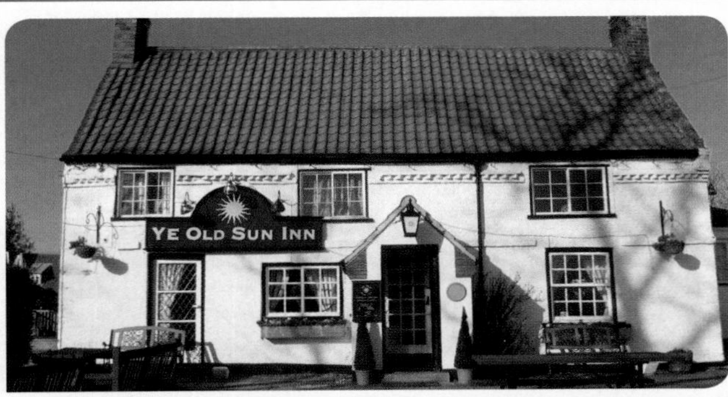

010 Ye Old Sun Inn

Main Street,
Colton LS24 8EP
Tel.: (01904) 744261
e-mail: kelly.mccarthy@btconnect.com - Website: www.yeoldsuninn.co.uk

John Smiths, Timothy Taylor's, Black Sheep and guest beers including Cropton, Deuchars, Copper Dragon, York Brewery, Rudgate

It's a family affair at Ye Old Sun Inn; he's in the kitchen, while she serves out front, and they also run a small deli selling homemade goodies including cheese, oils, jams, chutneys and freshly baked bread. The four small dining areas have a homely, rustic feel, with open coal fires and period prints and photos, and while the sun theme adds further charm inside, the spacious gardens and decked terrace provide somewhere to sit when it comes out for real. Cooking is classically based, with an international flavour, so menus might include Dales lamb or stuffed vine leaves, steak and ale pie or Thai BBQ chicken. Menus change on a monthly basis, and the food is tasty, seasonal and local – with some of the ingredients grown in the inn's own poly tunnel and herb garden. The selection of freshly churned ice creams will have you licking your lips in anticipation, while the chef's dinky dessert platter wins the prize for the best named pud.

Food serving times

Tuesday-Saturday:
12pm-2pm, 6.30pm-9.30pm

Sunday:
12pm-4pm, 6.30pm-9.30pm

Closed 26 December and 1-21 January

Prices

Meals: 14.95 (3 course Sunday lunch) and a la carte 17.00/25.00

Typical Dishes

Warm duck salad
Seafood trio
Chocolate cake

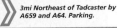

3mi Northeast of Tadcaster by A659 and A64. Parking.

011 Wyvill Arms

Constable Burton DL8 5LH
Tel.: (01677) 450581

Black Sheep, Theakstons, John Smiths

Lest you forget you're in the middle of the countryside, all areas of this ivy-clad stone pub contain a liberal sprinkling of rustically-themed decorative pictures, fabrics and ornaments. There's a choice of eating areas: a small bar with an open fire, a dining area with stone floors, banquette seating and linen laid tables, plus a more formal dining area, with high-backed leather chairs. Cooking is hearty and robust and menus make use of local ingredients such as black pudding and Wensleydale cheese, with moments of individuality among the more classic pub fare. If the weather's playing ball, the neat gardens, with resident wishing well, have a terrace for outside dining. Bedrooms here are simple but neat. Make use of your location to go walking, riding or cycling on the Dales and to view the gardens at Constable Burton Hall, or travel slightly further afield to Jervaulx Abbey, where Wensleydale cheese was reputedly created.

Food serving times

Monday-Sunday:
11.45am-2.15pm, 6pm-9pm

Prices

Meals: a la carte
22.00/29.00

2 rooms: 55.00/75.00

Typical Dishes

Dressed Whitby crab
Roast suckling pig
Passion fruit pannacotta

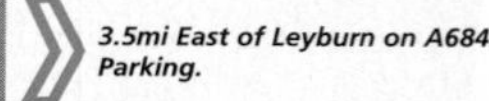

3.5mi East of Leyburn on A684. Parking.

012 The Durham Ox

Westway,
Crayke YO61 4TE
Tel.: (01347) 821506 - Fax: (01347) 823326
e-mail: enquiries@thedurhamox.com - Website: www.thedurhamox.com

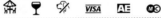

Theakstons Best Bitter, Timothy Taylor's Landlord, XXXB, Henry's IPA

Complete with curled up cat, the cosy, characterful interior of this 300 year old inn has a distinctly rustic feel with carved wood panels, flagstone floor and open fires. Homemade hampers are for sale in the deli shop and you can eat in either bar or in the boldly decorated, beamed dining room. Country style bedrooms are situated in the adjacent block of converted farm cottages and the rear courtyard with its fixed marquee has great views over the surrounding countryside. The famous Durham Ox, exhibited around the country in the early 19C, reportedly reached a maximum weight of 270 stone. If you consider yourself to have the constitution of an ox, then select a dish from the à la carte menu. You'll find hearty British cooking, with a wide-ranging choice including local meat and game. Available at both lunch and dinner, a snack from the 'bar bites' menu might be a better option for those of a more delicate disposition.

Food serving times

Monday-Friday:
12pm-2.30pm, 6pm-9.30pm

Saturday:
12pm-2.30pm, 6pm-10pm

Sunday:
12pm-3pm, 6pm-8.30pm

Closed meals 25 December

Prices

Meals: a la carte
17.95/29.95

4 rooms: 60.00/100.00

Typical Dishes

Carpaccio of Nidderdale beef
Slow-roast pork belly
Spotted dick

2 mi East of Easingwold on Helmsley rd. Parking.

013 The Travellers Rest

Dalton DL11 7HU
Tel.: (01833) 621225
e-mail: annebabsa@aol.com

 **Black Sheep Best Bitter**

This stone-built pub sits in a small rural hamlet, reached down the narrow country roads which branch off from the A66. Although its ivy-clad exterior suggests a traditional Yorkshire inn, inside it's actually quite plainly decorated, but the friendly welcome from staff and locals alike more than makes up for any neutrality of décor. Order your drinks at the copper-topped bar and soak up the atmosphere; with its beamed ceilings, open fire and pictures of local life hanging on the walls, you'll soon find this inn has retained plenty of old fashioned charm. Most people eat in the dining room, but you can also dine in the bar rooms. Casually-dressed staff are polite and keen, and serve classically based dishes from the constantly evolving blackboard menus, made with whatever's fresh in that day. After an hour or two, you should certainly feel well rested – and ready to explore the moors and Dales.

Food serving times

Tuesday-Saturday:
6pm-9.30pm

Sunday:
12pm-2.30pm

Closed 25-26 December and 1 January

Prices

Meals: a la carte
17.00/27.00

Typical Dishes

Duck filled spring rolls
Grilled fillet of turbot
Fine apple tart

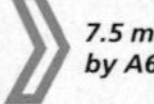

7.5 mi Northwest of Scotch Corner by A66. Parking.

014 The Blue Lion

East Witton DL8 4SN
Tel.: (01969) 624273 - Fax: (01969) 624189
e-mail: bluelion@breathe.net
Website: www.bluelion.co.uk

Theakstons, Black Sheep, Riggwelter, John Smith's

Standing on the main road of the small village of East Witton, this cosy country pub calls out to passing tourists exploring the peaceful Wensleydale countryside and beckons them inside, as it has done for several hundred years. The rustic main bar has flagstone floors, stone walls and an open fire while the candlelit tables create an intimate atmosphere in the dining room. You can dine al fresco in the lawned gardens too, but the modern menus are the same wherever you choose to sit and service from uniformed staff is friendly and attentive. Those who prefer their culinary influences to be closer to home will be happy to see the reassuring and heartwarming black pudding, bubble and squeak and steamed sponge pudding while those who like food of a more European provenance will like the sound of dishes involving Parma ham, brioche and chorizo. Sympathetically renovated bedrooms are comfortable and traditionally decorated.

Food serving times

Monday-Saturday:
12pm-2.15pm (bar meals), 7pm-9.15pm

Sunday:
12pm-2.15pm, 7pm-9.30pm

Booking essential

Prices

Meals: a la carte 11.15/38.85

15 rooms: 57.50/110.00

Typical Dishes

Warm goats' cheese salad
Slow-braised mutton
Apple tart Tatin

3mi Southeast of Leyburn on A6108. Parking.

015 The Plough Inn

Main Street,
Fadmoor YO62 7HY
Tel.: (01751) 431515 - Fax: (01751) 432492

 **Black Sheep Best Bitter, Tetleys Cask**

Set in a small village, overlooking the green, this is the sort of country pub people are happy to travel some distance to eat at, but it also goes down well with the hungry hikers who happen upon it. A friendly welcome greets you, service is informal yet organised, and the exposed beams, quarry tiled floors and open fires provide a characterful and relaxing environment in which to dine. There are various little rooms and snugs to choose from, with walls covered in framed maps and pictures, and a decked terrace and small garden for use when the sun has got his hat on. On the extensive table and blackboard menus you'll find the sort of classic pub food that would fill a hungry ploughman, like homemade steak and ale pie, a choice of warming soups, or rice pudding, and flavours range from the local, with dishes such as creamy Wensleydale mushrooms, to the more international with Thai fishcakes or seafood paella.

Food serving times

Monday-Saturday:
12pm-1.45pm, 6.30pm-8.45pm

Sunday:
12pm-1.45pm, 7pm-8.45pm

Closed 25-26 December and 1 January

Booking essential

Prices

Meals: 12.95 (2 course lunch & dinner) and a la carte 17.90/28.00

Typical Dishes

Deep-fried Brie
Escalopes of pork tenderloin
Warm pear and almond tart

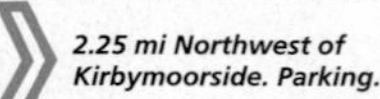

2.25 mi Northwest of Kirbymoorside. Parking.

016 The General Tarleton Inn

Boroughbridge Rd,
Ferrensby HG5 0PZ
Tel.: (01423) 340284 - Fax: (01423) 340288
e-mail: gti@generaltarleton.co.uk - Website: www.generaltarleton.co.uk

We most liked

Black Sheep Best Bitter, Timothy Taylor's Landlord

Set in the beautiful North Yorkshire countryside, this long-established 18C coaching inn is well-run and used to being busy. The bar area is split into four characterful rooms, with painted, beamed ceilings, bay windows and humorous pictures on the walls, while the glass-roofed enclosed courtyard is the brightest place to dine, and there is also a considerably more formal restaurant in the stone built extension. The menus are bursting with good value, locally sourced food, so you can choose from dishes such as Swaledale cheese and leek soufflé, Whitby crab and organic salmon fishcake, Birstwith farmed steak and Dales lamb. There's a bar brasserie menu and another labelled, 'More substantial dishes,' which provides exactly what it says; food that will fill you up like local steak and ale pudding and oxtail shepherd's pie. Bedrooms are comfortable and smart and the power showers provide a welcoming morning blast to wake you up.

Food serving times

Monday-Sunday:
12pm-2pm, 6pm-9.15pm

Bar meals lunch Monday-Saturday and dinner Sunday

Prices

Meals: 22.95/32.50 (3 course lunch Sunday & dinner) and a la carte 20.00/31.50

14 rooms:
85.00/120.00

Typical Dishes

Seafood in crisp pastry
Steak and ale pudding
Yorkshire rhubarb crumble

From A1 at Boroughbridge, take A6055 road towards Knaresborough; the inn is on the right hand side. Parking.

017 The Star Inn

High St,
Harome YO62 5JE
Tel.: (01439) 770397 - Fax: (01439) 771833
e-mail: starinn@btopenworld.com - Website: www.thestaratharome.co.uk

Black Sheep, Theakston's, Copper Dragon, Hambleton Real Ales

Still twinkling brightly in the firmament, this aptly named star's reputation precedes it, so book ahead. The acclaimed cooking is a celebration of the pub's Yorkshire roots; these balanced dishes combine traditional Northern flavours with more modern, original nuances and are produced using ingredients sourced from local estates and farms. How unusual, yet how welcome it is to see words such as woof, hare, lovage, scrumpy and parkin on a menu.The fine food is matched only by the delightful setting in which one dines; this beautiful part 14C thatched inn on the tip of the North York Moors exudes character and boasts a deliciously snug, beamed bar. Polished wood furniture features in the elegant dining room and the walls are filled with awards, books, glassware and other curios. The Star has been so successful that it has now even spawned a gastronomic empire in the area, including a herb garden, a butcher's shop and a deli.

Food serving times

Tuesday-Saturday: 11.30pm-2pm, 6.15pm-9.30pm

Sunday: 12pm-6pm

Closed 25 December and Bank Holidays

Booking essential

Prices

Meals: a la carte 25.00/35.00

15 rooms: 120.00/230.00

Typical Dishes

Soused Hartlepool halibut

Wild rabbit pie

Harrogate sponge fingers

2.75 mi Southeast of Helmsley by A170. Parking.

018 The Angel Inn

Hetton BD23 6LT
Tel.: (01756) 730263 - Fax: (01756) 730363
e-mail: info@angelhetton.co.uk
Website: www.angelhetton.co.uk

 **Black Sheep Bitter, Timothy Taylor's Landlord**

The awards hanging among the cartoons and pictures on the walls of this beamed 18C inn are a clue to the quality of the dining experience to be had here; just as the clusters of wine bottles on every flat surface, and the adjoining 'wine cave' where tastings are held, point to the exceptional calibre of the wine list. Such a pub does tend to get very busy, so make sure you book ahead – and avoid a table by the bar where drinkers waiting for a table in the dining room tend to stand. The kitchen makes good use of local produce to inform both the rustic bar menu and the à la carte, with choices including Swinton Park venison, Bolton Abbey mutton and Yorkshire lamb, beef and pheasant, and smartly dressed staff in waistcoats and ties provide polite, friendly service. Bedrooms are set in a converted stone built farm building. All are very individual and spacious with high quality furniture and fabrics and plenty of extra little touches.

Food serving times

Monday-Saturday:
12pm-2.15pm (bar meals only), 6pm-9.30pm

Sunday:12pm-2pm

Closed 25 December, 1 January and 1st week in January

Booking essential

Prices

Meals: 22.50/34.50 (3 course Sunday lunch / Saturday dinner) and a la carte 27.00/32.50

5 rooms: 130.00/155.00

Typical Dishes

Artichoke and leek risotto

Baked Goosnargh duck breast

Apple crumble cheesecake

5.75mi North of Skipton by B6265. Parking.

019 The Bay Horse Inn

Main St,
Kirk Deighton LS22 4DZ
Tel.: (01937) 580058 - Fax: (01937) 582443

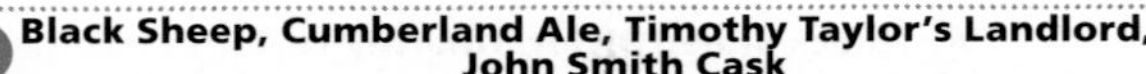

Black Sheep, Cumberland Ale, Timothy Taylor's Landlord, John Smith Cask

Pop up the road from Wetherby and you'll come upon a pub that's really making a name for itself locally. The Bay Horse is a busy place. Those in the know don't just come for the selection of real ales, good as it is. Nor for the spacey, eclectic interior bursting with country curios, such as fishing rods on the ceiling and charming old sepia prints on the walls. They don't even make the trip to stock up on homemade jams and pickles, though this is part of the appeal. They come mostly for the great food: local reputation is ensuring the Bay Horse is earning its spurs as a dining destination pub. Yorkshire ingredients are put to appealing use on a set menu with traditional undercurrent or daily specials board where local pheasant and mallard are typically popular choices, backed up by welcoming service from keen staff.

Food serving times

Tuesday-Saturday:
12pm-2pm, 6pm-9.15pm

Sunday:
12pm-2pm

Monday:
6pm-9.15pm

Booking essential

Prices

Meals: 13.95 (2 course lunch & dinner) and a la carte 18.00/35.00

Typical Dishes

Ginger & lime prawns
Daube of beef
Assiette of puddings

1.5mi North of Wetherby by B6164. Parking.

020 The Charles Bathurst Inn

Langthwaite DL11 6EN

Tel.: (01748) 884567 - Fax: (01748) 886233

e-mail: info@cbinn.co.uk - Website: www.cbinn.co.uk

 **John Smith's Best Bitter, Black Sheep Best and Riggwelter, Theakstons Best Bitter**

Set high on the hills of Arkengarthdale, with views out over the surrounding countryside, the CB inn, as it is known locally, enjoys a strong reputation in the area. Dating from the 18C, although sympathetically extended, the spacious bar has various timbered rooms and snugs to sit in. Photos and paintings of the region decorate the walls and the local servers are well-organised and chatty. Curiously and more curiously, the daily-changing menus are written on the mirrors above the fire - but thankfully there are no slithy toves on offer here. There is something to suit every taste though; modern British cooking blends with the classics and there's the odd sunny European influence too- from the tarts to the terrines, all making good use of local produce. For those staying overnight, bedrooms are large and individually styled with period furniture and two comfortable lounges are also available.

Food serving times

Monday-Sunday:
12pm-2pm, 6.30pm-9pm

Closed 25 December

Prices

Meals: a la carte
20.00/35.00

19 rooms:
92.50/115.00

Typical Dishes

Balsamic marinated chicken

Swale Hall rump of lamb

Honey ice cream

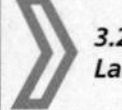

3.25mi Northwest of Reeth on Langthwaite rd. Parking.

021 The Sandpiper Inn

Market Pl,
Leyburn DL8 5AT
Tel.: (01969) 622206 - Fax: (01969) 625367
e-mail: hsandpiper99@aol.com - Website: www.sandpiperinn.co.uk

Black Sheep Bitter, Black Sheep Special, Copper Dragon and guest ale

A friendly Yorkshire welcome is extended to the Dale walkers who come to refuel at this stone built part 16C pub, situated just off the main square in the market town of Leyburn.Visitors can rest their blistered feet by the fire in the traditionally furnished, split-level, beamed bar, or plump for a seat in the neatly laid-out dining room with its polished wood furniture. A small enclosed terrace out the back provides a third alternative for when it's sunny, but you'll have to come inside to read the blackboard menus, found hanging on the walls amidst the general clutter of decorative pictures, books and ornaments. Influences from across Europe are found in the good sized daily-changing menus, so the chicken is Moroccan, the tomatoes are sunblushed and local lamb comes with a garlic sauce. Two pleasant bedrooms are upstairs on the first floor, with a third over the road in a converted cottage.

Food serving times

Tuesday-Saturday:
12pm-2.30pm, 6.30pm-9pm

Sunday:
12pm-2pm, 7pm-9pm

Closed 25 December and 1 January

Sometimes closed Tuesdays

Prices

Meals: a la carte 20.00/33.50

2 rooms: 65.00/75.00

Typical Dishes

Lambs' kidneys
Fillet of pork
Selection of pastries

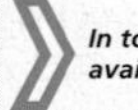

In town centre. Limited parking available in the Market Place.

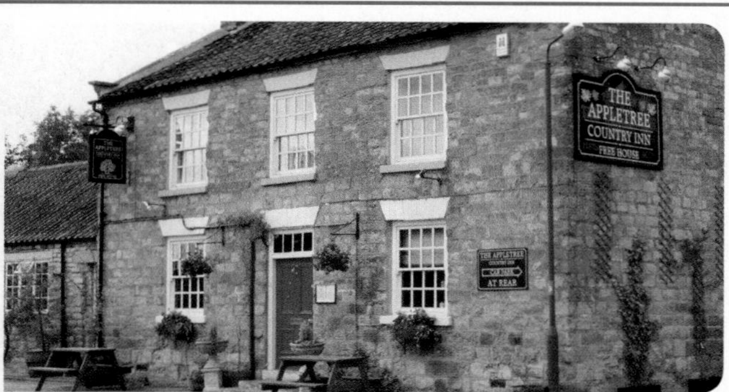

022 The Appletree

Marton YO62 6RD
Tel.: (01751) 431457 - Fax: (01751) 430190
e-mail: appletreeinn@supanet.com
Website: www.appletreeinn.co.uk

Moorhouses (Pendle) TJ's Tipple, Suddaby's (Malton) Windfall - both brewed especially for the Appletree

This spacious stone built pub is situated in a pretty rural village by the river Seven. Well-regarded locally, The Appletree is often busy, so it's advisable to book. It's run by a husband and wife team; he's in the kitchen, while she's in charge of the organised team out front. Having made changes and improvements, they've still managed to retain the sense of intimacy and friendliness. Wherever possible it's locally grown or reared produce that graces the menu, so you'll find Whitby crab fishcakes alongside braised Marton beef and hare; their exact provenance brought to your attention on the menu. Order as many mini desserts as you like – or just one big one - all are homemade, as are the chocolates that come with your coffee. There's a comprehensive selection of wines by the glass, two real ales brewed especially for the pub, plus a selection of homemade foodstuffs to purchase, such as pesto and chutney.

Food serving times

Wednesday-Saturday:
12pm-2pm, 6pm-9.30pm

Sunday:
12pm-2pm, 6.30pm-9pm

Closed 25 December and 2 weeks January

Prices

Meals: a la carte
17.00/25.00

Typical Dishes

Yorkshire Blue cheese soufflé

Roast fillet of hare

Yorkshire Golden treacle tart

7mi Southeast of Welshpool on B4386. Parking.

023 The Golden Lion

6 West End,
Osmotherley DL6 3AA
Tel.: (01609) 883526
Website: www.goldenlionosmotherley.co.uk

Timothy Taylor's Landlord, Daleside Brewery, Prior's Ale, North York Brew Co, Hambleton's Ales, North York Dales Brew Co

Walkers stopping off at this old, stone built inn for a simple, satisfying Yorkshire meal will not be disappointed. There's plenty of choice for everyone on the well-priced, seasonal menus; and while traditional British dishes such as fish and steaks are just the right type of food to fill you up, ready once more to face the moors, there are also salads, pasta dishes and vegetarian options if you're after something lighter. Ingredients are locally sourced - and even the burgers and the ice cream are homemade. Set in the centre of a picturesque rural market village, the beamed candlelit interior of the pub is rustic through and through. There's a first floor dining area decorated with potted plants, but the fire lit ground floor bar is the best place to sit. The pub is well-run, and keen, friendly service from staff in T-shirts and aprons suggests that they are used to being busy. Three delightful bedrooms have a spacious, modern feel.

Food serving times

Monday-Sunday:
12pm-2.30pm, 6pm-9.30pm

Closed 25 December

Prices

Meals: a la carte
16.00/27.00

3 rooms: 60.00/90.00

Typical Dishes

Salmon and tomoto risotto

Pork loin in Parma ham

Prune, apple and walnut cake

6 mi Northeast of Northallerton by A684. Parking in the village.

024 The Yorke Arms

Ramsgill-in-Nidderdale HG3 5RL
Tel.: (01423) 755243 - Fax: (01423) 755330
e-mail: enquiries@yorke-arms.co.uk
Website: www.yorke-arms.co.uk

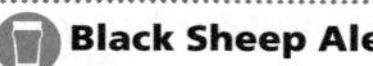
Black Sheep Ale

Set in unspoilt countryside near Gouthwaite reservoir, this part 17C, delightfully ivy clad former shooting lodge is quite simply one of England's most charming inns. Handsomely styled with carved wooden furniture, antiques, oriental rugs and bright, gilt-framed oils, two welcoming dining rooms feel closer in atmosphere to a country house than a village pub, and the formal, structured service is that of a restaurant rather than an inn, but as a dining experience it's calm, refined and, at its best, quite delightful. Precise and consistent seasonal cooking balances classical style with a subtle regional identity. Good value lunch Monday to Saturday and you can make the most of a lovely riverside terrace and gardens, or flop onto the squashy sofas in the lounge. Superlative, stylish and contemporary bedrooms have been recently refurbished.

Food serving times

Monday-Saturday:
12pm-2pm, 7pm-9pm

Sunday:
12pm-2pm

Accommodation rates include dinner

Prices

Meals: 21.00 (3 course lunch) and a la carte 45.00/55.00

14 rooms:
100.00/380.00

Typical Dishes

Potted beef, ham hock terrine
Hake & scallop ravioli
Coconut soufflé

5 mi Northwest of Pateley Bridge by Low Wath rd. Parking.

025 The Anvil Inn

Main St, Sawdon YO13 9DY

Tel.: (01723) 859896

e-mail: theanvilinnsawdon@btinternet.com

Website: www.theanvilinnsawdon.co.uk

VISA 

Black Sheep Best and 3 other guest ales in summer and 2 in winter

Twenty years ago, you would have found blacksmiths working in this solid stone building. Now the atmosphere is more sedate, though much evidence of former days lives on: an old furnace, bellows, tools and the original anvil are all in situ. Close by, in the village of Sawdon, stunning views over Dalby Dale prevail, and the rustic charm of the inn – all candle-lit tables, country style paraphernalia and log-burning stove - loses nothing by comparison. Yorkshire ales are pulled in the locals' bar and the intimate dining room is like a home-from-home. Mark, one of the owners and also the chef here, trained at local college and his roots are in evidence with seriously considered, good value dishes using dishes primarily sourced from the nearby moors and dales. And the portions are good, too!

Food serving times

Tuesday-Saturday:
12pm-2pm, 6.30pm-9pm

Sunday:
12pm-2pm

Closed lunch 25 December, 2 weeks in January and August Bank Holiday Monday

Prices

Meals: a la carte
16.00/24.25

Typical Dishes

Pigeon breast Wellington

Pan roast lamb loin eye

Trio of English puddings

12mi Southwest of Scarborough by A170 to Brompton and minor road north. Parking.

026 The Hare Inn

Scawton YO7 2HG
Tel.: (01845) 597769
e-mail: geoff@brucearms.com
Website: www.thehareinn.co.uk

 **Theakstons, Black Sheep**

One and a half miles from the beautiful Rievaulx Abbey and gardens, in the very rural location of Scawton, sits The Hare, with its smart yellow exterior. There is a spacious main dining room, whose walls are filled with photos, prints and hanging hop bines, and an adjacent room with linen-laid tables; although the best place to sit is probably in the main bar by the open fired stove, where you can become acquainted with the friendly resident Labrador, Teal. Cooking is satisfying, seasonal and freshly prepared with vibrant use of local ingredients. The menu has a classical base, but there's something here to suit every taste, with meat, seafood and vegetarian offerings as well as daily specials chalked up on the blackboard. Any visitor here will recognise the truth Samuel Johnson expressed so well when he said, 'There is nothing which has yet been contrived by man, by which so much happiness is produced as by a good tavern or inn.'

Food serving times
Tuesday-Saturday:
12pm-2pm, 6.30pm-9.30pm
Sunday:
12pm-2pm

Prices
Meals: a la carte
20.00/30.00

Typical Dishes
Red mullet & orange dressing
Fillet of beef
Chocolate fondant

Between Thirsk and Helmsley, off north side of A170. Parking.

027 Fox and Hounds

Main St, Sinnington YO62 6SQ

Tel.: (01751) 431577 - Fax: (01751) 432791

e-mail: foxhoundsinn@easynet.co.uk

Website: www.thefoxandhoundsinn.co.uk

Theakstons Best Bitter, Cask, Black Sheep Special

This extended 18C coaching inn is found on the river Seven, in the sleepy village of Sinnington, at the base of the North York moors. Its handsome stone exterior has long been a welcoming sight to tourists and locals alike, and inside there's a beamed bar and traditionally styled residents lounge, as well as a more modern, formal restaurant, set in the rear extension. Hungry as a hunter? Lunchtime menus offer classic dishes, such as steak or fish and chips, as well as lighter dishes, whilst the evening menu has a more international flavour to it, with dishes such as skewers of tiger prawns and king scallops or spiced monkfish. Uniformed staff provide polite, attentive service and the atmosphere is relaxed and friendly, with several open fires and a large garden. Weary as a woodlouse after all that walking? Retire to one of the compact bedrooms - quite cottagey in style, with flowery drapes and décor.

Food serving times

Summer:
Monday-Sunday: 12pm-2pm, 6.30pm-9pm

Winter:
Monday-Sunday: 12pm-2pm, 7pm-9pm

Closed 25-26 December

Prices

Meals: a la carte 20.00/28.00

10 rooms: 49.00/120.00

Typical Dishes

Roast quail
Escalope of veal
Dark chocolate marquise

Just off A170 between Pickering and Kirkymoorside. Parking.

028 The Bull

Broughton, Skipton BD23 3AE
Tel.: (01756) 792065 - Fax: (01756) 792065
e-mail: janeneil@thebullatbroughton.co.uk
Website: www.thebullatbroughton.co.uk

    MC

 **Bull Bitter, Copper Dragon Best Bitter and Black Gold**

Set within the grounds of the Broughton Hall Country Park Estate, just down the road from the bustling market town of Skipton, this spacious stone pub is rustic in character with its warren of little rooms and snugs, open fire, stone floors and timbered beams. The menu involves robust, classic British dishes such as shepherd's pie, fish of the day or duck breast, and the odd French touch too in the form of dishes such as cassoulet. If you're after something lighter, try fishcakes or a chicken breast ciabatta, or for a more economical option, go for the 'Early bird' set price 2 course menu. There's plenty of choice, it's all homemade, and local produce is well-used. The large terrace for outside dining, and the friendly welcome served up with the food add two more good reasons why this pub is a great stop off point on your way to or from the Yorkshire Dales, or indeed a destination in its own right.

Food serving times

Monday-Thursday:
12pm-2pm, 6pm-9pm

Friday-Saturday:
12pm-2pm, 6pm-9.30pm

Sunday and Bank Holidays:
12pm-6pm

Prices

Meals: 9.95 (2 course lunch & dinner (6-7pm)) and a la carte 18.48/27.00

Typical Dishes

Toasted goats' cheese salad
Home-made sausages
Vanilla crème brûlée

 *3mi West of Skipton town centre on A59. In the grounds of Broughton Hall Country Park Estate. Parking.* 

Yorkshire and The Humber • North Yorkshire

029 Coachman Inn

Pickering Road West,
Snainton YO13 9PL
Tel.: (01723) 859231 - Fax: (01723) 850008
e-mail: james@coachmaninn.co.uk - Website: www.coachmaninn.co.uk

    MC

 **Wold Top, Wold Gold, Falling Stone**

This Grade II listed building has stood on the same site just outside Snainton since 1776, providing sustenance for travellers on the York to Scarborough road. These days, lunchtime means a choice of sandwiches and traditional dishes such as sausage and mash or smoked salmon and prawns, while the evening menu offers more substantial dishes like lamb Wellington, roasted half of Gressingham duck or pan fried pork medallions. Inside, a contemporary dining room has a view over the lawn – if you're planning on a formal meal, this is probably better, not to mention more spacious, but the traditional flagstoned bar takes some beating for warmth and character. Individually styled bedrooms.

Food serving times

Tuesday:
7pm-9.30pm

Wednesday-Saturday:
12pm-2pm, 7pm-9.30pm

Sunday:
12pm-2pm, 6.30pm-8.30pm

Closed 25 December

Prices

Meals: a la carte
20.00/30.00

2 rooms: 50.00/66.00

Typical Dishes

Warm crispy duck salad
Venison steak
Chocolate fondant

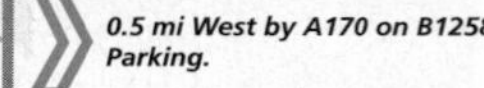
0.5 mi West by A170 on B1258.
Parking.

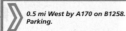

The Blackwell Ox Inn

030 The Blackwell Ox Inn

Huby Rd,
Sutton on the Forest YO61 1DT

Tel.: (01347) 810328 - Fax: (01347) 812738
e-mail: info@blackwelloxinn.co.uk - Website: www.blackwelloxinn.co.uk

 **John Smith's Cask, Black Sheep Ale**

If it's heaving in York and you're stuck for a place to wine, dine and rest your weary bones, then you could do a lot worse than head north a few miles to the picturesque village of Sutton on the Forest and try your luck at this recently enlarged country inn and restaurant, where you'll be immediately enticed by the sight of cosy sofas in the open-fired bar. But do stir yourself, as food is the main emphasis here. The two dining rooms are set out with formal linen-clad tables, yet are intimate enough to feel snug. Menus are based upon the southwest of France and the Catalan region of Spain, so expect tapas at one end of the culinary range, big cassoulets and rich Catalan stews at the other. Good value daily changing midweek set-price menus are another attraction. And for those weary bones, five comfy, individually decorated rooms are on offer.

Food serving times

Monday-Sunday:
12pm-2pm, 6pm-9.30pm

Closed meals 25 December and 1 January

Prices

Meals: 11.50/13.50 (3 course lunch/dinner menu) and a la carte 16.50/26.85

6 rooms: 95.00

Typical Dishes

Spanish delicacies
Roast halibut
Warm chocolate pudding

8mi North of York by B1363.
Parking.

031 Rose & Crown

Main St,
Sutton-on-the-Forest YO61 1DP
Tel.: (01347) 811333 - Fax: (01347) 811333
e-mail: ben-w@btconnect.com - Website: www.rosecrown.co.uk

Black Sheep Best, Timothy Taylor's Landlord and guest ales such as York Brewery Terrier

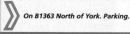

This is a relatively plain-looking pub from the outside, with a relatively plain-sounding name, but venture inside and you'll find that the food is anything but. The confident kitchen knows how to handle ingredients; dishes are refreshingly free from over-elaboration, with fish dishes being prepared in particular with care and precision, and prices are good when you consider the quality of the produce. Influences are predominantly European, but they're not afraid of throwing in the occasional Asian spice. The traditionally-styled, wood-floored bar has kept its original feature fireplaces and beams, while the dining room and conservatory have a stylishly informal feel to them, and the outside eating area and garden are delightful in the summer months. The Rose and Crown is situated in Sutton-on-the-Forest, a pretty village not far from York, where Laurence Sterne penned Tristram Shandy.

Food serving times

Tuesday-Saturday:
12pm-2pm, 6pm-9pm

Sunday:
12pm-2pm

Closed first 2 weeks in January

Prices

Meals: a la carte
23.00/27.00

Typical Dishes

Spiced tuna carpaccio
Pan-fried fillets of seabass
Sticky toffee pudding

On B1363 North of York. Parking.

032 The Bruce Arms

Main St,
West Tanfield HG4 5JJ
Tel.: (01677) 470325 - Fax: (01677) 470925
e-mail: info@bruce-arms.com - Website: www.bruce-arms.com

 **Black Sheep Bitter, Black Sheep Ale**

Situated on a roundabout between Masham and Ripon, its young owners are bringing their experience to bear at this 200 year old stone pub. Its characterful bar boasts flagstone floors and a wood burner while four vast port barrels above the bar make you question how on earth they got them up there in the first place. The bar area opens out into a traditional carpeted area with a mix of old pub chairs and a few leather armchairs, and you can either eat here or in the more formal, linen-laid burgundy-walled dining room. Blackboards display lunch dishes, some sandwiches and the day's specials, while the concise printed dinner menu offers starters such as scallops or terrine of ham hock and mains such as roast duck breast or salmon. The choice may be limited, but the food is well prepared, neatly presented and won't break the bank. There is a small decked terrace area at the front and two en suite bedrooms are available upstairs.

Food serving times
Tuesday-Sunday:
12pm-2pm, 6pm-9pm

Prices
Meals: a la carte
22.00/30.00
2 rooms: 35.00/70.00

Typical Dishes
Fresh Whitby crab
Roast rack of suckling pig
Glazed lemon tart

Between Masham and Ripon on A6108. Parking.

Yorkshire and The Humber • North Yorkshire

033 The Blacksmiths Inn

Main St,
Westow YO60 7NE
Tel.: (01653) 618365 - Fax: (01653) 618394
e-mail: info@blacksmithsinn.co.uk - Website: www.blacksmithsinn.co.uk

Jennings Bitter, Jennings Cumberland

Although it's fair to say that the Blacksmiths Inn is a modern dining pub, the move has taken it closer to, not further from, its country roots. There's a quiet glow from the wood-burning stove, and framed pictures, postcards, cartoons, Yorkshire landscapes and other themed artwork cover the walls. The local connection rings particularly true in the two trimly set dining rooms: vegetables from the pub's own farm, home-ground flour, and local sloe berries – in gin, jam, even chutneys and chocolates - play their part in a couple of specials and a concise, modern menu which changes by the week. Drinkers are made very welcome in the front lounge, with bowls of rustic, home-made nibbles like parsnip crisps and crackling set out on the bar. Knowledgeable and thoroughly pleasant service. Beamed, cottage-style bedrooms furnished in dark wood.

Food serving times

Wednesday-Saturday:
12pm-2pm, 5.30pm-9pm

Sunday:
12pm-4pm, 5.30pm-9pm

Closed 1 week in January

Prices

Meals: a la carte
15.00/30.00

6 rooms: 40.00/70.00

Typical Dishes

Goat's cheese crottin
Roast rack of Yorkshire lamb
White chocolate pannacotta

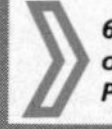

6.5 mi Southwest of Moulton off the A64 past Kirkham Priory. Parking.

034 The Stone Trough Inn

Kirkham Abbey,
Whitwell-on-the-Hill YO60 7JS
Tel.: (01653) 618713 - Fax: (01653) 618819
e-mail: info@stonetroughinn.co.uk - Website: www.stonetroughinn.co.uk

Tetley Cask Ale, Black Sheep Best Bitter, Theakstons Old Peculier, Timothy Taylor's Landlord, Copper Dragon Golden Pippin

On the Eastern end of the Howardian Hills, just off the A64, and near the ruins of Kirkham Abbey, sits the erroneously-named Stone Trough Inn. A large stone-built building, it has various little beamed rooms and charming snugs and the rustic feel is further enhanced by the pictures, ornaments, antiques and farm machinery which decorate the panelled walls. A games room with pool table offers welcome diversion should the conversation falter and the outside terrace is a great spot for fine weather dining. The extensive bar and restaurant menus offer traditional British favourites made with local produce, so you know that nothing has travelled too far to reach your plate; crab is from Whitby, beef is from Kilburn, lamb from Flaxton, and some fruit and herbs are even grown in the pub's own garden. More modern dishes also feature, with European flavours to the fore, and daily specials compete for your attention too.

Food serving times

Tuesday-Sunday and Bank Holidays:
12pm-2pm, 6.45pm-9.30pm

Closed 25 December and 2-5 January

Bar meals at lunchtime

Prices

Meals: a la carte 23.00/30.00

Typical Dishes

Home-cured gravadlax

Roast rump of Flaxton lamb

Apple & ginger sponge pudding

5mi Southwest of Malton off A64 following signs for Kirkham Priory. Parking.

035 The Fleece

152-154 Main St,
Addingham LS29 0LY
Tel.: (01943) 830491
e-mail: thefleece@mac.com - Website: www.fleeceaddingham.com

VISA 

Tetley's Cask, Timothy Taylor's Landlord, Copper Dragon Golden Pippin, Black Sheep

Set on the main street of the village of Addingham, this large, ivy-clad inn is a popular meeting place for locals who congregate to drink and discuss the day's events in its small public bar. Often equally as busy is the larger lounge and dining area; decorated with countryside pictures and knick-knacks, and whose beamed ceilings and stone floors and walls bear testament to the building's 18C genesis. The large blackboard menus displayed on the walls change frequently according to what's fresh and what's in season. Homely dishes with Yorkshire roots, such as locally sourced steak and meat pies offer lots of comfort appeal but the wide-ranging menus also include more contemporary dishes too. Service from friendly local staff remains efficient and polite, even when there's a rush on, and the hugely generous portions that they place in front of you present an enjoyable challenge you find you just have to conquer.

Food serving times

Monday-Saturday:
12pm-2.15pm, 6pm-9.15pm

Sunday:
12pm-8pm

Prices

Meals: a la carte
15.00/22.00

Typical Dishes

Whare Valley game terrine

Chris Haley's Exeter sirloin

Rhubarb & wild berry crumble

On the busy through road in the centre of Addingham. Parking.

Shibden Mill Inn

036 Shibden Mill Inn

Shibden Mill Fold, Halifax HX3 7UL
Tel.: (01422) 365840 - Fax: (01422) 362971
e-mail: glenpearson@shibdenmillinn.com
Website: www.shibdenmillinn.com

   AE

Shibden Mill Bitter, Theakstons XB, John Smiths and 2 regularly changing guest bitters

What was the mill pond many years hence is now the car park, and the mill has long since stopped grinding corn, but a sense of historic charm still inhabits this pub, with its cosy, cluttered rooms and snugs. The menus offer a little bit of everything, ranging from venison burger and chunky chips through to a six course gourmet dinner. While there are a few Mediterranean influences, traditional dishes such as fish pie, lamb casserole and roast Yorkshire beef dominate, and there is even a platter of 'British bites' on offer, including chicken pie, smoked salmon, and mini fish cakes. The chef's passion for food finds further expression in regular 'Guinea pig nights,' which involve the sampling of new dishes; thus named to refer to the fact that you are being 'experimented on,' rather than because you might actually find yourself feasting on one of the furry creatures, as popular as they may be fricasseed in some parts of the world.

Food serving times

Monday-Saturday:
12pm-2pm, 6pm-9.15pm

Sunday:
12pm-7.30pm

Closed dinner 25-26 December and dinner 1 January

Prices

Meals: a la carte
17.95/29.15

11 rooms: 75.00/90.00

Typical Dishes

Lincolnshire pigeon faggot

Red mullet and crayfish stew

Three chocolate terrine

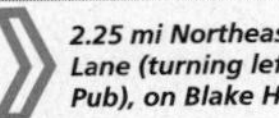

2.25 mi Northeast by A58 and Kell Lane (turning left at Stump Cross Pub), on Blake Hill Rd. Parking.

Yorkshire and The Humber • West Yorkshire

037 Olive Branch

Manchester Rd,
Marsden HD7 6LU
Tel.: (01484) 844487
e-mail: mail@olivebranch.uk.com - Website: www.olivebranch.uk.com

 **Greenfield Real Ales Dobcross Bitter**

Having built up an appetite with a bracing walk over Wessenden moor, prepare to pull up a pew next to the fire in the comfortingly rustic atmosphere of The Olive Branch, and peruse the blackboard menus. There's plenty to choose from, and the unconventional post-it note approach points to the freshness and seasonality of the food to be had here. Cooking is modern British with the emphasis on seafood and more than a hint of the Mediterranean, so your salad might be Lyonnaise, scallops might come with sunblushed tomato and spicy Spanish sausage, and your steak with snail, garlic and parsley butter. You can eat in one of the cosy beamed front rooms or in the contemporary rear dining room - the menu is the same throughout - and the decked terrace outside is a further alternative for when the weather's fine. Three well-kept bedrooms with modern en suites each have a style and a feel of their own.

Food serving times

Wednesday-Friday:
12pm-1.45pm, 6.30pm-9.30pm

Saturday:
6.30pm-9.30pm

Sunday: 12pm-8.30pm

Closed first 2 weeks January

Prices

Meals: 14.95/18.95 (3 course lunch/dinner) and a la carte 25.00/35.00

3 rooms: 55.00/70.00

Typical Dishes

Smoked salmon & quail's eggs
Tournedos Rossini
Classic lemon tart

1 mi Northeast on A62. Parking.

038 The Old Bore

Oldham Rd,
Rishworth HX6 4QU
Tel.: (01422) 822 291
e-mail: chefhessel@aol.com - Website: www.oldbore.co.uk

 **Old Bore Bitter, Timothy Taylor's Landlord, Black Sheep**

Here's a handy tip for drivers barrelling along the M62: do yourself a favour and turn off at J22 for a spot of R&R at the nearby Old Bore. Outside, there's a delightful terrace with stone walled border and good rural views. Inside, the relaxing main bar with its open fire, exposed rafters, red leather seats and hunting scene wallpaper is an ideal place to wind down – there's a good selection of real ales and plenty of top-notch wines by the glass, the walls are bursting with knick knacks, and pewter tankards hang from the beams. Two rustic-style main dining rooms are formally laid, and food takes a similarly luxurious approach, with truffles, foie gras and the like appearing on the restaurant-style menu alongside snails, mussels, rabbit saddle and Ryburn lamb; a mix of classic French and British cooking made using quality local ingredients, and supplemented with blackboard daily specials.

Food serving times

Wednesday-Friday:
12pm-2.15pm, 6pm-9.30pm

Saturday:
12pm-2.15pm, 6pm-10pm

Sunday:
12pm-4pm, 5.30pm-8pm

Closed first 2 weeks in January

Prices

Meals: 11.95 (3 course lunch & dinner) and a la carte 22.45/31.85

Typical Dishes

Home-smoked sea trout
Venison fillet
Baked egg custard

6mi Southwest of Halifax by A58 and A672. Parking.

039 The Millbank

Mill Bank,
Sowerby Bridge HX6 3DY
Tel.: (01422) 825588
e-mail: eat@themillbank.com - Website: www.themillbank.com

Timothy Taylor's Landlord, Tetley's Cask

From the outside, The Millbank looks to be your typical stone-built village local, and only the sign hints at the fact that it is actually a fully paid up member of the gastro gang, with a bright, contemporary interior, wooden floors and heavy wood tables. Modern art hangs for sale on the walls, there's a small area for drinkers and a smart conservatory overlooks the dining terrace, with views out over the Ryburn valley. People come from far and wide to taste the modern European cooking on the menu here, with choices ranging from parmesan polenta cake and goat's cheese ravioli to roast suckling pig, Yorkshire lamb, or ox tongue fritter. The chef is confident in his craft, and the well-balanced dishes taste as good as they read on the menus. Smart young staff offer friendly, efficient service and the atmosphere is relaxed. Every Thursday is fish night and every night is good-value-for-money night.

Food serving times

Monday:
6pm-9.30pm
Tuesday-Saturday:
12pm-2.30pm, 6pm-9.30pm
Sunday:
12.30pm-4.30pm, 6pm-8pm
Closed first week January, first 2 weeks October
Booking essential

Prices

Meals: 11.95 (2 courses lunch & dinner with coffee) and a la carte 20.50/35.00

Typical Dishes

Roast scallops
Beef Wellington
Chocolate fondant cake

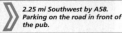

2.25 mi Southwest by A58. Parking on the road in front of the pub.

040 Woodman Inn

Thunderbridge HD8 0PX

Tel.: (01484) 605778 - Fax: (01484) 604110
e-mail: thewoodman@connectfree.co.uk
Website: www.woodman-inn.co.uk

Tetley's Bitter, Timothy Taylor's Best and Landlord and guest ales

This 19C stone inn stands in a wooded valley in the noisy-sounding yet in truth rather tranquil village of Thunderbridge, just south of Huddersfield in the heart of the Pennines. Its large open plan downstairs rooms are filled with polished wood tables and are set around a central horseshoe-shaped bar, while upstairs there's a comfortable lounge and large restaurant featuring the building's original beams. Extensive menus offer traditional British cooking, with classic dishes such as shepherd's pie, sausage and mash or fillet of sea trout fighting with the specials for your attention. Over a decade ago, the owners decided to convert the old weavers' cottages next door into simply decorated bedrooms for those wanting to stay overnight, so you can take the opportunity to explore the area, and of course pay homage to Compo, Cleggy et al at nearby Holmfirth, home of Last of the Summer Wine.

Food serving times

Sunday-Thursday:
12pm-3pm, 6.30pm-9pm

Friday-Saturday:
12pm-3pm, 6.30pm-9.30pm

Prices

Meals: a la carte
14.95/29.95

12 rooms: 45.00/65.00

Typical Dishes

Woodman duck liver parfait
Trio of fillets
Pear & apple tart Tatin

5.75mi Southeast of Huddersfield by A629, after Kirkburton follow signs to Thunderbridge. Parking.

041 The Fox and Hounds

Hall Park Road,
Walton LS23 7DQ
Tel.: (01937) 842192

 **Black Sheep, John Smith's Cask**

The same team that breathed recent life into the Bay Horse up the road in Kirk Deighton is also creating a stir at The Fox and Hounds, tucked away in a sleepy little West Yorkshire village east of Wetherby. You'll feel snug as soon as you enter the cosy bar, a stuffed fox tucked up in a basket typifying the relaxed mood. Pleasant country décor includes framed sepia prints, dried flowers and hop bines. Sit at rustic pine tables and tuck into very good value, wide ranging set menus underpinned by a solid Yorkshire base, served by an invariably cheerful and knowledgeable local waiting team. There are daily blackboard specials, too, and everything on them is home made, from rustic breads through to ice creams.

Food serving times

Monday-Saturday:
12pm-2pm, 5.30pm-9pm

Sunday:
12pm-2pm

Booking essential

Prices

Meals: 13.95 (2 course lunch & dinner) and a la carte 19.85/27.70

Typical Dishes

Home-made black pudding

Saddle of Dales lamb

Hazelnut chocolate brownie

3mi East of Wetherby by minor road; between A659 and B1224. Parking.

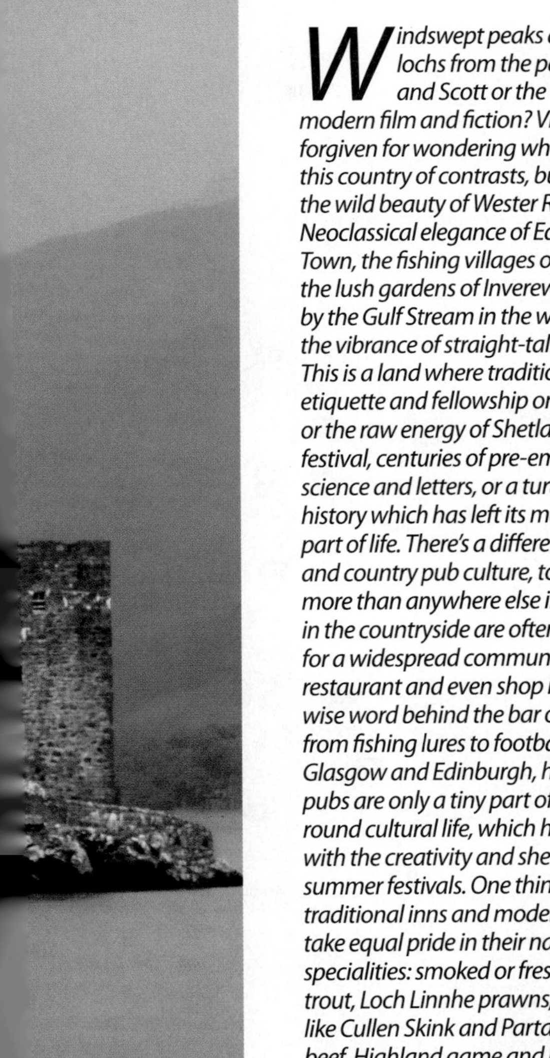

Windswept peaks and misty lochs from the pages of Burns and Scott or the urban grit of modern film and fiction? Visitors could be forgiven for wondering what to expect in this country of contrasts, but it's all here: the wild beauty of Wester Ross and the Neoclassical elegance of Edinburgh's New Town, the fishing villages of the East Neuk, the lush gardens of Inverewe, warmed by the Gulf Stream in the west, as well as the vibrance of straight-talking Glasgow. This is a land where tradition can mean etiquette and fellowship on the first tee or the raw energy of Shetland's Viking fire festival, centuries of pre-eminence in British science and letters, or a turbulent social history which has left its mark on every part of life. There's a difference in town and country pub culture, too. Perhaps more than anywhere else in Britain, inns in the countryside are often the centres for a widespread community: pub, hotel, restaurant and even shop in one, with a wise word behind the bar on anything from fishing lures to football scores. In Glasgow and Edinburgh, however, dining pubs are only a tiny part of a busy year-round cultural life, which hits fever pitch with the creativity and sheer variety of the summer festivals. One thing is for sure, traditional inns and modern gastropubs take equal pride in their national specialities: smoked or fresh salmon and trout, Loch Linnhe prawns, seafood soups like Cullen Skink and Partan Bree, prime beef, Highland game and haggis.

SCOTLAND
Northern Ireland
Ireland
North West
Lewis
Stornoway
St. Kilda
Tarbert
North Uist
Lochmaddy
South Uist
Lochboisdale
Barra
Castlebay
Uig
Dunvegan
Portree
Skye
Kyle of Lochalsh
Rhum
Mallaig
Coll
Tiree
Tobermory
Mull
Craignure
Fionnphort
Oban
Colonsay
Lochgilphead
Islay
Port Askaig
Jura
Port Ellen
Kintyre
Campbeltown
Arran
Brodick
Malin Head
Lochinver
Tongue
Lairg
Ullapool
Brora
Dornoch
Dingwall
Nairn
Inverness
Loch Ness
Newtonmore
Grantown
Fort William
Ben Nevis
Crianlarich
Crieff
Perth
Stirling
Kinross
Dumbarton
Dunoon
Greenock
Rothesay
GLASGOW
Ardrossan
Hamilton
Falkirk
EDINBURGH
Kilmarnock
Lanark
Peebles
Ayr
Moffat
Hawick
Dumfries
Kirkcudbright
Stranraer
Carlisle
Workington
Whitehaven
Keswick
Windermere
Man
Peel
Ramsey
Douglas
Giant's Causeway
Buncrana
Portrush
Coleraine
Ballycastle
Letterkenny
Londonderry
Donegal
Strabane
Omagh
Ballymena
Larne
Bundoran
Sligo
Enniskillen
Lisburn
BELFAST
Bangor
Armagh
Boyle
Monaghan
Newry
Newcastle
Dundalk
Longford
Dunnet

Yell
Unst
Shetland
Hillswick
Sandness
Mainland
Lerwick
Sumburgh
Bergen
Aberdeen
Stromness
Westray
Rousay
Sanday
Mainland
Stronsay
Kirkwall
Hoy
Aberdeen
Wick
NORTH SEA
MER DU NORD
Banff
Fraserburgh
Keith
A98
A96
A92
Peterhead
Bergen
Stromness
Lerwick
Aberdeen
Stonehaven
Montrose
Arbroath
Andrews
Forth
Berwick-upon-Tweed
Coldstream
North East
Blyth
Tynemouth
Bergen
Stavanger
South Shields
Sunderland
Gateshead
Durham
Hartlepool
Middlesbrough

Balmedie

001 Cock and Bull

Ellon Rd,
Blairton, Balmedie AB23 8XY
Tel.: (01358) 743249 - Fax: (01358) 742466
e-mail: info@thecockandbull.co.uk - Website: www.thecockandbull.co.uk

 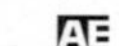  

 **Directors, Theakstons Old Peculier**

"Where ancient meets modern without so much as a jolt," it says in the Cock and Bull's promo blurb. And that's just the half of it. This former shepherds' watering hole looks over fields to the North Sea. Inside, there are three distinct areas: two of them, the lounge/bar and the restaurant, are delightfully atmospheric, cluttered with artefacts (some African themed), old record players, sewing machines, posters and fabrics (plus anything else you might care to mention). Open fires complete a feast for the eyes and the senses. A more contemporary conservatory with polished wood tables and chairs completes the picture. Extensive menus cover the full range from 'popular pub fare' to 'fine dining', as well as heartily ample one-course dishes with Scottish produce to the fore. Service is very friendly from staff used to being run off their feet.

Food serving times

Monday-Saturday:
12pm-9pm

Sunday:
12pm-7pm

Closed 25-26 December and 1-4 January

Prices

Meals: a la carte
15.50/33.45

Typical Dishes

Smooth duck liver parfait
Pan-fried fillet of pork
Dark chocolate fondant

6mi North of Aberdeen by A90. Parking.

002 The Steading

(at Lochside Lodge and Roundhouse restaurant),
Bridgend of Lintrathen DD8 5JJ

Tel.: (01575) 560340 - Fax: (01575) 560251

e-mail: enquiries@lochsidelodge.com - Website: www.lochsidelodge.com

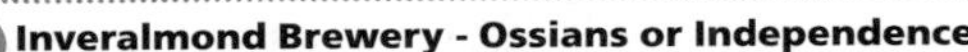

Inveralmond Brewery - Ossians or Independence

The more informal counterpart to the Roundhouse restaurant, the Steading's name is a reminder of its humble origins as an old farm building. The original stone walls are now decorated with all sorts of agricultural tools, rural fitments, and some country sports memorabilia, some of the mystery items look like they might fall into all three categories. Cushioned pews are pulled up to solid wood tables and a brasserie style lunch menu is served along with the same menu on offer in the Roundhouse restaurant at dinner. If you're just after a drink, there's a little bar to one side, with newspapers and magazines within easy reach of the leather seats. Four pine-fitted bedrooms, in the converted hayloft, all have a dash of tartan or floral colour and plenty in the way of thoughtful, homely touches.

Food serving times

Tuesday-Saturday: 12pm-1.30pm, 6.30pm-8.30pm

Sunday: 12pm-1.30pm

Closed 23-27 December, 1-25 January and 1 week October

Closed Sunday-Wednesday January-Easter

Prices

Meals: 19.00 (Sundays) and a la carte 16.00/37.00

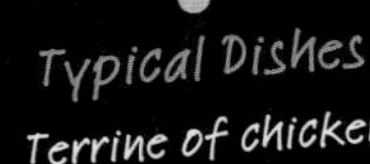

6 rooms: 70.00/120.00

Typical Dishes

Terrine of chicken

Grilled Shetland salmon

Glazed lemon tart

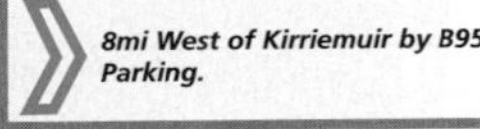

8mi West of Kirriemuir by B951.
Parking.

003 The Oyster Inn

Connel PA37 1PJ
Tel.: (01631) 710666 - Fax: (01631) 710042
e-mail: stay@oysterinn.co.uk
Website: www.oysterinn.co.uk

 VISA AE MC

 **Theakstons**

You get three for the price of one here: a restaurant, a neighbouring pub plus accommodation. Add to this the Falls of Lora – a naturally occurring spectacle of white water and whirlpools as the tides rise and fall - and you'll have to agree that Connel really is your oyster. The restaurant is spacious and contemporary in style, with a small terrace and a view of the loch. The adjacent pub, The Ferryman's, is much more traditional, with scrubbed wooden tables, log fires, real ales, a large range of malts and a pool table. Built in the 18C to serve the erstwhile ferry's passengers, it is known locally as The Glue Pot – be sure to touch the pot for luck. The same menu is served in both establishments – simple, seasonal homemade classics, daily specials with the emphasis on fresh seafood, plus a choice of homemade cakes and scones. Bedrooms are comfortable and modern, and bunk style budget rooms are also available for groups.

Food serving times

Monday-Sunday:
12.30pm-2.30pm, 6pm-9pm

Bar meals at lunch time

Prices

11 rooms:
52.00/104.00

Typical Dishes

Chicken liver paté
Seafood treasure
Cranachan with raspberries

5mi North of Oban by A85.
Parking.

004 **Crinan (Bar)**

Crinan PA31 8SR

Tel.: (01546) 830261 - Fax: (01546) 830292
e-mail: reservations@crinanhotel.com
Website: www.crinanhotel.com

Fyne Ales, Belhaven, Tennants Velvet

Run by the same family for nigh on forty years, this elegant, whitewashed building is superbly located in a commanding position with exceptional views of Loch Crinan and Sound of Jura, with picture windows that let guests take in superb views of fishing boats chugging out towards the Hebrides. Naturally enough, the bar has a nautical theme, while there are two homely lounges to sit and watch the world go by. There's a Gallery bar, too, which overlooks the loch. With all this natural beauty in abundance, make sure you get to eat where you can take in the vista. The split-level restaurant is smart with linen clad tables, and the menus have an interesting, modern feel to them. Large, local prawns are a speciality; other choices might include Loch Etive mussels, risotto of Shetland crab and cream cheese, or local Crinan seafood chowder. Stay in pleasant, bright bedrooms.

Food serving times

Monday-Sunday:
12pm-2.30pm, 7pm-8.30pm

Closed 25 December

Accommodation rates include dinner

Prices

Meals: a la carte 25.00/35.00

20 rooms:
95.00/300.00

Typical Dishes

Loch Crinan scallops

Loch Crinan seafood stew

Home-made tarte au citron

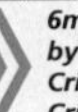

6mi Northwest of Lochgilphead by A816 and B841; at the end of Crinan canal on the edge of Loch Crinan. Parking.

005 The Kilberry Inn

Kintyre - Kilberry PA29 6YD
Tel.: (01880) 770223
e-mail: relax@kilberryinn.com
Website: www.kilberryinn.com

  MC

 **Loch Fyne Ales - Maverick, Vital Spark, Piper's Gold, Highlander**

Remotely set and reached along a scenic single track road, the team at the whitewashed, red-roofed Kilberry Inn extend a traditionally warm, Scottish welcome to any travellers who pass their way. A charming place, with high ceilings and log fires, its exposed stone walls are hung with artwork by local artists and there are two simply furnished main areas in which to dine, with banquette seating, wooden tables – some with tablecloths - and decorative orchids. Cooking here has a local base, with the emphasis on fresh seafood, and West Coast ingredients range from Loch Fyne langoustines and scallops to local cheeses and meats; carefully prepared, and good value for money. The comfortable bedrooms here are simple yet stylish, with all the facilities you will need. Whether you're travelling on foot, by bike or by boat, Kilberry is a great base for exploring this unspoilt area, and a trip to a whisky distillery is a must.

Food serving times

Tuesday-Sunday:
12.15pm-2.15pm, from 6.30pm

Closed January to mid-March; also Monday-Thursday, November-December

Prices

Meals: a la carte 19.50/29.50

 **4 rooms:** 45.00/90.00

Typical Dishes

Potted crab with lemon

Jura monkfish pan-fried

Kilberry crème brûlée

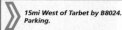

15mi West of Tarbet by B8024. Parking.

The Creggans Inn

006 The Creggans Inn

Strachur PA27 8BX
Tel.: (01369) 860279
e-mail: info@creggans-inn.co.uk
Website: www.creggans-inn.co.uk

 **Bitter and Twisted, Deuchars IPA, Fyne Ales, Fuller's London Pride, Timothy Taylor's Landlord, Coniston Bluebird**

This large, whitewashed building stands on the shores of Loch Fyne, with magnificent views out over the water and the surrounding hills, and if you wish to arrive by boat, there are two moorings at which to tie up. The interior is spacious, with a large, homely lounge. Traditional, home made meals are served in the cosy bar with its log fire, while a simple restaurant menu is offered at linen-clad tables in the main dining room, with views out over the water. Taking advantage of the natural larder of the Loch, the menus contain lots of local seafood, such as mussels, oysters and salmon, but might also include choices such as pigeon breast, partridge and steak. Food is sensibly priced and local ladies provide friendly service. Comfortable bedrooms are individually styled, and you can choose whether you would prefer to admire the view from the window in the residents' lounge, or get out amongst the flora and fauna yourself.

Food serving times
Monday-Sunday:
12pm-2.45pm, 6pm-8.45pm

Prices
Meals: 32.00 (3 course dinner) and a la carte 22.00/30.00

14 rooms:
65.00/170.00

Typical Dishes
Loch Fyne mussels
Local venison sausages
Caramelised walnut tart

21mi East and South of Inveraray by coast road A83 and A815.
Parking and 2 moorings for boats.

007 Tayvallich Inn

Tayvallich PA31 8PL
Tel.: (01546) 870282
e-mail: rfhanderson@aol.com - Website: www.tayvallich-inn.com

 VISA AE MC

 **Loch Fyne Ales: Maverick and Avalanche**

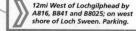

Driving up the single track road along the banks of Loch Sween, towards the quaintly isolated village of Tayvallich, population circa 100, you know that when you reach it, the view from this inn is going to be just as impressive. And you are not disappointed; sitting outside on the decked terrace there's not even a sheet of glass to separate you from the glorious tranquillity of the harbour. Running a business in such a location means that the owner gets the best local seafood delivered fresh to him. Not surprisingly, the very seasonal menu has a distinctly fishy flavour and simple dishes focused on prawns, lobster, scallops and the like dominate, with the odd steak or burger, made with meat sourced from a local farm, also thrown in. Now, when you survey the rustic, open bar and simply decorated dining room, it's hard to believe that this building was a bus garage until the 1970s. Young staff provide efficient service.

Food serving times

Monday-Sunday:
12.30pm-2pm, 6pm-9pm

Closed November to March, Monday-Thursday

Prices

Meals: a la carte
18.20/40.00

Typical Dishes

Pan-seared scallops
Roast monkfish
Figs roasted in honey & Port

12mi West of Lochgilphead by A816, B841 and B8025; on west shore of Loch Sween. Parking.

008 Black Bull

13-15 Market Place, Lauder TD2 6SR
Tel.: (01578) 722208 - Fax: (01578) 722419
e-mail: enquiries@blackbull-lauder.com
Website: www.blackbull-lauder.com

 **Broughton Ales and various guest beers**

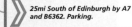

Can there be anything more satisfying than catching your own dinner? The owners of this former coaching inn, not too far from river, loch and coast will be more than happy to cook it for you - but beware fishy tales from the neighbouring table about the one that got away. Located on the busy main road between Newcastle and Edinburgh, this inn was built in the 1750s, with a former church hall added in the 19th century. Traditionally decorated, the bar area is comfortable and cosy whereas the dining room is slightly more formal. Friendly local staff serve home-cooked dishes throughout, from a menu that changes with the season, and if you're wanting a place to lay your head at the end of a hard day's fishing, there is a choice of comfortable bedrooms available, with good facilities. With its pretty window boxes and hanging baskets, this village inn will soon have you falling for its charms; hook, line and sinker.

Food serving times

Monday-Sunday:
12pm-2.30pm, 5pm-9pm

Closed 26 December and 1-28 February

Prices

Meals: a la carte 16.00/27.50

8 rooms: 60.00/90.00

Typical Dishes

Warm cheese croutons salad

Duck confit

Praline Armagnac mousse

25mi South of Edinburgh by A7 and B6362. Parking.

009 Burts

**Market Square,
Melrose TD6 9PL**

Tel.: (01896) 822285 - Fax: (01896) 822870
e-mail: burtshotel@aol.com - Website: www.burtshotel.co.uk

Caledonian, Deuchar's IPA and 1 guest ale: Timothy Taylor's Landlord

This immaculate black and white inn, with its pretty window boxes was built in 1722, and is situated on the main market square of the busy Borders town of Melrose, the spiritual home of Sevens rugby, on the banks of the Tweed. Rugby players, fishermen, golfers, walkers and other sporty types are made to feel most welcome, as are businesspeople, tourists and locals. Burts has been run by the same family for nearly forty years, and their dedication and hospitality is renowned. The traditional bar is always well-stocked, and there is also a more formal dining room with high-backed chairs, which opens out onto the lawned garden. The extensive, daily-changing menus encompass the traditional to the modern with some innovative twists. Seasonality is taken seriously, ingredients are sourced locally, and game, fish, Scottish beef and Border lamb feature highly. Bedrooms are small and unpretentious.

Food serving times

Monday-Sunday:
12pm-2pm, 7pm-9pm

Closed 26 December and 2-3 January

Prices

Meals: a la carte
22.00/30.00

20 rooms:
60.00/120.00

Typical Dishes

Smoked haddock crumble

Rump of Borders lamb

Hot chocolate fondant

In town centre on north side of A6091. Parking.

010 The Wheatsheaf

Main Street, Swinton TD11 3JJ
Tel.: (01890) 860257 - Fax: (01890) 860688
e-mail: reception@wheatsheaf-swinton.co.uk
Website: www.wheatsheaf-swinton.co.uk

 **Deuchars IPA, Broughton Reiver**

If fishing on the Tweed was good but your catching was bad, a meal at The Wheatsheaf is sure to assuage you. Well-run by a keen husband and wife team, this stone built inn is set on the main street in this Borders village, overlooking the green. Inside, there are numerous cosy little lounges in which to relax, with soft seating, suites and sofas and the obligatory log fire, although the fishing theme on the walls might well remind you of the one that got away. Classic, unfussy dishes with a modern twist bring out the flavour of local produce, with fish sourced from Eyemouth harbour, as well as Borders beef, and lamb and organic pork from traditional butchers. If you hope to try your luck again on the morrow, you'll rest well in modern, comfortable, individually furnished bedrooms, with good facilities and extra touches. And don't have nightmares, just remember; there are plenty more fish in the Tweed.

Food serving times

Monday-Sunday:
12pm-2pm, 6pm-9pm

Closed 25-26 December

Closed dinner Sunday December- February

Prices

Meals: a la carte
22.00/36.00

10 rooms:
69.00/102.00

Typical Dishes

Chilled hot-smoked salmon

Roast salmon & herb crust

Blancmange & saffron syrup

6mi North of Coldstream by A6112. Parking.

011 The Sorn Inn

35 Main St,
Sorn KA5 6HU
Tel.: (01290) 551305 - Fax: (01290) 553470
e-mail: craig@sorninn.com - Website: www.sorninn.com

 **No real ales offered**

The Sorn Inn throws up an interesting choice to the diner: do you mingle with the locals whilst eating in the 'Chop House' next to the bar, or would you rather dine in the more formal restaurant with its clothed tables, candles and flowers? Both have a pleasant – if very different - feel to them, and, although they offer separate menus, the same kitchen cooks for both, using the freshest and best of local produce – and at prices that won't put you into the red. Expect to eat grilled beef steaks, homemade burgers, pasta and fresh fish in the Chop House, or rabbit, pigeon and braised pork belly in the restaurant. This whitewashed village inn is family-run and the staff are friendly, welcoming and professional. Solve the dining conundrum by staying for the weekend; four good-sized bedrooms furnished in a modern style offer a very good value night's sleep - and breakfast is a tasty treat too.

Food serving times

Tuesday-Sunday:
12pm-2pm, 6.30pm-9pm

Closed 2 weeks in January

Prices

Meals: 14.95/25.00 (3 course lunch/dinner) and a la carte 15.00/25.00

4 rooms: 40.00/90.00

Typical Dishes

Smoked haddock ravioli
Soy braised pork belly
Glazed raspberries

2mi East of Catrine by B713.
Parking.

012 Iglu

2B Jamaica Street,
Edinburgh EH3 6HH
Tel.: (0131) 476 5333
e-mail: mail@theiglu.com - Website: www.theiglu.com

VISA  

 **Innis and Gunn, Black Isle Brewery Ales, Angel Organic, Broughton Ales**

It's hidden away in the old part of town, but once you're in the vicinity, there's no missing Iglu's vivid blue exterior. Inside, it's just as modern, with plasma screens, low tub chairs and funky music playing on the ground floor, and framed photos for sale, fish tanks and potted plants upstairs. Ethical eating is the ethos, and the motto is 'wild, organic and local,' so you can eat with a clear conscience, safe in the knowledge that your food has had a happy life and hasn't had to travel too far to your plate. And it's not just the food either; there are juices and smoothies, organic wines and fair trade coffee on offer too. Using the freshest and best seasonal ingredients available means that the menu changes frequently; dishes might include game pie, organic cod, wild boar burger stack and vegetarian haggis. Thus named because it's a snug place of tranquillity, Iglu can actually become pretty busy, so it's sensible to book ahead.

Food serving times

Monday-Sunday:
12pm-3pm, 6pm-10pm

Closed 25 December

Prices

Meals: 12.95/14.95 (2/3 course lunch) and a la carte 22.00/35.00

Typical Dishes

Seared breast of pigeon
Cod fillet with asparagus
Praline coated goats' cheese

 *In the New Town, off the west side of Howe Street.* 

013 The King's Wark

36 The Shore,
Leith EH6 6QU
Tel.: (0131) 554 9260

 **Caledonian IPA, Caledonian 80s and one guest ale**

At the mouth of the harbour in gentrified Leith stands The King's Wark, with its distinctive blue front. Originally built in 1434 as a royal armoury and store to hold wines and other provisions for King James I, the building has also been used as a naval yard and a royal palace, was later destroyed by fire and then rebuilt. Its history is reflected in its characterful interior, all exposed stone and beams; the welcome is effusive and a fireside seat nice and warm. Due to its popularity, it can get quite busy - misanthropes might call it cramped, while philanthropists would probably prefer cosy. Especially strong on fish and seafood, the handwritten, weekly-changing menu offers proper, unpretentious Scottish food to fill your belly, and what it might lack in presentation, it more than makes up for in flavour. Well-known for its special all-day weekend breakfasts, you'll have to book well in advance if you want join the fun.

Food serving times
Monday-Sunday:
12pm-3pm (bar meals),
6pm-10pm

Closed 25 December and 1 January

Prices
Meals: a la carte
18.00/28.00

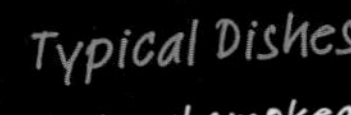

Typical Dishes
Natural smoked haddock
Medallions of venison saddle
Selection of Scottish cheeses

Off the south side of Bernard Street, A199. Parking across the street on the shore.

014 Babbity Bowster

16-18 Blackfriars St,
Glasgow G1 1PE
Tel.: (0141) 552 5055 - Fax: (0141) 552 7774

Deuchars IPA, Kelburn Misty Law and a regularly changing guest ale

'Wha learned you to dance, / Babbity Bowster, Babbity Bowster? / Wha learned you to dance, / Babbity Bowster, brawly?' It was the regular custom in Scotland to wind up every dancing-ball with a dance called the Babbity Bowster, and the framed musical score to it hangs here on the wall of the bar, although the only dancing likely to occur these days might be a jig along to the live music on Saturday afternoons. Something of a city institution, this double-fronted Georgian-style building stands in the Merchant City area, which is currently being regenerated. Food on the short bar menu is simple yet wholesome, with local dishes including cullen skink, neeps and tatties, but if you'd prefer something a little more adventurous, you might instead choose to dine upstairs in the small restaurant with its open plan kitchen, and away from the drinkers (although it's best to phone ahead and check it's open before booking).

Food serving times

Monday-Sunday:
12pm-10pm

Closed 25 December

Prices

Meals: a la carte
12.95/25.85

Typical Dishes

Seared scallops
Rack of Scottish lamb
Strawberry tart

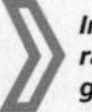

In city centre North of the Central railway station. Parking for hotel guests only.

015 Summer Isles (Bar)

Achiltibuie IV26 2YG
Tel.: (01854) 622282 - Fax: (01854) 622251
e-mail: info@summerisleshotel.co.uk
Website: www.summerisleshotel.co.uk

 **Red Cuillin, Young Pretender, Highland Gold**

An idyllically named establishment for an idyllic setting – this super bar and hotel faces the eponymous isles, far away from the madding crowd at the end of a 20 mile single track road. The bar is the 'village pub', attached to the hotel but separate from it. Its simple, rustic ambience is perfect for the setting: sit in wooden booths and take in the wild, untouched landscape. You'll dine on seafood platters and rustic dishes such as casseroles and lamb shank; in the summer, don't miss the chance to eat al fresco. If you plump for the hotel, you'll be sampling precisely judged cuisine which has earned a Michelin Star for its excellence. There's every chance you'll stay the night: look forward to bedrooms ranging from simple and restrained to smart and sophisticated.

Food serving times

Monday-Sunday:
12pm-3pm, 5.30pm-8.30pm

Closed mid-October to mid-March

- Seafood - Bookings not accepted

Prices

Meals: a la carte 18.00/35.00

13 rooms: 85.00/200.00

Typical Dishes

Platter of local langoustines
Roast fillet of hake
4 Scottish cheeses

15mi Northwest of Ullapool by A835 and minor road west from Drumrunie. Parking.

016 Applecross Inn

Shore St,
Applecross IV54 8LR

Tel.: (01520) 744262 - Fax: (01520) 744400
e-mail: applecrossinn@globalnet.co.uk - Website: www.applecross.uk.com

 **Isle of Skye Brewery - Red Cuillin, Blaven, Young Pretender**

Run by the aptly named Judith Fish, the remote Applecross Inn attracts people from far and wide wanting to sample the bountiful seafood and local meats, from local prawns and crab to venison, featured on their extensive blackboard menus. That this inn gets so busy seems even more miraculous when you take into account the journey involved in getting here, for the tiny hamlet of Applecross is reached either via a twenty-four mile single track costal road or via a hair-raising mountain pass with such steep gradients and sharp bends that learner drivers are advised not to attempt it. Anyone brave enough is rewarded with all the charm you would expect from a cosy Highland inn, plus stunning views across the water to the Island of Raasay and the distant hills of Skye. As befits an inn which used to be a row of fishermen's cottages, bedrooms are small, but all offer sea views and, after recent modernisation, are smart and comfortable.

Food serving times

Monday-Sunday:
12pm-9pm

Closed 25 December and 1 January

Booking essential

Prices

Meals: a la carte 20.00/26.00

7 rooms: 70.00/100.00

Typical Dishes

Prawns with Marie Rose dip

Applecross Bay crab salad

West Highland Dairy cheeses

From Kishorn via the Bealach nam Bo (Alpine pass), or round by Shieldaig and along the coast. Parking.

017 Badachro Inn

Badachro IV21 2AA
Tel.: (01445) 741255 - Fax: (01445) 741319
e-mail: lesley@badachroinn.com - Website: www.badachroinn.com

 **An Teallach, Caledonian 80, IPA and 6 nations Isle of Skye**

Nestled on the South shore of Loch Gairloch, this pub inhabits a superbly sheltered spot in a little secluded inlet, a stone's throw away from the jetty. Two moorings are available if you are arriving by boat and a smart decked area provides great views over the Loch. If the weather is being typically Scottish, you can still sit outside, as there's a canopy of sail cloth to protect you from the drizzle, but if the wind picks up or the temperatures drop too low, the conservatory is your next best bet. Inside, the atmosphere is cosily rustic, with a beamed bar, open fire and local maritime charts on the walls. Menus make good use of the local catch – lobsters, prawns and crabs are especially abundant in this area - and sandwiches and simple salads are available at lunchtimes. There are plenty of pre or post-prandial walks to be enjoyed, or you could take a boat trip and sail off into the scenery.

Food serving times

April-December:
Monday-Sunday: 12pm-3pm, 6pm-9pm

January-March:
Monday-Friday: 6pm-9pm

Saturday-Sunday:
12pm-3pm, 6pm-9pm

Closed 25 December

Prices

Meals: a la carte
12.00/34.70

Typical Dishes

Smoked venison
Salmon & monkfish kebabs
Cheese board

6mi South of Gairloch by A832 and B8056. Parking and 2 moorings for boats.

018 Cawdor Tavern

The Lane,
Cawdor IV12 5XP
Tel.: (01667) 404777 - Fax: (01667) 404777
e-mail: cawdortavern@btopenworld.com

 **Orkney Dark Island, Atlas Three Sisters**

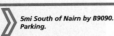

'All hail, Macbeth, hail to thee, thane of Cawdor!' Although in real life, Macbeth actually died a few centuries before it was built, the nearby tourist attraction of Cawdor Castle is famous for its role in Shakespeare's tragedy, and this pub was originally its joiners' workshop. Nowadays, with its exposed beams and wood panelling, it has the feel of a traditional country pub about it and, as the same menu is served throughout, there's a choice between the bar with a pool table, the characterful lounge bar or the restaurant. This is a smoothly run establishment and therefore tends to get busy, especially at weekends, so guarantee yourself a seat by booking ahead. A large menu provides lots of choice, with plenty of Scottish favourites and a selection of specials. Cooking is fresh and robust and a lighter menu is also available at lunch. 'Now, good digestion wait on appetite, / And health on both!'

Food serving times

Monday-Saturday:
12pm-2pm, 5.30pm-9pm

Sunday:
12.30pm-3pm, 5.30pm-9pm

Closed 25-26 December and 1 January

Booking essential Saturday-Sunday

Prices

Meals: a la carte
16.60/25.50

Typical Dishes

Scallop & smokey bacon salad

Collops of Highland Venison

Cappuccino crème brûlée

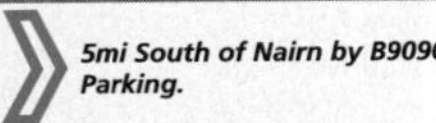

5mi South of Nairn by B9090.
Parking.

Glenelg

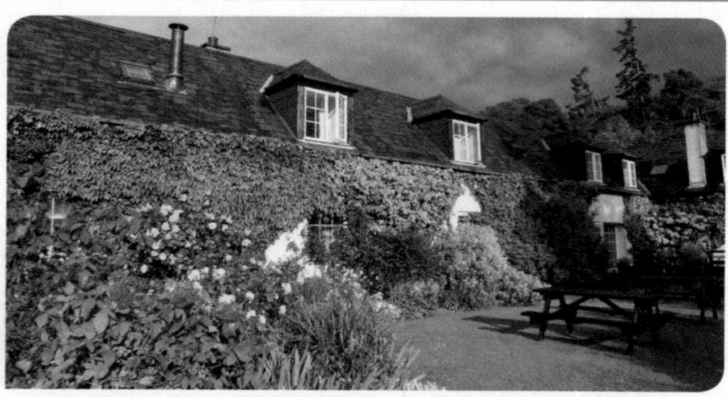

019 Glenelg Inn

Glenelg IV40 8JR
Tel.: (01599) 522273 - Fax: (01599) 522283
e-mail: christophermain7@glenelg-inn.com
Website: www.glenelg-inn.com

 **Several from the Skye Brewery**

Idyllically set off the beaten track in its own extensive grounds in a quiet hamlet by the lochside, this cosy inn was, in a previous incarnation, a couple of wee cottages. The Inn gloriously overlooks Glenelg Bay and the Isle of Skye. There's a very pubby bar, full of character: the locals have an amiable habit of turning it into the centre of the universe. It also boasts a beamed ceiling, dark wood panelling, and plenty of local photos on the walls. Blackboard menus offer a tried-and-tested, classic selection, utilising much local produce, of which fish and seafood are the speciality. If you're staying overnight, you can look forward to comfy, individually decorated bedrooms, followed by great Highland breakfasts in the morning.

Food serving times

Monday-Sunday:
12pm-2.30pm, 6pm-9pm

Closed lunch in winter; also Sunday dinner to non residents - Booking essential

Prices

Meals: 35.00 (3 course dinner) and a la carte 10.00/20.00

6 rooms: 40.00/160.00

Typical Dishes

Fresh local seafood chowder

Fillet of turbot

Rich bitter chocolate mousse

South of Kyle of Lochalsh: 10mi by toll bridge, A87 Southwest, minor road to Kylerhea and ferry or 20mi by A87 Southeast. Parking.

020 **Kylesku**

Kylesku IV27 4HW
Tel.: (01971) 502231 - Fax: (01971) 502313
e-mail: info@kyleskuhotel.co.uk
Website: www.kyleskuhotel.co.uk

 **No real ales offered**

With its genuinely unforgettable view of Loch Glencoul and the mountains, the temptation would be to keep all knowledge of Kylesku to yourself. The heart of the discovery is the old hotel itself, with a very comfortable lounge in pretty patterns, and simple bedrooms, but for anyone not staying, the bar's the place to be. It's got a nice, down-to-earth feeling to it: there's a pool table, all sorts of countryside objects ranged along the wall, and a stove burning all through the long Highland winter. A blackboard menu with a strong seasonal character concentrates on the local speciality: good, just-landed shellfish in simply prepared, nicely judged dishes. Tasty and fresh, and as authentic as you could wish for.

Food serving times

Monday-Sunday:
12pm-2.30pm, 6pm-9pm

Closed mid-October to end February

Bar snacks at lunchtime

Prices

Meals: 28.50 (3 course dinner) and a la carte 15.00/25.00

8 rooms: 60.00/88.00

Typical Dishes

Wild venison terrine
Grilled local langoustines
Bread and butter pudding

32mi North of Ullapool by A835, A837 and A894. Public car park in the village 50m walk.

021 **Plockton**

41 Harbour St,
Plockton IV52 8TN
Tel.: (01599) 544274 - Fax: (01599) 544475
e-mail: info@plocktonhotel.co.uk - Website: www.plocktonhotel.co.uk

VISA AE MC

Deuchar's IPA, Hebridean Gold and guest beers - Young Pretender, Bitter & Twisted

Fine views of Loch Carron are a more than adequate reason to visit this attractive little National Trust village near the Kyle of Lochalsh. The eponymous inn – a delightful pair of wee cottages on the lochside – is the place to indulge the views while supping a pint with the locals, who flock here. The bar's the centre of activity, but if you're after a quieter environment, then you can retreat to the small rear terrace or the recently installed restaurant, where it's quite possible you'll be able to order a corn on the cob, alongside an impressive list of local seafood. Plockton isn't renowned for its road network, so for those making the wise move of staying overnight, there are plenty of recently refurbished, well-kept, comfy bedrooms to tempt you.

Food serving times

Monday-Sunday:
12pm-2.15pm, 6pm-10pm

Closed 25 December and 1 January

Prices

Meals: a la carte
15.00/45.00

15 rooms:
45.00/100.00

Typical Dishes

Plockton smokies
Monkfish in Serrano ham
Achmore Dairy cheeses

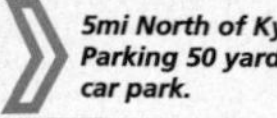

5mi North of Kyle of Lochalsh. Parking 50 yards away in Village car park.

022 Plockton Inn

Innes Street,
Plockton IV52 8TW
Tel.: (01599) 544222 - Fax: (01599) 544487
e-mail: info@plocktoninn.co.uk - Website: www.plocktoninn.co.uk

VISA 

Fuller's London Pride, Deuchar's IPA, Greene King Abbot Ale, Caley 80

If on arrival in the picturesque village of Plockton, you find that it looks familiar, it could be because this North West Highland village was the setting for the television series, 'Hamish Macbeth' in the 1990s, and is perennially popular with filmmakers, photographers and artists. The eponymous inn is situated at the seaward end of Loch Carron where the cottages hug the harbour, so it's no surprise to find out that the menu here is heavily slanted towards seafood, with freshly caught fish and shellfish. The inn has been run by the same family for over ten years and the relaxed atmosphere and warm hospitality attract locals and visitors alike. Twice-weekly live music evenings in the tourist season are particularly popular. The lounge bar is the centre of proceedings, but there's also a dining room, a rear garden and a little front terrace too. Bedrooms are well-kept and modern and some come with a sea view.

Food serving times
Monday-Sunday:
12pm-2.30pm, 6pm-9pm

Prices
Meals: a la carte
14.50/26.00

14 rooms: 35.00/88.00

Typical Dishes
Seafood platter
Plockton prawns
Lemon & ginger crunch pie

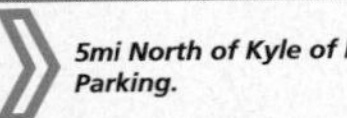
5mi North of Kyle of Lochalsh.
Parking.

023 Stein Inn

MacLeod Terr,
Stein, Isle of Skye, Waternish IV55 8GA
Tel.: (01470) 592362
e-mail: angus.teresa@steininn.co.uk - Website: www.steininn.co.uk

Deuchar's IPA, Red Cuillin, Trade Winds, Red MacGregor, Reeling Deck

In a breathtakingly beautiful spot on Loch Bay, the oldest inn on Skye is run with great warmth and dedication by a chatty husband and wife team. At the heart of the place is a tiny pine-clad locals bar and a lounge with rough stone walls, tall settles and an open fire; it's good for lunchtime soup, sandwiches and a local ale, but it would be a shame not to try something more substantial in the evening in the little dining room – well-prepared seafood dishes, like Skye scallops and Scottish salmon, are the pick of a tasty menu which also includes Highland venison. But for pure relaxation and peace of mind, take one of their 90 malts down to the grassy bank or the benches looking west over the bay and watch the sun set beyond the headland. Guests staying in the cosy, well-kept bedrooms – a snip at the price – can compare the view in the morning.

Food serving times

Monday-Sunday:
12pm-4pm, 6pm-9.30pm

Closed 25 December and 1 January; also lunch Monday-Friday November-March

- Seafood specialities -

Prices

Meals: a la carte
12.60/19.60

5 rooms: 27.00/54.00

Typical Dishes

Pan-fried scallop
Highland venison steak
Achmore Dairy cheeses

22mi West of Portree by A87, A850 and B886; on the shore of Loch Bay. Parking.

024 Ardeonaig

South Loch Tay,
By Killin, Ardeonaig FK21 8SU
Tel.: (01567) 820400 - Fax: (01567) 820282
e-mail: info@ardeonaighotel.co.uk - Website: www.ardeonaighotel.co.uk

No real ales on tap

This family-run inn has its origins in the 17C, standing serenely in a wooded meadow on the south shore of Loch Tay. Its tranquil aspect is enhanced with a large garden – an ideal spot to relax in – or the library, which offers fine views. The homely, snug bar has walls filled with fishing memorabilia, and if you wander into the welcoming dining room you'll understand why: freshwater fish is a key element to the menus, alongside interesting dishes with a South African influence: the owner himself is a Springbok. There's also an enclosed courtyard, which, on a sunny day, is an ideal place to dine. Afterwards, delight in Highland walks or a slow drive alongside the Loch.

Food serving times
Monday-Sunday:
12pm-3pm, 7pm-9pm

Accommodation rates include dinner, bed and breakfast

Prices
Meals: 26.50 (3 course lunch & dinner) and a la carte 32.50/50.00

20 rooms:
125.00/300.00

Typical Dishes
Loch Fyne black mussels
Local venison
Traditional Malva pudding

6mi East of Killin on south shore of Loch Tay. Parking.

025 Tormaukin Country Inn

Glendevon FK14 7JY

Tel.: (01259) 781252 - Fax: (01259) 781526

e-mail: enquiries@tormaukin.co.uk

Website: www.tormaukin.co.uk

   MC

Inveralmond Thrappledouser, Harviestoun Bitter & Twisted, Lia Fail

Its new owners have given the outside a lick of paint and improved the décor within, but with its stone floored, beamed bar and open fires, this 18C roadside drovers' inn has retained its rustic roots. Sit in the spacious main dining room, its whitewashed walls offset with vivid art, and enjoy food from the fiercely Scottish sourced à la carte or set menus, where the mix of traditional and more modern dishes might include gravadlax, langoustines and local beef. There is a good range of Scottish cheeses and a nice selection of real ales and wines by the glass; the welcome is extremely warm and the service by keen, local staff is impressive. Comfortable bedrooms provide a good night's rest, so you can sleep deeply, dreaming of the whopper you're going to catch, the pheasant you're going to shoot or the hole in one you are going to get next morning on your travels around the unspoilt Perthshire countryside.

Food serving times

Monday-Sunday:
12pm-3.30pm, 5.30pm-9.30pm

Closed 23-26 December

Prices

Meals: 13.95/19.95 (3 course lunch/dinner) and a la carte 18.00/50.00

14 rooms:
85.00/120.00

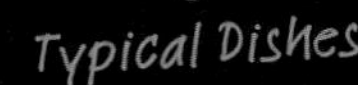

Typical Dishes

Ham hock terrine
Slow roasted belly of pork
Sticky toffee pudding

22mi Southwest of Perth by M90 to Junction 7, A91 and A823. Parking.

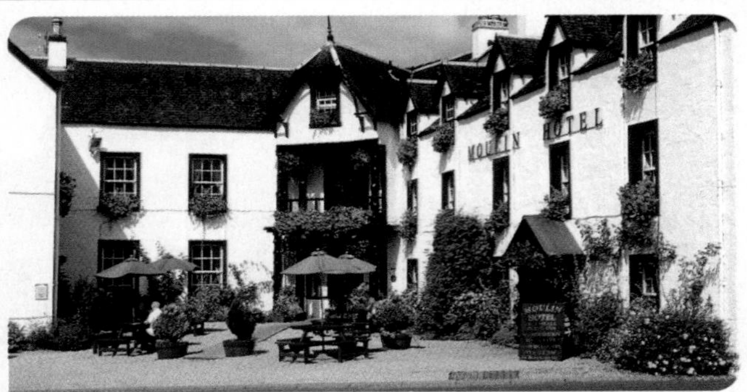

026 The Moulin Inn

Kirkmichael Road,
Pitlochry PH16 5EH

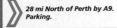

Tel.: (01796) 472196 - Fax: (01796) 474098
e-mail: enquiries@moulinhotel.co.uk - Website: www.moulinhotel.co.uk

VISA MC

Moulin Breweries - Braveheart, Old Remedial, Ale of Atholl, LIght Ale

Scottish hospitality has been dispensed on the site of this inn for more than three hundred years, during which time the hotel has grown up around it. Set in the centre of a conservation village, it's popular with tourists, walkers and locals, but if you were expecting to find a mill next door, you'll be disappointed – it is thus named simply as a derivation of the word 'Maohlinn.' The terrace is popular in clement weather, but it is equally, if not more relaxing to sit at one of the large tables in the cosy semi-booths and be warmed by the open fire. The neighbouring Moulin micro brewery supplies the real cask ales sold in the bar and, being Scotland, there's a fine selection of whiskies too. The chef may be French, but the food is Scottish through and through. Made with local Perthshire produce, the hearty steaks and casseroles, smoked meat platters and haggis are tasty and filling enough to mean that one course may be sufficient.

Food serving times

Monday-Sunday:
12pm-9.30pm

Bar snacks at lunchtime

Prices

Meals: 22.50 (3 course dinner) and a la carte 25.00/35.00

18 rooms: 45.00/85.00

Typical Dishes

Chestnut & wild mushroom soup

Sirloin steak with haggis

Whisky fudge cake

28 mi North of Perth by A9.
Parking.

Scotland • Perthshire and Kinross

027 The Inn at Kippen

Fore Rd,
Kippen FK8 3DT
Tel.: (01786) 871010 - Fax: (01786) 871011
e-mail: info@theinnatkippen.co.uk - Website: www.theinnatkippen.co.uk

 **Inveralmond Ossian, Thrappledouser**

Spacious, contemporary and open-plan, this fully refurbished village inn may not be quite what you were expecting. High-backed leather chairs and banquettes, smart glassware and casually uniformed staff set a determinedly modern tone, but it's not all out-with-the-old: framed black-and-white photos from the early 1900s show a very different way of life in this town on the edge of the Gargunnock Hills. The same wide choice is available at lunch and dinner, in the dining rooms and the rear bar, and ranges from surefire pub standards to slightly more elaborate restaurant dishes, still with a robust and straightforward style. Decorated in co-ordinated colours, the four bedrooms, named after local parishes, have a comfortable country feel to them.

Food serving times

Monday-Sunday:
12pm-2.30pm, 6pm-9pm

Closed 25 December and 1-2 January

Prices

Meals: 9.95 (3 course lunch/dinner) and a la carte 20.00/40.00

4 rooms: 40.00/85.00

Typical Dishes

Crabmeat & mango timbale
Roast loin of venison
Dark chocolate fondant

9mi West of Stirling by A811 and B822. Parking.

028 The Chop and Ale House

Champany,
Linlithgow EH49 7LU

Tel.: (01506) 834532 - Fax: (01506) 834302
e-mail: reception@champany.com - Website: www.champany.com

 **Belhaven Best**

Housed in a simple annex to the Champany inn, in what used to be its public bar, The Chop and Ale house provides a lighter alternative to dinner at the main restaurant, without losing any of its quality. Not the ideal place for teetotal vegetarians – the clue is in the name - the exposed stone walls are filled with shotguns, fishing rods and mounted animal heads. Meat is all important here, with Aberdeen Angus steaks, Scottish lamb chops, superior homemade sausages and spit-roasted chicken on offer; and of particular note are the homemade burgers. If you're the kind of person who would never normally eat a burger, make a point of trying one here. Homemade, from the same beef that provides the restaurant with its steaks, they come with a choice of toppings and taste just great. A fire burns in the grate, the tables are closely set and the atmosphere is one of relaxed conviviality.

Food serving times

Monday-Sunday:
12pm-2pm, 6.30pm-10pm

Closed 25-26 December and 1 January

Prices

Meals: a la carte
17.95/29.50

16 rooms:
105.00/135.00

Typical Dishes

Smoked duck fillet
Dornoch lamb loin chops
Lemon possett

2.5mi Northeast of town centre by A803; at the Champany Inn. Parking.

"Hiraeth" – the longing for home – and pride in the life of the nation take their source in many parts of Welsh identity. Unity is rooted in the very language of the Cymry, or "comrades", and the strength of community famously finds its voice in the songs of an eager rugby crowd. But above all, love of Wales is inseparable from a love of the land itself. The emblematic peaks of Snowdon and Cadair Idris and the steep streets of the Rhondda live long in the memory, but the full picture is wide enough to take in Lleyn's hidden coves and holy islands, the craggy stacks of the Pembrokeshire coast, the dominating towers of King Edward's castles and the fantasia of Portmerion, a playful dreamscape of domes and colonnades. Though long overlooked, Welsh cuisine is now making up for lost time and offering a taste of home, from rare delicacies like Wye and Usk salmon to world-famous lamb, Caerphilly, cawl cenin – a leek soup – and the humble Bara Brith; increasingly diverse real ales, and even Welsh whisky, mean there's always something new to try: Iechyd da!

BAILE ÁTHA CLIATH
Douglas (I. of Man)
Liverpool
Mostyn
Belfast
Dublin
LIVERPOOL
Liverpool Bay
Southport
Lytham St. Anne's
Preston
Chorley
Bury
Bolton
Wigan
St. Helens
Warrington
Widnes
Runcorn
Leigh
Altrincham
Ormskirk
Skelmersdale
Formby
Ainsdale
Bootle
Wallasey
Hoylake
Birkenhead
Bebington
Ellesmere Port
North West
Northwich
Winsford
Chester
Tarporley
Middlewich
Sandbach
Crewe
Nantwich
Newcastle under Lyme
Audlem
Market Drayton
Eccleshall
Newport
Hodnet
Wem
Whitchurch
Ellesmere
Oswestry
Llynclys
Shrewsbury
WREKIN
Telford
Iron-Bridge
Cruggington
SHROPSHIRE
West Midlands
WOLVERHAMPT
BIRMINGH
Bridgnorth
Stretton
Minsterley
Montgomery
Bishop's Castle
Wrexham / Wrecsam
Ruabon
Llangollen
Corwen
Mold / Yr Wyddgrug
Flint / Fflint
Queensferry
Holywell
Mostyn
Prestatyn
Rhyl
Colwyn Bay / Bae Colwyn
Llandudno
Great Ormes Head
Conwy
Abergele
St. Asaph
Denbigh / Dinbych
Ruthin / Rhuthun
Penmaenmawr
Llanfairfechan
Beaumaris
Bangor
Menai Bridge
Llangefni
Llanerchymedd
Amlwch
ANGLESEY
Holyhead / Caergybi
Holy Island
Rhosneigr
Isle of Anglesey
Newborough
Caernarfon
Caernarfon Bay
Bethesda
Carnedd Llewelyn
Llanberis
Capel Curig
Llanrwst
Betws-y-Coed
Pentrefoelas
Cerrigydrudion
Snowdon
Snowdonia
Beddgelert
Blaenau Ffestiniog
Ffestiniog
Porthmadog
Penrhyndeudraeth
Criccieth
Pwllheli
Nefyn
Lleyn Peninsula
Abersoch
Aberdaron
Harlech
GWYNEDD
SNOWDONIA National Park
Bala
Berwyn
Barmouth
Dolgellau
Cader Idris
Mallwyd
Llanfyllin
WALES
Welshpool / Y Trallwng
Tywyn
Aberdovey
Machynlleth
Caersws
Newtown / Drenewydd
Llanidloes
Severn
Aberystwyth

WALES
POWYS
CEREDIGION
CARMARTHENSHIRE
PEMBROKESHIRE
HEREFORD
South West
BRISTOL CHANNEL
Severn Estuary
Carmarthen Bay
St. Bride's Bay
Pembrokeshire Coast National Park
Brecon Beacons National Park
Black Mountain
Strumble Head
St. David's Head
St. Govan's Head
Worms Head
Lundy
Exmoor
Cork
Rosslare
Kidderminster
Worcester
Gloucester
Hereford
Ledbury
Leominster
Ludlow
Stroud
Bath
BRISTOL
Wells
Frome
Glastonbury
Bridgwater
Burnham
Weston-Super-Mare
Clevedon
Portishead
Avonmouth
Chepstow
Monmouth
Abergavenny
Ross-on-Wye
NEWPORT / CASNEWYDD
CARDIFF / CAERDYDD
Barry / Barri
Penarth
Caerphilly
Cwmbran
Pontypool
Merthyr Tydfil
Ebbw Vale
Brecon / Aberhonddu
Hay-on-Wye
Builth Wells / Llanfair-ym-Muallt
Llandrindod Wells
Rhayader / Rhaeadr
Aberdare
Rhondda
Pontypridd
Bridgend / Pen-y-bont
Cowbridge
Maesteg
Neath / Castell-nedd
Port Talbot
Porthcawl
Swansea / Abertawe
The Mumbles
Llanelli
Ammanford
Llandeilo
Llandovery / Llanymddyfri
Lampeter
Tregaron
Aberaeron
New Quay
Aberporth
Cardigan / Aberteifi
Newport
Fishguard / Abergwaun
St. David's
Haverfordwest / Hwlffordd
Milford Haven / Aberdaugleddau
Pembroke
Pembroke Dock / Doc Penfro
Tenby / Dinbych-y-pysgod
Saundersfoot
Narberth
Whitland
St. Clears / Sanclêr
Carmarthen / Caerfyrddin
Kidwelly
Burry Port
Minehead
Porlock
Lynmouth
Lynton
Combe Martin
Ilfracombe
Barnstaple
Braunton
Croyde

001 Ye Olde Bull's Head Inn

Castle St,
Beaumaris LL58 8AP

Tel.: (01248) 810329 - Fax: (01248) 811294
e-mail: info@bullsheadinn.co.uk - Website: www.bullsheadinn.co.uk

   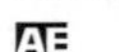

Bass, Hancocks and 1 weekly changing guest ale

A classic market town inn and a good start for anyone crossing the Menai Strait for the first time – smart and spacious rooms are nicely maintained, but the same right-minded professionalism is in evidence throughout and a devoted following gives the restaurant an even stronger local reputation. Unlike the well-kept bar, which retains much of its old-style pub character, the brasserie has been tastefully restyled; an airy and comfortable place with slate tile flooring, underfloor heating and lights around the sand-coloured beams. Sound, tasty cooking makes good use of seasonal Welsh produce; dishes like ravioli of tiger prawn and lobster, roasted turbot and loin of Welsh lamb whisked from the kitchen by an efficiently drilled team. Bookings are not accepted, so arrive early to ensure a seat. With its ample modern bedrooms it makes a good base from which to explore Anglesey, Snowdonia and the North Wales coast.

Food serving times

Monday-Sunday:
12pm-2pm, 7pm-9.30pm

Closed 25 December, meals
26 December, meals
1 January

Prices

Meals: a la carte
13.85/21.50

13 rooms:
77.00/105.00

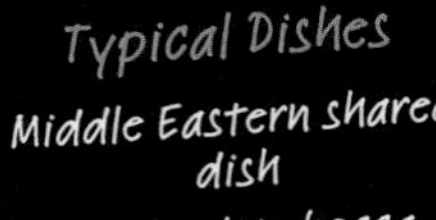

Typical Dishes

Middle Eastern shared dish
Pork saltimbocca
Local Welsh cheeses

On the east side of the town centre. Parking in town centre and other free car parks.

002 Y Polyn

Nantgaredig SA32 7LH
Tel.: (01267) 290000
e-mail: ypolyn@hotmail.com - Website: www.ypolyn.co.uk

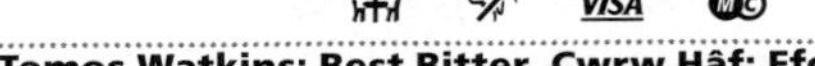

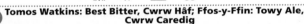

Tomos Watkins: Best Bitter, Cwrw Hâf; Ffos-y-Ffin: Towy Ale, Cwrw Caredig

Only a short drive from the National Botanic Gardens, this modest roadside pub doesn't look particularly eye-catching at first, but its interior gives a very different impression. Attention to detail and a love of food are clear to see in the fresh, bright interior, decorated with cookbooks, framed menus and pictures of the world's famous chefs, and in the relaxed and assured service. The food itself shows similar care and effort: classic rustic dishes – from French and Welsh traditions – are prepared to show local ingredients at their best and bring out their wholesome and natural flavours. You're welcome to stop for just a drink, though, and settle down in one of the bar's easy chairs: the pub was actually built over a stream, which was used to cool the beer in the old days.

Food serving times

Tuesday-Friday:
12pm-2pm, 7pm-9pm

Saturday:
7pm-9pm

Sunday:
12pm-2pm

Closed 2 weeks in October

Prices

Meals: 27.50 (3 course dinner) and a la carte 19.00/25.00

Typical Dishes

Duck rillettes
Fillets of John Dory
Treacle tart

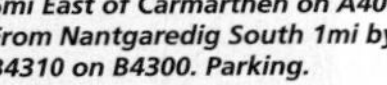

5mi East of Carmarthen on A40. From Nantgaredig South 1mi by B4310 on B4300. Parking.

003 The Angel Inn

Salem SA19 7LY
Tel.: (01558) 823394
e-mail: eat@angelsalem.co.uk

 **Towy Ale, Dylon's Choice**

You drive up a narrow, twisty road to reach this cream-coloured pub, which, fittingly, given its name, is located next to the village chapel. Inside, it's traditionally ornate, and well-kept by its keen young owners, if a little impervious to the modern world. The inviting bar lounge contains an assortment of comfy chairs and sofas in which to sink and the spacious Edwardian style dining room contains large, well-spaced tables. The chef -a former Welsh chef of the year-produces elaborate cooking which combines classic, modern and local influences. Welsh specialities offered might include lamb, salmon and cheeses, but, if you're on a time limit, beware- the wide choice available on the blackboard lunch menu might have you dawdling for far too long. The friendly atmosphere here attracts many locals as well as visitors, and you'll find the welcome extended here is as wide as the village of Salem is small.

Food serving times

Tuesday:
7pm-9pm

Wednesday-Saturday:
12pm-2pm, 7pm-9pm

Sunday and Bank Holidays:
12pm-2pm

Closed 1-2 weeks in January

Prices

Meals: a la carte
25.00/35.00

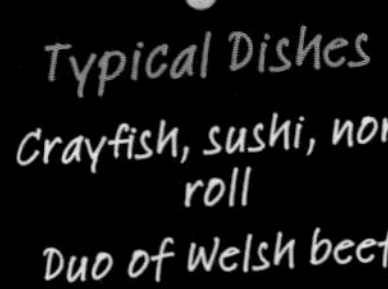

Typical Dishes

Crayfish, sushi, nori roll

Duo of Welsh beef

Assiette of mini desserts

3mi North of Llandeilo by A40 off Pen y bane road. Parking.

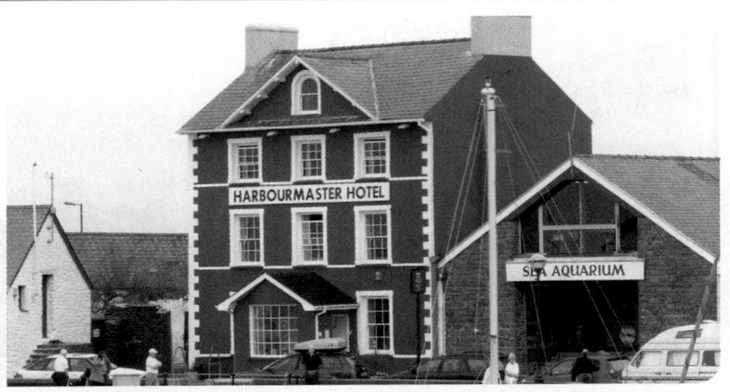

004 Harbourmaster

Quay Parade,
Aberaeron SA46 0BA
Tel.: (01545) 570755
e-mail: info@harbour-master.com - Website: www.harbour-master.com

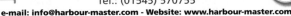

Thomas Watkin, Buckley's

Contemporary is the best word with which to describe the Harbourmaster; from its outer appearance – it is painted a striking shade of purple – to its interior, and indeed, its food. Originally the harbourmaster's house, this listed building occupies a prime position overlooking the quay, and is often deservedly busy. Eat in the restaurant or in the lively locals' bar – the same menus are served in both - before heading outside to watch the sun set over Cardigan Bay. With the emphasis firmly on seafood, the modern menus offer a selection of culinary delights and do not disappoint. The best local ingredients, including locally caught crab and lobster, are used, and if you're staying over, breakfast is also a treat for the taste buds, with delicious home-baked bread. The comfortable, stylish bedrooms are named after sailing boats and are situated up the spiral staircase in the main house, and in the cottage two doors down.

Food serving times

Monday-Sunday:
12pm-2.30pm, 6.30pm-9.15pm

Closed 25 December

Closed lunch Monday September-June

Prices

Meals: 16.50 (3 course lunch) and a la carte 20.00/30.00

9 rooms: 55.00/150.00

Typical Dishes

Cardigan Bay crab risotto
Welsh Black beef fillet
Chocolate fondant

In town centre overlooking the harbour. Parking on the harbour road.

005 Pen-y-Bryn

Pen-y-Bryn Rd,
Upper Colwyn Bay, Colwyn Bay LL29 6DD
Tel.: (01492) 533718 - Fax: (01492) 536127
Website: www.penybryn-colwynbay.co.uk

Flower's Original, Thwaite's Original, Castle Bitter Conwy, Young's Special

Just a little further down the road from the zoo, inside this unremarkable-looking building, you can actually observe urban man feeding in his natural habitat. This spacious, open-plan pub with wood floors, a central bar and low ceilings provides shelter for this animal, open fires provide warmth, and the framed pictures, posters and articles on the walls make him feel at home in his environment. The large rear gardens and terrace provide space for man to move about outside, and he enjoys nothing better than sunning himself out here on hot afternoons. A varied diet is on offer on the daily-changing blackboard menus, with dishes ranging from hearty Welsh lamb hotpot or fish pie to Thai green curry, and the not-so-naked ape likes to sit at the wooden tables provided in order to feast on the large portions. Being a sociable creature, man tends to gather in groups, and he is well looked after by the polite, organised staff.

Food serving times

Monday-Sunday:
12pm-9.30pm

Closed dinner 25-26 December and dinner 1 January

Prices

Meals: a la carte
17.20/32.35

Typical Dishes

Feta & date salad
Roast rib of Welsh Black beef
Baked custard & apple tart

1 mi Southwest of Colwyn Bay by B5113. Parking.

006 The Groes Inn

Tyn-y-Groes LL32 8TN
Tel.: (01492) 650545 - Fax: (01492) 650855
e-mail: reception@groesinn.com
Website: www.groesinn.com

 **Burton Ale, Great Orme**

This foliage-clad roadside inn is reputed to be the oldest in Wales, and it certainly has all the character you'd expect from a five-hundred year old. Old beams hang overhead, and the atmospheric bar and various little rooms and snugs are filled with bric-à-brac, ornaments, and pictures. The dining room is more formally laid out with smartly dressed tables, and the cooking offers a comprehensive mix of classic and traditional pub fare, supplemented by the blackboard menu. No reinvention of the wheel happens here – food is robust, satisfying and recognisable. The inn may be old, but the bedroom extensions are right up-to-date. Large, comfortable and individually decorated with warm fabrics, stylish furniture and good facilities, some also have terraces or balconies overlooking the surrounding countryside. With the foothills of Snowdonia on one side, and the Conwy river on the other, whichever way you're facing, the view will be good.

Food serving times

Monday-Sunday:
12pm-2.15pm (bar meals), 6.30pm-9pm

Closed 25 December

Prices

Meals: 17.50 (3 course Sunday lunch) and a la carte 22.00/28.00

14 rooms: 79.00/175.00

Typical Dishes

Groes smokie
Welsh lamb steak
Home-made ice creams

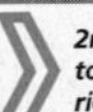

2mi from Conwy Castle by B5106 towards Trefriw; the inn is on the right. Parking.

007 **The Corn Mill**

Dee Lane,
Llangollen LL20 8PN
Tel.: (01978) 869555

   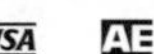 

A dozen or more regularly changing local and well known ales

This large, stone-built former corn mill enjoys an enviable position on banks of the river Dee, and its decked terrace, jutting out over the fast-flowing waters, is a popular spot on days offering even the merest hint of sunshine. From this vantage point, not only can you enjoy the delightful scenery, but you also hear the steam trains chugging slowly out of the nearby station. The charmingly restored, beamed interior with its enduring water wheel and picture frame-filled walls can become just as busy as outside, but happily the casually-attired staff are well used to being run off their feet, and provide polite, friendly and efficient service whatever the weather. Daily changing menus provide robust, classic dishes and the wide choice ensures something for everyone. July in Llangollen is the time to indulge a love of music at the International Eisteddfod; an annual music, song and dance festival which draws crowds from far afield.

Food serving times

Monday-Sunday:
12pm-9.30pm

Closed 25-26 December

Prices

Meals: a la carte
20.00/28.00

Typical Dishes

Tiger prawn salad
Shoulder of lamb
Banoffee pie

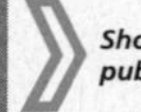

Short walk from railway and public parking.

008 Glas Fryn

Raikes Lane, Sychdyn, Mold CH7 6LR
Tel.: (01352) 750500 - Fax: (01352) 751923
e-mail: glasfryn@brunningandprice.co.uk
Website: www.glasfryn-mold.co.uk

 **Flower's Original, Snowdonia Ale, Timothy Taylor's Landlord, Brains, Deuchar's**

Another well-run pub from the Brunning and Price stable, bought in a dilapidated state, renovated, and now an imposing red-brick structure complete with extension. Inside it's all open plan spaciousness, wooden floors and furniture, neutral colour schemes and walls covered in neatly exhibited photos, pictures, books and the like, as well as the huge blackboard menus. You know that the food on offer will include wholesomely classic dishes, that the choice will be extensive and that the service will remain efficient even during busy periods, which is a good job seeing how many people come here. Situated a little way out of the town centre, right by the entrance to the Theatr Clwyd, residents of Mold and beyond mingle happily with customers ranging from theatregoers to farmers to ensure the atmosphere is buzzing, particularly at weekends. A seat on the terrace or in the large garden is recommended when the weather acquiesces.

Food serving times

Monday-Saturday:
12pm-9.30pm

Sunday:
12pm-9pm

Closed 25-26 December

Prices

Meals: a la carte
22.00/28.00

Typical Dishes

Hot smoked salmon
Braised shoulder of lamb
Spotted Dick

1 mi North by A5119 on Civic Centre rd. Parking.

009 The Stables (at Soughton Hall)

Mold CH7 6AB

Tel.: (01352) 840577 - Fax: (01352) 840872
e-mail: info@soughtonhall.co.uk
Website: www.soughtonhall.co.uk

 **Plassey, Stables, Honey Pot, Dick Turpin, Inn-Keepers**

Set in the grounds of a large 18C Italianate mansion, you can probably deduce from its name what part this attractive red brick building used to play in proceedings, but in case you missed the connection, the stalls are still here, the tables are named after racehorses and the menus divided into punters' starters and mains, owners' and trainers' starters and mains, and the final furlong (desserts). The characterful interior boasts rustic décor with beamed ceilings, heavy wood tables, open fires and cobbled and stone flooring. Upstairs is the restaurant and a large wine shop, and the terrace out the back is a great spot for al fresco summer dining. Modern British menus offer everything from lunchtime light bites to sandwiches, steaks, seafood and steamed pudding, while more elaborate dishes might include venison Wellington or pan-seared king scallops. Local staff provide friendly, informal service, but make sure you book ahead.

Food serving times

Monday-Sunday:
12pm-2.30pm, 6pm-9.30pm

Booking essential

Prices

Meals: a la carte
24.20/31.40

15 rooms:
130.00/180.00

Typical Dishes

Tempura of king prawns
Venison Wellington
Mascarpone cheesecake

2.5 mi North by A5119 on Alltami Rd. Parking

010 Penhelig Arms

Aberdovey LL35 0LT
Tel.: (01654) 767215 - Fax: (01654) 767690
e-mail: info@penheligarms.com
Website: www.penheligarms.com

 **HB Reverend James, Timothy Taylor, Abbot, Brains SA, Spitfire, Broadside, Old Speckled Hen**

At the Southern tip of Snowdonia National park lies the pretty coastal village of Aberdyfi, where 'The Pen' nobly surveys the Dyfi Estuary as it has done for three hundred years. Although now much extended, it still retains a rustic feel, and a seat by the fire in the wood-panelled bar is the perfect place to warm yourself up after a bracing coastal walk. Eat at one of the polished wood tables, or in the more formal adjoining dining room with its lighter décor and linen laid tables. Seafood unsurprisingly plays a starring role on the menus, with crab, lobster, scallops and fish on offer alongside burgers, steaks, sandwiches and even the odd chicken curry. The renowned wine list is well worth a long look too. The leather-furnished lounge provides welcome comfort at the end of the day and the bedrooms have all been refurbished to a good standard. Individually styled, and contemporary; all but one have an excellent view.

Food serving times

Monday-Sunday:
12pm-2pm, 7pm-9.30pm

Closed 25-26 December

Booking essential

Prices

Meals: 18.00/28.00 (3 course Sunday lunch / dinner) and a la carte 17.50/25.75

16 rooms:
55.00/130.00

Typical Dishes

Grilled fillet of mullet
Rack of salt marsh lamb
Dark chocolate brownie

On A493; 9mi West of Machynlleth. Parking.

011 The Hardwick

Old Raglan Rd,
Abergavenny NP7 9AA
Tel.: (01873) 854220 - Fax: (01873) 854623
e-mail: stephen@thehardwick.co.uk - Website: www.thehardwick.co.uk

We most liked

 VISA

Rhymney Brewery, Wye Valley

Modern signage is the only real hint at what to expect here. The rest of the exterior – roughly textured in white – is rather plain and unassuming. Venture inside, though, and you instantly get a good feel. The middle room is where you're drawn to: it has original beams, a wood burner and, the key element, a convivial atmosphere. Its unfussy décor feels very natural and uncluttered, providing the perfect backdrop for appreciating where the Hardwick's real talent lies: the kitchen. Chef (and owner) Stephen won a Michelin star at the famous Walnut Tree, and he knows his suppliers well. Menus evolve with the seasons, and their extensive range veers from classic British to modern European: the cooking's neat, wholesome and unafraid to throw in some powerful flavours. Desserts, helpfully, come in two sizes and there's a good variety of bottled local beers to try.

Food serving times

Tuesday-Saturday:
12pm-3pm, 6.30pm-10pm

Sunday and Bank Holiday Monday:
12pm-3pm

Closed 25 December

Prices

Meals: a la carte
20.40/36.85

Typical Dishes

Confit duck hash
Naturally smoked haddock
Panetone crème brûlée

2mi Southeast by A40 and B4598.
Parking.

012 Raglan Arms

Llandenny NP15 1DL
Tel.: (01291) 690800 - Fax: (01291) 690155
e-mail: raglanarms@aol.com - Website: www.raglanarms.com

 **Wye Valley Butty Bach, Brecon County Ales**

An Englishman, a Frenchman and a Swedish woman walked into The Raglan Arms, and the landlord said, "Is this some sort of joke?" No, of course he didn't, but the three of them took over the pub; out went the pool table, carpet and fruit machines, and in came a bit of charm in the form of mismatched pine furniture, an old settle, a dresser and a butcher's chopping block. Old wood beams and a stone tiled floor add to the rustic ambience, and there's enough room in the tardis-like interior to have several tables exclusively for drinkers, plus a lounge with comfy leather sofas and an open fireplace. Weekly-changing menus include dishes such as bangers and mash and Welsh rarebit as well as Chinese rack of rib and cep risotto, while the summer platters might be Scandinavian, Italian, or Spanish. Influences might be global, but ingredients are reassuringly local; sourced from nearby farms, and with their provenance often included on the menu.

Food serving times

Tuesday-Saturday:
12pm-3pm, 6.30pm-9.30pm

Sunday:
12pm-3pm

Closed meals 25 December; closed 26-27 December

Prices

Meals: 20.50 (3 course Sunday lunch) and a la carte 29.00/31.50

Typical Dishes

Imam Bayaldi & crème fraiche
Longhorn ribeye steak
Glazed lemon tart

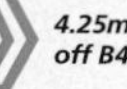

4.25mi Northeast of Usk by A472 off B4235. Parking.

013 The Foxhunter

Nant-y-Derry NP7 9DD
Tel.: (01873) 881101
e-mail: info@thefoxhunter.com - Website: www.thefoxhunter.com

 **Bath Ales, Old Speckled Hen, Butty Bach, Brains SA**

Having learned his skills in the big smoke, Matt Tebbutt made his way back to this unspoilt village in Wales in order to demonstrate them, and having acquired The Foxhunter has proceeded to do just that. The stone pub started life as the stationmaster's house but is now decked out in true gastropub style; all cheery and bright with foodie prints on the walls, dark wood floors, and solid wood tables, and Matt's wife Lisa ensures an informal, friendly atmosphere front of house. You'll find both bold British cooking and European dishes on the menus, but whether you're eating cottage pie or salmorejo, à la carte or table d'hôte, you can rest assured that the ingredients are fresh, seasonal and locally sourced. In fact, so passionate are they here about using local produce that you can even go out with a professional forager in order to search out some of the ingredients for your dinner – and it doesn't get more immediate than that.

Food serving times

Tuesday-Saturday, Mothering Sunday and some other Sundays:
12pm-2.30pm, 7pm-9.30pm

Closed 25-26 December, 2 weeks February and Bank Holidays

Prices

Meals: 21.95 (3 course lunch) and a la carte 21.95/35.00

Typical Dishes
Smoked eel
Marinated lamb rump
Quince & apple crumble

6.5mi South of Abergavenny by A4042 and minor road. Parking.

014 The Clytha Arms

Raglan NP7 9BW
Tel.: (01873) 840206 - Fax: (01873) 840209
e-mail: clythaarms@tiscali.co.uk

 **Rhymney Bitter, Hooky Bitter, Double Dragon, Thomas Watkins OSB, Freeminer BSH, Brains Dark**

Distinctive is a word that applies equally well to the appearance, the character and the cooking at the Clytha Arms. The walls of the pub are painted pink, the atmosphere is one of chaotic charm and the menu uncommonly eclectic. You'll receive a warm welcome and the interior is full of character, with open fires, wooden floors, bench seating and an old games board calling you to try your luck at traditional bar games such as dominoes and skittles. Food is of a high quality and the à la carte and set menus offer a choice of dishes, ranging from the Welsh to the international, with bar snacks and tapas also served in the bar. When the Welsh weather is fine, a seat in the extensive lawned grounds is imperative. Comfortable, individually-styled bedrooms are available if you are making a weekend of it; one has a four-poster bed, and in all, little extras such as magazines and toiletries are provided.

Food serving times

Monday: 7pm-9.30pm

Tuesday-Saturday:
12.30pm-3pm, 7pm-9.30pm

Sunday:
12.30pm-3pm

Closed 25 December

Prices

Meals: 19.95 (3 course lunch/dinner) and a la carte 25.40/32.50

4 rooms: 60.00/100.00

Typical Dishes

Goat cheese dumplings
Teriyaki fillet steak
Tequila & citrus iced soufflé

3mi West on the Clytha road (Old Abergavenny Road). Parking.

015 The Bell at Skenfrith

Skenfrith NP7 8UH

Tel.: (01600) 750235 - Fax: (01600) 750525

e-mail: enquiries@skenfrith.co.uk

Website: www.skenfrith.co.uk

VISA

Golden Valley, Timothy Taylor's Landlord, St Austell Tribute

Rather than the devil, here it's the angel that's in the detail. Nothing is too much trouble for the owners of our 2007 pub of the year. Bedrooms are the height of luxury, with home made biscuits, touchpad TVs, CD and DVD players, and local information guides are provided for your perusal. Dining tables resplendent with garden-picked flowers have been polished till they gleam, service is unhurriedly attentive and the extensive wine list is a delight for oenophiles. The daily-changing menu offers classic French cuisine, with a twist of innovation, you'll find the names of the local suppliers proudly posted on blackboards in the bar, and the kitchen garden produces its own organic vegetables and herbs. In the beamed interior, country meets contemporary, with flagstone floors and comfy sofas. All this plus the rolling Monmouthshire countryside dotted with sheep; a river, a bridge and a castle all begging to be explored.

Food serving times

Monday-Sunday:
12pm-2.30pm, 7pm-9.30pm

Closed 2 weeks late January to early February

Closed Monday November to March

Prices

Meals: a la carte
25.00/32.00

8 rooms: 75.00/180.00

Typical Dishes

Pan-roasted quail

Roast halibut & rocket crust

Plum Pithivier

11mi West of Ross-on-Wye by A49 on B4521. Parking.

016 The Newbridge

Tredunnock NP15 1LY
Tel.: (01633) 451000 - Fax: (01633) 451001
e-mail: eatandsleep@thenewbridge.co.uk
Website: www.thenewbridge.co.uk

Reverend James and 1 monthly changing guest beer

If at first you struggle to locate this gloriously rural pub, getting lost won't be a tragedy; firstly because of the wonderful scenery to be enjoyed in the area, and secondly because, when you do finally arrive, you'll find that everything about this place is that bit better than the norm. The rustic bar is smart and spacious and the relaxing lounge with its luscious leather sofa is the ideal place in which to have your pre-dinner drink. The dining areas are airy and comfortable, service is polite and prompt and several of the tables afford splendid views out over the River Usk and the eponymous bridge. Menus offer modern, seasonally-based meals made from locally-sourced ingredients, and the three course lunch menu represents especially good value for money. Bedrooms are elegant and contemporary yet unpretentious, and their sophistication extends to the bathrooms too, where you can even wash in style in a roll top bath.

Food serving times

Monday-Sunday:
12pm-2.30pm, 7pm-10pm

Closed 26-31 December

Booking advisable

Prices

Meals: a la carte
15.00/25.00

6 rooms: 95.00/120.00

Typical Dishes

Caerphilly cheese on mushroom

Herb crusted rump of lamb

Bread and butter pudding

Five minutes drive from the centre of Caerleon, on the banks of the River Usk. Parking.

017 The Felin Fach Griffin

Felin Fach, Brecon LD3 0UB

Tel.: (01874) 620111 - Fax: (01874) 620120

e-mail: enquiries@eatdrinksleep.ltd.uk

Website: www.eatdrinksleep.ltd.uk

Tomos Watkins OSB, Breconshire Breweries Golden Valley and Winter Beacons

As you enter this terracotta-coloured converted farmhouse, you get the feeling you've arrived somewhere special. Friendly, cool and with a style so laid back it's almost horizontal, this place will soon oblige you to join in its relaxed vibe and you'll find yourself curling up next to the fire in one of the large leather sofas. The chef has a notable C.V. and produces modern, seasonal food worth trekking over the Brecon Beacons to taste. Dishes are made using local produce and lunch menus offer quality food at decent prices. The owners' company is called EatDrinkSleep, and once they've ensured that you've had your fill of the first two, you'll be more than ready for the latter. Simply decorated, stylish rooms, several with four-posters and all containing books rather than televisions, will ensure that you do so like the proverbial baby. Breakfast next morning like a country lady or gent, soothed by the warmth of the Aga.

Food serving times

Monday: 6.30pm-9.30pm

Tuesday-Saturday: 12.30pm-2.30pm, 6.30pm-9.30pm

Sunday: 6.30pm-9pm

Closed 24-25 December and early January

Prices

Meals: 27.90 (3 course dinner) and a la carte 30.00/35.00

7 rooms: 67.50/125.00

Typical Dishes

Black Mountain smokery

Welsh ribeye steak

Vanilla crème brûlée

4.75mi Northeast of Brecon by B4602 off A470. Parking.

018 Nantyffin Cider Mill Inn

Brecon Rd,
Crickhowell NP8 1SG
Tel.: (01873) 810775 - Fax: (01873) 810986
e-mail: info@cidermill.co.uk - Website: www.cidermill.co.uk

Old Rosie, Addlestones and 2 regularly changing ales

One of the first Welsh pubs to get the 'gastro' treatment, this converted 16C cider mill is passionately run and serves fresh, modern food at decent prices. With its salmon-pink tinge, it's certainly hard to miss, and inside you'll find two charming bars which have an inviting feel to them. Eat in either of these or in the more formal cloth-clad dining room - it used to be the old apple store and is still home to the original cider press. Cooking is wholesome and full of flavour without being overpowering, and is made with seasonal ingredients, some of which come from the owners' farm. The produce may be local, but the menu is global, with British classics mixing with dishes from Europe and beyond. The blackboard menu changes according to what produce is available and the set lunch menu is particularly good value. Wines and ales are given serious regard here, too - and draft cider is also unsurprisingly a feature.

Food serving times

Tuesday-Sunday and Bank Holiday Monday: 12pm-2.30pm, 6.30pm-9.30pm

Closed 25-26 December

Closed dinner Sunday September-April

Prices

Meals: 16.95 (3 course lunch & dinner) and a la carte 19.95/40.00

Typical Dishes

Fresh ravioli
Confit of Uncle Martin's lamb
Sticky toffee pudding

1.5mi West of Crickhowell on A40.
Parking.

The Bear

019 The Bear

High St,
Crickhowell NP8 1BW

Tel.: (01873) 810408 - Fax: (01873) 811696
e-mail: bearhotel@aol.com - Website: www.bearhotel.co.uk

 **Bass, Ruddles Best, Reverend James, Evans and Jones**

Nestled between the Black Mountains and the Brecon Beacons, the pretty town of Crickhowell is home to the landmark that is the Bear. This former coaching inn's long-established owners know what the locals like and provide it for them in spades: good food, a warm welcome and a friendly atmosphere. Dating back to 1432, with its open fires and antiques, its busy beamed bar is an undeniably characterful place in which to eat, and there are also two separate dining rooms, each with a charm of their own. In summer, hanging baskets provide a blaze of colour and the garden comes alive. The popular bar menu offers a range of hearty dishes, plus lighter meals and sandwiches; the restaurant menu combines the traditional with the more modern, and a daily-changing specials menu also adds to the choice. Traditionally styled bedrooms are gradually being upgraded and given a more contemporary edge, whilst retaining their character and comfort.

Food serving times

Monday-Sunday:
12pm-2pm, 7pm-9.30pm

Closed 25 December

Prices

Meals: a la carte
17.95/25.00

34 rooms:
84.00/150.00

Typical Dishes

Welsh rarebit
Daube of black beef
Wild wimberry tart

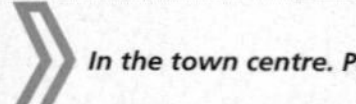
In the town centre. Parking.

020 Old Black Lion

26 Lion St,
Hay-on-Wye HR3 5AD
Tel.: (01497) 820841 - Fax: (01497) 822960
e-mail: info@oldblacklion.co.uk - Website: www.oldblacklion.co.uk

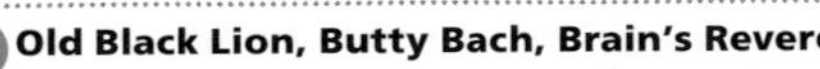
Old Black Lion, Butty Bach, Brain's Reverend James

'Some books are to be tasted, others to be swallowed, and some few to be chewed and digested,' said Francis Bacon. Bibliophiles may get their fill of books in the myriad second hand bookshops to be found in literary Hay-on Wye, but staying at Old Black Lion will ensure food for the body as well as for the soul. Long renowned for its competence in all things culinary, this pub serves traditional dishes as well as meals with a more international flavour, and lighter options are available on the bar menu. A part-13C inn which can reputedly count Oliver Cromwell among previous guests, its style is fittingly rustic with exposed timber beams and scrubbed pine tables, and the well-maintained bedrooms, part-furnished with antiques, maintain the historical feel. Whether you're here with the crowds for the town's annual festival or during a quieter spell, a pleasant service is provided by local staff and a warm welcome extended.

Food serving times

Monday-Sunday:
12pm-2.30pm, 6.30pm-8.30pm

Closed 24-26 December

Prices

Meals: a la carte
20.00/30.00

10 rooms:
42.50/115.00

Typical Dishes

Goat cheese salad
Beef Wellington
Chocolate nemesis

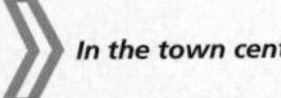
In the town centre. Parking.

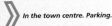

021 The Talkhouse

Pontdolgoch SY17 5JE
Tel.: (01686) 688919
e-mail: info@talkhouse.co.uk
Website: www.talkhouse.co.uk

 **No real ales offered**

The Talkhouse might be the talk of the town because of the quality of its food, but when you step inside this unassuming 17C former coaching inn, it's the surprising stylishness of its interior which is sure to become a talking point. Tastefully fitted out with the floral fabric and furnishings of Wales' famous daughter, Laura Ashley, on one side there is a comfortable lounge with sofas, and on the other, a cosy rustic beamed bar. This leads to dining areas which in turn overlook an immaculate garden, great for dining al fresco in the summer months. The charm doesn't stop there but also extends to the elegantly characterful bedrooms, each with very individual fittings and decoration, and the smooth service by the friendly young owners. Regularly changing blackboard menus offer bold, wholesome cooking, made from locally sourced, seasonal ingredients, and portions are generous, bordering on philanthropic.

Food serving times

Tuesday-Saturday:
6.30pm-8.45pm

Sunday:
12pm-1.30pm, 6.30pm-8.45pm

Closed 25-26 December and first 2 weeks of January

Prices

Meals: a la carte
21.00/30.00

 **3 rooms:** 70.00/95.00

Typical Dishes

Smoked haddock rarebit
Welsh rump of lamb
Berry cheesecake

 *1.5mi Northwest of Caersws on A470. Parking.* 

022 The Blue Anchor Inn

East Aberthaw CF62 3DD
Tel.: (01446) 750329
Website: www.blueanchoraberthaw.com

 **Wye Valley Pale Ale, Wadworth 6X, Theakstons Old Peculier**

Apart from a ten-month hiatus following a fire in 2004, when its loyal local following mourned its loss, this popular inn has purportedly been trading since 1380. The long-established family owners haven't been at the helm for quite this long, but they were never going to let a little fire see them off, and having re-thatched the inn, were soon back behind the bar, much to the relief of many. The extremely characterful interior, with its open fires, flagstone floors, hidden corners and soft lighting provides a charming backdrop for a meal, and local ladies provide amiable, chatty service. The bar menu offers baguettes and jacket potatoes, plus a selection of traditional meals, whilst the menu for the more formal upstairs restaurant brings an international flavour to the South coast, with an interesting mix of Asian and Welsh dishes. Dishes are cooked using locally grown produce and desserts are proudly homemade in the inn's pastry room.

Food serving times

Monday-Saturday:
12pm-2pm, 7pm-9.30pm

Sunday:
12.30pm-2.30pm, 7pm-9.30pm

Prices

Meals: 18.95 (dinner) and a la carte 15.00/26.00

Typical Dishes

Duck spring roll
Rump of Welsh lamb
Vanilla & lemon cheesecake

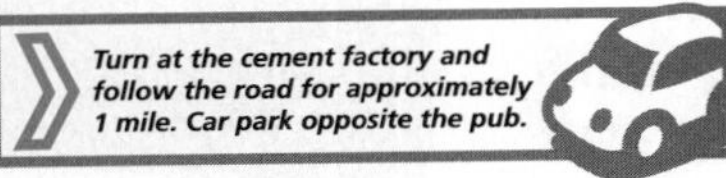

Turn at the cement factory and follow the road for approximately 1 mile. Car park opposite the pub.

023 Pant-yr-Ochain

Old Wrexham Rd, Gresford LL12 8TY
Tel.: (01978) 853525 - Fax: (01978) 853505
e-mail: pant.yr.ochain@brunningandprice.co.uk
Website: www.brunningandprice.co.uk

     MC

Timothy Taylor's Landlord, Flowers Original, Thwaites Original, Phoenix Arizona, Weetwood Eastgate

As old as it is large, you can still see the previous owners' coat of arms on the outside of the cream washed building, and the Tudor wattle and daub walls in the alcove behind its 16C inglenook fireplace. As large as it is popular, this spacious, open plan inn has plenty of different rooms for drinking and dining, and a buzzy, bustling atmosphere. Inside, there's a conservatory, a book-lined library, a dining room, and a large central bar, all stylishly furnished, with many nooks and crannies in which to nestle. This grand country house is also set in delightful gardens and the picnic tables overlooking the lake are in demand when the weather is fine. The extensive menu doesn't try to reinvent the wheel, sticking to classics like burgers and Ploughman's but the kitchen also does its thing with belly pork and seabass. The staff are masters of polite, friendly service which doesn't lose its edge when the pressure's on.

Food serving times

Monday-Sunday:
12pm-9.30pm

Closed 25-26 December

Booking essential

Prices

Meals: a la carte
17.70/26.95

Typical Dishes

Peppered beef salad
Venison steak
Sticky toffee pudding

3.5mi Northeast of Wrexham by A483 on B5445; then 1mi South from Gresford. Parking.

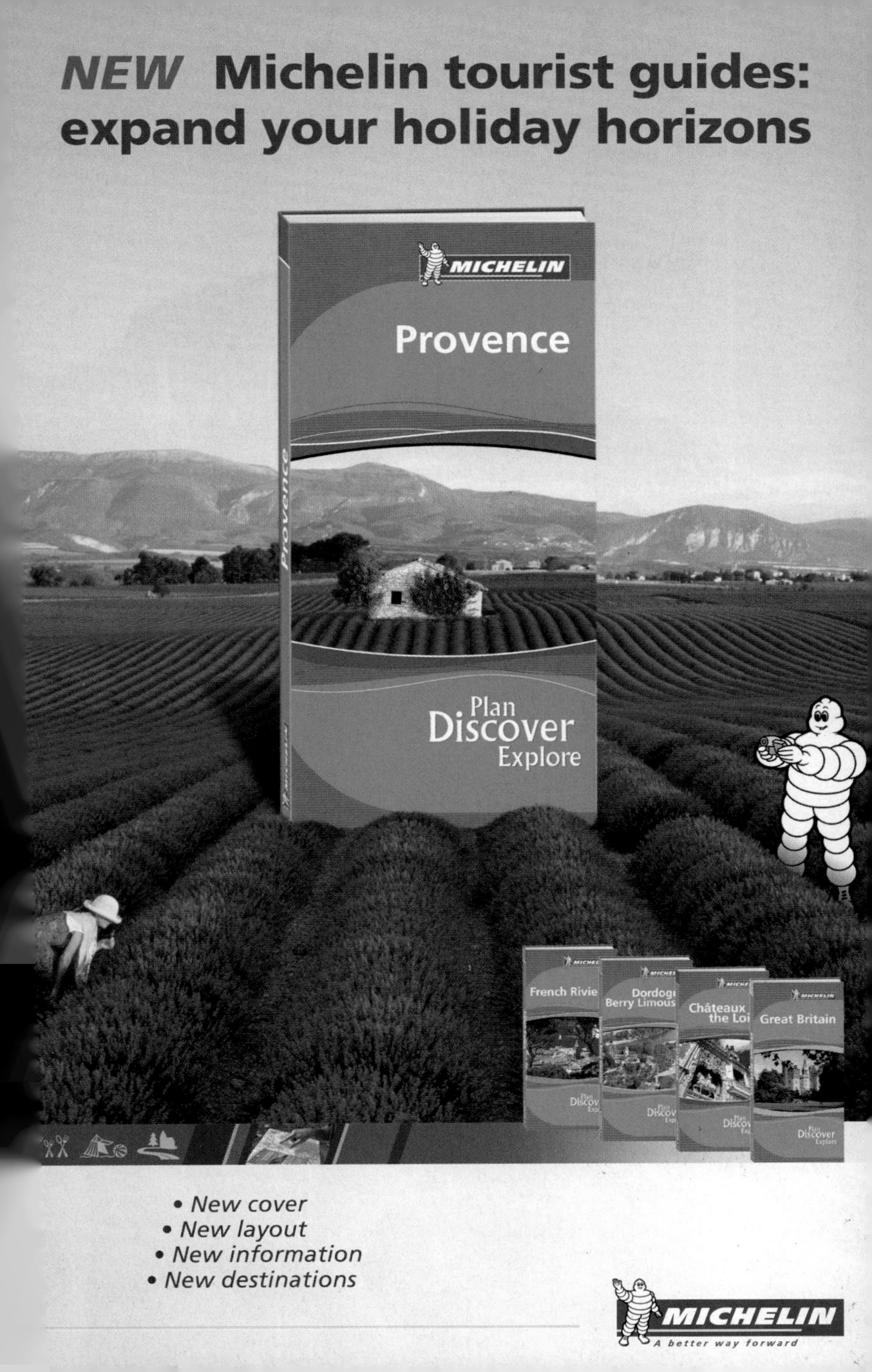
NEW Michelin tourist guides:
expand your holiday horizons
MICHELIN
Provence
Provence
Plan
Discover
Explore
French Rivie
Dordogı
Berry Limous
Châteaux
the Loi
Great Britain
• New cover
• New layout
• New information
• New destinations
MICHELIN
A better way forward

With over a third of the country's population living in and around, Belfast is truly the focus of Northern Irish life. As the only city in Ireland to feel the rise and heavy fall of Britain's industrial empire, it has worked bravely to re-establish itself with a busy cultural life and a wave of new building, and perhaps it is in part the attitudes in the rest of Britain and Ireland that make us look elsewhere for easier symbols and images of the country. Though less intensely marketed than the Southern Ireland experience, the six counties contain some of the finest landscapes in the island. The incredible, innumerable columns of the Giant's Causeway, formed 60 million years ago by volcanic eruptions, attract thousands of visitors every year, while to the east lie the quiet, wooded bays of the Antrim coast and the deep inland glens. The beautiful Mourne and Sperrin Mountains stand as great Ulster landmarks, while Lough Neagh, the largest body of fresh water in the British Isles, lies in repose, a vast blue mirror in the heart of the province: here you'll find the working landscapes and the working people richly explored in Seamus Heaney's poetic memories of his youth. From the cultivated splendour of Mount Stewart Gardens or Castle Coole to the earth-magic of Beaghmore, from the whale-backed islands of Strangford Lough to the leaping salmon and pike in Lough Erne, a feeling for the natural world of Northern Ireland goes straight to the heart.

Coll
Tiree
Tobermory
Loch Linnhe
Mull
Craignure
Fionnphort
Oban
Colonsay
Scotland
Lochgilphead
Loch Fyne
Islay
Port Askaig
Jura
Rothesay
Port Ellen
Malin Head
Kintyre
Brodick
Campbeltown
Arran
Firth of Clyde
Giant's Causeway
Buncrana
Lough Foyle
Portrush
Coleraine
Ballycastle
Letterkenny
Londonderry
Donegal
NORTHERN IRELAND
North Channel
Bundoran
Omagh
Larne
Stranraer
Lough Neagh
Bangor
Sligo
Enniskillen
Lisburn
BELFAST
Armagh
Boyle
Monaghan
Newry
Newcastle
Man
Peel
Cavan
Dundalk
Longford
Ardee
Roscommon
Lough Ree
Ireland
Drogheda
Athlone
Mullingar
Navan
Kinnegad
R. Boyne
IRL
Tullamore
DUBLIN
IRISH S
Naas
Dún Laoghaire
Anglesey
Birr
Portlaoise
Bray
Roscrea
Glendalough
Holyhead
Wicklow
Carlow
Kilkenny
Caernarfon
Snowdon
Wales
R. Suir
R. Barrow
Cashel
Arklow
Clonmel
Caher
New Ross
Enniscorthy

001 The Distillers Arms

140 Main St,
Bushmills BT57 8QE
Tel.: (028) 2073 1044 - Fax: (028) 2073 2843
e-mail: simon@distillersarms.com - Website: www.distillersarms.com

Situated at the top of the town, the traditional white-painted exterior of The Distillers Arms belies its spacious, modern interior. There's a comfortable lounge and airy bar where a tapas-style menu – from oysters to cold sausage and mustard - is served, and a horseshoe shaped restaurant where colourful, contemporary oil paintings hang on the stone walls. The dining area is large enough to accommodate groups of tourists fresh from the Giant's Causeway and the old whiskey distillery, and while they're here, they can take advantage of the new wine shop attached, to purchase beers, spirits and speciality wines. The bold, straightforward lunch menu offers robust cooking served in hearty, fulfilling portions with dishes such as steak and Guinness or seafood chowder, while dinner is a more elaborate affair with choices such as roasted seabass or fruits de mer. The owner takes a hands-on approach and service is enthusiastic and effective.

Food serving times

Monday-Sunday:
12.30pm-3pm, 5.30pm-9pm

Closed October to April, Monday-Friday

Prices

Meals: a la carte
17.00/25.00

Typical Dishes

Whiskey cured salmon
Irish shellfish platter
Honey & lavender crème brûlée

Close to the Bushmills whiskey distillery. Parking.

Northern Ireland • Antrim

002 The Pheasant

410 Upper Ballynahinch Rd,
Annahilt BT26 6NR

Tel.: (028) 9263 8056 - Fax: (028) 9263 8026

e-mail: pheasantinn@aol.com - Website: www.barretro.com/pheasant

No real ales offered

The Pheasant is a homily to the Irish generosity of spirit; a generously-sized establishment serving generously-sized portions. There's a larger than life stag painted on the wall, and even the car park is generously proportioned – but then it would need to be to fit in all its customers' cars. The bar manages to feel spacious yet cosy at the same time, with its flag and tiled flooring, colourful seating and soft lighting, and the well-established team dressed in black know the drill. The menus contain a little bit of everything, so there should be a dish or two to suit everybody's taste. Plump for a fajita or a wrap, perhaps a seafood dish, some pheasant or duck, or a steak from the grill. Get your thinking caps on if you're visiting on a Thursday, as it's quiz night and there are prizes to be won. Stick around till the Friday and you'll need your dancing shoes instead, when a variety of groups provide the live music.

Food serving times

Monday-Sunday :
12pm-2.30pm, 5pm-9pm

Closed 25-26 December and 12-13 July

Prices

Meals: 14.95/23.95 (lunch & dinner) and a la carte 15.00/25.00

Typical Dishes

Gorgonzola and pear galette

Venison and beef fillet

Rhubarb and custard brûlée

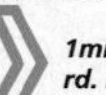

1mi North of Annahilt on Lisburn rd. Parking.

003 Coyle's

44 High St,
Bangor BT20 5AZ
Tel.: (028) 9127 0362 - Fax: (028 9127 0362

  VISA

No real ales offered

Northern Ireland's most popular coastal resort deserves a great venue to eat and drink, and at Coyle's it's hit paydirt. There's no mistaking the pubby appearance: a black exterior, advertising real music and hard liquor! The ground floor bar keeps that image intact. It's intimate and friendly with a welcoming ambience, and, apart from the liquor, there's an up-to-date menu where classics meet dishes with an international accent. A board directs you upstairs for the restaurant proper. This comes as a bit of a surprise: there's a touch of the art deco/ nouveau about it, with stained glass and old framed posters such as a '40s ad for Craven A cigarettes. Although the rather basic tables and chairs don't really do justice to their surroundings, the cooking ticks all the right boxes. It's a harmonious blend of safe, traditional styles with more ambitious, but well executed, dishes.

Food serving times

Monday-Friday:
12pm-3pm, 5pm-9pm
Saturday:
12pm-5pm, 5pm-9pm
Sunday:12pm-5pm, 5pm-8pm
Closed 25 December
Bar meals at lunch time.
Restaurant closed dinner Monday.

Prices

Meals: a la carte
14.00/25.30

Typical Dishes

Grilled red mullet
Rack of Irish lamb
Apple and pecan crumble

In the town centre. Pay and display parking 2min walk.

Donaghadee

004 Grace Neill's

33 High St,
Donaghadee BT21 0AH
Tel.: (028) 9188 4595 - Fax: (028) 9188 9631
e-mail: info@graceneills.com - Website: www.graceneills.com

We most liked

 **No real ales offered**

You'd expect a pub reputed to be the oldest in Ireland to have more character and atmosphere than most and Grace Neill's doesn't disappoint. In fact, if you listen very carefully, you might just be able to hear the faint echoes of the past over the creaking of the floorboards - tales of seafaring and smugglers, famous former customers and the figure of a ghost. The charmingly traditional beamed front snug leads through to a high-ceilinged library bar, which in turn leads through to the more modern dining space with its small open kitchen. Eclectic menus cover all bases, from the classics like beef and Guinness pie to the more contemporary dishes, such as king prawn tempura - but whatever dish you choose the food is wholesome and flavourful. Fancy making sweet music? Then borrow the guitar and tin whistles kept behind the bar. More discord than harmony? Perhaps it's best left to the professionals.

Food serving times

Monday-Thursday:
12pm-2.30pm, 5.30pm-9pm

Friday-Sunday:
12pm-9pm

Closed 25 December

Prices

Meals: a la carte
13.95/28.00

Typical Dishes

Strangford Lough mussels
Beef and Guinness pie
Mint crème brûlée

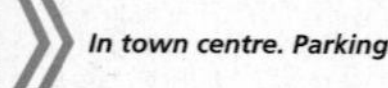
In town centre. Parking.

005 Pier 36

36 The Parade,
Donaghadee BT21 0HE
Tel.: (028) 9188 4466 - Fax: (028) 9188 4636
e-mail: info@pier36.co.uk - Website: www.pier36.co.uk

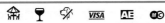

 **No real ales offered**

What will stay with you long after your trip to Pier 36 will be the hospitality offered by the hands-on family proprietors, and the personal service by their pleasant team of staff. That and the location – it's not every pub that can boast a harbourside position within spitting distance of an impressive lighthouse. Inside, it's all on one level, but spacious; there's a traditional front bar with open fire and stone floors, where meals are served all day, and a more modern area to the rear. Menus, including a list of specials, are longer than they need to be, but involve a real range of dishes, from the traditional – burgers, steak and the like - to dishes such as Moroccan chicken or fillet of Barbary duckling; and freshly caught seafood reels the regulars in time and time again. Add comfortable bedrooms with good facilities plus the pull of live jazz on Wednesday nights and you can see why this place is often full to the rafters.

Food serving times

Monday-Saturday:
12pm-2.30pm, 5pm-9.30pm

Sunday:
12pm-9pm

Closed 25 December

Seafood specialities

Prices

Meals: a la carte
17.00/35.00

4 rooms: 50.00/85.00

Typical Dishes

Sauté crab claws
Fresh lobster
Bread & butter pudding

On the harbour front. Parking in the street at the rear.

Northern Ireland • Down

006 Buck's Head Inn

77-79 Main St,
Dundrum BT33 0LU
Tel.: (028) 4375 1868 - Fax: (028) 4481 1033
e-mail: buckshead1@aol.com - Website: www.thebucksheaddundrum.co.uk

 **No real ales offered**

Situated in the historic village of Dundrum, best known for its ruined Norman castle, this mustard-coloured inn looks every inch the traditional pub from the front, with its window boxes and big gold signage. In contrast, the restaurant area overlooking the walled garden to the rear – open in the evening only - has a much more contemporary appearance. Lunch is served in the bar, as is high tea; a popular early evening choice with walkers fresh from Dundrum Bay or the Mourne Mountains, happy to warm themselves by the open fire and admire the oil paintings for sale on the walls. Seafood is the speciality on the modern, internationally-influenced menus, where Dundrum Bay mussels might come au naturel and oysters might come Thai style, while chicken might come as simple chicken supreme or spicy, with a noodle salad. The long-established owners take the wine list seriously and it's well worth investigating.

Food serving times

Monday-Sunday:
12pm-2.30pm, 5pm-9.30pm

Closed 25 December and Monday October-April

Seafood specialities

Prices

Meals: 26.50 (3 course dinner) and a la carte 17.20/24.95

Typical Dishes

Dundrum Bay oysters
Venison loin on beetroot
Buttermilk pannacotta

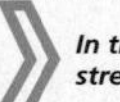

In the village. Parking on the street.

007 Mourne Seafood Bar

10 Main St,
Dundrum BT33 0LU

Tel.: (028) 4375 1377 - Fax: (028) 4375 1161
e-mail: bob@mourneseafood.com - Website: www.mourneseafood.com

 **Belfast Ale, Clotworthy Ale**

Standing over the road from the popular Buck's Head Inn, this rather untypical seafood bar was previously the current owner's home, and the name plaque 'Downshire Manor' can still be found on the front. He also runs an oyster and mussel farm in Carlingford Lough, source of many dishes here, while other produce is brought in from the local boats. Bob (the owner) is keen for people to try 'bi-catch' species rather than fish under pressure such as cod, and this simple, casual bar is a great place to give it a go: prices are reasonable and fair. There's a core menu: meanwhile, waiters take time to explain the six or seven daily blackboard specials. Wet fish is available to buy and chef is happy to suggest the best way to cook if asked. It's not just seafood on the menu here: locally reared chicken and steaks also make an appearance. An excellent local reputation is building, so, if it's summertime, do make sure you book first.

Food serving times

Summer:
Monday-Sunday: 12pm-9.30pm

Winter:
Wednesday-Sunday: 12pm-9pm or earlier

Closed 25 December

- Seafood - Booking essential in summer

Prices

Meals: a la carte 16.00/28.00

Typical Dishes

6 Mourne oysters
Grilled lobster with chips
Crème brûlée

In the village. Parking across the street and in the village.

008 The Plough Inn

3 The Square,
Hillsborough BT26 6AG
Tel.: (028) 9268 2985 - Fax: (028) 9268 2472
Website: www.barretro.com

  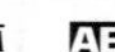  

A well-established, family-run inn, the vastly extended Plough Inn has a well-deserved local following. You get three for the price of one here; a pub, a bistro and a café, all serving slightly different menus, and appealing to slightly different people. The traditional dark wood bar area with its horse brass is still popular with older diners, younger ones head for the trendy bistro upstairs, whilst families tend to congregate in the café, where children are welcome. The bar serves traditional dishes such as sausage and mash as well as more modern dishes like Thai Green Curry or smoked goose and chorizo Caesar salad - and the older folks flock in for the good value specials to be had here. Upstairs, the bistro menu is similar, if a little more trendy, whilst the café serves food like burgers, wraps and paninis. Wherever you choose to eat, all dishes come in generous helpings and staff are only too happy to help.

Food serving times

Monday-Saturday:
12pm-2.30pm, 5pm-9.30pm

Sunday:
all day (bar meals)

Closed 25 December

Prices

Meals: a la carte
15.00/25.00

Typical Dishes

Marinated beef strips
Trio of local seafood
Rhubarb & ginger brûlée

At the top of the hill in The Square. Parking.

Well deserving of its old epithet, 'The Emerald Isle', Ireland conjures up images of dewy fields and distant mountains. Wondrous, ever-changing cloudscapes do haul in rainfall on an almost industrial scale, accounting for the fresh atmosphere and luminous look of the landscape, but this picture of gentle, unpeopled tranquillity does no justice to the country's variety: sandy strands, flora-rich peatland and, at the westernmost edge of Europe, the natural phenomenon of the Cliffs of Moher, a five mile spectacular of shale and sandstone bounded by the Atlantic breakers and the Burren. Peaceful Cashel and Clonmacnoise evoke the spirit of Celtic Christianity and kingship, while the Republic's towns and cities throb with life, culture and chatter: Galway has grown into a bustling university and cathedral city alongside its thriving port while Killarney, near the wild south-west tip, has been attracting visitors for over 200 years. Dublin remains the heart of the nation, a fascinating focus of literary association with a vital blend of street, café, bar and restaurant life: the addictive craic *of the "fair city" is played out to an accompaniment of Georgian elegance and the stunning background of the Wicklow Mountains. Away from the capital, too, friendly pubs serve up not only good stout and even better conversation, but also wholesome favourites like Irish stew, colcannon and coddle and imaginative new cuisine showcasing the finest produce the country has to offer.*

Northern Ireland
REP. OF IRELAND
IRL
DUBLIN
Malin Head
Giant's Causeway
Buncrana
Letterkenny
Londonderry
Portrush
Coleraine
Strabane
Donegal
Bundoran
Omagh
Enniskillen
Lisburn
Armagh
Monaghan
Newry
Newcastle
Belmullet
Achill
Ballina
Sligo
Castlebar
Boyle
Westport
Clifden
Connemara
Lough Mask
Lough Corrib
Roscommon
Longford
Cavan
Dundalk
Ardee
Drogheda
Navan
Mullingar
Athlone
Kinnegad
Galway
Ballinasloe
Loughrea
Aran
Cliffs of Moher
Ennistimon
Tullamore
Naas
Dún Laoghaire
Bray
Birr
Glendalough
Kilrush
River Shannon
Limerick
Listowel
Wicklow
Carlow
Kilkenny
Arklow
Dingle
Tralee
Tipperary
Cashel
Lakes of Killarney
Killarney
Clonmel
Caher
Mallow
Enniscorthy
New Ross
Cahersiveen
Macgillycuddy's Reeks
Fermoy
Carrick-on-Suir
Ring of Kerry
Kenmare
Wexford
Waterford
Dungarvan
Rosslare
Cork
Youghal
Glengarriff
Bantry
Cobh
Carnsore Point
Skibbereen
St. George's Channel
St. David's
Milford Haven
Islay
Port Ellen
Tiree

001 Vaughan's Anchor Inn

Main Street,
Liscannor
Tel.: (065) 708 1548 - Fax: (065) 706 8977
Website: www.vaughans.ie

  VISA MC

 **No real ales offered**

Conveniently placed for the cliffs of Moher and the beach, this is a long-standing pub, seriously well-regarded by the locals and now also offers accommodation. It boasts a charmingly unique interior: the front counter acts as a shop where you can buy corn flakes and coffee, while the walls are filled with fishing paraphernalia: nets, photos, ships' wheels and the like. Simple wooden tables make it seem like a bistro; a mix of simple and complex dishes means there's always something of interest on the menu. The more involved options might include seared scallops on a bed of crisp-fried smoked haddock and scallion mash with a white wine sauce. It gets very busy, so be prepared to wait for your dish to arrive.

Food serving times
Monday-Sunday:
12pm-9.30pm
Closed 25 December
- Seafood -

Prices
Meals: a la carte
22.00/36.00
3 rooms: 70.00

Typical Dishes
Lobster spring roll
Roast fillet of salmon
Chocolate fondant

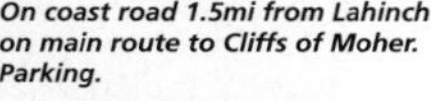
On coast road 1.5mi from Lahinch on main route to Cliffs of Moher. Parking.

002 Linnane's Bar

New Quay Pier,
Newquay
Tel.: (065) 707 8120
e-mail: linnaneslobsterbar@hotmail.com

 **No real ales offered**

On the crags overlooking Galway Bay, this little white-painted pub is traditional, friendly and totally relaxed. If the clouds are setting in, you can always find a table in the modest bar, decorated with black and white photos, but if there's even a hint of sun, make straight for the lovely terrace overlooking the water. A concise, all-seafood menu, concentrating on prime fresh shellfish, keeps it delightfully simple; they're open all day in summer, so you can while away the afternoon with open sandwiches, chowders, lobster, scallops, oysters, chilled Sancerre and plenty of fresh sea air! There's more seafood for sale at the pier shop. If you can tear yourself away, drive through the strange, barren Tolkien-scape of The Burren to Lahinch beach or the breathtaking Cliffs of Moher.

Food serving times
Monday-Sunday:
12.30pm-9pm
- Seafood -

Prices
Meals: a la carte
20.00/30.00

Typical Dishes
Fresh local lobster
Seafood platter
Apple crumble

About 2mi off N 67 between Kinvara and Ballyvaughan. Parking.

003 Mary Ann's

Castletownshend

Tel.: (028) 36146 - Fax: (028) 36920
e-mail: maryanns@eircom.net
Website: www.westcorkweek.com/maryanns

 **No real ales offered**

Don't go searching round this pub for someone called Mary Ann – it's actually named after a previous owner – the current ones have been here since 1988 and go by the names of Fergus and Patricia. Eat at simple wooden tables in the bar or head upstairs to dine on tablecloths; in the summer, it's the huge outside terrace which accommodates the crowds, when the pub gets busy with sailors stopping for the night in the harbour. Not too many pubs can boast their own art gallery, but this one can, and it attracts visitors up this steep, narrow street from far and wide. Called The Warren Gallery, it houses the owner's collection of modern Irish art, mostly bought at auction on his travels around the country. The food served here may not quite qualify as a work of art, but it's extremely tasty and there's plenty of it; portions are huge, with masses of vegetables, and the emphasis is firmly on fresh fish and seafood.

Food serving times

Monday-Sunday:
12pm-2.30pm, 6pm-9pm

Closed 24-26 December and 8-31 January; also Monday November-March

Bookings not accepted

Prices

Meals: a la carte
20.00/45.00

Typical Dishes

Seafood selection
Scallops Mary Ann
Crème brûlée

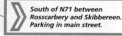

South of N71 between Rosscarbery and Skibbereen. Parking in main street.

004 An Súgán

**41 Wolfe Tone St,
Clonakilty**

Tel.: (023) 33498 - Fax: (023) 33825
e-mail: ansugan4@eircom.net - Website: www.ansugan.com

 **No real ales offered**

Located in the middle of a busy town, this colourful pub is popular with locals and visitors alike. It's spotless inside, and full of character: water jugs and old meat plates hang from the ceiling, and you can see hundreds of business cards which have been wedged into the old wood beams by visitors over the years. There are always plenty of locals enjoying the bar side banter, while the wood-panelled dining room upstairs, decorated with antique theatre programmes, tends to get busy in the evenings. Simple, home cooked food is served daily: the lunch menu is chalked up on a board, offering dishes such as seafood pie, smoked salmon and the famous Clonakilty black pudding, while the evening à la carte offers more choice, with fresh local seafood featuring heavily – including lobster when available - and daily-changing specials written on blackboards. Smartly dressed staff provide friendly service. Bedrooms are clean and comfortable.

Food serving times

Monday-Sunday:
12.30pm-9.30pm

Closed 25-26 December and Good Friday

Prices

Meals: a la carte
25.00/40.00

7 rooms: 35.00/70.00

Typical Dishes

Terrine of Clonakilty pudding

An Súgán seafood basket

Chocolate & amaretto pudding

 *East of town centre. Parking in the street.* 

005 Dalton's

3 Market St,
Kinsale
Tel.: (021) 477 8025
e-mail: fedalton@eircom.net

 **No real ales offered**

Moist, tasty crab cakes with pineapple salsa, chicken satay and Cajun popcorn prawns: here's a globe-trotting chef and landlord who is determined to bring a little unexpected variety to Kinsale's dining. A loyal local following suggests he must be doing something right, and while they still offer a good pie and pint for the traditionalist, it's the more ambitious dishes which set the place apart from the countless other pubs in town. It just goes to show that you can't go by appearances, for apart from the eyecatching purple façade, the line of bar stools, the tan banquettes, the tiled floor and the glowing fire are as traditional as the easygoing ambience and the cheerful welcome.

Food serving times

Monday-Saturday:
12pm-4pm

Closed 2 weeks at Christmas

Prices

Meals: a la carte
20.00/40.00

Typical Dishes

Chunky seafood chowder

Crab cakes

Chocolate brownie cake

 *In town centre. Parking 2 minutes away in St Multose car park at top of road.* 

006 Clarendon Café Bar

32 Clarendon Street,
Dublin D2

Tel.: (01) 679 2909 - Fax: (01) 670 6900
Website: www.clarendon.ie

 **No real ales offered**

The city's front-running gastropub, this sleek, metal-and-glass fronted destination has caused quite a stir since its refurbished doors were opened in 2004. Tourists, business suits, shoppers and, at nights, young clubbers all make a beeline for its shiny facade. You're free to eat or drink, and there are no 'time slots' weighing upon you. A distinct contemporary feel is adhered to so don't be surprised at sitting on chocolate leather boxes, augmented by a slight Moroccan edge courtesy of vivid scatter cushions. Tables are closely packed by the entrance; you might like to go upstairs and grab an intimate window table instead. The modern menus drift temptingly between casual favourites and serious restaurant dishes, all of which can be washed down with a choice from the extensive list of cocktails or wine by the glass.

Food serving times

Monday-Thursday:
12pm-3pm, 5pm-9.30pm

Friday-Sunday:
12pm-6pm

Closed 25-26 December,
1 January and Good Friday

Bookings not accepted

Prices

Meals: a la carte
15.00/41.80

Typical Dishes

Tiger prawn open sandwich

Braised lamb shank

Mixed berry crumble

In town centre, west of Grafton Street. Drury Street or Brown Thomas car park.

007 The Cellar Bar

**Upper Merrion St,
Dublin D2**

Tel.: (01) 603 0600 - Fax: (01) 603 0700

e-mail: info@merrionhotel.com - Website: www.merrionhotel.com

 **No real ales offered**

One of Dublin's favourite places for lunch is hidden away behind the elegant façade of an old Georgian town house, now the Merrion Hotel. The superbly restored wine vaults are now a smart destination bar by night, a bar-brasserie by day, and a city institution all round, so beat the lunchtime rush and find an alcove table under the brick and granite arches or pull up a spare stool at the long bar. Even on the busiest days, smiling, super-efficient bar staff keep things moving, serving up everything from hot roast beef sandwiches and Caesar salad to bacon and cabbage or Irish stew; plum frangipane tart with deliciously smooth ice cream is an occasional special and deserves to be tried.

Food serving times

Monday-Saturday:
12pm-3pm, 6pm-10pm

Closed 25 December

Prices

Meals: a la carte
35.00/50.00

Typical Dishes

Torchon of foie gras

Irish West Coast seafood pie

Iced passion fruit parfait

At the Merrion Hotel; in town centre, between Merrion Square and St Stephen's Green. Parking available in Merrion Square.

008 John J Burke

Mount Gable House,
Clonbur
Tel.: (094) 954 6175
e-mail: tibhurca@eircom.net - Website: www.burkes-clonbur.com

 **No real ales offered**

Between two of Ireland's finest fishing waters, it's no surprise to find cabinets and cases displaying the ones that didn't get away. The brown trout in Lough Corrib and Lough Mask are legendary, the perch and pike no less so, and where better for food and drink after a long day out than this friendly pub, still owned by the Burke family. The tiny, unassuming shopfront opens up into a big, characterful bar and simply set rear dining room, as popular with the locals as with the anglers who flock to the West Coast in the height of the season. Simple, fortifying meals will set you up for the great outdoors: try cod and chips, a pint of stout and a generous slice of home-made apple pie.

Food serving times

Monday-Sunday:
10am-3pm (bar meals only), 6.30pm-9pm

Closed 25 December and Good Friday; October to March bar meals only

Live music Sunday

Prices

Meals: a la carte 23.00/40.00

4 rooms: 40.00/80.00

Typical Dishes

Home-made soup
Irish sirloin steak
Home-made apple tart

 *West of Cong. On street parking.* 

009 Moran's Oyster Cottage

The Weir,
Kilcolgan
Tel.: (091) 796113
e-mail: moranstheweir@eircom.net

 **No real ales offered**

Situated in a tiny hamlet, and accessed via country lanes, unless you'd heard of this inn, you'd never know it was there. Chances are, though, if you're in this part of the world, you most definitely will have heard of it, as its reputation for all things edible and from the sea tends to precede it - and the pictures on the walls show in whose famous footsteps you follow. In the summer, the place gets packed out; and don't be too surprised if you see the odd coach driving up here, for the place is now virtually a tourist attraction. What's the big deal? Well, it makes for a very pleasant spot on a sunny day, watching the swans glide by, and with its 18C origins, thatched roof and cosy front bar, it certainly has plenty of character. It's well-run and the service is friendly, but primarily people come here for the oysters. The seafood is fresh and simply prepared, and includes smoked salmon, crabs, prawns - and oysters. Always oysters.

Food serving times

Monday-Sunday:
12pm-10pm

Closed 24-26 December and Good Friday

- Seafood -

Prices

Meals: a la carte
26.00/60.00

Typical Dishes

Native Irish oysters
Seafood special
Baileys Cheesecake

5 minutes from the village of Clarenbridge. Parking in road.

010 Keogh's Bar

Main St,
Kinvara

Tel.: (091) 637145 - Fax: (091) 637028

e-mail: keoghsbar@eircom.net - Website: www.kinvara.com/keoghs

 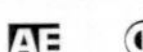 

 **No real ales offered**

Kinvara is a pretty harbour village on the Galway coast, renowned for the quality of its Atlantic fishing catch. Gateway to the Burren, its colourful character is echoed in this bright yellow-fronted pub whose busy bar constantly buzzes to the sound of locals chattering over a pint of dark stout. At the back is a spacious, slightly more formal dining room, which still maintains a warm, pubby ambience. The Keoghs have been here for many years, and they serve simple, well-prepared and tasty dishes, based around the plentiful supplies of local seafood. On offer, typically, are prawns, salmon, crab, mussels and seafood chowder, cooked in a hearty and traditional style.

Food serving times

Monday-Sunday:
from 9am (bar meals),
6pm-10pm

Closed 25-26 December

Prices

Meals: a la carte
16.00/30.00

Typical Dishes

Country terrine
Spicy chicken parcels
Bread & butter pudding

 *In town centre. Parking in the square outside.* 

011 O'Neill's (The Point) Seafood Bar

Renard Point,
Cahersiveen
Tel.: (066) 947 2165 - Fax: (087) 259 2165
e-mail: oneillsthepoint@eircom.net

 **No real ales offered**

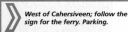

As the beautiful Ring of Kerry runs south, hold your course to the tip of the Iveragh peninsula: down at the quay, looking out across the harbour to Valencia Island, is a neatly kept little bar that's definitely worth going a little further for. Between them, a charming couple, owners of long standing, keep the place shipshape, pull the pints and prepare a short hot and cold supper menu of local seafood; all well chosen and as fresh as it comes, as you'd expect with a fish shed next door! It's a good place for a relaxed pint and a chat – there's no food at all at lunchtime – but if you arrive in the afternoon with time to spare, just take a seat on the little pavement terrace and wait for 6pm to roll around!

Food serving times

April to end September:
Monday-Saturday: 12.30pm-3.30pm, 5.30pm-10pm
Sunday:5.30pm-10pm
Closed November to mid December; January-April, Monday-Thursday, lunch Friday-Sunday; lunch April to mid-May - Seafood - Bar lunch. Bookings not accepted

Prices

Meals: a la carte approx. 30.00

Typical Dishes

Deep-fried Atlantic squid
Monkfish casserole
Irish coffee

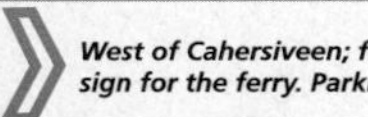

West of Cahersiveen; follow the sign for the ferry. Parking.

012 Allo's Bar

41 Church St,
Listowel
Tel.: (068) 22880 - Fax: (068) 22803
e-mail: allos@eircom.net

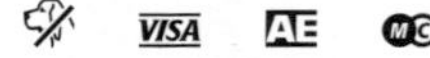

No real ales offered; extensive selection of Irish whiskeys

A discreetly set institution in the centre of Listowel, this is a wonderfully relaxed pub that proves very popular with locals and tourists alike. It's the other half of Allo's restaurant with rooms, the two gelling in a smooth and seamless symmetry. The bar is a narrow room with lots of original 19C charm. Walls feature exposed brick and the wooden bar and floor are thickly varnished; small booths and stools at the bar provide a most convivial and traditional feel. Menus change on a weekly basis and offer a good range of popular snacks and sandwiches alongside hearty daily specials. Booking really is a must, as it invariably gets packed here.

Food serving times
Tuesday-Saturday:
12pm-7pm, 7pm-9pm
Closed 25 December
Booking essential

Prices
Meals: a la carte
18.00/70.00
3 rooms: 60.00/120.00

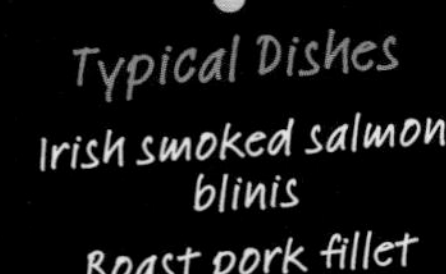

Typical Dishes
Irish smoked salmon blinis
Roast pork fillet
Vanilla bean pannacotta

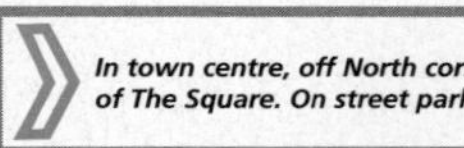

In town centre, off North corner of The Square. On street parking.

013 The Oarsman

Bridge St,
Carrick-on-Shannon
Tel.: (071) 962 1733 - Fax: (071) 962 1734
e-mail: info@theoarsman.com - Website: www.theoarsman.com

No boating experience necessary, of course, but the town's club eights have been known to drop in, along with sea-anglers and tour rowers, back from a long day's pull up to Lough Key. They come for the spirited, upbeat atmosphere, light lunches and fresh, tasty dinners combining modern classics and a few popular Irish favourites; even when it's busy, alert and helpful staff will do their best find you a table in the main bar or up in the mezzanine, though propping up the bar for a half is no hardship here. Refurbished in traditional style, with some unlikely bits of bric-à-brac hanging from its exposed timbers and stone, it's an enjoyable place and worth seeking out.

Food serving times

Tuesday-Wednesday:
12pm-8.30pm (bar meals)

Thursday-Saturday:
12pm-5.30pm, 6.45pm-9.30pm

Closed 25 December and Good Friday

Prices

Meals: a la carte
25.00/45.00

Typical Dishes

Smoked salmon and scallops

Pan-fried Thornhill duck

Apricot and plum pudding

In town centre. Nearby parking close to river and bridge.

014 Larkins

Garrykennedy

Tel.: (067) 23232 - Fax: (067) 23933

e-mail: info@larkinspub.com - Website: www.larkinspub.com

 **No real ales offered**

This thatched, whitewashed inn at the end of the lane looks barely big enough to swing the proverbial pussycat, leave alone house a whole troop of Irish dancers, but Larkins is actually a lot larger on the inside than it appears from the out, and plenty big enough to accommodate the local live music groups who entertain from Wednesday to Sunday. Whitewashed walls covered with old pictures and classic adverts spark off nostalgia, as do the cabinets behind the bar full of old food packets and tins. There is a simple lunch menu and a longer evening version, both of which offer wholesome, hearty cooking served in portions which will satisfy the healthiest of appetites. Homemade soda bread is served at the start of your meal, and you can choose from dishes ranging from steak burger and stew to sea bass and salmon, via seafood chowder and spicy chicken salad. The rear garden and dining room overlook the shores of Lough Derg.

Food serving times

Monday-Sunday:
12pm-4pm, 5pm-10pm

Closed 25 December, Good Friday, lunch October-March

Prices

Meals: a la carte
22.95/40.00

Typical Dishes

Golden fried Brie
Honey roast duckling
Warm chocolate cake

9km west of Nenagh by R494 and minor road north. Free public car park opposite.

015 The Glencairn Inn

Lismore

Tel.: (058) 56232 - Fax: (058) 55840
e-mail: info@glencairninn.com
Website: www.glencairninn.com

 **No real ales offered**

This "pretty as a picture" cottage style inn is most homely: it even has a picket fence. A country pub writ large, it boasts everything from a little fire-lit bar to charming bedrooms with an old-world feel. The quaint bar is a good place to settle down with a pint of stout and enjoy freshly prepared dishes off a limited choice menu; or, if you prefer, the same options are on offer in a couple of small dining rooms, charmingly set up with a stylish country informality. The food is heartily rustic in nature: on the menu, you might find pot-roasted fillet of pork and apricots, or fish landed at Helvick, cooked in butter, olive oil and lemon juice. The owner is a talented artist, and it's easy to appreciate just how much of his inspiration has gone into the pub's appeal, not to mention his popular menus.

Food serving times

Wednesday-Saturday:
6.30pm-9.30pm

Sunday:
1pm-6pm

Closed 25 December, 2 weeks mid January, Good Friday, 1-15 November

Prices

Meals: a la carte
35.00/45.00

4 rooms: 80.00/120.00

Typical Dishes

Crispy duck roll
Pan-seared seabass
Pot au chocolat

2mi west of Lismore on the road to Ballyduff and Glencairn. Parking.

016 The Lobster Pot

Carne
Tel.: (053) 913 1110 - Fax: (053) 913 1401

   VISA AE

 **No real ales offered**

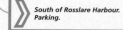

Engagingly quirky and genuinely welcoming, this personally owned seaside pub has been over 20 years in the making: it's now covered with old metal signs on the outside, and the intimate snugs and parlours are crammed with nauticalia and pasted with old posters and advertisements from days gone by. There's also a dining room at the back and, come the evening, they add an extensive list of grills, steaks and locally landed fish to the lunchtime chowders, salads and sandwiches. The real treat, though, is the huge seafood platter, an aquarium's worth of home-smoked salmon and mackerel, freshly dressed crab, poached salmon and prawns Marie Rose, served with bushels of salad. Try it with freshly baked brown scones and a glass of stout!

Food serving times

Tuesday-Sunday and Bank Holiday Monday: 6pm-9pm

Sunday: 12.30pm-8.30pm (7.30pm out of season)

Closed 25-26 December, all January, 1 week of February, Good Friday; also Tuesday after Bank Holiday Monday

- Seafood -

Prices

Meals: a la carte 35.00/55.00

Typical Dishes

Crab Mornay
Grilled Dover sole
Pear and almond pie

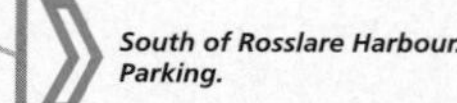
South of Rosslare Harbour. Parking.

A

B

C

D

E

Y

Z

A

B

C

D

E

F

G

H

I

J

P

Q

R

S

eating out in pubs

Michelin Maps & Guides

*Michelin Maps & Guides
Hannay House,
39 Clarendon Rd
Watford WD17 1JA
Tel: (01923) 205247
Fax: (01923) 205241
www.ViaMichelin.com
eatingoutinpubs-gbirl@
uk.michelin.com*

Manufacture française des pneumatiques Michelin

*Société en commandite
par actions au capital de
304 000 000 EUR.
Place des Carmes-Déchaux
63 Clermont-Ferrand (France)
R.C.S. Clermont-Fd B 855 200 507*

*Dépôt légal Septembre 2007
Printed in France 07-07*

Typesetting:

*Nord Compo, Villeneuve-d'Ascq
Printing and binding:
Clerc, St Amand-Montrond*

Photography

*Project manager: Alain Leprince
Agence ACSI – A Chacun Son Image
242, bd. Voltaire– 75011 Paris*

Location Photographs:

Jérôme Berquez, Frédéric Chales, Ludivine Boizard, Jean-Louis Chauveau/ACSI

Thanks to:

Pandora Inn, Mylor Bridge and The Lickfold Inn, Lickfold for the front cover images.

p 12: John A Rizzo/Photodisc Vert/Getty Images

p 14: www.britainonview.com

p 200: britainonview/Rod Edwards

p 456: britainonview/Martin Brent

YOUR OPINION MATTERS!

To help us constantly improve this guide, please fill in this questionnaire and return to:

Eating out in Pubs 2008
Michelin Maps & Guides,
Hannay House, 39 Clarendon Road,
Watford, WD17 1JA, UK

First name: ....

Surname: ....

Address: ....

Profession: ....

< 25 years old	☐	25-34 years old	☐
35-50 years old	☐	> 50 years	☐

1. How often do you use the Internet to look for information on pubs?

Never ☐
Occasionally (once a month) ☐
Regularly (once a week) ☐
Very frequently (more than once a week) ☐

2. Have you ever bought Michelin guides?

☐ Yes ☐ No

3. If yes, which one(s)?

Eating out in Pubs ☐
The Michelin Guide Great Britain & Ireland ☐
The Green Guide (please specify titles) ☐

....

Other (please specify titles) ☐

....

4. If you have previously bought Eating out in Pubs, what made you purchase this new one?

....

....

5. If you buy the Michelin Guide Great Britain & Ireland, how often do you buy it?

Every year ☐
Every 2 years ☐
Every 3 years ☐
Every 4 years or more ☐

ABOUT EATING OUT IN PUBS :

6. Did you buy this guide:

For holidays? ☐
For a weekend/short break? ☐
For business purposes? ☐
As a gift? ☐
For everyday use ☐

How do you rate these different elements of this guide?

NB: 1. Very Poor 2. Poor 3. Average 4. Good 5. Very Good

	1	2	3	4	5
Selection of pubs	☐	☐	☐	☐	☐
Number of pubs in London	☐	☐	☐	☐	☐
Geographical spread of pubs	☐	☐	☐	☐	☐
Menu Prices	☐	☐	☐	☐	☐
Practical information (services, menus)	☐	☐	☐	☐	☐
Photos	☐	☐	☐	☐	☐
Description of the pubs	☐	☐	☐	☐	☐
Cover	☐	☐	☐	☐	☐
The format & size of the guide	☐	☐	☐	☐	☐
Guide Price	☐	☐	☐	☐	☐

8. How easily could you find the information you were looking for ?

....

....

9. Please rate the guide out of 20 ..../20

10. Which aspects could we improve?

....

....

....

....

....

....

11. Was there a pub you particularly liked or a choice you didn't agree with? Perhaps you have a favourite address of your own that you would like to tell us about? Please send us your remarks and suggestions.

....

....

....

....

....

....

....

....

....

....